THE PURITANS

VOLUME II

Nov'r 2. Midweek, went again, and found Mrs.
Alden there, who quickly went out. Gave her
ab't a pound of Sugar Almonds, cost 3s per l.
Carried it on Monday. She seemed pleas'd with
them, ask'd what they cost. Spake of giving her a
Hundred pounds per annum if I dy'd before her. Ask'd
her what sum she would give me, if she should dy
first? Said I would give her time to Consider of
it. She [said] she would not be beholden as if I had given all to
my Children by Deeds of Gift. I told her 'twas
a mistake, Point-Judith was mine &c. That
in England, I found, my Father's desire was yt
it should go to my eldest Son; 'twas 20ol per annum
tho that 'twas forty. I think when I spake to excuse pressing this; she seemed to think 'twas best to
speak of it, a long winter was coming on. Gave
me a Glass or two of Canary. Nov. 4th Friday.
Went again ab't 7 a-clock, found there Mr.
John Walley and his wife: Sat discoursing
pleasantly. I shew'd ym Isaac Moses's Writ-
ting. Madam W. served Comfats to us. After
a-while a Table was spread, & Supper was set.
I urg'd mr. Walley to Crave a Blessing; but he
put it upon me. About 9 they went away.
I ask'd Madam what fashion Neck-lace
I should present her with, She s. None at
all. I ask'd her whereabout we left off last
time, mention'd what I had offer'd to give
her; ask'd her what she would give me:
She said she could not change her condition
She had said so from ye beginning; could not
be so far from her children, the Picture.
Quoted the Apostle Paul affirming that a
single Life was better than a Married. I
answer'd That was for the present Distress.
Said she had not pleasure in things of that
nature as formerly: I said, you are the
fitter to make me a Wife. If she held
in yt mind, I must go home and bewail my
Rashness in making more haste than good
Speed. However, Considering ye Supper, I
desired her to be within, might lie so long. Allowed

Page of Samuel Sewall's *Diary*. (For text, see p. 526.)

THE PURITANS

VOLUME II   Revised Edition

PERRY MILLER

AND

THOMAS H. JOHNSON

Bibliographies Revised for the Torchbook Edition
by George McCandlish

HARPER TORCHBOOKS ▼ THE ACADEMY LIBRARY

HARPER & ROW, PUBLISHERS, NEW YORK, EVANSTON, AND LONDON

CONTENTS
Volume II

Chapter IV

MANNERS, CUSTOMS, AND BEHAVIOR

Chapter V

BIOGRAPHIES AND LETTERS

Chapter VI

POETRY 545

Readings

Chapter VII

LITERARY THEORY 665

Readings

Chapter VIII

EDUCATION 695

Readings

Chapter IX

SCIENCE

NOTES

Illustrations

Volume II

The page of Taylor's manuscript is reproduced through the courtesy of Yale University Library. All the other reproductions are by courtesy of the Massachusetts Historical Society.

MANNERS, CUSTOMS, AND BEHAVIOR

W HEN John Josselyn, naturalist and traveler, returned to England in 1671, he wrote of the civil and ecclesiastical "great masters" whom he met in the Bay Colony that some of them were "damnable rich." His objurgations went even farther:

> . . . inexplicably covetous and proud, they receive your gifts but as an homage or tribute due to their transcendency, which is a fault their Clergie are also guilty of, whose living is upon the bounty of their hearers. . . . The chiefest objects of discipline, Religion, and morality they want, some are of a *Linsie-woolsie* disposition, of several professions in Religion, all like *Aethiopians* white in the Teeth, only full of ludification and injurious dealing, . . . and savagely factious amongst themselves. . . .[1]

Some forty years had elapsed since Governor Winthrop led his earnest followers to New England, and doubtless times had changed. The authority of the earlier magistrates, most of whom by Josselyn's time had been "laid asleep in their beds of rest till the day of doom," [2] was passing; even the clergy, alarmed at the defection from high seriousness which they believed was spreading among the coming generation, had cautioned them "always to remember, that Originally they are a *Plantation Religious*, not a plantation of Trade." [3] But a clergyman's privilege of straight speaking and a traveler's presumption in criticizing are two different things. Perhaps Josselyn was right, even if his censure went unheeded, for though sketched in pique his outline does not seriously misrepresent the composite Yankee.

Josselyn was one of the first among many observers of American manners who have found much to bewilder them and not a little to criticize. Colonizers as a rule do not combine high ideals with shrewd clear-sightedness, self-discipline with passion. If the leaders among the second generation of New Englanders accepted Josselyn's gifts as homage, they were but receiving a tribute due the "*Plantation Religious*"; if they were proud, then Josselyn had misjudged them in expecting servility.

Factiousness was indeed an infirmity to which early New Eng-

[1] *An Account of Two Voyages to New-England* (London, 1674), pp. 180, 181. Linsey-woolsey is a coarse fabric of linen and wool; by extension, a term of depreciation.

[2] *Ibid.*, p. 183.

[3] John Norton, *The Heart of N-England rent* (1659), p. 58. The same phrase is repeated in John Higginson's Massachusetts Election Sermon for 1663, *The Cause of God* (Cambridge), p. 11.

landers were peculiarly prone. The relative isolation of each village group compelled its members to associate in vexatious yet unavoidable propinquity. The era when "Good fences make good neighbors" had not yet arrived, and the "commonage," or unfenced village land, was shared. When horses and cattle strayed, as they might do with exasperating ease, tempers flared, and only the greatest self-control prevented bitter contention, as the diary of Joseph Green vividly testifies (see p. 448). The colonists did not welcome lawyers as a class—wisely perhaps, for the issues which made the townsmen so "savagely factious amongst themselves" could be as equitably resolved by private agreement. Petty gossip and meanness, bickering and contentiousness were the "little foxes" all too often lurking in the Puritan vineyard. We encounter them in journals and diaries, and they were the texts for innumerable sermons and "lectures." The godly were as much embroiled as the unregenerate. John Pike, the minister at Dover, New Hampshire, was prevented by the town from collecting his salary in 1702 because a large part of his congregation discovered they could get Quaker preachers "who should Preach to them freely without any Cost or Charge, not like their hireling Minister, who put them to great charge to maintain him." [1] We are glad to record, however, that the town finally came to its senses when the minister was about to depart, repudiated its heresies, and paid the arrears of Master Pike's salary.

Larger centers, such as Boston and Salem, provided a greater diversity of interests; their ministers were often quicker to perceive the smoldering embers of disaffection, and wiser in blanketing them. It was the provincial town usually that let "mighty contests rise from trivial things." The "bad book" controversy in Northampton, as late as 1744, is a case in point; [2] even more incomprehensibly serio-comic was the question of "dignifying the seats" in Deerfield in 1701. Pews were allotted townspeople according to their rank. The third meeting-house in Deerfield was newly built, and the citizens, united though they were against the very present danger of Indian attacks, split into two acrimonious parties in their views of social precedence regarding the dignity of the pews. The matter was settled only by recourse to statutory fiat:

As to estimation of Seats yᵉ Town agreed and voted yᵗ yᵉ fore seat in yᵉ front Gallery shall be equall in dignity with yᵉ 2ᵈ seat in yᵉ Body of yᵉ meeting house:

[1] Sibley, *Biographical Sketches*, II, 451.
[2] See Thomas H. Johnson, "Jonathan Edwards and the 'Young Folks' Bible,'" *New England Quarterly*, V (1932), 37–54.

That yᵉ fore seats in yᵉ side Gallerys shall be equall in dignity with yᵉ 4th seats in yᵉ Body of yᵉ meeting house: [1]

The town record continues to specify in detail the ranking of the seats, and implies the status of the families which could expect to occupy them!

The characteristics observed by Josselyn were undoubtedly, for better or worse, a part of the Yankee make-up. They resulted from a way of life, and determined certain qualities of behavior peculiarly Puritan. Twentieth-century philosophy, based upon principles of toleration for religious, political, social differences; equality for all in the pursuit of happiness—often conceived as the equal ability of all to achieve "the more abundant life":—such a concept is immeasurably removed from that which obtained in the Puritan era. Clearly if Puritans believed that in the Bible lay all true and proper laws for governing human conduct, if they voluntarily relinquished to magistrates and ministers the power of interpreting the code, if they had not yet conceived the doctrine of laissez faire, then in questions of behavior the governors would tend to become "covetous and proud," the governed gradually to develop "a *Linsie-woolsie* disposition," and all men come to be their brother's keeper. The germ of the failure of Puritanism lay concealed within its fruit. The ways of the Puritan are not our ways, and it is easy for us, removed in time and point of view, to see the failure. It were wiser for us, nevertheless, not to accept Josselyn's verdict until we have observed one final aspect of the reaction of highly conceived ideals on human frailty. A glance, then, at their mode of life.

Most of the families, especially those from among the twenty thousand emigrants who left England during the 1630's, were recruited from the lesser gentry and yeoman stock, with a sprinkling of artisans and indentured servants. Frequently the servants were adventurers who departed England to escape imprisonment for debt by covenanting with another emigrant or the skipper of a sailing vessel for the amount of their passage. Their debt discharged, they could be admitted "inhabitants," and then, if they became church members, they could secure complete "citizenship." The magistrates and ministers almost without exception were university trained gentlemen of good family. Though church membership was a necessary preliminary to the franchise, all men were recognized as equal before the law, all were freeholders, and

[1] Quoted from George Sheldon, *A History of Deerfield, Massachusetts* (Deerfield, 1895–1896), I, 205.

all except the indentured servants owned their farms. Indeed, whatever trade or calling a New England settler might follow, he was
always of necessity a farmer.

The severities of pioneer life, to which the rigors of a New England
winter and the fear of Indian attacks were added, determined the mode
of communal life. It was best that the village be closely knit, with no
outlying farms. Except for a few settlements established up the Connecticut River as far as Deerfield and Northfield, the population was
spread along the seacoast, from which the forest stretched almost
unbroken north to Canada and west to Albany. The General Court
appropriated the arable land: the fresh and salt marshes, intervales,
meadows, and Indian clearings, and granted it to communities—to
"proprietors" who held the "commonage." [1] The grantees were appor-
tioned their holdings not on a basis of share and share alike, but upon
principles less democratic perhaps, though equitable enough. The proprietors distributed the land according to the size of families, the
number of their livestock, the wealth and position of the settler. None
of the holdings was large, consequently no landed gentry established
itself on great estates, as in New Netherlands or in the South. In a few
instances, land was granted directly to individuals—to the ministers,
for example, who received much larger apportionments, together with
certain rights and privileges, in part payment as salary.

Each farm, tilled by its owner, was self-sustaining. The land was
planted to such staples as wheat, rye, and Indian corn; barley for beer,
oats for stock; hemp and flax for clothing. In the garden plots the
husbandman grew beans, white and green peas, hops, squash, "pum-
pions," "pasneps," and "turneps." Potatoes were not raised until the
eighteenth century. Governor Bradford left the most comprehensive
picture of the subsistence that New England furnished in the first
decades of the settlements. Not only were there native herbs, fruits,
and vegetables, but whatever was to be found in England, he says,
had been brought to the colonies, where it thrived well:

> All sorts of grain which our own land doth yield,
> Was hither brought, and sown in every field:
> As wheat and rye, barley, oats, beans, and pease
> Here all thrive, and they profit from them raise,
> All sorts of roots and herbs in gardens grow,
> Parsnips, carrots, turnips, or what you'll sow,
> Onions, melons, cucumbers, radishes,

[1] For a brief account, see especially Robert R. Walcott, "Husbandry in Colonial
New England," *New England Quarterly*, IX (1936), 218–252.

Skirets,[1] beets, coleworts, and fair cabbages.
Here grows fine flowers many, and 'mongst those,
The fair white lily and sweet fragrant rose.
Many good wholesome berries here you'll find,
Fit for man's use, almost of every kind,
Pears, apples, cherries, plumbs, quinces, and peach,
Are *now* no dainties; you may have of each.
Nuts and grapes of several sorts are here,
If you will take the pains them to seek for.[2]

After 1650, horses were bred in sufficient numbers for general use,—exported, in fact, to the West Indies, where they were used in the sugar industry,—and hay was therefore grown plentifully. As summers must be devoted chiefly to raising crops, winters were free for tending the herd. Stock raising often supplied the principal income or credit with which the settler could trade. There were goats in abundance, cattle, horses, sheep, swine, poultry, and bees; hence the larder was amply stocked with native produce. In addition, a good supply of wild game depended only upon a practiced eye and a quick trigger, and such luxuries as maple sugar depended, after 1700, only upon the industry of each farmer (see p. 747). Fish were so common that along the coast, then as now, they provided fertilizer. Only spices and condiments, principally salt, sugar, and molasses, needed to be imported. Apples were abundant, and no cellar but contained enough cider—ten to forty barrels—to last out the season. Cider and beer were the universal drinks, served to all with every meal; while cider-brandy and rum, distilled at Boston and Newport, made headier beverages.

The "selling points" by which promoters for the New England Company attracted settlers had not overstated the advantages. If their literature omitted any reference to the ravages and annoyances of hostile Indians, wolves, field mice, and sparrows, it assumed that they could soon be overcome by industry and the favor of God. The customer owned his home, he could raise a large family, and he had plenty to eat. On the whole he was satisfied.

The New England emigrants brought comparatively few furnishings with them: ship space was dear, and in mid-seventeenth century pas-

---

[1] A skirret is a species of water-parsnip, long cultivated in Europe for its succulent root. Like the parsnip, which it resembles in flavor, it was boiled and served in butter, or half-boiled and fried. At present it is very little used.

[2] "A Descriptive and Historical Account of New England in verse," *Collections of the Massachusetts Historical Society*, III (1794), 77–84; quoted from pp. 77, 78. Bradford died in 1657.

sage alone—and very crowded quarters at that—cost four or five pounds. Besides, why go to the expense of moving freight when all trades were represented among every shipload of passengers? Carvers and joiners, masons, coopers, and blacksmiths—all knew they would find plenty of native material on which to exercise their skill. Though some metal, bog iron particularly, was founded, wood, brick, or stone was chiefly used for building needs. The indentured servant labored as he could; and there were the negro slaves, sold directly by the ship's captain at Boston or Newport, for those who could afford them; but on the whole few servants found their way to any one household. The skilled artisan, except in the smaller towns, was supremely important. Young men learned their business as apprentices; trades flourished, and some substantial incomes were acquired by owners of sawmills, breweries, and ships, by shipbuilders, and exporters of lumber, furs, and fish. The mint-master, John Hull of Boston, held the corner on silver; from 1652 until 1686 he minted the only native coin that the General Court allowed in the colonies—the famous "Pine Tree Shilling"—on which his profit was considerable. Paper money was introduced only in 1690, in the same year that the name *dollar* (Ger. *thaler*) was given to the Spanish peso or "piece of eight."

As population increased, land values rose; a speculative fever that accompanied the subsequent prosperity forced men gradually to abandon the use of "commons" under a claim of ownership by proprietors. Thus in the early years of the eighteenth century a new town ceased to be a congregation formed about a new church; it was "a planting by land speculators of persons forced out from the old settlements by economic necessity." [1] With expansion came a demand for "cheap money," but Puritans of property and standing vehemently opposed any economic theory which argued that men were naturally equal or that a democratic government was the best. The brilliant arguments of "the first great American democrat" John Wise (see pp. 257–269) do not reflect the temper of orthodox Puritan economic theory, except in so far as he advocated the dignity of labor, the sanctity of property, and the virtue of saving. [2]

[1] James T. Adams, *Revolutionary New England* (Boston, 1927), p. 89.
[2] See for example, John Blackwell, *A Discourse in Explanation of the Bank of Credit . . . to be Erected in Boston*, Boston, 1687; *idem, Some Additional Considerations Addressed unto the Worshipful Elisha Hutchinson*, Boston, 1691; Cotton Mather, *Some Considerations on the Bills of Credit now passing in New-England*, Boston, 1691; *idem, Fair Dealing between Debtor and Creditor*, Boston, 1716. See further, Edgar A. J. Johnson, *American Economic Thought in the Seventeenth Century*, London, 1932. For the Puritan, private property was deemed necessary in a world of men actuated by self-love and incapable of achieving an ideal commonwealth. Only by labor was a decent state possible. Thus idleness was

Manners, Customs, and Behavior

Trade with the West Indies, begun in the 1640's, was always brisk. Lumber, horses, grain, meat, and tobacco were exchanged for wines, liquor, cheeses, sugar, tropical woods, slaves, and other merchandise not native to the colonies. From the West Indies silver coins had been first introduced during the seventeenth century, though musket balls and wampum continued to have value in barter; wampum as well as farm produce was accepted in payment for college tuition. Though the Puritans were not originally a seafaring people, their new environment gave opportunity for a development of trade that by the 1650's made New England ships, commanded by the "Bible-quoting Yankee skipper," a familiar sight in Atlantic and European waters; one which by 1676 had extended to the Levant and the Far East.[1] Pay was good, and whether the enterprise involved legitimate commerce, smuggling, or privateering, owners found adventurous fellows who were glad to take up before the mast. But the "down-Easters" who manned the vessels were not always young romantics; very often they were deserters, runaway servants, and "beach combers": a sinewy, hard-working, heavy-drinking, picturesque crew that lent color to the thriving seaport towns of Marblehead, Salem, Boston, and Newport; and caused grave concern to the ministers.

Few professions were represented in any one town. Lawyers were held in contempt,[2] and for the first ten years unrestricted judicial powers were exercised by the Court of Assistants, that is, the magistrates— the Governor, Deputy-Governor, and twelve Assistants, annually elected by the freemen on the last Wednesday in Easter Term. Legal administration was brought more into line with English precedent in 1641 by a codification of the "Body of Liberties," or "Abstract of Laws," mainly adopted from the legal books of the Old Testament. Thenceforth a codified fundamental law existed to which the magis-

---

wrong both morally and socially, for it bred disrespect, fostered contention, and restricted production; the amassing of wealth was justified and desirable in that God could thereby be further glorified. (See Cotton Mather, *Durable Riches* (Boston, 1695), pp. 13, 14.)

[1] See especially John W. McElroy, "Seafaring in Seventeenth-Century New England," *New England Quarterly*, VIII (1935), 331–364.

[2] For a summary of the legal aspects of the Puritan colonies, see the introduction by Zechariah Chafee, Jr., to *Records of the Suffolk County Court, 1671–1680*, in *Publications of the Colonial Society of Massachusetts*, Vols. XXIX, XXX (1933). The theory obtained that those who drew fees for representing their fellow men in court were usurers; but more fundamentally the objection to lawyers was simply that the colonists thought every man should be able to plead his own cause. The litigious character of the colonists, noted by travelers, was encouraged by magistrates and juries who disregarded legal precedent to the extent that lawsuits were sometimes protracted for two or three generations.

trates were bound, though as compared with the judicial procedure in English courts New England judges still exercised a wide discretionary power. Law and order were the rule, though punishments in the Puritan colonies were less severe than in England. Pirates and murderers were hanged at a public execution during which the prisoner was excoriated by the minister, his felonious life reviewed, and a plea for forgiveness entertained (see p. 413). Few survivals of medieval practices are known: two cases of burning at the stake for arson and poisoning; at least one "ordeal of touch" [1] as a means of giving evidence. The witchcraft delusion of 1692 (see pp. 758–762) was brief, very local, and is not now regarded as a phenomenon particularly Puritan. Lesser offences were punished by the customary English methods: stocking, whipping, branding, and cutting off ears.

No settlement but had a well organized town government, together with its church presided over by a college-bred minister; the wealthier towns or churches often divided the ministerial function of pastor and teacher between two equally distinguished men: the "pastor" was to concern himself with the administration of the society, and the "teacher" to devote himself primarily to expounding and maintaining the purity of doctrine. Increase Mather and his son Cotton, for example, served as pastor and teacher respectively of the Old North Church in Boston.

Physicians were scarce in the colonies. It frequently fell to the lot of the minister, who might well be the only liberally educated resident, to practice medicine in what Cotton Mather described as "Angelical Conjunction" [2] with his spiritual office. Michael Wigglesworth, in fact, was both the minister and the physician of Malden during his long occupation of the pulpit. On the whole, residents were far more dependent upon their own knowledge of herbs and simples than is commonly imagined. Midwives attended the lying-in; a few herbals, based on the writings of Galen, circulated from hand to hand; some quacks, —"chemists," or followers of Paracelsus—compounded drugs; but infant mortality was high, childbirth fever claimed many young mothers, consumption took heavy toll among adolescents, the ravages of smallpox destroyed young and old indiscriminately, and now and then one encounters what appears to have been a fatal attack of appendicitis, recorded simply as "a prodigious belly-ache." Though several reputable physicians practiced in New England, the slow development of medi-

---

[1] The superstition which required the person suspected of murder to touch the neck of the deceased with the index finger of the left hand; if blood appeared to flow from the corpse, the suspect was deemed guilty.   [2] *Magnalia*, III, 26.

cine itself was basically responsible for much ignorant procedure. Usually doctors learned their profession as apprentices; it is significant that but one physician in the colonies in 1716, William Douglass of Boston, held the degree of Doctor of Medicine.[1]

Surprisingly little is known of the customs and practices in the ordinary routine of Puritan life, for the journals and diaries, so numerous in the period, seldom or but incidentally record what to them were the commonplaces of existence.[2] Except in the very earliest years of the emigrations, it would appear that the colonists as a whole lived in a degree of luxury. The story of the hardships and lack of decencies among the Plymouth Pilgrims during the early years is too well known to need rehearsing; we are aware also that a few of the early settlers lived for a brief time in tents, huts, or dug-outs, heated by wooden chimneys, and lighted with oil-paper windows. But as soon as thrifty pioneers had won a foothold, aided by neighbors or servants they raised clapboarded frame houses, similar in architecture to those they knew in England. No log cabins ever were erected, though logs served for garrison houses as defense against Indian attacks. Many seventeenth-century houses survive today in New England: usually two-storey frame dwellings built around an enormous brick chimney with openings for large fireplaces in several rooms. The large kitchen, with its enormous fireplace, served often as dining room in winter, when a nor'easter penetrated through to the marrow, and thin clapboards could not repel the cold. In summer a back room or "summer kitchen" could be opened up to accommodate a more expansive way of living. The "foreroom" or parlor, occasionally plastered with "painted paper," was large and pleasant; it was probably not heated in winter except for occasional social gatherings or for funerals. In winter, especially in provincial New England, the foreroom was doubtless used for "bundling" or "tarrying"—that curious custom wherein young men courted their girls in cold weather by lying with them upon bed or couch wrapped between heavy blankets sewed together on three sides and down through the middle.

A brickworks was established at Salem in 1629, and now and then as the colonists prospered, well-to-do residents abandoned frame houses —so easily destroyed by fire—for more substantial brick edifices. A glance within the house indicates that forks were unknown to most and

[1] John Clark (1667–1728) of Boston, brother-in-law of Cotton Mather, was a talented physician. He was third in a direct line of seven generations of that name who practiced medicine in Massachusetts for over one hundred and fifty years.

[2] The best gleanings are to be found in George F. Dow, *Every Day Life in the Massachusetts Bay Colony* (Boston, 1935).

seldom used by any, though Winthrop brought one from England, perhaps as a curiosity. The food was plain: fresh meat in season, boiled or roasted, and salted at other times; corn meal, stews, and such vegetables as were ripened or could be stored in winter. The diet perhaps lacked sufficient balance, for Josselyn noticed that "Men and Women keep their complexions, but lose their Teeth: the Women are pittifully Tooth-shaken; whether through the coldness of the climate, or by sweetmeats of which they have store, I am not able to affirm." [1] False teeth were not common, and the toothbrush was only introduced in 1718; but the salt and water solution used as a dentrifice was no doubt quite as adequate as any devised today. Bathing was a luxury,— at least, observers of colonial manners gave it scant notice. As for ventilation, quite possibly the bedrooms in winter received only such circulation of air as large fireplaces supply, since chilly air was thought to be poisonous. Indeed, the modern insistence upon wide-thrown windows on winter nights would have been incomprehensible to a Puritan.

Only the wealthy could afford the imported craft or fabric of silversmith, cabinetmaker, linen draper, or tailor; furniture was plain, dishes of wood or pewter, clothing homespun though plentiful. [2] In dress decorum was preserved. Workmen wore leather; their betters, both men and women, indulged a taste for latest fashions both in clothes and in jewelry and trinkets; for, said Master Oakes, "one end of Apparel is to distinguish and put a difference between persons according to their Places and Conditions, . . . provided it carry nothing of Immodesty in it, or Contrariety to the Rules of Moral Honesty. The civil Customs of the place where we live is that which must regulate in this case." [3] In the light of Oakes's sensible opinion we may better understand why the sumptuary laws to preserve a Puritan plainness were not enforced. Such advice would not support a view that Puritans of the upper classes lived drab and colorless lives. On the contrary, too many inventories bear witness to the presence of finery, and ministers other than Oakes so often addressed congregations on the subject of dress, citing scripture and verse (see p. 454), that we know there must have been color aplenty. Ministers of the first generation thought long hair was unscriptural, and thus short hair became a party badge.

---

[1] *Account of Two Voyages*, p. 185.

[2] The American wing of the Metropolitan Museum of Art gives a most complete and accurate idea of colonial architecture, furniture, and decorations. One must keep in mind, nevertheless, that the art of the painter, carver, and silversmith belongs rather to the eighteenth century than to the seventeenth. The Puritan period in the colonies was substantially over by the end of Queen Anne's reign.

[3] Urian Oakes, *New-England Pleaded with* (Cambridge, 1673), p. 34.

By the end of the century, when the new fashion of periwigs came into style, the more conservative pillars of state and society transferred their animus to wigs. "Mr Chievar died this last night . . .," Judge Sewall entered briefly in his *Diary* for August 20, 1708; "The Wellfare of the Province was much upon his Spirit. He abominated Perriwigs." It is doubtful whether the naive *non sequitur* of Sewall's views obtained very widely after 1710. Times were changing, the older views seemed stuffy, and such laws as had been enacted to preserve the decorum of an earlier day were forgotten. The first generations of Yankees, never "timid souls," had been as independent in action and as restive under petty restraints as their descendants now seemed. By the close of the century the patriarchs that remained were merely exercising an old man's prerogative of plain speaking. Laws that had been enacted were not always enforced. The Puritan was opinionated, and it is inevitable that he sometimes made himself ridiculous.

marriage

Puritans were married young, though by no means so young as we often suppose. Revealing data on that matter can be gleaned from the vital records—lists of births, marriages, and deaths—relating to colonial towns. The average age for first marriages in early New England strikingly parallels that of today. Girls were almost never given in marriage under eighteen, and more often not until they had passed their twentieth or twenty-first birthday. Men were usually somewhat older. The average holds true for the colonies as a whole; certain classes, ministers' children, for instance, or those whose education was longer pursued, sometimes were well along in their twenties before they assumed the responsibilities of matrimony. Isolation doubtless compelled delay: five of the six daughters of the Reverend Solomon Stoddard of Northampton were married rather late. Furthermore, properly qualified suitors were not always at hand—the four daughters of Joseph Dudley were well into their twenties before they wed. Bachelors were uncommon, for the Biblical injunction to marry and increase was literally observed; food was ample, and there was work for all. Besides, the death rate was very high, so that oversupply of labor was no serious problem. Some have concluded that Puritan families were not very large, and it is true that no very great number reached maturity. The statement regarding Judge Sewall may fairly be considered representative: "Sewall had issue by his first wife only. There were seven sons and seven daughters, of whom only six lived to maturity, and only three survived him." [1]

[1] Sibley, *Biographical Sketches*, II, 359.

The marriage ceremony was simple and regarded as a civil, not a religious rite; banns were published and after a brief but appropriate interval the intending couple appeared before a magistrate. Elopements were uncommon, and divorces, though rare, were less so among Puritans than Anglicans, for the latter group flatly refused to sanction such a step.[1] Those who raise large families do not have time to humor their caprices; besides, man was the master and woman his helpmate; death so often separated partners that men and women often married twice, thrice, and sometimes even oftener. The choice of mate was by no means exclusively a parental matter. The florid love letter which the Reverend Edward Taylor (see p. 650) addressed to the young lady of his choice in 1674, Elizabeth Fitch of Norwich, is still preserved: [2]

. . . Looke not (I entreate you) on it as one of Loves Hyperboles, if I borrow the Beams of some Sparkling Metaphors to illustrate my Respects vnto your selfe by. For you having made my breast the Cabbinet of your Affections (as I yours, mine) I know not how to vse a fitter Comparison to set out my Love by, than to Compare it vnto a Golden Ball of pure Fire rowling vp and down my Breast, from which there flies now, and then a Sparke like a Glorious Beam from the Body of the Flaming Sun . . .

The ardent lover then goes on to prove syllogistically that "Conjugall Love ought to exceed all other," with the conclusion that "it must be kept within bounds too. For it must be Subordinate to Gods Glory." The conception was surely orthodox, and perhaps the expression of it seemed a model proposal. At any rate, it is poles removed from the courtship of Mary Stoddard of Northampton by the young Wethersfield pastor, Stephen Mix. Tradition has it that Stephen first approached the daughter by way of the father. Stoddard's consent obtained, the couple met and chatted, Mary asking simply for a brief time to consider the proposal. Her reply by letter shortly after reads as follows:

Northampton, 1695

Rev. Stephen Mix:

Yes.

Mary Stoddard.[3]

[1] See Chilton L. Powell, "Marriage in Early New England," *New England Quarterly*, I (1928), 323–334.

[2] In his MS "Poetical Works," Yale University Library; printed in part in Frances M. Caulkins, *History of Norwich, Connecticut* (Hartford, 1866), p. 154.

[3] Charles Stoddard, *Anthony Stoddard of Boston, Mass., and His Descendants* (New York, 1865), p. 4.

Letters of the period exchanged between husband and wife, parents and children, or brothers and sisters, show a tender but not effusive regard: "My dear Companion," "Dear Spouse," "My service to my sisters," "Your affectionate Friend and Father," "Your most tender and affectionate Father." For all that religion and the church played an important role in Puritan affairs, the home was the center of their lives, and for most, their love towards it must have been as deep as Anne Bradstreet's, if less expressive.

The attitude of the Puritans toward death and suffering is hardest to interpret in modern terms. Though not fatalists, they seem curiously insensitive to any great bereavement. It is not merely that they looked upon translation from the flesh to the spirit as a welcome change, though such an attitude was a principle in their ethics. It is rather the curiously immobile acceptance of a *fait accompli*. Sewall's diary for May 26, 1720 points the case: "About midnight my dear wife expired to our great astonishment, especially mine." To be sure, death stalked too frequently among people of all ages to be an uncommon sight. For that reason perhaps, and because the rites were regarded in a secular light, funerals were seized upon as occasions for impressive assembly, extravagant display, and excessive drinking. The gloves, rings, and scarves provided in nearly every will for the bearers were likewise distributed to the clergy, and the number they accumulated must have been reckoned in scores. So florid and diffuse was the stream of elegies and sermons that poured forth on such occasions that the Reverend James Fitch of Norwich wrote: "The Abusive, and justly to be Condemned practice of too too many, who in Preaching Funeral Sermons, by mis-representing the Dead, have dangerously misled the living, and by flatteries corrupted many, hath occasioned not a few to question (if not conclude against) the lawfulness of Preaching at such seasons. . . ." [1] Many of the old burying grounds are still to be seen, with their simple freestone, syenite, or slate markers undisturbed. Flat marble slabs, imported from England, occasionally dot the quiet landscape, or low brick and marble tombs; vaults were a late innovation.

Whoever wishes to learn about the sports and diversions of Puritan children should turn to Miss Earle's delightful study.[2] Dolls and toys there were; as the child matured he participated in sports: football, ball and bat, stoolball, and cricket. We nowhere encounter any objec-

---

[1] *Peace The End of the Perfect and Vpright* (Cambridge, 1672), preface, sig. A 1ᵛ.
[2] Alice M. Earle, *Child Life in Colonial Days* (2d ed., New York, 1927).

tion to pleasant, healthful divertisement, which indeed was encouraged.
So too was a sense of humor. Colman said:

A great deal of *Pleasantry* there is in the *Town*, and very graceful
and charming it is so far as it is Innocent and Wise. Our *Wit* like
our *Air* is clear and *Keen*, and in very Many 'tis exalted by a *Polite
Education* meeting with good *Natural Parts* . . . We daily need some
respite & diversion, without which we dull our Powers; a little intermission sharpens 'em again. It spoils the *Bow* to keep it always bent,
and the *Viol* if always strain'd up. Mirth is some loose or relaxation
to the labouring Mind or Body, it lifts up the hands that hang down
in weariness, and strengthens the feeble knees that cou'd stand no
longer to work: it renews our strength, and we resume our labours
again with vigour. 'Tis design'd by nature to chear and revive us
thro' all the toils and troubles of life, and therefore equally a benefit
with the other Rests which Nature has provided for the same end. 'Tis
in our present Pilgrimage and Travel of Life refreshing as the *Angels
provision for Elijah* in his sore travel.[1]

Doubtless the genial pastor knew men and times, and that wit
whereof he spoke. In the next century the characteristics of "Yankee
humor" are seen more clearly, though even in the seventeenth century
we perceive it occasionally. At its best it is seldom worldly, though it
understood the way of the world; it was quiet usually and slow, sometimes solemn and resigned, often sardonic; yet at its core never without
warmth—the dry, crackling wit that mulls along, seldom breaking
into flame.[2]

But all merriment was not innocent, and against such sports or games
as fostered gambling, rows, immorality, drunkenness, or Sabbath-
breaking strong voice was raised, and penalties enacted. Mixed dancing
was condemned by some (see p. 411), as were card playing, shuffle-

[1] Benjamin Colman, *The Government & Improvement of Mirth* (Boston, 1707), preface, and p. 29. Colman's book indicates that the colonial ministers, by allying
themselves with such reformers as Jeremy Collier, were establishing a respectable
point of contact with England. At the same time they were keeping up with an important current of public opinion at home and demonstrating that they were not
merely a provincial stock concerned with abstract theology. Cotton Mather's *Essays to do Good* was written for the same reason, and likewise shows the desire of New
Englanders to co-operate with moral reforms. Colman's conception of mirth and
its government is that of traditional Puritanism, but the spirit informing it is of the
eighteenth-century English nonconformist and Low-Church piety.

[2] See, for instance, the letter which Timothy Cutler wrote his classmate George
Curwin in 1711, quoted in Sibley, *Biographical Sketches*, V, 46, 47. But for another interpretation of early "Yankee humor"—one which gives in this writer's opinion too
much weight to its broad, farcical play—see George F. Horner, *A History of American
Humor to 1765* (Dissertation, University of North Carolina, 1936).

board, billiards, and bowling. Yet many diversions, if moderately in-dulged, were willingly countenanced as long as they did not lead to "waste of time." In the privacy of one's own home much passed un-noticed—even dancing, card playing, and other such "frolicks." A public bowling green was advertised at the present Bowdoin Square in Boston in 1700. All Yankees have had an eye for good horses, and horse racing, especially after 1715, was featured in many towns. There were pig-runs as well, and bearbaiting—sports which were never wholly approved even in England; but the tolerant colonial parson may sometimes have deemed it wise to drive with slackened rein.

Holidays were times of hilarity: training-days for militia review, commencements—then as now,—and November Fifth or "Pope's Night,"—three occasions especially licenced. But such times of public festivity by no means exhaust the tally. Puritans found excuse as well for private merrymaking in baptisms, weddings, funerals, barn-rais-ings, cornhuskings, quilting-parties, church-raisings, house-raisings, ship launchings, and, in truth, ministers' ordinations. Thanksgiving was a peculiarly New England holiday, observed from the first with fitting solemnity. Christmas was associated in the Puritan mind with the "Lords of Misrule," with riot and drunkenness. Though commemorated outside New England, and by the Anglicans in Boston as early as 1686, it never came to be regarded generally as a day of joy and good will until the mid-nineteenth century.

The Anglo-Saxon race has never been regarded an abstemious stock. "I will tell you," Samuel Nowell remarked in the course of an Artillery Election address,

> I will tell you how we breed up Souldiers, both in old England and New, every Farmers Son, when he goes to the Market-Town, must have money in his purse; and when he meets with his Companions, they goe to the Tavern or Ale-house, and seldome away before Drunk, or well tipled. It is rare to find men that we can call Drunkards, but there are abundance of Tiplers in *New-England*. [1]

Colman spoke his mind even more eloquently: "But above all kinds of vain Mirth deliver me from the *Drunken Club*, who belch out noisy *Ribaldry* rank of the foul lees within." [2] Taverns, though maintained for travelers, were too often the gathering places for idle drinkers. Unlike their English counterparts, they were not famous for their plenty and their genial comfort. No better account survives of the poor

---

[1] *Abraham in Arms* (Boston, 1678), p. 15.
[2] *Government . . . of Mirth*, p. 48.

appearance and slatternly service of early New England inns than
Madam Knight's *Journal* (see p. 425). It is easy to understand why
travelers preferred to lodge with friends or acquaintances along the way
when business compelled them to set out upon a journey. Those who
could do so went by water; the rest stayed home.

A final word on the attitude of the Puritans toward the arts. Drama
they banned, because they evidently gave great weight to the injunc-
tions urged against it by the primitive church, and also because they
knew it in their day as an art supported by a court which they disap-
proved, and as a theater which, in the words of Chesterfield on decorum,
combined the useful appearance of virtue with the solid satisfaction of
vice. There was still bitter with them the caricatures of Puritans in Mal-
volio and Zeal-of-the-Land Busy. The Restoration stage was scarcely
one to attract God-centered men; but in the eighteenth century, with
the return of sentimental drama, we find *The New-England Weekly Journal*
printing Lillo's *George Barnwell* (1731) within a year of its appearance in
London, defending the work on the grounds that it tended to promote
virtue and piety.[1]

Because Puritans held to the older tradition of *a cappella* singing in
their churches, while Anglicans admitted instrumentalists, an idea has
passed current that they were hostile to music. The truth is otherwise.
Puritans produced the first Italian opera in England, Cromwell supported an orchestra at court, and in this country music, both secular
and sacred, was encouraged (see p. 451), as Sewall's Diary often indicates.[2]

Possession of fine architecture, tapestries, painting, and sculpture
depends as much upon the wealth as the taste of the purchaser. As
money increased, the arts followed. An inventory of Peter Sargent's
property in 1714 lists a tapestry. The great house of William Clark
of Boston, with its fluted pilasters, is known to have contained at his
death in 1715, oil paintings, a mosaic floor of wood, and painted ara-
besques.[3] It may be that Puritan inventories list few works of art because the fathers had seldom been men of property; besides, taste itself
needs training. Yet we cannot be far wrong if we see the typical Puri-

[1] It is well to note that even outside New England drama revived slowly. No
professional actors performed in any of the colonies until the eighteenth century,
when a play was given in Charleston, South Carolina, in 1703. Professionals were
not established in New York until 1732.

[2] See Percy A. Scholes, *The Puritans and Music in England and New England* (London,
1934). The organ owned by Thomas Brattle, and willed by him in 1713 to the church
which he founded, was rejected solely on grounds of polity.

[3] George F. Dow, *Every Day Life, passim.*

tan as one dedicated to the glory of God, though living in this world; accepting its fashions as long as they did not run counter to God's Word—and sometimes interpreting that Word to fit his own taste.

JOHN SMITH, 1580–1631

[No Puritan, John Smith was of that company of Elizabethan sea dogs, the story of whose lives, written both in word and deed, is treasured up in Hakluyt's famous *Voyages*. Smith's career is too well known to need rehearsing. The "sometimes Governour of Virginia, and Admirall of New-England" was a promoter whose conscious purpose was to enlarge the King's dominions. He left several vivid and picturesque accounts of his travels. *Advertisement For the unexperienced Planters of New-England, or anywhere. Or, The Path-way to experience to erect a Plantation* (London, 1631) was his last work, dedicated to the archbishops of Canterbury and York, and prefaced by the pathetic stanzas called "The Sea Marke," wherein the aging traveler pictures himself as a battered hulk and a warning to after-comers.

Smith's description of the founding of Massachusetts Bay is a memorable account and deserves to be better known. The author tells his story with dramatic force, in crisp and racy diction, pausing in the onward rush only to limn the portrait of some founder or to exclaim over the natural beauties of the newly discovered wilderness.

The text is from a copy of the original edition in the New York Public Library (pp. 18–29, with omissions indicated). See Tyler, *A History of American Literature*, I, 18–38; *Dictionary of American Biography;* and especially Samuel E. Morison, *Builders of the Bay Colony*, chap. I.]

THE SEA MARKE.

Aloofe, aloofe, and come no neare,[1]
    the dangers doe appeare;
Which if my ruine had not beene
    you had not seene:
I onely lie upon this shelfe
    to be a marke to all
    which on the same might fall,
That none may perish but my selfe.

If in or outward you be bound,
    doe not forget to sound;
Neglect of that was cause of this
    to steare amisse.

The Seas were calme, the wind was faire,
      that made me so secure,[2]
      that now I must indure
All weathers be they foule or faire.

The Winters cold, the Summers heat,
            alternatively beat
Upon my bruised sides, that rue
            because too true
That no releefe can ever come.
      But why should I despaire
      being promised so faire
That there shall be a day of Dome.

ADVERTISEMENT FOR THE UNEXPERIENCED PLANTERS

CHAP. 8.

EXTREMITY NEXT DESPAIRE, GODS GREAT MERCY, THEIR ESTATE, THEY MAKE GOOD SALT, AN UNKNOWNE RICH MYNE.

1623.

AT *New-Plimoth*, having planted there Fields and Gardens, such an extraordinary drought insued, all things withered, that they expected no harvest; and having long expected a supply, they heard no newes, but a wracke split upon their Coast, they supposed their Ship: thus in the very labyrinth of despaire, they solemnly assembled themselves together nine houres in prayer. At their departure, the parching faire skies all overcast with blacke clouds, and the next morning, such a pleasant moderate raine continued fourteene daies, that it was hard to say, whether their withered fruits or drooping affections were most revived; not long after came two Ships to supply them, with all their Passengers well, except one, and he presently recovered; for themselves, for all their wants, there was not one sicke person amongst them: the greater Ship they returned fraught with commodities. This yeare went from *England*, onely *Five and forty saile to fish.* to fish, five and forty saile, and have all made a better voyage than ever.

1624.

In this Plantation there is about an hundred and fourescore persons, some Cattell, but many Swine and Poultry: their Towne containes two and thirty houses,

wherof seven were burnt, with the value of five or six
hundred pounds in other goods, impailed about halfe
a mile, within which within a high Mount, a Fort, with
a Watch-tower, well built of stone, lome, and wood,
their Ordnance well mounted, and so healthfull, that
of the first Planters not one hath died this three yeares:
yet at the first landing at *Cape Cod*, being an hundred
passengers, besides twenty they had left behind at *Pli-
moth* for want of good take heed, thinking to finde all
things better than I advised them, spent six or seven
weekes in wandring up and downe in frost and snow,
wind and raine, among the woods, cricks, and swamps,
forty of them died, and threescore were left in most
miserable estate at *New-Plimoth*, where their Ship left
them, and but nine leagues by Sea from where they
landed, whose misery and variable opinions, for want
of experience, occasioned much faction, till necessity
agreed them. These disasters, losses, and uncertainties,
made such disagreement among the Adventurers in *England*, who beganne to repent, and rather lose all, than
longer continue the charge, being out of purse six or
seven thousand pounds, accounting my bookes and their
relations as old Almanacks. But the Planters, rather than
leave the Country, concluded absolutely to supply themselves, and to all their adventurers pay them for nine
yeares two hundred pounds yearely without any other
account; where more than six hundred Adventurers for
Virginia, for more than two hundred thousand pounds,
had not six pence. Since they have made a salt worke, *They make*
wherewith they preserve all the fish they take, and have *store of good*
fraughted this yeare a ship of an hundred and foure- *salt.*
score tun, living so well they desire nothing but more
company, and what ever they take, returne commodities
to the value.

This you may plainly see, although many envying I
should bring so much from thence, where many others
had beene, and some the same yeare returned with
nothing, reported the Fish and Bevers I brought home,
I had taken from the French men of *Canada*, to discourage any from beleeving me, and excuse their owne
misprisions, some onely to have concealed this good
Country (as is said) to their private use; others taxed
me as much of indiscretion, to make my discoveries and
designes so publike for nothing, which might have beene
so well managed by some concealers, to have beene all

rich ere any had knowne of it. Those, and many such like wise rewards, have beene my recompences, for which I am contented, so the Country prosper, and Gods name bee there praised by my Country-men, I have my desire; and the benefit of this salt and fish, for breeding Mariners and building ships, will make so many

An incredible rich mine.

fit men to raise a Common-wealth, if but managed, as my generall history will shew you; it might well by this have beene as profitable as the best Mine the King of *Spaine* hath in his West Indies. . . .

Chap. 11.

The planting Bastable or Salem and Charlton, a description of the Massachusets.

1629. The Planting Salem.

In all those plantations, yea, of those that have done least, yet the most will say, we were the first; and so every next supply, still the next beginner: But seeing history is the memory of time, the life of the dead, and the happinesse of the living; because I have more plainly discovered, and described, and discoursed of those Countries than any as yet I know, I am the bolder to continue the story, and doe all men right so neere as I can in those new beginnings, which hereafter perhaps may bee in better request than a forest of nine dayes pamphlets.

Their provisions for Salem.

In the yeare 1629. about March, six good ships are gone with 350. men, women, and children, people professing themselves of good ranke, zeale, meanes and quality: also 150. head of cattell, as horse, mares, and neat beasts; 41. goats, some conies, with all provision for houshold and apparell; six peeces of great Ordnance for a Fort, with Muskets, Pikes, Corslets, Drums and Colours, with all provisions necessary for the good of man. They are seated about 42. degrees and 38. minutes, at a place called by the natives *Naemkecke*, by our Royall King *Charles*, *Bastable;* but now by the planters, *Salem;* where they arrived for most part exceeding well, their cattell and all things else prospering exceedingly, farre beyond their expectation.

The planting Salem and Charlton.

At this place they found some reasonable good provision and houses built by some few of *Dorchester*, with whom they are joyned in society with two hundred men, an hundred and fifty more they have sent to the *Massachusets*, which they call *Charlton*, or *Charles* Towne: I

tooke the fairest reach in this Bay for a river, whereupon
I called it *Charles* river, after the name of our Royall
King *Charles;* but they find that faire Channell to divide
it selfe into so many faire branches as make forty or
fifty pleasant Ilands within that excellent Bay, where
the land is of divers and sundry sorts, in some places
very blacke and fat, in others good clay, sand and gravell,
the superficies neither too flat in plaines, nor too high
in hils. In the Iles you may keepe your hogs, horse,
cattell, conies or poultry, and secure for little or nothing,
and to command when you list, onely having a care
of provision for some extraordinary cold winter. In those
Iles, as in the maine, you may make your nurseries for
fruits and plants where you put no cattell; in the maine
you may shape your Orchards, Vineyards, Pastures,
Gardens, Walkes, Parkes, and Corne fields out of the
whole peece as you please into such plots, one adjoyning
to another, leaving every of them invironed with two,
three, foure, or six, or so many rowes of well growne
trees as you will, ready growne to your hands, to defend
them from ill weather, which in a champion you could
not in many ages; and this at first you may doe with
as much facility, as carelessly or ignorantly cut downe
all before you, and then after better consideration make
ditches, pales, plant young trees with an excessive charge
and labour, seeing you may have so many great and
small growing trees for your maine posts, to fix hedges,
palisados, houses, rales, or what you will; which order
in *Virginia* hath not beene so well observed as it might:
where all the woods for many an hundred mile for the
most part grow streight, like unto the high grove or
tuft of trees, upon the high hill by the house of that
worthy Knight Sir *Humphrey Mildmay*,[3] so remarkable in
Essex in the Parish of *Danbery*, where I writ this discourse,
but much taller and greater, neither grow they so thicke
together by the halfe, and much good ground betweene
them without shrubs, and the best is ever knowne by the
greatnesse of the trees and the vesture it beareth. Now
in *New-England* the trees are commonly lower, but much
thicker and firmer wood, and more proper for shipping,
of which I will speake a little, being the chiefe engine
wee are to use in this worke, and the rather for that
within a square of twenty leagues, you may have all,
or most of the chiefe materials belonging to them, were
they wrought to their perfection as in other places. . . .

A description of the Massachusets Bay.

CHAP. 13.

THEIR GREAT SUPPLIES, PRESENT ESTATE
AND ACCIDENTS, ADVANTAGE.

1630.
Their present
estate.

Who would not thinke but that all those trials had beene sufficient to lay a foundation for a plantation, but we see many men many mindes, and still new Lords, new lawes: for those 350. men with all their cattell that so well arived and promised so much, not being of one body, but severall mens servants, few could command and fewer obey, lived merrily of that they had, neither planting or building any thing to any purpose, but one faire house for the Governour, till all was spent and the winter approached; then they grew into many diseases, and as many inconveniences, depending only of a supply from *England*, which expected Houses, Gardens, and Corne fields ready planted by them for their entertainment.

It is true, that Master *Iohn Wynthrop*,[4] their now Governour, a worthy Gentleman both in estate and esteeme, went so well provided (for six or seven hundred people went with him) as could be devised, but at Sea, such an extraordinarie storme encountred his Fleet, continuing ten daies, that of two hundred Cattell which were so tossed and brused, threescore and ten died, many of their people fell sicke, and in this perplexed estate, after ten weekes, they arrived in *New-England* at severall times, where they found threescore of their people dead, the rest sicke, nothing done, but all complaining, and all things so contrary to their expectation, that now every monstrous humor began to shew it selfe. And to second this, neare as many more came after them, but so ill provided, with such multitudes of women and children, as redoubled their necessities.

The fruits of
counterfeits.

This small triall of their patience, caused among them no small confusion, and put the Governour and his Councell to their utmost wits; some could not endure the name of a Bishop, others not the sight of a Crosse nor Surplesse, others by no meanes the booke of common Prayer. This absolute crue, only of the Elect, holding all (but such as themselves) reprobates and cast-awaies, now make more haste to returne to *Babel*, as they tearmed *England*, than stay to enjoy the land they called *Canaan;* somewhat they must say to excuse themselves. . . .

THOMAS LECHFORD, *fl.* 1629–1642

[Thomas Lechford was the first professional lawyer in Massachusetts Bay. Refusing preferment abroad, he emigrated to New England in 1638, but he was not in sympathy with affairs, and, never becoming a church member, could not vote or hold public office. Debarred from practice in 1641 for trying to influence a jury, he returned to England in disgust, leaving his wife and household goods behind.

Lechford's pique found expression in a volume published in London after his return: *Plain Dealing: or, Newes from New-England* (1642). It is salutary, perhaps, to see the Bay Colony through the eyes of one whose opinions were not colored by close attachments.

Plain Dealing was shortly reissued with a new title and was reprinted twice in the nineteenth century. A "Notebook" which he kept from 1638 to 1641 is also available. See *Dictionary of American Biography.*]

PLAIN DEALING

FOR THE STATE OF THE COUNTRY IN THE BAY AND THEREABOUTS.

THE LAND is reasonable fruitfull, as I think; they have cattle, and goats, and swine good store, and some horses, store of fish and fowle, venison, and * corne, both *English* and *Indian*. They are indifferently well able to subsist for victuall. They are setting on the manufacture of linnen and cotton cloath, and the fishing trade, and they are building of ships, and have good store of barks, catches, lighters, shallops, and other vessels. They have builded and planted to admiration for the time. There are good masts and timber for shipping, planks, and boards, clap-board, pipe-staves, bever, and furres, and hope of some mines. There are Beares, Wolves, and Foxes, and many other wilde beasts, as the Moose, a kind of Deere, as big as some Oxen, and Lyons, as I have heard. The Wolves and Foxes are a great annoyance. There are Rattlesnakes, which sometimes doe some harme, not much; He that is stung with any of them, or bitten, he turnes of the colour of the Snake, all over his body, blew, white, and greene spotted; and swelling, dyes, unlesse he timely get some Snake-weed;[1] which if he eate, and rub on the wound, he may haply recover, but feele it a long while in his bones and body. Money is wanting, by reason of the failing of passengers these two last yeares, in a manner. They want help to goe

State of the Countrey of New-England.
*Wheat and Barley are thought not to be so good as those grains in England; but the Rye and Pease are as good as the English: the Pease have no wormes at all. Beanes also there are very good.

forward, for their subsistance in regard of cloathing: And great pity it would be, but men of estates should help them forward. It may bee, I hope, a charitable worke. The price of their cattell, and other things being fallen, they are not at present able to make such returns to *England*, as were to be wished for them: God above direct and provide for them. There are multitudes of godly men among them, and many poore ignorant soules. Of late some thirty persons went in two small Barks for the *Lords Isle of Providence*,[2] and for the Maine thereabout, which is held to be a beter countrey and climate by some: For this being in about 46. degrees of northerne latitude, yet is very cold in winter, so that some are frozen to death, or lose their fingers or toes every yeere, sometimes by carlesnes, sometimes by accidents, and are lost in snowes, which there are very deepe sometimes, and lye long: Winter begins in October, and lasts till Aprill. Sixty leagues Northerly it is held not habitable, yet again in Summer it is exceeding hot. If shipping for conveyance were sent thither, they might spare divers hundreds of men for any good design. The jurisdiction of the *Bay* Patent reacheth from *Pascattaqua* Patent Northeast to *Plymouth* Patent Southward. And in my travailes there, I have seene the towns of *Newberry*, *Ipswich*, *Salem*, *Lynne*, *Boston*, *Charlestowne*, *Cambridge*, *Watertowne*, *Concord*, *Roxbury*, *Dorchester*, and *Braintree* in the *Bay* Patent, *New Taunton* in *Plymouth* Patent, the Island *Aquedney*, and the two townes therein, *Newport* and *Portsmouth*, and *New Providence* within the *Bay* of *Narhiggansets*. This for the satisfaction of some that have reported I was no Travailer in *New-England*. . . .

WHEN I WAS TO COME AWAY, ONE OF THE CHIEFEST
IN THE COUNTRY WISHED ME TO DELIVER HIM
A NOTE OF WHAT THINGS I MISLIKED IN
THE COUNTRY, WHICH I DID, THUS:

I doubt,

1. Whether so much time should be spent in the publique Ordinances, on the Sabbath day, because that thereby some necessary duties of the Sabbath must needs be hindred, as visitation of the sick, and poore, and family.

2. Whether matters of offence should be publiquely handled, either before the whole Church, or strangers.

3. Whether so much time should be spent in particular catechizing those that are admitted to the communion of the Church, either men or women; or that they should make long speeches; or when they come publiquely to be admitted, any should speak contradictorily, or in recommendation of any, unlesse before the Elders, upon just occasion.

4. Whether the censures of the Church should be ordered, in publique, before all the Church, or strangers, other then the denunciation of the censures, and pronunciation of the solutions.

5. Whether any of our *Nation* that is not extremely ignorant or scandalous, should bee kept from the Communion, or his children from *Baptisme*.

6. That many thousands in this Countrey have forgotten the very principles of Religion, which they were daily taught in *England*, by set forms and Scriptures read, as the Psalmes, first and second Lesson, the ten Commandments, the Creeds, and publique catechizings. And although conceived Prayer be good and holy, and so publike explications and applications of the Word, and also necessary both in and out of season: yet for the most part it may be feared they dull, amaze, confound, discourage the weake and ignorant, (which are the most of men) when they are in ordinary performed too tediously, or with the neglect of the Word read, and other premeditated formes inculcated, and may tend to more ignorance and inconvenience, then many good men are aware of.

7. I doubt there hath been, and is much neglect of endeavours, to teach, civilize, and convert the *Indian Nation*, that are about the Plantations.

8. Whether by the received principles, it bee *possible* to teach, civilize, or convert them, or when they are converted, to maintain Gods worship among them.

9. That electorie courses will not long be safe here, either in Church or Common-wealth.

JASPER DANCKAERTS, 1639–*ca.* 1703

[During the last quarter of the seventeenth century a sect of the Dutch Reformed Church called Labadists settled in Maryland and Delaware. With evangelical earnestness the small group, which ceased to exist by 1727, lived a communal existence, sustained principally by agriculture. In 1679 two representatives from the central church in Friesland, Jasper Danckaerts and Peter Sluyter (1645–1722), crossed the ocean to transact business with the provincial associates. Their mission accomplished, the two men traveled north through New York to Boston before returning to Holland. They remained in Boston from June 19 to July 23, 1680, and the *Journal* of their voyage, especially of their sojourn in Cambridge and vicinity, makes delightful reading.

The manuscript in Danckaerts's handwriting is in the possession of the Long Island Historical Society. It was first printed by the Society in 1867, soon after its discovery. The text, together with the notes, is from the *Journal of Jasper Danckaerts, 1679–1680*, ed. by B. B. James and J. F. Jameson (New York, 1913), pp. 254, 255, 258–269, 272–275.]

JOURNAL OF JASPER DANCKAERTS

JUNE, 1680] About three o'clock we caught sight of the main land of Cape Cod, to which we sailed northerly. We arrived inside the cape about six o'clock, with a tolerable breeze from the west, and at the same time saw vessels to the leeward of us which had an east wind, from which circumstance we supposed we were in a whirlwind. These two contrary winds striking against each other, the sky became dark, and they whirled by each other, sometimes the one, and sometimes the other being strongest, compelling us to lower the sails several times. I have never seen such a twisting and turning round in the air as at this time, the clouds being driven against each other, and close to the earth. At last it became calm and began to rain very hard, and to thunder and lighten heavily. We drifted along the whole night in a calm, advancing only twelve or sixteen miles.

23d, Sunday. A breeze blew up from the northeast. It was fortunate for us that we arrived inside of Cape Cod yesterday evening, before this unfavorable weather, as we should otherwise have been compelled to put back to Rhode Island. We could now still proceed; and we laid our course northwest to Boston. We arrived at the entrance of the harbor at noon, where we found a considerable rolling sea caused by the ebb tide and wind being against each other. There are about thirty islands here, not large ones, through which we sailed, and reached Boston at four o'clock in the afternoon, our captain running with his yacht quite up to his house in the Milk-ditch.[1]

The Lord be praised, who has continued in such a fatherly manner to conduct us, and given us so many proofs of His care over us; words are wanting to express ourselves properly, more than occasions for them, which we have had abundantly.

We permitted those most in haste to go ashore before us, and then went ourselves. The skipper received us politely at his house, and so did his wife; but as it was Sunday, which it seems is somewhat strictly observed by these people, there was not much for us to do today. Our captain, however, took us to his sister's where we were welcome, and from there to his father's, an old corpulent man, where there was a repetition of the worship, which took place in the kitchen while they were turning the spit, and busy preparing a good supper. We arrived while they were engaged in the service, but he did not once look up. When he had finished, they turned round their backs, and kneeled on chairs or benches. The prayer was said loud enough to be heard three houses off, and also long enough, if that made it good. This done, he wished us and his son welcome, and insisted on our supping with him, which we did. . . .

24*th, Monday.* We walked with our captain into the town, for his house stood a little one side of it, and the first house he took us to was a tavern. From there, he conducted us to the governor, who dwelt in only a common house, and that not the most costly. He is an old man, quiet and grave.[2] He was dressed in black silk, but not sumptuously. Paddechal explained the reasons of our visit. The governor inquired who we were, and where from, and where we were going. Paddechal told him we were Hollanders, and had come on with him from New York, in order to depart from here for England. He asked further our names, which we wrote down for him. He then presented us a small cup of wine, and with that we finished. We went then to the house of one John Tayller, or merchant tailor,[3] to whom William van Cleyf had recommended us; but we did not find him. We wanted to obtain a place where we could be at home, and especially to ascertain if there were any Dutchmen. They told us of a silversmith who was a Dutchman, and at whose house the Dutch usually went to lodge. We went in search of him, but he was not at home. At noon we found this merchant tailor, who appeared to be a good sort of a person. He spoke tolerably good French, and informed us there was a ship up for England immediately, and another in about three weeks. The first was too soon for us, and we therefore thought it best to wait for the other. We also found the silversmith, who bade us welcome. His name was Willem Ros, from Wesel. He had married an Englishwoman, and carried on his business here. He told us we might come and lodge with him, if we wished, which we determined to do; for to lie again in our last night's nest was not agreeable to us. We exchanged some of our money, and obtained six shillings and six-pence each for our ducatoons, and ten shillings each for the ducats. We went accordingly to lodge at the goldsmith's, whom my comrade knew well, though he did not recollect my comrade.[4] We were better off at his house, for although his wife was an Englishwoman, she was quite a good housekeeper.

25*th, Tuesday.* We went in search of Mr. Paddechal this morning and paid him for our passage here, twenty shillings New England currency, for each of us. We wanted to obtain our goods, but they were all too busy then, and promised they would send them to us in the city the next day. We inquired after Mr. John Pigon, to whom Mr. Robert Sanders, of Albany, promised to send Wouter the Indian, with a letter, but he had received neither the letter nor the Indian; so that we must offer up our poor Indian to the pleasure of the Lord. We also went to look after the ship, in which we were going to leave for London. We understood the name of the captain was Jan Foy. The ship was called the *Dolphin*, and mounted sixteen guns.[5] Several passengers were engaged. There was a surgeon in the service of the ship from Rotterdam, named Johan Owins, who had been to Surinam [6] and afterwards to the island of Fayal,[7] from whence he had come here, and now wished to go home. There was also a sailor on board the ship who spoke Dutch, or was a Dutchman. The carpenter was a Norwegian who lived at Flushing.

26*th, Wednesday.* We strove hard to get our goods home, for we were fearful, inasmuch as our trunk was on deck, and it had rained, and a sea now and then had washed over it, that it might be wet and ruined; but we did not succeed, and Paddechal in this exhibited again his inconsiderateness, and little regard for his promise. We resolved to take it out the next day, go as it would.

27*th, Thursday.* We went to the Exchange in order to find the merchant tailor, and also the skipper, which we did. We agreed for our passage at the usual price of six pounds sterling for each person, with the choice of paying here or in England; but as we would have less loss on our money here, we determined to pay here. After 'change was over there was preaching,[8] to which we had intended to go; but as we had got our goods home, after much trouble, and found several articles wet and liable to be spoiled, we had to stay and dry them.

28*th, Friday.* One of the best ministers in the place being very sick, a day of fasting and prayer was observed in a church near by our house. We went into the church, where, in the first place, a minister made a prayer in the pulpit, of full two hours in length; after which an old minister delivered a sermon an hour long, and after that a prayer was made, and some verses sung out of the Psalms. In the afternoon, three or four hours were consumed with nothing except prayers, three ministers relieving each other alternately; when one was tired, another went up into the pulpit.[9] There was no more devotion than in other churches, and even less than at New York; no respect, no reverence; in a word, nothing but the name of Independents; and that was all. . . .

7th, Sunday. We heard preaching in three churches, by persons who seemed to possess zeal, but no just knowledge of Christianity. The auditors were very worldly and inattentive. The best of the ministers whom we have yet heard is a very old man, named Mr. John Eliot,[10] who has charge of the instruction of the Indians in the Christian religion. He has translated the Bible into their language. After we had already made inquiries of the booksellers for this Bible, and there was none to be obtained in Boston, and they told us if one was to be had, it would be from Mr. Eliot, we determined to go on Monday to the village where he resided, and was the minister, called Rocsberry [Roxbury]. Our landlord had promised to take us, but was not able to do so, in consequence of his having too much business. We therefore thought we would go alone and do what we wanted.

JULY *8th, Monday.* We went accordingly, about six o'clock in the morning, to Rocxberry, which is three-quarters of an hour from the city, in order that we might get home early, inasmuch as our captain had informed us, he would come in the afternoon for our money, and in order that Mr. Eliot might not be gone from home. On arriving at his house, he was not there, and we therefore went to look around the village and the vicinity. We found it justly called Rocxberry, for it was very rocky, and had hills entirely of rocks. Returning to his house we spoke to him, and he received us politely. As he could speak neither Dutch nor French, and we spoke but little English, we were unable to converse very well; however, partly in Latin, partly in English, we managed to understand each other. He was seventy-seven years old,[11] and had been forty-eight years in these parts. He had learned very well the language of the Indians, who lived about there. We asked him for an Indian Bible. He said in the late Indian war, all the Bibles and Testaments were carried away, and burnt or destroyed, so that he had not been able to save any for himself; but a new edition was in press, which he hoped would be much better than the first one, though that was not to be despised. We inquired whether any part of the old and new edition could be obtained by purchase, and whether there was any grammar of their language in English. Thereupon he went and brought us one of the Old Testaments in the Indian language, and also almost the whole of the New Testament, made up with some sheets of the new edition of the New Testament, so that we had the Old and New Testaments complete. . . .[12]

He deplored the decline of the church in New England, and especially in Boston, so that he did not know what would be the final result. We inquired how it stood with the Indians, and whether any good fruit had followed his work. Yes, much, he said, if we meant true conversion of the heart; for they had in various countries, instances of conversion, as they called it, and had seen it amounted to nothing at all; that they must not endeavor, like scribes and Pharisees, to make Jewish proselytes, but true Christians. He could thank God, he continued, and God be praised for it, there were Indians whom he knew, who were truly converted of heart to God, and whose profession, he believed, was sincere. It seemed as if he were disposed to know us further, and we therefore said to him, if he had any desire to write to our sort of people, he could use the names which stood on the title-page of the *Declaration*, and that we hoped to come and converse with him again. He accompanied us as far as the jurisdiction of Roxbury extended, where we parted from him.

9th, Tuesday. We started out to go to Cambridge, lying to the north-east of Boston, in order to see their college and printing office. We left about six o'clock in the morning, and were set across the river at Charlestown. We followed a road which we supposed was the right one, but went full half an hour out of the way, and would have gone still further, had not a negro who met us, and of whom we inquired, disabused us of our mistake. We went back to the right road, which is a very pleasant one. We reached Cambridge about eight o'clock. It is not a large village, and the houses stand very much apart. The college building is the most conspicuous among them. We went to it, expecting to see something unusual, as it is the only college, or would-be academy of the Protestants in all America, but we found ourselves mistaken. In approaching the house we neither heard nor saw anything mentionable; but, going to the other side of the building, we heard noise enough in an upper room to lead my comrade to say, "I believe they are engaged in disputation." We entered and went up stairs, when a person met us, and requested us to walk in, which we did. We found there eight or ten young fellows, sitting around, smoking tobacco, with the smoke of which the room was so full, that you could hardly see; and the whole house smelt so strong of it that when I was going up stairs I said, "It certainly must be also a tavern."[13] We excused ourselves, that we could speak English only a little, but understood Dutch or French well, which they did not. However, we spoke as well as we could. We inquired how many professors there were, and they replied not one, that there was not enough money to support one. We asked how many students there were. They said at first, thirty, and then came down to twenty; I afterwards understood there are probably not ten. They knew hardly a word of Latin, not one of them, so that my comrade could not converse with them. They took us to the library where there was nothing particular. We looked over it a little. They presented us with a glass of wine. This is all we ascertained there. The minister of the place goes there morning and evening to make prayer, and has charge over them; besides him, the students are under tutors or masters.[14] Our visit was soon over, and we left them to go and look at the land about there. We found the place beautifully situated on a large plain, more than eight miles square, with a fine stream in the middle of it, capable of bearing heavily laden vessels. As regards the fertility of the soil, we consider the poorest in New York superior to the best here. As we were tired, we took a mouthful to eat, and left. We passed by the printing office, but there was nobody in it; the paper sash however being broken, we looked in, and saw two presses with six or eight cases of type. There is not much work done there. Our printing office is well worth two of it, and even more.[15] We went back to Charlestown, where, after waiting a little, we crossed over about three o'clock. . . .

But before going further to sea we must give a brief description of New England, and the city of Boston in particular.

When New Netherland was first discovered by the Hollanders, the evidence is that New England was not known; because the Dutch East India Company then sought a passage by the west, through which to sail to Japan and China; and if New England had been then discovered, they would not have sought a passage there, knowing it to be the main land; just as when New Netherland and New England did become known, such a passage was sought no longer through them, but farther to the north through Davis and Hudson straits. The Hollanders, when they discovered New Netherland, embraced under that name and title all the coast from Virginia or Cape Hinloopen eastwardly to Cape Cod, as it was then and there discovered by them and designated by Dutch names, as sufficiently appears by the charts. The English afterwards discovered New England and settled there.[16] They increased so in consequence of the great liberties and favorable privileges which the king granted to the Independents, that they went to live not only west of Cape Cod and Rhode Island, but also on Long Island and other places, and even took possession of the whole of the Fresh River,[17] which the Hollanders there were not able to prevent, in consequence of their small force in New Netherland, and the scanty population. The English went more readily to the west, because the land was much better there, and more accessible to vessels, and the climate was milder; and also because they could trade more conveniently with the Hollanders, and be supplied by them with provisions. New England is now described as extending from the Fresh River to Cape Cod and thence to Kennebec, comprising three provinces or colonies: Fresh River or Connecticut, Rhode Island and the other islands to Cape Cod, and Boston, which stretches from thence north. They are subject to no one, but acknowledge the king of England for their lord,[18] and therefore no ships enter unless they have English passports or commissions. They have free trade with all countries; but the return cargoes from there to Europe go to England, except those which go secretly to Holland. There is no toll or duty paid upon merchandise exported or imported, nor is there any impost or tax paid upon land. Each province chooses its own governor from the magistracy, and the magistrates are chosen from the principal inhabitants, merchants or planters. They are all Independents in matters of religion, if it can be called religion; many of them perhaps more for the purposes of enjoying the benefit of its privileges than for any regard to truth and godliness. I observed that while the English flag or color has a red ground with a small white field in the uppermost corner, where there is a red cross, they have here dispensed with this cross in their colors, and preserved the rest.[19] They baptize no children except those of the members of the congregation. All their religion consists in observing Sunday, by not working or going into the taverns on that day; but the houses are worse than the taverns. No stranger or traveller can therefore be entertained on a Sunday, which begins at sunset on Saturday, and continues until the same time on Sunday. At these two hours you see all their countenances change. Saturday evening the constable goes round into all the taverns of the city for the purpose of stopping all noise and debauchery, which frequently causes him to stop his search, before his search causes the debauchery to stop. There is a penalty for cursing and swearing, such as they please to impose, the witnesses thereof being at liberty to insist upon it. Nevertheless you discover little difference between this and other places. Drinking and fighting occur there not less than elsewhere; and as to truth and true godliness, you must not expect more of them than of others. When we were there, four ministers' sons were learning the silversmith's trade.

The soil is not as fertile as in the west. Many persons leave there to go to the Delaware and New Jersey. They manure their lands with heads of fish. They gain their living mostly or very much by fish, which they salt and dry for selling; and by raising horses, oxen, and cows, as well as hogs and sheep, which they sell alive, or slaughtered and salted, in the Caribbean Islands and other places. They are not as good farmers as the Hollanders about New York.

INCREASE MATHER

["Seasonable merriment" was a phrase the Puritans often used approvingly, but they interpreted it after their own fashion. "Dancing (yea though mixt) I would not simply condemn." John Cotton had written a friend in 1625, justifying it from the Old Testament: "Only lascivious dancing to wanton ditties" (*Collections of the Massachusetts Historical Society*, second series, X (1823), 183). The thirty-page essay which Increase Mather published in Boston in 1684: *An Arrow against Profane and Promiscuous Dancing. Drawn out of a Quiver of the Scriptures*, resulted from a ministers' discussion. It is stricter in tone than Cotton's letter, and in the eyes of twentieth-century readers seems to lay a disproportionate stress on moral inessentials. By 1716, at least, dancing was taught in Boston by Edward Euston, the organist of the Episcopal King's Chapel, who thus augmented his salary, and he met with no interference. See *Diary of Samuel Sewall*, III, 111 note.

For Mather, see p. 334. The text is from pp. 1–3, 27–30, with omissions indicated.]

AN ARROW AGAINST PROFANE AND PROMISCUOUS DANCING

CONCERNING the Controversy about *Dancing*, the Question is not, whether all *Dancing* be in it self sinful. It is granted, that *Pyrrhical* or *Polemical Saltation:* i.e. when men vault in their Armour, to shew their strength and activity, may be of use. Nor is the question, whether a sober and grave *Dancing* of Men with Men, or of Women with Women, be not allowable; we make no doubt of that, where it may be done without offence, in due season, and with moderation. The Prince of Philosophers has observed truly, that *Dancing* or *Leaping*, is a natural expression of joy: So that there is no more Sin in it, than in laughter, or any outward expression of inward Rejoycing.

But our question is concerning *Gynecandrical Dancing*, or that which is commonly called *Mixt* or *Promiscuous Dancing, viz.* of Men and Women (be they elder or younger persons) together: Now this we affirm to be utterly unlawful, and that it cannot be tollerated in such a place as *New-England*, without great Sin. And that it may appear, that we are not transported by Affection without Judgment, let the following Arguments be weighed in the Ballance of the Sanctuary.

Arg. 1. *That which the Scripture condemns is sinful.* None but Atheists will deny this *Proposition:* But the Scripture condemns *Promiscuous Dancing.* This *Assumption* is proved, 1. *From the Seventh Commandment.* It is an Eternal Truth to be observed in expounding the Commandments, that whenever any sin is forbidden, not only the highest acts of that sin, but all degrees thereof, and all occasions leading thereto are prohibited. Now we cannot find one Orthodox and Judicious Divine, that writeth on the Commandments, but mentions *Promiscuous Dancing*, as a breach of the seventh Commandment, as being an occasion, and an incentive to that which is evil in the sight of God. Yea, this is so manifest as that the *Assembly* in the *larger Catechism*, do expresly take notice of *Dancings*, as a violation of the Commandments. It is sad, that when in times of Reformation, Children have been taught in their C[a]techism, that such *Dancing* is against the Commandment of God, that now in *New-England* they should practically be learned the contrary. The unchast Touches and Gesticulations used by *Dancers*, have a palpable tendency to that which is evil. Whereas some object, that they are not sensible of any ill motions occasioned in them, by being Spectators or Actors in such *Saltations;* we are not bound to believe all which some pretend concerning their own Mortification. . . .

Now they that frequent Promiscuous Dancings, or that send their Children thereunto, walk disorderly, and contrary to the Apostles Doctrine. It has been proved that such a practice is a *Scandalous Immorality*, and therefore to be removed out of Churches by Discipline, which is the Broom of Christ, whereby he keeps his Churches clean. . . .

And shall Churches in *N[ew] E[ngland]* who have had a Name to be stricter and purer than other Churches, suffer such a scandalous evil amongst them? if all that are under Discipline be made sensible of this matter, we shall not be much or long infested with a *Choreutical Dæmon.* . . .

The Catechism which Wicked men teach their Children is to Dance and to Sing. Not that Dancing, or Musick, or Singing are in themselves sinful: but if the Dancing Master be wicked they are commonly abused to lasciviousness, and that makes them to become abominable. But will you that are Professors of Religion have your Children to be thus taught? the Lord expects that you should give the Children who are Baptized into his Name another kind of Education, that you should bring them up in the nurture and admonition of the Lord: And do you not hear the Lord Expostulating the case with you, and saying, you have taken my Children, the Children that were given unto me; the Children that were solemnly engaged to renounce the Pomps of Satan; but is this a light matter that you have taken these my Children, and initiated them in the Pomps and Vanities of the Wicked one, contrary to your Covenant? What will you say in the day of the Lords pleading with you? we have that charity for you as to believe that you have erred through Ignorance, and not wickedly: and we have therefore accounted it our Duty to inform you in the Truth. If you resolve not on Reformation, you will be left inexcusable. However it shall be, we have now given our Testimony and delivered our own Souls. *Consider what we say, and the Lord give you understanding in all things.*

JOHN DUNTON, 1659–1733

[John Dunton was an eccentric bookseller of London who came to Boston in 1686 to collect bad debts, dispose of excess stock, and perhaps to escape the dangers of the Monmouth rising. He remained in New England but eight months, during which time he wrote a series of entertaining but unreliable letters, published by the Prince Society of Boston in 1867 in two volumes: *John Dunton's Letters from New-England.*

The selections chosen for the text deal in part with sermons delivered by Cotton Mather, Joshua Moody, and Increase Mather in the presence of the condemned murderer James Morgan. Dunton's version of the sermons is quite accurate, in some portions *verbatim*. Of the prisoner little is known save that he lived in Boston. All three sermons, each of which required at least an hour to expound, were published within a year of their delivery, and represent a class of literature which publishers willingly undertook in anticipation of profitable sales. Such accounts supplied the public with what we might call the murder novels of their day. They presented the horrors of sin with enough lurid detail to arouse interest, and concluded with edifying advice. The custom of publicly addressing the condemned man in the presence of the gallows was brought from England; the twentieth-century mind revolts from the barbaric practice, yet the rite was universal in English-speaking communities till well into the eighteenth century.

For accounts of Moody and the Mathers, see pp. 162, 334, and 367.

Dunton's "Ramble" from Charlestown through Medford and Cambridge, and his chat with the college librarian, John Cotton, about
books, offer a pleasanter side of people and customs.

The text of the *Letters* is from I, 118–137; II, 154–163, with omissions
indicated. The selections are chosen from the more reliable passages.
For a discussion of the general untrustworthiness of the *Letters*, see
Chester N. Greenough, "John Dunton's Letters from New England,"
Publications of the Colonial Society of Massachusetts, XIV (1913), 212–257;
idem, "John Dunton Again," *ibid.*, XXI (1920), 232–251.

LETTERS

To Mr. George Larkin, Printer, at the Two Swans, without Bishopsgate, London.

Boston, in New-England, March 25, 1686.

ANOTHER Occurrence that happened, whilst I was here, was the
Execution of Morgan, which I may send you as a Piece of News,
for there has not (it seems) been seen an Execution here this seven
years. So that some have come 50 miles to see it: And I do confess,
Considering what serious care the two Mathers and Mr. Moody took
to prepare the Dying Criminal for Death, the Relation may be worth
relateing in my Summer Rambles; and in this Occurrence, I shall relate
nothing but what I saw my self.

And first, I went to view the Prison, in Prison-Lane;[1] and here I
think it will not be amiss, if I first give you the Character of a Prison:
A Prison is the Grave of the Living, where they are shut up from the
World and their Friends, and the Worms that gnaw upon them are
their own Thoughts and the Jayler. 'Tis a House of meagre Looks,
and ill smells: for Lice, Drink, and Tobacco, are the Compound: Or,
if you will, 'tis the Subburbs of Hell; and the Persons much the same
as there: You may ask, as Manippas in Lucian, which is Nevius, which
Thirsites; which the Beggar, and which the Knight: for they are all
suited in the same kind of nasty Poverty. The only fashion here, is to
be out at the Elbows; and not to be thread-bare, is a great Indecorum.

Every Man shews here like so many Wrecks upon the Sea: here the
Ribs of a thousand Pound; and there, the Relicks of so many Manners
is only a Doublet without Buttons; and 'tis a Spectacle of more Pity
than Executions are. Men huddle up their Lives here, as a thing of no
use, and wear it out like an old suit, the faster the better; and he that
deceives the time best, best spends it. Men see here much sin, and

much calamity; and where the last does not mortifie, the other hardens: And those that are worse here, are desperately worse, as those from whom the Horror of sin is taken off, and the Punishment familiar. This is a School, in which much Wisdom is learnt, but it is generally too late, and with danger; and it is better to be a fool, than come here to learn it.

Here it was that I saw poor Morgan; who seem'd to be very sorrowful and penitent, and confessed that he had in his rage murdered the Man whose Death and Blood has been laid to his Charge: He told me that the other gave him some ill Language whereby he was provoked, and that he said to him, If he came within the door, he wou'd run the spit into his Bowels, and he was as wicked as his Word; and so confessed himself guilty of Murder. . . .

But to return to Morgan, whose Execution being appointed on the 11th of March, there was that Care taken for his Soul that three Excellent Sermons [2] were preached before him, before his Execution; Two on the Lord's Day, and one just before his Execution. The first was preached by Mr. Cotton Mather, who preached upon that Text in *Isa.* 45 : 22, *Look unto Me and be ye saved, all the Ends of the Earth.* He declar'd that when the no less unexpected than undeniable Request of a Dying Man, who (says he) now stands in this Assembly, that he wou'd allow him this morning, a Discourse proper to his Uncomfortable Circumstances, was brought to him, he cou'd not think of a more proper Text; Telling the poor Wretch, That he was now listening to one of the three last Sermons that ever he was like to sit under before his incounter with the King of Terrors. And then said, "Poor Man! Do you hearken diligently, and I'll study to make this whole hour very particularly suitable and serviceable to you; and methinks a Man that knows himself about to take an Eternal Farewel of all Sermons, shou'd Endeavour to hear with most Earnest heed. And a little after, "The Faithful and True Witness saith unto us, *I will give you rest;* O let the poor fetter'd Prisoner recollect himself! James! Thy Name is not excepted in these Invitations."

"I am glad for the seemingly penitent Confession of your monstrous Miscarriages, which yesterday I obtain'd in writing from you, and which indeed was no more than there was need of: But it remains yet, that you give your Dying Looks to the Lord Jesus Christ; for Salvation from all your Guilt, and from all the Plagues in the flying Roll." And a little after, "My request unto you is, That you wou'd at this hour think of an Interest in Christ.—Surely when the Executioner is laying the Cold Cloth of Death over your Eyes, the Look, with the

Shriek of your Soul, will then say, "O now a Thousand Worlds for an Interest in Jesus Christ!" Surely a few minutes after that, when your naked Soul shall appear before the Judgment-Seat of the Most High, you will again say, an Interest in Jesus Christ, is worth whole Mountains of Massive Gold!

You have murder'd the Body and (no thanks to you, if not) the Soul of your Neighbour too: And O that the Rock in your Bosom might flow with Tears at such a thought! If the Court shou'd say unto you, Beg hard, and you shall live; O, how affectionate wou'd you be! Poor dying man, The Lord Jesus Christ saith the same thing to you, If thou canst heartily look and beg, thou shalt not be hang'd up among the Monuments of my Vengeance, in Chains for Evermore.

"The sharp Ax of Civil Justice will speedily cut you down; O for a little good Fruit before the Blow! Manifest your penitence for your Iniquities by a due care to excel in Tempers quite contrary to those ill habits and Customs whereby you have heretofore blasphemed the Worthy Name of Christ and Christianity: Especially employ the last minutes of your Life, in giving a Zealous Warning unto others, to take heed of those things which have been destructive unto you. Tell them what wild Gourds of Death they are, by which you have got your Bane; point out before them those Paths of the Destroyer which have led you down So near unto the Congregation of the Dead.

"When the numerous Crowd of Spectators are, three or four days hence, throng'd about the Place where you shall then breathe your last before them all, then do you with the heart-piercing-groans of a deadly wounded Man, beseech of your Fellow-sinners, That they wou'd turn now every one from the Evil of his way. Beseech them to keep clear of ill haunts and ill houses, with as much dread of them, as they cou'd have of lying down in a Nest of poysonous Snakes: Beseech them to abhor all Uncleanness, as they wou'd the Deep Ditch which the abhorred of the Lord do fall into. Beseech of them to avoid all Excess in Drinking, as they wou'd not rot themselves with more bitter Liquors than the Waters of Jealousie. Beseech them to mortifie and moderate all inordinate Passions, as they wou'd not surrender themselves into the hands of Devils, that will hurry them down into deeper Deeps than they are aware of. Beseech them to shun Idle Swearing, as a Prophanity that the God to whom vengeance belongeth will not permit to go unpunished. Beseech them to avoid Curses on themselves or others, least whilst they like Madmen so throw about Firebrands, Arrows, and Death, they bring upon their own heads, as you have done, the things which they are apt to be wishing. Beseech them to beware of Lying, as they wou'd not be put to need, and Crave, and be deny'd, a drop of Water, to cool their Tongues in the place of Torment. Beseech of them to be as averse to all stealing, as they wou'd be to carry coals of Fire into those Nests that they so feather by their dishonesty. Beseech of them to prize the means of Grace; to sleep at, or keep from sermons no more: To love the Habitation of GOD's House, and the place where his Honour dwells; lest GOD soon send their barren, froward souls to dwell in silence, where there shall never be a Gospel-Sermon heard; Never, Never, as long as the Almighty sits upon his Christal Throne.

"And when you have given these Warnings, upon the Ladder from whence you shall not come off without taking an Irrecoverable step into Eternity; O remember still, you give unto Jesus Christ the Honour of Looking to him for his salvation. Remember, that if you wou'd do a work highly for the Honour of Him, this is The Work of GOD, that you believe on Him. Even after your Eyes are so covered, as to take their leave of all sights below, still continue Looking unto Him whom you have heard saying, *Look unto me*. And now let the Everlasting Saviour look down in much mercy upon you: O that he wou'd give this Murderer and Extraordinary Sinner, a place among the Wonders of Free Grace! O that this Wretched Man might be made meet for the Inheritance among the Saints in Light; being kept from an un-repenting and deluded Heart as unquenchable Fire will find fewel in."

This was the Substance of what Mr. Cotton Mather address'd to the Prisoner, in his Sermon in the Morning. . . .

In the Evening of the same Lord's Day, Mr. Joshua Moodey preach'd before him; his Text was *Isa.* 12 : 1.—*Tho' thou wast angry with me, thine anger is turned away.*—He told the Poor condemned Prisoner, That what he had to say to him, shou'd be under these two Heads, 1. By way of Conviction and awakening: 2. By way of Encouragement and Counsel. He told him also, That he shou'd use all Plainness and Free-dom, taking it for Granted that Dying Men are past all Expectation of Flatteries or Complements; and that plain Dealing, which will do the most Good, will find the best Acceptance. . . .

"You seem to bewail your Sin of Sabbath-breaking: Well, know that you shall never have another Sabbath to break.—The Lord help you to keep this as you ought.—It is a very awful thing to us to look on you, a Person in your Youth, Health, and Strength, Brests full of Milk, and Bones moistened with Marrow, and then to think that within so many Days, this Man, tho' in his full strength, must Dye: And methinks it shou'd be much more awful to you.—Consider, You have no time to get Sin pardoned, and Wrath turn'd away, (if it be not done already) but between this and Death, into the very Borders, and under the Sentence of which, you now are. In the Grave there is no Repentance, no Remission, *Eccles.* 9: 10. Before four Days more pass over your head, (and O how swiftly do they fly away!) you will be entered into an Eternal and Unchangeable state, of Weal or Wo; and of wo it will be, if speedy, thorough Repentance prevent it not.

"But yet know, That notwithstanding all that has been spoken, there is yet hope in Israel concerning this thing. There is a way found out, and revealed by GOD for the Turning of his Anger even from such Sinners. Paul was a Murderer, and yet Pardon'd; Manasseh made the streets of Jerusalem to swim with Innocent Blood, and yet was forgiven. . . ."

Then addressing himself to the Congregation, he said: "You may not expect to have any come from the Dead to warn you, but here is one that is just going to the Dead, who bequeaths you this Warning, lest you also be in like manner hung up as Monuments of GOD's Wrath. I lived near twenty years in this Countrey, before I heard an Oath or a Curse: But now as you pass along the Streets, you may hear Children curse and swear, and take the great and dreadful name of GOD in vain. This they have learnt from Elder Persons, but wo to them that taught them, if they repent not.—I remember what Pious Herbert saith, in his Advice to young Men, That the Swearer has neither any fair pretence for doing it, nor Excuse when done, either from Pleasure or Profit, &c., and says, That if he were an Epicure, he cou'd forbear Swearing.

"And O you Drunkards, Let trembling take hold of you, Especially you Drunkards of Ephraim, *Isa.* 28: 1. I mean Church-Member Drunkards. I wish there were none such, that hear me this Day, who neither are Church-Members now, nor were, till Dismembred for that Sin. . . .

He then said, "I shall conclude, in a few words more to this Dying Bloody Sinner":—And then addressing himself to the Prisoner, he said, —"Poor Man! Consider, That all who live under the Gospel, are brought to JESUS, *the Mediator of the New Covenant; to the Blood of Sprinkling, that speaketh better things than that of Abel.—Heb.* 12: 24. And thereupon it is presently added, *vers.* 25, *See that ye refuse not him that speaks from Heaven.* Abel's Blood cried for Vengeance upon the Murderer, but Christ's Blood cries for Pardon, and Christ himself calls on thee, to receive, and not refuse him; unto which Call, if thou yield the obedience of Faith, his Blood will speak on thy Behalf. Thy sins speak bitter things, old sins, sins of youth, a Course of Sin; and this bloody Sin cries aloud, and speaks most bitterly; but that blood of Christ can out-speak, out-cry all these. It was from hence, that David, when under the Anguish of Soul, for his Blood-guiltiness, expected Pardon, and had it, and so mayst thou. *Psal.* 51. . . ."

This was the substance of Mr. Moody's Address to the Prisoner; who was remanded to Prison, where he continued till Thursday Morning, (the Day of his Execution) and then another Sermon (the last he ever heard) was preached before him by the Reverend Mr. Increase Mather, just before his going to Execution. . . .

"I have spoken so often to you in private, since your being apprehended, that I shall not need to say much now: Only a few Words:—

"1. Consider what a Sinner you have been; The Sin which you are to dye for, is as red as Scarlet; and many other Sins has your wicked Life been filled with. You have been a stranger to me; I never saw you; I never heard of you, until you had committed the Murder, for which you must dye this Day; but I hear by others that have known you, how wicked you have been; and you have your self confessed to the World, That you have been guilty of Drunkenness, guilty of Cursing and Swearing, guilty of Sabbath-breaking, guilty of Lying, guilty of Secret Uncleanness; as Solomon said to Shimei, *Thou knowest the Wickedness which thine own heart is privy to;* so I say to you: and that which aggravates your guiltiness not a little, is, That since you have been in Prison you have done Wickedly: You have made your self drunk several Times since your Imprisonment; yea, and you have been guilty of Lying since your Condemnation.

"2. Consider what misery you have brought upon your self: on your Body, that must dye an accursed Death; you must hang between Heaven and Earth, as it were forsaking of both, and unworthy to be in either. And what misery have you brought upon your poor Children? You have brought an Everlasting Reproach upon them. How great will their shame be, when it shall be said to them that their Father was hang'd? Not for his Goodness, as many in the World have been; but for his Wickedness: Not as a Martyr, but as a Malefactor: But that which is Ten thousand thousand times worse than all this, is, That you have (without Repentance,) brought undoing Misery upon your poor, yet precious Soul: Not only Death on your Body, but a second Death on your never-dying Soul: O tremble at that! . . ."

This, Mr. Larkin, is a part of what I heard preached at Mr. Willard's Meeting in an Auditory of near 5000 People; they went first to the New Church, but the Gallery crack'd, and so they were forced to remove to Mr. Willard's.[3] They were all preach'd with so much Awfulness, and so pathetically apply'd to the Poor Condemned Man, that all the Auditory (as well as my self) were very much affected thereat: And tho' I have been pretty long in the Rehearsal, yet you being an old Dissenter, I did not think the Reading of them wou'd be unacceptable to you. And remember this, I am rambling still, tho' it be from one subject to another.—But before I leave off this subject, I must bring Morgan to his Execution, whither I rid with Mr. Cotton Mather, after the Sermon was ended. Some thousands of the People following to see the Execution. As I rid along I had several glimpses of poor Morgan, as he went.

He seem'd penitent to the last: Mr. Cotton Mather pray'd with him at the place of Execution, and conferred with him about his Soul all the way thither, which was about a mile out of Boston. After being ty'd up, standing on the Ladder, he made the following Speech:—

"I pray GOD that I may be a Warning to you all, and that I may be the last that ever shall suffer after this manner. In the fear of GOD I warn you to have a Care of the Sin of Drunkenness, for that's a Sin that leads to all manner of Sins and Wickedness: (Mind and have a Care of breaking the Sixth Commandment, where it is said, *Thou shalt do no Murder*.) For when a Man is in drink, he is ready to commit all manner of Sin, till he fill up the Cup of the Wrath of GOD, as I have done, by committing that Sin of Murder. I beg of GOD, as I am a Dying Man, and to appear before the LORD within a few Minutes, that you may take notice of what I say to you: Have a Care of Drunkenness and ill Company, and mind all good Instruction, and don't turn your back upon the Word of GOD, as I have done. When I have been at a Meeting, I have gone out of the Meeting-House to commit sin, and to please the Lust of my flesh: and don't make a mock at any poor Object of Pity, but bless GOD, that he hath not left you, as he hath justly done me, to commit that horrid Sin of Murder. . . ."

After he had been about an hour at the Gallows, and had prayed again, his Cap was pulled over his Eyes, and then having said, "O Lord, Receive my Spirit; I come unto thee, O Lord; I come, I come, I come"; he was Turned off, and the multitude by degrees dispers'd. I think, during this Mournful Scene, I never saw more serious nor greater Compassion.

But from the House of Mourning, I rambled to the House of Feasting; for Mr. York, Mr. King, with Madam Brick, Mrs. Green, Mrs. Toy, the Damsell and my self, took a Ramble to a place call'd Governour's Island, about a mile from Boston, to see a whole Hog roasted, as did several other Bostonians. We went all in a Boat; and having treated the Fair Sex, returned in the Evening. . . .

[RAMBLE TO MEDFORD]

This was nothing near so pleasant a Ramble as the other; and that for three Reasons; for first, the Weather wasn't so good: For tho' the Sun flatter'd me in the Morning, and made me believe it wou'd be a fair day, yet before noon he grew sullen, drew in his exhilerating Beams, and muffl'd up his Face in a Cloud, so that there was no getting sight of him all the Day after: Nor was the Clouds' obscuring of the Sun's bright face, the only mischief that they did me; but to make my Rambling more uncomfortable yet, they pour'd down such a Prodigious Shower of Rain upon me, that if I wasn't wet to th' Skin, it was because my kinder Fate provided a good Shelter near at hand. For the chief kindness I receiv'd at Medford, was to be shelter'd by it from a Swinging shower of Rain, which only wet my Upper Garment,— and no more.

But Secondly, Neither was my Company so good; for I had only with me a young Bostonian for my Guide, who when he saw that it began to rain, turn'd a Deserter, and foolishly turn'd back again, fast as his Legs cou'd carry him; by which means he was catch'd in all the Shower, whilst I was shelter'd by making haste to Medford. Nor thirdly, Did I meet with such kind Entertainment at Medford as at Charles Town: For here I had no Acquaintance, but took Sanctuary in a Publick,[4] where there was extraordinary good Cyder, and tho' I hadn't such a Noble Treat as at Captain Jenner's; yet with the Cyder and such other Entertainment as the House afforded, (together with my Landlord and my Landlady's good Company,) I made a very pretty thing on't.

I ask'd my Landlady whether if the rain continu'd, there was any Lodging to be had, and she was pleas'd to tell me I shou'dn't want for that, tho' she set up all night her self; I told her before she shou'd do so, I'd seek a Lodging out among the Indians: And ask'd my Landlord whether he thought the Indians wou'd entertain me? My Landlord told me there was no need of my going among them, for he had Lodging enough; but as to the Indians Entertaining of me, he said that he had often known them (in the Summer time Especially) lie abroad themselves, to make room for Strangers, either English or others. I ask'd him what Beds they had, and he told me either Mats, or else Straw; and that when they lay down to sleep, they generally, both in Summer and Winter, made a great Fire, which serves them instead of Bedcloaths; and he that finds himself a-cold, must turn to the Fire to warm him; and they that wake first, must repair the Fire;

For as they have abundance of Fewel, so they don't spare in laying of it on. He told me also that when they had a Bad Dream, they look'd upon it as a threatening from God, and that on such occasions they wou'd rise and fall to Prayer, at any time of the Night.

By this time, the rain was over, tho' it still remain'd Cloudy; and therefore I thought it was best taking Time by the Fore-lock, and go back to Boston while it held up, there being nothing remarkable to be seen at Medford, which is but a small Village, consisting of a few Houses; And so paying my Reckoning, I came back to Boston in good time: For I had not been long at home, before it fell a raining again very hard.

My Third Ramble was to a Town called New-Town, which is situated three Miles from Charles-Town, on the North Side of the River, a league and a half by Water: This Town was first intended for a City, and is one of the neatest and best compacted Towns in the whole Countrey: It has many stately structures, and well-contrived Streets; Which for handsomness and beauty out-does Boston it self: The Inhabitants are generally rich, and have many hundred Acres of Land paled with one common Fence,—a mile and half long, affording store of Cattel.

You will the less wonder, Cousin, at what I have said about this Town, when you shall know this Town, that at first was called New Town, is now made an University, and called Cambridge, there being a colledge Erected there by one Mr. John Harvard, who gave £700 for the Erecting of it, in the year 1638. I was invited hither by Mr. Cotton,[5] a fellow of the Colledge, by whom I was very handsomely Treated, and shewn all that was remarkable in it. He discours'd with me about my Venture of Books; and by his means I sold many of my Books to the Colledge.

Among other Discourse that we had, he ask'd me, Who I look'd upon in England to be the best Authors, and Men of greatest Name and Repute? I told him, This was a very Comprehensive Question; For there were Authors famous in their several Faculties, some for Divinity, others for Philosophy, and some for the Mathematics; and several other Arts and Sciences; and therefore without he was more particular, 'twould be an Endless Task to answer him. He then reply'd he did intend chiefly Divinity; but since 'twas necessary for a Scholar to be universal in his knowledge, so 'twou'd be necessary for him to know who were the best Authors in every several Faculty I mention'd: I then told him I wou'd Endeavour to serve him, as far as my Memory wou'd give me leave: And as to Divinity, in England I must make a Distinction between the Establish'd Church-men and the Dissenters. . . .

"Nor must I omit [I said,] amongst these great Names, to mention that of Mr. John Bunyan, who tho' a Man of but very ordinary Education, yet was a Man of great Natural Parts, and as well known for an Author thro'out England, as any I have mention'd, by the many Books he has Publish'd, of which the Pilgrim's Progress bears away the Bell.

"But as I said of the Church-men, so I must of the Dissenters, these are scarce a Tythe of the Eminent Authors among 'em. You see Sir," said I, "what a Task you have put me upon, and therefore if I have been too tedious, and worn your Patience out, you must thank your self, since 'tis the Deference I pay to your Commands that has occasion'd it. But I shall Dispatch the others quickly.

"As to Philosophy, especially Experimental Philosophy, there are the Transactions of the Royal Society, published by Dr. Grew; and the Celebrated Works of the Honourable Robert Boyle, Esq., who is also as great a Divine as a Philosopher, as his style of the Scriptures, Occasional Reflections, and his Seraphic Love will Witness.

"For Law, Fleta, Bracton, and Cook upon Littleton, are Eminent. There are also the Reports of Sir Geoffery Palmer, and divers other Learned Judges, Eminent in their times. Among which Sir Mathew Hale, late Lord Chief Justice of England, must not be forgotten, who was the Perfect Pattern of an Upright Judge, and as great a Philosopher and Divine as a Lawyer; as Divine Origination of Mankind in Folio, and his Meditations and Contemplations, in Octavo, which are Excellent things, do abundantly Evidence.

"For Physick, the Learned Dr. Willett is a Famous Author, and Dr. Salmon by his Dispensatory, and several other Books, is very well known.

"For the Mathematicks, Sir Jonas Moore and Mr. William Leybourn are both very Eminent Authors.

"And for Poetry, the Immortal Cowley, who first brought in the use of Pindarick Poetry in English. Besides whom we have Dryden, Shadwel, Tate, Settle, and several others, very Eminent Authors.

Nor must we here forget to do justice to the Fair Sex, Mrs. Katharine Philips having made herself deservedly Famous for her Excellent Poetical Pieces; Mrs. Behn also has approved her self a Devotee to the Muses; and not the least, tho' the last, is the Incomparable Philomela; than whom, none has drunk a larger Draught at the Heliconian Spring, or been a greater Favourite of the Muses."

Mr. Cotton gave me many thanks for the Account I had given him of our English Authors; many of whom he said he had before heard on, and had some of their Works; but others of them were till now altogether unknown to him; but now that he knew them, he intended to enlarge his study with some of their Writings. I told him I was very glad I had in any measure gratified his Curiosity: And added, That since I had given him an Account of some of the most Eminent of our Old English Authors, he wou'd by way of Retaliation give me some little Account of their New-England Authors, for I did not doubt but there were many that had done worthily in this Countrey.

To this Mr. Cotton reply'd: "That I cou'd not expect New-England cou'd compare with Old, either for the Number of Authors, or the Excellency of their Parts and Endowments; New-England being only a Colony; and all their Learning but as springs from those two Fountains in Old England, Oxford and Cambridge: However, we have not been without Excellent Men in this Countrey: And amongst the first Planters here, Mr. John Cotton, and Mr. Seaborn Cotton, his Son, are deservedly Famous; and Mr. Shepherd for the many Excellent Tracts written by him, has his Praise in all the Churches: The many impressions that have been made of his Sincere Convert and Sound Believer, both at London, and here at Boston, shews what acceptance they have mett with in the World; his Parable of the Ten Virgins also, tho' in Folio, has been several times printed.

"Nor must the Famous Mr. Elliot (who is still living, tho' very aged,) [6] be Omitted; whose indefatigable Zeal and Industry, both by Printing and Preaching, for the Conversion of the Indians, has given Place to none.

"And as to our Modern Authors, the Reverend Mr. Increase Mather, the Present Rector of our Colledge, holds the chief Rank, whose Universal knowledge, both in Divine and Humane Learning, is very well known both in New-England and Old too: And his Worthy Son, Mr. Cotton Mather, does not come much short of his Father; and his Works do also praise him in the Gate: And to the Honour of our Colledge do I speak it, he was brought up in it. And tho' our Colledge does not pretend to compare it self with any either in Oxford or Cambridge, yet has there been brought up in it since its Foundation, 122 Ministers; of which Ten are dead, seventy-one remain still in the Country, and Forty-one are removed to England.

"As to the other of our Boston-Ministers, I believe you have heard 'em, and know 'em to be good Preachers, and men of great Parts; There are also several eminent Ministers in several Parts of the Countrey, but of them, I can give you but a small Account, having little Acquaintance with them, and therefore shall pass them by."

I then gave Mr. Cotton many thanks for the Trouble I had put him to, and promised him a Catalogue of my Books as soon as I cou'd write it out, and so took my leave of him.

SARAH KEMBLE KNIGHT, 1666–1727

[The most sprightly and graphic picture of rustic manners in the early eighteenth century has been left in the record of a journey made by Sarah Kemble Knight from Boston to New York in 1704. The intrepid business woman, who at one time kept a writing-school which young Benjamin Franklin is said to have attended, had interests to look after in New York. On October 2 she left Boston on horseback and alone, except for the companions she hired or fell in with along the way. The route she chose led through Rhode Island and New Haven, and she followed the same roads home in March, 1705. Such a trip, hazardous for anyone, was extraordinary for a woman. The discomforts and annoyances of the journey she met with tolerant humor and a certain mocking resignation.

Madam Knight's husband was a Boston merchant about whom little is known. In later life she removed to New Haven where she died, leaving an estate valued at £1800. Her *Journal* was first published, along with that of the Reverend Mr. Thomas Buckingham of Hartford, in New York, 1825, by Theodore Dwight. It has most recently been printed with an introduction by George P. Winship (Boston, 1920; facsimile reprint, 1935). In no other published journal of the period will the student of colonial dialect find a more racy idiom recorded.

The text is here given entire from the first edition. For an account of Madam Knight, see *Dictionary of American Biography;* also Anson Titus, "Madam Sarah Knight, Her Diary and Her Times," *Bostonian Society Publications*, IX (1912), 99–126.]

THE JOURNAL OF MADAM KNIGHT.

MONDAY, Octb'r. ye second, 1704.—About three o'clock afternoon, I begun my Journey from Boston to New-Haven; being about two Hundred Mile. My Kinsman, Capt. Robert Luist, waited on me as farr as Dedham, where I was to meet ye Western post.

I vissitted the Reverd. Mr. Belcher,[1] ye Minister of ye town, and tarried there till evening, in hopes ye post would come along. But he not coming, I resolved to go to Billingses where he used to lodg, being 12 miles further. But being ignorant of the way, Mad^m Billings,[2] seing no persuasions of her good spouses or hers could prevail with me to Lodg there that night, Very kindly went wyth me to yᵉ Tavern, where I hoped to get my guide, And desired the Hostess to inquire of her guests whether any of them would go with mee. But they being tyed by the Lipps to a pewter engine, scarcely allowed themselves time to say what clownish ******

[*Here half a page of the MS. is gone.*]

*** Peices of eight, I told her no, I would not be accessary to such extortion.

Then John shan't go, sais shee. No, indeed, shan't hee; And held forth at that rate a long time, that I began to fear I was got among the Quaking tribe, beleeving not a Limbertong'd sister among them could out do Madm. Hostes.

Upon this, to my no small surprise, son John arrose, and gravely demanded what I would give him to go with me? Give you, sais I, are you John? Yes, says he, for want of a Better; And behold! this John look't as old as my Host, and perhaps had bin a man in the last Century. Well, Mr. John, sais I, make your demands. Why, half a pss. of eight and a dram, sais John. I agreed, and gave him a Dram (now) in hand to bind the bargain.

My hostess catechis'd John for going so cheep, saying his poor wife would break her heart *****

[*Here another half page of the MS is gone.*]

His shade on his Hors resembled a Globe on a Gate post. His habitt, Hors and furniture, its looks and goings Incomparably answered the rest.

Thus Jogging on with an easy pace, my Guide telling mee it was dangero's to Ride hard in the Night, (whᶜʰ his horse had the sence to avoid,) Hee entertained me with the Adventurs he had passed by late Rideing, and eminent Dangers he had escaped, so that, Remembring the Hero's in Parismus and the Knight of the Oracle,[3] I didn't know but I had mett wᵗʰ a Prince disguis'd.

When we had Ridd about an how'r, wee come into a thick swamp, wch. by Reason of a great fogg, very much startled mee, it being now very Dark. But nothing dismay'd John: Hee had encountered a thousand and a thousand such Swamps, having a Universall Knowledge in the woods; and readily Answered all my inquiries wch. were not a few.

In about an how'r, or something more, after we left the Swamp, we come to Billinges, where I was to Lodg. My Guide dismounted and very Complasantly help't me down and shewd the door, signing to me wᶜʰ his hand to Go in; wᶜʰ I Gladly did—But had not gone many steps into the Room, ere I was Interogated by a young Lady I understood afterwards was the Eldest daughter of the family, with these, or words to this purpose, (viz.) Law for mee—what in the world brings You here at this time a night?—I never see a woman on the Rode so Dreadfull late, in all the days of my versall life. Who are You? Where are You going? I'me scar'd out of my witts—with much now of the same Kind. I stood aghast, Prepareing to reply, when in comes my Guide—to him Madam turn'd, Roreing out: Lawfull heart, John, is it You?—how de do! Where in the world are you going with this woman? Who is she? John made no Ansr. but sat down in the corner, fumbled out his black Junk,[4] and saluted that instead of Debb; she then turned agen to mee and fell anew into her silly questions, without asking me to sitt down.

I told her shee treated me very Rudely, and I did not think it my duty to answer her unmannerly Questions. But to get ridd of them, I told her I come there to have the post's company with me to-morrow on my Journey, &c. Miss star'd awhile, drew a chair, bid me sitt, And then run up stairs and putts on two or three Rings, (or else I had not seen them before,) and returning, sett herself just before me, showing the way to Reding, that I might see her Ornaments, perhaps to gain the more respect. But her Granam's new Rung [5] sow, had it appeared, would affected me as much. I paid honest John wth money and dram according to contract, and Dismist him, and pray'd Miss to shew me where I must Lodg. Shee conducted me to a parlour in a little back Lento,[6] wch was almost fill'd wth the bedsted, wch was so high that I was forced to climb on a chair to gitt up to ye wretched bed that lay on it; on wch having Stretcht my tired Limbs, and lay'd my head on a Sad-coloured pillow, I began to think on the transactions of ye past day.

Tuesday, October ye third, about 8 in the morning, I with the Post proceeded forward without observing any thing remarkable; And about two, afternoon, Arrived at the Post's second stage, where the western Post mett him and exchanged Letters. Here, having called for something to eat, ye woman bro't in a Twisted thing like a cable, but something whiter; and laying it on the bord, tugg'd for life to bring it into a capacity to spread; wch having wth great pains accomplished, shee serv'd in a dish of Pork and Cabage, I suppose the remains of Dinner. The sause was of a deep Purple, wch I tho't was boil'd in her dye Kettle; the bread was Indian, and every thing on the Table service Agreeable to these. I, being hungry, gott a little down; but my stomach was soon cloy'd, and what cabbage I swallowed serv'd me for a Cudd the whole day after.

Having here discharged the Ordnary for self and Guide, (as I under-

stood was the custom,) About Three afternoon went on with my Third
Guide, who Rode very hard; and having crossed Providence Ferry,
we come to a River wch they Generally Ride thro'. But I dare not
venture; so the Post got a Ladd and Cannoo to carry me to tother side,
and hee rid thro' and Led my hors. The Cannoo was very small and
shallow, so that when we were in she seem'd redy to take in water,
which greatly terrified mee, and caused me to be very circumspect,
sitting with my hands fast on each side, my eyes stedy, not daring so
much as to lodg my tongue a hair's breadth more on one side of my
mouth then tother, nor so much as think on Lott's wife, for a wry
thought would have oversett our wherey: But was soon put out of
this pain, by feeling the Cannoo on shore, wch I as soon almost saluted
with my feet; and Rewarding my sculler, again mounted and made
the best of our way forwards. The Rode here was very even and y^e
day pleasant, it being now near Sunsett. But the Post told mee we had
neer 14 miles to Ride to the next Stage, (where we were to Lodg.)
I askt him of the rest of the Rode, foreseeing wee must travail in the
night. Hee told mee there was a bad River we were to Ride thro',
wch was so very firce a hors could sometimes hardly stem it: But it
was but narrow, and wee should soon be over. I cannot express The
concern of mind this relation sett me in: no thoughts but those of the
dang'ros River could entertain my Imagination, and they were as
formidable as varios, still Tormenting me with blackest Ideas of my
Approaching fate—Sometimes seing my self drowning, otherwhiles
drowned, and at the best like a holy Sister Just come out of a Spiritual
Bath in dripping Garments.

Now was the Glorious Luminary, wth his swift Coursers arrived at
his Stage, leaving poor me wth the rest of this part of the lower world
in darkness, with which *wee* were soon Surrounded. The only Glimer-
ing we now had was from the spangled Skies, Whose Imperfect Reflections rendered every Object formidable. Each lifeless Trunk, with
its shatter'd Limbs, appear'd an Armed Enymie; and every little
stump like a Ravenous devourer. Nor could I so much as discern my
Guide, when at any distance, which added to the terror.

Thus, absolutely lost in Thought, and dying with the very thoughts
of drowning, I come up wth the post, who I did not see till even with
his Hors: he told mee he stopt for mee; and wee Rode on Very de-
liberatly a few paces, when we entred a Thickett of Trees and Shrubbs,
and I perceived by the Hors's going, we were on the descent of a Hill,
w^ch, as wee come neerer the bottom, 'twas totaly dark wth the Trees
that surrounded it. But I knew by the Going of the Hors wee had

entred the water, w^ea my Guide told mee was the hazzardos River he had told me off; and hee, Riding up close to my Side, Bid me not fear— we should be over Imediatly. I now ralyed all the Courage I was mistriss of, Knowing that I must either Venture my fate of drowning, or be left like ye Children in the wood. So, as the Post bid me, I gave Reins to my Nagg; and sitting as Stedy as Just before in the Cannoo, in a few minutes got safe to the other side, which hee told mee was the Narragansett country.

Here We found great difficulty in Travailing, the way being very narrow, and on each side the Trees and bushes gave us very unpleasent welcomes wth their Branches and bow's, wch wee could not avoid, it being so exceeding dark. My Guide, as before so now, putt on harder than I, wth my weary bones, could follow; so left mee and the way beehind him. Now Returned my distressed aprehensions of the place where I was: the dolesome woods, my Company next to none, Going I knew not whither, and encompased wth Terrifying darkness; The least of which was enough to startle a more Masculine courage. Added to which the Reflections, as in the afternoon of ye day that my Call was very Questionable, wch till then I had not so Prudently as I ought considered. Now, coming to ye foot of a hill, I found great difficulty in ascending; But being got to the Top, was there amply recompenced with the friendly Appearance of the Kind Conductress of the night, Just then Advancing above the Horisontall Line. The Raptures wch the Sight of that fair Planett produced in mee, caus'd mee, for the Moment, to forgett my present wearyness and past toils; and Inspir'd me for most of the remaining way with very divirting tho'ts, some of which, with the other Occurances of the day, I reserved to note down when I should come to my Stage. My tho'ts on the sight of the moon were to this purpose:

> Fair Cynthia, all the Homage that I may
> Unto a Creature, unto thee I pay;
> In Lonesome woods to meet so kind a guide,
> To Mee's more worth than all the world beside.
> Some Joy I felt just now, when safe got or'e
> Yon Surly River to this Rugged shore,
> Deeming Rough welcomes from these clownish Trees,
> Better than Lodgings wth Nereidees.
> Yet swelling fears surprise; all dark appears—
> Nothing but Light can disipate those fears.
> My fainting vitals can't lend strength to say,
> But softly whisper, O I wish 'twere day.

The murmer hardly warm'd the Ambient air,
E're thy Bright Aspect rescues from dispair:
Makes the old Hagg her sable mantle loose,
And a Bright Joy do's through my Soul diffuse.
The Boistero's Trees now Lend a Passage Free,
And pleasent prospects thou giv'st light to see.

From hence wee kept on, with more ease y^n before: the way being smooth and even, the night warm and serene, and the Tall and thick Trees at a distance, especially w^n the moon glar'd light through the branches, fill'd my Imagination wth the pleasent delusion of a Sumpteous citty, fill'd wth famous Buildings and churches, wth their spiring steeples, Balconies, Galleries and I know not what: Granduers wch I had heard of, and wch the stories of foreign countries had given me the Idea of.

Here stood a Lofty church—there is a steeple,
And there the Grand Parade—O see the people!
That Famous Castle there, were I but nigh,
To see the mote and Bridg and walls so high—
They'r very fine! sais my deluded eye.

Being thus agreably entertain'd without a thou't of any thing but thoughts themselves, I on a suden was Rous'd from these pleasing Imaginations, by the Post's sounding his horn, which assured mee hee was arrived at the Stage, where we were to Lodg: and that musick was then most musickall and agreeable to mee.

Being come to mr. Havens', I was very civilly Received, and courteously entertained, in a clean comfortable House; and the Good woman was very active in helping off my Riding clothes, and then ask't what I would eat. I told her I had some Chocolett, if shee would prepare it; which with the help of some Milk, and a little clean brass Kettle, she soon effected to my satisfaction. I then betook me to my Apartment, wch was a little Room parted from the Kitchen by a single bord partition; where, after I had noted the Occurrances of the past day, I went to bed, which, tho' pretty hard, Yet neet and handsome. But I could get no sleep, because of the Clamor of some the of Town tope-ers in next Room, Who were entred into a strong debate concerning ye Signifycation of the name of their Country, (viz.) *Narraganset*. One said it was named so by ye Indians, because there grew a Brier there, of a prodigious Highth and bigness, the like hardly ever known, called by the Indians Narragansett; And quotes an Indian of so Barberous a name for his Author, that I could not write it. His Antagonist Replyed no—It was from a Spring it had its name, wch hee well knew where it was, which was extreem cold in summer, and as Hott as could be imagined in the winter, which was much resorted too by the natives, and by them called Narragansett, (Hott and Cold,) and that was the originall of their places name—with a thousand Impertinances not worth notice, wch He utter'd with such a Roreing voice and Thundering blows with the fist of wickedness on the Table, that it peirced my very head. I heartily fretted, and wish't 'um tongue tyed; but wth as little succes as a freind of mine once, who was (as shee said) kept a whole night awake, on a Jorny, by a country Left.[7] and a Sergent, Insigne and a Deacon, contriving how to bring a triangle into a Square. They kept calling for tother Gill, wch while they were swallowing, was some Intermission; But presently, like Oyle to fire, encreased the flame. I set my Candle on a Chest by the bed side, and setting up, fell to my old way of composing my Resentments, in the following manner:

> I ask thy Aid, O Potent Rum!
> To Charm these wrangling Topers Dum.
> Thou hast their Giddy Brains possest—
> The man confounded wth the Beast—
> And I, poor I, can get no rest.
> Intoxicate them with thy fumes:
> O still their Tongues till morning comes!

And I know not but my wishes took effect, for the dispute soon ended w^th 'tother Dram; and so Good night!

Wedensday, Octob^r 4th. About four in the morning, we set out for Kingston (for so was the Town called) with a french Docter in our company. Hee and ye Post put on very furiously, so that I could not keep up with them, only as now and then they'd stop till they see mee. This Rode was poorly furnished wth accommodations for Travellers, so that we were forced to ride 22 miles by the post's account, but neerer thirty by mine, before wee could bait so much as our Horses, wch I exceedingly complained of. But the post encourag'd mee, by saying wee should be well accommodated anon at mr. Devills, a few miles further. But I questioned whether we ought to go to the Devil to be helpt out of affliction. However, like the rest of Deluded souls that post to ye Infernal denn, Wee made all posible speed to this Devil's Habitation; where alliting, in full assurance of good accommodation, wee were going in. But meeting his two daughters, as I suposed twins, they so neerly resembled each other, both in features and habit, and look't as old as the Divel himselfe, and quite as Ugly, We desired entertainm't, but could hardly get a word out of 'um, till with our

Importunity, telling them our necesity, &c. they call'd the old Sophister, who was as sparing of his words as his daughters had bin, and no, or none, was the reply's hee made us to our demands. Hee differed only in this from the old fellow in to'ther Country: hee let us depart. However, I thought it proper to warn poor Travailers to endeavour to Avoid falling into circumstances like ours, wch at our next Stage I sat down and did as followeth:

> May all that dread the cruel feind of night
> Keep on, and not at this curs't Mansion light.
> 'Tis Hell; 'tis Hell! and Devills here do dwell:
> Here dwells the Devill—surely this's Hell.
> Nothing but Wants: a drop to cool yo'r Tongue
> Cant be procur'd these cruel Feinds among.
> Plenty of horrid Grins and looks sevear,
> Hunger and thirst, But pitty's bannish'd here—
> The Right hand keep, if Hell on Earth you fear!

Thus leaving this habitation of cruelty, we went forward; and arriving at an Ordinary about two mile further, found tollerable accommodation. But our Hostes, being a pretty full mouth'd old creature, entertain'd our fellow travailer, ye french Docter, wth Inumirable complaints of her bodily infirmities; and whispered to him so lou'd, that all ye House had as full a hearing as hee: which was very divirting to ye company, (of which there was a great many,) as one might see by their sneering. But poor weary I slipt out to enter my mind in my Jornal, and left my Great Landly with her Talkative Guests to themselves.

From hence we proceeded (about ten forenoon) through the Narragansett country, pretty Leisurely; and about one afternoon come to Paukataug River, wch was about two hundred paces over, and now very high, and no way over to to'ther side but this. I darid not venture to Ride thro, my courage at best in such cases but small, And now at the Lowest Ebb, by reason of my weary, very weary, hungry and uneasy Circumstances. So takeing leave of my company, tho' wth no little Reluctance, that I could not proceed wth them on my Jorny, Stop at a little cottage Just by the River, to wait the Waters falling, wch the old man that lived there said would be in a little time, and he would conduct me safe over. This little Hutt was one of the wretchedest I ever saw a habitation for human creatures. It was suported with shores enclosed with Clapbords, laid on Lengthways, and so much asunder, that the Light come throu' every where; the doore tyed on wth a cord in ye place of hinges; The floor the bear earth; no windows but such as the thin covering afforded, nor any furniture but a Bedd wth a glass Bottle hanging at ye head on't; an earthan cupp, a small pewter Bason, A Bord wth sticks to stand on, instead of a table, and a block or two in ye corner instead of chairs. The family were the old man, his wife and two Children; all and every part being the picture of poverty. Notwithstanding both the Hutt and its Inhabitance were very clean and tydee: to the crossing the Old Proverb, that bare walls make giddy hows-wifes.[8]

I Blest myselfe that I was not one of this misserable crew; and the Impressions their wretchedness formed in me caused mee on ye very Spott to say:

> Tho' Ill at ease, A stranger and alone,
> All my fatigu's shall not extort a grone.
> These Indigents have hunger wth their ease;
> Their best is wors behalfe then my disease.
> Their Misirable hutt wch Heat and Cold
> Alternately without Repulse do hold;
> Their Lodgings thyn and hard, their Indian fare,
> The mean Apparel which the wretches wear,
> And their ten thousand ills wch can't be told,
> Makes nature er'e 'tis midle age'd look old.
> When I reflect, my late fatigues do seem
> Only a notion or forgotten Dreem.

I had scarce done thinking, when an Indian-like Animal come to the door, on a creature very much like himselfe, in mien and feature, as well as Ragged cloathing; and having 'litt, makes an Awkerd Scratch wth his Indian shoo, and a Nodd, sits on ye block, fumbles out his black Junk,[9] dipps it in ye Ashes, and presents it piping hott to his muscheeto's, and fell to sucking like a calf, without speaking, for near a quarter of an hower. At length the old man said how do's Sarah do? who I understood was the wretches wife, and Daughter to ye old man: he Replyed —as well as can be expected, &c. So I remembred the old say, and suposed I knew Sarah's case. Butt hee being, as I understood, going over the River, as ugly as hee was, I was glad to ask him to show me ye way to Saxtons, at Stoningtown; wch he promising, I ventur'd over wth the old mans assistance; who having rewarded to content, with my Tattertailed guide, I Ridd on very slowly thro' Stoningtown, where the Rode was very Stony and uneven. I asked the fellow, as we went, divers questions of the place and way, &c. I being arrived at my country Saxtons, at Stonington, was very well accommodated both as to victuals and Lodging, the only Good of both I had found since my setting out. Here I heard there was an old man and his Daughter

to come that way, bound to N. London; and being now destitute of
a Guide, gladly waited for them, being in so good a harbour, and
accordingly, Thursday, Octob^r ye 5th, about 3 in the afternoon, I sat
forward with neighbour Polly and Jemima, a Girl about 18 Years old,
who hee said he had been to fetch out of the Narragansetts, and said
they had Rode thirty miles that day, on a sory lean Jade, wth only a
Bagg under her for a pillion, which the poor Girl often complain'd
was very uneasy.

Wee made Good speed along, wch made poor Jemima make many a
sow'r face, the mare being a very hard trotter; and after many a hearty
and bitter Oh, she at length Low'd out: Lawful Heart father! this bare
mare hurts mee Dingeely, I'me direfull sore I vow; with many words
to that purpose: poor Child sais Gaffer—she us't to serve your mother
so. I don't care how mother us't to do, quoth Jemima, in a pasionate
tone. At which the old man Laught, and kik't his Jade o' the side, which
made her Jolt ten times harder.

About seven that Evening, we come to New London Ferry: here,
by reason of a very high wind, we mett with great difficulty in getting
over—the Boat tos't exceedingly, and our Horses capper'd at a very
surprizing Rate, and set us all in a fright; especially poor Jemima, who
desired her father to say so jack to the Jade, to make her stand. But
the careless parent, taking no notice of her repeated desires, She Rored
out in a Passionate manner: Pray suth father, Are you deaf? Say so
Jack to the Jade, I tell you. The Dutiful Parent obey's; saying so Jack,
so Jack, as gravely as if hee'd bin to saying Catechise after Young
Miss, who with her fright look't of all coullers in ye Rain Bow.

Being safely arrived at the house of Mrs. Prentices in N. London, I
treated neighbour Polly and daughter for their divirting company, and
bid them farewell; and between nine and ten at night waited on the
Rev^d Mr. Gurdon Saltonstall,[10] minister of the town, who kindly Invited
me to Stay that night at his house, where I was very handsomely and
plentifully treated and Lodg'd; and made good the Great Character
I had before heard concerning him: viz. that hee was the most affable,
courteous, Genero's and best of men.

Friday, Octo^r 6th. I got up very early, in Order to hire somebody to
go with mee to New Haven, being in Great parplexity at the thoughts
of proceeding alone; which my most hospitable entertainer observing,
himselfe went, and soon return'd wth a young Gentleman of the town,
who he could confide in to Go with mee; and about eight this morning,
wth Mr. Joshua Wheeler my new Guide, takeing leave of this worthy
Gentleman, Wee advanced on towards Seabrook. The Rodes all along

this way are very bad, Incumbred wth Rocks and mountainos passages, wch were very disagreeable to my tired carcass; but we went on with a moderate pace wch made ye Journy more pleasent. But after about eight miles Rideing, in going over a Bridge under wch the River Run very swift, my hors stumbled, and very narrowly 'scaped falling over into the water; wch extreemly frightened mee. But through God's Goodness I met with no harm, and mounting agen, in about half a miles Rideing, come to an ordinary, were well entertained by a woman of about seventy and vantage, but of as Sound Intellectuals as one of seventeen. Shee entertain'd Mr. Wheeler wth some passages of a Wedding awhile ago at a place hard by, the Brides-Groom being about her Age or something above, Saying his Children was dredfully against their fathers marrying, wch shee condemned them extreemly for.

From hence wee went pretty briskly forward, and arriv'd at Saybrook ferry about two of the Clock afternoon; and crossing it, wee call'd at an Inn to Bait, (foreseeing we should not have such another Opportunity till we come to Killingsworth.) Landlady come in, with her hair about her ears, and hands at full pay scratching. Shee told us shee had some mutton wch shee would broil, wch I was glad to hear; But I supose forgot to wash her scratchers; in a little time shee brot it in; but it being pickled, and my Guide said it smelt strong of head sause, we left it, and p^d sixpence a piece for our Dinners, wch was only smell.

So wee putt forward with all speed, and about seven at night come to Killingsworth, and were tollerably well with Travillers fare, and Lodgd there that night.

Saturday, Oct. 7th, we sett out early in the Morning, and being something unaquainted wth the way, having ask't it of some wee mett, they told us wee must Ride a mile or two and turne down a Lane on the Right hand; and by their Direction wee Rode on but not Yet comeing to ye turning, we mett a Young fellow and ask't him how farr it was to the Lane which turn'd down towards Guilford. Hee said wee must Ride a little further, and turn down by the Corner of uncle Sams Lott. My Guide vented his Spleen at the Lubber; and we soon after came into the Rhode, and keeping still on, without any thing further Remarkabell, about two a clock afternoon we arrived at New Haven, where I was received with all Posible Respects and civility. Here I discharged Mr. Wheeler with a reward to his satisfaction, and took some time to rest after so long and toilsome a Journey; And Inform'd myselfe of the manners and customs of the place, and at the same time employed myselfe in the afair I went there upon.

They are Govern'd by the same Laws as wee in Boston, (or little differing,) thr'out this whole Colony of Connecticot, And much the same way of Church Government, and many of them good, Sociable people, and I hope Religious too: but a little too much Independant in their principalls, and, as I have been told, were formerly in their Zeal very Riggid in their Administrations towards such as their Lawes made Offenders, even to a harmless Kiss or Innocent merriment among Young people. Whipping being a frequent and counted an easy Punishment, about wch as other Crimes, the Judges were absolute in their Sentences. They told mee a pleasant story about a pair of Justices in those parts, wch I may not omit the relation of.

A negro Slave belonging to a man in ye Town, stole a hogs head from his master, and gave or sold it to an Indian, native of the place. The Indian sold it in the neighbourhood, and so the theft was found out. Thereupon the Heathen was Seized, and carried to the Justices House to be Examined. But his worship (it seems) was gone into the feild, with a Brother in office, to gather in his Pompions.[11] Whither the malefactor is hurried, And Complaint made, and satisfaction in the name of Justice demanded. Their Worships cann't proceed in form without a Bench: whereupon they Order one to be Imediately erected, which, for want of fitter materials, they made with pompions—which being finished, down setts their Worships, and the Malefactor call'd, and by the Senior Justice Interrogated after the following manner. You Indian why did You steal from this man? You sho'dn't do so—it's a Grandy wicked thing to steal. Hol't Hol't, cryes Justice Junr, Brother, You speak negro to him. I'le ask him. You sirrah, why did You steal this man's Hoggshead? Hoggshead? (replys the Indian,) me no stomany. No? says his Worship; and pulling off his hatt, Patted his own head with his hand, sais, Tatapa—You, Tatapa—you; all one this. Hoggshead all one this. Hah! says Netop, now me stomany that. Whereupon the Company fell into a great fitt of Laughter, even to Roreing. Silence is comanded, but to no effect: for they continued perfectly Shouting. Nay, sais his worship, in an angry tone, if it be so, *take mee off the Bench.*

Their Diversions in this part of the Country are on Lecture days and Training days mostly: [12] on the former there is Riding from town to town.

And on training dayes The Youth divert themselves by Shooting at the Target, as they call it, (but it very much resembles a pillory,) where hee that hitts neerest the white has some yards of Red Ribbin presented him, wch being tied to his hattband, the two ends streeming down his back, he is Led away in Triumph, wth great applause, as the winners of the Olympiack Games. They generally marry very young: the males oftener as I am told under twentie than above; they generally make public wedings, and have a way something singular (as they say) in some of them, viz. Just before Joyning hands the Bridegroom quitts the place, who is soon followed by the Bridesmen, and as it were, dragg'd back to duty—being the reverse to ye former practice among us, to steal m^s Pride.

There are great plenty of Oysters all along by the sea side, as farr as I Rode in the Collony, and those very good. And they Generally lived very well and comfortably in their famelies. But too Indulgent (especially ye farmers) to their slaves: sufering too great familiarity from them, permitting y^m to sit at Table and eat with them, (as they say to save time,) and into the dish goes the black hoof as freely as the white hand. They told me that there was a farmer lived nere the Town where I lodgd who had some difference wth his slave, concerning something the master had promised him and did not punctualy perform; wch caused some hard words between them; But at length they put the matter to Arbitration and Bound themselves to stand to the award of such as they named—wch done, the Arbitrators Having heard the Allegations of both parties, Order the master to pay 40^s to black face, and acknowledge his fault. And so the matter ended: the poor master very honestly standing to the award.

There are every where in the Towns as I passed, a Number of Indians the Natives of the Country, and are the most salvage of all the salvages of that kind that I had ever Seen: little or no care taken (as I heard upon enquiry) to make them otherwise. They have in some places Landes of their owne, and Govern'd by Law's of their own making;— they marry many wives and at pleasure put them away, and on the ye least dislike or fickle humour, on either side, saying *stand away* to one another is a sufficient Divorce. And indeed those uncomely *Stand aways* are too much in Vougue among the English in this (Indulgent Colony) as their Records plentifully prove, and that on very trivial matters, of which some have been told me, but are not proper to be Related by a Female pen, tho some of that foolish sex have had too large a share in the story.

If the natives committ any crime on their own precincts among themselves, ye English takes no Cognezens of. But if on the English ground, they are punishable by our Laws. They mourn for their Dead by blacking their faces, and cutting their hair, after an Awkerd and frightfull manner; But can't bear You should mention the names of their dead Relations to them: they trade most for Rum, for wch they^d hazzard

their very lives; and the English fit them Generally as well, by seasoning it plentifully with water.

They give the title of merchant to every trader; who Rate their
Goods according to the time and spetia they pay in: viz. Pay, mony,
Pay as mony, and trusting. *Pay* is Grain, Pork, Beef, &c. at the prices
sett by the General Court that Year; *mony* is pieces of Eight, Ryalls,
or Boston or Bay shillings (as they call them,) or Good hard money,
as sometimes silver coin is termed by them; also Wampom, vizt. Indian
beads wch serves for change. *Pay as mony* is provisions, as afores^d one
Third cheaper then as the Assembly or Gene^l Court sets it; and *Trust*
as they and the merch^t agree for time.

Now, when the buyer comes to ask for a comodity, sometimes before
the merchant answers that he has it, he sais, *is Your pay redy?* Perhaps
the Chap Reply's Yes: what do You pay in? say's the merchant. The
buyer having answered, then the price is set; as suppose he wants a
sixpenny knife, in pay it is 12d—in pay as money eight pence, and hard
money its own price, viz. 6d. It seems a very Intricate way of trade and
what Lex Mercatoria [13] had not thought of.

Being at a merchants house, in comes a tall country fellow, w^th
his alfogeos [14] full of Tobacco; for they seldom Loose their Cudd, but
keep Chewing and Spitting as long as they'r eyes are open,—he advanc't to the midle of the Room, makes an Awkward Nodd, and spitting
a Large deal of Aromatick Tincture, he gave a scrape with his shovel
like shoo, leaving a small shovel full of dirt on the floor, made a full
stop, Hugging his own pretty Body with his hands under his arms,
Stood staring rown'd him, like a Catt let out of a Baskett. At last, like
the creature Balaam Rode on, he opened his mouth and said: have
You any Ribinen for Hatbands to sell I pray? The Questions and
Answers about the pay being past, the Ribin is bro't and opened.
Bumpkin Simpers, cryes its confounded Gay I vow; and beckning to
the door, in comes Jone Tawdry, dropping about 50 curtsees, and
stands by him: hee shows her the Ribin. *Law, You,* sais shee, *its right
Gent,*[15] do You, take it, *tis dreadfull pretty.* Then she enquires, *have You
any hood silk I pray?* wch being brought and bought, Have You any
thred silk to sew it wth says shee, wch being accomodated wth they Departed. They Generaly stand after they come in a great while speach-
less, and sometimes dont say a word till they are askt what they want,
which I Impute to the Awe they stand in of the merchants, who they
are constantly almost Indebted too; and must take what they bring
without Liberty to choose for themselves; but they serve them as well,
making the merchants stay long enough for their pay.

We may Observe here the great necessity and bennifitt both of Education and Conversation; for these people have as Large a portion of mother witt, and sometimes a Larger, than those who have bin brought up in Citties; But for want of emprovements, Render themselves almost Ridiculos, as above. I should be glad if they would leave such follies, and am sure all that Love Clean Houses (at least) would be glad on't too.

They are generaly very plain in their dress, throuout all yᵉ Colony, as I saw, and follow one another in their modes; that You may know where they belong, especially the women, meet them where you will.

Their Cheif Red Letter day is St. Election,[16] wᶜʰ is annualy Observed according to Charter, to choose their Govenʳ: a blessing they can never be thankfull enough for, as they will find, if ever it be their hard fortune to loose it. The present Govenor in Conecticott is the Honˡᵇᵉ John Winthrop Esq.[17] A Gentleman of an Ancient and Honourable Family, whose Father was Govenor here sometime before, and his Grand father had bin Govʳ of the Massachusetts. This gentleman is a very curteous and afable person, much Given to Hospitality, and has by his Good services Gain'd the affections of the people as much as any who had bin before him in that post.

Decʳ 6th. Being by this time well Recruited and rested after my Journy, my business lying unfinished by some concerns at New York depending thereupon, my Kinsman, Mr. Thomas Trowbridge of New Haven, must needs take a Journy there before it could be accomplished, I resolved to go there in company wᵗʰ him, and a man of the town wᶜʰ I engaged to wait on me there. Accordingly, Dec. 6ᵗʰ we set out from New Haven, and about 11 same morning came to Stratford ferry; wᶜʰ crossing, about two miles on the other side Baited our horses and would have eat a morsell ourselves, But the Pumpkin and Indian mixt Bred had such an Aspect, and the Bare-legg'd Punch so awkerd or rather Awfull a sound, that we left both, and proceeded forward, and about seven at night come to Fairfield, where we met with good entertainment and Lodg'd; and early next morning set forward to Norowalk, from its halfe Indian name *North-walk*, when about 12 at noon we arrived, and Had a Dinner of Fryed Venison, very savoury. Landlady wanting some pepper in the seasoning, bid the Girl hand her the spice in the little *Gay* cupp on yᵉ shelfe. From hence we Hasted towards Rye, walking and Leading our Horses neer a mile together, up a prodigios high Hill; and so Riding till about nine at night, and there arrived and took up our Lodgings at an ordinary, wᶜʰ a French family kept. Here being very hungry, I desired a fricasee, wᶜʰ the Frenchman undertakeing, mannaged so contrary to my notion of Cookery, that

I hastned to Bed superless; And being shewd the way up a pair of stairs wch had such a narrow passage that I had almost stopt by the Bulk of my Body; But arriving at my apartment found it to be a little Lento Chamber furnisht amongst other Rubbish with a High Bedd and a Low one, a Long Table, a Bench and a Bottomless chair,—Little Miss went to scratch up my Kennell wch Russelled as if shee'd bin in the Barn amongst the Husks, and supose such was the contents of the tickin— nevertheless being exceeding weary, down I laid my poor Carkes (never more tired) and found my Covering as scanty as my Bed was hard. Annon I heard another Russelling noise in Y^e Room—called to know the matter—Little miss said shee was making a bed for the men; who, when they were in Bed, complained their leggs lay out of it by reason of its shortness—my poor bones complained bitterly not being used to such Lodgings, and so did the man who was with us; and poor I made but one Grone, which was from the time I went to bed to the time I Riss, which was about three in the morning, Setting up by the Fire till Light, and having discharged our ordinary [18] wch was as dear as if we had had far Better fare—wee took our leave of Monsier and about seven in the morn come to New Rochell a french town, where we had a good Breakfast. And in the strength of that about an how'r be- fore sunsett got to York. Here I applyd myself to Mr. Burroughs, a merchant to whom I was recommended by my Kinsman Capt. Prout, and received great Civilities from him and his spouse, who were now both Deaf but very agreeable in their Conversation, Diverting me with pleasant stories of their knowledge in Brittan from whence they both come, one of which was above the rest very pleasant to me viz. my Lord Darcy had a very extravagant Brother who had mortgaged what Estate hee could not sell, and in good time dyed leaving only one son. Him his Lordship (having none of his own) took and made him Heir of his whole Estate, which he was to receive at the death of his Aunt. He and his Aunt in her widowhood held a right understanding and lived as become such Relations, shee being a discreat Gentlewoman and he an Ingenios Young man. One day Hee fell into some Company though far his inferiors, very freely told him of the Ill circumstances his fathers Estate lay under, and the many Debts he left unpaid to the wrong of poor people with whom he had dealt. The Young gentleman was put out of countenance—no way hee could think of to Redress himself—his whole dependance being on the Lady his Aunt, and how to speak to her he knew not—Hee went home, sat down to dinner and as usual sometimes with her when the Chaplain was absent, she desired him to say Grace, wch he did after this manner:

> Pray God in Mercy take my Lady Darcy
> Unto his Heavenly Throne,
> That little John may live like a man,
> And pay every man his own.

The prudent Lady took no present notice, But finishd dinner, after wch having sat and talk't awhile (as Customary) He Riss, took his Hatt and Going out she desired him to give her leave to speak to him in her Clossett, Where being come she desired to know why hee prayed for her Death in the manner aforesaid, and what part of her deportment towards him merritted such desires. Hee Reply'd, none at all, But he was under such disadvantages that nothing but that could do him service, and told her how he had been affronted as above, and what Impressions it had made upon him. The Lady made him a gentle reprimand that he had not informed her after another manner, Bid him see what his father owed and he should have money to pay it to a penny, And always to lett her know his wants and he should have a redy supply. The Young Gentleman charm'd with his Aunts Discrete management, Beggd her pardon and accepted her kind offer and retrieved his fathers Estate, &c. and said Hee hoped his Aunt would never dye, for shee had done better by him than hee could have done for himself.—Mr. Burroughs went with me to Vendue [19] where I bought about 100 Rheem of paper wch was retaken in a flyboat from Holland and sold very Reasonably here—some ten, some Eight shillings per Rheem by the Lott wch was ten Rheem in a Lott. And at the Vendue I made a great many acquaintances amongst the good women of the town, who curteosly invited me to their houses and generously entertained me.

The Cittie of New York is a pleasant, well compacted place, situated on a Commodius River wch is a fine harbour for shipping. The Buildings Brick Generaly, very stately and high, though not altogether like ours in Boston. The Bricks in some of the Houses are of divers Coullers and laid in Checkers, being glazed look very agreeable. The inside of them are neat to admiration, the wooden work, for only the walls are plasterd, and the Sumers and Gist [20] are plained and kept very white scowr'd as so is all the partitions if made of Bords. The fire places have no Jambs (as ours have) But the Backs run flush with the walls, and the Hearth is of Tyles and is as farr out into the Room at the Ends as before the fire, wch is Generally Five foot in the Low'r rooms, and the peice over where the mantle tree should be is made as ours with Joyners work, and as I supose is fasten'd to iron rodds inside. The House where the Vendue was, had Chimney Corners like ours, and they and the hearths were laid wth the finest tile that I ever see, and the stair cases laid all with white tile which is ever clean, and so are the walls of the Kitchen wch had a Brick floor. They were making Great preparations to Receive their Govenor, Lord Cornbury [21] from the Jerseys, and for that End raised the militia to Gard him on shore to the fort.

They are Generaly of the Church of England and have a New England Gentleman for their minister, and a very fine church set out with all Customary requsites. There are also a Dutch and Divers Conventicles as they call them, viz. Baptist, Quakers, &c. They are not strict in keeping the Sabbath as in Boston and other places where I had bin, But seem to deal with great exactness as farr as I see or Deall with. They are sociable to one another and Curteos and Civill to strangers and fare well in their houses. The English go very fasheonable in their dress. Dut the Dutch, especially the middling sort, differ from our women, in their habitt go loose, were French muches wch are like a Capp and a head band in one, leaving their ears bare, which are sett out wth Jewells of a large size and many in number. And their fingers hoop't with Rings, some with large stones in them of many Coullers as were their pendants in their ears, which You should see very old women wear as well as Young.

They have Vendues very frequently and make their Earnings very well by them, for they treat with good Liquor Liberally, and the Customers Drink as Liberally and Generally pay for't as well, by paying for that which they Bidd up Briskly for, after the sack has gone plentifully about, tho' sometimes good penny worths are got there. Their Diversions in the Winter is Riding Sleys about three or four Miles out of Town, where they have Houses of entertainment at a place called the Bowery, and some go to friends Houses who handsomely treat them. Mr. Burroughs cary'd his spouse and Daughter and myself out to one Madame Dowes, a Gentlewoman that lived at a farm House, who gave us a handsome Entertainment of five or six Dishes and choice Beer and metheglin,[22] Cyder, &c. all which she said was the produce of her farm. I believe we mett 50 or 60 slays that day—they fly with great swiftness and some are so furious that they'le turn out of the path for none except a Loaden Cart. Nor do they spare for any diversion the place affords, and sociable to a degree, they'r Tables being as free to their Naybours as to themselves.

Having here transacted the affair I went upon and some other that fell in the way, after about a fortnight's stay there I left New-York with no Little regrett, and Thursday, Dec. 21, set out for New Haven wth my Kinsman Trowbridge, and the man that waited on me about one afternoon, and about three come to half-way house about ten miles out of town, where we Baited and went forward, and about 5 come to Spiting Devil, Else Kings bridge,[23] where they pay three pence for passing over with a horse, which the man that keeps the Gate set up at the end of the Bridge receives.

We hoped to reach the french town and Lodg there that night, but unhapily lost our way about four miles short, and being overtaken by a great storm of wind and snow which set full in our faces about dark, we were very uneasy. But meeting one Gardner who lived in a Cottage thereabout, offered us his fire to set by, having but one poor Bedd, and his wife not well, &c. or he would go to a House with us, where he thought we might be better accommodated—thither we went, But a surly old shee Creature, not worthy the name of woman, who would hardly let us go into her Door, though the weather was so stormy none but shee would have turnd out a Dogg. But her son whose name was gallop, who lived Just by Invited us to his house and shewed me two pair of stairs, viz. one up the loft and tother up the Bedd, wch was as hard as it was high, and warmed it with a hott stone at the feet. I lay very uncomfortably, insomuch that I was so very cold and sick I was forced to call them up to give me something to warm me. They had nothing but milk in the house, wch they Boild, and to make it better sweetened wth molasses, which I not knowing or thinking oft till it was down and coming up agen wch it did in so plentifull a manner that my host was soon paid double for his portion, and that in specia. But I believe it did me service in Cleering my stomach. So after this sick and weary night at East Chester, (a very miserable poor place,) the weather being now fair, Friday the 22^d Dec. we set out for New Rochell, where being come we had good Entertainment and Recruited ourselves very well. This is a very pretty place well compact, and good handsome houses, Clean, good and passable Rodes, and situated on a Navigable River, abundance of land well fined and Cleerd all along as wee passed, which caused in me a Love to the place, wch I could have been content to live in it. Here wee Ridd over a Bridge made of one entire stone of such a Breadth that a cart might pass with safety, and to spare—it lay over a passage cutt through a Rock to convey water to a mill not farr off. Here are three fine Taverns within call of each other, very good provision for Travailers.

Thence we travailed through Merrinak, a neet, though little place, wth a navigable River before it, one of the pleasantest I ever see—Here were good Buildings, Especialy one, a very fine seat, wch they told me was Col. Hethcoats, who I had heard was a very fine Gentleman.

From hence we come to Hors Neck, where wee Baited, and they told me that one Church of England parson officiated in all these three towns once every Sunday in turns throughout the Year; and that they all could but poorly maintaine him, which they grudg'd to do, being a poor and quarelsome crew as I understand by our Host; their Quarelling about their choice of Minister, they chose to have none—But caused the Government to send this Gentleman to them. Here wee took leave of York Government, and Descending the Mountainos passage that almost broke my heart in ascending before, we come to Stamford, a well compact Town, but miserable meeting house, wch we passed, and thro' many and great difficulties, as Bridges which were exceeding high and very tottering and of vast Length, steep and Rocky Hills and precipices, (Buggbears to a fearful female travailer.) About nine at night we come to Norrwalk, having crept over a timber of a Broken Bridge about thirty foot long, and perhaps fifty to ye water. I was exceeding tired and cold when we come to our Inn, and could get nothing there but poor entertainment, and the impertinant Bable of one of the worst of men, among many others of which our Host made one, who, had he bin one degree Impudenter, would have outdone his Grandfather. And this I think is the most perplexed night I have yet had. From hence, Saturday, Dec. 23, a very cold and windy day, after an Intolerable night's Lodging, wee hasted forward only observing in our way the Town to be situated on a Navigable river wth indiferent Buildings and people more refind than in some of the Country towns wee had passed, tho' vicious enough, the Church and Tavern being next neighbours. Having Ridd thro a difficult River wee come to Fairfield where wee Baited and were much refreshed as well with the Good things wch gratified our appetites as the time took to rest our wearied Limbs, wch Latter I employed in enquiring concerning the Town and manners of the people, &c. This is a considerable town, and filled as they say with wealthy people—have a spacious meeting house and good Buildings. But the Inhabitants are Litigious, nor do they well agree with their minister, who (they say) is a very worthy Gentleman.[24]

They have aboundance of sheep, whose very Dung brings them great gain, with part of which they pay their Parsons sallery, And they Grudg that, prefering their Dung before their minister. They Lett out their sheep at so much as they agree upon for a night; the highest Bidder always caries them, And they will sufficiently Dung a Large quantity of Land before morning. But were once Bitt by a sharper who had them a night and sheared them all before morning—From hence we went to Stratford, the next Town, in which I observed but few houses, and those not very good ones. But the people that I conversed with were civill and good natured. Here we staid till late at night, being to cross a Dangerous River ferry, the River at that time full of Ice; but after about four hours waiting with great difficulty wee got over. My fears and fatigues prevented my here taking any particular observation. Being got to Milford, it being late in the night, I could go no further; my fellow travailer going forward, I was invited to Lodg at Mrs. ——, a very kind and civill Gentlewoman, by whom I was handsomely and kindly entertained till the next night. The people here go very plain in their apparel (more plain than I had observed in the towns I had passed) and seem to be very grave and serious. They told me there was a singing Quaker lived there, or at least had a strong inclination to be so, His Spouse not at all affected that way. Some of the singing Crew come there one day to visit him, who being then abroad, they sat down (to the woman's no small vexation) Humming and singing and groneing after their conjuring way—Says the woman are you singing quakers? Yea says They—Then take my squalling Brat of a child here and sing to it says she for I have almost split my throat wth singing to him and cant get the Rogue to sleep. They took this as a great Indignity, and mediately departed. Shaking the dust from their Heels left the good woman and her Child among the number of the wicked.

This is a Seaport place and accomodated with a Good Harbour, But I had not opportunity to make particular observations because it was Sabbath day—This Evening.

December 24. I set out with the Gentlewomans son who she very civilly offered to go with me when she see no parswasions would cause me to stay which she pressingly desired, and crossing a ferry having but nine miles to New Haven, in a short time arrived there and was Kindly received and well accommodated amongst my Friends and Relations.

The Government of Connecticut Collony begins westward towards York at Stanford (as I am told) and so runs Eastward towards Boston (I mean in my range, because I dont intend to extend my description beyond my own travails) and ends that way at Stonington—And has a great many Large towns lying more northerly. It is a plentiful Country for provisions of all sorts and its Generally Healthy. No one that can and will be dilligent in this place need fear poverty nor the want of food and Rayment.

January 6th. Being now well Recruited and fitt for business I discoursed the persons I was concerned with, that we might finnish in

order to my return to Boston. They delay^d as they had hitherto done
hoping to tire my Patience. But I was resolute to stay and see an End
of the matter let it be never so much to my disadvantage—So January
9th they come again and promise the Wednesday following to go
through with the distribution of the Estate which they delayed till
Thursday and then come with new amusements. But at length by the
mediation of that holy good Gentleman, the Rev. Mr. James Pierpont,[25]
the minister of New Haven, and with the advice and assistance of other
our Good friends we come to an accommodation and distribution,
which having finished though not till February, the man that waited
on me to York taking the charge of me I sit out for Boston. We went
from New Haven upon the ice (the ferry being not passable thereby)
and the Rev. Mr. Pierpont wth Madam Prout Cuzin Trowbridge and
divers others were taking leave wee went onward without any thing
Remarkabl till wee come to New London and Lodged again at Mr.
Saltonstalls—and here I dismist my Guide, and my Generos entertainer provided me Mr. Samuel Rogers of that place to go home with
me—I stayed a day here Longer than I intended by the Commands
of the Honble Govenor Winthrop to stay and take a supper with him
whose wonderful civility I may not omitt. The next morning I Crossed
ye Ferry to Groton, having had the Honor of the Company, of Madam
Livingston (who is the Govenors Daughter) and Mary Christophers and
divers others to the boat—And that night Lodg^d at Stonington and had
Rost Beef and pumpkin sause for supper. The next night at Haven's
and had Rost fowle, and the next day wee come to a river which by
Reason of Y^e Freshetts coming down was swell'd so high wee fear^d
it impassable and the rapid stream was very terryfying—However we
must over and that in a small Cannoo. Mr. Rogers assuring me of his
good Conduct, I after a stay of near an how'r on the shore for consultation went into the Cannoo, and Mr. Rogers paddled about 100 yards
up the Creek by the shore side, turned into the swift stream and dexter-
ously steering her in a moment wee come to the other side as swiftly
passing as an arrow shott out of the Bow by a strong arm. I staid on
ye shore till Hee returned to fetch our horses, which he caused to
swim over himself bringing the furniture in the Cannoo. But it is past
my skill to express the Exceeding fright all their transactions formed
in me. Wee were now in the colony of the Massachusetts and taking
Lodgings at the first Inn we come too had a pretty difficult passage the
next day which was the second of March by reason of the sloughy ways
then thawed by the Sunn. Here I mett Capt. John Richards of Boston
who was going home, So being very glad of his Company we Rode

something harder than hitherto, and missing my way in going up a very steep Hill, my horse dropt down under me as Dead; this new surprize no little hurt me meeting it Just at the Entrance into Dedham from whence we intended to reach home that night. But was now obliged to gett another Hors there and leave my own, resolving for Boston that night if possible. But in going over the Causeway at Dedham the Bridge being overflowed by the high waters comming down I very narrowly escaped falling over into the river Hors and all wch twas almost a miracle I did not—now it grew late in the afternoon and the people having very much discouraged us about the sloughy way wch they said wee should find very difficult and hazardous it so wrought on mee being tired and dispirited and disapointed of my desires of going home that I agreed to Lodg there that night wch wee did at the house of one Draper, and the next day being March 3d wee got safe home to Boston, where I found my aged and tender mother and my Dear and only Child in good health with open arms redy to receive me, and my Kind relations and friends flocking in to welcome mee and hear the story of my transactions and travails I having this day bin five months from home and now I cannot fully express my Joy and Satisfaction. But desire sincearly to adore my Great Benefactor for thus graciously carying forth and returning in safety his unworthy handmaid.

JOSEPH GREEN, 1675–1715

[After graduation from college in 1695, Joseph Green, the son of a Cambridge tailor, experienced a religious conversion while teaching school at Roxbury. Thereupon he returned to college, secured his Master's degree, and was settled as pastor at Salem Village (Danvers) in 1698. He did great service restoring calm after the witchcraft panic, and fostered education in the somewhat backward town. His "Diary," kept intermittently from March 4, 1700, to June 18, 1715—five months before his death—is largely a record of the domestic contentment of a country parson who loved gardening, fishing, hunting, and dispensing quiet hospitality. His account of the *aurora borealis* on December 18, 1700, is probably the earliest notice of the phenomenon in New England.

See Samuel P. Fowler, "Biographical Sketch and Diary of Rev. Joseph Green, of Salem Village," *Essex Institute Historical Collections*, VIII (1868), 91–96, 165–174, 215–224; X (1869), pt. I, 73–104; XXXVI (1900), 325–330. The text is from *idem*, X, 86–89. See Sibley, *Biographical Sketches*, IV, 228–233.]

EXTRACTS FROM GREEN'S "DIARY."

M AY 19, 1710] I went down to ye mouth of ye harbour and lay in ye boat at an anchor.

May 20. I rowed over ye Sound and got on to Mr. Gardner's Island.[1] Ye Indian's carried me over and set me on shore at Fire Place. At sunset I travelled eight miles to E. H.[2]

21. *Sab.* I preached at East Hampton in forenoon, from Luke 7, 2, and P.M., Luke 10, 41. I was very faint with my travelling.

22. I visited ye people and found them very kind.

24. I visited Mr. White[3] at Sag [Harbor] and Mr. Whiting[4] at S. Hampton.

25. I prepared to come home.

26. After 2 o'clock I came with my mother, first to Mr. Gardner's Island, and then in a whale boat; about sun one hour and one half high. I arrived safe at New London about 11 o'clock at night. We lodged at Mr. Coits.[5]

27. We travelled heavy laden to Major Fitches at Canter.

28. *Sab.* I preached, P.M., at Canterbury.

29. My horse ran away, which hindered us two hours. Mr. Easton came eight miles and brought my mother; we travelled to Providence.

30. I hired men to bring my mother. 30 inst. we came to brother Jonathan's.

31. I came home and found all well and have had much experience of God's goodness to me abroad and to mine at home.

June 8. I went with my wife to Wenham on J. Gansons horse.

18. *Sab.* Mr. Blowers[6] was ill, and sent me word he could not exchange as he expected.

July 5. Dined at Zach. Hicks and went to Boston in Calash to brother S. Green's.

6. Bought a brass kettle, 3£. 6 shil. 6 d.; and went to Cambridge and brought my mother home with me at 6 o'clock.

9. Went to Wenham; ye most plentiful rain we have had these three summers.

10. I came home; training, half ye company pricked.

28. I tried first to catch pigeons.

Aug. 2. I got two dozen of pigeons. Mr. Blowers here.

7. Rain. Nine men 'listed for Port Royal.

8. Catched pigeons.

10. Pubb. thanksgiving, especially for rain.

16. Rain. Catched eight dozen and one half pigeons.

28. Catched eight dozen pigeons.

Sept. 1. Catched six dozen pigeons.

Sept. 4. I went to Boston to visit Br. Sam. Gerrish [7] sick. He was very bad at night. Saw old Mr. Mather.[8] Visited Mr. Wadsworth.[9]

Sept. 6. I carried my mother to Salem Lecture, dined with Maj. Sewell.

18. Our fleet of 36 sail set out for Port Royall.

28. Pubb. Fast for ye fleet against P. Royall.

Oct. 3. I went to Wenham at ye ministers meeting, and then met Mr. Rogers [10] of Ipswich and Mr. Blowers. We had deacon Fitches case.

4. I went to Wenham with my wife. Mr. Noyes [11] and I wrote over ye ministers determination. Boiled Syder.

22. *Sab.* News from Port Royall; rain A.M.

Nov. 6. Preparing for winter. Ben. H [utchinson] in my orchard.

7. Storm at night. Capt. Eastes' brother here. I went to Benj. H. and prayed him to keep his horses out of my orchard. He told me if my feed was not eaten quickly ye snow would cover it, &c.

8. B. Hu. horses in every night this week.

Nov. 11. I at study. Sent for Benj. H. and prayed him to mend up his fence, which he did and kept them out this one night.

Nov. 17. Benj. H. three jades having been here in my orchard every night this week, had got such a hank [ering] that they would not easily be drove out, so that J. H. tried last night at 9 o'clock to get them out till he was cold and tired, and forced to leave them in. And as we wer trying to get them out this morning, the two jades trying to jump out at once by ye well, one pressed another so as he jumped into my well, and altho. we got him out with Mr. Hutchinson's help, yet he soon dyed. Snow.

18. Snow. I went to Mr. H. he said I might pay for one-half of his colt, and that he could by the law force me to pay all. I told him I was no ways to blame about his colt being killed; but I looked it as a Providential rebuke unto him for suffering his jades to afflict me. I told him he only was to blame, because I had spake and sent to him ten times to look to his horses. He told me no body desired him to fetter his horses in the winter, and that folks fields was mostly common.

25. I went to Mrs. Walcuts and urged her to pole her wall.

27. I told Benj. Hutch. I would give his boys 20 shil. for his colt that fell into my well, and also ye damage his horses had done me this month, which I valued 20 shil. more. And he said that would satisfy *him* and all his family. I told him I gave it to him to make him easy and

if that end was not obtained, I should account my money thrown away. For I knew no law did oblige me to pay for his colt, that came over a lawful fence into my well.

Dec. 5. I had ground ploughed. Killed four hogs, in all 350 pounds.

23. I at study; not well. Clear and cold.

28. Killed three hogs 316 pounds, so that we have this year killed 666 pounds of pork.

1711. Jan. 2. Boys cyphering at home.

22. I was called up at 4 o'clock to pray with Benj. Hutchinson's child; it died at 6 o'clock.

26. Killed a calf; sent John Hicks to Salem with 21 3-4 lbs. to Mr. Kitchen. He bought ginger, starch, molasses and wine.

Feb. 23. Cold. I wrote deeds for J. Ross. Brewed.

25. *Sab.* Snowed hard all day; a thin assembly.

March 1. Cold. Ye church kept a Fast at ye house of Dea. Benj. Putnam's, to pray for ye pouring out of ye spirit on us, &c. a g. d.; my wife ill.

4. *Sab.* 100 communicants.

14. I went to Salem, paid 24 shil. to Mr. Noyes. Bought a hat for Nedd at Mr. K's.

19. I bought 3 acres of woodland of Benj. Hutchinson for 15£. I paid him 5£. and gave him a bond for 10£., to be paid in paper or silver, April 10, 1712.

27. Meeting of ye Inhabitants about covering ye house &c. I had three men making wall.

COTTON MATHER

[It was customary for the congregations in New England churches to use metrical versions of the Psalms during the service, alternately singing and reading line by line. But the congregations knew hardly ten tunes by ear, and few could sing words to more than five. During the first quarter of the eighteenth century discontent arose over the manner of singing, some of the more fastidious claiming that without the aid of musical notations the zeal of the worshippers often betrayed them into sounds "which made a Jar in the ears" (letter of Cotton Mather, *Collection of the Massachusetts Historical Society*, seventh series, VIII, 693). Several entered into the controversy whether singing by note, that is, "Regular Singing," should not supplant the old method of singing by ear.

Cotton Mather was among the first to champion the newer way,

with a tract published in Boston in 1721 called *The Accomplished Singer.
Instructions . . . How the Melody of Regular Singing, and the Skill of doing it,
according to the Rules of it, may be easily arrived unto.* As most ministers
heartily favored "Regular Singing," doubtless the older psalmodies
lacking notations were less and less used thenceforth.

See Matt B. Jones, "Some Bibliographical Notes on Cotton Mather's
'The Accomplished Singer,'" *Publications of the Colonial Society of Massachusetts,* XXVIII (1935), 186–193.]

THE ACCOMPLISHED SINGER.

§ 1. It is the Concern of every one that would enjoy *Tranquillity* in
this World, or obtain *Felicity* in the World to come, to follow that Holy
Direction of Heaven, *Exercise thy self in* PIETY. And there is no *Exercise*
of PIETY more unexceptionable than that of *making a Joyful* Noise of
SINGING in the Praises of our GOD; That of signifying our *Delight* in
Divine *Truths* by SINGING of them; That of *Uttering* the Sentiments of
Devotion, with the *Voice,* and such a *Modulation of the Voice,* as will
naturally express the *Satisfaction* and *Elevation* of the *Mind,* which a
Grave SONG shall be expressive of. 'Tis indeed a very *Ancient Way* of
Glorifying the Blessed GOD; As *Ancient* as the Day *when the Foundations
of the Earth were fastened,* and *the Corner-Stone thereof was laid.* The *Morning-
Stars* then *Sang together.* And it is as *Extensive* an one; For it is Remarkable, That *All Nations* make SINGING to be one part of the *Worship*
which they pay unto their GOD. Those Few *Untuned Souls,* who affect
upon Principle to distinguish themselves from the rest of Mankind
by the Character of *Non-Singers,* do seem too much to divest themselves
of an *Humanity,* whereof it may be said unto them, *Doth not Nature it self
teach it you?* Be sure, they sufficiently differ from the *Primitive Christians;*
For, though the *Eastern* Churches were at first Superiour to the *Western,*
for the *Zeal of the House of* GOD in this matter, yet both betimes Con-
curr'd in it. Not only *Justin* the *Martyr,* and *Clemens* of *Alexandria,* as
well as *Tertullian,* and several others of the *Primitive Writers,* but also
Governour *Pliny* himself will tell us, what *Singers to their* GOD, the Faithful were then known to be; and how much they *Worshipped* Him in
these *Beauties of Holiness.*

§ 2. BUT this piece of *Natural Worship* is further Confirmed by a
positive Institution of GOD our SAVIOUR for it. The *Sacred Scriptures* with
which the Holy SPIRIT of GOD has Enriched us, have directed us unto
this *Way* of Worshipping. In our *Old Testament* we there find it as a
Command of GOD; but Calculated particularly for Times under the

New-Testament: Psal. LXVIII. 32. *Sing Praises unto* GOD, *ye Kingdoms of the Earth, O Sing Praises unto the Lord.* And Psal. C. 1, 2. *Make a Joyful Noise unto the Lord, All ye Lands; Come into his Presence with Singing.* The *Ninety-fifth Psalm* in our Psalter, does according to the Interpretation of our Apostle *Paul,* an *Interpreter, One of a Thousand,* certainly to be relied upon!——Prescribe the *Duties* of a *Sabbath* in the Days of the Gospel. But what is the *First* of those Duties? *O come, Let us sing unto the Lord, Let us with Psalms make a Joyful Noise unto Him.* In our *New-Testament* it self 'tis a Thing so positively enjoined, that it must be a wonder, if any Christian can make any Question of it. How plainly is it commanded? Jam. V. 13. *Is any cheerful among you, Let him sing Psalms.* Yea, In the *Pauline* Epistles, we have it; how frequently, how earnestly inculcated! This Exercise is none of those *Intrusions* into our *Worship,* which the *Worshippers in the Inner-Court,* wou'd see a *Quo Warranto* serv'd upon, 'Tis *Warranted* with a most Incontestible *Institution.* . . .

IT would follow from hence, that such a *Version* of the PSALMS, as keeps most *Close to the Original,* were most of all to be wished for. Of about Three Times seven Translations of the *Psalms,* which we have seen fitted for the Tunes of our *Sacred Songs* there is not one, but what for the sake of a needless *Rhyme,* does *Leave out* very much of what the Holy SPIRIT has inserted in the *Original,* and *put in* as much of what is not *there* to be met withal. Of these Translations, there are some *Nearer* to the *Original* than others, and have more of *That* in it, with least of Diversion from it, or Addition to it: And the *Nearest* are certainly the most worthy to have our Meditations employed upon them. After all, of what Consequence is (the *Similis Desimentia* of) *Rhyme,* to our *Psalmody,* when even to *Poetry* it self, it is not Essential? The *Psalms* might easily be so turned into *Blank Verse,* that there should be ALL, and ONLY, what it has pleased the Holy One to give us in the *Original.* And no doubt there will a Time come, when Myriads of Christians will chuse to Serve GOD with such a *Pure Offering,* and present unto Him what is *purely His own,* rather than have their Devotions in Danger of being palled, by the sense of *Humane Debasements,* upon what they Address unto Him. An Honourable Counsellor in the Low-Countries, Mynheer *Bruyne,* published in Dutch, the PSALMS in such *Blank Verse.* But because his Translation differed, as it must, from what was in the *Common Bible,* another who was a Master of Musick, fitted a variety of Tunes to the Psalter, without changing a word in the *Common Bible.* However the Tunes were so various, and the necessary Repetition of the same Word so frequent, that this did not much mend the matter. . . .

The Skill of *Regular Singing,* is among the *Gifts* of GOD unto the Chil-

dren of Men, and by no means unthankfully to be Neglected or Despised. For the Congregations, wherein 'tis wanting, to recover a
Regular Singing, would be really a *Reformation*, and a Recovery out of
an *Apostacy*, and what we may judge that Heaven would be pleased
withal. We ought certainly to Serve our GOD with our *Best*, and *Regular
Singing* must needs be *Better* than the confused Noise of a Wilderness.
GOD is not for Confusion in the Churches of the Saints; but requires, *Let all
things be done decently.* 'Tis a Great Mistake of some weak People, That
the *Times* regulated with the *Notes* used in the *Regular Singing* of our
Churches are the same that are used in the Church of *Rome*. And
what if they were? Our *Psalms* too are used there. But the *Tunes* used
in the *French Psalmody*, and from Them in the *Dutch* also, were set by
a famous Martyr of JESUS CHRIST; And when *Sternhold* and *Hopkins* [1]
illuminated *England*, with their Version of the *Psalms*, the *Tunes* have
been set by such as a Good Protestant may be willing to hold Communion withal. The *Tunes* commonly used in our Churches, are *Few;*
T'were well if there were *more*. But they are also *Grave*, and such as
well *become the Oracles of GOD*, and such as do Steer clear of the Two
Shelves, which *Austin* was afraid of; when he did, *In cantu Sacro fluctuare,
inter Periculum Voluptatis, et Experimentum Salubritatis;* in danger of too
much *Delicacy* on the one side, and *Asperity* on the other.

THE *Musick* of the Ancient Hebrews, an Adjustment whereto seems
to be all the *Measure* of their *Poetry*, (after all the Attempts of *Gomarus*,
and other Learned Men otherwise to *Measure* it,) being utterly Lost;
and as *Aben-Ezra* [2] observes, of the *Musical Instruments* in the *Hundred
and Fiftieth Psalm*, wholly Irrecoverable; we have no way Left us now,
but with *Tunes* composed by the *Chief Musicians* for us, to *do as well as
we can.*

SOLOMON STODDARD, 1643–1729

[It was expected of ministers, to the extent they were dialecticians
and arbiters of public morals, that they should decide questions of
behavior as well as polity. The ministers certainly never shirked such
responsibility. When custom or logic failed, there remained the firm
rock of the Bible from which to cite precedent, and thus, it was hoped,
end counter-argument. A tract written by Solomon Stoddard was published in 1722, on matters of morals, called *An Answer to Some Cases
of Conscience Respecting the Country.* Stoddard, the grandfather of Jonathan
Edwards, had been pastor of the Northampton church since 1672,
and was a man held in great esteem.

The fashion of wearing long hair, attacked by the General Court and by ministers during the mid-seventeenth century, had fallen into disfavor later in the century when periwigs came into style. The General Court condemned periwigs in 1675. But as time passed, such questions of minor morals agitated the country less and less. By 1710, though the laws forbidding long hair and periwigs continued on the statutes, enforcement was negligible.

On Stoddard, see Sibley, *Biographical Sketches*, II, 111–122. The text is from *An Answer, etc.*, pp. 4–7, 12, 13.]

AN ANSWER TO SOME CASES OF CONSCIENCE

Q. IV. Is it Lawfull to wear long Hair?

ANSW. It was the Custom in *England* to cut their Hair all off, in imitation of King *Henry* the Eighth, who out of an humour, as Dr. *Fuller* [1] says, cut off his Hair. This custom continued for about three-score years: but by degrees, Men took a greater liberty; tho some Men placed Religion in it: yet in length of time, they were not so scrupulous as formerly. And some wore their Hair very long. And many of those that wear Periwigs, use such as are of a very great length. And the custom doth now prevail among Pious People. But it seems utterly Unlawful to wear their Hair long; It is a great Burden and Cumber; it is Effiminacy, and a vast Expence.

One Scripture that condemns it, 1 Cor. 11. 14. *Doth not even nature it self teach you, that if a man wear long hair, it is a shame to him?* That which the light of Nature condemns, is a Moral Evil. The light of Nature is to be our Rule in ordinary cases. The reason why it is a shame to wear long Hair is, because it is a Sin: the light of Nature doth condemn it; therefore it is sinfull.

The principal Objection that is brought to evade the Authority of this Place, is, That by *Nature*, Custom is meant. So Dr. *Hammond* [2] expounds it: I judge he doth it, that he may strengthen himself in his *Arminianism*, that he may have the better pretence to expound it so, *Eph.* 2. 3. where it is said, *We are by nature children of wrath, even as others*. His Exposition there is contrary to the Rule of *Faith;* and in this Place, contrary to the Rule of *Life*. We sometimes say that Custom is a second nature: yet it is never so used in the Scripture: the Interpretation is without Precedent: and the Apostle being presently after to speak of Custom, useth another word: 1 *Cor.* 11. 16. He saith, We have no such *Custom*. The Apostles Expression is very remarkable, He saith, *even Nature it self*, as if he had foreseen that Men would put a false interpretation on his words. He doth not content himself to say, *Nature;* but that they may not suppose he meant *Custom.* He saith, *Even Nature it self.* Undoubtedly he was guided therein by the Spirit of GOD. Besides, it was not true, that *Custom* taught them that it was a shame for a Man to wear long Hair: for it was the *Custom* of the *Greeks* to wear their Hair *long:* The *Romans* wore their Hair *short;* but the *Greeks* wore their Hair *long. Homer* calls the Grecians *Comati Achivi.*[3] And when *Alexander* was in a rage with *Cassander* one of his Nobles; he took him by the Hair, and knocked his head against the wall. Moreover in the next verse, 1 *Cor.* 11. 13. The Apostle to shew, that Nature teaches Women to wear their Hair *long;* He saith, *If a woman have long hair, it is a glory to her; for her hair is given her for a covering.* GOD gave it to *Women* for a covering, but not to *Men.*

Another Scripture doth also condemn it, *viz.* Ezek. 44. 20. *Neither shall they shave their heads, nor suffer their locks to grow long, they shall only poll their heads.* Here are two Extreams forbid; *Shaving the head,* and *suffering their locks to grow long.* This must either signify some spiritual thing; but no Man can devise what; or some Gospel Institution; and if so, why is it not enjoyned unto Ministers in the New Testament, or else it is a Moral Law: and so it must be. One part of it, is surely Moral; *They shall not shave their heads;* therefore the other part is Moral also; *They shall not suffer their locks to grow long.*

The Command of GOD requiring the Nazarites to nourish their Hair, is no vindication of long Hair; but a forcible reason against it; which will appear, if we consider two things.

1. SUCH Actions, as under their *ordinary* circumstances, are Moral Evils; under *extraordinary* circumstances, be very good: So for *Brothers* and *Sisters* to joyn in Wedlock, as *Adam's* Children did: For the *Brother,* among the *Jews,* to Marry his *Brother's* Wife: So, for a Physician, to give an intoxicating Potion: to do that which ordinarily, is contrary to a Rule of Modesty. One Command, in many cases, must give way to another.

2. The Nazarites were to deny themselves many comforts, to shew us that we should be mortified to the things of this World. Upon a Religious account, they were to abstain from Wine & Raisins, *&c.* and upon that account, they were to deny themselves of that neatness and comeliness in wearing their Hair, that was a duty in other Men.

It was a part of the Calamity that came upon *Nebuchadnezzar,* that his Hairs were grown like Eagles Feathers, *and his Nailes like birds claws,* Dan. 4. 33.

[*The following Letter, written by the same learned Author many years ago, may be here inserted.*]

Sir,

In compliance with your desire, I now send you my Thoughts concerning *Periwigs*. I cannot see sufficient Reason to condemn them Universally. God does allow Man, by *Art* to supply the defects of *Nature*. Hair artificially prepared may supply as fully & innocently, the want of Hair, as any other matter artificially prepared.

But yet I judge that there is abundance of Sin, in this Country, in wearing *Periwigs*. Particularly, in these two things;

First, When Men do wear them needlessly, in compliance with the Fashion. Their own Hair is sufficient for all those Ends that God has given Hair for. One Man's Hair is comlier than another's. And so it is with their Faces, and Bodies. Some cut off their Own because of the Colour; it is *Red* or *Grey;* Some, because it is *Streight;* Some, because it is *Frizel'd;* and some, only, because it is their *Own*.

Secondly, When those that may have just occasion to wear them, doe wear them in such a Ruffianly way, as it would be utterly unlawfull to wear their own Hair in. Some of them are of an unreasonable *Length;* and generally, they are extravagant as to their *Bushyness*. . . .

The *Practice* seems, to me, to have these four *Evils* in it:

1. It is an *Uncontentedness* with that Provision that God has made for Men. God has generally given Men such Hair as is comly; and a sufficiency of it. And when it is so, Men have cause to be well satisfyed. When God has given to Men such Hair as is sutable to answer the Ends of Hair; It seems to be a *Despising* of the Goodness of God, to cut it off, in compliance with a Vain Fashion. . . .

2. It is *Wastefullness*. Abundance of Money is *needlessly* spent in maintaining this *Practice*. Some of the Men that use it, have need enough of the Money other ways; and lay themselves under Temptation by this *Extravagancy;* either to oppress Men in their Dealings; or to be more Pinching in other Cases, than they ought to be. And those Men that have more plentiful Estates, have no Liberty to use them according to their own Pleasure. That Money that may be laid out to *Advantage*, should not be spent *Unprofitably*.

3. It is *Pride:* they do it to make a great *Shew;* It is from an Affectation of *Swaggering;* it is an Affecting of *Finery* that there is no just occasion for. They count it *Brave* to be in the Fashion; crave the honour of being counted as *Gallant* as others. It is too much *Flanting*.

4. It is *contrary to Gravity*. There is a Masculine Gravity that should

appear in the Countenances of Men, discovering a Solemnity of Spirit. But this *Practice* is *Light*, and *Effeminat*. Thô it make a *Shew;* yet it takes much away from the Presence of Men. Such *Curiosity* discovers much *Vanity* in the Mind; and makes others to esteem the more lightly of them; and not to shew that Respect to them. This *Practice* makes them look, as if they were more dispos'd *to Court a Maid;* than to bear upon their Hearts the weighty Concernments of GOD's Kingdom.

But I am fearful that the Stream runs so strong this way, that no Endeavours will work a Publick Reformation; until GOD does give Men another Spirit; or lay them under other Dispensations. Yet it may not be without good Effect on some particular Persons, if a Testimony be born against the *Practice;* if not to *Reduce* any; yet to *Prevent* some that were in danger.

Thus Sir, I have endeavoured to give some Satisfaction to your Desires; which I hope you will take in good part, from your Servant.

N——*H. July,* 29. 1701.

Q. VIII. DID WE ANY WRONG TO THE *INDIANS* IN BUYING THEIR LAND AT A SMALL PRICE?

A. 1. There was some part of the Land that was not purchased, neither was there need that it should; it was *vacuum domicilium;* [4] and so might be possessed by vertue of GOD's grant to Mankind, Gen. 1. 28. *And God blessed them, and God said unto them, Be fruitful and multiply and replenish the earth, and subdue it: and have dominion over the fish of the sea, and over the fowl of the air, and over every living thing that moveth upon the earth.* The *Indians* made no use of it, but for Hunting. By GOD's first Grant Men were to subdue the Earth. When *Abraham* came into the Land of *Canaan*, he made use of vacant Land as he pleased: so did *Isaac* and *Jacob*.

2. The Indians were well contented that we should sit down by them. And it would have been for great Advantage, both for this World, and the Other; if they had been wise enough to make use of their Opportunities. It has been common with many People, in planing this World since the Flood, to admit Neighbours, to sit down by them.

3. Tho' we gave but a small Price for what we bought; we gave them their demands, we came to their Market, and gave them their price; and indeed, it was worth but little: And had it continued in their hands, it would have been of little value. It is our dwelling on it, and our Improvements, that have made it to be of Worth.

Letter of Margaret Winthrop to Her Husband. (For text, see p. 467.)

Chapter V

BIOGRAPHIES AND LETTERS

Among the three or four scamps and scalawags who somehow strayed into the holy communities of New England, and whose disreputable figures add a welcome touch of comic relief to the high seriousness of the Puritan drama, was Captain John Underhill. He was a soldier, brought along by the Massachusetts Bay Company more for his usefulness than for his piety; he did yeoman service in drilling farm boys and apprentices into soldiers and Indian fighters, but he succumbed to the insidious influence of Mrs. Anne Hutchinson, and gave a spectacular example of the worst implications of her teachings. Being assured that he was united to Christ by an immediate joining of spirits, he became confident he could do no wrong and need no longer respect the rules and regulations of civilized society. In 1638 he was arraigned before the General Court on the charge, among others, of calling the authorities of Massachusetts Scribes and Pharisees. A witness further deposed that he had told her how he had sought five years for grace, "and could get no assurance, till at length, as he was taking a pipe of tobacco, the Spirit set home an absolute promise of free grace with such assurance and joy, as he never since doubted of his good estate, neither should he, though he should fall into sin." Thereupon he proceeded not simply to fall, but more accurately to plunge into a considerable quantity of sin, without so much as a single qualm of conscience.

Underhill was dealt with by the usual machinery of Puritan justice. The ministers explained the nature of his sins, and the magistrates passed such sentence as those sins deserved. His ethical theories were of course exposed as dangerous fallacies; John Cotton also took occasion to point out that any sense of assurance obtained while he was occupied in so trivial and worldly a practice as smoking his pipe was suspect to begin with, and further declared that except in a few special cases, as with St. Paul, the experience of regeneration does not come upon a man in a sudden flash, but slowly and by degrees. Assurance of salvation does not hit the saint like a brickbat on the head, but is gradually and industriously acquired by his diligent pursuit of religious ordinances and strenuous meditation upon God's word. Therefore Cotton seriously "advised him well to examine the revelation and joy which he had."[1] Captain Underhill made a pretense of profiting

---

[1] *Winthrop's Journal*, ed. J. K. Hosmer (New York, 1908), I, 275–276.

by this advice, but still went from bad to worse, and at last the government and churches breathed a long sigh of relief when he and his erroneous assurance went off to New Amsterdam to take service with the Dutch.

It is probable that the Puritans in England had been more ready to conceive of regeneration as a clap of thunderous illumination, but in New England the heresy of the Antinomians and the whole task of holding religious passion within the limits of control and orderly procedure accentuated the tendency to regard the experience not as a sudden convulsion of the soul wrought in the twinkling of an eye, but as a laborious process. Too many of these cataclysmic conversions turned out like Captain Underhill's. Consequently the standard doctrine in New England very soon was crystallized in the statement that though in rare instances the Holy Ghost might overwhelm a soul without any previous preparation, still for most persons the call of Christ would come through a long succession of sermons carefully and inwardly digested, long conferences with ministers and saints, years of self-examination and sustained endeavor to live the saintly life. Samuel Willard explained that those who "Commence Believers" (using the academic phrase, by which a student given a degree was said "to commence") without an antecedent and long-drawn out conviction and period of humiliation were apt to prove apostates, that God carries his decree of election in secret ways "under ground a great while, before it rise and break out in effectual Calling." [1] The whole process was mysterious, it was something that happened to men and women, not something they brought about of their own volition. Another minister, seeking for a metaphor to illustrate it, hit upon one of the happier figures of Puritan sermonizing:

It fares here, as when persons by some unobserved and unforeseen emanations of spirits from the heart, and pressing through the optick nerves flow into their mutual eyes, and dart themselves into one anothers breasts, whence they become suddenly taken, and as it were inkindled by certain lineatures in their feitures; and are rapt into deep admiration of somewhat in each other, which neither themselves nor the wisest Philosopher in being can give reason sagacious enough to unfold the surprizing influence when they are constellated to conjugal union.[2]

Some couples may indeed fall in love at first sight, but the average pair of lovers advance somewhat less precipitously, what with emanations of spirits pressing through the optic nerves, and are less aware of what

[1] *Mercy Magnified on a Penitent Prodigal*, A 3 recto.
[2] Samuel Lee, Χαρὰ της Πιστεως, *The Joy of Faith*, pp. 119-120.

is happening to them, up to the very point of proposal; so the normal saints become aware only after a time of doubt and bewilderment that the seeds of grace have been sown in their hearts.

It is necessary to keep this doctrine in mind when we come to the reading of Puritan journals, diaries, and biographies, for it explains the purpose of the Puritan's study of his own life, or of the lives of others. The ways of grace were manifold and no two men ever underwent the crisis in a perfectly similar fashion; in order that we might know the nature and manifestations of the disease, it was necessary to peruse the records of those who had undergone it, and to keep a full medical chart upon our own pulse and temperature. The art of biography as understood by the Puritans was the preparation of case histories. And every man who was concerned about his own plight should take down a daily record of his fluctuations and his symptoms, so that he could view himself with the complete objectivity demanded for accurate diagnosis of his spiritual health or sickness. A journal covering several years' experience could, when critically perused, offer the best evidence as to whether or not the secret decree of God had been operating "under ground" during that time. Accounts of individuals' own lives, or of the lives of great men and conspicuous saints, were not to be descriptions of their appearances or of the clothes they wore or of what they ate for breakfast, but of the works of grace in their hearts and the exemplifications of the spirit in their conduct. The masterpiece of autobiography in this vein is Bunyan's *Grace Abounding*, and in *The Pilgrim's Progress* is the type figure for all Puritan journeys from birth to death, the supreme exemplar of which the biography of each particular Christian is but the individual variant.

It is probable that almost every literate Puritan kept some sort of journal; the number of diaries that remain from the seventeenth and eighteenth centuries is legion, and the habit became so thoroughly ingrained in the New England character that it remained a practice with various Yankees long after they had ceased to be Puritans, to the great enrichment of our political and literary history, as witness the diaries of John Quincy Adams and Gideon Welles, or the journals of Emerson, Thoreau, and Hawthorne. Henry Adams, dissecting his career in the search for "education," is writing in the true New England tradition, and undertakes no more than countless Puritans had done when they submitted their lives to microscopic examination to discover if they had at any time found that vision of the unity and meaning of the universe which they called regeneration and for which he endeavored to substitute a dynamic theory of history.

The preoccupation with the subjective life and the essential sameness of the experiences recorded make most of these early journals monotonous and unrevealing. Very few of them tell us anything of what people did or what they said or how they occupied their time, and of what they thought there appears but one reiterated strain. Most of them are not of great interest to the historian and of less to the general reader, but there is a brilliant exception, both for its literary charm and historical value, in that of Samuel Sewall. The reasons for its pre-eminence are in part the result of the times and circumstances in which Sewall made his jottings. He lived through the transition from the religious seventeenth century to the more wordly eighteenth, and though he was a conservative in doctrinal belief and disinclined to many new customs and ideas, whether periwigs or the Copernican hypothesis, still he was bound to move with his age. Consequently, though the early pages of his journal are concerned with probings into the state of his soul and with pious meditations, and though he continues to the end of his days "improving" occasions with spiritual moralizings, yet even with him the religious preoccupation perceptibly lessened, and for the last thirty or forty years he recorded more and more of his secular employments and worldly fortunes. In his old age, after his first wife died, he went a-courting, and put down the story of his successes and rebuffs with an attention to incidentals that would hardly have been possible in a diary of the seventeenth century. The result was that he created, all unknowingly, two minor literary triumphs, the stories of his failure to acquire the hand of either the timorous widow Denison or of the supremely competent widow Winthrop.

Sewall's journal is also exceptional because of his own prominence in the political affairs of the colony, Though trained for the ministry, his bent was for business and administration; he married the daughter of John Hull, the mintmaster and one of the wealthiest men of the community; he inherited property from his father-in-law, and always had a considerable estate to manage. He served the colony in many official capacities, as magistrate, judge, and at last chief justice. Inevitably he recorded his meetings with leading men of the colony, of discussions in the council, of squabbles among the politicians, of good dinners enjoyed by the judges while riding the circuit, and of crises in the state. He was appointed by Governor Phips to serve on the special court that tried and condemned the witches at Salem; he concurred in the decisions at the time, but a few years later he realized, along with most intelligent opinion in the colony, that the community had been stampeded by panic and that innocent men and women had been slaughtered. The chief justice of that particular court, William Stoughton, in whose address before the General Court of 1668 had glowed the confidence that New England was the apple of the divine eye (pp. 243–246), never repented his share in the executions, but Sewall was of larger mold. The custom in the churches was for anyone who wanted the prayers of the congregation during affliction, or their sympathy during repentance, to post a notice of the request before the assembly; Sewall put up the sheet which he transcribes in his diary, announcing his humiliation and repentance for misjudging the innocent, and sat during this Sabbath not in the pew to which he, as a pillar of the church and the leader of the singing, was entitled, but on the mourners' bench, where convicted sinners were customarily exhibited to the admonition and censure of the godly.

This act indicates that there is still a further reason for the quality of Sewall's diary besides the times and his official prominence. He was a limited and prosaic man, but there is an honesty about him that shines through his pages, even where he himself least intended it or where it does not show him to advantage. The unconscious humor and the unwitting self-portraiture of the story of the courtships elevate those portions of the journal into the realm of classic confessionals. His meditation, in 1727, upon the death of his classmate, when he himself was seventy-five and had but three years to live, reveals the essential depth of the man, for all his crotchets and shortcomings.

Thomas Shepard, the great preacher who succeeded Hooker at Cambridge, wrote the narrative of his life for the edification of his children. John Williams, pastor at Deerfield, told of the massacre and his captivity in Canada for the edification of all the righteous; his book was bought and read not only by them, but, one suspects, by many others, for he managed to tell a good adventure story that sold to a tune which must have warmed his publishers' hearts. Shepard was much the greater man of the two, with a larger breadth of education and vision; Williams was a back-country minister, a provincial figure with a limited imagination and not much taste, but his courage was invincible and his devotion to what he believed very little short of incredible. The two narratives reveal much about the Puritan character, and a comparison of them indicates some of the features that remained constant in a hundred years of development, and some that changed.

The literary value of letters written by Puritans is naturally fugitive. Thousands of papers survive from the seventeenth century, and most of them concern immediate affairs. Those of John Winthrop to his wife, particularly at the time of the departure for New England, not only throw light upon the circumstances of that expedition, but reveal certain depths of the Puritan spirit and the nature of conjugal affection in Puritan households. Mrs. Winthrop was to remain in England until a home was prepared in America; on Mondays and Fridays at five in the afternoons they agree to drop all distractions and to think of each other; in another letter, written on St. Valentine's Day, he closes by assuring his Margaret she is his Valentine. Tenderness and love undoubtedly existed here, but side by side with it there was religious passion, so that he mingles exhortation with his affection, and she, pining in his absence, welcomes his love letters because they serve her instead of a sermon. The letters of Roger Williams are clear revelations of the spirit of the man, and proclaim his greatness and his nobility as no panegyrics could do. The correspondence with Mrs. Sadleir furnishes a commentary upon his theories of religious liberty; it also illustrates that this splendid radical had something in him of the tactless intrusiveness of the doctrinaire, who sees nothing amiss in forcing his well-meaning attentions upon those who want none of them.

The art of formal biography is here represented by the work of Increase and Cotton Mather. Increase proposed the task of writing his father's life immediately after the old gentleman died, telling himself "it would be a service not only honorable to my Father, but acceptable & honorable to the name of God." As Professor Murdock has said, the biography reaches "a simple dignity that comes close to art." [1] Cotton Mather provided in the *Magnalia* a complete list of New England leaders and supplied their biographies; the faults of his work have already been commented upon (p. 90), and are indeed all too obvious, but it is a mine of information and a storehouse of Puritan beliefs. The life of Eliot is one of his happier efforts; it is at least an excellent illustration of the values which were to be perceived according to Puritan standards in the life of a saint, and of the manner in which the moral of a holy career was to be pointed up. The chapter on Eliot's birth, early life, and marriage makes "no more than an entrance in the history," which becomes really significant with the account of his conversion; episodes are stressed not for themselves, but for their meanings, and are shamelessly taken as occasions for generalization; the death scene is draped in the phrases appropriate to the saint's certain translation from earth to heaven.

The pilgrimage of man and woman from earth to heaven is still the theme of Parson Ebenezer Turell when he relates the lives of his

[1] Kenneth B. Murdock, *Increase Mather* (Cambridge, 1925), pp. 96–97.

father-in-law and of his wife. Jane Turell evidently possessed the authentic Puritan conscience, and agonized in the approved abasement of spirit over her salvation. But in these works a new note begins to sound; the title page proclaims the life of a lady who was not only "pious" but "ingenious"; she had "digested" English poetry, and was versed in "polite pieces in prose"; her husband was first attracted to her not only by her sanctity but by her "taste," which he feared so much that even at her request he would not venture to translate a psalm lest he do violence to her sensibilities by the grossness of his masculine meters. When such criteria began to creep into the judgment of biographers, the Puritan age was on the wane.

JOHN WINTHROP, 1588–1649

[For Winthrop's life see p. 125. Margaret Winthrop was John's third wife; they were married in 1618. She died in 1647 (see Winthrop's notice, p. 142). Texts are from *Winthrop Papers*, Vol. II (Massachusetts Historical Society, Boston, 1931).]

LETTERS OF THE WINTHROPS

John Winthrop to His Wife

THE LARGNESSE and trueth of my loue to thee makes me allwayes mindfull of thy wellfare, and settes me on to worke to beginne to write, before I heare from thee: the verye thought of thee affordes me many a kynde refreshinge, what will then the enioyinge of thy sweet societye, which I prize aboue all worldly comfortes?

Yet such is the folye and miserye of man, as he is easylye brought to contemne the true good he enioyes, and to neglect the best thinges which he holdes onely in hope, and bothe vpon an vngrounded desire of some seeminge good which he promiseth to himselfe: and if it be thus with vs, that are Christians, who haue a sure worde to directe vs, and the holy Faith to liue by, what is the madnesse and bondage of those who are out of Christ? O: the riches of Christ! O: the sweetnesse of the worde of Grace! it rauisheth my soule in the thought heerof, so as when I apprehende but a glimpse of the dignitye and felicitye of a Christian, I can hardly perswade my heart, to hope for so great happynesse: let men talke what they will of riches, honors pleasures etc.; let vs haue Christ crucified, and let them take all besides: for indeed, he who hath Christ hath all thinges with him, for he enioyeth an allsufficiencie which makes him abundantly riche in pouertye, honorable in the lowest abasementes, full of ioye and consolation in the sharpest Afflictions, liuinge in death, and possessinge aeternitye in this vale of miserye: therefore blesse we God, for his free and infinite mercye, in bestowinge Christ vpon vs: let vs entertaine and loue him with our whole heartes: let vs trust in him, and cleaue to him, with denyall of our selues, and all thinges besides, and account our portion the best in the world: that so beinge strengthned and comforted in his loue, we may putt forth our selues, to improue our life and meanes, to doe him seruice: there are very fewe howers lefte of this daye of our labour, then comes the night, when we shall take our rest, in the morninge we shall awake vnto glorye and immortalitye, when we shall haue no more worke to doe, no more paines or griefe to endure, no more care, feare, want, reproach, or infirmitye; no more sinne, corruption or temptation.

I am forced to patch vp my lettres, heer a peece and there another. I haue now receiued thine, the kyndly fruites of thy most sweet Affection. Blessed be the Lorde for the wellfare of thy selfe and all our familye. I receiued lettres from my 2: sonnes with thee, remember my loue and blessinge to them, and to my daughter Winth[rop] for whose safetye I giue the Lord thankes: I haue so many lettres to write as I cannot write to them now: our freindes heer are in reasonable health, and desire to be kindly remembered to you all. Commende me to all my good freindes, my louinge neighbours goodman Cole and his wife, to whom we are allwayes much behouldinge. I will remember M[ary] her gowne and petticoate, and the childrens girdles. So with my most affectionate desires of thy wellfare, and my blessinge to all our children, I kisse my sweet wife, and comende thee and all ours to the gratious protection of our heauenly father, and rest Thy faithfull husbande still present with thee in his most vnkinde absence

                                                          Jo: Winthrop.
May 8 1629.

I am sorye for my neighbour Bluetes horse, but he shall loose nothinge by him. tell my sonne Hen: I will pay the mony he writes of.

John Winthrop to His Wife

My good wife, I prayse the Lorde for the wished newes of thy wellfare and of the rest of our Companye, and for the continuance of ours heer: it is a great favour, that we may enioye so much comfort and peace in these so euill and declininge tymes and when the increasinge of our sinnes giues vs so great cause to looke for some heauye Scquorge and Judgment to be comminge vpon us: the Lorde hath admonished, threatened, corrected, and astonished vs, yet we growe worse and worse, so as his spirit will not allwayes striue with vs, he must needs giue waye to his furye at last: he hath smitten all the other Churches before our eyes, and hath made them to drinke of the bitter cuppe of tribulation, euen vnto death; we sawe this, and humbled not our-selues, to turne from our euill wayes, but haue prouoked him more then all the nations rounde about vs: therefore he is turninge the cuppe towards vs also, and because we are the last, our portion must be, to drinke the verye dreggs which remaine: my deare wife, I am veryly perswaded, God will bringe some heauye Affliction vpon this lande, and that speedylye: but be of good Comfort, the hardest that can come shall be a meanes to mortifie this bodye of Corruption, which is a thousand tymes more dangerous to vs then any outward tribulation, and to bringe vs into neerer communion with our Lo: Jes: Christ, and more Assurance of his kingdome. If the Lord seeth it wilbe good for vs, he will prouide a shelter and a hidinge place for vs and ours as a Zoar for Lott,[1] Sarephtah for his prophet etc: if not, yet he will not forsake vs: though he correct vs with the roddes of men, yet if he take not his mercye and louinge kindnesse from vs we shalbe safe. He onely is allsufficient, if we haue him, we haue all thinges: if he seeth it not good, to cutt out our portion in these thinges belowe equall to the largnesse of our desires, yet if he please to frame our mindes to the portion he allottes vs, it wilbe as well for vs.

I thanke thee for thy kinde lettre, I am goinge to Westm[inster], and must heere breake of. I would haue my sonne H[enry] to be heere on teusdaye that I may goe out of towne on wensdaye or thursdaye next. If marye her gowne be made I will send it down by Smith this weeke, or els next, with other thinges: all our freindes heer are indif-ferent well, and desire to be comended to thee, so with my hearty salut[ation]s to all our freindes with thee, my loue and blessinge to my sonnes and daughteres, In very much hast, I ende and commende thee and all ours to the gratious protection and blessinge of the Lorde so I kisse my sweet wife, and thinke longe till I see thee farewell. Thine

Jo: Winthrop.

I thanke thee for our Turkye
May 15 1629

MARGARET WINTHROP TO HER HUSBAND

To my very loueinge Husband John Winthrope Esquire theese dd.

Most louinge and good Husband, I haue receued your letters. the true tokens of your loue and care of my good, now in your abcence as well as when you are present, it makes me thinke that sayinge falce out of sight out of minde. I am sure my hart and thoughts are all wayes neere you to doe you good and not euill all the dayse of my life.

I hope through gods blessinge your paynes will not be all together lost which you bestow vpon me in rightinge those serious thoughts of your owne which you sent me did make a very good supply in stead of a sarmon. I shall often reade them and desyre to be of gods famyle to home so many blessinges be-longe and pray that I may not be one separated from god whose concience is always accusinge them. I shall not neede to right to you of any thing this weke my sonne and brother Goslinge can tell you how we are. and I shall thinke longe for your cominge home. and thus with my best loue to you I beseech the lord to send vs a comfortable meetinge in his good time I commit you to the Lord. Your louinge and obedient wife

Margaret Winthrope.

[*Ca.* May 18, 1629.]

MARGARET WINTHROP TO HER HUSBAND

To hir very louinge and deare Husban John Winthrope Esquire at
mr. Downings house in fleet strete neere thee Condite these dd.

My deare Husband, I knowe thou art desyrus to heere often from vs which makes me take plesure in rightinge to thee, and in relatinge my true affections to thee and desyers of your wished welfayer. the good lord be euer with thee and prosper all thy affayres [in] this great and waytty busines which is now in hand, that it may be for the glory of his most holy name and furtherance of his gospell, but I must part with my most deare Husban, which is a uery hard tryall for me to vndergoe, if the lord doe not supporte and healpe me in it, I shalbe vnable to beare it. I haue now receiued thy kinde letter which I cannot reade without sheding a great many teares, but I will resine thee and giue thee into the hands of the almyti god who is all soficient for thee, whome I trust will keepe thee and prosper thee in the way thou art to goe, if thou walke before him in truth and vprightnesse of hart, he will neuer fayle of his promise to thee. therefore my good Husban chere vp thy hart in god and in the expectation of his fauors and blessings in this thy change, with asurance of his loue in Crist Jesus our lord for our change heare after when we shall liue with him in glory for euer. as for me his most vnworthy seruant I will cleaue to my Husban Crist as neere as I can though my infirmytes be great he is able to heale them and wil not forsake me in the time of neede. I know I shall haue thy prayers to god for me that what is wanting in thy presence may be supplyed by the comfort of gods spirit. I am now full of passion haueinge nuly receiued thy letter and not able to right much. my sonne F[orth] will right about other busines. I begine to feare I shall see thee no more before thou goest which I should be very sory for and earnestly intreat thee that thou wilt com once more downe if it be possible. and thus with my due respect to thy selfe brother and sister D. thankes for my leamers to my sister, my loue to my sonnes, I commit thee to god and rest Your faythfull and obedient wife

Margaret Winthrope.

My good sister F. remembers hir loue.

[Groton, February 2, 1630.]

JOHN WINTHROP TO HIS WIFE

To my very louinge wife mrs. Winthrop the Elder at Groton in Suffolk dd.

My sweet wife, Thy loue is such to me, and so great is the bonde betweene vs, that I should neglect all others to hold correspondencye of lettres with thee: but I knowe thou art willinge to dispense with somewhat of thine owne right, to giue me lib[er]ty to satisfie my other occasions for the present, which call me to much writinge this eueninge, otherwise I would haue returned a larger answeare to thy sweet lettre. I prayse God we are all in health, and we goe on cheerfully in our businesse: I purpose (if God will) to be with thee vpon thursdaye come sennight, and then I must take my Farewell of thee, for a summers daye and a winters daye, the Lorde our good God will (I hope) sende vs a happye meetinge againe in his good tyme: Amen. Comende me kindly to my good sister F[ones] I would haue written to her, but I cannot, havinge 6: Lettres to write. I wrote to mr. P[aynter] tell my sister that her mother is brought in bedd and the child dead, and she in great danger. among other thinges let the brassen quart in the Larder howse be putt vp: and my grey cloake and the coate which was my brother Fones. and let this warrant inclosed be sent to Colchester to mr. Samuell Borrowes by the next tyme the carte goes. The Lord blesse thee my sweet wife with all our children: my brother and sister salute you all: my sonnes remember their loue and dutye: comend my loue to all: farewell Thy faithfull husband,

Jo: Winthrop.

[London,] Feb: 5. 1630.

remember to putt me vp some Cardam[ons] and Cardam[on] seed.

Beinge now ready to sende away my lettres; I receiued thine, the readinge of it hath dissolued my head into tears, I can write no more, if I liue I will see thee ere I goe. I shall parte from thee with sorrowe enough, be comfortable my most sweet wife, our God wilbe with thee Farewell.

JOHN WINTHROP TO HIS WIFE

To M. W. the Elder at Groton

My faithfull and deare wife, It pleaseth God that thou shouldest once againe heare from me before our departure, and I hope this shall come safe to thy hands, I knowe it wilbe a great refreshinge to thee: And blessed be his mercye, that I can write thee so good newes, that we are all in verye good health, and hauinge tryed our shipps entertainment now more then a weeke, we finde it agree very well with vs, our boyes are well and cheerfull, and haue no minde of home, they lye both with me, and sleepe as soundly in a rugge (for we vse no sheets heer) as euer they did at Groton, and so I doe my selfe (I prayse God). the winde hath been against vs this weeke and more, but this day it is come faire to the North, so as we are preparinge (by Godes assistance) to sett sayle in the morninge: we haue onely 4: shippes ready, and some 2: or 3: hollandes goe alonge with vs: the rest of our fleet (beinge 7: shippes) will not be ready this senight. we haue spent now 2: sabbaths on shipp board, very comfortably (God be praysed) and are daylye more and more incouraged to looke for the Lords presence to goe alonge with vs: Hen: Kingesburye hath a childe or 2: in the Talbott sicke of the measells, but like to doe well: one of my men had them at Hampton, but he was soone well againe. we are in all our 11: shippes, about 700: persons passengers; and 240 Cowes, and about 60: horses. the shippe which went from Plimouth carried about 140: persons, and the shippe which goes from Bristowe, carrieth about 80: persons. And now (my sweet soule) I must once againe take my last farewell of thee in old England, it goeth verye neere to my heart to leaue thee, but I know to whom I haue committed thee, euen to him, who loues the[e] much better than any husband can, who hath taken account of the haires of thy head, and putts all thy teares in his bottle, who can, and (if it be for his glorye) will bringe vs togither againe with peace and comfort. oh how it refresheth my heart to thinke that I shall yet againe see thy sweet face in the lande of the liuinge: that louely countenance, that I haue so much delighted in, and beheld with so great contente! I haue hetherto been so taken vp with businesse, as I could seldome looke backe to my former happinesse, but now when I shalbe at some leysure, I shall not auoid the remembrance of thee, nor the greife for thy absence: thou hast thy share with me, but I hope, the course we haue agreed vpon wilbe some ease to vs both, mundayes and frydayes at 5: of the clocke at night, we shall meet in spiritt till we meet in person. yet if all these hopes should faile, blessed be our God, that we are assured, we shall meet one day, if not as husband and wife, yet in a better condition, let that staye and comfort thy heart, neither can the sea drowne thy husband, nor enemyes destroye, nor any adversity depriue thee of thy husband or children. therefore I will onely take thee now and my sweet children in mine armes, and kisse and embrace you all, and so leaue you with my God. farewell farewell. I blesse you all in the name of the Lord Jesus; I salute my daughter Winth: Matt, Nan and the rest, and all my good neighbors and freindes pray all for vs. farewell.

Comende my blessinge to my sonne John. I cannot now write to him, but tell him I haue committed thee and thine to him, labour to drawe him yet nearer to God, and he wilbe the surer staffe of comfort to thee. I cannot name the rest of my good freinds, but thou canst supply it. I wrote a weeke since to thee and mr. Leigh and diuerse others. Thine wheresoever

Jo: Winthrop.

From Aboard the Arbella rydinge at the Cowes march 28. 1630.

I would haue written to my brother and sister Gostlinge, but it is neer midnight, let this excuse and commende my love to them and all theirs.

THOMAS SHEPARD, 1605–1649

[For Shepard's life see p. 117. The autobiography was written for the benefit of his son. This text is from *The Autobiography of Thomas Shepard*, edited by Allyn B. Forbes, *Publications of the Colonial Society of Massachusetts*, XXVII (1932), 321–400.]

THE AUTOBIOGRAPHY OF THOMAS SHEPARD

THE FIRST two yeares I spent in Cambridge was in studying & in my neglect of god & priuate prayer which I had sometime vsed. & I did not regard the Lord at all vnless it were at some fits; the 3ᵈ yeare wherin I was Sophister I began to be foolish & proud & to shew my selfe in the publike Schooles; & there to be a disputer about things which now I see I did not know then at all but only prated about them; & toward the end of this yeare when I was most vile (after I had bin next vnto the gates of Death by the [*small*] Pox the yeare before) the Lord began to Call me home to the fellowship of his grace; which was in this manner

1. I doe remember that I had many good affections (but blind & vnconstant) oft cast into me since my fathers sicknes by the spirit of god wrastling with me, & hence I would pray in secret & hence when I was at Cambridge I heard old Doctor Chadderton [1] the master of the Colledge when I came & the first yeare I was there to heare him vpon a Sacrament day my hart was much affected but I did breake loose from the Lord agayne & halfe a yeare after I heard m[r] Dickinson common place in the chappell vpon those woords I will not destroy it for tens sake. Gen: 19. & then agayne was much affected, but I shooke this off also & fell from god to loose & lewd company to lust & pride & gaming & bowling & drinking; & yet the Lord left me not but a godly Scholler walking with me, fell to discourse about the misery of euery man out of Christ viz: that what euer they did was sin; & this did much affect me; & at another time when I did light in godly company I heard them discourse about the wrath of god, & the terrour of it & how intollerable it was which they did present by fire how intollerable the torment of that was for a time what then would æternity be; & this did much awaken me; & I began to pray agayne; but then by loose company I came to dispute in the Schooles & there to joyne to loose schollers of other colledges & was fearfully left of god & fell to drinke with them; & I dranke so much on day that I was dead drunke & that vpon a saturday night & so was carryed from the place I had drinke at & did feast at, vnto a Schollers chamber on Basset of Christs Colledge; & knew not where I was vntill I awakened late on that sabboth & sick with my beastly carriage; & when I awakened I went from him in shame & confusion, & went out into the feelds & there spent that sabboth lying hid in the corne feelds where the Lord who might justly haue cut me off in the mids of my sin; did meet me with much sadnes of hart & troubled my soule for this & other my sins which then I had cause & laysure to thinke of: & now when I was woorst he began to be best vnto me & made me resolue to set vpon a course of dayly meditation about the euill of sin & my own wayes; yet although I was troubled for this sin I did not know my sinfull nature all this while. . . .

At this time I cannot omit the goodnes of god as to my selfe so to all the cuntry in deliuering vs from the Pekoat furies; [2] these Indians were the stoutest proudest & most successefull in there wars of all the

Indians; there cheefe Sachem was Sasakus, a proud cruell vnhapy & headstrong prince, who not willing to be guided by the perswasions of his fellow an aged Sachem Momanattuck nor fearing the reuenge of the English, hauing first suckt the blood of captaine Ston & m^r Oldam found it so sweet & his proceedings for on whole winter so successefull that hauing beseeged & kild about 4 men that kept Seabrook fort he aduentured to fall vpon the English vp the riuer at Wethersfeed where he slew 9 or 10. men women & children at vnawares, & tooke two maids prisoners carrying them away captiue to the Pekoat cuntry herevpon those vpon the riuer first gathered about 70 men & sent them into Pekoat cuntry, to make that the seat of war, & to reuenge the death of those innocents whom they barbarously & most vnnaturally slew; these men marched two dayes & nights from the way of the Naraganset vnto Pekoat; being guided by those Indians then the ancient enemies of the Pekoats they intended to assault Sasakus Fort but falling short of it the second night the prouidence of god guided them to another nearer, full of stout men & their best souldiers being as it were coopt vp there to the number of 3 or 400 in all for the diuine slaughter by the hand of the English; these therfore being all night making merry & singing the death of the English the next day, toward breake of the day being very heauy with sleepe the English drew neare within the sight of the fort, very weary with trauayle & want of sleepe, at which time 500 Naragansets fled for feare & only 2 of the company stood to it to conduct them to the fort & the dore & entrance thereof; the English being come to it awakened the fort with a peale of muskets directed into the midst of there wigwams; & after this some vndertaking to compasse the fort without some aduentured into the fort vpon the very faces of the enemy standing ready with there arrowes ready bent to shoot who euer should aduenture; but the English casting by there peeces tooke there swoords in there hands (the Lord doubling there strength & courage) & fell vpon the Indians where a hot fight continued about the space of an houre, at last by the direction of on Captayne Mason there wigwams were set on fire which being dry & contiguous on to another was most dreadfull to the Indians, some burning some bleeding to death by the swoord some resisting till they were cut off some flying were beat down by the men without vntill the Lord had vtterly consumed the whole company except 4 or 5. girles they tooke prisoners & dealt with them at Seabrooke as they dealt with ours at Wethersfeeld, & tis verily thought scarce on man escaped vnles on or two to carry foorth tydings of the lamentable end of there fellowes; & of the English not on man was kild but on by the

musket of an Englishman (as was conceiued) some were wounded
much but all recouered & restored agayne. . . .

But the Lord hath not bin woont to let me liue long without some
affliction or other, & yet euer mixt with some mercy, & therefore Aprill
the 2ᵈ: 1646. as he gaue me another son, John. so he tooke away my
most deare precious meeke & louing wife, in childbed, after 3 weekes
lying in, hauing left behind her two hopefull branches my deare children, Samuell, & John: this affliction was very heauy to me, for in it
the Lord seemd to withdraw his tender care for me & mine, which
he graciously manifested by my deare wife; also refused to heare
prayer, when I did thinke he would haue hearkned & let me see his
bewty in the land of the liuing, in restroring of her to health agayne;
also in taking her away in the prime time of her life when shee might
haue liued to haue glorifyed the Lord long. also in threatning me to
proceed in rooting out my family, & that he would not stop hauing
begun here as in Ely for not being zealous enough agaynst the sins
of his son; & I saw that if I had profited by former afflictions of this
nature I should not haue had this scourge; but I am the Lords, & he
may doe with me what he will, he did teach me to prize a little grace
gained by a crosse as a sufficient recompense for all outward losses;
but this losse was very great; shee was a woman of incomparable
meeknes of spirit, toward my selfe especially & very louing; of great
prudence to take care for & order my family affayres being neither
too lauish nor sordid in any thing so that I knew not what was vnder
her hands; shee had an excellency to reprooue for sin & discerned the
euills of men; shee loued gods people dearly & studious to profit by
there fellowship, & therefore loued there company shee loued gods
woord exceedingly & hence was glad shee could read my notes which
shee had to muse on euery weeke; shee had a spirit of prayer beyond
ordinary of her time & experience shee was fit to dy long before shee
did dy, euen after the death of her first borne which was a great
affliction to her, but her woorke not being done then shee liued almost
9. yeares with me & was the comfort of my life to me & the last Sacrament before her lying in seemd to be full of Christ & thereby fitted
for heauen; shee did oft say shee should not outliue this child; & when
her feuer first began (by taking some cold) shee told me soe, that we
should loue exceedingly together because we should not liue long together; her feuer tooke away her sleepe, want of sleepe wrought much
distemper in her head, & filled it with fantasies & distractions but
without raging; the night before shee dyed, shee had about 6 houres
vnquiet sleepe; but that so coold & setled her head, that when shee

knew none else so as to speake to them, yet shee knew Jesus Chri.
could speake to him, & therefore as soone as shee awakened out of
sleepe shee brake out into a most heauenly hartbreaking prayer after
Christ her deare redeemer for the sparing of life; & so continued
praying vntill the last houre of her death: Lord tho I vnwoorthy Lord
on woord on woord &c. & so gaue vp the ghost; thus god hath visited
& scourged me for my sins & sought to weane me from this woorld,
but I haue euer found it a difficult thing to profit euer but a little by
the sorest & sharpest afflictions.

ROGER WILLIAMS, 1604–1683

[For Williams's life see p. 214. The text of these letters is from
Publications of the Narragansett Club, Vol. VI (Providence, R. I., 1874),
edited by John Russell Bartlett.]

LETTERS OF ROGER WILLIAMS

To his much honored Governor John Winthrop.

Providence, [April 16, 1638.]

MUCH HONORED SIR,—I kindly thank you for your loving inclination
to receive my late protestation concerning myself, ignorant of
Mr. Greene's letter. I desire unfeignedly, to rest in my appeal to the
Most High in what we differ, as I dare not but hope you do: it is no
small grief that I am otherwise persuaded, and that sometimes you say
(and I can say no less) that we differ: the fire will try your works and
mine: the Lord Jesus help us to make sure of our persons that we seek
Jesus that was crucified: however it is and ever shall be (the Lord
assisting) my endeavor to pacify and allay, where I meet with rigid
and censorious spirits, who not only blame your actions but doom
your persons . . .

Sir, there will be new Heavens and a new Earth shortly but no more
Sea. (Revel. 21. 2.) the most holy God be pleased to make us willing
now to bear the tossings, dangers and calamities of this sea, and to
seal up to use upon his own grounds, a great lot in the glorious state
approaching. So craving pardon for prolixity, with mine and my wife's
due respect to Mrs. Winthrop, Mr. Deputy, Mr. Bellingham, &c., I
rest

Your worship's desirous to be ever yours unfeigned

Roger Williams.

THE CORRESPONDENCE OF ROGER WILLIAMS AND
MRS. SADLEIR, 1652.

[Mrs. Sadleir was the daughter of the famous lawyer, Sir Edward Coke, who had been the benefactor and patron of Roger Williams before Williams came to New England. Though the father had been one of the great maintainers of Parliamentary government against the absolutism of James I, the daughter had obviously come to feel by 1652 that constitutional opposition had long since passed into overt rebellion, and no longer held with any of the programs of the Protectòrate. When Williams came to England in 1652, having published opinions that were identified with the most radical wing of the revolutionary forces, he innocently attempted to pay his respects to the daughter of his old friend, and the following correspondence ensued.]

For my much honored kind friend, Mistress Sadleir, at Stondon,
Puckridge, these.

From my lodgings near St. Martin's, at Mr. Davis his house, at the sign
of the Swan.
                                                   [London, 1652]

MY MUCH HONORED FRIEND, MRS. SADLEIR,—The never-dying honor and respect which I owe to that dear and honorable root and his branches, and, amongst the rest, to your much honored self, have emboldened me, once more, to enquire after your dear husband's and your life, and health, and welfare. This last winter I landed, once more, in my native country, being sent over from some parts of New England with some addresses to the Parliament.

My very great business, and my very great straits of time, and my very great journey homeward to my dear yoke-fellow and many children, I greatly fear will not permit me to present my ever-obliged duty and service to you, at Stondon, especially if it please God that I may despatch my affairs to depart with the ships within this fortnight. I am, therefore, humbly bold to crave your favorable consideration, and pardon, and acceptance, of these my humble respects and remembrances. It hath pleased the Most High to carry me on eagles' wings, through mighty labors, mighty hazards, mighty sufferings, and to vouchsafe to use, so base an instrument—as I humbly hope—to glorify himself, in many of my trials and sufferings, both amongst the English and barbarians.

I have been formerly, and since I landed, occasioned to take up the two-edged sword of God's Spirit, the word of God, and to appear in public in some contests against the ministers of Old and New England, as touching the true ministry of Christ and the soul freedoms of the people. Since I landed, I have published two or three things, and have a large discourse at the press, but 'tis controversial, with which I will not trouble your meditations; only I crave the boldness to send you a plain and peaceable discourse, of my own personal experiments, which, in a letter to my dear wife—upon the occasion of her great sickness near death—I sent her, being absent myself amongst the Indians.[1] And being greatly obliged to Sir Henry Vane, junior—once Governor of New England—and his lady, I was persuaded to publish it in her name, and humbly to present your honorable hands with one or two of them. I humbly pray you to cast a serious eye on the holy Scriptures, on which the examinations are grounded. I could have dressed forth the matter like some sermons which, formerly, I used to pen. But the Father of lights hath long since shown me the vanity and soul-deceit of such points and flourishes. I desire to know nothing, to profess nothing, but the Son of God. the King of souls and consciences; and I desire to be more thankful for a reproof for ought I affirm than for applause and commendation. I have been oft glad in the wilderness of America, to have been reproved for going in a wrong path, and to be directed by a naked Indian boy in my travels. How much more should we rejoice in the wounds of such as we hope love us in Christ Jesus, than in the deceitful kisses of soul-deceiving and soul-killing friends.

My much honored friend, that man of honor, and wisdom, and piety, your dear father, was often pleased to call me his son; and truly it was as bitter as death to me when Bishop Laud pursued me out of this land, and my conscience was persuaded against the national church and ceremonies, and bishops, beyond the conscience of your dear Father. I say it was as bitter as death to me, when I rode Windsor way, to take ship at Bristow, and saw Stoke House, where the blessed man was; and I then durst not acquaint him with my conscience, and my flight. But how many thousand times since have I had honorable and precious remembrance of his person, and the life, the writings, the speeches, and the examples of that glorious light. And I may truly say, that beside my natural inclination to study and activity, his example, instruction, and encouragement, have spurred me on to a more than ordinary, industrious, and patient course in my whole course hitherto.

What I have done and suffered—and I hope for the truth of God according to my conscience—in Old and New England, I should be a fool in relating, for I desire to say, not to King David—as once Mephibosheth—but to King Jesus, "What is thy servant, that thou shouldest look upon such a dead dog?" And I would not tell yourself of this, but that you may acknowledge some beams of his holy wisdom and goodness, who hath not suffered all your own and your dear father's smiles to have been lost upon so poor and despicable an object. I confess I have many adversaries, and also many friends, and divers eminent. It hath pleased the general [2] himself to send for me, and to entertain many discourses with me at several times; which, as it magnifies his christian nobleness and courtesy, so much more doth it magnify *His* infinite mercy and goodness, and wisdom, who hath helped me, poor worm, to sow that seed in doing and suffering—I hope for God—that as your honorable father was wont to say, he that shall harrow what I have sown, must rise early. And yet I am a worm and nothing, and desire only to find my all in the blood of an holy Savior, in whom I desire to be

Your honored,

Most thankful, and faithful servant,

Roger Williams.

My humble respects presented to Mr. Sadleir.

From Mrs. Sadleir to Roger Williams.

Mr. Williams,—Since it hath pleased God to make the prophet David's complaint ours (Ps. lxxix.): "O God, the heathen," &c., and that the Apostle St. Peter has so long ago foretold, in his second epistle, the second chapter, by whom these things should be occasioned, I have given over reading many books, and, therefore, with thanks, have returned yours. Those that I now read, besides the Bible, are, first, the late King's book; Hooker's Ecclesiastical Polity; Reverend Bishop Andrew's Sermons, with his other divine meditations; Dr. Jer. Taylor's works; and Dr. Tho. Jackson upon the Creed.[3] Some of these my dear father was a great admirer of, and would often call them the glorious lights of the church of England. These lights shall be my guide; I wish they may be yours: for your new lights that are so much cried up, I believe, in the conclusion, they will prove but dark lanterns: therefore I dare not meddle with them.

Your friend in the old way,

Anne Sadleir.

For his much honored, kind friend, Mrs. Anne
Sadleir, at Stondon, in Hartfordshire,
near Puckridge.

My much honored, kind Friend, Mrs. Sadleir,—

. . . You were pleased to direct me to divers books, for my satisfaction. I have carefully endeavoured to get them, and some I have gotten; and upon my reading, I purpose, with God's help, to render you an ingenuous and candid account of my thoughts, result, &c. At present, I am humbly bold to pray your judicious and loving eye to one of mine.

'Tis true, I cannot but expect your distaste of it; and yet my cordial desire of your soul's peace here, and eternal, and of contributing the least mite toward it, and my humble respects to that blessed root of which you spring, force me to tender my acknowledgments, which if received or rejected, my cries shall never cease that one eternal life may give us meeting, since this present minute hath such bitter partings.

For the scope of this *rejoinder*, if it please the Most High to direct your eye to a glance on it, please you to know, that at my last being in England, I wrote a discourse entitled, "*The Bloudy Tenent of Persecution for Cause of Conscience.*" I bent my charge against Mr. Cotton especially, your standard bearer of New English ministers. That discourse he since answered, and calls his book, "*The Bloody Tenent made white in the Blood of the Lamb.*" This rejoinder of mine, as I humbly hope, unwasheth his washings, and proves that in soul matters no weapons but soul weapons are reaching and effectual.

I am your most unworthy servant, yet unfeignedly respective,

Roger Williams.

Mrs. Sadleir in reply to Roger Williams.

Sir,—I thank God my blessed parents bred me up in the old and best religion, and it is my glory that I am a member of the Church of England, as it was when all the reformed churches gave her the right hand. When I cast mine eye upon the frontispiece of your book, and saw it entitled "The Bloudy Tenent," I durst not adventure to look into it, for fear it should bring into my memory the much blood that has of late been shed, and which I would fain forget; therefore I do, with thanks, return it. I cannot call to mind any blood shed for conscience:—some few that went about to make a rent in our once well-governed church were punished, but none suffered death. But this I know, that since it has been left to every man's conscience to fancy what religion he list, there has more christian blood been shed than was in the ten persecutions. And some of that blood, will, I fear, cry till the day of judgment. But you know what the Scripture says, that when there was no king in Israel, every man did that which was right in his own eyes,—but what became of that, the sacred story will tell you.

Thus entreating you to trouble me no more in this kind, and wishing
you a good journey to your charge in New Providence, I rest
                    Your Friend in the Old and Best Way.

From Roger Williams to Mrs. Sadleir.

My honored, kind Friend, Mrs. Sadleir,—

. . . That you admire the king's book, and Bp. Andrews his sermons,
and Hooker's Polity, &c., and profess them to be your lights and guides,
and desire them mine, and believe the new lights will prove dark
lanterns, &c. I am far from wondering at it, for all this have I done
myself, until the Father of Spirits mercifully persuaded mine to swal-
low down no longer without chewing : to chew no longer without
tasting; to taste no longer without begging the Holy Spirit of God
to enlighten and enliven mine against the fear of men, tradition of
fathers, or the favor or custom of any men or times. . . .

I have read those books you mention, and the king's book, which
commends two of them, Bishop Andrews's and Hooker's—yea, and a
third also, Bishop Laud's: and as for the king, I knew his person,
vicious, a swearer from his youth, and an oppressor and persecutor
of good men (to say nothing of his own father), and the blood of so
many hundred thousands English, Irish, Scotch, French, lately charged
upon him. Against his and his blasphemous father's cruelties, your own
dear father, and many precious men, shall rise up shortly and cry for
vengeance. . . .

The Turks—so many millions of them—prefer their Mahomet before
Christ Jesus, even upon such carnal and worldly respects, and yet
avouch themselves to be the only Muselmanni or true believers. The
catholics account us heretics, diabloes, &c.; and why? but because
we worship not such a golden Christ and his glorious vicar and lieutenant. The several sects of common protestants content themselves
with a traditional worship, and boast they are no Jews, no Turks,
(Matt. vii. 21, 22.) nor catholics, and yet forget their own formal dead
faith, (2 Tim. iii. 9.) dead hope, dead joys, and yet, *nescio vos*, I know
you not, depart from me, which shall be thundered out to many gallant
professors and considents, who have held out a lamp and form of religion, yea, and possibly of godliness too, and yet have denied the power
and life of it. . . .

God's Spirit persuadeth the hearts of his true servants: First, to be
willing to be searched by him, which they exceedingly beg of him,
with holy fear of self-deceit and hypocrisy.

Second. To be led by him in the way everlasting: (Ps. cxxxix.), whether it seem old in respect of institution, or new in respect of restoration. This I humbly pray for your precious soul, of the God and Father of mercies, even your eternal joy and salvation. Earnestly desirous to be in the old way, which is the narrow way, which leads to life, which few find.

Your most humble, though most unworthy servant,

Roger Williams.

My honored Friend, since you please not to read mine, let me pray leave to request your reading of one book of your own authors. I mean the "Liberty of Prophesying," penned by (so called) Dr. Jer. Taylor. In the which is excellently asserted the toleration of different religions, yea, in a respect, that of the papists themselves, which is a new way of soul freedom, and yet is the old way of Christ Jesus, as all his holy Testament declares.

I also humbly wish that you may please to read over impartially Mr. Milton's answer to the king's book.[4]

Mrs. Sadleir in reply to Roger Williams.

Mr. Williams,—I thought my first letter would have given you so much satisfaction, that, in that kind, I should never have heard of you any more; but it seems you have a face of brass, so that you cannot blush. But since you press me to it, I must let you know, as I did before (Ps. lxxix.), that the Prophet David there complains that the heathen had defiled the holy temple, and made Jerusalem a heap of stones. And our blessed Saviour, when he whipped the buyers and sellers out of the temple, told them that they had made his Father's house a den of thieves. Those were but material temples, and commanded by God to be built, and his name there to be worshipped. The living temples are those that the same prophet, in the psalm before mentioned (verse the 2nd and 3rd), "The dead bodies of thy servants have they given to the fowls of the air, and the flesh of thy saints to the beasts of the land. Their blood have they shed like water," &c. And these were the living temples whose loss the prophet so much laments; and had he lived in these times, he would have doubled these lamentations. For the foul and false aspersions you have cast upon that king, of ever-blessed memory, Charles, the martyr, I protest I trembled when I read them, and none but such a villain as yourself would have wrote them . . .

For Milton's book, that you desire I should read, if I be not mistaken, that is he that has wrote a book of the lawfulness of divorce; and, if report says true, he had, at that time, two or three wives living. This, perhaps, were good doctrine in New England; but it is most abominable in Old England. For his book that he wrote against the late king that you would have me read, you should have taken notice of God's judgment upon him, who stroke him with blindness, and, as I have heard, he was fain to have the help of one Andrew Marvell,[5] or else he could not have finished that most accursed libel. God has began his judgment upon him here—his punishment will be hereafter in hell. . . .

I cannot conclude without putting you in mind how dear a lover and great an admirer my father was of the liturgy of the church of England, and would often say, no reform church had the like. He was constant to it, both in his life and at his death. I mean to walk in his steps; and, truly, when I consider who were the composers of it, and how they sealed the truth of it with their blood, I cannot but wonder why it should now of late be thus contemned. By what I have now writ, you know how I stand affected. I will walk as directly to heaven as I can, in which place, if you will turn from being a rebel, and fear God and obey the king, there is hope I may meet you there; howsoever, trouble me no more with your letters, for they are very troublesome to her that wishes you in the place from whence you came.

                                                              Anne Sadleir.

[Near the direction, on the outside, of Williams's first letter, there is the following note by Mrs. Sadleir:]—

This Roger Williams, when he was a youth, would, in a short hand, take sermons and speeches in the Star Chamber and present them to my dear father. He, seeing so hopeful a youth, took such liking to him that he sent him in to Sutton's Hospital, and he was the second that was placed there; full little did he think that he would have proved such a rebel to God, the king, and his country. I leave his letters, that, if ever he has the face to return into his native country, Tyburn may give him welcome.

To John Winthrop, Jr.

To my honored, kind friend, Mr. John Winthrop, [Jr.] Governor,
at Hartford, on Connecticut.

                    Providence, 6, 12, 59–60. [6th February, 1660.]

Sir,—Loving respects to yourself and Mrs. Winthrop, &c. Your loving lines in this cold, dead season, were as a cup of your Connecticut cider, which we are glad to hear abounds with you, or of that western metheglin, which you and I have drunk at Bristol together, &c. Indeed, it is the wonderful power and goodness of God, that we are preserved in our dispersions among these wild, barbarous wretches. . . .

Sir, you were, not long since, the son of two noble fathers, Mr. John

Winthrop and Mr. H. Peters.[6] It is said they are both extinguished. Surely, I did ever, from my soul, honor and love them even when their judgments led them to afflict me. Yet the Father of Spirits spares us breath, and I rejoice, Sir, that your name (amongst the New England magistrates printed, to the Parliament and army, by H. Nort. Rous, &c.,) is not blurred, but rather honored, for your prudent and moderate hand in the late Quakers' trials amongst us. And it is said, that in the late Parliament, yourself were one of the three in nomination for General Governor over New England, which however that design ripened not, yet your name keeps up a high esteem, &c. I have seen your hand to a letter to this colony, as to your late purchase of some land at Narragansett. The sight of your hand hath quieted some jealousies amongst us, that the Bay, by this purchase, designed some prejudice to the liberty of conscience amongst us. We are in consultations how to answer that letter, and my endeavor shall be, with God's help, to welcome, with both our hands and arms, your interest in these parts, though we have no hope to enjoy your personal residence amongst us. I rejoice to hear that you gain, by new plantations, upon this wilderness. I fear that many precious souls will be glad to hide their heads, shortly, in these parts. Your candle and mine draws towards its end. The Lord graciously help us to shine in light and love universally, to all that fear his name, without that monopoly of the affection to such of our own persuasion only; for the common enemy, the Romish wolf, is very high in resolution, and hope, and advantage to make a prey on all, of all sorts that desire to fear God. Divers of our neighbors thankfully re-salute you We have buried, this winter, Mr. Olney's son, whom, formerly, you heard to be afflicted with a lethargy. He lay two or three days wholly senseless, until his last groans. My youngest son, Joseph, was troubled with a spice of an epilepsy. We used some remedies, but it hath pleased God, by his taking of tobacco, perfectly, as we hope, to cure him. Good Mr. Parker, of Boston, passing from Prudence Island, at his coming on shore, on Seekonk land, trod awry upon a stone or stick, and fell down, and broke the small bone of his leg. He hath lain by of it all this winter, and the last week was carried to Boston in a horse litter. Some fears there was of a gangrene. But, Sir, I use too much boldness and prolixity. I shall now only subscribe myself

Your unworthy friend,
Roger Williams.

Sir, my loving respects to Mr. Stone, Mr. Lord, Mr. Allen, Mr. Webster, and other loving friends.

To Major Mason

[In 1670 Connecticut and Rhode Island were involved in a dispute concerning the boundary between the two colonies; committees were appointed and in May held a stormy conference that produced no agreement; Connecticut men thereupon seized control of the town of Westerly. The Rhode Island government retaliated by capturing some of the invaders and sending them to jail at Newport. At this juncture Williams wrote the following letter to Major Mason, one of the magistrates of Connecticut:]

Providence, June 22, 1670.

Major Mason,—My honored, dear and ancient friend, my due respects and earnest desires to God, for your eternal peace, &c.

I crave your leave and patience to present you with some few considerations, occasioned by the late transactions between your colony and ours. The last year you were pleased, in one of your lines to me, to tell me that you longed to see my face once more before you died. I embraced your love, though I feared my old lame bones, and yours, had arrested traveling in this world, and therefore I was and am ready to lay hold on all occasions of writing, as I do at present.

The occasion, I confess, is sorrowful, because I see yourselves, with others, embarked in a resolution to invade and despoil your poor countrymen, in a wilderness, and your ancient friends, of our temporal and soul liberties.

It is sorrowful, also, because mine eye beholds a black and doleful train of grievous, and, I fear, bloody consequences, at the heel of this business, both to you and us. The Lord is righteous in all our afflictions, that is a maxim; the Lord is gracious to all oppressed, that is another; he is most gracious to the soul that cries and waits on him; that is silver, tried in the fire seven times.

Sir, I am not out of hopes, but that while your aged eyes and mine are yet in their orbs, and not yet sunk down into their holes of rottenness, we shall leave our friends and countrymen, our children and relations, and this land, in peace, behind us. To this end, Sir, please you with a calm and steady and a Christian hand, to hold the balance and to weigh these few considerations, in much love and due respect presented:

First. When I was unkindly and unchristianly, as I believe, driven from my house and land and wife and children, (in the midst of a New England winter, now about thirty-five years past,) at Salem, that ever honored Governor, Mr. Winthrop, privately wrote to me to steer my course to Narragansett Bay and Indians, for many high and heavenly and public ends, encouraging me, from the freeness of the place from any English claims or patents. I took his prudent motion as a hint and voice from God, and waving all other thoughts and motions, I steered my course from Salem (though in winter snow, which I feel yet) unto these parts, wherein I may say Peniel, that is, I have seen the face of God.

Second, I first pitched, and began to build and plant at Seekonk, now Rehoboth, but I received a letter from my ancient friend, Mr. Winslow,[7] then Governor of Plymouth, professing his own and others love and respect to me, yet lovingly advising me, since I was fallen into the edge of their bounds, and they were loath to displease the Bay, to remove but to the other side of the water, and then, he said, I had the country free before me, and might be as free as themselves, and we should be loving neighbors together. These were the joint understandings of these two eminently wise and Christian Governors and others, in their day, together with their counsel and advice as to the freedom and vacancy of this place, which in this respect, and many other Providences of the Most Holy and Only Wise, I called *Providence.*

Third. Sometime after, the Plymouth great Sachem, (Ousamaquin,) upon occasion, affirming that Providence was his land, and therefore Plymouth's land, and some resenting it, the then prudent and godly Governor, Mr. Bradford, and others of his godly council, answered, that if, after due examination, it should be found true what the barbarian said, yet having to my loss of a harvest that year, been now (though by their gentle advice) as good as banished from Plymouth as from the Massachusetts, and I had quietly and patiently departed from them, at their motion to the place where now I was, I should not be molested and tossed up and down again, while they had breath in their bodies; and surely, between those, my friends of the Bay and Plymouth, I was sorely tossed, for one fourteen weeks, in a bitter winter season, not knowing what bread or bed did mean, beside the yearly loss of no small matter in my trading with English and natives, being debarred from Boston, the chief mart and port of New England. God knows that many thousand pounds cannot repay the very temporary losses I have sustained. It lies upon the Massachusetts and me, yea, and other colonies joining with them, to examine, with fear and trembling, before the eyes of flaming fire, the true cause of all my sorrows and sufferings. It pleased the Father of spirits to touch many hearts, dear to him, with some relentings; amongst which, that great and pious soul, Mr. Winslow, melted, and kindly visited me, at Providence, and put a piece of gold into the hands of my wife, for our supply.

Fourth. When the next year after my banishment, the Lord drew the bow of the Pequod war against the country, in which, Sir, the Lord made yourself, with others, a blessed instrument of peace to all New England, I had my share of service to the whole land in that Pequod business, inferior to very few that acted, for,

1. Upon letters received from the Governor and Council at Boston, requesting me to use my utmost and speediest endeavors to break and hinder the league labored for by the Pequods against the Mohegans, and Pequods against the English, (excusing the not sending of company and supplies, by the haste of the business,) the Lord helped me immediately to put my life into my hand, and, scarce acquainting my wife, to ship myself, all alone, in a poor canoe, and to cut through a stormy wind, with great seas, every minute in hazard of life, to the Sachem's house.

2. Three days and nights my business forced me to lodge and mix with the bloody Pequod ambassadors, whose hands and arms, methought, wreaked with the blood of my countrymen, murdered and massacred by them on Connecticut river, and from whom I could not but nightly look for their bloody knives at my own throat also. . . .

9. However you satisfy yourselves with the Pequod conquest, with the sealing of your charter some weeks before ours; with the complaints of particular men to your colony; yet upon a due and serious examination of the matter, in the sight of God, you will find the business at bottom to be,

First, a depraved appetite after the great vanities, dreams and shadows of this vanishing life, great portions of land, land in this wilderness, as if men were in as great necessity and danger for want of great portions of land, as poor, hungry, thirsty seamen have, after a sick and stormy, a long and starving passage. This is one of the gods of New England, which the living and most high Eternal will destroy and famish.

2. An unneighborly and unchristian intrusion upon us, as being the weaker, contrary to your laws, as well as ours, concerning purchasing of lands without the consent of the General Court. . . .

From these violations and intrusions arise the complaint of many privateers, not dealing as they would be dealt with, according to law of nature, the law of the prophets and Christ Jesus, complaining against others, in a design, which they themselves are delinquents and wrong doers. I could aggravate this many ways with Scripture rhetoric and similitude, but I see need of anodynes, (as physicians speak,) and not of irritations. Only this I must crave leave to say, that it looks like a prodigy or monster, that countrymen among savages in a wilderness;

that professors of God and one Mediator, of an eternal life, and that this is like a dream, should not be content with those vast and large tracts which all the other colonies have, (like platters and tables full of dainties,) but pull and snatch away their poor neighbors' bit or crust; and a crust it is, and a dry, hard one, too, because of the natives' continual troubles, trials and vexations.

10. Alas! Sir, in calm midnight thoughts, what are these leaves and flowers, and smoke and shadows, and dreams of earthly nothings, about which we poor fools and children, as David saith, disquiet ourselves in vain? Alas? what is all the scuffling of this world for, but, *come, will you smoke it?* What are all the contentions and wars of this world about, generally, but for greater dishes and bowls of porridge, of which, if we believe God's Spirit in Scripture, Esau and Jacob were types? Esau will part with the heavenly birthright for his supping, after his hunting, for god belly: and Jacob will part with porridge for an eternal inheritance. O Lord, give me to make Jacob's and Mary's choice, which shall never be taken from me.

11. How much sweeter is the counsel of the Son of God, to mind first the matters of his kingdom; to take no care for to-morrow; to pluck out, cut off and fling away right eyes, hands and feet, rather than to be cast whole into hell-fire; to consider the ravens and the lilies, whom a heavenly Father so clothes and feeds; and the counsel of his servant Paul, to roll our cares, for this life also, upon the most high Lord, steward of his people, the eternal God: to be content with food and raiment; to mind not our own, but every man the things of another; yea, and to suffer wrong, and part with what we judge is right, yea, our lives, and (as poor women martyrs have said) as many as there be hairs upon our heads, for the name of God and the son of God his sake. This is humanity, yea, this is Christianity. The rest is but formality and picture, courteous idolatry and Jewish and Popish blasphemy against the Christian religion, the Father of spirits and his Son, the Lord Jesus. Besides, Sir, the matter with us is not about these children's toys of land, meadows, cattle, government, &c. But here, all over this colony, a great number of weak and distressed souls, scattered, are flying hither from Old and New England, the Most High and Only Wise hath, in his infinite wisdom, provided this country and this corner as a shelter for the poor and persecuted, according to their several persuasions. . . .

16. Sir, I lament that such designs should be carried on at such a time, while we are stripped and whipped, and are still under (the whole country) the dreadful rods of God, in our wheat, hay, corn, cattle,

shipping, trading, bodies and lives; when on the other side of the water, all sorts of consciences (yours and ours) are frying in the Bishops' pan and furnace; when the French and Romish Jesuits, the firebrands of the world for their god belly sake, are kindling at our back, in this country, especially with the Mohawks and Mohegans, against us, of which I know and have daily information.

17. If any please to say, is there no medicine for this malady? Must the nakedness of New England, like some notorious strumpet, be prostituted to the blaspheming eyes of all nations? Must we be put to plead before his Majesty, and consequently the Lord Bishops, our common enemies, &c. I answer, the Father of mercies and God of all consolations hath graciously discovered to me, as I believe, a remedy, which, if taken, will quiet all minds, yours and ours, will keep yours and ours in quiet possession and enjoyment of their lands, which you all have so dearly bought and purchased in this barbarous country, and so long possessed amongst these wild savages; will preserve you both in the liberties and honors of your charters and governments, without the least impeachment of yielding one to another; with a strong curb also to those wild barbarians and all the barbarians of this country, without troubling of compromisers and arbitrators between you; without any delay, or long and chargeable and grievous address to our King's Majesty, whose gentle and serene soul must needs be afflicted to be troubled again with us. If you please to ask me what my prescription is, I will not put you off to Christian moderation or Christian humility, or Christian prudence, or Christian love, or Christian self-denial, or Christian contention or patience. For I design a civil, a humane and political medicine, which, if the God of Heaven please to bless, you will find it effectual to all the ends I have proposed. Only I must crave your pardon, both parties of you, if I judge it not fit to discover it at present. I know you are both of you hot; I fear myself, also. If both desire, in a loving and calm spirit, to enjoy your rights, I promise you, with God's help, to help you to them, in a fair, and sweet and easy way. My receipt will not please you all. If it should so please God to frown upon us that you should not like it, I can but humbly mourn, and say with the prophet, that which must perish must perish. And as to myself, in endeavoring after your temporal and spiritual peace, I humbly desire to say, if I perish, I perish. It is but a shadow vanished, a bubble broke, a dream finished. Eternity will pay for all.

Sir, I am your old and true friend and servant,

Roger Williams.

INCREASE MATHER, 1639–1723

[For life of Increase Mather see p. 334. This text is from *The Life and Death of that Reverend Man in God, Mr. Richard Mather* (Cambridge, 1670), pp. 8–11, 25–33.]

THE LIFE OF RICHARD MATHER

B EING as hath been related, setled in the Ministry at *Toxteth*, he resolved to change his single condition: And accordingly he became a Suitor to Mrs. *Katharine Hoult*, Daughter to *Edmund Hoult* Esq; of *Bury* in *Lancashire*. She had (and that deservedly) the repute of a very godly and prudent Maid. The Motion for several years met with Obstructions, by reason of her Fathers not being affected towards Non-conformable Puritans: But at last he gave his Consent that Mr. *Mather* should marry his Daughter; the Match therefore was Consummated *Septemb.* 29. 1624. God made her to become a rich Blessing to him, continuing them together for the space of above 30 years. By her God gave him six Sons; four whereof (*viz. Samuel, Timothy, Nathaniel* and *Joseph*) were born in *England*, and two (*viz. Eleazar* and *Increase*) in *New-England*. After his Marriage he removed his Habitation three miles from *Toxteth*, to *Much-Woolton*, having there purchased an House of his own; yet he was wont constantly Summer and Winter to Preach the Word at *Toxteth* upon the Lords-dayes. During his abode there, he was abundant in Labours in the Gospel: For every Lords-day he Preached twice at *Toxteth*, and once in a Fortnight on the Third day of the Week he kept a *Lecture* at the Town of *Prescot*. Also, faithful and powerful Preaching being then rare in those parts, he did frequently Preach upon the *Holy dayes* (as they are called) being often thereunto desired by godly Christians of other Parishes in that Country: And this he did, not as thinking that there was any Holiness in those times (or in any other day besides the Lords-day) beyond what belongs to every day; but because then there would be an opportunity of great Assemblies,[1] and it is good casting the Net where there is much Fish: for which cause it might be that the Apostles Preached mostly in Populous Towns and Cities, and also (which suiteth with what we are speaking) on the *Jewish Sabbaths* after their abrogation as to any Religious tye upon Conscience for their observation. Yea and besides all this, he often Preached at *Funerals*. It is true that *Cartwright, Sherwood, Hildersham,* and many other Renowned Non-Conformists, have scrupled Preaching *Funerall Sermons;* Also in some Reformed Churches that

practice is wholly omitted, yea and Decrees of Councils have sometimes been against it; but that hath been chiefly upon account of that
Custome of *Praising the dead* upon such occasions, and that many times
untruly: Which *Custome* (as many Learned men have observed) is
Ethnicall, having its rise from the Funeral Orations of the Heathen.
Publicola made an excellent Oration in Praise of *Brutus*, which the People
were so taken with, that it became a Custome that Famous men dying
should be so praised, and when (as *Plutarch* saith in the Life of *Camillus*)
the Women amongst the *Romans* parted with their Golden Ornaments
for the Publick Good, the Senate decreed, That it should be lawful to
make Funeral Orations for them also. *Hinc mortuos laudandi mos fluxit
quem nos hodiè servamus.*[2] *Pol. Verg. de Rer. Invent. lib. 3. cap.* 10. Nor indeed
was this Rite practised in the Church afore the *Apostacy* began. *Vide
Magd. Cent. 4. Cap.* 6. wherefore this faithful Servant of the Lord avoided
that practice, his speech at Funerals being taken up not with Praising
the Dead, but with *Instructing the Living* concerning Death, the Resurrection, the Judgement to come, and the like seasonable Truths. Thus did
he Preach the Word, being instant in season and out of season; reprov-
ing, rebuking, exhorting, with all long-suffering and doctrine. In his
publick Ministry in *England* he went over 2 *Samuel, Chap.* 24. *Psalm* 4.
and *Psalm* 16. *Proverbs, Chap.* 1. *Isaiah, Chap.* 1. and *Chap.* 6. *Luke,* 22
and 23 *Chapters. Romans, Chap.* 8. 2 *Epist.* to *Timothy;* 2. *Epist.* of *John;*
and the *Epistle* of *Jude.*

After that he had thus painfully and faithfully spent fifteen years
in the Work of the Ministry, He that holds the Stars in his right hand,
had more work for him to do elswhere; and therefore the rage of
Satan and wrath of men must be suffered to break forth, untill this
choice Instrument had his mouth stopped in unrighteousness. The *Lecture* which he kept at *Prescot* caused him to be much taken notice of,
and so was the more unto the Adversaries of the Truth an object of
Envy. *Magnam famam & magnam quietem eodem tempore nemo potest acquirere.*
Quint.[3] Wherefore Complaints being made against him for Non-
Conformity to the Ceremonies, he was by the *Prelates Suspended.* This
was in *August, Anno* 1633. Under this Suspension he continued untill
November following: But then, by means of the Intercession of some
Gentlemen in *Lancashire*, and by the Influence of *Simon Byby* (a near
Alliance of the Bishops) he was restored again to his Publick Ministry.
After his Restauration he more fully searched into, and also in his
Ministry handled the Points of *Church-Discipline.* And God gave him
in those dayes not onely to see, but also to Instruct others in the Sub-
stance of the *Congregationall-Way*, which came to pass by his much

reading of the holy Scriptures, and his being very conversant in the Writings of *Cartwright, Parker, Baynes,* and *Ames.*[4] But this restored Liberty continued not long; for *Anno* 1634. Bishop *Neal* (he who was sometimes by King *James* pleasantly admonished of his Preaching Popery, because by his carriage he taught the people to pray for a blessing upon his dead Predecessor) being now become *Archbishop of York,* sent his Visitors into *Lancashire;* of whom Doctor *Cousins* (whose *Cozening Devotions* Mr. *Pryn*[5] hath made notorious to the world) was one: These Visitors being come into the Country . . . kept their Courts at *Wigan;* where, amongst many other unrighteous proceedings, & having Mr. *Mather* convened before them, they passed a Sentence of *Suspension* against him, meerly for his *Non-Conformity* to the Inventions of men in the Worship of God. It was marvellous to see how God was with him, causing a Spirit of Courage and of Glory to rest upon him, and filling him with wisdome when he stood before those Judges, who were not willing that he should speak for himself, or declare the Reasons which convinced his Conscience of the unlawfulness of that *Conformity* which they required. Concerning the Lords presence with him at that time, himself doth in a Manuscript left in his Study thus express it: *In the passages of that day, I have this to bless the Name of God for, that the terrour of their threatning words, of their Pursevants, and of the rest of their Pomp, did not so terrifie my minde, but that I could stand before them without being daunted in the least measure, but answered for my self such words of truth and soberness as the Lord put into my mouth, not being afraid of their faces at all: which supporting and comforting presence of the Lord I count not much less mercy, then if I had been altogether preserved out of their hands.*

Being thus silenced from Publick Preaching the Word, means was again used by Mr. *Mathers* friends to obtain his Liberty; but all in vain. The Visitor asked how long he had been a Minister? Answer was made, That he had been in the Ministry fifteen years. And (said he) how often hath he worn the Surpless? Answer was returned, That he had never worn it. *What* (said the *Visitor,* swearing as he spake it) *preach Fifteen years and never wear a Surpless? It had been better for him that he had gotten Seven Bastards.* This was a Visitors judgement. . . .

Wherefore the case being thus, he betook himself to a private life: and no hope being left of enjoying Liberty again in his Native Land; foreseeing also (*Sapiens Divinat*)[6] the approaching Calamities of *England,* he meditated a Removall into *New-England.* . . .

During the time of his Pilgrimage in *New-England* he under-went not so many Changes, as before that he had done; for he never removed his Habitation out of *Dorchester,* albeit he had once serious thoughts that way, by reason that his old people in *Toxteth*, after that the *Hierarchy* was deposed in *England*, sent to him, desiring his return to them: But *Dorchester* was in no wise willing to forgoe their interest in him, therefore he left them not. Nevertheless, he did in *New-England* (as in a Wilderness might be expected) experience many Trials of his Faith and Patience. That which of outward Afflictions did most agrieve him, was the Death of his dear Wife, who had been for so many years the greatest outward Comfort and Blessing which he did enjoy: Which Affliction was the more grievous, in that she being a Woman of singular Prudence for the Management of Affairs, had taken off from her Husband all Secular Cares, so that he wholly devoted himself to his Study, and to Sacred Imployments. After he had continued in the state of Widowhood a year and half, he again changed his Condition, and was Married to the pious Widow of that deservedly Famous Man of God Mr. *John Cotton;* [7] and her did God make a Blessing and a Comfort to him during the remainder of his dayes.

Old Age now being come upon him, he was sensible of the Infirmities thereof, being in his latter years something thick of Hearing: Also (as it was with great *Zanchy*) [8] the sight in one of his Eyes failed, seven years before his Death. Yet God gave him Health of Body and Vigour of Spirit in a wonderful measure, so as that in fifty years together, he was not by Sickness detained so much as one Lords-day from Publick Labours. Which continued Health (as to Natural causes) proceeded partly from his strong Constitution of Body, and partly from his accustoming himself to a plain and wholsome Diet. *Bona Diata est potior quovis Hippocrate.*[9] He never made use of any Physician, nor was he ever in all his life sick of any acute Disease. Onely the two last years of his *Life* he was sorely afflicted with that Disease which some have called *Flagellum Studiosorum,* viz.[10] *The Stone,* which at last brought him to an end of all his Labours and Sorrows.

Concerning the Time and Manner of his Sickness and Death, thus it was. There being some Differences in *Boston,*[11] Counsel from Neighbour-Churches was by some desired, to direct them in the Lord what should be done: Accordingly the Churches sent their Messengers; and *Dorchester* Church, amongst others, sent Mr. *Mather* their aged *Teacher,* who Assembled in *Boston, April* 13. 1669. He was, because of his Age, Gravity, Grace and Wisdome wherewith the Lord had endowed and adorned him, chosen the *Moderator* in that *Reverend Assembly*. For divers dayes after his being thus in *Consultation,* he enjoyed his Health as formerly, or rather better then for some time of late. But as *Luther* when Assembled in a *Synod* was surprized with a violent Fit of the Stone, whence he was forced to return home, his Friends having little hopes of his life; so it was with this holy man. For *April* 16. 1669. he was in the night, being then in his Sons house in *Boston*, taken exceeding ill through a totall stoppage of his Urine. The next morning he therefore returned home to *Dorchester*. Great was the favour of God towards him, that he should be *found about* such *a blessed Work* as then he was ingaged in, for the Lord found him sincerely and earnestly endeavouring to be a Peace-maker. His being thus taken when at a Synod, brings to minde that of the *German Phoenix;*

Viximus in Synodis, & jam moriemur in illis.[12]

Now as usually Providence so ordereth, that they who have been speaking all their lives long, shall not say much when they come to die: Blessed *Hooker* in his last Sickness, when Friends would have had him answered to some Enquiries which might have made for their Edification after he was gone, he referred them wholly to the things which he had taught them in his health, because then he had enough to do to grapple with his own bodily weakness, *&c.* Neither did this good man speak much in his last Sickness either to Friends or to his Children. Onely his Son who is now *Teacher* of a Church in *Boston*, coming to visit his Father, and perceiving the Symptomes of Death to be upon him, said unto him, *Sir, if there be any speciall thing which you would recommend unto me to do, in case the Lord should spare me upon the Earth, after you are in Heaven, I would intreat you to express it.* At the which, his Father making a little pause, and lifting up his eyes and hands to Heaven, replied, *A speciall thing which I would commend to you, is, Care concerning the Rising Generation in this Country, that they be brought under the Government of Christ in his Church; and that when grown up and qualified, they have Baptism for their Children. I must confess I have been defective as to practise, yet I have publickly declared my judgement, and manifested my desires to practise that which I think ought to be attended, but the Dissenting of some in our Church discouraged me. I have thought that persons might have Right to Baptism, and yet not to the Lords Supper; and I see no cause to alter my judgement as to that particular. And I still think that persons qualified according to the Fifth Proposition of the late Synod-Book, have Right to Baptism for their Children.*[13]

His bodily Pains continued upon him untill *April* 22. when in the Morning his Son aforementioned, coming to visit him, asked his Father if he knew him; to whom he Replied that he did, but was not able to speak any more to him: Whereupon his Son saying, *Now you will speedily be in the joy of your Lord;* His Father lifted up his hands, but could not speak. Not long after his Son again spoke to him, saying,

*You will quickly see Jesus Christ, and that will make amends for all your pains
and sorrows:* At which words his Father again lifted up his hands; but
after that he took notice of no person or thing, but continuing speechless untill about 10 *h. P.M.* he quietly breathed forth his last. Thus did
that Light that had been shining in the Church above Fifty years,
Expire.

As he was a man faithful and fearing God above many, so the Lord
shewed great faithfulness unto him, both in making him serviceable
unto the last, yea and continuing the vigour of his Spirit, and power
of his Ministry. Few men, though young, are known to Preach with
such vigour as he did but ten dayes before his death. Also the Lord
was faithful and gracious to him, in respect of his Children. It was a
special token of Divine favour unto some of the Ancients, that their
Sons after them succeeded in the Ministry; so was it with the Fathers
of *Gregory Nazianzen, Gregory Nyssen, Basil, Hilary, &c.* And the Lord
cheered the heart of this his Servant in his old Age, by giving him to
see most of his Sons imployed in the Ministry many years before their
precious Father's decease. He left four Sons in that Work; one of whom,
viz. Mr. *Eleazar Mather*, late Pastor of the Church at *Northampton* in
New-England, went to his rest about three Moneths after his Father,
with him to sound forth the praises of God amongst the Spirits of just
men made perfect. The other three are yet surviving, *viz.* Mr. *Samuel
Mather*, Teacher of a Church in *Dublin;* Mr. *Nathaniel Mather*, late
Minister of *Barnstable* in *Devon*, and since in *Rotterdam* in *Holland;* and
Increase Mather of *Boston* in *New-England.* . . .

His way of Preaching was plain, aiming to shoot his Arrows not over
his peoples heads, but into their Hearts and Consciences. Whence he
studiously avoided obscure phrases, Exotick words, or an unnecessary
citation of Latine Sentences, which some men addict themselves to the
use of. Mr. *Dod* was wont to say, That *so much Latine was so much flesh
in a Sermon:* So did this humble man look upon the affectation of such
things in a *Popular Auditory* to savour of Carnal wisdome. The Lord
gave him an excellent faculty in making abstruse things plain, that in
handling the deepest Mysteries he would accommodate himself to
Vulgar Capacities, that even the meanest might learn something. He
knew how to express καινὰ κοινῶς καὶ κοινὰ καινῶς.[14] He would often
use that Saying, *Artis est celare Artem.*[15] And much approved that of
Austin; If (said he) *I preach Learnedly, then onely the Learned and not the
Unlearned can understand and profit by me; but if I preach plainly, then Learned
and Unlearned both can understand, so I may profit all.* He was *Mighty in the
Scriptures:* Whence Mr. *Hooker* would say of him, *My Brother* Mather *is

a mighty man. Also his usuall way of Delivery was very Powerful, Awakening, and Zealous; especially in his younger years, there being few men of so great strength of body as he, which together with his natural fervour of Spirit, being sanctified, made his Ministry the more powerful. And the Lord went forth with his Labours to the Conversion of many, both in *England* and in *New-England.* Yet though his way of Preaching was plain and zealous, it was moreover Substantial and very Judicious. Even in his beginning times, Mr. *Gillebrand* (a famous Minister in *Lancashire;* and the more famous, for that though he did exceedingly Stammer in his ordinary discourse, he would Pray and Preach as fluently as any man) once having heard him Preach, asked what his Name might be? And answer being made that his Name was *Mather;* Nay (said Mr. *Gillebrand*) call him *Matter,* for believe it this man hath Substance in him. Yea, such was his *Solidity of Judgement,* that some who were his Opposites, yet did therefore greatly respect and honour him. Doctor *Parr* (then Bishop in the Isle of *Man*) having heard Mr. *Mather* was Silenced, lamented it, saying, *If* Mather *be Silenced I am sorry for it, for he was a solid man, and the Church of God hath then a great loss.* . . .

It might be said of him, as was said of that blessed *Martyr,* that he was *sparing in his Diet, sparing in his Speech, most sparing of all of his Time.* He was very diligent both as to duties of general and particular Calling, which are indeed the two Pillars upon which Religion stands. As to his general Calling; He was much in Prayer, especially in his Study, where he oft-times spent whole dayes with God in suing for a Blessing upon himself and Children, and upon the people to whom he was related, and upon the whole Country where he lived. The Requests which upon such occasions he put up to God in Jesus Christ, and also how his heart was moved to believe that God heard him, he left (many of them) in writing amongst his private Papers, I suppose that so himself might have recourse unto those *Experiences* in a time of darkness and Temptation; also that his Sons after him might see by their Fathers Example, what it is to *walk before God.* Now what a loss is it to the world when such a Righteous man is taken away! Well might *Philo* and *Jerome* weep bitterly, when they heard of the death of any such men, because it portended evil to the places where they had lived, and served God. As he was much in Prayer, so he was very frequent in *Hearing the Word.* It was his manner to attend several Lectures in Neighbour-Congregations, untill his Disease made him unable to ride; yea and usually even to his old Age (as did Mr. *Hildersham* [16]) he took Notes from those whom he heard, professing that he found profit in it.

As to his particular Calling, he was even from his youth a hard Student. Yea his minde was so intent upon his Work and Studies, that the very morning before he died, he importuned those Friends that watched with him to help him into his Study: They urging that he was not able to go so farre, he desired them to help him and try; which they did: but ere he was come to the door of his Lodging-room, *I see* (saith he) *I am not able, yet I have not been in my Study several dayes, and is it not a lamentable thing that I should lose so much time?* After his entrance upon the Ministry, he was not onely in *England* (as hath been said) but in *New-England* abundant in Labours: for except when he had an Assistant with him (which was seldome) he Preached twice every Lords-day; and a Lecture once a fortnight, besides many occasionall Sermons both in Publick and in Private. Also he was much exercised in answering many practical *Cases of Conscience*, and in Polemical, especially Disciplinary Discourses. In his Publick Ministry in *Dorchester* he went over *The Book of Genesis to Chap.* 38. *Psalm* 16. *The whole Book of the Prophet Zechariah. Matthews Gospel*, to *Chap.* 15. 1. *Epist. to Thess. Chap.* 5. *And the whole Second Epistle of* Peter; *his Notes whereon he reviewed, and Transcribed for the Press*, not many years before his decease.

Notwithstanding those rare Gifts and Graces wherewith the Lord had adorned him, he was exceeding low and little in his own eyes. Some have thought that his greatest errour was, that he did not magnifie his Office, as he might and sometimes should have done. If a man must erre, it is good erring on that hand. *Humble enough, and good enough*, was the frequent saying of a great Divine. And another observeth, *That every man hath just as much and no more true worth in him, as he hath Humility. Austine* being asked which was the most excellent grace, answered, *Humility;* and which was the next, answered, *Humility;* and which was the third, replied again, *Humility.* That indeed is *Comprehensively All*, being of great price in the sight of God; And if so, Mr. Mather was a man of much Reall Worth.

COTTON MATHER, 1663–1728

[For Cotton Mather's life see p. 162. This text is from *Magnalia Christi Americana* (London, 1702), Book III. John Eliot was born at Widford, Herts, 1604; emigrated in 1631 and was ordained teacher of the church at Roxbury in 1632; he died May 21, 1690. As Mather's account makes clear, he was a leader of New England Puritanism, not because like Cotton and Hooker he was a profound intellect, but because he incarnated the Puritan ideal of saintly piety.]

LIFE OF JOHN ELIOT

The Birth, Age, and Family of Mr. Eliot.

The inspired *Moses*, relating the Lives of those Anti Diluvian Patriarchs, in whom the Church of God, and Line of Christ was continued, through the first Sixteen hundred Years of Time, recites little but their *Birth*, and their *Age*, and their *Death*, and their *Sons* and *Daughters*. If those Articles would satisfie the Appetites and Enquiries of such as come to read the Life of our *Eliot*, we shall soon have dispatch'd the Work now upon our Hands.

The *Age*, with the *Death* of this Worthy Man, has been already terminated, in the Ninetieth Year of the present Century, and the Eighty sixth Year of his own Pilgrimage. And for his *Birth*, it was at a Town in *England;* the Name whereof I cannot presently recover; nor is it necessary for me to look back so far as the place of his *Nativity;* any more than 'tis for me to recite the Vertues of his *Parentage*, of which he said, *Vix ea nostra voco:* [1] Tho' indeed the pious Education which they gave him, caused him in his Age, to write these Words: *I do see that it was a great Favour of God unto me, to season my first Times with the Fear of God, the Word, and Prayer.*

The *Atlantick Ocean*, like a River of *Lethe*, may easily cause us to forget many of the things that happened on the other side. Indeed the *Nativity* of such a Man, were an Honour worthy the Contention of as many *Places*, as laid their Claims unto the famous *Homer's:* But whatever *Places* may challenge a share in the Reputation of having enjoy'd the *first Breath* of our *Eliot*, it is *New-England* that with most Right can call him *Hers;* his *best Breath*, and afterwards his *last Breath* was here; and here 'twas, that God bestow'd upon him *Sons and Daughters.*

He came to *New-England* in the Month of *November, A.D.* 1631. among those blessed old Planters, which laid the Foundations of a remarkable Country, devoted unto the Exercise of the Protestant Religion, in its purest and highest Reformation. He left behind him in *England*, a Vertuous young Gentlewoman, whom he had pursued and purposed a *Marriage* unto; and she coming hither the Year following, that Marriage was consummated in the Month of *October, A.D.* 1632.

This *Wife of his Youth* lived with him until she became to him also the *Staff of his Age;* and she left him not until about three or four Years before his own Departure to those Heavenly Regions, where they now together *see Light.* She was a Woman very eminent, both for *Holiness* and *Usefulness*, and she excelled most of the *Daughters that have done vertuously*. Her Name was *Anne*, and *Gracious* was her Nature. God made her a rich Blessing, not only to her *Family*, but also to her *Neighbourhood;* and when at last she died, I heard and saw her Aged Husband, who else very rarely wept, yet now with Tears over the Coffin, before the Good People, a vast Confluence of which were come to her Funeral, say, *Here lies my dear, faithful, pious, prudent, prayerful Wife; I shall go to her, and she not return to me.* My Reader will of his own accord excuse me, from bestowing any further *Epitaphs* upon that *gracious* Woman. . . .

Mr. Eliot's Early Conversion, Sacred Employment, and Just Removal into America.

But all that I have hitherto said, is no more than an entrance into the History of our *Eliot*. Such an *Enoch* as he, must have something more than these things recorded of him; his *Walk with God*, must be more largely laid before the World, as a thing that would bespeak us all to be *Followers* no less than we shall be *Admirers* of it.

He had not passed many *Turns* in the World, before he knew the meaning of a saving *Turn* from the Vanities of an Unregenerate State, unto God in Christ, by a true Repentance; he had the singular Happiness and Privilege of an *early Conversion* from the Ways, which *Original Sin* disposes all Men unto. One of the principal Instruments which the God of Heaven used in tingeing, and filling the Mind of this *chosen Vessel*, with good Principles, was that Venerable *Thomas Hooker*, whose Name in the Churches of the Lord Jesus, is, *As an Ointment poured forth;* even that *Hooker*, who having *Angled* many Scores of Souls into the Kingdom of Heaven, at last laid his Bones in our *New England;* it was an Acquaintance with *him*, that contributed more than a little to the Accomplishment of our *Elisha*, for that Work unto which the most High designed him. His liberal *Education*, having now the Addition of *Religion* to direct it, and improve it, it gave such a *Biass* to his young Soul, as quickly discovered it self in very signal Instances. His first Appearance in the World after his Education in the *University*, was in the too *difficult* and *unthankful* but very *necessary* Employment of a *School-Master*, which Employment he discharged with a good Fidelity. And as this *first Essay* of his Improvement was no more Disgrace unto him, than it was unto the famous *Hieron, Whitaker, Vines*, and others, that they *thus* began to be serviceable; so it rather prepared him, for the further Service, which his Mind was now set upon. He was of worthy Mr. *Thomas Wilson's* [2] Mind, that the calling of a *Minister* was the only one wherein a Man might be more serviceable to the Church of God, than in that of a *School-Master:* And with *Melchior Adam*, he reckoned, the Calling of a *School-Master, Pulverulentam, ac Molestissimam quidem, sed Deo longe gratissimam Functionem.*[3] Wherefore having dedicated himself unto God betimes, he could not reconcile himself to any lesser way of serving his Creator and Redeemer, than the Sacred *Ministry* of the Gospel; but alas, where should he have Opportunities for the Exercising of it? The *Laudian, Grotian,*[4] and *Arminian* Faction in the Church of *England,* in the Prosecution of their Grand Plot, for the reducing of *England* unto a moderate sort of *Popery,* had pitched upon *this* as one of their Methods for it; namely, to *creeple* as fast as they could, all the Learned, Godly, Painful Ministers of the Nation; and invent certain *Shibboleths* for the detecting and the destroying of such Men as were cordial Friends to the Reformation. 'Twas now a time when there were every day multiplied and imposed those unwarrantable *Ceremonies* in the Worship of God, by which the Conscience of our Considerate *Eliot* counted the *second Commandment* notoriously violated; 'twas now also a time, when some Hundreds of those Good People which had the Nick-name of *Puritans* put upon them, transported themselves, with their whole Families and Interests, into the Desarts of *America,* that they might here peaceably erect *Congregational Churches,* and therein attend and maintain all the pure Institutions of the Lord Jesus Christ; having the Encouragement of *Royal Charters,* that they should never have any Interruption in the Enjoyment of those *precious and pleasant things.* Here was a Prospect which quickly determined the devout Soul of our young *Eliot,* unto a Remove into *New-England,* while it was yet a *Land not sown;* he quickly lifted himself among those valiant Souldiers of the Lord Jesus Christ, who cheerfully encountred first the Perils of the *Atlantick Ocean,* and then the Fatigues of the *New-English Wilderness,* that they might have an undisturbed Communion with him in his Appointments here. And thus did he betimes procure himself the Consolation of having afterwards and for ever a Room in that Remembrance of God, *I remember thee, the Kindness of thy Youth, and the Love of thine Espousals, when thou wentest after me into the Wilderness.*

On his first Arrival to *New-England,* he soon joined himself unto the Church at *Boston;* 'twas *Church-work* that was his Errand hither, Mr. *Wilson,* the Pastor of that Church, was gone back into *England,* that he might perfect the Settlement of his Affairs; and in his Absence, young Mr. *Eliot* was he that supplied his place. Upon the Return of Mr. *Wilson,* that Church was intending to have made Mr. *Eliot* his Collegue, and their Teacher; but it was diverted. Mr. *Eliot* had engaged unto a select Number of his Pious and Christian Friends in

England, that if they should come into these Parts before he should be in the Pastoral Care of any other People, he would give himself to *Them*, and be for *Their* Service. It happened, that these Friends transported themselves hither, the Year after him; and chose their Habitation at the Town which they called *Roxbury*. A Church being now gathered at this place, he was in a little while *Ordained* unto the Teaching and Ruling of that Holy Society. So, 'twas in the Orb of that Church that we had him as a *Star fixed* for very near Threescore Years; it only remains that we now observe what was his *Magnitude* all this while, and how he performed his *Revolution*. . . .

HIS FAMILY-GOVERNMENT.

The Apostle *Paul*, reciting and requiring Qualifications of a *Gospel Minister*, gives Order, that he be *The Husband of one Wife, and one that ruleth well his own House, having his Children in subjection with all gravity.* It seems, that a Man's Carriage in his *own House* is a *part*, or at least a *sign*, of his due Deportment in the *House of God;* and then, I am sure, our *Eliot*'s was very Exemplary. That *one Wife* which was given to him truly *from the Lord*, he loved, prized, cherished, with a *Kindness* that notably represented the Compassion which he (thereby) taught his Church to expect from the Lord Jesus Christ; and after he had lived with her for more than half an Hundred Years, he followed her to the Grave with *Lamentations* beyond those, which the Jews from the figure of a Letter in the Text, affirm, that *Abraham* deplored his aged *Sarah* with; her Departure made a deeper Impression upon him than what any common Affliction could. His whole Conversation with her, had that *Sweetness*, and that *Gravity* and *Modesty* beautifying of it, that every one called them *Zachary* and *Elizabeth*. His Family was a little *Bethel*, for the Worship of God constantly and exactly maintained in it; and unto the daily Prayers of the Family, his manner was to prefix the *Reading* of the *Scripture;* which being done, 'twas also his manner to make his young People to chuse a certain Passage in the Chapter, and give him some *Observation* of their own upon it. By this Method he did mightily *sharpen* and *improve*, as well as *try*, their Understandings, and endeavour to make them *wise unto Salvation*. He was likewise very strict in the Education of his Children, and more careful to mend any *error* in their Hearts and Lives, than he could have been to cure a *Blemish* in their Bodies. No *Exorbitancies* or *Extravagancies* could find a Room under his Roof, nor was his House any other than a *School of Piety;* one might have there seen a perpetual mixture of a *Spartan* and a *Christian* Disciple. Whatever Decay there might be upon *Family-Religion*

among us, as for our *Eliot*, we *knew him, that he would command his Chil-*
dren, and his Houshold after him, that they should keep the Way of the Lord.

His Way of Preaching.

Such was he in his *lesser Family!* And in his *greater Family*, he manifested still more of his Regards to the Rule of a *Gospel-Ministry*. To his
Congregation, he was a *Preacher* that made it his Care, to *give every*
one their Meat in due Season. It was *Food* and not *Froth;* which in his
publick Sermons, he entertained the Souls of his People with, he did
not *starve* them with empty and windy Speculations, or with such
things as *Animum non dant, quia non habent;* [5] much less did he *kill* them
with such *Poyson* as is too commonly exposed by the *Arminian* and
Socinian Doctors that have too often sat in *Moses*'s Chair. His way of
Preaching was very *plain;* so that the very *Lambs* might wade, into his
Discourses on those Texts and Themes, wherein *Elephants* might *swim;*
and herewithal, it was very *powerful*, his Delivery was always very
graceful and grateful; but when he was to use reproofs and warnings
against any *Sin*, his Voice would rise into a *Warmth* which had in it
very much of *Energy* as well as *Decency;* he would sound the *Trumpets*
of God against all *Vice*, with a most penetrating Liveliness, and make
his Pulpit another Mount *Sinai*, for the Flashes of Lightning therein
display'd against the Breaches of the *Law* given upon that *Burning*
Mountain. And I observed, that there was usually a special Fervour in
the Rebukes which he bestow'd upon *Carnality*, a carnal Frame and
Life in Professors of Religion; when he was to brand the Earthly-
mindedness of *Church-Members*, and the Allowance and the Indulgence
which they often gave unto themselves in sensual Delights, here he was
a right *Boanerges;* he then spoke, as 'twas said one of the Ancients did,
Quot verba tot Fulmina, as many *Thunderbolts* as *Words*.

It was another Property of his *Preaching*, that there was evermore
much of CHRIST in it; and with *Paul*, he could say, *I determined to know*
nothing but Jesus Christ; having that Blessed Name in his Discourses,
with a Frequency like that, with which *Paul* mentions it in his *Epistles.*
As 'twas noted of Dr. *Bodly*, that whatever Subject he were upon, in
the Application still his Use of it would be, *to drive Men unto the Lord*
Jesus Christ; in like manner, the Lord Jesus Christ was the Loadstone
which gave a touch to all the Sermons of our *Eliot;* a Glorious, Precious,
Lovely *Christ* was the Point of Heaven which they still verged unto.
From this *Inclination* it was, that altho' he Printed several *English* Books
before he dy'd, yet his Heart seemed not so much in any of them, as in
that serious and savoury Book of his, Entituled, *The Harmony of the*

Gospels, in the Holy History of Jesus Christ.[6] From hence also 'twas, that he would give that Advice to young Preachers, *Pray let there be much of Christ in your Ministry;* and when he had heard a Sermon, which had any special Relish of a Blessed Jesus in it, he would say thereupon, *O blessed be God, that we have Christ so much and so well preached in poor* New-England!

Moreover, he lik'd no *Preaching,* but what had been *well studied* for; and he would very much commend a Sermon which he could perceive had required some good *Thinking* and *Reading* in the Author of it. I have been present, when he has unto a Preacher then just come home from the Assembly with him, thus expressed himself, *Brother, there was Oyl required for the Service of the Sanctuary; but it must be beaten Oyl; I praise God, that I saw your Oyl so well beaten to day; the Lord help us always by good Study to beat our Oyl, that there may be no knots in our Sermons left undissolved, and that there may a clear light be thereby given in the House of God!* And yet he likewise look'd for something in a Sermon beside and beyond the meer *Study* of *Man;* he was for having the *Spirit* of *God,* breathing in it and with it; and he was for speaking *those* things, from *those* Impressions and with *those* Affections, which might compel the Hearer to say, *The Spirit of God was here!* I have heard him complain, *It is a sad thing, when a Sermon shall have that one thing,* The Spirit of God wanting in it. . . .

Eliot as an Evangelist.

The Titles of a *Christian* and of a *Minister,* have rendred our *Eliot* considerable; but there is one memorable Title more, by which he has been signalized unto us. An Honourable Person [7] did once in Print put the Name of an *Evangelist* upon him; whereupon in a Letter of his to that Person afterwards Printed, his Expressions were, "There is a *Redundancy,* where you put the Title of *Evangelist* upon me; I beseech you to suppress all such things; let us do and speak and carry all things with Humility; it is the Lord who hath done what is done; and it is most becoming the Spirit of Jesus Christ to lift up him, and lay our selves low; I wish that Word could be obliterated." My Reader sees what a Caution Mr. *Eliot* long since entred against our giving him the Title of an *Evangelist;* but his *Death* has now made it safe, and his *Life* had long made it just, for us to acknowledge him with such a Title. I know not whether that of an *Evangelist,* or one separated for the Employment of Preaching the Gospel in such Places whereunto Churches have hitherto been gathered, be not an *Office* that should be continued in our Days; but this I know, that our *Eliot* very notably did the *Service* and *Business* of such an Officer.

Cambden [8] could not reach the Heighth of his Conceit, who bore in his *Shield* a Salvage of *America*, with his Hand pointing to the *Sun*, and this Motto, *Mihi Accessu, Tibi Recessu*. Reader, Prepare to behold this *Device* Illustrated!

The Natives of the Country now Possessed by the *New-Englanders*, had been forlorn and wretched *Heathen* ever since their first herding here; and tho' we know not *When* or *How* those *Indians* first became Inhabitants of this mighty Continent, yet we may guess that probably the Devil decoy'd those miserable Salvages hither, in hopes that the Gospel of the Lord Jesus Christ would never come here to destroy or disturb his *Absolute Empire* over them. But our *Eliot* was in such ill Terms with the Devil, as to alarm him with sounding the *Silver Trumpets* of Heaven in his Territories, and make some Noble and Zealous Attempts towards outing him of his Ancient Possessions here. There were, I think, Twenty several *Nations* (if I may call them so) of *Indians* upon that spot of Ground, which fell under the Influence of our *Three United Colonies;* and our *Eliot* was willing to rescue as many of them as he could, from that old usurping *Landlord* of *America*, who is *by the Wrath of God, the Prince of this World*.

I cannot find that any besides the Holy Spirit of God, first moved him to the blessed Work of *Evangelizing* these perishing *Indians;* 'twas that Holy Spirit which laid before his Mind the Idea of that which was on the *Seal* of the Massachuset Colony; *A poor Indian having a Label going from his Mouth, with a,* COME OVER AND HELP US. It was the Spirit of our Lord Jesus Christ, which enkindled in him a *Pitty* for the dark Souls of these Natives, whom the *God of this World had blinded*, through all the By-past Ages. He was none of those that make, *The Salvation of the Heathen*, an Article of their *Creed;* but (setting aside the unrevealed and extraordinary Steps which the *Holy one of Israel* may take out of his *usual Paths*) he thought men to be *lost* if our *Gospel* be hidden from them; and he was of the same Opinion with one of the Ancients, who said, *Some have endeavoured to prove* Plato *a Christian, till they prove themselves little better than Heathens*. It is indeed a Principle in the Turkish *Alcoran*, That *Let a Man's Religion be what it will, he shall be saved, if he conscientiously live up to the Rules of it:* But our *Eliot* was no *Mahometan*. He could most heartily subscribe to that Passage in the Articles of the Church of *England*. "They are to be held accursed, who presume to say, that every Man shall be saved by the Law or Sect which he professeth, so that he be diligent to frame his Life according to that Law, and Light of Nature; for Holy Scripture doth set out unto us, only the Name of Jesus Christ, whereby Men must be saved."

And it astonished him to see many dissembling Subscribers of those Articles, while they have grown up to such a *Phrensy*, as to deny peremptorily all *Church-state*, and all *Salvation* to all that are not under *Diocesan Bishops*, yet at the same time to grant that the *Heathen* might be saved without the Knowledge of the Lord Jesus Christ. . . .

The exemplary *Charity* of this excellent Person in this important Affair, will not be seen in its due Lustres, unless we make some Reflections upon several Circumstances which he beheld these forlorn *Indians* in. Know then, that these doleful Creatures are the veriest *Ruines of Mankind*, which are to be found any where upon the Face of the Earth. No such *Estates* are to be expected among them, as have been the *Baits* which the pretended *Converters* in other Countries have snapped at. One might see among them, what an *hard Master* the Devil is, to the most devoted of his *Vassals!* These abject Creatures, live in a Country full of *Mines;* we have already made entrance upon our *Iron;* and in the very Surface of the Ground among us, 'tis thought there lies *Copper* enough to supply all this World; besides other Mines hereafter to be exposed; but our shiftless *Indians* were never Owners of so much as a *Knife*, till we come among them; their Name for an *English-man* was a *Knife-man;* Stone was instead of Metal for their *Tools;* and for their *Coins*, they have only little *Beads* with Holes in them to string them upon a *Bracelet*, whereof some are *white;* and of these there go six for a Penny; some are *black* or *blew;* and of these, go *three* for a Penny; this *Wampam*, as they call it, is made of the *Shell-fish*, which lies upon the Sea Coast continually.

The[y] live in a Country, where *we* now have all the Conveniencies of human Life: But as for *them*, their *housing* is nothing but a few *Mats* ty'd about *Poles* fastened in the Earth, where a good *Fire* is their *Bed Clothes* in the coldest Seasons; their *Clothing* is but a Skin of a Beast, covering their *Hind-parts*, their *Fore-parts* having but a little Apron, where Nature calls for Secrecy; their *Diet* has not a greater Dainty than their *Nokehick*, that is a spoonful of their *parch'd meal*, with a spoonful of *Water*, which will strengthen them to travel a Day together; except we should mention the Flesh of *Deers*, *Bears*, *Mose*, *Rackoons*, and the like, which they have when they can *catch* them; as also a little *Fish*, which if they would preserve, 'twas by *drying*, not by *salting;* for they had not a grain of *Salt* in the World, I think, till we bestow'd it on them. Their *Physick* is, excepting a few odd *Specificks*, which some of them Encounter certain Cases with, nothing hardly, but an *Hot-House*, or a *Powaw;* their *Hot-House* is a little *Cave* about eight foot over, where after they have terribly heated it, a Crew of·them go sit and sweat and smoke for an Hour together, and then immediately run into some very cold adjacent Brook, without the least Mischief to them; 'tis this way they recover themselves from some Diseases, particularly from the *French;* but in most of their dangerous Distempers, 'tis a *Powaw* that must be sent for; that is, a *Priest*, who has more Familiarity with Satan than his Neighbours; this Conjurer comes and Roars, and Howls, and uses Magical Ceremonies over the Sick Man, and will be well paid for it, when he has done; if this don't effect the Cure, the *Man's Time is come, and there's an end.*

They live in a Country full of the best *Ship-Timber* under Heaven: But never saw a *Ship*, till some came from *Europe* hither; and then they were scar'd out of their Wits, to see the *Monster* come sailing in, and spitting Fire with a mighty noise, out of her floating side; they cross the Water in *Canoo's*, made sometimes of *Trees*, which they burn and hew, till they have hollow'd them: and sometimes of *Barks*, which they stitch into a light sort of a Vessel, to be easily carried over Land; if they over-set, it is but a little paddling like a Dog, and they are soon where they were.

Their way of living, is infinitely Barbarous: The Men are most abominably *slothful;* making their poor *Squaws*, or Wives, to plant and dress, and barn, and beat their Corn, and build their *Wigwams* for them; which perhaps may be the reason of their extraordinary Ease in Childbirth. In the mean time, their chief Employment, when they'll *condescend* unto any, is that of *Hunting;* wherein they'll go out some scores, if not Hundreds of them in a Company, driving all before them.

They continue in a Place, till they have burnt up all the *Wood* thereabouts, and then they pluck up Stakes; to follow the *Wood*, which they cannot fetch home unto themselves; hence when they enquire about the *English, Why come they hither!* They have themselves very Learnedly determined the Case, *'Twas because we wanted Firing.* No *Arts* are understood among them, unless just so far as to maintain their Brutish Conversation, which is little more than is to be found among the very *Bevers* upon our Streams. . . .

This was the miserable People, which our *Eliot* propounded unto himself, to teach and save! And he had a double Work incumbent on him; he was to make Men of them, e'er he could hope to see them *Saints;* they must be *civilized* e'er they could be *Christianized;* he could not, as *Gregory* once of our Nation, see any thing *Angelical* to bespeak his Labours for their Eternal Welfare, all among them was *Diabolical.* To think on raising a Number of these hideous Creatures, unto the *Elevations* of our Holy Religion, must argue more than common or little Sentiments in the Undertaker; but the Faith of an *Eliot* could encounter it! . . .

The *First Step* which he judg'd necessary now to be taken by him, was to learn the *Indian* Language; for he saw them so stupid and sense-less, that they would never do so much as enquire after the Religion of the Strangers now come into their Country, much less would they so far imitate us, as to leave off their beastly way of living, that they might be Partakers of any Spiritual Advantage by us: Unless we could first address them in a *Language* of their own. Behold, new Difficulties to be surmounted by our indefatigable *Eliot!* He hires a Native to teach him this exotick Language, and with a laborious Care and Skill, reduces it into a *Grammar* which afterwards he published. There is a Letter or two of our Alphabet, which the *Indians* never had in *theirs;* tho' there were enough of the *Dog* in their *Temper,* there can scarce be found an R in their *Language;* (any more than in the Language of the *Chinese,* or of the *Greenlanders*) save that the *Indians* to the North-ward, who have a peculiar *Dialect,* pronounce an R where an N is pronounced by our *Indians;* but if their *Alphabat* be *short,* I am sure the *Words* composed of it are long enough to tire the Patience of any Scholar in the World; they are *Sesquipedalia Verba,*[9] of which their *Lingua* is composed; one would think, they had been growing ever since *Babel,* unto the Dimensions to which they are now extended. For instance, if my Reader will count how many Letters there are in this one Word, *Nummatchekodtantamooonganunnonash,* when he has done, for his Reward I'll tell him, it signifies no more in *English,* than *our Lusts,* and if I were to translate, *our Loves;* it must be nothing shorter than *Noowomantammooonkanunonnash.* Or, to give my Reader a longer Word than either of these, *Kummogkodonattoottummooetiteaongannunnonash,* is in English, *Our Question:* But I pray, Sir, count the Letters! Nor do we find in all this Language the least Affinity to, or Derivation from any *European* Speech that we are acquainted with. I know not what Thoughts it will produce in my Reader, when I inform him, that once finding that the *Dæmons* in a possessed young Woman, understood the *Latin* and *Greek* and *Hebrew* Languages, my Curiosity led me to make Trial of this *Indian* Language, and the *Dæmons* did seem as if they did not understand it. This tedious Language our *Eliot* (the Anagram of whose Name was ToiLE) quickly became a Master of; he employ'd a pregnant and witty *Indian,* who also spoke *English* well, for his Assistance in it; and compiling some Discourses by his Help, he would single out a *Word,* a *Noun,* a *Verb,* and pursue it through all its Variations: Having finished his Grammar, at the close he writes, *Prayers and Pains thro'*

Faith in Christ Jesus will do any thing! And being by his *Prayers* and *Pains* thus furnished, he set himself in the Year 1646. to preach the Gospel of our Lord Jesus Christ, among these Desolate Outcasts. . . .

MR. ELIOT'S WAY OF OPENING THE MYSTERIES OF THE GOSPEL, TO OUR INDIANS.

'Twas in the Year 1646, that Mr. *Eliot*, accompany'd by three more, gave a Visit unto an Assembly of *Indians*, of whom he desired a Meeting at such a Time and Place, that he might lay before them the Things of their Eternal Peace. After a serious *Prayer*, he gave them a *Sermon* which continued about a Quarter above an Hour, and contained the principal Articles of the Christian Religion, applying all to the Condition of the *Indians* present. Having done, he asked of them, Whether *they understood?* And with a General Reply they answered, *They understood all.* He then began what was his usual Method afterwards in treating with them; that is, he caused them to propound such *Questions* as they pleas'd unto himself; and he gave wise and good *Answers* to them all. Their *Questions* would often, tho' not always, refer to what he had newly preached; and he this way not only made a *Proof* of their profiting by his Ministry, but also gave an Edge to what he delivered unto them. Some of their *Questions* would be a little *Philosophical*, and required a good Measure of Learning in the Minister concerned with them; but for this our *Eliot* wanted not. He would also put proper *Questions* unto them, and at one of his first Exercises with them, he made the Young Ones capable of regarding those three Questions,

Q. 1. *Who made you and all the World?*
Q. 2. *Who do you look should save you from Sin and Hell?*
Q. 3. *How many Commandments has the Lord given you to keep?*

It was his Wisdom that he began with them upon such Principles as they themselves had already some Notions of; such as that of an *Heaven* for good, and *Hell* for bad People, when they dy'd. It broke his gracious Heart within him to see, what Floods of Tears fell from the Eyes of several among those degenerate Salvages, at the first Addresses which he made unto them; yea, from the very worst of them all. He was very inquisitive to learn who were the *Powawes*, that is, the *Sorcerers*, and *Seducers*, that maintained the Worship of the Devil in any of their Societies; and having in one of his first Journeys to them, found out one of those Wretches, he made the *Indian* come unto him, and said, *Whether do you suppose* God, *or* Chepian (i.e. *the Devil) to be the Author of all Good?* The Conjurer answered, *God.* Upon this he added with a stern

Countenance, *Why do you pray to* Chepian *then?* And the poor Man was not able to stand or speak before him; but at last made Promises of Reformation. . . .

The Conclusion: or, Eliot Expiring.

By this time, I have doubtless made my Readers loth to have me tell what now remains of this little History; doubtless they are wishing that this *John* might have *Tarried unto the Second Coming of our Lord.* But, alas, All-devouring *Death* at last snatch'd him from us, and slighted all those Lamentations of ours, *My Father, My Father, the Chariots of Israel, and the Horsemen thereof!*

When he was become a sort of *Miles Emeritus,*[10] and began to draw near his *End,* he grew still more Heavenly, more Savoury, more Divine, and scented more of the Spicy Country at which he was ready to put ashore. As the Historian observes of *Tiberius,* That when his *Life* and *Strength* were going from him, his *Vice* yet remained with him; on the contrary, the *Grace* of this Excellent Man rather increased than abated, when every thing else was dying with him. 'Tis too usual with *Old Men,* that when they are past *Work,* they are least sensible of their Inabilities and Incapacities, and can scarce endure to see another succeeding them in any part of their Office. But our *Eliot* was of a Temper quite contrary thereunto; for finding many Months before his Expiration, That he had not Strength enough to Edify his Congregation with Publick *Prayers,* and *Sermons,* he importun'd his People with some Impatience to call another Minister; professing himself unable to die with Comfort, until he could see a good Successor ordained, settled, fixed among them. For this Cause, he also cry'd mightily unto the Lord Jesus Christ our *Ascended Lord,* that he would give such a *Gift* unto *Roxbury,* and he sometimes call'd his whole Town together to join with him in a *Fast* for such a Blessing. As the Return of their Supplications, our Lord quickly bestow'd upon them, a Person young in Years, but old in Discretion, Gravity, and Experience; and one whom the Church of *Roxbury* hopes to find, *A Pastor after God's own Heart.*

It was Mr. *Nehemiah Walter,* who being by the Unanimous Vote and Choice of the Church there, become the *Pastor* of *Roxbury,* immediately found the Venerable *Eliot* Embracing and Cherishing of him, with the tender Affections of a Father. The good Old Man like Old *Aaron,* as it were disrobed himself, with an unspeakable Satisfaction, when he beheld his Garments put upon a Son so dear unto him. After this, he for a Year or two before his Translation, could scarce be perswaded unto any *Publick Service*, but humbly pleaded, what none but he would ever have said, *It would be a Wrong to the Souls of the People, for him to do any thing among them, when they were supply'd so much to their Advantage otherwise.* If I mistake not, the last that ever he Preached was on a Publick *Fast;* when he fed his People with a very distinct and useful *Exposition* upon the Eighty Third Psalm; and he concluded with an Apology, begging his Hearers to pardon the *Poorness*, and *Meanness*, and *Brokenness*, (as he called it) of his *Meditations*; but added he, *My dear Brother here, will by'nd by mend all.*

But altho' he thus dismissed himself as one so near to the Age of *Ninety*, might well have done, from his Publick *Labours*; yet he would not give over his Endeavours, in a more private Sphere, to *Do good unto all*. He had always been an Enemy to *Idleness;* any one that should look into the little *Diary* that he kept in his *Almanacks*, would see that there was with him, *No Day without a Line;* and he was troubled particularly, when he saw how much *Time* was devoured by that Slavery to *Tobacco*, which too many debase themselves unto; and now he grew old, he was desirous that his *Works* should hold pace with his *Life;* the less *Time* he saw *left*, the less was he willing to have *lost*. He imagined that he could now do nothing to any purpose in any Service for God; and sometimes he would say with an Air peculiar to himself, *I wonder for what the Lord Jesus Christ lets me live; he knows that now I can do nothing for him!* And yet he could not forbear Essaying to *Do something* for his Lord; he conceived, that tho' the *English* could not be benefited by any *Gifts* which he now fancied himself to have only the *Ruines* of, yet who can tell but the *Negro's* might! He had long lamented it with a Bleeding and a Burning Passion, that the *English* used their *Negro's* but as their *Horses* or their *Oxen*, and that so little Care was taken about their immortal Souls; he look'd upon it as a Prodigy, that any wearing the *Name* of *Christians*, should so much have the *Heart* of *Devils* in them, as to prevent and hinder the Instruction of the poor *Blackamores*, and confine the Souls of their miserable Slaves to a *Destroying Ignorance*, meerly for fear of thereby losing the Benefit of their Vassalage; but now he made a Motion to the *English* within two or three Miles of him, that at such a time and Place they would send their *Negro's* once a Week unto him: For he would then *Catechise* them, and *Enlighten* them, to the utmost of his Power in the Things of their Everlasting Peace; however, he did not live to make much Progress in this Undertaking. . . .

He fell into some Languishments attended with a *Fever*, which in a few days brought him into the *Pangs* (may I say? or *Joys*) of Death;

and while he lay in these, Mr. *Walter* coming to him, he said unto him, *Brother, Thou art welcome to my very Soul. Pray retire to thy Study for me, and give me leave to be gone;* meaning that he should not, by Petitions to Heaven for his Life, detain him here. It was in these Languishments, that speaking about the Work of the Gospel among the *Indians*, he did after this Heavenly manner express himself, *There is a Cloud* (said he) *a dark Cloud upon the Work of the Gospel among the poor* Indians. *The Lord revive and prosper that Work, and grant it may live when I am Dead. It is a Work, which I have been doing much and long about. But what was the Word I spoke last? I recal that Word,* My Doings *Alas, they have been poor and small, and lean Doings, and I'll be the Man that shall throw the first Stone at them all.*

It has been observed, That they who have spoke many considerable things in their *Lives*, usually speak few at their *Deaths*. But it was otherwise with our *Eliot*, who after much Speech of and for God in his *Life-time*, uttered some things little short of *Oracles* on his *Death-Bed*, which, 'tis a thousand Pities, they were not more exactly regarded and recorded. Those Authors that have taken the pains to Collect, *Apophthegmata Morientum*, have not therein been unserviceable to the Living; but the *Apophthegms* of a Dying *Eliot* must have had in them a *Grace* and a *Strain* truly extraor[di]nary; and indeed the *vulgar Error* of the signal sweetness in the Song of a *Dying Swan*, was a very Truth in our Expiring *Eliot;* his last Breath smelt strong of Heaven, and was Articled into none but very gracious Notes; one of the last whereof, was, *Welcome Joy!* and at last it went away calling upon the standers-by, to *Pray, pray, pray!* Which was the thing in which so vast a Portion of it, had been before Employ'd.

This was the Peace in the End of this *Perfect and upright Man;* thus was there another *Star* fetched away to be placed among the rest that the third Heaven is now enriched with. He had once, I think, a pleasant Fear, that the Old Saints of his Acquaintance, especially those two dearest Neighbours of his, *Cotton* of *Boston*, and *Mather* of *Dorchester*, which were got safe to Heaven before him, would suspect him to be gone the wrong way, because he staid so long behind them. But they are now together with a Blessed Jesus, *beholding of his Glory*, and celebrating the High Praises of him that has *call'd them into his marvellous Light*. Whether *Heaven* was any more *Heaven* to him, because of his finding there, so many *Saints*, with whom he once had his Desireable Intimacies, yea, and so many *Saints* which had been the Seals of his own Ministry in this lower World, I cannot say; but it would be *Heaven* enough unto him, to go unto that *Jesus*, whom he had lov'd,

preach'd, serv'd, and in whom he had been long assured, ther
All Fullness dwell. In that Heaven I now leave him: Not without
Grynæus's Pathetical Exclamations [*O beatum illum diem!*] "Blessed will
be the Day, O Blessed the Day of our Arrival to the Glorious Assembly
of Spirits, which this great Saint is now rejoicing with!"

Bereaved *New-England*, where are thy Tears, at this Ill-boding
Funeral? We had a Tradition among us, "That the Country could
never perish, as long as *Eliot* was alive." But into whose Hands must this
Hippo fall, now the *Austin* of it is taken away? Our *Elisha* is gone, and
now who must *next Year invade the Land?* The *Jews* have a Saying,
Quando Luminaria patiuntur Eclipsin, malum signum est mundo; [11] But I
am sure, 'tis a dismal *Eclipse* that has now befallen our *New-English*
World. I confess, many of the Ancients fell into the Vanity of esteeming
the Reliques of the *Dead Saints*, to be the *Towers* and *Ramparts* of the
Places that enjoy'd them; and the *Dead Bodies* of two Apostles in the
City, made the Poet cry out,

> *A Facie Hostili duo propugnacula præsunt.* [12]

If the Dust of *dead Saints* could give us any Protection, we are not
without it; here is a Spot of *American* Soyl that will afford a rich Crop
of it, at the *Resurrection of the Just.* Poor *New-England* has been as *Glasten-
bury* of Old was called, *A Burying-place of Saints.* But we cannot see a
more terrible Prognostick, than Tombs filling apace with such *Bones*,
as those of the Renowned *Eliot*'s; the whole Building of this Country
trembles at the Fall of such a Pillar.

SAMUEL SEWALL, 1652–1730

[For Sewall's life see p. 376. Text from *Collections of the Massachusetts
Historical Society*, Fifth Series, Vols. V–VII.]

DIARY

JAN. 13, 1677. Giving my chickens meat, it came to my mind that I
gave them nothing save Indian corn and water, and yet they eat it
and thrived very well, and that that food was necessary for them,
how mean soever, which much affected me and convinced what need
I stood in of spiritual food, and that I should not nauseat daily duties
of Prayer, &c.

Nov. 6, 1692. Joseph threw a knop of Brass and hit his Sister Betty
on the forehead so as to make it bleed and swell; upon which, and for
his playing at Prayer-Time, and eating when Return Thanks, I

whipd him pretty smartly. When I first went in (call'd by his Grandmother) he sought to shadow and hide himself from me behind the
head of the Cradle: which gave me the sorrowfull remembrance of
Adam's carriage.

April 29, 1695. The morning is very warm and Sunshiny; in the
Afternoon there is Thunder and Lightening, and about 2. P.M. a very
extraordinary Storm of Hail, so that the ground was made white with
it, as with the blossoms when fallen; 'twas as bigg as pistoll and
Musquet Bullets; It broke of the Glass of the new House about 480
Quarrels [Squares] of the Front; of Mr. Sergeant's about as much;
Col. Shrimpton, Major General, Govr. Bradstreet, New Meetinghouse,
Mr. Willard, &c. Mr. Cotton Mather dined with us, and was with me
in the new Kitchen when this was; He had just been mentioning that
more Ministers Houses than others proportionably had been smitten
with Lightening; enquiring what the meaning of God should be in it.
Many Hail-Stones broke throw the Glass and flew to the middle of
the Room, or farther: People afterward Gazed upon the House to see
its Ruins. I got Mr. Mather to pray with us after this awfull Providence;
He told God He had broken the brittle part of our house, and prayd
that we might be ready for the time when our Clay-Tabernacles should
be broken. Twas a sorrowfull thing to me to see the house so far undon
again before twas finish'd.

Jan. 13, 1696. When I came in, past 7. at night, my wife met me in
the Entry and told me Betty had surprised them. I was surprised with
the abruptness of the Relation. It seems Betty Sewall had given some
signs of dejection and sorrow; but a little after dinner she burst out
into an amazing cry, which caus'd all the family to cry too; Her
Mother ask'd the reason; she gave none; at last said she was afraid
she should goe to Hell, her Sins were not pardon'd. She was first
wounded by my reading a Sermon of Mr. Norton's, about the 5th
of Jan. Text Jno 7. 34. Ye shall seek me and shall not find me. And
those words in the Sermon, Jno 8. 21. Ye shall seek me and shall die
in your sins, ran in her mind, and terrified her greatly. And staying at
home Jan. 12. she read out of Mr. Cotton Mather—Why hath Satan
filled thy heart, which increas'd her Fear. Her Mother ask'd her whether
she pray'd. She answer'd, Yes; but feared her prayers were not heard
because her Sins not pardon'd. Mr. Willard though sent for timelyer,
yet not being told of the message, . . . He came not till after I came
home. He discoursed with Betty who could not give a distinct account,
but was confused as his phrase was, and as had experienced in himself.
Mr. Willard pray'd excellently. The Lord bring Light and Comfort

out of this dark and dreadful Cloud, and Grant that Christ's being formed in my dear child, may be the issue of these painfull pangs.

Dec. 25, 1696. We bury our little daughter. In the chamber, Joseph in course reads Ecclesiastes 3^d a time to be born and a time to die— Elisabeth, Rev. 22. Hanah, the 38th Psalm. I speak to each, as God helped, to our mutual comfort I hope. I order'd Sam. to read the 102. Psalm. Elisha Cooke, Edw. Hutchinson, John Baily, and Josia Willard bear my little daughter to the Tomb.

Note. Twas wholly dry, and I went at noon to see in what order things were set; and there I was entertain'd with a view of, and converse with, the Coffins of my dear Father Hull, Mother Hull, Cousin Quinsey, and my Six Children: for the little posthumous was now took up and set in upon that that stands on John's: so are three, one upon another twice, on the bench at the end. My Mother ly's on a lower bench, at the end, with head to her Husband's head: and I order'd little Sarah to be set on her Grandmother's feet. 'Twas an awfull yet pleasing Treat; Having said, The Lord knows who shall be brought hether next, I came away.

Jan. 14, 1697. Copy of the Bill I put up on the Fast day; giving it to Mr. Willard as he pass'd by, and standing up at the reading of it, and bowing when finished; in the Afternoon.

Samuel Sewall, sensible of the reiterated strokes of God upon himself and family; and being sensible, that as to the Guilt contracted upon the opening of the late commission of Oyer and Terminer at Salem (to which the order for this Day relates) he is, upon many accounts, more concerned than any that he knows of, Desires to take the Blame and shame of it, Asking pardon of men, And especially desiring prayers that God, who has an Unlimited Authority, would pardon that sin and all other his sins; personal and Relative: And according to his infinite Benignity, and Sovereignty, Not Visit the sin of him, or of any other, upon himself or any of his, nor upon the Land: But that He would powerfully defend him against all Temptations to Sin, for the future; and vouchsafe him the efficacious, saving Conduct of his Word and Spirit.

Jan. 26, 1697. I lodged at Charlestown, at Mrs. Shepards, who tells me Mr. Harvard built that house. I lay in the chamber next the street. As I lay awake past midnight, In my Meditation, I was affected to consider how long agoe God had made provision for my comfortable Lodging that night; seeing that was Mr. Harvards house: And that led me to think of Heaven the House not made with hands, which God for many Thousands of years has been storing with the richest furniture (saints that are from time to time placed there), and that I had some hopes of being entertain'd in that Magnificent Convenient Palace, every way fitted and furnished. These thoughts were very refreshing to me.

Oct. 1, 1697. Jer. Balchar's sons came for us to go to the Island. My Wife, through Indisposition, could not goe: But I carried Sam. Hannah, Elisa, Joseph, Mary and Jane Tapan: I prevail'd with Mr. Willard to goe, He carried Simon, Elisabeth, William, Margaret, and Elisa Tyng: Had a very comfortable Passage thither and home again; though against Tide: Had first Butter, Honey, Curds and Cream. For Dinner, very good Rost Lamb, Turkey, Fowls, Applepy. After Dinner sung the 121 Psalm. Note. A Glass of spirits my Wife sent stood upon a Joint-Stool which, Simon W. jogging, it fell down and broke all to shivers: I said twas a lively Emblem of our Fragility and Mortality. . . .

Jan. 14, 1701. Having been certified last night about 10. oclock of the death of my dear Mother at Newbury, Sam. and I set out with John Sewall, the Messenger, for that place. Hired Horses at Charles-town: set out about 10. aclock in a great Fogg. Din'd at Lewis's with Mr. Cushing of Salisbury. Sam. and I kept on in 'Ipswich Rode, John went to accompany Bro^r from Salem. About Mr. Hubbard's in Ipswich farms, they overtook us. Sam. and I lodg'd at Cromptons in Ipswich. Bro^r and John stood on for Newbury by Moon-shine. Jany. 15th Sam. and I set forward. Brother Northend meets us. Visit Aunt Northend, Mr. Payson. With Bro^r and sister we set forward for Newbury: where we find that day appointed for the Funeral: twas a very pleasant Comfortable day.

Bearers, Jno Kent of the Island, Lt Cutting Noyes, Deacon William Noyes, Mr. Peter Tappan, Capt. Henry Somersby, Mr. Joseph Wood-bridge. I follow'd the Bier single. Then Bro^r Sewall and sister Jane, Bro^r Short and his wife, Bro^r Moodey and his wife, Bro^r Northend and his wife, Bro^r Tappan and sister Sewall, Sam. and cous. Hannah Tappan. Mr. Payson of Rowley, Mr. Clark, Minister of Excester, were there. Col. Pierce, Major Noyes &c. Cous. John, Richard and Betty Dummer. Went ab^t 4. p.m. Nathan^l Bricket taking in hand to fill the Grave, I said, Forbear a little, and suffer me to say That amidst our bereaving sorrows We have the Comfort of beholding this Saint put into the rightfull possession of that Happiness of Living desir'd and dying Lamented. She liv'd commendably Four and Fifty years with her dear Husband, and my dear Father: And she could not well brook the being divided from him at her death; which is the cause of our taking leave of her in this place. She was a true and constant

Lover of Gods Word, Worship, and Saints: And she always, with a patient cheerfullness, submitted to the divine Decree of providing Bread for her self and others in the sweat of her Brows. And now her infinitely Gracious and Bountiful Master has promoted her to the Honor of higher Employments, fully and absolutely discharged from all manner of Toil, and Sweat. My honoured and beloved Friends and Neighbours! My dear Mother never thought much of doing the most frequent and homely offices of Love for me; and lavish'd away many Thousands of Words upon me, before I could return one word in Answer: And therefore I ask and hope that none will be offended that I have now ventured to speak one word in her behalf; when shee her self is become speechless. Made a Motion with my hand for the filling of the Grave. Note, I could hardly speak for passion and Tears.

Jan. 24, 1704. Took 24ˢ in my pocket, and gave my Wife the rest of my cash £4. 3–8, and tell her she shall now keep the Cash; if I want I will borrow of her. She has a better faculty than I at managing Affairs: I will assist her; and will endeavour to live upon my Salary; will see what it will doe. The Lord give his Blessing.

April 3, 1711. I dine with the Court at Pullin's. Mr. Attorney treats us at his house with excellent Pippins, Anchovas, Olives, Nuts. I said I should be able to make no Judgment on the Pippins without a Review, which made the Company Laugh. Spake much of Negroes; I mention'd the problem, whether [they] should be white after the Resurrection: Mr. Bolt took it up as absurd, because the body should be void of all Colour, spake as if it should be a Spirit. I objected what Christ said to his Disciples after the Resurrection. He said twas not so after his Ascension.

April 11, 1712. I saw Six Swallows together flying and chippering very rapturously.

May 5, 1713. Dr. Cotton Mather makes an Excellent Dedication-Prayer in the New Court-Chamber. Mr. Pain, one of the Overseers of the Work wellcom'd us, as the Judges went up Stairs. Dr. Cotton Mather having ended Prayer, The Clark went on and call'd the Grand-Jury: Giving their Charge, which was to enforce the Queen's Proclamation, and especially against Travailing on the Lord's Day; God having return'd to give us Rest. [In the margin: My speech to Grand jury in new Court House.] I said, You ought to be quickened to your Duty, in that you have so Convenient, and August a Chamber prepared for you to doe it in. And what I say to you, I would say to my self, to the Court, and to all that are concern'd. Seeing the former decay'd Building is consum'd, and a better built in the room, Let us pray, May that Proverb, Golden Chalices and Wooden Priests, never be transfer'd to the Civil order; that God would take away our filthy Garments, and cloath us with Change of Raiment; That our former Sins may be buried in the Ruins and Rubbish of the former House, and not be suffered to follow us into this; That a Lixivium may be made of the Ashes, which we may frequently use in keeping ourselves Clean: Let never any Judge debauch this Bench, by abiding on it when his own Cause comes under Trial; May the Judges always discern the Right, and dispense Justice with a most stable, permanent Impartiality; Let this large, transparent, costly Glass serve to oblige the Attornys alway to set Things in a True Light, And let the Character of none of them be *Impar sibi;* Let them Remember they are to advise the Court, as well as plead for their clients. The Oaths that prescribe our Duty run all upon Truth; God is Truth. Let Him communicat to us of His Light and Truth, in Judgment, and in Righteousness. If we thus improve this House, they that built it, shall inhabit it; the days of this people shall be as the days of a Tree, and they shall long enjoy the work of their hands. The Terrible Illumination that was made, the third of October was Twelve moneths, did plainly shew us that our GOD is a Consuming Fire: but it hath repented Him of the Evil. And since He has declar'd that He takes delight in them that hope in his Mercy, we firmly believe that He will be a Dwelling place to us throughout all Generations.

Saturday, Feb. 6, 1714 [Queen Anne's birthday]. . . . My neighbour Colson knocks at our door about 9. or past to tell of the Disorders at the Tavern at the Southend in Mr. Addington's house, kept by John Wallis. He desired me that I would accompany Mr. Bromfield and Constable Howell thither. It was 35. Minutes past Nine at Night before Mr. Bromfield came; then we went. I took Æneas Salter with me. Found much Company. They refus'd to go away. Said were there to drink the Queen's Health, and they had many other Healths to drink. Call'd for more Drink: drank to me, I took notice of the Affront to them. Said must and would stay upon that Solemn occasion. Mr. John Netmaker drank the Queen's Health to me. I told him I drank none; upon that he ceas'd. Mr. Brinley put on his Hat to affront me. I made him take it off. I threaten'd to send some of them to prison; that did not move them. They said they could but pay their Fine, and doing that they might stay. I told them if they had not a care, they would be guilty of a Riot. Mr. Bromfield spake of raising a number of Men to Quell them, and was in some heat, ready to run into Street. But I did not like that. Not having Pen and Ink, I went to take their Names with my Pensil, and not knowing how to Spell their Names, they themselves of their own accord writ them. Mr. Netmaker, reproaching the Province, said they had not made one good Law.

At last I address'd myself to Mr. Banister. I told him he had been longest an Inhabitant and Freeholder, I expected he should set a good Example in departing thence. Upon this he invited them to his own House, and away they went; and we, after them, went away. The Clock in the room struck a pretty while before they departed. I went directly home, and found it 25. Minutes past Ten at Night when I entred my own House. . . .

Monday, Feb. 8. Mr. Bromfield comes to me, and we give the Names of the Offenders at John Wallis's Tavern last Satterday night, to Henry Howell, Constable, with Direction to take the Fines of as many as would pay; and warn them that refus'd to pay, to appear before us at 3. p.m. that day. Many of them pay'd. The rest appear'd; and Andrew Simpson, Ensign, Alexander Gordon, Chirurgeon, Francis Brinley, Gent. and John Netmaker, Gent., were sentenc'd to pay a Fine of 5^s each of them, for their Breach of the Law Entituled, An Act for the better Observation, and Keeping the Lord's Day. They all Appeal'd, and Mr. Thomas Banister was bound with each of them in a Bond of 20^s upon Condition that they should prosecute their Appeal to effect.

Capt. John Bromsal, and Mr. Thomas Clark were dismiss'd without being Fined. The first was Master of a Ship just ready to sail, Mr. Clark a stranger of New York, who had carried it very civilly, Mr. Jekyl's Brother-in-Law.

Dec. 23, 1714. Dr. C. Mather preaches excellently from Ps. 37. Trust in the Lord &c. only spake of the Sun being in the centre of our System. I think it inconvenient to assert such Problems.

Oct. 15, 1717. My Wife got some Relapse by a new Cold and grew very bad; Sent for Mr. Oakes, and he sat up with me all night.

Oct. 16. The Distemper increases; yet my Wife speaks to me to goe to Bed.

Oct. 17. Thursday, I asked my wife whether twere best for me to go to Lecture: She said, I can't tell; so I staid at home. put up a Note. It being my Son's Lecture, and I absent, twas taken much notice of. Major Genl Winthrop and his Lady visit us. I thank her that she would visit my poor Wife.

Oct. 18. My wife grows worse and exceedingly Restless. Pray'd God to look upon her. Ask'd not after my going to bed. Had the advice of Mr. Williams and Dr. Cutler.

Oct. 19. Call'd Dr. C. Mather to pray, which he did excellently in the Dining Room, having Suggested good Thoughts to my wife before he went down. After, Mr. Wadsworth pray'd in the Chamber when 'twas suppos'd my wife took little notice. About a quarter of an hour past four, my dear Wife expired in the Afternoon, whereby the Chamber was fill'd with a Flood of Tears. God is teaching me a new Lesson; to live a Widower's Life. Lord help me to Learn; and be a Sun and Shield to me, now so much of my Comfort and Defense are taken away.

Oct. 20. I goe to the publick Worship forenoon and Afternoon. My Son has much adoe to read the Note I put up, being overwhelm'd with tears.

Feb. 6, 1718. This morning wandering in my mind whether to live a Single or a Married Life; I had a sweet and very affectionat Meditation Concerning the Lord Jesus; Nothing was to be objected against his Person, Parentage, Relations, Estate, House, Home! Why did I not resolutely, presently close with Him! And I cry'd mightily to God that He would help me so to doe!

March 14, 1718. Deacon Marion comes to me, sits with me a great while in the evening; after a great deal of Discourse about his Courtship—He told [me] the Olivers said they wish'd I would Court their Aunt [Mrs. Winthrop]. I said little, but said twas not five Moneths since I buried my dear Wife. Had said before 'twas hard to know whether best to marry again or no; whom to marry.

June 9, 1718. . . . Mrs. D[eniso]n came in the morning about 9 aclock, and I took her up into my Chamber and discoursed thorowly with her; She desired me to provide another and better Nurse. I gave her the two last News-Letters—told her I intended to visit her at her own house next Lecture-day. She said, 'twould be talked of. I answer'd, In such Cases, persons must run the Gantlet. Gave her Mr. Whiting's Oration for Abijah Walter, who brought her on horseback to Town. I think little or no Notice was taken of it.

June 17, 1718. Went to Roxbury Lecture, visited Mr. Walter. Mr. Webb preach'd. Visited Govr Dudley, Mrs. Denison, gave her Dr. Mather's Sermons very well bound; told her we were in it invited to a Wedding. She gave me very good Curds.

July 25, 1718. I go in the Hackny Coach to Roxbury. Call at Mr. Walter's who is not at home; nor Govr Dudley, nor his Lady. Visit Mrs. Denison: she invites me to eat. I give her two Cases with a knife and fork in each; one Turtle shell tackling; the other long, with Ivory handles, Squar'd, cost 4^s 6^d; Pound of Raisins with proportionable Almonds.

Oct. 15, 1718. Visit Mrs. Denison on Horseback; present her with a pair of Shoe-buckles, cost 5ˢ 3ᵈ.

Nov. 1, 1718. My Son from Brooklin being here I took his Horse, and visited Mrs. Denison. Sat in the Chamber next Majʳ Bowls. I told her 'twas time now to finish our Business: Ask'd her what I should allow her; she not speaking; I told her I was willing to give her Two [Hundred] and Fifty pounds per annum during her life, if it should please God to take me out of the world before her. She answer'd 'she had better keep as she was, than give a Certainty for an uncertainty; She should pay dear for dwelling at Boston. I desired her to make proposals, but she made none. I had Thoughts of Publishment next Thorsday the 6th. But I now seem to be far from it. May God, who has the pity of a Father, Direct and help me!

Nov. 28, 1718. I went this day in the Coach; had a fire made in the Chamber where I spake with her before, 9ʳ the first: I enquired how she had done these 3 or 4 weeks; Afterwards I told her our Conversation had been such when I was with her last, that it seem'd to be a direction in Providence, not to proceed any further; She said, It must be what I pleas'd, or to that purpose. Afterward she seem'd to blame that I had not told her so 9ʳ 1. . . . I repeated her words of 9ʳ 1. She seem'd at first to start at the words of her paying dear, as if she had not spoken them. But she said she thought twas Hard to part with *All*, and have nothing to bestow on her Kindred. I said, I did not intend any thing of the Movables, I intended all the personal Estate to be to her. She said I seem'd to be in a hurry on Satterday, 9ʳ 1., which was the reason she gave me no proposals. Whereas I had ask'd her long before to give me proposals in Writing; and she upbraided me, That I who had never written her a Letter, should ask her to write. She asked me if I would drink, I told her Yes. She gave me Cider, Apples and a Glass of Wine: gathered together the little things I had given her, and offer'd them to me; but I would take none of them. Told her I wish'd her well, should be glad to hear of her welfare. She seem'd to say she should not again take in hand a thing of this nature. Thank'd me for what I had given her and Desired my Prayers. I gave Abijah Weld an Angel. Mr. Stoddard and his wife came in their Coach to see their Sister which broke off my Visit. Upon their asking me, I dismiss'd my Coach, and went with them to see Mr. Danforth, and came home by Moon-shine. Got home about 9. at night. *Laus Deo*.

My bowels yern towards Mrs. Denison: but I think God directs me in his Providence to desist. . . .

Nov. 30, 1718. Lord's-day. In the evening I sung the 120. Psalm in

the family. About 7 a-clock Mrs. Dorothy Denison comes in, her
Cousin Weld coming first, saying she desired to speak with me in
privat. I had a fire in the new Hall, and was at prayer; was very much
startled that she should come so far a-foot in that exceeding Cold
Season; She enter'd into discourse of what pass'd between us at Roxbury last Friday; I seem'd to be alter'd in my affection; ask'd pardon
if she had affronted me. Seem'd to incline the Match should not break
off, since I had kept her Company so long. Said Mr. Denison spake to
her after his Signing the Will, that he would not make her put all
out of her Hand and power, but reserve somwhat to bestow on his
Friends that might want. I told her She might keep all. She excus'd,
and said 'twas not such an all. I Commended the estate. I could not
observe that she made me any offer of any part all this while. She
mention'd two Glass Bottles she had. I told her they were hers, and the
other small things I had given her, only now they had not the same
signification as before. I was much concern'd for her being in the Cold,
would fetch her in a plate of somthing warm; (for I had not sup'd),
she refus'd. However I Fetched a Tankard of Cider and drank to her.
She desired that no body might know of her being here. I told her they
should not. Sam. Hirst went to the door, who knew not her Cousin
Weld; and not so much as he might stay in the room while we talked
together. She went away in the bitter Cold, no Moon being up, to
my great pain. I Saluted her at parting.

April 1, 1719. In the morning I dehorted Sam. Hirst and Grindal
Rawson from playing Idle Tricks because 'twas first of April; They
were the greatest fools that did so. N[ew] E[ngland] Men came hither
to avoid anniversary days, the keeping of them, such as the 25th of
Decr. How displeasing must it be to God, the giver of our Time, to
keep anniversary days to play the fool with ourselves and others. . . .

[The courtship of the widow Denison having unhappily come to
naught, Sewall looked about him once more, and in August, 1719,
began calling upon the widow Abigail Tilly. His overtures were more
acceptable in this quarter, and on October 29 they were married by
Sewall's son, the Reverend Joseph. The new Mrs. Sewall, however,
was soon taken ill, and in the night of May 26, 1720, as Sewall records,
"About midnight my dear wife expired to our great astonishment,
especially mine."]

Sept. 5, 1720. Going to Son Sewall's I there meet with Madam Winthrop, told her I was glad to meet her there, had not seen her a great
while; gave her Mr. Homes's Sermon.

Sept. 30, 1720. Mr. Colman's Lecture: Daughter Sewall acquaints

Madam Winthrop that if she pleas'd to be within at 3. p.m. I would wait on her. She answer'd she would be at home.

Oct. 1, 1720. Satterday, I dine at Mr. Stoddard's: from thence I went to Madam Winthrop's just at 3. Spake to her, saying, my loving wife died so soon and suddenly, 'twas hardly convenient for me to think of Marrying again; however I came to this Resolution, that I would not make my Court to any person without first Consulting with her. Had a pleasant discourse about 7 Single persons sitting in the Fore-seat 7ʳ 29ᵗʰ, viz. Madᵐ Rebekah Dudley, Catharine Winthrop, Bridget Usher, Deliverance Legg, Rebekah Loyd, Lydia Colman, Elizabeth Bellingham. She propounded one and another for me; but none would do, said Mrs. Loyd was about her Age.

Oct. 3, 1720. Waited on Madam Winthrop again; 'twas a little while before she came in. Her daughter Noyes being there alone with me, I said, I hoped my Waiting on her Mother would not be disagreeable to her. She answer'd she should not be against that that might be for her Comfort. I Saluted her, and told her I perceiv'd I must shortly wish her a good Time; (her mother had told me, she was with Child, and within a Moneth or two of her Time). By and by in came Mr. Airs, Chaplain of the Castle, and hang'd up his Hat, which I was a little startled at, it seeming as if he was to lodge there. At last Madam Winthrop came too. After a considerable time, I went up to her and said, if it might not be inconvenient I desired to speak with her. She assented, and spake of going into another Room; but Mr. Airs and Mrs. Noyes presently rose up, and went out, leaving us there alone. Then I usher'd in Discourse from the names in the Fore-seat; at last I pray'd that Katharine [Mrs. Winthrop] might be the person assign'd for me. She instantly took it up in the way of Denyal, as if she had catch'd at an Opportunity to do it, saying she could not do it before she was asked. Said that was her mind unless she should Change it, which she believed she should not; could not leave her Children. I express'd my Sorrow that she should do it so Speedily, pray'd her Consideration, and ask'd her when I should wait on her agen. She setting no time, I mention'd that day Sennight. Gave her Mr. Willard's Fountain open'd with the little print and verses; saying, I hop'd if we did well read that book, we should meet together hereafter, if we did not now. She took the Book, and put it in her Pocket. Took Leave.

Oct. 6, 1720. A little after 6. p.m. I went to Madam Winthrop's. She was not within. I gave Sarah Chickering the Maid 2ˢ, Juno, who brought in wood, 1ˢ. Afterward the Nurse came in, I gave her 18ᵈ, having no other small Bill. After awhile Dr. Noyes came in with his

Mother; and quickly after his wife came in: They sat talking, I think, till eight a-clock. I said I fear'd I might be some Interruption to their Business: Dr. Noyes reply'd pleasantly: He fear'd they might be an Interruption to me, and went away. Madam seem'd to harp upon the same string. Must take care of her Children; could not leave that House and Neighbourhood where she had dwelt so long. I told her she might doe her children as much or more good by bestowing what she laid out in Hous-keeping, upon them. Said her Son would be of Age the 7ᵗʰ of August. I said it might be inconvenient for her to dwell with her Daughter-in-Law, who must be Mistress of the House. I gave her a piece of Mr. Belcher's Cake and Ginger-Bread wrapped up in a clean sheet of Paper; told her of her Father's kindness to me when Treasurer, and I Constable. My Daughter Judith was gon from me and I was more lonesom—might help to forward one another in our Journey to Canaan.—Mr. Eyre came within the door; I saluted him, ask'd how Mr. Clark did, and he went away. I took leave about 9 aclock. I told [her] I came now to refresh her Memory as to Monday-night; said she had not forgot it. In discourse with her, I ask'd leave to speak with her Sister; I meant to gain Madᵐ Mico's favour to per-suade her Sister. She seem'd surpris'd and displeas'd, and said she was in the same condition!

Oct. 10, 1720. In the Evening I visited Madam Winthrop, who treated me with a great deal of Curtesy; Wine, Marmalade. I gave her a News-Letter about the Thanksgiving Proposals, for sake of the verses for David Jeffries. She tells me Dr. Increase Mather visited her this day, in Mr. Hutchinson's Coach.

Oct. 11, 1720. I writ a few Lines to Madam Winthrop to this purpose: "Madam, These wait on you with Mr. Mayhew's Sermon, and Account of the state of the Indians on Martha's Vinyard. I thank you for your Unmerited Favours of yesterday; and hope to have the Happiness of Waiting on you to-morrow before Eight a-clock after Noon. I pray God to keep you, and give you a joyfull entrance upon the Two Hundred and twenty ninth year of Christopher Columbus his Dis-covery; and take Leave, who am, Madam, your humble Servᵗ. S.S.

Oct. 12, 1720. Mrs. Anne Cotton came to door (twas before 8.) said Madam Winthrop was within, directed me into the little Room, where she was full of work behind a Stand; Mrs. Cotton came in and stood. Madam Winthrop pointed to her to set me a Chair. Madam Winthrop's Countenance was much changed from what 'twas on Mon-day, look'd dark and lowering. At last, the work, (black stuff or Silk) was taken away, I got my Chair in place, had some Converse, but very Cold and indifferent to what 'twas before. Ask'd her to acquit me of Rudeness if I drew off her Glove. Enquiring the reason, I told her twas great odds between handling a dead Goat, and a living Lady. Got it off. I told her I had one Petition to ask of her, that was, that she would take off the Negative she laid on me the third of October; She readily answer'd she could not, and enlarg'd upon it; She told me of it so soon as she could; could not leave her house, children, neighbours, business. I told her she might do som Good to help and support me. Mentioning Mrs. Gookin, Nath, the widow Weld was spoken of; said I had visited Mrs. Denison. I told her Yes! Afterward I said, If after a first and second Vagary she would Accept of me returning, Her Victorious Kindness and Good Will would be very Obliging. She thank'd me for my Book, (Mr. Mayhew's Sermon), But said not a word of the Letter. When she insisted on the Negative, I pray'd there might be no more Thunder and Lightening, I should not sleep all night. I gave her Dr. Preston, The Church's Marriage and the Church's Carriage, which cost me 6^s at the Sale. The door standing open, Mr. Airs came in, hung up his Hat, and sat down. After awhile, Madam Winthrop moving, he went out. Jno Eyre look'd in, I said How do ye, or, your servant Mr. Eyre: but heard no word from him. Sarah fill'd a Glass of Wine, she drank to me, I to her, She sent Juno home with me with a good Lantern, I gave her 6^d and bid her thank her Mistress. In some of our Discourse, I told her I had rather go to the Stone-House adjoining to her, than to come to her against her mind. Told her the reason why I came every other night was lest I should drink too deep draughts of Pleasure. She had talk'd of Canary, her Kisses were to me better than the best Canary. Explain'd the expression Concerning Columbus.

Oct. 13. I tell my Son and daughter Sewall, that the Weather was not so fair as I apprehended.

Oct. 17. In the Evening I visited Madam Winthrop, who Treated me Courteously, but not in Clean Linen as somtimes. She said, she did not know whether I would come again, or no. I ask'd her how she could so impute inconstancy to me. (I had not visited her since Wednesday night being unable to get over the Indisposition received by the Treatment received that night, and *I must* in it seem'd to sound like a made piece of Formality.) Gave her this day's Gazett. Heard David Jeffries say the Lord's Prayer, and some other portions of the Scriptures. He came to the door, and ask'd me to go into Chamber, where his Grandmother was tending Little Katee, to whom she had given Physick; but I chose to sit below. Dr. Noyes and his wife came in, and sat a Considerable time; had been visiting Son and dâter Cooper. Juno came home with me.

Oct. 18, 1720. Visited Madam Mico, who came to me in a splendid Dress. I said, It may be you have heard of my Visiting Madam Winthrop, her Sister. She answered, Her Sister had told her of it. I ask'd her good Will in the Affair. She answer'd, If her Sister were for it, she should not hinder it. I gave her Mr. Homes's Sermon. She gave me a Glass of Canary, entertain'd me with good Discourse, and a Respectfull Remembrance of my first Wife. I took Leave.

Oct. 19, 1720. Midweek, Visited Madam Winthrop; Sarah told me she was at Mr. Walley's, would not come home till late. I gave her Hannah 3 oranges with her Duty, not knowing whether I should find her or no. Was ready to go home: but said if I knew she was there, I would go thither. Sarah seem'd to speak with pretty good Courage, She would be there. I went and found her there, with Mr. Walley and his wife in the little Room below. At 7 a-clock I mentioned going home; at 8. I put on my Coat, and quickly waited on her home. She found occasion to speak loud to the servant, as if she had a mind to be known. Was Courteous to me; but took occasion to speak pretty earnestly about my keeping a Coach: I said 'twould cost £100. per annum: she said twould cost but £40. . . . Exit. Came away somewhat late.

Oct. 20, 1720. . . . Madam Winthrop not being at Lecture, I went thither first; found her very Serene with her dâter Noyes, Mrs. Dering, and the widow Shipreev sitting at a little Table, she in her arm'd Chair. She drank to me, and I to Mrs. Noyes. After awhile pray'd the favour to speak with her. She took one of the Candles, and went into the best Room, clos'd the shutters, sat down upon the Couch. She told me Madam Usher had been there, and said the Coach must be set on Wheels, and not by Rusting. She spake somthing of my needing a Wigg. Ask'd me what her Sister said to me. I told her, She said, If her Sister were for it, She would not hinder it. But I told her, she did not say she would be glad to have me for her Brother. Said, I shall keep you in the Cold, and asked her if she would be within to morrow night, for we had had but a running Feat. She said she could not tell whether she should, or no. I took Leave. As were drinking at the Governour's, he said: In England the Ladies minded little more than that they might have Money, and Coaches to ride in. I said, And New-England brooks its Name. At which Mr. Dudley smiled. Govr said they were not quite so bad here.

Oct. 21, 1720. Friday, My Son, the Minister, came to me p.m by appointment and we pray one for another in the Old Chamber; more especially respecting my Courtship. About 6. a-clock I go to Madam Winthrop's; Sarah told me her Mistress was gon out, but did not tell me whither she went. She presently order'd me a Fire; so I went in, having Dr. Sibb's Bowels with me to read. I read the two first Sermons, still no body came in: at last about 9. a-clock Mr. Jn° Eyre came in; I took the opportunity to say to him as I had done to Mrs. Noyes before, that I hoped my Visiting his Mother would not be disagreeable to him; He answered me with much Respect. When twas after 9. a-clock He of himself said he would go and call her, she was but at one of his Brothers: A while after I heard Madam Winthrop's voice, enquiring something about John. After a good while and Clapping the Garden door twice or thrice, she came in. I mentioned something of the lateness; she banter'd me, and said I was later. She receiv'd me Courteously. I ask'd when our proceedings should be made publick: She said They were like to be no more publick than they were already. Offer'd me no Wine that I remember. I rose up at 11 a-clock to come away, saying I would put on my Coat, She offer'd not to help me. I pray'd her that Juno might light me home, she open'd the Shutter, and said twas pretty light abroad; Juno was weary and gon to bed. So I came hôm by Star-light as well as I could. At my first coming in, I gave Sarah five Shillings. I writ Mr. Eyre his Name in his book with the date Octobʳ 21. 1720. It cost me 8ˢ. Jehovah jireh! Madam told me she had visited M. Mico, Wendell, and Wᵐ Clark of the South [Church].

Oct. 22, 1720. Dâter Cooper visited me before my going out of Town, staid till about Sun set. I brought her going near as far as the Orange Tree. Coming back, near Leg's Corner, Little David Jeffries saw me, and looking upon me very lovingly, ask'd me if I was going to see his Grandmother? I said, Not to-night. Gave him a peny, and bid him present my Service to his Grandmother.

Oct. 24, 1720. I went in the Hackny Coach through the Common, stop'd at Madam Winthrop's (had told her I would take my departure from thence). Sarah came to the door with Katee in her Arms: but I did not think to take notice of the Child. Call'd her Mistress. I told her, being encourag'd by David Jeffries loving eyes, and sweet Words, I was come to enquire whether she could find in her heart to leave that House and Neighbourhood, and go and dwell with me at the South-end; I think she said softly, Not yet. I told her It did not ly in my Lands to keep a Coach. If I should, I should be in danger to be brought to keep company with her Neighbour Brooker, (he was a little before sent to prison for Debt). Told her I had an Antipathy against those who would pretend to give themselves; but nothing of their Estate. I would a proportion of my Estate with my self. And I suppos'd she would do so. As to a Perriwig, My best and greatest Friend, I could not possibly have a greater, began to find me with Hair before I was born, and had continued to do so ever since; and I could not find in my heart to go to another. She commended the book I gave her, Dr. Preston, the Church Marriage; quoted him saying 'twas inconvenient keeping out of a Fashion commonly used. I said the Time and Tide did circumscribe my Visit. She gave me a Dram of Black-Cherry Brandy, and gave me a lump of the Sugar that was in it. She wish'd me-a good Journy. I pray'd God to keep her, and came away. Had a very pleasant Journy to Salem.

Oct. 31, 1720. At night I visited Madam Winthrop about 6. p.m. They told me she was gon to Madam Mico's. I went thither and found she was gon; so return'd to her house, read the Epistles to the Galatians, Ephesians in Mr. Eyre's Latin Bible. After the Clock struck 8. I began to read the 103. Psalm. Mr. Wendell came in from his Warehouse. Ask'd me if I were alone? Spake very kindly to me, offer'd me to call Madam Winthrop. I told him, She would be angry, had been at Mrs. Mico's; he help'd me on with my Coat and I came home: left the Gazett in the Bible, which told Sarah of, bid her present my Service to Mrs. Winthrop, and tell her I had been to wait on her if she had been at home.

Nov. 1, 1720. I was so taken up that I could not go if I would.

Nov. 2, 1720. Midweek, went again, and found Mrs. Alden there, who quickly went out. Gave her about ½ pound of Sugar Almonds, cost 3ˢ per £. Carried them on Monday. She seem'd pleas'd with them, ask'd what they cost. Spake of giving her a Hundred pounds per anum if I dy'd before her. Ask'd her what sum she would give me, if she should dy first? Said I would give her time to Consider of it. She said she heard as if I had given all to my Children by Deeds of Gift. I told her 'twas a mistake, Point-Judith was mine &c. That in England, I own'd, my Father's desire was that it should go to my eldest Son; 'twas 20£ per anum; she thought 'twas forty. I think when I seem'd to excuse pressing this, she seem'd to think twas best to speak of it; a long winter was coming on. Gave me a Glass or two of Canary.

Nov. 4, 1720. Friday, Went again about 7. a-clock; found there Mr. John Walley and his wife: sat discoursing pleasantly. I shew'd them Isaac Moses's [an Indian] Writing. Madam W. serv'd Comfeits to us. After awhile a Table was spread, and Supper was set. I urg'd Mr. Walley to Crave a Blessing; but he put it upon me. About 9. they went away. I ask'd Madam what fashioned Neck-lace I should present her with, She said, None at all. I ask'd her Whereabout we left off last time; mention'd what I had offer'd to give her; Ask'd her what she would give me; She said she could not Change her Condition: She had said so from the beginning; could not be so far from her Children, the Lecture. Quoted the Apostle Paul affirming that a single Life was better than a Married. I answer'd That was for the present Distress. Said she had not pleasure in things of that nature as formerly: I said, you are the fitter to make me a Wife. If she hald in that mind, I must go home and bewail my Rashness in making more haste than good Speed. However, considering the Supper, I desired her to be within next Monday night, if we liv'd so long. Assented. She charg'd me with saying, that she must put away Juno, if she came to me: I utterly deny'd it, it never came in my heart; yet she insisted upon it; saying it came in upon discourse about the Indian woman that obtained her Freedom this Court. About 10. I said I would not disturb the good orders of her House, and came away. She not seeming pleas'd with my Coming away. Spake to her about David Jeffries, had not seen him.

Nov. 7, 1720. My Son pray'd in the Old Chamber. Our time had been taken up by Son and Daughter Cooper's Visit; so that I only read the 130th and 143 Psalm. Twas on the Account of my Courtship. I went to Mad. Winthrop; found her rocking her little Katee in the Cradle. I excus'd my Coming so late (near Eight). She set me an arm'd Chair and Cusheon; and so the Cradle was between her arm'd Chair and mine. Gave her the remnant of my Almonds; She did not eat of them as before; but laid them away; I said I came to enquire whether she had alter'd her mind since Friday, or remained of the same mind still. She said, Thereabouts. I told her I loved her, and was so fond as to think that she loved me: She said had a great respect for me. I told her, I had made her an offer, without asking any advice; she had so many to advise with, that twas a hindrance. The Fire was come to one short Brand besides the Block, which Brand was set up in end; at last it fell to pieces, and no Recruit was made: She gave me a Glass of Wine. I think I repeated again that I would go home and bewail my Rashness in making more haste than good Speed. I would endeavour to contain myself, and not go on to sollicit her to do that which she could not Consent to. Took leave of her. As came down the steps she bid me have a Care. Treated me Courteously. Told her she had

enter'd the 4th year of her Widowhood. I had given her the News-
Letter before; I did not bid her draw off her Glove as sometime I had
done. Her Dress was not so clean as somtime it had been. Jehovah
jireh!

Nov. 9, 1720. Dine at Bro^r Stoddard's: were so kind as to enquire
of me if they should invite M'^m Winthrop; I answer'd No. Thank'd
my Sister Stoddard for her Courtesie; . . . She sent her servant home
with me with a Lantern. Madam Winthrop's Shutters were open as
I pass'd by.

[The courtship of Madam Winthrop having failed still more disas-
trously than that of Mrs. Denison, Sewall gave over the attack in
November, 1720; in January, 1722, he turned his attentions toward
Mrs. Mary Gibbs, whom he married for his third wife on March 29.]

March 5, 1721. Lord's Day, Serene, and good but very cold, yet
had a comfortable opportunity to celebrate the Lord's Supper. Mr.
Prince, p.m. preach'd a Funeral Sermon from Psal. 90. 10. Gave
Capt. Hill a good character. Just as I sat down in my Seat, one of my
Fore-teeth in my under Jaw came out, and I put it in my pocket. This
old servant and daughter of Musick leaving me, does thereby give
me warning that I must shortly resign my Head: the Lord help me to
do it cheerfully!

June 15, 1725. I accompanied my Son to Mad. Winthrop's. She
was a-bed about 10. *mane.* I told her I found my Son coming to her
and took the Opportunity to come with him. She thank'd me kindly,
enquired how Madam Sewall did. Ask'd my Son to go to Prayer.
Present Mr. John Eyre, Mrs. Noyes, Mrs. Walley and David Jeffries.
At coming I said, I kiss your hand Madame (her hand felt very dry).
She desired me to pray that God would lift up upon her the Light of
his Countenance.

Apr. 14, 1726. Mr. Coney died more than three years ago; and now
his widow Mrs. Mary Coney died somwhat suddenly on Tuesday
morning April, 12. and was inter'd in one of the new Tombs of the
South-burying place; Bearers, Sam. Sewall, John Clark esqr; Sam.
Brown esqr, Thomas Fitch esqr; Sam. Checkley esqr. Capt. John
Ballantine. Was buried from her daughter Bromfield's. His Honour
the Lieut Govr follow'd his Aunt as a Mourner and his Lady. Thus
death, by its regardless stroke, mows down all before it, making no
distinction between our most prudent and Charming Friends, and
others; May we learn more entirely to delight and trust in God who
is Altogether Lovely and Lives for Ever. Three Sams being Bearers

together on the right side, occasion'd my binding all the Bearers up together in this band,

> Three Sams, two Johns, and one good Tom
> Bore Prudent Mary to her Tomb.

July 26, 1726. Rode in Mr. Sheriff's Calash to Cambridge. Mr. Appleton prays. Entring upon the Charge to the Grand-Jury, I said, Since men's departure from God, there was such an aversion in them to return, that every kind of Authority was necessary to reclaim them. Notwithstanding the singular advantage Cambridge had enjoy'd in their excellent Pastors, and Presidents of the College—yet it must be said, *Venimus ipsam Cantabrigiam ad stabiliendos, et corrigendos mores.*[1]—

Dec. 17, 1727. I was surprised to hear Mr. Thacher of Milton, my old Friend, pray'd for as dangerously Sick. Next day. Decr 18. 1727. I am inform'd by Mr. Gerrish, that my dear friend died last night; which I doubt bodes ill to Milton and the Province, his dying at this Time, though in the 77th year of his Age. *Deus avertat Omen!*

Dec. 22, 1727. the day after the Fast, was inter'd. Bearers, Rev^d Mr. Nehemiah Walter, Mr. Joseph Baxter; Mr. John Swift, Mr. Saml Hunt; Mr. Joseph Sewall, Mr. Thomas Prince. I was inclin'd before, and having a pair of Gloves sent me, I determined to go to the Funeral, if the Weather prov'd favourable, which it did, and I hired Blake's Coach with four Horses; my Son, Mr. Cooper and Mr. Prince went with me. Refresh'd there with Meat and Drink; got thither about half an hour past one. It was sad to see [death] triumphed over my dear Friend! I rode in my Coach to the Burying place; not being able to get nearer by reason of the many Horses. From thence went directly up the Hill where the Smith's Shop, and so home very comfortably and easily, the ground being mollified. But when I came to my own Gate, going in, I fell down, a board slipping under my Left foot, my right Legg raised off the skin, and put me to a great deal of pain, especially when 'twas washed with Rum. It was good for me that I was thus Afflicted that my spirit might be brought into a frame more suitable to the Solemnity, which is apt to be too light; and by the loss of some of my Skin, and blood I might be awakened to prepare for my own Dissolution. Mr. Walter prayed before the Corps was carried out. I had a pair of Gloves sent me before I went, and a Ring given me there. . . . I have now been at the Interment of 4 of my Class-mates. . . . Now I can go to no more Funerals of my Class-mates; nor none be at mine; for the survivers, the Rev'd Mr. Samuel Mather at Windsor, and the Rev^d Mr. Taylor at Westfield, [are] one Hundred Miles off, and are entirely enfeebled. I humbly pray that Christ may be graciously present with us all Three both in Life, and in Death, and then we shall safely and Comfortably walk through the shady valley that leads to Glory.

JOHN WILLIAMS, 1664–1729

[John Williams was born at Roxbury, his father being a deacon in John Eliot's church, a shoemaker by trade; he was helped through college by his grandfather, and graduated in 1683. He taught school at Dorchester for two years, and settled as minister at Deerfield in 1686. The massacre occurred on February 29, 1704. Williams was redeemed in October, 1706, and returned to Boston; all his children were redeemed except a daughter, Eunice, who married an Indian and lost all memory of any other way of life. The town was resettled in 1707, and Williams went back to his post, saying, "I must return and look after my sheep in the wilderness." This text is from *The Redeemed Captive Returning to Zion* (Boston, 1707), pp. 2–9, 22–25.]

THE REDEEMED CAPTIVE

ON THE Twenty-ninth of *February* [1704] Not long before break of day, the Enemy came in like a Flood upon us; our Watch being unfaithful: an evil, whose awful effects, in a surprizal of our Fort, should bespeak all Watchmen to avoid, as they would not bring the charge of blood upon themselves. They came to my House in the beginning of the Onset, and by their violent endeavours to break open Doors, and Windows, with *Axes*, and *Hatchets*, Awaken'd me out of Sleep; on which I leapt out of bed, and running toward the door, perceived the Enemy making their entrance into the House: I called to awaken two Souldiers, in the Chamber; and returned towards my bedside, for my Arms: the Enemy immediately brake into the Room, I judge to the number of Twenty, with *Painted Faces*, and hideous Acclamations. I reach'd up my hands to the Bed-tester, for my Pistol, uttering a short Petition to God, *For Everlasting Mercies for me & mine, on the account of the Merits of our Glorify'd Redeemer;* Expecting a present passage through the Valley of the shadow of Death: Saying in my self, as *Isaiah* 38. 10, 11. *I said, in the cutting off my days, I shall go to the gates of the grave: I am deprived of the residue of my years. I said, I shall not see the Lord, even the Lord, in the land of the Living: I shall behold man no more with the inhabitants of the World.* Taking down my Pistol, I Cockt it, and put it to the breast of the first Indian who came up; but my Pistol missing fire, I was seized by Three Indians, who disarmed me, and bound me Naked, as I was in my Shirt, and so I stood for near the space of an hour: binding me, they told me they would carry me to *Quebeck*. My Pistol missing fire, was an occasion of my Life's being preserved: Since which I have also found it profitable to be cross'd in my own Will. The judgment of God did not long slumber against one of the Three which took me, who was a Captain, for by Sun-rising he received a Mortal Shot, from my next Neighbours house; who opposed so great a number of *French* & *Indians* as Three hundred, and yet were no more than Seven men in an Ungarison'd house.

I cannot relate the distressing care I had for my dear Wife, who had lien-In but a few Weeks before, and for my poor Children, Family, and Christian Neighbours. The Enemy fell to riffling the house, and entred in great numbers into every room of the house. I beg'd of God, to Remember Mercy in the midst of Judgment: that He would so far restain their Wrath, as to prevent their Murdering of us: that we might have *Grace to Glorify His Name, whether in Life or Death;* and as I was able committed our State to God. The Enemies who entred the House were all of them *Indians* and *Macqua's*, insulted over me a while, holding up Hatchets over my head, threatning to burn all I had, but yet God beyond expectation made us in a great measure to be Pityed: for tho' some were so cruel and barbarous as to take & carry to the door, Two of my Children and Murder them, as also a Negro Woman; yet they gave me liberty to put on my Clothes, keeping me bound with a Cord on one arm, till I put on my Cloths to the other; and then changing my Cord, they let me dress my self and then Pinioned me again. Gave liberty to my dear Wife to dress her self, & our Children. About Sun an hour high, we were all carryed out of the house, for a March, and saw many of the Houses of my Neighbours in Flames, perceiving the whole Fort, one house excepted, to be taken. Who can tell, what Sorrows pierced our Souls, when we saw our selves carryed away from Gods Sanctuary, to go into a strange Land, exposed to so many Trials? the journey being at least Three hundred Miles we were to Travel; the Snow up to the Knees, and we never inur'd to such hardships and fatigues, the place we were to be carryed to, a Popish Country. Upon my parting from the Town they fired my House & Barn. We were carryed over the river, to the foot of the *Mountain*, about a Mile from my House, where we found, a great number of our Christian Neighbours, Men, Women & Children, to the number of an hundred, Nineteen of which were afterward Murdered by the Way, and two starved to Death, near *Cowass*, in a time of great scarcity or Famine, the Salvages underwent there. When we came to the foot of our Mountain, they took away our Shoes, and gave us, in the room of them Indian-Shoes, to prepare us for our Travel. Whilst we were there the English beat out a Company, that remained in the Town, and pursued them to the River, Killing and Wounding many of them; but the body of the Army, being Alarm'd, they repulsed those few *English* that pursued them.

I am not able to give you an account of the number of the Enemy Slain, but I observed after this night, no great insulting Mirth, as I expected; and saw many Wounded Persons, and for several days together they buryed of their party, & one of chief Note among the *Macqua's*. The Governour of *Canada*, told me, his Army had that Success with the loss but of Eleven men, Three French-men, One of which was the *Lieutenant* of the Army, Five *Macqua's*, and Three *Indians:* but after my Arrival at *Quebeck*, I spake with an English man, who was taken the last War, and Married there, and of their Religion; who told me, they lost above Forty, and that many were Wounded: I replyed the Governour of *Canada* said, they lost but Eleven men: He answered, 'tis true, That there were but Eleven killed out-right at the taking of the Fort, but that many others were Wounded, among whom was the *Ensign* of the *French;* but said he, they had a fight in the Meadow, and that in both Engagements, they lost more than Forty. Some of the Souldiers, both *French* and *Indians* then present told me so (said he) adding, That the French always endeavour, to conceal the number of their Slain.

After this, we went up the Mountain, and saw the smoak of thè Fires in the Town, and beheld the awful desolations of our Town: And before we marched any farther, they kill'd a Sucking Child of the English. There were slain by the Enemy of the Inhabitants of our Town to the number of Thirty-eight, besides Nine of the Neighbouring Towns. We Travel'd not far the first day; God made the Heathen, so to Pity our Children, that though they had several Wounded Persons, of their own to carry, upon their Shoulders, for Thirty Miles, before they came to the River, yet they carryed our Children, uncapable of Travelling upon their Shoulders and in their Arms. When we came to our Lodging place, the first Night, they dugg away the snow, and made some Wigwams, cut down some of the small branches of *Spruce-trees* to lye down on, and gave the Prisoners some-what to eat; but we had but little Appetite. I was Pinioned, and bound down that Night, and so I was every Night whilst I was with the Army. Some of the Enemy who brought drink with them, from the Town, fell to drinking, and in their Drunken fit, they kill'd my Negro man, the only dead Person, I either saw at the Town, or in the Way. In the Night an *English* Man made his escape: in the Morning I was call'd for, and ordered by the General to tell the English, That if any more made their escape, they would burn the rest of the Prisoners. He that took me was unwilling to let me speak with any of the Prisoners, as we March'd; but on the Morning of the Second day, he being appointed to guard the rear, I was put into the hands of my other Master, Who permitted me to speak to my Wife, when I overtook her, and to Walk with her to help her in her Journey. On the Way we discoursed of the happiness of them who had a right to *an House not made with Hands, Eternal in the Heavens;* and *God for a Father, and Friend;* as also, That it was our reasonable Duty, quietly to submit, to the Will of God, and to say, *The Will of the Lord be done.* My Wife told me her strength of body began to fail, So that I must expect to part with her; Saying, She hoped God would preserve my Life, and the Life of some, if not of all of our Children, with us; and commended to me, under God, the care of them. She never spake any discontented Word as to what had befal'n us, but with suitable expressions justified God, in what had befal'n us. We soon made a halt, in which time my chief Surviving Master came up, upon which I was put upon Marching with the foremost, and so made to take my last fare-well of my dear Wife, *the desire of my Eyes,* and companion in many Mercies and Afflictions. Upon our Separation from each other, we askt for each other Grace sufficient, for what God should call us to. After our being parted from one another, she spent the few remaining Minutes of her stay, in Reading the Holy Scriptures; which she was wont Personally every day to delight her Soul in Reading, Praying, Meditating of, and over, by her self, in her Closet, over and above what she heard out of them in our Family Worship. I was made to Wade over a small River, and so were all the English, the Water above Knee-deep, the Stream very Swift; and after that, to Travel up a small Mountain, my Strength was almost spent, before I came to the top of it: No sooner had I overcome the difficulty of that ascent but I was permitted to sit down, & be unburthened of my Pack; I sat pitying those who were behind and intreated my Master, to let me go down, and help up my Wife, but he refused, and would not let me stir from him. I ask'd each of the Prisoners (as they passed by me) after her, and heard that in passing through the abovesaid River, she fell down and was plunged over Head and Ears in the Water after which she travelled not far, for at the Foot of this Mountain, the cruel and blood thirsty Salvage who took her, slew her with his

Hatchet, at one stroak; the tidings of which were very awful: and yet such was the hard-heartedness of the Adversary, that my Tears were reckoned to me as a reproach. My loss, and the loss of my Children was great, our hearts were so filled with Sorrow, that nothing but the comfortable hopes of her being taken away in Mercy, to her self, from the evils we were to see, feel and suffer under; (and joyn'd to the Assembly of the *Spirits of just men made perfect*, to rest in Peace, and *joy unspeakable, and full of glory;* and the good Measure of God thus to exercise us,) could have kept us from sinking under, at that time. That Scripture, *Job* 1. 21.—*Naked came I out of my Mothers womb, and Naked shall I return thither: the Lord gave, and the Lord hath taken away, blessed be the Name of the Lord:* Was brought to my Mind, and from it, That an *Afflicting God was to be Glorifyed;* with some other places of Scripture, to perswade to a Patient bearing my Afflictions. . . .

[At Quebec:] The next Morning the *Bell Rang* for *Mass:* My Master *bid me go to Church:* I refused: he threatned me, and went away in a rage. At Noon the *Jesuit* sent for me, to dine with them; for I eat at their Table all the time I was at the Fort. And after Dinner, they told me, *the Indians would not allow of any of their Captives staying in their Wigwams, whilst they were at Church; and were resolved by force and violence to bring us all to Church, if we would not go without.* I told them it was highly unreasonable so to impose upon those who were of a contrary Religion; and to force us to be present at such Service, as we *Abhor'd,* was nothing becoming Christianity. They replyed, *They were Salvages, and would not hearken to reason, but would have their Wills:* Said also, *If they were in* New-England *themselves, they would go into the Churches to see their Wayes of Worship.* I answered, the case was far different, for there was nothing (them selves being judges) as to matter or manner of *Worship,* but what was according to the Word of God, in our Churches; and therefore it could not be an offence to any mans Conscience. But among those there were *Idolatrous Superstitions* in *Worship:* they said, *Come and see, and offer us Conviction, of what is superstitious in Worship.* To which I answered, *That I was not to do Evil that Good might come on it;* and that forcing in matters of Religion was hateful. They answered, *The Indians were resolved to have it so, & they could not pacify them without my coming; and they would engage they should offer no force or violence to cause any compliance with their Ceremonies.*

The next Mass, my Master bid me go to *Church:* I objected; he arose and forcibly pulled me out by head and Shoulders out of the *Wigwam* to the *Church,* that was nigh the door. So I went in and sat down behind the door, and there saw a great confusion, instead of any *Gospel*

Order. For one of the *Jesuits* was at the Altar, saying *Mass* in a Tongue *Unknown* to the Salvages, and the other, between the Altar & the door, saying and singing *Prayers* among the *Indians* at the same time; and many others were at the same time saying over their *Pater Nosters*, and *Ave Mary*, by tale from their *Chapelit*, or *Beads* on a string. At our going out we smiled at their Devotion so managed; which was offensive to them: for they said, *We made a Derision of their Worship.* When I was here, a certain Salvagess dyed; one of the *Jesuits* told me, *She was a very holy Woman, who had not committed One Sin in Twelve Years.* After a day or two the *Jesuits* ask'd me, *What I thought of their Way, how I saw it?* I told them, I thought Christ said of it, as *Mark* 7. 7, 8, 9. *Howbeit, in vain do they Worship me, teaching for doctrines the Commandments of men. For laying aside the Commandment of God, ye hold the tradition of men, as the washing of pots, and cups: and many other such like things ye do. And he said unto them, Full well ye reject the commandment of God, that ye may keep your own tradition.* They told me, *They were not the Commandments of men,* but *Apostolical Traditions*, of equal authority with the Holy Scriptures. And that after my Death, I would bewail my not Praying to the Virgin *Mary;* and that I should find the want of her Intercession for me, *with her Son;* judging me to Hell for asserting, the Scriptures to be a perfect rule of Faith: and said, I abounded in my own sense, entertaining explications contrary to the sense of the *Pope*, regularly sitting with a general Council, explaining Scripture, and making Articles of Faith. I told them, It was my Comfort that Christ was to be my *Judge*, and not they at the *Great Day:* And as for their censuring and judging of me, I was not moved with it. One day a certain Salvage, taken Prisoner in *Philips* War, who had lived at Mr. *Buckleys* at *Wethersfield*, called *Ruth*, who could speak *English* very well; who had been often at my House but was now proselyted to the *Romish Faith*, came into the *Wigwam*, and with her an *English* Maid who was taken the last War, who was dress'd up in *Indian* Apparel, could not speak one word of *English*, who said she could neither tell her own name, or the name of the place from whence she was taken. These two talked in the *Indian* Dialect with my Master a long time; after which my Master bad me *Cross my self;* I told him I would not he commanded me several times, and I as often refused. *Ruth* said, Mr. *Williams* you know the Scripture, and therefore act against your own light, for you know the Scripture saith, *Servants obey your Masters;* he is your Master, and you his Servant. I told her she was ignorant, and knew not the meaning of the Scripture, telling her, *I was not to disobey the Great God to obey any Master, and that I was ready to suffer for God if called thereto:* On which she talked to my

Master, I suppose she interpreted what I said. My Master took hold of my hand to force me to *Cross my self*, but I strugled with him, and would not suffer him to guide my hand; upon this he pulled off a *Crucifix* from his own neck, and bad me *Kiss* it; but I refused once and again; he told me *he would dash out my brains with his Hatchet if I refused.* I told him I should sooner chuse death then to Sin against God; then he ran and catcht up his Hatchet, and acted as tho' he would have dashed out my Brains; seeing I was not moved, he threw down his Hatchet, saying, *he would first bite off all my nails if I still refused;* I gave him my hand and told him, I was ready to suffer, he set his teeth in my thumb nails and gave a gripe with his teeth, and then said, *no good Minister, no love God, as bad as the Devil;* and so left off. I have reason to bless God who strengthened me to withstand; by this he was so discouraged as never more to meddle with me about my **Religion.**

EBENEZER TURELL, 1702–1778

[Ebenezer Turell was born in Boston, graduated from Harvard College in 1721, married the daughter of Benjamin Colman, and served as minister at Medford, 1724–1778. He published *The Life and Character of the Reverend Benjamin Colman, D.D.* in Boston, 1749; this text is from pp. 5–7, 26–28, 166–167, 182–184, 210–211. The biography of his wife, *Memoirs of the Life and Death of the Pious and Ingenious Mrs. Jane Turell*, was published at Boston, 1735, and in London, 1741; this text is from the edition of 1735, pp. 60–61, 78–79, 116–119.]

BENJAMIN COLMAN

IT was after the Twentieth Day of *July* in the year 1695 that Mr. *Colman* imbarked for *London* (by the Will of God) on board the Ship *Swan* Capt. *Thomas Gilbert* Commander—For the whole three first Days he was on Shipboard he endured the Extremity of Sea Sickness, and at times through the Voyage. On the fourth Day the Vessel sprang a Leek, and the Water was heard to pour in on the Star-board Tack, which alarmed the Sailors, and made some of them remark his Eveness and Calmness when they expected he should have been much affrighted. When the Winds blew a Storm afterward, he governed his Fears by looking on the Captain, Mate, and Sailors to discover what he saw in their Faces. When they came into the warm Seas, a *Dolphin* which they had marked with a Scar on his shining Back, kept Company with the Ship for Ten or Twelve Days together, feeding on her Bottom.

At the End of seven Weeks a *Seeker* made after them, and soon came up with them. She was a Privateer of 20 Guns and an 100 Men, a light and fleet Ship; The Swan was heavy laden, twelve Guns and 24 Men, Sailors and Passengers together. The Swan's Company bore their Broad-sides and Vollies of small Arms six or seven Times that Afternoon, defending themselves and annoying the Enemy; but were taken the next Morning, having their Boltsprit shot away, and the Mast, and Rigging so torn and cut, that the Masts fell all together an Hour after; by which means the Ship became a perfect Wreck, and the Company were much looked at by the French when they came into Port. The French had a great Number of Men killed, for they were so full that if a shot entered it must do Execution.

God graciously preserved Mr. *Colman* in the Fight, exposed all the while on the Quarter-Deck, where four out of seven were wounded, and one mortally. He was much praised for his Courage when the Fight was over; but though he charged and discharged like the rest, yet he declared he was sensible of no Courage but of a great deal of Fear; and when they had reecived two or three Broadsides he wondered when his Courage would come, as he had heard others talk. In short, he fought like a Philosopher and a Christian. He looked Death in the Face, and prayed all the while he charged and fired,——while the Boatswain and others made a Frolick and Sport of it.

There was a young *Rake*, a Passenger on board, that lisped at Atheism, and spit at Religion every Day of the Voyage, who was now in the Terrors of Death,—when he saw Mr. *Colman* take a Musket, he was ashamed to leave the Deck; but the first Volley of small Arms laid him flat on his Belly without being touched: when the great Guns roared he would have crept through the Boards to hide himself; he lay as one Dead, and let the Men tread on him or kick him as they pleased. At last he peeped up when the firing ceased for a Minute, and asked where they were? Mr. *Colman* told him they lay by to charge again; and in a Moment he flew down into the Doctor's Room, and was seen no more till the Ship was taken. Yet this Spark when safe in *France* was ridiculing Religion again, and scorning the Ministers of it as much as ever. . . .

He took Coach on *Christmas* Day, and found in it a Gentlewoman of very good Fashion and Sense, with her little Daughter, and was much delighted in the Journey with the agreeable Conversation of the Lady and Prattle of Miss.

At *Cambridge* Mr. *Colman* found a small Congregation of inferior People, the Shadow of the University, like that of all Cathedrals, stunting the Growth of the Dissenters.

They liked illiterate Preachers, and when *Davis* and others of that Sort came to Town, he was left by one half of his Hearers. They were also sadly tinged with *Antinomian* Principles, and his Texts were too legal for them.*—So he was ashamed of his Post, and wrote earnestly to *London* to be released from it.—He saw all the Colleges there after a Sort, but had none of those honorary Advantages for doing it as he had at *Oxford*.

At twelve Weeks End he returned to *London*, and some of the City Ministers resolved to take a Turn down themselves. The Reverend and zealous Mr. *Pomfret* went first for a Month, and others followed him.

But at length they got a handsom Subscription at *London* to the ingenious and learned Mr. *Pearse*, an excellent Preacher, to fix him at *Cambridge* for two or three Years. He went; and being already well entred into the Mathematicks, soon made himself known to the learned Mr. *Whiston*,[1] and became his most esteemed Friend. A fatal Friendship! for then he also drank in Mr. *Whiston's* Arrian Principles, which has since been the Spring of so much Strife and Confusion and every evil Work among the Dissenters.

Within a few Weeks after Mr. *Colman* was invited to the great Town of *Ipswich* in *Suffolk*.—In his Way thither God graciously preserved him from a very dangerous Snare, which three ill Women laid for him. He found them in the Stage-Coach, supped with them in the Evening, and was retired to his Chamber: But as he was going to Bed one of them knocked at his Door, and told him that they had mulled a Glass of Wine, chiefly because of the Cold that was upon him, and he must needs take Part of it with them. In their Chamber were two Beds, and he heard one of them gigling behind the Curtains of the furthermost Bed. He began now to suspect them, when one of them told him, that truly they were afraid to lie in the Chamber alone; that the furthest Bed would hold them three; and they begged of him to lodge in the nearest Bed. He told them he was greatly surprised at their Motion, and ashamed of it, that their Fear was groundless; no Danger would happen to them in the Inn; if there were any he should make a poor Defence; and that in short, they utterly forgot what they owed to their Reputation and Virtue, or to his. So they begged his Pardon, and he suddenly stept into his own Chamber.

* Like as at this Day in some Places of *New-England*. [*Turell's* note.]

At *Ipswich* he spent eleven Weeks very pleasantly, and with much Satisfaction; but they needed a Preacher only every other Lord's Day. The excellent Mr. *Fairfax* divided his Time with them and some neighbouring Congregations, as the Bishop of them all. Being now got to a plentiful Fish-market, and near to the Oyster-Banks, he began to think himself again in *New-England*. . . .

Reading, and close Application of Mind to Study was early, and ever his Delight—He read much, and digested well the various Authors he perused; and often collected from them what was curious and useful, as appears by many Sheets left, and numerous Quotations in his Sermons.*

In his *younger* Times he was a Night-Student, by which his Health was greatly impaired, and he experienced the Truth of that Saying in Erasmus, *Nocturnae Lucubrationes longe periculosissimæ habentur.*[2] In his latter Years he plied his Studies chiefly in the Forenoon, and ordinarily spent the whole of it in them. And he has been heard to say on the Verge of *Seventy*, "That he found himself best in Health and Spirit, at his Table with a Book or Pen in his Hand.—All must be hushed and still when he was there employed either in Reading, writing Letters or composing Sermons—He wrote many Hundred Epistles in a Year— (*Nulla Dies sine Epistolis* [3]) to all Ranks of Persons; on all Occasions and Businesses, and with greatest Ease imaginable, to the vast Pleasure and Profit of his Friends, the Benefit of his Country and the Churches in it; and the Good of Mankind.—His Letters to his Correspondents abroad being seen and admired, created him new Friends and were a happy Means of raising up new Benefactors to these Provinces . . . —I need not therefore here observe to my Readers, how good a Master he was of the Epistolary Stile—The Letters already inserted and others to be published in our Narrative shall speak for themselves.†

When he was about making a Sermon, after he had first looked up to Heaven for Assistance, he chose a Text, and consulted the best Expositors upon it (particularly the Rev. Mr. *Matthew Henry*, for whose Writings he seems to have had the greatest Value next to the sacred Scriptures) and then drew the Scheme of it on loose Papers, and noted down not only general Heads and Subdivisions, but also some of the most leading Thoughts and brightest Quotations from Authors (around

---

* He had a good Library, not large, but wisely collected of the best Authors ancient and modern. He retained considerable of his School-Learning to the last— I find him to have read over Horace in his Old Age, by his Collections of some of the most beautiful Lines and Sentiments from it. [*Turell's note.*]

† And yet as I observed in my Introduction, all or the most of them are printed off from the first rough Draught. [*Turell's note.*]

him) with many Passages of Scripture for Proof and Illustration.—Thus prepared he proceeded to write his Sermon on a Sheet of Paper neatly folded and stitched, which he sometimes finished with a Celerity and Exactness incredible. I have known him begin and compleat a Discourse that would last an Hour at one Sitting in a Forenoon.* Few Interlines or Emendations were afterward inserted or needed.† . . .

The *Doctor* as became a vigilant Overseer made frequent Visits to the several Families of his Charge, not only *common* and *civil* to cultivate Friendship and Good Will, but proper *Pastoral* Ones to enquire into and know their State and Circumstances in Order to treat them agreably, wisely and faithfully, and that he might the better adapt his publick Exercises, and give to every one their Portion in due Season.

He made Conscience of visiting the Poor as well as the Rich (especially in their Afflictions) instructing, advising, admonishing and comforting as he saw Occasion: And this he did Night and Day as long as his Strength lasted, and oftentimes to the no small Hazard of his Health and Life.

And when he gave Visits to any of his Congregation or received Visits from them (or other his Friends) he generally and generously bestowed Books of Piety on them, either his own Sermons, or the Publications of others.—When he was called to minister to the Souls of the Poor at their own Dwellings, he ordinarily enquired of their bodily Wants, which were soon supplied either by himself, or charitable Friends to whom he instantly applyed on their Behalf.

His Prayers over sick and dying Ones, were not only very affectionate and fervent, but also most instructive and edifying—By a Train of excellent Thoughts he led them into the Knowledge of Sin and Duty, of God and Christ, and from Earth to Heaven.‡

When he could not conveniently visit his People or other his Friends in distant Places, he sent his Thoughts to them in Writing, suted to the various Providences he heard they were under—A few § of the Copies which are found, and which exhibit the bright Image of his Mind, the Reader shall be entertained withal after I have just added

---

* One of his Twenty Sacramental Sermons in Print. [*Turell's note.*]

† And yet he saw Cause to destroy many of his Sermons. On one and another of them he has wrote—The first three or five Sermons on this Text, are burnt. [*Turell's note.*]

‡ Some of the Members (I might say Ministers) of the Church of *England* have declared themselves more raised and edified by them than by all the devout and pious Forms of their own Church. [*Turell's note.*]

§ Alas, that so few are found; for he seldom kept Copies of his familiar Letters. A large and valuable Collection of them might be obtained if sought for, equally entertaining with those that follow. [*Turell's note.*]

a Word or two (for a Close to this Chapter) on his gentlemanly Carriage and Behaviour, and other *Homiletical* Virtues which adorned him,
and were so conspicuous to all he conversed with.—He was a good
Master of Address, and carried all the Politeness of a Court about
him.—And as he treated Mankind of various Degrees and Ranks with
a Civility, Courtesy, Affability, Complaisance and Candor scarce to
be equalled. So all but the Base and Mean showed him an high Degree
of Respect and Reverence, Love and Affection.—Particularly Men of
Figure and Parts of our own Nation and Foreigners, whom he failed not
to visit upon their coming among us, greatly valued and admired him.

It has been said (perhaps not without some seeming Grounds for it)
that he sometimes went too far in complemental Strains both in Word
and Writing—but if he did, I am perswaded such Flights took their
Rise rather from an Exuberance or Excrescence (if the Phrase be allowable) of the before-mentioned homiletical Virtues, and a too high
Complacency in the appearing Excellencies of others, than from faulty
Insincerity and designed Flattery in the Time of it.—As he took a
sincere Pleasure in the Gifts of others, and had a natural Proneness to
think favourably of all Men, and construed every Thing in the most
candid Sense, it is not much to be wondered at if he sometimes exceeded
in his Expressions.—And it is to be lamented that some have swollen
with Pride, and made an ill Use of the Doctor's high Esteem and good
Opinion of them.

JANE TURELL

HER *Father* the Reverend Dr. *Benjamin Colman* (thro' the gracious
Favour of *God*) is still living among us, one universally acknowleg'd to be even from his younger Times (at Home and Abroad) a bright
Ornament and Honour to his Country, and an Instrument in *God*'s
Hand of bringing much Good to it.

Her *Mother* Mrs. *Jane Colman* was a truly gracious Woman, Daughter
of Mr. *Thomas Clark* Gentleman.

Mrs. *Turell* was their *third* Child, graciously given them after they
had mourn'd the Loss of the two former; and for *seven* Years their *only*
one. Her Constitution from her early Infancy was wonderful weak and
tender, yet the Organs of her Body so form'd as not to obstruct the
free Operations of the active and capacious Spirit within. The Buddings
of Reason and Religion appear'd on her sooner than usual.—Before her
second Year was compleated she could speak distinctly, knew her Letters,
and could relate many Stories out of the Scriptures to the Satisfaction

and Pleasure of the most Judicious. I have heard that Governour *Dudley*, with other Wise and Polite *Gentlemen*, have plac'd her on a Table and setting round it own'd themselves diverted with her Stories.— Before she was *four* Years old (so strong and tenacious was her Memory) she could say the greater Part of the *Assembly's Catechism*, many of the *Psalms*, some hundred Lines of the best *Poetry*, read distinctly, and make pertinent Remarks on many things she read.—

She grew in *Knowlege* (the most useful) day by day, and had the *Fear* of *God* before her Eyes.

She *pray'd* to *God* sometimes by excellent *Forms* (recommended to her by her Father and suited to her Age & Circumstances) and at other times *ex corde*, the *Spirit of God* helping her Infirmities. When her Father upon a Time enquir'd of her what Words she used in Prayer to God, she answer'd him,—"*That when she was upon her Knees God gave her Expressions.*

Even at the Age of *four, five*, & *six* she ask'd many astonishing *Questions* about divine Mysteries, and carefully laid up and hid the *Answers* she received to them, in her Heart. . . .

Before She had seen *Eighteen*, she had read, and (in some measure) digested all the English *Poetry*, and polite Pieces in *Prose*, printed and Manuscripts in her Father's well furnish'd Library, and much she borrow'd of her Friends and Acquaintance. She had indeed such a Thirst after Knowledge that the Leisure of the Day did not suffice, but she spent whole Nights in reading.

I find she was sometimes fir'd with a laudable Ambition of raising the honour of her *Sex*, who are therefore under Obligations to her; and all will be ready to own she had a fine *Genius*, and is to be placed among those who have excell'd.

When I was first inclin'd (by the Motions of God's Providence and Spirit) to seek her Acquaintance (which was about the Time she entred her *nineteenth* Year) I was surpriz'd and charm'd to find her so accomplish'd. I found her in a good measure Mistress of the politest *Writers* and their Works; could point out the Beauties in them, and had made many of their best Tho'ts her own: And as she went into more free Conversation, she discours'd how admirably on many Subjects!

I grew by Degrees into such an Opinion of her good *Taste*, that when she put me upon translating a *Psalm* or two, I was ready to excuse my Self, and if I had not fear'd to displease her should have deny'd her Request.

After her *Marriage* which was on *August* 11th. 1726, her Custom was once in a Month or two, to make some *new Essay* in Verse or Prose, and to read from Day to Day as much as a faithful Discharge of the Duties of her new Condition gave Leisure for: and I think I may with Truth say, that she made the writing of Poetry a *Recreation* and not a *Business*.

What greatly contributed to increase her Knowlege in *Divinity, History, Physick, Controversy,* as well as *Poetry,* was her attentive hearing most that I read upon those Heads thro' the long Evenings of the Winters as we sat together. . . .

Having related these Things, you will not wonder if I now declare my self a *Witness* of her daily close Walk with God during her married State, and of her Retirements for Reading, Self-Examination and Devotion.

It was her Practice to read the *Bible* out in Course, once in a Year, the Book of *Psalms* much oftner, besides many *Chapters* and a Multitude of *Verses* which she kept turn'd down in *a Bible,* which she had been the Owner and Reader of more than *twenty* Years. If I should only present my *Readers* with a *Catalogue* of these *Texts,* I doubt not but that they would admire the Collection, be gratified with the Entertainment; and easily conjecture many of her holy Frames and Tempers from them.—I must own, considering her tender Make and often Infirmities she *exceeded* in Devotion. And I have tho't my self oblig'd sometimes (in Compassion to her) to call her off, and put her in mind of God's *delighting in Mercy more than in Sacrifice.*

How often has she lain whole *Nights* by me mourning for Sin, calling upon God, and praising him, or discoursing of Christ and Heaven? And when under Doubts intreating me to help her (as far as I could) to a full Assurance of God's Love. Sometimes she would say, "Well, I am content if you will shew me that I have the Truth of Grace." And I often satisfy'd her with one of Mr. *Baxter*'s Marks of Love to Christ, namely, *Lamenting & panting after him;* for this kind of Love she was sure she exercis'd in the most cloudy Hours of her Life.

I may not forget to mention *the strong and constant Guard she plac'd at the Door of her Lips.* Who ever heard her call an ill Name? or *detract* from any Body? When she apprehended she receiv'd Injuries, *Silence* and *Tears* were her highest Resentments. But I have often heard her *reprove* others for rash and angry Speeches.

In every *Relation* she sustain'd she was truly *Exemplary,* sensible how much of the Life and Power of Religion consists in the conscientious Practice and Performance of *Relative Duties.*

No *Child* had a greater Love to and Reverence for her *Parents,* she even exceeded in Fear and Reverence of her *Father,* notwithstanding all his Condescentions to her, and vast Freedoms with her.

As a *Wife* she was dutiful, prudent and diligent, not only content but joyful in her Circumstances. She *submitted as is fit in the Lord, look'd well to the Ways of her Houshold, and her own Works praise her in the Gates.*

Her very Apparel discover'd Modesty and Chastity: She lov'd to appear neat and clean, but never gay and fine.

To her *Servants* she was good and kind, and took care of them, especially of the Soul of a *Slave* who dy'd (in the House) about a Month before her.

She respected all her *Friends* and *Relatives*, and spake of them with Honour, and never forgot either their Counsels or their Kindnesses.

She often spake of her Obligations to her *Aunt Staniford*, which were great living and dying.

She honour'd all Men, and lov'd every Body. *Love and Goodness was natural to her*, as her *Father* expresses it in a Letter Years ago.

Her tender Love to her only *Sister*, has been already seen; and was on all Occasions manifested, and grew exceedingly to her Death. A few Days before it, I heard her speak to her particularly of preparing for another World. "Improve (said she) the Time of Health, 'tis the *only* Time for doing the great Work in."

And in Return for her Love and amiable Carriage, *She had the Love and Esteem of all that knew her.* Those that knew her *best* lov'd her best, and praise her most.

Her *Humility* was so great, that she could well bear (without being elated) such *Praises* as are often found in her *Father's* Letters to us. viz. "*I greatly esteem as well as highly love you: The best of Children deserves all that a Child can of a Father: My Soul rejoyces in you: My Joy, my Crown. I give Thanks to God for you daily. I am honour'd in being the Father of such a Daughter.*"

Her *Husband* also, and he *praiseth* her as a *Meet Help* both in Spirituals and Temporals.

Her *Relations* and Acquaintance ever manifested the highest Value for her.

The *People*, among whom she liv'd the last *eight* Years of her Life, both *Old* and *Young* had a Love and *Veneration* for her; as a Person of the strictest Virtue and undefil'd Religion. Her *Innocence, Modesty, Ingenuity*, & *Devotion* charm'd all into an Admiration of her. And I question whether there has been *more Grief and Sorrow* shown at the Death of any private Person, by People of all Ranks, to whom her Virtues were known; *Mourning*, for the Loss sustain'd by our selves, *not for her*, nor *as others who have no Hope.* For it is beyond Doubt that she *died in the Lord*, and is *Blessed*.

Chapter VI

POETRY

IT IS a commonplace that the literature of any given period too often is judged by succeeding generations according to their own standards of taste. Now and then an injudicious verdict is quickly reversed, especially when no strong sentiments—sectional prejudices or violently emotional antipathies—prevent judicial appraisal. An equitable evaluation of colonial Puritan poetry has been difficult to make until recent years because, for one thing, the era as a whole in its relation to the English background has been neglected; and again, because much that seems intolerably arid today was extravagantly praised in its time; and finally, because many earlier verdicts have so long passed unchallenged that they have at last been accepted as true. For instance, the general reader has probably known colonial poetry only through a few extracts from Anne Bradstreet, Michael Wigglesworth, and the Bay Psalm Book. Beyond that triad even scholars have not easily penetrated, for modern editions of the seventeenth-century colonial poets have rarely appeared;[1] and critical estimates of Puritan verse are almost nonexistent.[2] The conjunction of two factors might be cited to explain the neglect: very little colonial verse has literary importance; that little, executed by writers who sometimes imitated only the superficialities of their models, was conceived according to standards which soon came into disfavor. The colonial Puritàns, if they wrote at all, invariably tried their hand at versifying, and a really formidable amount of poetry was issued,—sometimes, as in the case of Wigglesworth, Anne Bradstreet, and Benjamin Tompson, in book form; but more often scattered informally through almanacs, histories, biographies, funeral sermons, and broadsides in the form of elegies, anagrams, epitaphs, and occasional "effusions." A few words, then, to bring the era into focus.

The cultivated Puritan was in no sense an implacable foe to the arts, for, like the Anglicans, he expected to win from life such mental and spiritual comfort as it could be made to offer. He studied in the same universities, read the same authors, discussed the same philosophies, and attempted to live, as they, "A sweet self-privacy in a right soul."[3]

---

[1] For recently published texts of Puritan verse, usually in limited editions, see Bibliography, p. 818, and the headings to the poetry selections.

[2] Moses C. Tyler, *A History of American Literature During the Colonial Period, 1607–1765* (New York, 1878), chapters X and XI, first essayed a judicious criticism of Puritan verse. After Tyler's *History*, no re-examination was made until Kenneth B. Murdock published his brief introduction to *Handkerchiefs from Paul* (Cambridge, 1927).

[3] Henry Vaughan, *Rules and Lessons, Poems* (The Muses' Library), I, 96.

His traditions were likewise Renaissance and Elizabethan, and as there was no law or reason to the contrary in the tenets of his particular faith, he was educated by way of the classics. Though the Bible was for him

> the Sacred *Grammar*, where
> The Rules of speaking well, contained are,[1]

the Puritan expected that the example set by the classical poets might guide him to achieve a higher virtue in life; therefore exercises in imitation of Vergil and Horace were part of his school training, as they were for all liberally educated English boys; and among the modern poets Spenser, Sidney, and Du Bartas (by way of Sylvester), and later Milton were his favorites. In one respect only can we detect in his attitude a view of poetry different from that held by other Englishmen. The Puritan centered his mind on God with a keener intensity, and thus more consciously withdrew his attention from "fleshly schools." The Anglican poets juxtaposed the flesh and spirit: Herrick's "Pious Pieces," *His Noble Numbers,* are no more colorful and sincere than his *Hesperides;* Donne's secular verses occupy a greater place even in his works than the *Divine Poems;* and the same can be said of the Catholic poet Crashaw, whose fame was spread as far by *The Delights of the Muses* as by *Carmen Deo Nostro.* But for the Puritans, and especially for those who came to New England, God, not the' world, inspired their "noble numbers," and they many times chose verse the better to honor Him. They were still Elizabethan enough to live intensely, though their ardor took a new direction. It is clear therefore that since the Puritan did not cut himself off from the realities which a poetic art can summon, he made such use of them as seemed to him most fitting. Fundamentally Spenser, Sidney, and Milton, the real precursors of lesser Puritan bards, are ethical poets, and it is the moral import of their art which appealed to the Puritan mind; broadly speaking, those great writers conceived poetry as a philosophy—the highest philosophy, in fact; one which taught men virtue by example, not through mere didacticism, but by the embodiment of every knowledge. Above all else, poetry, they felt, should not be written merely to delight; it should be, as Du Bartas's *Divine Week* had shown, a speculum or compendium of the profoundest spiritual mysteries drawn from the most diverse learnings. Thus the subject matter of poetry was regarded as of highest consequence to men. To such a literary ideal the Puritans clung, even when they lacked the creative fire of their originals.

[1] Cotton Mather, *Corderius Americanus* (Boston, 1708), p. 29.

All this is not to say that the Puritans developed a conscious theory by which they judged poets and fashioned verses of their own. On the contrary, most of them probably gave it little consideration as an art; they thought of it simply as a means to an end, and remained curiously indifferent to the quintessential breath and finer spirit of the poetic idiom. It remains true, nevertheless, that they display an awareness of the art even though few had the talent to rise above mediocrity. It would seem wise to distinguish between the artistry they lacked, and the honor in which they held the poet's high office. The colonial Puritans seldom produced fine verse, because authentic talent among them was rare, and that which did manifest itself was perhaps neglected because of the tacit assumption—followed to extremes—that matter counted for more than manner. Learning was all, because it led past the world to God. The marvel of Milton is not that a Puritan wrote sensuously, but that a scholar could be a poet. If lesser Puritans adopted only the machinery of conceits, puns, and mythological fancies, they did so because they lacked the feeling, not the will, to achieve a higher reality.

The great poets searched for profitable doctrine which would teach great precepts when molded into spacious lines. Among Puritans, who as a class evidenced deep interest in historical and scientific matters, we find in extreme form the will to teach. Others before Puritans had written verse for the purpose designed by John Wilson, and in like manner,—the authors of *A Mirror for Magistrates*, for instance,—yet Wilson's poem, *A Song or, Story For . . . Remembrance* (see p. 552), is typical of much Puritan verse in style and content. Written to teach children the providential shaping of English history under Protestant rule, it is done into fourteeners to help them memorize it. For his matter Wilson drew upon Speed, Camden, and current tracts on the Gunpowder Plot. The doggerel ballad meter, universally familiar as that employed in the Sternhold and Hopkins version of the Psalms, hardly seems worthy of a gentleman who had shown a talent for Latin verse, and who had been nurtured at King's College, where the Fellows were encouraged to study poetry and music; but the poem is a product of the times, and its hold during the seventeenth century was unbroken, for it was republished in 1680, with a preface recalling "how excedingly pretious the remembrance of this heavenly man of God is. . . . He was another sweet singer of Israel, whose heavenly Verses passed like to the handkerchief carryed from Paul to help and uphold disconsolate ones, and to heal their wracked Souls, by the effectual prisence of Gods holy Spirit."

Probably no body of Puritan verse has seemed to modern readers more insensible to poetic feeling than that contained in the Bay Psalm Book (see p. 555). Composed as it was by ministers who labored to fashion suitable translations of the Psalms for vocal use in the churches, its angularity has often been judged either hopelessly uninspired or consciously hostile to grace and measure. Of course, such paraphrases now are out of style; and any metrical translation of the Psalms, in addition to being shaped to a familiar tune, must compete with the sustained felicity of the Bible rendering. The reader who compares the Bay Psalm Book with versions similarly adapted by Sandys, Donne, Milton, and Dryden need not single out the colonial versifiers for apology. Evidently the metric flaws troubled the authors, for their revision ten years later was undertaken with the idea of smoothing the lines. One cannot claim for either rendering more than its authors intended: an exact translation with as much grace as they knew how to give it. Their ideal, quite defensible, proved an extreme example of matter heeded at the expense of art.

No Puritan more clearly exemplifies the ideals which Puritan poets strove to reach than Anne Bradstreet (see pp. 561–579). Her ambitious discourses of Man, Monarchies, Seasons, and Elements, modeled on Du Bartas, pay homage to the poet as philosopher, even though Mistress Bradstreet's muse soars with a middle-flight. The mythological machinery and conventional praise of nature, not as she saw it, but as she had often encountered it in others' verse, were flaws which she acquired by poetic, not Puritan, tradition. It was, after all, the ingenious display of erudition in a woman which made her a "best seller" in England for a short time, and won for her the appellation of "Tenth Muse." For us she lives rather in the moments when her contemplative spirit stirs to life a theme which touched her heart. A tender wistfulness plays through the lines which she wrote "vpon the burning of our house":

> Here stood that Trunk, and there that chest;
> There lay that store I covnted best:
> My pleasant things in ashes lye,
> And them behold no more shall I.[1]

Except it be Jonathan Edwards, no Puritan has more often been cited as the embodiment of repulsive joylessness than Michael Wigglesworth; his *Day of Doom* is still reckoned a monstrous example of unre-- lieved horror. Yet Wigglesworth's purpose was similar to that of Wilson. When Cotton Mather preached the funeral sermon for Wigglesworth,

[1] See p. 578.

he recalled that the late Malden pastor had written "several Com-posures, wherein he proposed the Edification of such Readers, as are for Truth's dressed up in a *Plain Meeter*." [1] Indeed, the "Little Feeble *Shadow of a Man*," as Mather called him, whose health was so poor that he gave up his college tutorship, preached but seldom, and turned down the Harvard presidency in 1684, had written an epic that was also a "best seller." The grim intensity of its vivid descriptions must have struck terror in the hearts of many a child who was compelled to memorize its doggerel staves, and belied the character of the country parson and doctor whose nature was essentially guileless and gentle. The verses in his second published volume, *Meat out of the Eater*, rivaled in popularity *The Day of Doom*. The songs and meditations are written in the same monotonous fourteeners adopted in the earlier epic, but though rude, the stanzas are alive and occasionally touching. The merits of Wigglesworth's poetry today are more clearly felt in the tonal quality of such lines as those from *A Song of Emptiness*, fashioned on the *ubi sunt* theme:

> If *Beauty* could the beautiful defend
> From Death's dominion, than slain *Absalom*
> Had not been brought to such a shameful end:
> But fair and foul unto the Grave must come.
>
> If *Wealth* or *Scepters* could Immortal make,
> Then wealthy *Croesus*, wherefore art thou dead?
> If *Warlike force*, which makes the World to quake,
> Then why is *Julius Caesar* perished?
>
> Where are the *Scipio's* Thunder-bolts of War?
> Renowned *Pompey*, *Caesars* Enemie?
> Stout *Hannibal*, *Romes* Terror known so far?
> Great *Alexander*, what's become of thee?
>
> If *Gifts* and *Bribes* Death's favour might but win, . . .
> All these, and more, had still surviving been: . . . [2]

We must bear in mind that the doctrines of God's immutable justice, which Wigglesworth "dressed up in a *Plain Meeter*," were not in their day considered unlovely. Cotton Mather tells how John Cotton felt about the matter: "And being asked, why in his Latter Dayes, he In-

---

[1] *A Faithful Man, Described and Rewarded* (Boston, 1705), p. 24.

[2] With the somewhat prolix second and fourth lines removed, the resulting couplet produces, with the preceding three stanzas, a highly creditable sonnet.

dulged *Nocturnal Studies,* more than formerly, he pleasantly Replied, *Because I Love to Sweeten my mouth with a piece of* Calvin, *before I go to sleep.*" [1] Jonathan Edwards later described in his "Personal Narrative" how he found the doctrine of God's absolute sovereignty and justice with respect to salvation and damnation exceedingly pleasant, bright, and sweet.

The Puritans wrote their most ambitious poems for "edification," but some of the most appealing and sprightly lines are the commendatory pieces written, in the current fashion, sometimes to launch an author before the public (see p. 580), or perhaps, spontaneously conceived—as the stalwart lines of Edward Johnson,—to hymn God's wonder-working providence (see p. 630). Much of the beauty of Johnson's verse lies hidden in the elusive overtones of passionate conviction and half-realized felicities that are felt rather than heard. Even less purposeful than any verses yet discussed were those "composures" of the young college graduates who during the seventeenth century prepared the yearly almanacs, and were allowed to fill any blank spaces as a remuneration for the fussy task; the authors chose usually to write an essay on science, or perhaps a poem. The theme in either case was appropriate to the work in hand, and the resulting verses derived their inspiration from Vergilian themes wherein the signs of the zodiac intertwine with classic mythology:—often the ornate narrative recounts Apollo's wooing of the earth goddess Tellus. The imagery by which Thomas Shepard allegorized September in the *Almanack* for 1656 is unusually tempered and graceful:

> The glorious Monarch of the Sky,
> Times moderator, keep's his Court,
> The Scoales of Justice hanging by
> The golden Mean. And here resort
> Pomona bringing mellow fruit,
> And Ceres corn upon her back,
> And kind Silvanus spread's this bruit;
> His budget's full of nutts to crack.

The florid style sometimes gave way to allegory on contemporary events, as for instance the lines of Samuel Danforth in the *Almanack* for 1647, where the stanza for September offers the suggestion that

> Four heads should meet and counsell have,
> The chickens from the kite to save,

[1] *Johannes in Eremo* (Boston, 1695), p. 54.

> The idle drones away to drive,
> The little Bees to keep i' th' hive.
> How honey may be brought to these
> By making fish to dance on trees.[1]

"Thus the Cambridge Almanac became the annual poetry magazine of Harvard College." [2]

It has been queried why the Puritans so delighted in conceits and strained rhetorical figures, in anagrams and acrostics; [3] indeed, the fad at times was carried to extravagant lengths. As its worst it produced such verses as Benjamin Tompson's "Funeral Tribute" to Governor Winthrop of Connecticut, opening thus:

> Another Black Parenthesis of woe
> The *Printer* wills that all the World should know
> Sage *Winthrop* prest with publick sorrow Dies
> As the sum total of our Miseries.[4]

But the Puritan elegy at its best, as in Oakes's lament for Shepard (see p. 641), achieves a dignity and heartfelt simplicity, a tender pathos that goes far to redeem Puritan elegiac verse from the oblivion into which most of it has fallen. Tompson (see p. 635) was a poet of very local reputation, at his best in satire, whose achievements were evidently modeled on the extravagant commonplaces of Quarles; they reflect one popular literary fashion shaped to native material.

Of the colonial writers whose poetic accomplishments fall within the later Puritan era, Roger Wolcott and Mather Byles won some recognition. The verse of Wolcott (see p. 657), like that of Tompson, has small merit. The meditations of the future statesman and soldier on Biblical themes ally him with the Puritans of the seventeenth century, and his ambitious narrative of the agency of Winthrop at King Charles's court is the first colonial epic in patriotic strain. The couplets,

---

[1] The allegory is not very clear, but the "four heads" evidently refer to the united colonies of New England; the "hive" is Harvard College; the last two lines suggest that the college should be aided by a tax on the fishing industry. For interpretation, see K. B. Murdock, *Handkerchiefs from Paul*, pp. 101–111.

[2] Samuel E. Morison, *Harvard College in the Seventeenth Century*, p. 133.

[3] See Murdock, *op. cit.*, p. liv. A possible explanation is suggested by the Puritan's exaggerated desire to find God's shaping hand in all affairs, and by all symbolic, implicit, or elaborate means. "A Glass of spirits my Wife sent stood upon a Joint-Stool which, Simon W[illard] jogging, it fell down and broke all to shivers: I said twas a lively Emblem of our Fragility and Mortality" (*Diary of Samuel Sewall*, I, 460). It is an easy transfer, once the mind is thinking "emblematically," to heighten any figure by elaborate device.

[4] *Benjamin Tompson . . . His Poems*, ed. Howard J. Hall (Boston, 1924), p. 99; from a unique broadside.

sad rubbish though they be, seem to look forward to the more pretentious American epics of the late eighteenth century written by Humphrey, Dwight, Barlow, and Trumbull. The greater part of Byles's verses fall outside the Puritan era both in time and in spirit. "An Hymn to Christ" (see p. 663) is in some measure a link between the earlier period when men wrote to honor Christ, and the later more urbane decades when English literary fashions, set by Pope, Thomson, and Watts, were cleaving to new molds. Those who would seek representative selections of the punster's ready wit, or enjoy the light vein of his pleasant humor, must turn to such verses as he published after the Puritan years had passed.

The intrinsic value of Puritan poetry, even when the best of it is singled out for commendation, is apparent only in snatches. Two Puritans only were distinguished in their own time, Anne Bradstreet and Michael Wigglesworth; and such characteristics of their verses as were praised by their contemporaries are now more harshly judged. To modern eyes the undigested narrative summaries, the severe theology, and the edifying tone are frankly boring. Moments of inspiration they have in a phrase, a line, or a single poem. Perhaps we scrutinize too closely if we expect to discover finished poets in a country so remote from literary inspiration, among people whose purpose in writing was generally to edify. The one poet whose stature may well develop as time reveals him has been—at his own wish—forgotten; yet Edward Taylor (see p. 650) speaks perhaps with a more genuinely inspired voice than any other colonial poet. His fertility in image-making, his rapture, tenderness, delicacy, and intense devotion communicate something of the fervor which the man himself derived from his sacramental meditations. They give us one authentic indication that the indigenous Puritan muse, even when tied down to the fashions of an earlier style, soared with metaphoric brilliance.

JOHN WILSON, 1588–1667

[John Wilson, one of the two ministers who emigrated with Winthrop in 1630, is now chiefly remembered for his opposition to the Antinomian heresy and for his persecution of Anne Hutchinson. He was, in fact, a scholar eminent for his learning and attainments. Admitted to King's College, Cambridge, in 1605, he became three years later a Fellow of that royal institution. For a short time he devoted himself to the law, but through the influence of his friends Richard Rogers and William Ames—distinguished Puritans both,—he adopted the Congregational way. In trouble for nonconformity, he came to Boston as minister of the church which he served for the remaining thirty-seven years of his life.

In 1626, he published in London *A Song or, Story, For the Lasting Remembrance of diuerse famous works, which God hath done in our time*, a second edition of which appeared in Boston in 1680, entitled *A Song of Deliverance for the Lasting Remembrance of Gods Wonderful Works never to be Forgotten*. Few of his sermons were ever published. Cotton Mather wrote his Life in 1695, *Memoria Wilsoniana* (bound into his Life of the Reverend John Cotton, *Johannes in Eremo*), later incorporated in the *Magnalia* (1702). The 1680 edition of the poem is available in complete form in Kenneth B. Murdock, *Handkerchiefs from Paul* (Cambridge, 1927), together with a biographical and critical introduction. See also Savage, *Genealogical Dictionary;* and Samuel E. Morison, *The Founding of Harvard College* (Cambridge, 1935), *passim*. The text below is from a photostat copy of the first edition (pp. 37–40) in the British Museum.]

THE LONDON PLAGUE

From *A Song or, Story, For the Lasting Remembrance of diuerse famous works.*

1625

IN THE one thousand yeare of God,
  Sixe hundred twenty fiue,
Was sent the Pestilentiall rod,
  Our rockie hearts to riue.
In the chiefe City of the Realme,
  It had the chiefest seate:
There like a sea to ouerwhelme,
  Pride that was growne so great;
Or like a fire to purge away,
  The drosse of hatefull sinne;
Or like a trumpet thence to fray,
  The sleepe that soules were in.
The Queene of Cities wont to sit,
  In Chaire of highest state,
Now sate in dust and lowest pit,
  All sad and desolate:
The highest Court of Parlament,
  To Oxford did remooue.
The Tearmers were to Redding sent,
  Their Titles there to prooue.

Nor were the strangers strange alone,
   To the infected City;
But her best louers all were gone,
   And left her without pitty.
I meane, the rich did flocke away,
   And bad her streetes adew,
Except the poore (which needes must stay)
   There stayed but a few.
Nothing was heard but passing-bels,
   And friends their friends lamenting,
Nothing but heauy dolefull-knells.
   (Death not at all relenting)
Nothing was seene but heapes of dead,
   To feede the hungrie graue;
Or others lying sicke a bed,
   (No way their life to saue.)
Some looked pale, and some with paine,
   Were forc't to raue and roare,
Some did the deadly markes sustaine,
   And some the deadly sore:
In one yeares space, or lesse then so,
   (From time the Plague began)
To what a number did they grow,
   That death grip't in his spanne?
Sixtie two thousand at the least,
   Sixe hundred seuenty seuen,
Were made appeare by deaths arrest,
   Before the God of heauen.
Yea, do but from Iunes second looke
   Vnto Decembers last,
Scarse shall you reade in English-booke
   Of like doome euer past.
Within this three months space alone,
   As hath bin duly counted,
Fiftie three thousand ninetie one,
   By Bills report amounted.[1]
In London and the Liberties,[2]
   (Sixe moe [3] neere Parishes adde,)
All the forenamed clos'd their eies,
   And made their friends full sad.
More dyde in *this* than *former* pest,
   By th'heauy hand of God;
In thirteene weekes (to say the lest)
   Eleuen thousand fortie and odde.

Of all which summes, the greatest part
   By death departed thence,
Were pearced through with fire dart,
   Of raging Pestilence.
If within and without one Cittie Walls,
   Were found of men such lacke,
More then six myriades of soules
   Brought to so heauy wracke:
Oh then what was the wrecke and spoile,
   Of all the land beside,
In Cities and in Country soyle,
   Throughout the kingdome wide?
Trading grew dead, and mony scant,
   The rich doubting their state,
The poore were pinched sore with want,
   All fear'd the dismall fate.

THE BAY PSALM BOOK

[Only ten known copies survive of *The Whole Booke of Psalmes Faithfully Translated into English Metre* (Cambridge, 1640), from an edition that numbered seventeen hundred. The volumes were worn threadbare with use; a second printing was issued in 1647, and within the next hundred years twenty-five more printings were necessary. Generally known as the Bay Psalm Book, it was the first book issued in the American colonies—preceded only by a broadside sheet, the Freeman's Oath, and by the 1639 Alamanac—and is probably the first book in English printed in North America.

Typographically it bears marks of hasty or unskilled workmanship; its prosodic merits are few, but not quite so few as Tyler implied when he called it "a poetic phenomenon, happily unique, we may hope, in all the literatures of English speech" (*A History of American Literature*, I, 274, 275). The authors, Thomas Weld, John Eliot, and Richard Mather, were university-trained ministers who perhaps "for the meetre sake" should not have refused Francis Quarles's offer to help in the composition. But they were translating the Hebrew with what seemed to them fitting exactness. "Neither let any think," Mather explains in the preface (see p. 670), "that for the meetre sake wee have taken liberty or poeticall licence to depart from the true and proper sence of Davids words in the hebrew verses, noe; . . . Gods Altar needs not our pollishings." Indeed, its purpose was to replace the Sternhold and Hopkins version currently used, a text which, because of its departure from the

original and its sacrifice of a literal rendering for poetic effect, troubled
the straightforward Puritan's scholarly conscience.

But even from the beginning the rude lines of the Bay Psalms were
not regarded as sacrosanct. The first two editions (1640, 1647) having
run out, what was in effect a third appeared in 1651: *The Psalms Hymns
And Spiritual Songs Of the Old and New Testament, faithfully translated into
English metre.* President Dunster of Harvard, assisted by a Mr. Richard
Lyon, took the work over, "having a special ey," as the preface
explains, "both to the gravity of the phrase" and "sweetnes of the
verse." The new editors added translations from other books of the
Bible, principally from the Songs of Solomon. The changes they effected are occasionally an improvement.

"It was thought," Cotton Mather said a half-century later (*Magnalia,*
III, 100), "that a little more of Art was to be employ'd upon the verses";
and this edition, thus "Revised and Refined," continued to be standard
until the aged Reverend John Barnard of Marblehead brought forth
A New Version of the Psalms of David at Boston in 1752. He states by
way of preface that the older version "is generally very good, and few of
the same Age may be compar'd with it; yet the Flux of Languages has
rendered several Phrases in it obsolete . . ." His ideal, however, was
still that of the first generation. "My great Care has been to keep as
close to the Original as I could . . . And all in a Stile . . . adapted to
the Capacity of our Christian Assemblies; neither in such Flights of
Poetry as soar above them, nor yet so low, I trust, as to be contemptible." His version, in turn, was superseded by one published by Thomas
Prince in 1758.

The 1640 edition was reprinted at Cambridge in 1862, and reproduced in facsimile with an introduction by Wilberforce Eames at New
York in 1903. The text of the Dunster-Lyon selections below follows the
unique copy in the New York Public Library. The verses are from the
1640 edition, however, unless otherwise stated.]

THE PSALMS

23 A PSALME OF DAVID.

THE LORD to mee a shepheard is, want therefore shall not I.
    2 Hee in the folds of tender-grasse, doth cause mee downe to lie:
To waters calme me gently leads (3) Restore my soule doth hee:
he doth in paths of righteousnes: for his names sake leade mee.
4 Yea though in valley of deaths shade I walk, none ill I'le feare:
because thou art with mee, thy rod, and staffe my comfort are.

5 For mee a table thou hast spread, in presence of my foes:
  thou dost annoynt my head with oyle, my cup it over-flowes.
6 Goodnes & mercy surely shall all my dayes follow mee:
  and in the Lords house I shall dwell so long as dayes shall bee.

Psal: XXIII. A Psalm of David.

THE LORD to me a shepheard is: want therfore shall not I.
  2 Hee in the foulds of tender grass doth make me down to ly:
Hee leads me to the waters still. (3) Restore my soul doth hee;
In paths of righteousness, he will for his names sake lead mee.

4 In valley of deaths shade although I walk I'le fear none ill:
For thou with me thy rod, also thy staff me comfort will.
5 Thou hast 'fore me a table spread, in presence of my foes:
Thou dost anoint with oyle my head, my cup it ouer-flowes.

6 Goodness and mercy my dayes all shall surely follow mee:
And in the LORDS house dwell I shall so long as dayes shall bee.

[From Dunster-Lyon revision, 1651]

Psalme 107.

O GIVE yee thanks unto the Lord, because that good is hee:
  because his loving kindenes lasts to perpetuitee.
2 So let the Lords redeem'd say: whom hee freed from th'enemies
  hands:
3 And gathred them from East, & West, from South, & Northerne
  lands.
4 I'th desart, in a desart way they wandred: no towne finde,
5 to dwell in. Hungry & thirsty: their soule within them pinde.
[6] Then did they to Iehovah cry when they were in distresse:
  who did them set at liberty out of their anguishes.
7 In such a way that was most right he led them forth also:
  that to a citty which they might inhabit they might go.
8 O that men would Iehovah prayse for his great goodnes *then:*
  & for his workings wonderfull unto the sonnes of men.
9 Because that he the longing soule doth throughly satisfy:
  the hungry soule he also fills with good abundantly.

(2)

10 Such as in darknes' and within the shade of death abide;
  who are in sore affliction, also in yron tyde:
11 By reason that against the words of God they did rebell;
  also of him that is most high contemned the counsell.
12 Therefore with molestation hee did bring downe their heart:
  downe did they fall, & none their was could help to them impart.

13 Then did they to Iehovah cry when they were in distress:
    who did them set at liberty out of their anguishes.
14 He did them out of darknes bring, also deaths shade from under:
    as for the bands that they were in he did them break asunder.
15 O that men would Iehovah prayse for his great goodnes *then:*
    and for his workings wonderfull unto the sonnes of men.
16 For he hath all to shivers broke the gates that were of brasse:
    & hee asunder cut each barre that made of yron was.

(3)

17 For their transgressions & their sins, fooles doe affliction beare.
18 All kinde of meate their soule abhorres: to deaths gate they draw
    neare.
19 Then did they to Iehovah cry when they were in distress:
    who did them set at liberty out of their anguishes.
20 He, sent his word, & therewithall healing to them he gave:
    from out of their destructions he did them also save.
21 O that men would Iehovah prayse, for his great goodnes *then:*
    & for his workings wonderfull unto the sons of men.
22 And sacrifices sacrifice let them of thanksgiving:
    & while his works they doe declare let them for gladnes sing.

(4)

23 They that goe downe to'th sea in ships: their busines there to doo
24 in waters great. The Lords work see, i'th deep his wonders too.
25 Because that he the stormy winde commandeth to arise:
    which lifteth up the waves therof, (26) They mount up to the skyes:
    Downe goe they to the depths againe, their soule with ill doth
    quaile.
27 They reele, & stagger, drunkard like, and all their witt doth faile.
28 Then did they to Iehovah cry when they were in distress:
    and therupon he bringeth them out of their anguishes.
29 Hee makes the storme a calme: so that the waves therof are still.
30 Their rest then glads them; he them brings to'th hav'n which they
    did will.
31 O that men would Iehovah prayse for his great goodnes *then:*
    & for his workings wonderfull unto the sons of men.
32 Also within the peoples Church him let them highly rayse:
    where Elders are assembled, there him also let them prayse.

(5)

33 He rivers to a desart turnes, to drought the springing well:
34 A fruitfull soyle to barrennes; for their sin there that dwell.
35 The desart to a poole he turnes; and dry ground to a spring.

36 Seates there the hungry; who prepare their towne of habiting,
37 Vineyards there also for to plant, also to sow the field;
   which may unto them fruitfull things of much revenue yield.
38 Also he blesseth them, so that they greatly are increast:
   and for to be diminished he suffers not their beast.
39 Againe they are diminished & they are brought downe low,
   by reason of their pressing-streights, affliction & sorrow.

(6)

40 On Princes he contempt doth powre; and causeth them to stray
   i'th solitary wildernes, wherin there is no way.
41 Yet hee out of affliction doth make the poore to rise:
   & like as if it were a flock.doth make him families.
42 The righteous shall it behold, and he shall joyfull bee:
   in silence stop her mouth also shall all iniquitee.
43 Who so is wise, & who so will these things attentive learne:
   the loving kindenes of the Lord they clearely shall discerne.

PSAL: CVII.

Gods goodnes to Travellers.

(1)

WITH thanks unto yᵉ LORD confess, because that good is hee:
   Because his loving kindnesses last to eternitie.
2 So say the LORDS redeem'd, whom bought he hath from th'enemys
   hands.
3 And from the East, & west hath brought from South, and northern
   lands.
4 I'th desert stray'd in desert way, no dwelling Town they find.
5 They hungry were, and thirstie they, their souls within them pin'd.
6 Then did they to Jehovah cry, when they were in distress:
Who did them set at liberty, out of their anguishes.

7 In such a way as was most right, he led them forth also:
That to a Citty which they might inhabit, they might go.
8 O that men praise Jehovah would, for his great goodnes then!
And for his wonders manifold unto the sonns of men!

[From Dunster-Lyon revision, 1651]

PSALME 141. A PSALME OF DAVID.

O GOD, my Lord, on thee I call, doe thou make hast to mee:
   and harken thou unto my voice, when I cry unto thee.
2 And let my pray'r directed be as incense in thy sight:
   and the up-lifting of my hands as sacrifice at night.

3 Iehovah: oh that thou would'st set a watch my mouth before:
as also of my lips with care o doe [thou] keepe the dore.
4 Bow not my heart to evill things; to doe the wicked deed
with wicked workers: & let not mee of their dainties feed.
5 Let just-men smite mee, kindenes 'tis; let him reprove mee eke,
it shall be such a pretious oyle, my head it shall not breake:
For yet my prayr's ev'n in their woes. (6) When their judges are cast

on rocks, then shall they heare my words, for they are sweet to taste.
7 Like unto one who on the earth doth cutt & cleave the wood,
ev'n so our bones at the graves mouth are scattered abroad.
8 But unto thee o God, the Lord directed are mine eyes:
my soule o leave not destitute, on thee my hope relyes.
9 O doe thou keepe mee from the snare which they have layd for mee;
& also from the grins of those that work iniquitee.
10 Together into their owne nets o let the wicked fall:
untill such time that I escape may make from them withall.

Solomons Song Chap: 6.

FAIREST of women, whither is thy loved gone away:
Where is thy love by-turn'd, that so seek him with thee wee may.
2 My love to's gardens down is gone: into the beds of spice,
To feed in gardens, and to get the lilly-flowrs likewise.

3 I am for my beloved one, and my belov'd for mee:
And feed among the lilly-flowers continually doth hee.
4 Thou art my love as Tirza neat, fair as Jerusalem,
Yea, terrible, as is an hoast, that doth with banners stream.

5 Turn thou from me thine eyes, because they have me overcome:
Thine hair is as a flock of goats, which look from Gilead down.
6 Thy teeth are as a flock of sheep, up from the washing gone,
Wherof each one bears twinns, of them ther's not a barren one.

7 And in such wise within thy locks, thy temples placed are:
That to a piece of Pomgranate, the same I may compare.
8 Of Queens threescore, and fourscore is of concubins the count,
There are so many Virgins as all number do surmount.

9 My dove, my undefiled one, shee is her mothers one:
Of her that did her bear alone, shee is the choicest one:
The daughters, when they her beheld, they did her blessed call,
Yea both the Queens, and concubins, they praysed her withall.

10 Who's shee y^t looks as morning forth, fair as the Moon so bright?
Clear as the Sun, and terrible as hoasts with banners dight?
11 To'th garden of the nuts I went down, valley fruits to see:
To see, if Vines did bud, if bloom did the Pomgranate tree.

12 My soul had placed me before I ever was aware,
Upon the charriots of them that my willing people are.
13 Turn, turn, O Shulamite, turn, turn, that wee may look on thee:
What will you see i'th Shulamite, as two camps company.

[From Dunster-Lyon revision, 1651]

ANNE BRADSTREET, 1612–1672

[*The Tenth Muse Lately sprung up in America. or Severall Poems, compiled
with great variety of Wit and Learning, full of delight* (London, 1650),
by Anne Bradstreet, was the first important book of poems written in
America. Daughter of Thomas Dudley, who later became governor
of the Bay Colony, she married at sixteen Simon Bradstreet, emigrated
with him in 1630, and lived a frontier life in North Andover, Massachusetts, on a farm near the Merrimac River. Here, as devoted wife
to the man who advanced to governor and royal councillor, she raised
her large family, and in moments of leisure wrote a long poem in praise
of the seasons, "together with an exact epitome of the four monarchies,"
and songs honoring Queen Elizabeth, Sidney, Spenser, and Du Bartas.
These somewhat frigid manuscript verses were taken to London by her
brother-in-law and published without her knowledge. They won the
attention of the public to such a degree that Edward Phillips in *Thea-
trum Poetarum* (1675) pronounced them "not yet wholly extinct."

Her best lyrics, however, were inspired by native settings of the
world about her or the homely events of her daily life, and a second
edition: *Several Poems Compiled . . . By a Gentlewoman in New-England
. . . Corrected by the Author* was issued posthumously at Boston in 1678.
It incorporated the "Contemplations," "The Flesh and the Spirit,"
and the delightful verses upon her husband and children. A few poems,
including the "Meditations," remained in manuscript until John H.
Ellis brought out the definitive edition of her *Works* at Charlestown,
Massachusetts, in 1867 (reprinted in New York, 1932). Her burial place
is unknown, and no portrait of her is known to exist.

See Oscar Wegelin, *comp.*, "A List of Editions of the Poems of
Anne Bradstreet, with Several Additional Books Relating to Her,"
American Book Collector, IV (1933), 15–16. See Bibliography (p. 814) for
titles of biographies. Accounts also appear in Cotton Mather, *Magnalia*,

Book II, 17; Tyler, *A History of American Literature*, I, 277–292; and *Dictionary of American Biography*. See especially the sketch in Samuel E. Morison, *Builders of the Bay Colony*, chapter XI. The text of all but "Meditations," "Verses vpon the burning of our house," and "Longing for Heaven" is from the second edition; the above named are from *Works*, ed. Ellis, 1932.]

THE TENTH MUSE

THE FOUR SEASONS OF THE YEAR.

Spring.

ANOTHER four I've left yet to bring on,
   Of four times four the last *Quaternion*,
The Winter, Summer, Autumn & the Spring,
In season all these Seasons I shall bring:
Sweet Spring like man in his Minority,
At present claim'd, and had priority.
With smiling face and garments somewhat green,
She trim'd her locks, which late had frosted been,
Nor hot nor cold, she spake, but with a breath,
Fit to revive, the nummed earth from death.
Three months (quoth she) are 'lotted to my share
March, April, May of all the rest most fair.
Tenth of the first, *Sol* intò *Aries* enters,
And bids defiance to all tedious winters,
Crosseth the Line, and equals night and day,
(Stil adds to th' last til after pleasant *May*)
And now makes glad the darkned northern wights
Who for some months have seen but starry lights.
Now goes the Plow-man to his merry toyle,
He might unloose his winter locked soyl:
The Seeds-man too, doth lavish out his grain,
In hope the more he casts, the more to gain:
The Gardner now superfluous branches lops,
And poles erects for his young clambring hops.
Now digs then sowes his herbs, his flowers & roots
And carefully manures his trees of fruits.
The *Pleiades their influence* now give,
And all that seem'd as dead afresh doth live.
The croaking frogs, whom nipping winter kil'd
Like birds now chirp, and hop about the field,
The Nightingale, the black bird and the Thrush
Now tune their layes, on sprayes of every bush.

The wanton frisking Kid, and soft-fleec'd Lambs
Do jump and play before their feeding Dams,
The tender tops of budding grass they crop,
They joy in what they have, but more in hope:
For though the frost hath lost his binding power,
Yet many a fleece of snow and stormy shower
Doth darken *Sol*'s bright eye, makes us remember
The pinching North-west wind of cold *December*.
My second moneth is *April*, green and fair,
Of longer dayes, and a more temperate Air:
The Sun in *Taurus* keeps his residence,
And with his warmer beams glanceth from thence.
This is the month whose fruitful showrs produces
All set and sown for all delights and uses:
The Pear the Plum, and Apple tree now flourish
The grass grows long the hungry beast to nourish.
The Primrose pale, and azure violet
Among the virduous grass hath nature set,
That when the Sun on's Love (the earth) doth shine,
These might as lace set out her garment fine.
The fearfull bird his little house now builds
In trees and walls, in Cities and in fields.
The outside strong, the inside warm and neat;
A natural Artificer compleat:
The clocking hen her chirping chickins leads
With wings & beak defends them from the gleads.[1]
My next and last is fruitfull pleasant *May*,
Wherein the earth is clad in rich aray,
The Sun now enters loving *Gemini*,
And heats us with the glances of his eye,
Our thicker rayment makes us lay aside
Lest by his fervor we be torrifi'd.
All flowers the Sun now with his beams discloses,
Except the double pinks and matchless Roses.
Now swarms the busy, witty, honey-Bee,
Whose praise deserves a page from more then me
The cleanly Huswifes Dary's now in th' prime,
Her shelves and firkins [2] fill'd for winter time.
The meads with Cowslips, Honey-suckles dight,
One hangs his head, the other stands upright:
But both rejoyce at th' heavens clear smiling face,
More at her showers, which water them a space.
For fruits my Season yields the early Cherry,
The hasty Peas, and wholsome cool Strawberry.
More solid fruits require a longer time,

Each Season hath his fruit, so hath each Clime:
Each man his own peculiar excellence,
But none in all that hath preheminence.
Sweet fragrant Spring, with thy short pittance fly
Let some describe thee better then can I.
Yet above all this priviledg is thine,
Thy dayes still lengthen without least decline.

CONTEMPLATIONS.

S OME time now past in the Autumnal Tide,
    When *Phœbus* wanted but one hour to bed,
The trees all richly clad, yet void of pride,
Where gilded o're by his rich golden head.
Their leaves & fruits seem'd painted, but was true
Of green, of red, of yellow, mixed hew,
Rapt were my sences at this delectable view.

2

I wist not what to wish, yet sure thought I,
If so much excellence abide below;
How excellent is he that dwells on high?
Whose power and beauty by his works we know.
Sure he is goodness, wisdome, glory, light,
That hath this under world so richly dight:
More Heaven then Earth was here, no winter & no night.

3

Then on a stately Oak I cast mine Eye,
Whose ruffling top the Clouds seem'd to aspire;
How long since thou wast in thine Infancy?
Thy strength, and stature, more thy years admire,
Hath hundred winters past since thou wast born?
Or thousand since thou brakest thy shell of horn,
If so, all these as nought, Eternity doth scorn.

4

Then higher on the glistering Sun I gaz'd,
Whose beams was shaded by the leavie Tree,
The more I look'd, the more I grew amaz'd,
And softly said, what glory's like to thee?
Soul of this world, this Universes Eye,
No wonder, some made thee a Deity:
Had I not better known, (alas) the same had I.

5

Thou as a Bridegroom from thy Chamber rushes,
And as a strong man, joyes to run a race,
The morn doth usher thee, with smiles & blushes,
The Earth reflects her glances in thy face.
Birds, insects, Animals with Vegative,
Thy heart from death and dulness doth revive:
And in the darksome womb of fruitful nature dive.

6

Thy swift Annual, and diurnal Course,
Thy daily streight, and yearly oblique path,
Thy pleasing fervor, and thy scorching force,
All mortals here the feeling knowledg hath.
Thy presence makes it day, thy absence night,
Quaternal Seasons caused by thy might:
Hail Creature, full of sweetness, beauty & delight.

7

Art thou so full of glory, that no Eye
Hath strength, thy shining Rayes once to behold?
And is thy splendid Throne erect so high?
As to approach it, can no earthly mould.
How full of glory then must thy Creator be?
Who gave this bright light luster unto thee:
Admir'd, ador'd for ever, be that Majesty.

8

Silent alone, where none or saw, or heard,
In pathless paths I lead my wandring feet,
My humble Eyes to lofty Skyes I rear'd
To sing some Song, my mazed Muse thought meet.
My great Creator I would magnifie,
That nature had, thus decked liberally:
But Ah, and Ah, again, my imbecility!

9

I heard the merry grashopper then sing,
The black clad Cricket, bear a second part,
They kept one tune, and plaid on the same string,
Seeming to glory in their little Art.
Shall Creatures abject, thus their voices raise?
And in their kind resound their makers praise:
Whilst I as mute, can warble forth no higher layes.

10

When present times look back to Ages past,
And men in being fancy those are dead,
It makes things gone perpetually to last,
And calls back moneths and years that long since fled.
It makes a man more aged in conceit,
Then was *Methuselah*, or's grand-sire great:
While of their persons & their acts his mind doth treat.

11

Sometimes in *Eden* fair, he seems to be,
Sees glorious *Adam* there made Lord of all,
Fancyes the Apple, dangle on the Tree,
That turn'd his Sovereign to a naked thral.
Who like a miscreant's driven from that place,
To get his bread with pain, and sweat of face:
A penalty impos'd on his backsliding Race.

12

Here sits our Grandame in retired place,
And in her lap, her bloody *Cain* new born,
The weeping Imp oft looks her in the face,
Bewails his unknown hap, and fate forlorn;
His Mother sighs, to think of Paradise,
And how she lost her bliss, to be more wise,
Believing him that was, and is, Father of lyes.

13

Here *Cain* and *Abel* come to sacrifice,
Fruits of the Earth, and Fatlings each do bring,
On *Abels* gift the fire descends from Skies,
But no such sign on false *Cain's* offering;
With sullen hateful looks he goes his wayes.
Hath thousand thoughts to end his brothers dayes,
Upon whose blood his future good he hopes to raise

14

There *Abel* keeps his sheep, no ill he thinks,
His brother comes, then acts his fratricide,
The Virgin Earth, of blood her first draught drinks
But since that time she often hath been cloy'd;
The wretch with gastly face and dreadful mind,
Thinks each he sees will serve him in his kind,
Though none on Earth but kindred near then could he find.

15

Who fancyes not his looks now at the Barr,
His face like death, his heart with horror fraught,
Nor Male-factor ever felt like warr,
When deep dispair, with wish of life hath sought,
Branded with guilt, and crusht with treble woes,
A Vagabond to Land of *Nod* [3] he goes.
A City builds, that wals might him secure from foes.

16

Who thinks not oft upon the Fathers ages.
Their long descent, how nephews sons they saw,
The starry observations of those Sages,
And how their precepts to their sons were law,
How Adam sigh'd to see his Progeny,
Cloath'd all in his black sinfull Livery,
Who neither guilt, nor yet the punishment could fly.

17

Our Life compare we with their length of dayes
Who to the tenth of theirs doth now arrive?
And though thus short, we shorten many wayes,
Living so little while we are alive;
In eating, drinking, sleeping, vain delight
So unawares comes on perpetual night,
And puts all pleasures vain unto eternal flight.

18

When I behold the heavens as in their prime,
And then the earth (though old) stil clad in green,
The stones and trees, insensible of time,
Nor age nor wrinkle on their front are seen;
If winter come, and greeness then do fade,
A Spring returns, and they more youthfull made;
But Man grows old, lies down, remains where once he's laid.

20 [19]

By birth more noble then those creatures all,
Yet seems by nature and by custome curs'd,
No sooner born, but grief and care makes fall
That state obliterate he had at first:
Nor youth, nor strength, nor wisdom spring again
Nor habitations long their names retain,
But in oblivion to the final day remain.

20

Shall I then praise the heavens, the trees, the earth
Because their beauty and their strength last longer
Shall I wish there, or never to had birth,
Because they're bigger, & their bodyes stronger?
Nay, they shall darken, perish, fade and dye,
And when unmade, so ever shall they lye,
But man was made for endless immortality.

21

Under the cooling shadow of a stately Elm
Close sate I by a goodly Rivers side,
Where gliding streams the Rocks did overwhelm;
A lonely place, with pleasures dignifi'd.
I once that lov'd the shady woods so well,
Now thought the rivers did the trees excel,
And if the sun would ever shine, there would I dwell.

22

While on the stealing stream I fixt mine eye,
Which to the long'd for Ocean held its course,
I markt, nor crooks, nor rubs that there did lye
Could hinder ought, but still augment its force:
O happy Flood, quoth I, that holds thy race
Till thou arrive at thy beloved place,
Nor is it rocks or shoals that can obstruct thy pace

23

Nor is't enough, that thou alone may'st slide,
But hundred brooks in thy cleer waves do meet,
So hand in hand along with thee they glide
To *Thetis* house,[4] where all imbrace and greet:
Thou Emblem true, of what I count the best,
O could I lead my Rivolets to rest,
So may we press to that vast mansion, ever blest.

24

Ye Fish which in this liquid Region 'bide,
That for each season, have your habitation,
Now salt, now fresh where you think best to glide
To unknown coasts to give a visitation,
In Lakes and ponds, you leave your numerous fry,
So nature taught, and yet you know not why,
You watry folk that know not your felicity.

25

Look how the wantons frisk to tast the air,
Then to the colder bottome streight they dive,
Eftsoon to *Neptun*'s glassie Hall repair
To see what trade they great ones there do drive,
Who forrage o're the spacious sea-green field,
And take the trembling prey before it yield,
Whose armour is their scales, their spreading fins their shield.

26

While musing thus with contemplation fed,
And thousand fancies buzzing in my brain,
The sweet-tongu'd Philomel [5] percht ore my head,
And chanted forth a most melodious strain
Which rapt me so with wonder and delight,
I judg'd my hearing better then my sight,
And wisht me wings with her a while to take my flight.

28 [27]

O merry Bird (said I) that fears no snares,
That neither toyles nor hoards up in thy barn,
Feels no sad thoughts, nor cruciating cares
To gain more good, or shun what might thee harm
Thy cloaths ne're wear, thy meat is every where,
Thy bed a bough, thy drink the water cleer,
Reminds not what is past, nor whats to come dost **fear**.

28

The dawning morn with songs thou dost prevent,[6]
Sets hundred notes unto thy feathered crew,
So each one tunes his pretty instrument,
And warbling out the old, begin anew,
And thus they pass their youth in summer season,
Then follow thee into a better Region,
Where winter's never felt by that sweet airy legion.

29

Man at the best a creature frail and vain,
In knowledg ignorant, in strength but weak,
Subject to sorrows, losses, sickness, pain,
Each storm his state, his mind, his body break,
From some of these he never finds cessation,
But day or night, within, without, vexation,
Troubles from foes, from friends, from dearest, near'st Relation.

30

And yet this sinfull creature, frail and vain,
This lump of wretchedness, of sin and sorrow,
This weather-beaten vessel wrackt with pain,
Joyes not in hope of an eternal morrow;
Nor all his losses, crosses and vexation,
In weight, in frequency and long duration
Can make him deeply groan for that divine Translation.

31

The Mariner that on smooth waves doth glide,
Sings merrily, and steers his Barque with ease,
As if he had command of wind and tide,
And now become great Master of the seas;
But suddenly a storm spoiles all the sport,
And makes him long for a more quiet port,
Which 'gainst all adverse winds may serve for fort.

32

So he that saileth in this world of pleasure,
Feeding on sweets, that never bit of th' sowre,
That's full of friends, of honour and of treasure,
Fond fool, he takes this earth ev'n for heav'ns bower.
But sad affliction comes & makes him see
Here's neither honour, wealth, nor safety;
Only above is found all with security.

33

O Time the fatal wrack of mortal things,
That draws oblivions curtains over kings,
Their sumptuous monuments, men know them not,
Their names without a Record are forgot,
Their parts, their ports, their pomp's all laid in th' dust
Nor wit nor gold, nor buildings scape times rust;
But he whose name is grav'd in the white stone [7]
Shall last and shine when all of these are gone.

THE FLESH AND THE SPIRIT. [8]

IN secret place where once I stood
     Close by the Banks of *Lacrim* flood
I heard two sisters reason on
Things that are past, and things to come;
One flesh was call'd, who had her eye
On worldly wealth and vanity;

The other Spirit, who did rear
Her thoughts unto a higher sphere:
Sister, quoth Flesh, what liv'st thou on
Nothing but Meditation?
Doth Contemplation feed thee so
Regardlesly to let earth goe?
Can Speculation satisfy
Notion without Reality?
Dost dream of things beyond the Moon
And dost thou hope to dwell there soon?
Hast treasures there laid up in store
That all in th' world thou count'st but poor?
Art fancy sick, or turn'd a Sot
To catch at shadowes which are not?
Come, come, Ile shew unto thy sence,
Industry hath its recompence.
What canst desire, but thou maist see
True substance in variety?
Dost honour like? acquire the same,
As some to their immortal fame:
And trophyes to thy name erect
Which wearing time shall ne're deject.
For riches dost thou long full sore?
Behold enough of precious store.
Earth hath more silver, pearls and gold,
Then eyes can see, or hands can hold.
Affect's thou pleasure? take thy fill,
Earth hath enough of what you will.
Then let not goe, what thou maist find,
For things unknown, only in mind.
Spir. Be still thou unregenerate part,
Disturb no more my setled heart,
For I have vow'd, (and so will doe)
Thee as a foe, still to pursue.
And combate with thee will and must,
Untill I see thee laid in th' dust.
Sisters we are, ye[a] twins we be,
Yet deadly feud 'twixt thee and me;
For from one father are we not,
Thou by old Adam wast begot,
But my arise is from above,
Whence my dear father I do love.
Thou speakst me fair, but hatst me sore,
Thy flatt'ring shews Ile trust no more.
How oft thy slave, hast thou me made,

when I believ'd, what thou hast said,
And never had more cause of woe
Then when I did what thou bad'st doe.
Ile stop mine ears at these thy charms,
And count them for my deadly harms.
Thy sinfull pleasures I doe hate,
Thy riches are to me no bait,
Thine honours doe, nor will I love;
For my ambition lyes above.
My greatest honour it shall be
When I am victor over thee,
And triumph shall, with laurel head,
When thou my Captive shalt be led,
How I do live, thou need'st not scoff,
For I have meat thou know'st not off;
The hidden Manna I doe eat,
The word of life it is my meat.
My thoughts do yield me more content
Then can thy hours in pleasure spent.
Nor are they shadows which I catch,
Nor fancies vain at which I snatch,
But reach at things that are so high,
Beyond thy dull Capacity;
Eternal substance I do see,
With which inriched I would be:
Mine Eye doth pierce the heavens, and see
What is Invisible to thee.
My garments are not silk nor gold,
Nor such like trash which Earth doth hold,
But Royal Robes I shall have on,
More glorious then the glistring Sun;
My Crown not Diamonds, Pearls, and gold,
But such as Angels heads infold.
The City [9] where I hope to dwell,
There's none on Earth can parallel;
The stately Walls both high and strong,
Are made of pretious *Jasper* stone;
The Gates of Pearl, both rich and clear,
And Angels are for Porters there;
The Streets thereof transparent gold,
Such as no Eye did e're behold,
A Chrystal River there doth run,
Which doth proceed from the Lambs Throne:
Of Life, there are the waters sure,
Which shall remain for ever pure,

Nor Sun, nor Moon, they have no need,
For glory doth from God proceed:
No Candle there, nor yet Torch light,
For there shall be no darksome night.
From sickness and infirmity,
For evermore they shall be free,
Nor withering age shall e're come there,
But beauty shall be bright and clear;
This City pure is not for thee,
For things unclean there shall not be:
If I of Heaven may have my fill,
Take thou the world, and all that will.

To my Dear and loving Husband.

IF EVER two were one, then surely we.
  If ever man were lov'd by wife, then thee;
If ever wife was happy in a man,
Compare with me ye women if you can.
I prize thy love more then whole Mines of gold,
Or all the riches that the East doth hold.
My love is such that Rivers cannot quench,
Nor ought but love from thee, give recompence.
Thy love is such I can no way repay,
The heavens reward thee manifold I pray.
Then while we live, in love lets so persever,
That when we live no more, we may live ever.

A Letter to her Husband, absent upon Publick employment.

MY HEAD, my heart, mine Eyes, my life, nay more,
  My joy, my Magazine of earthly store,
If two be one, as surely thou and I,
How stayest thou there, whilst I at *Ipswich* lye?
So many steps, head from the heart to sever
If but a neck, soon should we be together:
I like the earth this season, mourn in black,
My Sun is gone so far in's Zodiack,
Whom whilst I 'joy'd, nor storms, nor frosts I felt,
His warmth such frigid colds did cause to melt.
My chilled limbs now nummed lye forlorn;
Return, return sweet *Sol* from *Capricorn;* [10]
In this dead time, alas, what can I more
Then view those fruits which through thy heat I bore?

Which sweet contentment yield me for a space,
True living Pictures of their Fathers face.
O strange effect! now thou art *Southward* gone,
I weary grow, the tedious day so long;
But when thou *Northward* to me shalt return,
I wish my Sun may never set, but burn
Within the Cancer [11] of my glowing breast,
The welcome house of him my dearest guest.
Where ever, ever stay, and go not thence,
Till natures sad decree shall call thee hence;
Flesh of thy flesh, bone of thy bone,
I here, thou there, yet both but one.

MEDITATIONS WHEN MY SOUL HATH BEEN REFRESHED WITH THE CONSOLATIONS WHICH THE WORLD KNOWES NOT

I.

LORD, why should I doubt any more when thov hast given me such assured Pledges of thy Loue? First, thov art my Creator, I thy creature; thov my master, I thy servant. But hence arises not my comfort: Thov art my Father, I thy child. Yee shall [be] my Sons and Daughters, saith the Lord Almighty. Christ is my Brother; I ascend vnto my Father and your Father, vnto my God and your God. But least this should not bee enough, thy maker is thy husband. Nay, more, I am a member of his Body; he, my head. Such Priviledges, had not the Word of Truth made them known, who or where is the man that durst in his heart haue presumed to haue thought it? So wonderfull are these thoughts that my spirit failes in me at the consideration thereof; and I am confovnded to think that God, who hath done so much for me, should haue so little from me. But this is my comfort, when I come into Heaven, I shall vnderstand perfectly what he hath done for me, and then shall I bee able to praise him as I ovght. Lord, haueing this hope, let me purefie myself as thou art Pure, and let me bee no more affraid of Death, but even desire to bee dissolved, and bee with thee, which is best of All. . . .

IX.

Sweet words are like hony, a little may refresh, but too much gluts the stomach.

X.

Diuerse children haue their different natures; some are like flesh which nothing but salt will keep from putrefaction; some again like tender fruits that are best preserued with sugar: those parents are wise that can fit their nurture according to their Nature.

XI.

That town which thousands of enemys without hath not been able to take, hath been deliuered vp by one traytor within; and that man, which all the temptations of Sathan without could not hurt, hath been foild by one lust within.

XII.

Authority without wisedome is like a heavy axe without an edg, fitter to bruise then polish.

XIII.

The reason why christians are so loth to exchang this world for a better, is because they haue more sence then faith: they se what they injoy, they do but hope for that which is to Come.

XIV.

If we had no winter the spring would not be so pleasant: if we did not sometimes tast of adversity, prosperity would not be so welcome.

XV.

A low man can goe vpright vnder that door, wher a taller is glad to stoop; so a man of weak faith and mean abilities, may vndergo a crosse more patiently then he that excells him, both in gifts and graces.

XVI.

That house which is not often swept, makes the cleanly inhabitant soone loath it, and that heart which is not continually purifieing it self, is no fit temple for the spirit of god to dwell in.

XVII.

Few men are so humble as not to be proud of their abilitys; and nothing will abase them more then this,—What hast thou, but what thou hast receiued? come giue an account of thy stewardship. . . .

XXVII.

It is a pleasant thing to behold the light, but sore eyes are not able to look vpon it; the pure in heart shall se God, but the defiled in conscience shall rather choose to be buried vnder rocks and mountains then to behold the presence of the Lamb.

XXVIII.

Wisedome with an inheritance is good, but wisedome without an inheritance is better then an inheritance without wisedome.

XXIX.

Lightening doth vsually preceed thunder, and stormes, raine; and stroaks do not often fall till after threat'ning.

XXX.

Yellow leaues argue want of sap, and gray haires want of moisture; so dry and saplesse performances are simptoms of little spiritall vigor.

XXXI.

Iron till it be throughly heat is vncapable to be wrought; so God sees good to cast some men into the furnace of affliction, and then beats them on his anuile into what frame he pleases.

XXXII.

Ambitious men are like hops that neuer rest climbing soe long as they haue any thing to stay vpon; but take away their props and they are, of all, the most dejected.

XXXIII.

Much Labour wearys the body, and many thoughts oppresse the minde: man aimes at profit by the one, and content in the other; but often misses of both, and findes nothing but vanity and vexation of spirit.

XXXIV.

Dimne eyes are the concomitants of old age; and short sightednes, in those that are eyes of a Republique, foretels a declineing State.

XXXV.

We read in Scripture of three sorts of Arrows,—the arrow of an enemy, the arrow of pestilence, and the arrow of a slanderous tongue; the two first kill the body, the last the good name; the two former leaue a man when he is once dead, but the last mangles him in his graue. . . .

LXIII.

He that would keep a pure heart, and lead a blamlesse life, must set himself alway in the awefull presence of God, the consideration of his all-seeing eye will be a bridle to restrain from evill, and a spur to quicken on to good dutys: we certainly dream of some remotnes betwixt God and vs, or else we should not so often faile in our whole Course of life as we doe; but he, that with David, sets the Lord alway in his sight, will not sinne against him.

LXIV.

We see in orchards some trees soe fruitfull, that the waight of their Burden is the breaking of their limbes; some again are but meanly loaden; and some haue nothing to shew but leaues only; and some among them are dry stocks: so is it in the church, which is Gods orchard, there are some eminent Christians that are soe frequent in good dutys, that many times the waight therof impares both their bodys and estates; and there are some (and they sincere ones too) who haue not attained to that fruitfullnes, altho they aime at perfection: And again there are others that haue nothing to commend them but only a gay proffession, and these are but leavie christians, which are in as much danger of being cut down as the dry stock, for both cumber the ground.

LXV.

We see in the firmament there is but one Sun among a multitude of starres, and those starres also to differ much one from the other in regard of bignes and brightnes, yet all receiue their light from that one Sun: so is it in the church both militant and triumphant, there is but one Christ, who is the Sun of righteousnes, in the midest of an innumerable company of Saints and Angels; those Saintes haue their degrees euen in this life, some are Stars of the first magnitude, and some of a lesse degree; and others (and they indeed the most in number), but small and obscure, yet all receiue their luster (be it more or lesse) from that glorious sun that inlightens all in all; and, if some of them shine so bright while they moue on earth, how transcendently splendid shall they be, when they are fixt in their heauenly spheres!

HERE FOLLOWES SOME VERSES VPON THE BURNING OF OUR HOUSE, JULY IOTH, 1666. COPYED OVT OF A LOOSE PAPER.

> In silent night when rest I took,
> For sorrow neer I did not look,
> I waken'd was with thundring nois
> And Piteovs shreiks of dreadfull voice.
> That fearfull sound of fire and fire,
> Let no man know is my Desire.
>
> I, starting vp, the light did spye,
> And to my God my heart did cry
> To strengthen me in my Distresse
> And not to leaue me succourlesse.
> Then coming ovt beheld a space,
> The flame consvme my dwelling place.

And, when I could no longer look,
I blest his Name that gave and took,
That layd my goods now in the dvst:
Yea so it was, and so 'twas jvst.
It was his own: it was not mine;
Far be it that I should repine.

He might of All justly bereft,
But yet sufficient for us left.
When by the Ruines oft I past,
My sorrowing eyes aside did cast,
And here and there the places spye
Where oft I sate, and long did lye.

Here stood that Trunk, and there that chest;
There lay that store I covnted best:
My pleasant things in ashes lye,
And them behold no more shall I.
Vnder thy roof no gvest shall sitt,
Nor at thy Table eat a bitt.

No pleasant tale shall 'ere be told,
Nor things recovnted done of old.
No Candle 'ere shall shine in Thee,
Nor bridegroom's voice ere heard shall bee.
In silence ever shalt thou lye;
Adeiu, Adeiu; All's vanity.

Then streight I gin my heart to chide,
And did thy wealth on earth abide?
Didst fix thy hope on mouldring dvst,
The arm of flesh didst make thy trvst?
Raise vp thy thovghts above the skye
That dunghill mists away may flie.

Thou hast an house on high erect,
Fram'd by that mighty Architect,
With glory richly furnished,
Stands permanent though: this bee fled.
It's purchaséd, and paid for too
By him who hath enovgh to doe.

A Prise so vast as is vnknown,
Yet, by his Gift, is made thine own.
Ther's wealth enovgh, I need no more;
Farewell my Pelf, farewell my Store.

The world no longer let me Love,
My hope and Treasure lyes Above.

[LONGING FOR HEAVEN]

As WEARY pilgrim, now at rest,
  Hugs with delight his silent nest
His wasted limbes, now lye full soft
  That myrie steps, haue troden oft
Blesses himself, to think vpon
  his dangers past, and travailes done
The burning sun no more shall heat
  Nor stormy raines, on him shall beat.
The bryars and thornes no more shall scratch
  nor hungry wolues at him shall catch
He erring pathes no more shall tread
  nor wild fruits eate, in stead of bread,
for waters cold he doth not long
  for thirst no more shall parch his tongue
No rugged stones his feet shall gaule
  nor stumps nor rocks cause him to fall
All cares and feares, he bids farwell
  and meanes in safity now to dwell.
A pilgrim I, on earth, perplext
  wth sinns wth cares and sorrows vext
By age and paines brought to decay
  and my Clay house mouldring away
Oh how I long to be at rest
  and soare on high among the blest.
This body shall in silence sleep
  Mine eyes no more shall ever weep
No fainting fits shall me assaile
  nor grinding paines my body fraile
Wth cares and fears ne'r cumbred be
  Nor losses know, nor sorrowes see
What tho my flesh shall there consume
  it is the bed Christ did perfume
And when a few yeares shall be gone
  this mortall shall be cloth'd vpon
A Corrupt Carcasse downe it lyes
  a glorious body it shall rise
In weaknes and dishonour sowne
  in power 'tis rais'd by Christ alone
Then soule and body shall vnite
  and of their maker haue the sight

NATHANIEL WARD, JOHN ROGERS, AND
JOHN NORTON

[It was customary for publishers to invite poets and scholars to write commendatory verses by way of introducing an author to the public. The aged and distinguished "simple cobler," Nathaniel Ward, who returned to England in 1646, had been a neighbor of Mrs. Bradstreet, and contributed his sprightly lines to the first edition of *The Tenth Muse*. Since Ward had previously expressed contempt for women's talents, his praise may have attracted particular notice. For an account of Ward, see *ante* p. 225. The text is from the first edition.

In the Boston edition of Mrs. Bradstreet's *Several Poems* (1678), new commendatory offerings were included, among which the verses "Vpon Mrs. Anne Bradstreet Her Poems, etc." by John Rogers (1631–1684) of Ipswich, and "A Funeral Elogy" by the Rev. John Norton (1651–1716) of Hingham deserve to be remembered. Rogers's wife was a niece of Mrs. Bradstreet. He was son of the Rev. Nathaniel Rogers of Ipswich, and though he studied divinity, he was never ordained. Offered the presidency of Harvard in 1677, he declined it to devote himself to medicine, but he later reconsidered, and served in that office the two years before his death. See Tyler, *A History of American Literature*, II, 12–15; Sibley, *Biographical Sketches*, I, 166–171; and Samuel E. Morison, *Harvard College in the Seventeenth Century*, 430–445.

John Norton, ancestor of Charles Eliot Norton, was nephew of the famous Rev. John Norton of Boston and grand-nephew of Governor Winthrop. He published, besides the poem below, but one sermon, yet this "Elogy" will keep his memory alive, for as Tyler remarks (*ibid.*, p. 10), "here is something more than mechanic poetry, something other than inspiration of the thumb-nail." It has been suggested that Norton may have edited *Several Poems* (*New England Historical and Genealogical Register*, IX, 113 note). See also Sibley, *op. cit.*, II, 394–396; Tyler, *op. cit.*, II, 9–11. The text of both the Rogers and Norton selections is from *Several Poems*, 1678.]

ON MRS. BRADSTREET'S TENTH MUSE

MERCURY shew'd *Apollo, Bartas* Book,[1]
    Minerva this, and wisht him well to look,
And tell uprightly, which, did which excell;
He view'd, and view'd, and vow'd he could not tell.
They bid him Hemisphear his mouldy nose,
With's crackt leering-glasses, for it would pose

The best brains he had in's old pudding-pan,
Sex weigh'd, which best, the Woman, or the Man?
He peer'd, and por'd, and glar'd, and said for wore,[2]
I'me even as wise now, as I was before:
They both 'gan laugh, and said, it was no mar'l [3]
The Auth'resse was a right *Du Bartas* Girle.
Good sooth quoth the old *Don*, tel ye me so,
I muse whither at length these Girls wil go;
It half revives my chil frost-bitten blood,
To see a woman, once, do ought that's good;
And chode buy [4] *Chaucers* Boots, and *Homers* Furrs,
Let men look to't, least women weare the Spurs.

N. Ward.

VPON
MRS. ANNE BRADSTREET

HER POEMS, &c.

MADAM, twice through the Muses Grove I walkt,
    Under your blissfull bowres, I shrowding [5] there,
It seem'd with Nymphs of *Helicon* I talkt:
For there those sweet-lip'd Sisters sporting were,
Apollo with his sacred Lute sate by,
On high they made their heavenly Sonnets flye,
Posies around they strow'd, of sweetest Poesie.

2

Twice have I drunk the Nectar of your lines,
Which high sublim'd my mean born phantasie,
Flusht with these streams of your *Maronean* wines [6]
Above my self rapt to an extasie:
Methought I was upon Mount *Hiblas* top,[7]
There where I might those fragrant flowers lop,
Whence did sweet odors flow, and honey spangles drop.

3

To *Venus* shrine no Altars raised are,
Nor venom'd shafts from painted quiver fly,
Nor wanton Doves of *Aphrodites* Carr,
Or fluttering there, nor here forlornly lie,
Lorne Paramours, not chatting birds tell news
How sage *Apollo*, *Daphne* hot pursues,
Or stately *Jove* himself is wont to haunt the stews.

4

Nor barking Satyrs breath, nor driery [8] clouds
Exhal'd from *Styx*, their dismal drops distil
Within these *Fairy*, flowry fields, nor shrouds
The screeching night Raven, with his shady quill:
But Lyrick strings here *Orpheus* nimbly hitts,
Orion on his sadled Dolphin sits,
Chanting as every humour, age & season fits.

5

Here silver swans, with Nightingales set spells,
Which sweetly charm the Traveller, and raise
Earths earthed Monarchs, from their hidden Cells,
And to appearance summons lapsed dayes,
There heav'nly air, becalms the swelling frayes,[9]
And fury fell of Elements allayes,
By paying every one due tribute of his praise.

6

This seem'd the Scite [10] of all those verdant vales,
And purled springs, whereat the Nymphs do play,
With lofty hills, where Poets rear their tales,
To heavenly vaults, which heav'nly sound repay
By ecchoes sweet rebound, here Ladyes kiss,
Circling nor songs, nor dances circle miss;
But whilst those Syrens sung, I sunk in sea of bliss.

7

Thus weltring in delight, my virgin mind
Admits a rape; truth still lyes undiscri'd,
Its singular, that plural seem'd, I find,
'Twas Fancies glass alone that multipli'd;
Nature with Art so closely did combine,
I thought I saw the Muses trebble trine,
Which prov'd your lonely Muse, superiour to the nine.

8

Your only hand those Poesies did compose,
Your head the source, whence all those springs did flow,
Your voice, whence changes sweetest notes arose,
Your feet that kept the dance alone, I trow:
Then vail your bonnets, Poetasters all,
Strike, lower amain, and at these humbly fall,
And deem your selves advanc'd to be her Pedestal.

9

Should all with lowly Congies [11] Laurels bring,
Waste *Floraes* Magazine to find a wreathe;
Or *Pineus* [12] Banks 'twere too mean offering,
Your Muse a fairer Garland doth bequeath
To guard your fairer front; here 'tis your name
Shall stand immarbled; this your little frame
Shall great *Colossus* be, to your eternal fame.

I'le please my self, though I my self disgrace,
What errors here be found, are in *Errataes* place.

J. Rogers.

A FUNERAL ELOGY,

Upon that Pattern and Patron of Virtue, the truely pious,
peerless & matchless Gentlewoman

Mrs. Anne Bradstreet,

right Panaretes, [13]

Mirror of Her Age, Glory of her Sex, whose Heaven-born-Soul
leaving its earthly Shrine, chose its native home, and was
taken to its Rest, upon 16th. Sept. 1672.

Ask not why hearts turn Magazines of passions,
And why that grief is clad in sev'ral fashions;
Why She on progress goes, and doth not borrow
The smallest respite from th' extreams of sorrow,
Her misery is got to such an height,
As makes the earth groan to support its weight,
Such storms of woe, so strongly have beset her,
She hath no place for worse, nor hope for better;
Her comfort is, if any for her be,
That none can shew more cause of grief then she.
Ask not why some in mournfull black are clad;
The Sun is set, there needs must be a shade.
Ask not why every face a sadness shrowdes;
The setting Sun ore-cast us hath with Clouds.
Ask not why the great glory of the Skye
That gilds the starrs with heavenly Alchamy,
Which all the world doth lighten with his rayes,
The *Perslan* [14] God, the Monarch of the dayes;
Ask not the reason of his extasie,
Paleness of late, in midnoon Majesty,

Why that the palefac'd Empress of the night
Disrob'd her brother of his glorious light.
Did not the language of the starrs foretel
A mournfull Scœne when they with tears did swell?
Did not the glorious people of the Skye
Seem sensible of future misery?
Did not the lowring heavens seem to express
The worlds great lose, and their unhappiness?
Behold how tears flow from the learned hill,
How the bereaved Nine do daily fill
The bosome of the fleeting Air with groans,
And wofull Accents, which witness their moanes.
How doe the Goddesses of verse, the learned quire
Lament their rival Quill, which all admire?
Could *Maro*'s [15] Muse but hear her lively strain,
He would condemn his works to fire again.
Methinks I hear the Patron of the Spring,
The unshorn Deity abruptly sing.
Some doe for anguish weep, for anger I
That Ignorance should live, and Art should die.
Black, fatal, dismal, inauspicious day,
Unblest for ever by *Sol*'s precious Ray,
Be it the first of Miseries to all;
Or last of Life, defam'd for Funeral.
When this day yearly comes, let every one,
Cast in their urne, the black and dismal stone.
Succeeding years as they their circuit goe,
Leap o're this day, as a sad time of woe.
Farewell my Muse, since thou hast left thy shrine,
I am unblest in one, but blest in nine.
Fair *Thespian* Ladyes, light your torches all,
Attend your glory to its Funeral,
To court her ashes with a learned tear,
A briny sacrifice, let not a smile appear.
Grave Matron, whoso seeks to blazon thee,
Needs not make use of witts false Heraldry;
Whoso should give thee all thy worth would swell
So high, as 'twould turn the world infidel.
Had he great *Maro*'s Muse, or *Tully*'s [16] tongue,
Or raping numbers like the *Thracian* Song,
In crowning of her merits he would be
Sumptuously poor, low in Hyperbole.
To write is easie; but to write on thee,
Truth would be thought to forfeit modesty.
He'l seem a Poet that shall speak but true;

Hyperbole's in others, are thy due.
Like a most servile flatterer he will show
Though he write truth, and make the subject, You.[17]
Virtue ne're dies, time will a Poet raise
Born under better Starrs, shall sing thy praise.
Praise her who list, yet he shall be a debtor
For Art ne're feign'd, nor Nature fram'd a better.
Her virtues were so great, that they do raise
A work to trouble fame, astonish praise.
When as her Name doth but salute the ear,
Men think that they perfections abstract hear.
Her breast was a brave Pallace, a *Broad-street*,
Where all heroick ample thoughts did meet,
Where nature such a Tenement had tane,
That others souls, to hers, dwelt in a lane.
Beneath her feet, pale envy bites her chain,
And poison Malice, whetts her sting in vain.
Let every Laurel, every Myrtel bough
Be stript for leaves t' adorn and load her brow.
Victorious wreathes, which 'cause they never fade
Wise elder times for Kings and Poets made.
Let not her happy memory e're lack
Its worth in Fames eternal Almanack,
Which none shall read, but straight their loss deplore,
And blame their Fates they were not born before.
Do not old men rejoyce their Fates did last,
And infants too, that theirs did make such hast,
In such a welcome time to bring them forth,
That they might be a witness to her worth.
Who undertakes this subject to commend
Shall nothing find so hard as how to end.

      Finis & non. John Norton.

  Omnia Romanæ *sileant Miracula Gentis.*[18]

MICHAEL WIGGLESWORTH, 1631–1705

[The eighteen hundred copies of *The Day of Doom: or A Poetical Description of the Great and Last Judgement* (Cambridge, 1662), were exhausted within a year, and no copy of the first edition is known to survive. It was immediately re-issued here and in England. It was published in broadside and hawked about the country. In the next two centuries it appeared frequently, and was last printed as recently as 1929. In the same year that it was first published Michael Wigglesworth wrote "Gods Controversy with New-England. Written in the time of the great drought," wherein the backslidings of the time are indicated as the reason that New England has become "A waste and howling wilderness." The poem has been published in *Proceedings of the Massachusetts Historical Society*, XII (1873), 83–93, from which the present selection has been taken. Wigglesworth's last verses appeared in *Meat out of the Eater or Meditations Concerning The Necessity, End, and Usefulness of Affliction unto Gods Children*. The only known copy of the first edition of 1670 is in the Yale University Library.

See Matt B. Jones, "Notes for a Bibliography of Michael Wigglesworth's *Day of Doom* and *Meat out of the Eater*," *Proceedings of the American Antiquarian Society*, N.S. XXXIX (1929), 77–84; and *idem*, "Michael Wigglesworth's *Meat Out of the Eater:* The hitherto unknown First Edition," *Yale University Gazette*, V (1931), 45–47. See also Francis O. Matthiessen, "Michael Wigglesworth, A Puritan Artist," *New England Quarterly*, I (1928), 491–504; Kenneth B. Murdock, *ed.*, *The Day of Doom*, with introduction (New York, 1929); John W. Dean, *Memoir of Rev. Michael Wigglesworth*, second ed., Albany, 1871; "Letters of Michael Wigglesworth to Increase Mather," *Collections of the Massachusetts Historical Society*, fourth series, VIII, 645–647; Moses C. Tyler, *A History of American Literature*, II, 23–35; John L. Sibley, *Biographical Sketches*, I, 259–286; and especially Samuel E. Morison, *Harvard College in the Seventeenth Century, passim*. Several unpublished Wigglesworth MSS are in possession of the New England Historical Genealogical Society and of the Massachusetts Historical Society. The text of *Meat out of the Eater* here reproduced is from the fourth edition of 1689; that of *The Day of Doom* is from the fifth edition (1701), the last to appear in the author's lifetime.]

A PRAYER UNTO CHRIST THE JUDGE
OF THE WORLD.

O DEAREST Dread, most glorious King,
   I'le of thy justest Judgments sing:
Do thou my head and heart inspire,
To Sing aright, as I desire.
Thee, thee alone I'le invocate,
For I do much abominate
To call the *Muses* to mine aid:
Which is th' Unchristian use, and trade
Of some that Christians would be thought,

And yet they worship worse then nought.
Oh! what a deal of Blasphemy,
And Heathenish Impiety,
In Christian Poets may be found,
Where Heathen gods with praise are Crown'd,
They make *Jehovah* to stand by,
Till *Juno, Venus, Mercury,*
With frowning *Mars,* and thundering *Jove,*
Rule Earth below, and Heaven above.
But I have learnt to pray to none,
Save unto God in Christ alone.
Nor will I laud, no not in jest,
That which I know God doth detest.
I reckon it a damning evil
To give Gods Praises to the Devil.
Thou, *Christ,* art he to whom I pray,
Thy Glory fain I would display.
Oh! guide me by thy sacred Sprite
So to indite, and so to write,
That I thine holy Name may praise,
And teach the Sons of men thy wayes.

[Prefatory lines to *The Day of Doom*]

THE DAY OF DOOM.

(1)

STILL was the night, Serene and Bright, when all Men *The Security*
   sleeping lay; *of the World*
Calm was the season, and carnal reason thought so 'twould *before Christs*
   last for ay. *coming to*
    Judgment.
Soul, take thine ease, let sorrow cease, much good thou *Luk.* 12: 19.
   hast in store:
This was their Song, their Cups among, the Evening
   before.

(2)

Wallowing in all kind of sin, vile wretches lay secure:[1]
The best of men had scarcely then their Lamps kept in *Mat.* 25: 5.
   good ure.[2]
Virgins unwise, who through disguise amongst the best
   were number'd,
Had clos'd their eyes; yea, and the wise through sloth
   and frailty slumber'd.

(3)

Mat. 24:
37, 38.
Like as of old,[3] when Men grow bold Gods' threatnings
    to contemn,
Who stopt their Ear, and would not hear, when Mercy
    warned them:
But took their course, without remorse, till God began
    to powre
Destruction the World upon in a tempestuous showre.

(4)

They put away the evil day, And drown'd their care
    and fears,
Till drown'd were they, and swept away by vengeance
    unawares:
1 *Thes.* 5: 3.
So at the last, whilst Men sleep fast in their security,
Surpriz'd they are in such a snare as cometh suddenly.

(5)

*The Sud-
denness,
Majesty,
& Terror
of Christ's
appearing.*
Mat. 25: 6.
2 Pet. 3: 10.
For at midnight brake forth a Light, which turn'd the
    night to day,
And speedily an hideous cry did all the world dismay.
Sinners awake, their hearts do ake, trembling their loynes
    surprizeth;
Amaz'd with fear, by what they hear, each one of them
    ariseth.

(6)

They rush [4] from Beds with giddy heads, and to their
    windows run,
Mat. 24:
29, 30.
Viewing this light, which shines more bright then doth
    the Noon-day Sun.
Straightway appears (they see't with tears) the Son of
    God most dread;
Who with his Train comes on amain to Judge both
    Quick and Dead.

(7)

2 *Pet.* 3: 10.
Before his face the Heav'ns gave place, and Skies are
    rent asunder,
With mighty voice, and hideous noise, more terrible than
    Thunder.
His brightness damps heav'ns glorious lamps and makes
    them hide their heads,
As if afraid and quite dismay'd, they quit their wonted
    steads.

(8)

Ye sons of men that durst contemn the Threatnings of
    Gods Word.

How cheer you now? your hearts, I trow, are thrill'd
    as with a sword.

Now Atheist blind, whose brutish mind a God could
    never see,

Dost thou perceive, dost now believe that Christ thy
    Judge shall be?

(9)

Stout Courages, (whose hardiness could Death and Hell
    out-face)

Are you as bold now you behold your Judge draw near
    apace?

They cry, no, no: Alas! and wo! our Courage all is gone:

Our hardiness (fool hardiness) hath us undone, undone.

(10)

No heart so bold, but now grows cold and almost dead
    with fear:

No eye so dry, but now can cry, and pour out many a   *Rev.* 6 : 16.
    tear.

Earths Potentates and pow'rful States, Captains and Men
    of Might

Are quite abasht, their courage dasht at this most dread-
    ful sight.

(11)

Mean men lament, great men do rent their Robes, and
    tear their hair:

They do not spare their flesh to tear through horrible   *Mat.* 24 : 30.
    despair.

All Kindreds wail: all hearts do fail: horror the world
    doth fill

With weeping eyes, and loud out-cries, yet knows not
    how to kill.

(12)

Some hide themselves in Caves and Delves, in places   *Rev.* 6 : 15, 16.
    under ground:

Some rashly leap into the Deap, to scape by being
    drown'd:

Some to the Rocks (O sensless blocks!) and woody
    Mountains run,

That there they might this fearful sight, and dreaded
    Presence shun.

(13)

In vain do they to Mountains say, Fall on us, and us
    hide
From Judges ire, more hot than fire, for who may it
    abide?
No hiding place can from his Face sinners at all conceal,
Whose flaming Eyes hid things doth 'spy, and darkest
    things reveal.

(14)

Mat. 25 : 31.   The Judge draws nigh, exalted high upon a lofty
    Throne,
Amidst the throng of Angels strong, lo, Israel's Holy
    One!
The excellence of whose presence and awful Majesty,
Amazeth Nature, and every Creature, doth more than
    terrify.

(15)

Rev. 6 : 14.   The Mountains smoak, the Hills are shook, the Earth is
    rent and torn,
As if she should be clean dissolv'd, or from the Center
    born.
The Sea doth roar, forsakes the shore, and shrinks away
    for fear;
The wild Beasts flee into the Sea, so soon as he draws
    near.

(16)

Whose Glory bright, whose wondrous might, whose Power
    Imperial,
So far surpass whatever was in Realms Terrestrial;
That tongues of men (nor Angels pen) cannot the same
    express,
And therefore I must pass it by, lest speaking should
    transgress.

(17)

1 *Thes.* 4 : 16.   Before his Throne a Trump is blown, Proclaiming th'
Resurrection of   Day of Doom:
the Dead.   Forthwith he cries, *Ye Dead arise, and unto Judgment come.*
John 5 : 28, 29.   No sooner said, but 'tis obey'd; Sepulchers open'd are:
Dead Bodies all rise at his call, and's mighty power de-
    clare.

(18)

Both Sea and Land, at his Command, their Dead at
    once surrender:
The Fire and Air constrained are also their dead to
    tender.
The mighty word of this great Lord links Body and Soul
    together
Both of the Just, and the unjust, to part no more for
    ever.

(19)

The same translates, from Mortal states to Immortality, *The living*
All that survive, and be alive, i' th' twinkling of an *Changed.*
    eye:
That so they may abide for ay to endless weal or woe; *Luk.* 20 : 36.
Both the Renate [5] and Reprobate are made to dy no more. 1 *Cor.* 15 : 52.

(20)

His winged Hosts flie through all Coasts, together gather- *All brought*
    ing *to Judgment.*
Both good and bad, both quick and dead, and all to *Mat.* 24 : 31.
    Judgment bring.
Out of their holes those creeping Moles, that hid them-
    selves for fear,
By force they take, and quickly make before the Judge
    appear.

(21)

Thus every one before the Throne of Christ the Judge 2 *Cor.* 5 : 10.
    is brought, *The Sheep*
Both righteous and impious that good or ill had wrought. *separated from*
A separation, and diff'ring station by Christ appointed *the Goats.*
    is *Mat.* 25 : 32.
(To sinners sad) 'twixt good and bad, 'twixt Heirs of
    woe and bliss.

(22)

At Christ's right hand the Sheep do stand, his holy *Who are*
    Martyrs, who *Christ's*
For his dear Name suffering shame, calamity and woe. *Sheep.*
Like Champions stood, and with their Blood their testi- *Mat.* 5 : 10, 11.
    mony sealed;
Whose innocence without offence, to Christ their Judge
    appealed.

(23)

Heb. 12 : 5, 6, 7.   Next unto whom there find a room all Christ's afflicted
      ones,
      Who being chastised, neither despised nor sank amidst
      their groans:
      Who by the Rod were turn'd to God, and loved him
      the more,
      Not murmuring nor quarrelling when they were chast'ned
      sore.

(24)

Luke 7 : 41, 47.   Moreover, such as loved much, that had not such a
      tryal,
      As might constrain to so great pain, and such deep self
      denyal:
      Yet ready were the Cross to bear, when Christ them
      call'd thereto,
      And did rejoyce to hear his voice, they're counted Sheep
      also.

(25)

Joh. 21 : 15.   Christ's Flock of Lambs there also stands, whose Faith
Mat. 19 : 14.   was weak, yet true;
Joh. 3 : 3.
      All sound Believers (Gospel receivers) whose Grace was
      small, but grew:
      And them among an Infant throng of Babes, for whom
      Christ dy'd;
      Whom for his own, by wayes unknown to men, he sanc-
      tify'd.

(26)

Rev. 6 : 11.   All stand before their Saviour in long white Robes yclad,
Phil. 3 : 21.   Their countenance full of pleasance, appearing wondrous
      glad.
      O glorious sight! Behold how bright dust heaps are made
      to shine,
      Conformed so their Lord unto, whose Glory is Divine.

(27)

The Goats   At Christ's left hand the Goats do stand, all whining
described or the   hypocrites,
several sorts of
Reprobates on   Who for self-ends did seem Christ's friends, but foster'd
the left hand.   guileful sprites:
Mat. 24 : 51.   Who Sheep resembled, but they dissembled (their hearts
      were not sincere)
      Who once did throng Christ's Lambs among, but now
      must not come near.

(28)

Apostates and Run-awayes, such as have Christ forsaken, *Luk.* 11 : 24, 26.
Of whom the Devil, with seven more evil, hath fresh *Heb.* 6 : 4, 5, 6.
possession taken: *Heb.* 10 : 29.
Sinners in grain, reserv'd to pain and torments most
severe:
Because 'gainst light they sinn'd with spight, are also
placed there.

(29)

There also stand a num'rous band, that no Profession *Luk.* 12 : 47.
made *Prov.* 1 : 24, 26.
Of Godliness, nor to redress their wayes at all essay'd: *Joh.* 3 : 19.
Who better knew, but (sinful Crew) Gospel and Law
despised;
Who all Christ's knocks withstood like blocks and would
not be advised.

(30)

Moreover, there with them appear a number, numberless
Of great and small, vile wretches all, that did Gods Law *Gal.* 3 : 10.
transgress: 1 *Cor.* 6 : 9.
Idolaters, false worshippers, Prophaners of Gods Name, *Rev.* 21 : 8.
Who not at all thereon did call, or took in vain the
same.

(31)

Blasphemers lewd, and Swearers shrewd, Scoffers at
Purity,
That hated God, contemn'd his Rod, and lov'd Security; *Exod.* 20 :
Sabbath-polluters, Saints persecuters, Presumptuous men 7, 8.
and Proud,
Who never lov'd those that reprov'd; all stand amongst 2 *Thes.* 1 :
this Crowd. 6, 8, 9.

(32)

Adulterers and Whoremongers were [6] there, with all un- *Heb.* 13 : 4.
chast: 1 *Cor.* 6 : 10.
There Covetous, and Ravenous, that Riches got too fast:
Who us'd vile ways themselves to raise t' Estates and
worldly wealth,
Oppression by, or Knavery, by force, or fraud, or stealth.

(33)

Moreover, there together were Children flagitious,
And Parents who did them undo by Nurture vicious.

Zach. 5 : 3, 4.
Gal. 5 : 19,
·20, 21.

False-witness-bearers, and self-forswearers, Murd'rers,
and Men of blood,

Witches, Inchanters, & Ale house-haunters, beyond account there stood.

(34)

Their place there find all Heathen blind, that Natures
light abused,

Rom. 2 : 13.

Although they had no tydings glad of Gospel-grace refused.

There stands all Nations and Generations of *Adam*'s
Progeny,

Whom Christ redeem'd not, who Christ esteem'd not
through Infidelity.

(35)

Act. 4 : 12.

Who no Peace-maker, no Undertaker, [7] to shrow'd them
from Gods ire

Ever obtain'd; they must be pained with everlasting
fire.

These num'rous bands wringing their hands, and weeping all stand there,

Filled with anguish, whose hearts do languish through
self-tormenting fear.

(36)

Fast by them stand at Christ's left hand the Lion fierce
and fell,

The Dragon bold, that Serpent old, that hurried Souls
to Hell.

1 *Cor.* 6 : 3.

There also stand, under command, Legions of Sprights
unclean,

And hellish Fiends, that are no friends to God, nor unto
Men.

(37)

With dismal chains, and strongest reins, like Prisoners
of Hell,

Jude 6.

They're held in place before Christ's face, till He their
Doom shall tell.

These void of tears, but fill'd with fears, and dreadful
expectation

Of endless pains, and scalding flames, stand waiting for
Damnation.

(38)

All silence keep both Goats and Sheep before the Judge's
    Throne:
With mild aspect to his Elect then spake the Holy One;   *The Saints*
My Sheep draw near, your Sentence hear, which is to   *cleared &*
    you no dread,   *justified.*
Who clearly now discern, and know your sins are par-
    doned.

(39)

'Twas meet that ye should judged be, that so the world   *2 Cor.* 5 : 10.
    may spy   *Eccles.* 3 : 17.
No cause of grudge, when as I Judge and deal im-   *Joh.* 3 : 18.
    partially.
Know therefore all, both great and small, the ground
    and reason why
These Men do stand at my right hand, and look so
    chearfully.

(40)

These Men be those my Father chose before the worlds   *Joh.* 17 : 6.
    foundation,   *Eph.* 1 : 4.
And to me gave, that I should save from Death and
    Condemnation.
For whose dear sake I flesh did take, was of a Woman
    born.
And did inure my self t' indure, unjust reproach and
    scorn.

(41)

For them it was that I did pass through sorrows many
    one:
That I drank up that bitter Cup, which made me sigh   *Rev.* 1 : 5.
    and groan.
The Cross his pain I did sustain; yea more, my Fathers
    ire
I underwent, my Blood I spent to save them from Hell
    fire.

(42)

Thus I esteem'd, thus I redeem'd all these from every
    Nation,
That they may be (as now you see) a chosen Genera-
    tion.
What if ere-while they were as vile, and bad as any be,   *Eph.* 2 :
And yet from all their guilt and thrall at once I set   1, 3.
    them free?

(43)

Mat. 20 :
13, 15.
Rom. 9 : 20, 21.

My grace to one is wrong to none: none can Election claim,
Amongst all those their souls that lose, none can Rejection blame.
He that may chuse, or else refuse, all men to save or spill,
May this Man chuse, and that refuse. redeeming whom he will.

(44)

Isa. 53 : 4,
5, 11.

But as for those whom I have chose Salvations heirs to be,
I underwent their punishment, and therefore set them free;
I bore their grief, and their relief by suffering procur'd,
That they of bliss and happiness might firmly be assur'd.

(45)

Acts 13 : 48.
Jam. 2 : 18.
Heb. 12 : 7.
Mat. 19 : 29.

And this my grace they did imbrace, believing on my Name;
Which Faith was true, the fruits do shew proceeding from the same:
Their Penitence, their Patience, their Love and Self-denial
In suffering losses, and bearing Crosses, when put upon the tryal.

(46)

1 John 3 : 3.
Mat. 25 : 39, 40.

Their sin forsaking, their chearful taking my yoke, their Charity
Unto the Saints in all their wants, and in them unto me,
These things do clear, and make appear their Faith to be unfaigned,
And that a part in my desert and purchase they have gained.

(47)

Isa. 53 : 11, 12.
Rom. 8 : 16, 17,
33, 34.
John 3 : 18.

Their debts are paid, their peace is made, their sins remitted are;
Therefore at once I do pronounce, and openly declare
That Heav'n is theirs, that they be Heirs of Life and of Salvation!
Nor ever shall they come at all to Death or to Damnation.

(48)

Come, Blessed Ones, and sit on Thrones, Judging the
    World with me:
Come, and possess your happiness, and bought felicitie.
Henceforth no fears, no care, no tears, no sin shall you
    annoy,
Nor any thing that grief doth bring: Eternal Rest enjoy.

Luk. 22 :
29, 30.
Mat. 19 : 28.

(49)

You bore the Cross, you suffered loss of all for my Names
    sake:
Receive the Crown that's now your own; come, and a
    Kingdom take.
Thus spake the Judge, the wicked grudge, and grind
    their teeth in vain;
They see with groans these plac't on Thrones which
    addeth to their pain:

Mat. 25 : 34.
*They are
placed on
Thrones to
joyn with
Christ in
judging the
wicked.*

(50)

That those whom they did wrong and slay, must now their
    judgment see!
Such whom they slighted, and once despighted, must now
    their Judges be!
Thus 'tis decreed, such is their meed, and guerdon
    glorious!
With Christ they sit, Judging is fit to plague the Impious.

1 *Cor.* 6 : 2.

(51)

The wicked are brought to the Bar, like guilty Male-
    factors,
That oftentimes of bloody Crimes and Treasons have
    been Actors.
Of wicked Men, none are so mean as there to be neg-
    lected:
Nor none so high in dignity, as there to be respected.

*The wicked
brought to the
Bar.*
Rom. 2 : 3,
6, 11.

(52)

The glorious Judge will priviledge nor Emperour, nor
    King:
But every one that hath mis-done doth into Judgment
    bring.
And every one that hath mis-done, the Judge impartially
Condemneth to eternal wo, and endless misery.

Rev. 6 :
15, 16.
Isa. 30 : 33.

(53)

Thus one and all, thus great and small, the Rich as well
    as Poor,
And those of place as the most base, do stand the Judge
    before.
They are arraign'd, and there detain'd, before Christ's
    Judgment-seat
With trembling fear, their Doom to hear, and feel his
    angers heat.

(54)

Eccles. 11 :
9 & 12 : 14.

There Christ demands at all their hands a strict and
    strait account
Of all things done under the Sun, whose number far
    surmount
Man's wit and thought: yet all are brought unto this
    solemn Tryal;
And each offence with evidence, so that there's no denial.

(55)

There's no excuses for their abuses, since their own Con-
    sciences
More proof give in of each Man's sin, than thousand
    Witnesses,
Though formerly this faculty had grosly been abused,
Men could it stifle, or with it trifle, when as it them
    accused.

(56)

Now it comes in, and every sin unto Mens charge doth
    lay:
It judgeth them, and doth condemn, though all the world
    say nay.
It so stingeth and tortureth, it worketh such distress,
That each Man's self against himself, is forced to confess.

(57)

Secret sins and
works of dark-
ness brought
to light.
Psal. 139 :
2, 4, 12.
Rom. 2 : 16.

It's vain, moreover, for Men to cover the least iniquity:
The Judge hath seen, and privy been to all their villany.
He unto light, and open sight the works of darkness
    brings:
He doth unfold both new and old, both known and
    hidden things.

(58)

All filthy facts, and secret acts, however closly done,   *Eccles.* 12 : 14.
And long conceal'd, are there reveal'd before the mid-
   day Sun.
Deeds of the night shunning the light, which darkest
   corners sought,
To fearful blame, and endless shame, are there most
   justly brought.

(59)

And as all facts and grosser acts, so every word and   *Mat.* 12 : 36.
   thought,   *Rom.* 7 : 7.
Erroneous notion, and lustful motion, are unto judgment
   brought.
No sin so small and trivial but hither it must come:
Nor so long past, but now at last it must receive a
   doom.

.   .   .

(188)

The Judge is strong, doers of wrong cannot his power   *Mat.* 28 : 18.
   withstand: *Psal.* 139 : 7.
None can by flight run out of sight, nor scape out of his
   hand.
Sad is their state: for Advocate to plead their Cause
   there's none:
None to prevent their punishment, or misery bemone.

(189)

O dismal day! whither shall they for help and succour
   flee?
To God above, with hopes to move their greatest Enemee:
His wrath is great, whose burning heat no floods of tears   *Isa.* 33 : 14.
   can slake: *Psal.* 11 : 6.
His word stands fast, that they be cast into the burning   *Numb.* 23 : 19.
   Lake.

(190)

To Christ their Judge, he doth adjudge them to the   *Matt.* 25 : 41.
   Pit of Sorrow;
Nor will he hear, or cry, or tear, nor respite them one
   morrow.
To Heav'n alas, they cannot pass, it is against them shut;   *Matt.* 25 :
To enter there (O heavy cheer) they out of hopes are   10, 11, 12.
   put.

(191)

Luk. 12 : 20.   Unto their Treasures, or to their Pleasures, all these
Psal. 49 : 7, 17.   have them forsaken:
                  Had they full Coffers to make large offers, their Gold
                      would not be taken
Deut. 32 : 22.   Unto the place where whilome was their Birth and Edu-
                      cation?
                  Lo! Christ begins for their great sins to fire the Earths
                      Foundation:

(192)

2 Pet. 3 : 10.   And by and by the flaming Sky shall drop like molten
                      Lead
                  About their ears, t'increase their fears, and aggravate
                      their dread.
                  To Angels good that ever stood in their integrity,
                  Should they betake themselves, and make their sute in-
                      cessantly?

(193)

Matt. 13 :   They neither skill,[8] nor do they will to work them any
41, 42.   ease:
                  They will not mourn to see them burn, nor beg for their
                      release.
                  To wicked men, their bretheren, in sin and wickedness,
Rev. 20 : 13, 15. Should they make mone? their case is one, they're in
                      the same distress.

(194)

                  Ah, cold comfort, and mean support from such like Com-
                      forters!
                  Ah, little joy of Company, and fellow-sufferers!
Luk. 16 : 28.   Such shall increase their hearts disease, and add unto
                      their woe,
                  Because that they brought to decay themselves and many
                      moe.[9]

(195)

                  Unto the Saints with sad complaints should they them-
                      selves apply?
Rev. 21 : 4.   They're not dejected, nor ought affected with all their
                      misery.
Psal. 58 : 10.   Friends stand aloof, and make no proof what Prayers
                      or Tears can do:
                  Your godly friends are now more friends to Christ than
                      unto you.

(196)

Where tender love mens hearts did move unto a sym-
    pathy,
And bearing part of others smart in their anxiety;
Now such compassion is out of fashion, and wholly laid   *1 Cor.* 6 : 2.
    aside:
No Friends so near, but Saints to hear their Sentence
    can abide.

(197)

One natural Brother beholds another in this astonied fit,
Yet sorrows not thereat a jot, nor pitties him a whit.   *Compare*
The godly wife conceives no grief, nor can she shed a   *Prov* 1 : 26.
    tear   *with* 1 *Joh.* 3 :
For the sad state of her dear Mate, when she his doom   2. & 2 *Cor.*
    doth hear.   5 : 16.

(198)

He that was erst a Husband pierc't with sense of Wives
    distress,
Whose tender heart did bear a part of all her griev-
    ances,
Shall mourn no more as heretofore because of her ill
    plight;
Although he see her now to be a damn'd forsaken wight.

(199)

The tender Mother will own no other of all her numerous
    brood,
But such as stand at Christ's right hand acquitted
    through his Blood.
The pious Father had now much rather his graceless   *Luk.* 16 : 25.
    Son should ly
In Hell with Devils, for all his evils burning eternally,

(200)

Then God most high should injury, by sparing him
    sustain;
And doth rejoyce to hear Christ's voice adjudging him   *Psal.* 58 : 10.
    to pain;
Who having all, both great and small, convinc'd and
    silenced,
Did then proceed their Doom to read, and thus it uttered:

(201)

The Judge
pronounceth
the Sentence
of condemna-
tion.
Mat. 25 : 41.

Ye sinful wights, and cursed sprights, that work Iniquity,
Depart together from me for ever to endless Misery;
Your portion take in yonder Lake, where Fire and Brimstone
  flameth:
Suffer the smart, which your desert as it's due wages claimeth.

(202)

Oh piercing words more sharp than swords! what, to
  depart from *Thee,*
The terrour of it. Whose face before for evermore the best of Pleasures be!
What? to depart (unto our smart) from thee *Eternally:*
To be for aye banish'd away, with *Devils* company!

(203)

What? to be sent to *Punishment,* and flames of *Burning*
  Fire,
To be surrounded, and eke confounded with Gods *Re-*
  vengeful ire.
What? to abide, not for a tide these Torments, but for
  Ever:
To be released, or to be eased, not after years, but *Never.*

(204)

Oh, *fearful Doom!* now there's no room for hope or help
  at all:
Sentence is past which aye shall last, Christ will not it
  recall.
There might you hear them rent and tear the Air with
  their out-cries:
The hideous noise of their sad voice ascendeth to the
  Skies.

(205)

Luk. 13 : 28. They wring their hands, their caitiff-hands and gnash
  their teeth for terrour;
They cry, they roar for anguish sore, and gnaw their
  tongues for horrour.
But get away without delay, Christ pitties not your cry:
Prov. 1 : 26. Depart to Hell, there may you yell, and roar Eternally.

(206)

It is put in
Execution.
That word, *Depart,* maugre their heart, drives every
  wicked one,
With mighty pow'r, the self-same hour, far from the
  Judge's Throne.

Away they're chased [10] by the strong blast of his Death-   *Mat.* 25 : 46.
    threatning mouth:
They flee full fast, as if in haste, although they be full
    loath.

(207)

As chaff that's dry, and dust doth fly before the Northern
    wind:
Right so are they chased away, and can no Refuge find.
They hasten to the Pit of Wo, guarded by Angels stout;   *Matt.* 13 : 41,
Who to fulfil Christ's holy will, attend this wicked Rout.   42.

(208)

Whom having brought, as they are taught, unto the   *HELL.*
    brink of Hell   *Mat.* 25 : 30.
(That dismal place far from Christ's face, where Death   *Mark.* 9 : 43.
    and Darkness dwell: *Isa.* 30 : 33.
Where Gods fierce Ire kindleth the fire, and vengeance   *Rev.* 21 : 8.
    feeds the flame
With piles of Wood, and Brimstone Flood, that none
    can quench the same,)

(209)

With Iron bands they bind their hands, and cursed feet   *Wicked Men*
    together,   *and Devils*
And cast them all, both great and small, into that Lake   *cast into it for*
    for ever.   *ever.*
Where day and night, without respite, they wail, and   *Mat.* 22 : 13. &
    cry, and howl   25 : 46.
For tort'ring pain, which they sustain in Body and in
    Soul.

(210)

For day and night, in their despight, their torments   *Rev.* 14 : 10, 11.
    smoak ascendeth.
Their pain and grief have no relief, their anguish never
    endeth.
There must they ly, and never dy, though dying every
    day:
There must they dying ever ly, and not consume away.

(211)

Dy fain they would, if dy they could, but Death will
    not be had;
God's direful wrath their bodies hath for ev'r Immortal
    made.

They live to ly in misery, and bear eternal wo;
And live they must whilst God is just, that he may plague
them so.

(212)

The unsufferable
torments of the
damned.
Luk. 16 : 24.
Jude 7.

But who can tell the plagues of Hell, and torments
exquisite?
Who can relate their dismal state, and terrours infinite?
Who fare the best, and feel the least, yet feel that punishment
Whereby to nought they should be brought, if God did
not prevent.

(213)

The least degree of miserie there felt's incomparable,

Isa. 33 : 14.
Mark 9 :
43, 44.

The lightest pain they there sustain more than intolerable.
But God's great pow'r from hour to hour upholds them
in the fire,
That they shall not consume a jot, nor by it's force
expire.

(214)

But ah, the wo they undergo (they more than all besides)

Luk. 12 : 47.

Who had the light, and knew the right, yet would not
it abide.
The sev'n-fold smart, which to their part, and portion
doth fall,
Who Christ his Grace would not imbrace, nor hearken
to his call.

(215)

Mat. 11 : 24.

The *Amorites* and *Sodomites* although their plagues be sore,
Yet find some ease, compar'd to these, who feel a great
deal more.
Almighty God, whose Iron Rod, to smite them never lins,[11]
Doth most declare his Justice rare in plaguing these mens
sins.

(216)

Luk. 16 :
23, 25.
Luk. 13 : 28.

The pain of loss their Souls doth toss, and wond'rously
distress,
To think what they have cast away by wilful wickedness.
We might have been redeem'd from sin, think they, and
liv'd above,
Being possest of heav'nly rest, and joying in God's love.

(217)

But wo, wo, wo our Souls unto! we would not happy be;   *Luk.* 13 : 34.
And therefore bear Gods Vengeance here to all Eternitee.
Experience and woful sense must be our painful teachers
Who n'ould [12] believe, nor credit give, unto our faithful
    Preachers.

(218)

Thus shall they ly, and wail, and cry, tormented, and   *Mark* 9 : 44.
    tormenting   *Rom.* 2 : 15.
Their galled hearts with pois'ned darts but now too late
    repenting.
There let them dwell i'th' Flames of Hell; there leave we
    them to burn,
And back agen unto the men whom Christ acquits, re-
    turn.

(219)

The Saints behold with courage bold, and thankful   *The Saints*
    wonderment,   *rejoyce to see*
To see all those that were their foes thus sent to punish- *Judgment*
    ment: *executed upon*
                                                      the wicked
Then do they sing unto their King a Song of endless   *World.*
    Praise: *Ps.* 58 : 10.
They praise his Name, and do proclaim that just are   *Rev.* 19 : 1, 2, 3.
    all his ways.

(220)

Thus with great joy and melody to Heav'n they all as- *They ascend*
    cend,   *with Christ*
Him there to praise with sweetest layes, and Hymns that *into Heaven*
    never end,   *triumphing.*
                                                       Mat. 25 : 46.
Where with long Rest they shall be blest, and nought   1 *Joh.* 3 : 2.
    shall them annoy: 1 *Cor.* 13 : 12.
Where they shall see as seen they be, and whom they
    love enjoy.

(221)

O glorious Place! where face to face Jehovah may be   *Their Eternal*
    seen,   *happiness and*
                                                      incomparable
By such as were sinners whilere and no dark vail between. *Glory there.*
Where the Sun shine, and light Divine, of Gods bright
    Countenance,
Doth rest upon them every one, with sweetest influence.

(222)

O blessed state of the Renate! O wondrous **Happiness**,
To which they're brought, beyond what thought can
    reach, or words express!
Rev. 21 : 4.   Griefs water-course, and sorrows sourse, are turn'd to
    joyful streams.
Their old distress and heaviness are vanished like dreams.

(223)

For God above in arms of love doth dearly them em-
    brace,
Psal. 16 : 11.   And fills their sprights with such delights, and pleasures
    in his grace;
As shall not fail, nor yet grow stale through frequency
    of use:
Nor do they fear Gods favour there, to forfeit by abuse.

(224)

Heb. 12 : 23.   For there the Saints are perfect Saints, and holy ones
    indeed,
From all the sin that dwelt within their mortal bodies
    freed:
Rev. 1 : 6.   Made Kings and Priests to God through Christs dear
& 22 : 5.   loves transcendency,
There to remain, and there to reign with him Eternally.

[The End]

A SHORT DISCOURSE ON ETERNITY.

(1)

WHAT mortal man can with his Span mete out
    Eternity?
Isa. 57 : 15.   Or fathom it by depth of Wit, or strength of Memory?
Mark 3 : 29.   The lofty Sky is not so high, Hells depth to this is
Mat. 25 : 46.   small:
The World so wide is but a stride, compared therewithall.

(2)

It is a main great Ocean, withouten bank or bound:
A deep Abyss, wherein there is no bottom to be found.

This World hath stood now since the Flood, four thousand years well near,
And had before endured more than sixteen hundred
year.

．　　．　　．

(19)

Then, Ah poor men! what, not till then? No, not an
hour before:
For God is just, and therefore must torment them evermore.
ETERNITY! ETERNITY! thou mak'st hard hearts to bleed:
The thoughts of thee in misery, do make men wail indeed.

(20)

When they remind what's still behind, and ponder this   *Mark* 9 : 43, 44,
word NEVER,   45, 46, *&c.*
That they must here be made to bear Gods Vengeance
for EVER:
The thought of this more bitter is, then all they feel
beside:
Yet what they feel, nor heart of steel, nor Flesh of Brass
can bide.

(21)

To lye in wo, and undergo the direful pains of Hell,   2 *Thes.* 1 :
And know withall, that there they shall for aye, and ever   8, 9.
dwell;
And that they are from rest as far when fifty thousand   *Mat.* 25 : 46.
year,   *Rev.* 14 :
Twice told, are spent in punishment, as when they first   10, 11.
came there.

(22)

This, Oh! this makes Hells fiery flakes much more intolerable;
This makes frail wights and damned sprights, to bear their
plagues unable.
This makes men bite, for fell despite, their very tongues
in twain:
This makes them rore for great horror, and trebleth all
their pain.

[The End]

A SONG OF EMPTINESS,

To fill up the Empty Pages following.

Vanity of Vanities.

Vain, frail, short liv'd, and miserable Man,
  Learn what thou art when thine estate is best:
A restless Wave o'th' troubled Ocean,
A Dream, a lifeless Picture finely drest:

A Wind, a Flower, a Vapour, and a Bubble,
A Wheel that stands not still, a trembling Reed,
A rolling Stone, dry Dust, light Chaff, and Stubble,
A Shadow of Something, but nought indeed.

Learn what deceitful Toyes, and empty things,
This World, and all its best Enjoyments bee:
Out of the Earth no true Contentment springs,
But all things here are vexing Vanitee.

For what is *Beauty*, but a fading Flower?
Or what is *Pleasure*, but the Devils bait,
Whereby he catcheth whom he would devour,
And multitudes of Souls doth ruinate?

And what are *Friends* but mortal men, as we?
Whom Death from us may quickly separate;
Or else their hearts may quite estranged be,
And all their love be turned into hate.

And what are *Riches* to be doted on?
Uncertain, fickle, and ensnaring things;
They draw Mens Souls into Perdition,
And when most needed, take them to their wings.

Ah foolish Man! that sets his heart upon
Such empty Shadows, such wild Fowl as these,
That being gotten will be quickly gone,
And whilst they stay increase but his disease.

As in a Dropsie, drinking draughts begets,
The more he drinks, the more he still requires:
So on this World whoso affection sets,
His Wealths encrease encreaseth his desires.

O happy Man, whose portion is above,
Where Floods, where Flames, where Foes cannot
   bereave him,
Most wretched man, that fixed hath his love
Upon this World, that surely will deceive him!

For, what is *Honour?* What is *Sov'raignty,*
Whereto mens hearts so restlesly aspire?
Whom have they Crowned with Felicity?
When did they ever satisfie desire?

The Ear of Man with hearing is not fill'd:
To see new sights still coveteth the Eye:
The craving Stomack though it may be still'd,
Yet craves again without a new supply.

All Earthly things, man's Cravings answer not,
Whose little heart would all the World contain,
(If all the World should fall to one man's Lot)
And notwithstanding empty still remain.

The *Eastern Conquerour* was said to weep,
When he the *Indian* Ocean did view,
To see his Conquest bounded by the Deep,
And no more Worlds remaining to subdue.

Who would that man in his Enjoyments bless,
Or envy him, or covet his estate,
Whose gettings do augment his greediness,
And make his wishes more intemperate?

Such is the wonted and the common guise
Of those on Earth that bear the greatest Sway:
If with a few the case be otherwise
They seek a Kingdom that abides for ay.

Moreover they, of all the Sons of men,
That Rule, and are in highest places set,
Are most inclin'd to scorn their Bretheren
And God himself (without great grace) forget.

For as the Sun doth blind the gazer's eyes,
That for a time they nought discern aright:
So Honour doth befool and blind the Wise,
And their own Lustre 'reaves them of their sight.

Great are their Dangers, manifold their Cares;
Thro' which, whilst others Sleep, they scarcely Nap:
And yet are oft surprized unawares,
And fall unweeting into Envies Trap!

The mean Mechanick finds his kindly rest,
All void of fear Sleepeth the Country-Clown,
When greatest Princes often are distrest,
And cannot Sleep upon their Beds of Down.

Could *Strength* or *Valour* men Immortalize,
Could *Wealth* or *Honour* keep them from decay,
There were some cause the same to Idolize,
And give the lye to that which I do say.

But neither can such things themselves endure
Without the hazard of a Change one hour,
Nor such as trust in them can they secure
From dismal dayes, or Deaths prevailing pow'r.

If *Beauty* could the beautiful defend
From Death's dominion, than fair *Absalom*
Had not been brought to such a shameful end:
But fair and foul unto the Grave must come.

If *Wealth* or *Scepters* could Immortal make,
Then wealthy *Crœsus*, wherefore art thou dead?
If *Warlike force*, which makes the World to quake,
Then why is *Julius Cæsar* perished?

Where are the *Scipio's* Thunder-bolts of War?
Renowned *Pompey*, *Cæsars* Enemie?
Stout *Hannibal*, *Romes* Terror known so far?
Great *Alexander*, what's become of thee?

If *Gifts* and *Bribes* Death's favour might but win,
If *Power*, if force, or *Threatnings* might it fray,
All these, and more, had still surviving been:
But all are gone, for Death will have no Nay.

Such is this World with all her Pomp and Glory,
Such are the men whom worldly eyes admire:
Cut down by Time, and now become a Story,
That we might after better things aspire.

Go boast thy self of what thy heart enjoyes,
Vain Man! triumph in all thy worldly Bliss:
Thy best enjoyments are but Trash and Toyes:
Delight thy self in that which worthless is.

Omnia praetereunt praeter amare Deum.[13]

GOD'S CONTROVERSY WITH NEW-ENGLAND

WRITTEN IN THE TIME OF THE GREAT DROUGHT ANNO *1662.*

[GOD SPEAKS AGAINST THE LANGUISHING STATE OF NEW-ENGLAND]

. . .

ARE THESE the men that erst at my command
   Forsook their ancient seats and native soile,
To follow me into a desart land,
   Contemning all the travell and the toile,
Whose love was such to purest ordinances
   As made them set at nought their fair inheritances?

Are these the men that prized libertee
   To walk with God according to their light,
To be as good as he would have them bee,
   To serve and worship him with all their might,
Before the pleasures which a fruitfull field,
   And country flowing-full of all good things, could yield,

Are these the fold whom from the brittish Iles,
   Through the stern billows of the watry main,
I safely led so many thousand miles,
   As if their journey had been through a plain?
Whom having from all enemies protected,
   And through so many deaths and dangers well directed,

I brought and planted on the western shore,
   Where nought but bruits and salvage wights did swarm
(Untaught, untrain'd, untam'd by vertue's lore)
   That sought their blood, yet could not do them harm?
My fury's flaile them thresht, my fatall broom
   Did sweep them hence, to make my people elbow-room.

Are these the men whose gates with peace I crown'd,
   To whom for bulwarks I salvation gave,
Whilst all things else with rattling tumults sound,
   And mortall frayes send thousands to the grave?
Whilest their own brethren bloody hands embrewed
   In brothers blood, and fields with carcases bestrewed?

Is this the people blest with bounteous store,
   By land and sea full richly clad and fed,
Whom plenty's self stands waiting still before,
   And powreth out their cups well tempered?
For whose dear sake an howling wildernes
   I lately turned into a fruitfull paradeis?

Are these the people in whose hemisphere
   Such bright-beam'd, glist'ring, sun-like starrs I placed,
As by their influence did all things cheere,
   As by their light blind ignorance defaced,
As errours into lurking holes did fray,
   As turn'd the late dark night into a lightsome day?

Are these the folk to whom I milked out
   And sweetnes stream'd from consolations brest;
Whose soules I fed and strengthened throughout
   With finest spirituall food most finely drest?
On whom I rained living bread from Heaven,
   Withouten Errour's bane, or Superstition's leaven?

With whom I made a Covenant of peace,
   And unto whom I did most firmly plight
My faithfulness, If whilst I live I cease
   To be their Guide, their God, their full delight;
Since them with cords of love to me I drew,
   Enwrapping in my grace such as should them ensew.

Are these the men, that now mine eyes behold,
   Concerning whom I thought, and whilome spake,
First Heaven shall pass away together scrold,
   Ere they my lawes and righteous wayes forsake,
Or that they slack to runn their heavenly race?
   Are these the same? or are some others come in place?

If these be they, how is it that I find
   In stead of holiness Carnality,

In stead of heavenly frames an Earthly mind,
    For burning zeal luke-warm Indifferency,
For flaming love, key-cold Dead-heartedness,
    For temperance (in meat, and drinke, and cloaths) excess?

Whence cometh it, that Pride, and Luxurie
    Debate, Deceit, Contention, and Strife,
False-dealing, Covetousness, Hypocrisie
    (With such like Crimes) amongst them are so rife,
That one of them doth over-reach another?
    And that an honest man can hardly trust his Brother?

How is it, that Security, and Sloth,
    Amongst the best are Common to be found?
That grosser sins, in stead of Graces growth,
    Amongst the many more and more abound?
I hate dissembling shews of Holiness.
    Or practise as you talk, or never more profess.

Judge not, vain world, that all are hypocrites
    That do profess more holiness then thou:
All foster not dissembling, guilefull sprites,
    Nor love their lusts, though very many do.
Some sin through want of care and constant watch,
    Some with the sick converse, till they the sickness catch.

Some, that maintain a reall root of grace,
    Are overgrown with many noysome weeds,
Whose heart, that those no longer may take place,
    The benefit of due correction needs.
And such as these however gone astray
    I shall by stripes reduce into a better way.

Moreover some there be that still retain
    Their ancient vigour and sincerity;
Whom both their own, and others sins, constrain
    To sigh, and mourn, and weep, and wail, & cry:
And for their sakes I have forborn to powre
    My wrath upon Revolters to this present houre.

To praying Saints I always have respect,
    And tender love, and pittifull regard:
Nor will I now in any wise neglect
    Their love and faithfull service to reward;

Although I deal with others for their folly,
   And turn their mirth to tears that have been too jolly.

For thinke not, O Backsliders, in your heart,
   That I shall still your evill manners beare:
Your sinns me press as sheaves do load a cart,
   And therefore I will plague you for this geare
Except you seriously, and soon, repent,
   Ile not delay your pain and heavy punishment.

And who be those themselves that yonder shew?
   The seed of such as name my dreadfull Name!
On whom whilere compassions skirt I threw
   Whilest in their blood they were, to hide their shame!
Whom my preventing love did neer me take!
   Whom for mine own I mark't, lest they should me forsake!

I look't that such as these to vertue's Lore
   (Though none but they) would have Enclin'd their ear:
That they at least mine image should have bore,
   And sanctify'd my name with awfull fear.
Let pagan's Bratts pursue their lusts, whose meed
   Is Death: For christians children are an holy seed.

But hear O Heavens! Let Earth amazed stand;
   Ye Mountaines melt, and Hills come flowing down:
Let horro^r seize upon both Sea and Land;
   Let Natures self be cast into a stown.
I children nourisht, nurtur'd and upheld:
   But they against a tender father have rebell'd.

What could have been by me performed more?
   Or wherein fell I short of your desire?
Had you but askt, I would have op't my store,
   And given what lawfull wishes could require.
For all this bounteous cost I lookt to see
   Heaven-reaching-hearts, & thoughts, Meekness, Humility. . . .

        One wave another followeth,
          And one disease begins
        Before another cease, becaus
          We turn not from our sins.
        We stopp our ear against reproof,
          And hearken not to God:
        God stops his ear against o^r prayer,
          And takes not off his rod.

Our fruitful seasons have been turnd
  Of late to barrenness,
Sometimes through great & parching drought,
  Sometimes through rain's excess.
Yea now the pastures & corn fields
  For want of rain do languish:
The cattell mourn, & hearts of men
  Are fill'd with fear & anguish.

The clouds are often gathered,
  As if we should have rain:
But for oʳ great unworthiness
  Are scattered again.
We pray & fast, & make fair shewes,
  As if we meant to turn:
But whilst we turn not, God goes on
  Our field, & fruits to burn.

And burnt are all things in such sort,
  That nothing now appears,
But what may wound our hearts with grief,
  And draw foorth floods of teares.
All things a famine do presage
  In that extremity,
As if both men, and also beasts,
  Should soon be done to dy.

This O New-England hast thou got
  By riot, & excess:
This hast thou brought upon thy self
  By pride & wantonness.
Thus must thy worldlyness be whipt.
  They, that too much do crave,
Provoke the Lord to take away
  Such blessings as they have.

We have been also threatened
  With worser things then these:
And God can bring them on us still,
  To morrow if he please.
For if his mercy be abus'd,
  Which holpe us at our need
And mov'd his heart to pitty us,
  We shall be plagu'd indeed.

Beware, O sinful Land, beware;
    And do not think it strange
That sorer judgements are at hand,
    Unless thou quickly change.
Or God, or thou, must quickly change;
    Or else thou art undon:
Wrath cannot cease, if sin remain,
    Where judgement is begun.

Ah dear New England! dearest land to me;
    Which unto God hast hitherto been dear,
And mayst be still more dear than formerlie,
    If to his voice thou wilt incline thine ear.

Consider wel & wisely what the rod,
    Wherewith thou art from yeer to yeer chastized,
Instructeth thee. Repent, & turn to God,
    Who wil not have his nurture be despized.

Thou still hast in thee many praying saints,
    Of great account, and precious with the Lord,
Who dayly powre out unto him their plaints,
    And strive to please him both in deed & word.

Cheer on, sweet souls, my heart is with you all,
    And shall be with you, maugre Sathan's might:
And whereso'ere this body be a Thrall,
    Still in New-England shall be my delight.

[The End]

MEAT OUT OF THE EATER [14]

MEDITATION V.

The fifth perswades to Patience,
From that Rich future Recompense;
Minding us of our Heavenly Rest,
Which should revive vs when distrest.

[1]

MEEKLY to bear Christ's yoke it is an Honour high:
    Thou Christ wilt surely them reward who
    bear it patiently.

2 *Cor.* 4 : 17.   For this short Grief of ours, and our Affliction light
Shall work of glorious Happiness a far more lasting
    weight.

[2]

For just men light is sown (reward laid up in store) *Psal.* 97 : 11.
Who sow in tears shall reap in joy, and after mourn no *Psal.* 126 : 5.
    more.
  They'll one day wear a Crown, who now the Cross
    sustain:
In Christ our Lord no suffering, nor labour shall be *1 Cor.* 15 : 58.
    vain.

[4]

Reign with him long shall they, with him that suffer *1 Tim.* 2 : 12.
    do:
Who follow him in's Death, partake shall of his Glory
    too.
  Not that our services, deserve such Recompence: *Isa.* 64 : 6.
But he resolveth to set forth his own Munificence. *2 Thess.* 1 : 10.

[4]

Who can expect a Crop or Harvest to obtain,
That breaks no ground, that sows no feed, that under-
    goes no pain?
  To triumph who can hope that doth the Battel shun?
Eternal Glory whoso findes, must first through rough
    ways run.

[5]

Thou art a Pilgrim here; this world is not thy *Psal.* 39 : 12.
    home:
Then be content with Pilgrims fare, till thou to Heaven
    come.
  What if thou tossed art with boisterous winds and
    seas?
Behold the Haven where thou shalt enjoy long rest and *Heb.* 4 : 9.
    ease.

[6]

What if thy conflict with the roaring Lion be?
If thou be call'd to fight against World, Flesh, and Devil,
    all three.
  Stronger is Christ in thee then strongest Enemy, *Joh.* 4 : 4.
Who Satan under thy Souls feet shall tread down *Rom.* 16 : 20.
    speedily.

[7]

Heb. 2 : 10.   Souldier be strong, who fightest under a Captain
                        Stout:
                    Dishonour not thy conquering Head by basely giving
                        out.
                    Endure a while, Bear up, and hope for better things:
                    War ends in peace; and Morning light mounts up on
                        Midnights wing.

[8]

                    Through Changes manifold, and Dangers perilous,
Isa. 43 : 2.   Through fiery flames, and water-floods, through ways
Heb. 11 :   calamitous.
14, 16.   We travel towards Heaven a quiet Habitation:
Mat. 25 : 34.   Christ shews a Kingdom there prepar'd ev'n from the
                        worlds foundation.

[9]

2 Cor. 2 : 4, 8.   O Heaven, most holy place, which art our country
                        dear!
                    What cause have I to long for thee, and Beg with many
                        a tear.
                    Earth is to me a Prison; this Body an useless wight:
                    And all things else vile, vain, and nought, to one in
                        such ill plight.

[10]

                    O Christ make haste, from bands, of Sin and Death
                        me free;
                    And to those Heavenly Mansions, be pleas'd to carry
                        me.
1 Thes. 4 : 17.   Where glorified Saints for ever are possest,
                    Of God in Christ their chiefest Good. And from all
                        troubles Rest.

MEDITATION VIII.

Saints happier be when most distrest,
Then wicked men are at the best.

[1]

WE HAVE the wicked view'd, and seen his best
                        estate
                    And who would chuse with him to share, except a Rep-
                        robate?
Prov. 1 : 32.   For sure the Simple's ease shall turn to his decay:
                    And the Prosperity of Fools shall utterly them slay.

[2]

When wicked men like Grass do springing up arise, *Psal.* 92 : 7.
When they are in a flourishing case that work iniquities:
   'Tis for their cutting down to perpetuity;
It's but to ripen them for woe, and endless Misery.

[3]

The less Affliction here they feel, the more's to come: *Luk.* 16 :
The greater Blessings they abuse, the heavier is their 23, 24, 25.
   Doom.
Now let us take a Saint whom men account accurst,
Because they judge him plagu'd of God, and view him
     at his worst.

[4]

Suppose his case as bad, as bad it well can be:
And his Calamity more sad then commonly we see.
   Dispose him where you will, do with him what you
   can:
Yet God is present with him still; he is a happy man.

[5)

Let Sickness come upon him, or great Tormenting *Jam.* 5 : 11.
   Pain: *Act.* 23 : 11.
God will not lose him, but a Saint a Saint shall still
    remain.
   In Prison him immure, all comforts from him take:
You cannot rob him of his God, nor him unhappy make.

[6]

Plunge him into the mire, or water; God is near: *Isa.* 43 : 2.
Cast him into the burning Fire; God will be with him *Psal.* 42 : 7, 8.
   there.
   If many roaring waves of great Affliction roll
Over his head: God so supports they cannot sink his
    Soul.

[7]

(*Jacob* in servitude. *Joseph* in Prison Chains,
Moses in his long Banishment Heaven's Favourite still
    remains.
   Three Children in the Fire *Daniel* i'th' Lions Den
Have God to guard them: so had *Paul* when Shipwrack'd.
    Happy Men!)

[8]

Deut. 33 :
27.

The Everlasting Arms are underneath his head
To bear him up; and hence it comes he is not swal-
    lowed,

Psal. 44 :
17, 18, 22.

Nor suffered wickedly from God to turn aside:
As by his carriage will appear when troubles him betide.

MEDITATION IX.

The Carriage of a Child of God
Under his Fathers smarting Rod,

(1)

Job 1 : 21.
& 2 : 20.
2 Sam. 16 : 11.

HE sees a hand of God in his Afflictions all,
    And owns it for to be his Rod, Whatever Cross
    befall.
For whosoever be th'immediate instrument,
He knows right well that God himself was the Efficient.

(2)

Job 5 : 6.
1 Kings 22 :
48, 49.

And that Afflictions rise not out of the Dust:
Nor are they order'd by the will of Man, or Devils
    lust.
If that the Grief be small or the Chastisement light:
Yet since God finds it not in vain, light strokes he dare
    not slight.

(3)

Heb. 12 : 6.
Joel 2 : 12.
Amos 4 : 12.

If greater be the Blow, it doth not him dismay:
Because he knows a Fathers hand such stripes may on
    him lay,
But he prepares himself betimes to meet the Lord
By true Repentance, as he hath commanded in his Word.

(4)

Lam. 3 : 40.
Job 10 : 2.

Job 34 :
31, 32.
Job 42 : 6.

To search and try his wayes to find out what's
    amiss,
To leave his sins, to loath himself his first great Business
    is.
And having once found out what sin hath God of-
    fended;
He seriously bewails it, and endeavours to amend it.

(5)

Unto the cleansing Blood of Jesus Christ he flies;   *Heb.* 6 : 18.
And to his wounded Conscience that Soveraign Balm   *Psal.* 51 : 7.
    applies: *Job.* 2 : 2.
Which can both cleanse and heal; both pacifie God's   *Heb.* 9 : 14.
    wrath,   *Rev.* 1 : 5.
And cure a guilty sin-sick Soul, when 'tis improv'd by
    Faith.

(6)

And though he be unworthy to look God in the face;   *Heb.* 4 :
Yet through the Merits of his Son he begs and hopes   15, 16.
    for Grace: *Job* 19 :
Being right well assur'd that though the Lord chastise   25, 26, 27.
    him;   *Lam.* 3 : 31,
Yet will he not cast off his Soul, nor utterly despise him.   32.

[7]

But if by all his search he cannot find the cause
For which the Lord afflicteth him, or from his Soul
    withdraws:
Yet he believeth, that for just and holy ends,
To humble, purge, and better him the Lord Affliction
    sends.

[8]

And though he cannot say, I have at random run,   *Job* 10 : 2, 7.
Or wickedly by some known sin away from God have   *Job* 7 : 2.
    gon: *Job* 9 : 3.
Yet so much sin he sees both in his heart and wayes,
As God may judge it meet therefore to scourge him all
    his dayes.

[9]

Himself he humbleth under the mighty hand of God: 1 *Pet.* 5.
And for the sake of that sweet hand doth kiss the sharpest   1 *Sam.* 3 :
    Rod.   18.
He taketh up his Cross, denieth his own will,   *Job* 2 : 10.
Advanceth God's above his own, and yieldeth to him
    still.

[10]

Unto the yoke of Christ he doth his neck submit: *Lam.* 3 : 29, 30.
He turns his cheek to him that smites, and meekly
    taketh it.
Yea when his grief is most, and sorest is his pain: *Lam.* 3 :
He still endeavoureth good thoughts of God for to retain.   22, 23, 25.

[11]

His earnest care and prayer when greatest is his smart,
Is that he never may blaspheme God with his mouth
    or heart.
He beggeth Patience in his extremities
To bear Gods hand, that so his heart may not against
    him rise.

[12]

Psal. 73 :   If murmuring thoughts do rise (or hearts begin to
13, 14,   swell)
15, 22.   He strives to beat them down again; he hates such
                thoughts like Hell.
             God he resolves to love, deal with him as he will:
Job 13 : 15.   And in his mercy to confide although he should him kill.

[13]

             To God that smiteth him he strives to get more near
             He will not cease to pray, although God seem to stop
                his ear.
Psal. 88 :   Though God hath long delay'd to answer his request,
1, 2, 9, 13.   Yet will he seek, and never cease, whilst life is in his
Psal. 42 : 7, 8, 9.   brest.

[14]

Psal. 40 :   He waiteth patiently untill deliverance come,
1, 2, 4.   And will not use dishonest means to shun what's trouble-
Isa. 28 : 16.   some.
Psal. 116 : 16.   He hates all sinful sleights to get his Cross from under:
             And will not break his Bonds, but stay till God them
                cut asunder.

[15]

Gen. 8 :   *Noah* would not leave his Ark, nor out of Prison break,
13, 14, 16.   Although he saw the Ground was dry, till God did to him
                speak.
1 *Samuel*   *David* refus'd to kill, King *Saul* his mortal Foe,
26 : 9, 11.   That persecuted him to Death, and wrought him so
                much woe.

[16]

             He rather chose to wait, till God should plead his
                Cause,
             And of his Enemy him avenge, then for to break God's
                Laws.

Thus every Saint will rather, chuse Suffering, then to *Job* 36 : 21.
Sin,
He will not God offend Self-ease, or safety for to win.

[17]

But if through Humane frailty, and over-bearing *Mat.* 26 :
power,   70, 75.
Of Strong Temptation, he do swerve, and fall i'th evil
hour:
(As sometimes *Peter* did,) it grieveth him full sore, *Luke* 22 : 32.
He weeps and mourns, repents, returns, grows stronger
then before,

[18]

The longer God afflicts him, the better he is for it, *Psal.* 119 :
Love's Holiness the more, loath's sin and learneth to 67, 71.
abhor it.   *Eccles.* 7 : 3.
The more he is bereft, and stript of outward things:
The less he dotes on these wild Fowl, that take them to
their wings.

[19]

When creature comforts fail, when sorrows him sur-
round,
He takes the faster hold of God, in whom true Comfort's
found.
When Conduit-pipes are stopt, when Streams are
vanished,
The more he to the Fountain hastes, and lives at the
well-head.

[20]

Thus *David* comforted and cheer'd himself in God, 1 *Sam.* 30 : 6.
When all was gone, although he felt the anguish of the *Gen.* 32 :
Rod.   26, 28.
Thus *Jacob* took fast hold, and wrestled with the Lord,
When as he was distrest for fear of cruel *Esau's* sword.

[21]

Prince-like he wrestled and would not let him go,
Until he had a Blessing got to shield him from his Foe.
Thus every suffering Saint by wrestling shall prevail,
And having overcome at last be styled *Israel*.

LIGHT IN DARKNESS [15]

Song V.

A Dialogue between the Flesh *and* Spirit.

Flesh.   [1]

B UT OH methinks the Lord is angry with my Prayers,
      The more I cry to him for help the worse it with
          me fares.
   The more I sue for grace and beg for some relief:
   The more he lets me be distrest, and doubled is my
          grief.

[2]

   I fear he reckoneth my Prayers to me for sin,
   And rather is displeas'd therewith then takes delight
          therein.
   If God reject my Prayer, I fear he me rejects.
   For how can he despise their Prayer whose persons he
          respects?

Spirit.   [3]

Psal. 80 : 4.   Against his People's Prayers the Lord sometimes may
Psal. 66 : 18.   smoke,
                        When some sin unrepented of his anger doth provoke.
Lam. 3 : 40.   If *David* sin regard God will not hear his Prayer:
                        To search for, find out, mourn for sin, my Soul make
                              this thy care.

[4]

Josh. 7 :   God puts thee upon search, would have thee diligent
13, 14.   To find out what offensive is and to be Penitent.
Jer. 3.   Be thou displeas'd with sin, and he'll be pleas'd with
4 : 13, 14, 17.   thee:
Chap. 3 : 19, 20.   He'll turn to thee his face, if thou turn from iniquitie.

[5]

Mat. 15 :   Some-Times the Lord delayes, and makes us long to
23, 24, 29.   wait,
                        For other ends; as for to make us more importunate;
                          To try our Self-denial, our Faith, Love, Patience.
                        Sometimes to make his Power shine forth in our de-
                              liverance.

[6]

He lets our troubles grow unto the greater height,   *Exod.* 14 & 15
That his Salvation might appear more glorious in our *chapters*
    sight.
  For these, and other more, such great and gracious
    Ends
The Lord defers to hear our prayer, for he no hurt in-
    tends.

[7]

  Our Prayers are sometimes heard, not just unto our *Gen.* 18 : 19.
    mind,
Yet heard they are, and answered in some far better
    kind.
  God may deny to grant that thing that we request, *2 Cor.* 12 : 8, 9.
Yet answer in a better thing, for he knows what is best.

[8]

  Be silent then frail Flesh, thou favourest not these
    things:
Thy wisdom doth but vex my Soul; leave off thy Rea-
    sonings.
  Satan by Serpents mouth mankind did undermine: *Gen.* 3.
And I perceive he now assayes to ruine me by thine.

Song VI.

Another Combate between the Flesh *and* Spirit.

Flesh.   [1]

S OUL thou hast cause to fear thy Faith will not hold
    out:
And that it is but counterfeit thou do'st so often doubt.
  See what a mighty power of Unbelief prevails
From time to time! and how thine heart and Faith thee
    often fails!

Spirit.   [2]

  Oh sly and sinful flesh! Thou art a treacherous Thief,
That robs me of my Faith, and then condemns for Un-
    belief.
    They're thy suggestions vile (that do'st with Hell
      comply)
That make me doubt, who otherwise on Christ alone
    rely.

[3]

Joh. 1 :
12.
Act. 8 : 37.
1 *Cor.* 1 : 30.
Phil. 3 :
9, 10.
Heb. 12 : 14.

Whole Christ with all my heart I earnestly Embrace;
And for my whole Salvation I relie upon his grace:
Renouncing all my own both Righteousness, and Sin;
Endeav'ring Holiness, as well as Happiness to win.

[4]

Phil. 1 : 6.
1 *Pet.* 1 : 5.
Mat. 16 : 18.

And blessed be the Lord, who will compleat my Faith,
Weak though it be, as he the same at first begotten hath:
Mean while he it supports; and as himself doth tell,
It never shall be vanquished by all the force of Hell.

STRENGTH IN WEAKNESS

Song IV

[1]

Isai. 40:
27,

W HY say'st thou *Jacob*, and, O *Israel* spoken hast,
My way is hidden from the Lord, my judgment
from him past?

28,

Hast thou not known nor heard, th'Eternal God, the
Lord
Who hath the Ends of all the Earth created by his Word.

[2]

He never waxeth faint, nor wearied is he:
His understanding is so deep it cannot searched be.

29,

He giveth strength unto the faint and feeble wight:
And he bestows increase of strength on such as have no
might.

[3]

30,

The youth shall faint and tire, and young men wholly
fall:

31.

But those that wait upon the Lord their strength recover
shall.
They shall mount up with wings like Eagles; run shall
they
And not be weary: they shall walk and shall not faint
away.

POOR MENS WEALTH

T O talk of Poor mens Wealth, or Rich mens Poverty,
Seems to the World an Old Wives Tale, or idle foolery:
But whoso reads our Lines, if God but give him eyes,
Shall see that these things are no Tales, but Spiritual Mysteries.

MEDITATION I.

[1]

What means this Paradox? How can the Rich be poor?
Or Poor men Rich? What is their Wealth? Or where is
   all their store?
I know thy Poverty, saith Christ, yet thou art Rich, *Rev. 2.*
To *Smyrna's* undefiled Church: thou seest there may be
   such.

[2]

But to *Laodicea;* thou say'st that I am rich,
But thou art naked, blind and poor, a miserable wretch. *Rev. 3 : 17, 18.*
I counsel thee to buy Eye-salve that thou may'st see,
Of me; try'd Gold to make thee rich, white Robes to
   cover thee.

[3]

The Beggar *Lazarus* laid at the Rich man's doores *Luk. 16 :*
To beg relief, all Ulcerous, and full of running sores; 20, 22,
   When once his Body dies with many griefs opprest:
His Soul by Angels carried is unto that Heavenly Rest.

[4]

The Riotous Epicure, that feasted every day,
That cloath'd himself with Purple, and most gorgeous
   array:
He dy'd and went to Hell, suff'ring Eternal Pain. 23.
What thinkest thou my Soul? which was the richer of
   these twain?

[5]

He was a Rich Poor man, whose Poverty prepar'd
   him
For Heav'n: But he a Poor Rich man whose Worldly
   Wealth ensnar'd him.
That man is Poor indeed both when he lives and dies,
That hath some Treasure here on Earth, but none above
   the Skies.

[6]

He that enlarg'd his Barns to treasure up his store, *Luk. 12 :*
Was fetch'd away to Hell that night, and died worse 18, 20, 21.
   then poor.
And so is every man, that being worldly-wise
Provides for th' outward man, but doth the Heavenly
   wealth despise.

[7]

All Poor men are not Rich ('twere happy if they were)
But such as Christ enriched hath, and unto God brought
    near.
All Rich men are not Poor (that were a woful case)
But such as have no part in Christ, nor any saving grace.

[8]

Let not the poorest Saint despond; for thou art rich:

Mat. 9 : 33.
Luk. 16 : 9.
Luk. 12 : 33.

Nor richest Worldling bless himself; for thou may'st be a
    wretch.
But let both Rich and Poor endeavour to make sure
Of Heavenly Treasure, Spiritual Wealth. This only will
    endure.

[9]

If others will be fools and no true wisdom learn:
Yet what belongs unto my peace, Lord, help me to
    discern.
To have my portion here Oh never let me chuse,

Psal. 17 : 4.

Not for the sake of trifling Toyes eternal Joyes refuse.

[10]

My Soul craves better things then this World can
    afford:

Psal. 73 :.
25, 26.

Thou art the Portion that I chuse, give me thy self, O
    Lord.
I shall be richer then, then if I were possest
Of all the Riches, that are found both in the East and
    West.

*HEAVENLY CROWNS FOR THORNY
WREATHS.*

Song I.

[1]

Mat. 27 :
29, 30.

WHEN Christ was crown'd with Thorns, and smitten
    with a Reed
Upon the Thorns, to wound his Head and for to make
    him bleed;
The world did little think this was the King of Glory:
So when we speak of Crowns for Thorns, they think
    it's but a story.

[2]

But as our Lord doth now his Crown of Glory wear;
Who for our sake did wear those Thorns, and such
     Abuses bear:
So shall th' Afflicted Saints that suffer for his sake
E're long be Crowned like their Head, and of his Joyes
     partake.

[3]

Those that for doing well, for keeping Christ's Com-
     mands,
For bearing witness to his Truth suffer Reproach or
     Bands,
Or any other Pain to keep their Conscience pure;   *Rev.* 7 : 14, 15,
Such of a glorious Recompence and rich Reward are 16, 17.
     sure.

[4]

Those that are persecuted because of Righteousness,
Are Blessed ones, saith Christ, for they Heav'ns Kingdom *Mat.* 5 : 10, 11,
     shall possess.   12.
And Blest are ye whom men revile and persecute,
To whom for my sake heinous Crimes they wrongfully
     impute.

[5]

Rejoyce and be ye glad hereat exceedingly;
Because there is a great Reward laid up for you on high.
For thus they persecuted the Prophets that of old
Reprov'd their sins, and faithfully God's Counsel to them
     told.

[6]

Who Father, Mother Wife, for love of Christ forsakes *Mark* 10 :
Or of his houses, Lands Estate for him small reckoning 29, 30.
     makes.
Shall here an hundred fold with persecutions gain;
And in the world that is to come eternal Life obtain.

[7]

If in a suff'ring state of Christ we followers be,   2. *Tim.* 2 :
We shall be unto him conform'd in Royal dignitie.   11, 12.
Those that have stuck to Christ in Tribulations great *Mat.* 19 : 28.
Shall reign with Christ, and sit with him, upon his
     Judgment seat.

[8]

But those that suffer pain foul Errours to defend,
That for vile Fancies of their own dread not their lives
    to spend
  Such do in vain suppose they suffer for Christ's sake.
'Tis not the Suff'ring but the cause that doth a Martyr
    make.

EDWARD JOHNSON

[The narrative of Edward Johnson's *Wonder-working Providence* (1654)
(see p. 143) is interspersed with many short verse tributes celebrating
men and events. One of the best is the epitaph for Roger Harlackenden (1611–1638), the young assistant who emigrated with his eighteen-
year-old wife in the company of his close friend Thomas Shepard. His
early death deprived the Bay Colony of one of its sturdiest leaders. The
lines praising the new churches established in 1648 at Haverhill (Andover), Malden, and Boston are picturesque and touching in their
sincerity.

The text is from the edition of J. Franklin Jameson (New York,
1910), pp. 103, 249, 250. The lines on Harlackenden have been re-
fashioned to conform to the original stanzaic arrangement. The meter
throughout is thoroughly correct by Johnson's standards.]

TWO EPITAPHS FROM WONDER–WORKING
PROVIDENCE

[ROGER HARLACKENDEN]

Harlackenden,
  Among these men
Of note Christ hath thee seated:
    In warlike way
    Christ thee aray
With zeal, and love well heated.
    As generall
    Belov'd of all,
Christ Souldiers honour thee:
    In thy young yeares,
    Courage appeares,
And kinde benignity.
    Short are thy days
    Spent in his praise,

Whose Church work thou must aid,
His work shall bide,
Silver tride,
But thine by death is staid.

[To the New Churches]

Thou Sister young, Christ is to thee a wall
Of flaming fire, to hurt thee none may come,
In slipp'ry paths and dark wayes shall they fall,
His Angels might shall chase their countless sum.
Thy Shepheard with full cups and table spread,
Before thy foes in Wilderness thee feeds,
Increasing thy young lambs in bosom bred,
Of Churches by his wonder-working deeds:
To countless number must Christ's Churches reach,
The day's at hand, both Jew and Gentile shall
Come crowding in his Churches, Christ to preach,
And last for aye, none can cause them to fall.

SAMUEL BRADSTREET and DANIEL RUSSELL

[*An Almanack for The Year of Our Lord 1657* was issued in Cambridge by Samuel Bradstreet (1633?–1682), eldest son of Governor Simon and Anne Bradstreet, a graduate of Harvard in 1653, and a Fellow of the college. He appropriated the second page of the Almanac for a six-stanza account of Apollo's wooing of the earth-goddess Tellus. Bradstreet later spent four years abroad, and upon his return in 1661 practiced medicine in Boston. In 1670 he removed to Jamaica in the West Indies, where he died. See Sibley, *Biographical Sketches*, I, 360–361.

To Daniel Russell (1642–1679), son of the Hon. Richard Russell of Charlestown, was given the opportunity of preparing *An Almanack of Coelestiall Motions for the year of the Christian Aera, 1671.* At the foot of each page he placed an eight-line eclogue on the Tellurian theme appropriate to the calendar month. Florid in style, the verses nevertheless are in the Vergilian tradition, and it was the first almanac poetry after 1664 to draw upon the classics. Russell was elected a Fellow of the college in 1675. Two years later he was called to the Charlestown church, but he died before his installation. See Sibley, *ibid.*, II, 284–287.]

TWO ALMANAC POEMS

AN ALMANACK FOR THE YEAR OF OUR LORD, 1657

Aspice venturo latentur ut omnia Seclo.[1]

I T WAS, when scarce had rang the morning bells
   That call the dead to rise from silent tombes,
Whilst yet they were lockt up in darker Cells,
Ne had the light posses'd their shady roomes,
    That slumbring Tellus [2] in a dream did see
    Apollo [3] come to cure her Lethargee.

Strait shee awoke, and lifting up her eyes
To top of tall Mount-Æthers [4] burning brow;
From flaming Globes, the Titans Herauld spies
Herward approach; Then 'fore her shrine to bow;
    Who bids her in great Phæbus name to cheer,
    For he was coming, and would soon be heer.

Now rapt with joy, she takes her mantle soft,
On colder Couch ne longer will shee lie;
But decks her self by christall glass aloft
That hangs above her spangled Canopie,
    With pearly drops that fall from Limpid stilles
    She dights her too, and then with pleasance smiles.

Whilst fleet-fire-foming-steeds from farre appear
In speedy race the lofty hills to stride:
They Scout the smoaking Plaines, and then draw near
With burning Carre, that none but he can guide
    Who baulks their course with curb & gars [5] them bound
    Whilst he steps down to Sublunary-round:

To greet his Tellus then he hies apace,
Whom sprusely deckt he findes i'th verdant gown
He whilom sent. Each other doth embrace
In loving armes, and then they sitten down
    Whilst high-born states, and low Tellurean bands
    Rejoyce to see sage Hymen joyn their hands.

Eftsoones Apollo gives a Girlond rare
With flowers deckt (for Tellus front alone)
To her: and sayes in mind of me this weare
And Babyes deft will thence arise anon.
    She dons it strait: And buds that erst were green
    Now sucklings at her milkey papps they been.

Samuel Bradstreet

AN ALMANACK OF COELESTIAL MOTIONS FOR THE YEAR OF THE CHRISTIAN AERA, 1671.

By D. R. Philomathemat.

March:[6]

The Starry Monarch now to's full careere,
Comes marching up to our North Hemisphere,
And by his burning Beams, our Frigid Zone
Doth Metamorphize to a temperate one;
Re-animating with Celestial Fire,
Those liveless Natures *Hyem*'s [7] caus'd t'expire:
And causing *Tellus* t'doff her Winter Yest,
For joy of th'Spring; her new-come, welcome guest.

April:

The Airy Choristers, they now begin
To warble forth their Native Musick in
The new-leaf'd Boughs; and in each pleasant Field,
By Natures Art their curious Nests do build.
Now big with hopes, the toyling Country Swain
Buries in th'Earth his multiplying Grain,
On which the Heavens do fertile Showers distill,
Which th'Earth with fruits, the Swain with joy doth fill.

May:

Dame *Tellus* cloathed in a grass-green Coat,
By *Flora*'s curious Needle-work well wrought,
'Gins to appear; for now the Meads abound
With fragrant Roses, and with Lillies Crown'd.
The Proverb's verified, that *April* Showers
On *Maia*'s Fields do rain down glittering Flowers;
And now the croaking Crew, late *All a-Mort*,
By their Night-chantings, their new life report.

June:

The smiling Fields, attired in their Suits
Of Taste-delighting, and Eye-pleasing Fruits;
Their Strawb'ry Mantles now begin to wear,
And many Orchards Cherry-cheekt appear.
Now *Sol* in's Crabbed Throne doth take his place,
Where he performs his Longest daily Race:
Soon after which, the dayes length 'gins to fade,
And *Phoebus*, *Cancer*-like turns Retrograde.[8]

July:
>   Now *Ceres* Offspring's numerous every where,
>   And mighty Armies of Tall Blades appear
>   In many Fields, all Rank'd and Fil'd they stand
>   Ready for Battel: With whom hand to hand
>   Fierce Husbandmen with crooked Cutlash meet,
>   And being Victors lay them at their feet.
>   This don't suffice; together th'Blades are bound,
>   Transported home, and soundly thresh'd on th'ground.

August:
>   Now *Sol* and *Mercury* near th'*Virgin* [9] meet,
>   Where in Conjunction they each other greet,
>   The best of Aspects; which doth signify,
>   Advancement to the Sons of *Mercury*.
>   And now the verdant Meads begin to feel
>   The sharp encounter of the Mowers Steel:
>   The Noble Vines with Grapes, the Grapes begin
>   To swell with *Bacchus*, which is Barell'd in.

September:
>   The *Indian* Stalks, now richly fraught with store
>   Of golden-colour'd Ears, seem to implore
>   By humble bowing of their lofty Head,
>   From this their load to be delivered.
>   *Pomona*'s Daughters now at age, and dight
>   With pleasing Beauty, Lovers do invite
>   In multitudes: it's well if they escape
>   From each of these, without a cruel Rape.

October:
>   Now the *Aeolian* Lords and Commons meet
>   In Parliament, where it is Voted fit,
>   Yea and Resolv'd upon, what-ere it cost,
>   They'll King it over all, and rule the Rost.
>   Which to effect, it is Agreed by all,
>   That blustring *Boreas* shall be Generall
>   Of their great Forces; and then to't they go,
>   And *Tellus* Kingdom first they'll overthrow.

November:
>   Where thundring *Boreas*, with his Troops, doth shake
>   The trembling Woods, and makes the Trees to quake:
>   The Leaves for very fear the Trees have left,
>   Which of their July garb, now're quite bereft:

The Fruits, those pleasant Fruits, the painted Flowers,
The Flow'ry Meads, gay Fields, and shady Bowers,
Are now destroy'd; and th'Earths depriv'd of all
Her Summer glory by this Wasting FALL.

December:
    Exit Autumnus: Winter now draws neare,
    Armed with Frost i'th'Van, with Snow i'th'Rere;
    Whose freezing Forces cause men to retire,
    For help to th'Fortress of a well-made Fire.
    Phoebus himself, as if with pannick fear
    Hereat affrighted, now in's full Careere
    Doth poste away, and speeds him from our sight
    In greatest haste, bidding the World good-night.

January:
    The Northern Captains Siege still fiercely lasts,
    And still the Roaring Canons of his Blasts
    Are fired off; which brings both Land and Sea
    His Chained Captives quickly for to be:
    And lest they should rebell, if load they lack,
    Mountains of Snow are heap'd on *Tellus* back;
    The lofty swelling Waves, stout *Neptunes* pride,
    Are made a packhorse on which men may ride.

February:
    And now the Worlds bright Torch, whose radiant Light
    Dispels the gloomy Mists of black-fac'd Night:
    The Twelve *Herculean* Labours of his *Sphere*,
    Compleated hath, and Periodiz'd the Year,
    But not his Motion: Natures Law commands
    That fiery *Phoebus* Charriot never stands,
    Without a Miracle; but that it be,
    Still termed *Certus: semper Mobile.*[10]

                       Daniel Russell

BENJAMIN TOMPSON, 1642–1714

[Benjamin Tompson, first native-born colonial poet, was the youngest son of the Reverend Mr. William Tompson of Braintree, Massachusetts. After graduation from college in 1662, he taught school and studied medicine; in 1670 he was chosen assistant to Ezekiel Cheever, headmaster of the "Free Schoole" in Boston, (known since 1690 as the Boston Latin School), but he left shortly to teach and practice medicine

in Charlestown. In 1674 he removed to Braintree, and in 1700 he took
up residence in Roxbury, where his tombstone records him as "Learned
Schoolmaster & Physician & yᵉ Renouned Poet of N: Engl:."

His most ambitious poetic flight, a narrative of King Philip's War,
appeared in Boston and London in 1676: *New Englands Crisis. Or a
Brief Narrative, Of New-Englands Lamentable Estate at present, compar'd
with the former (but few) years of Prosperity . . . Poetically Described. By
a Well wisher to his Countrey.* Much of the contents he repeated in *New-
Englands Tears for her Present Miseries,* issued in the same year, written
probably as an afterthought.

The best edition of his works is that of Howard J. Hall, *Benjamin
Tompson . . . His Poems Collected with an Introduction* (Boston, 1924).
Kenneth B. Murdock, *Handkerchiefs from Paul* (Cambridge, 1927), offers
minor corrections and two additions. See also Tyler, *A History of
American Literature,* II, 21–23; Sibley, *Biographical Sketches,* II, 103–111;
and *Dictionary of American Biography.* The text is from the 1676 Boston
edition.]

NEW ENGLANDS CRISIS

Marlburyes Fate [1]

WHEN *Londons* fatal bills [2] were blown abroad
    And few but Specters travel'd on the road,
Not towns but men in the black bill enrol'd
Were in *Gazetts* by *Typographers* sold:
But our *Gazetts* without *Errataes* must
Report the plague of towns reduct to dust:
And feavers formerly to tenants sent
Arrest the timbers of the tenement.
Ere the late ruins of old *Groton*'s cold,
Of *Marlbury*'s peracute disease we're told.
The feet of such who neighbouring dwellings urnd
Unto her ashes, not her doors return'd.
And what remaind of tears as yet unspent
Are to its final gasps a tribute lent.
If painter overtrack my pen let him
An olive colour mix these elves to trim;
Of such an hue let many thousand thieves
Be drawn like Scare-crows clad with oaken leaves,
Exhausted of their verdant life and blown
From place to place without an home to own.
Draw Devils like themselves, upon their cheeks
The banks for grease and mud, a place for leeks.

Whose locks *Medusaes* snakes, do ropes resemble,
And ghostly looks would make *Achilles* tremble.
Limm them besmear'd with Christian Bloud & oild
With fat out of white humane bodyes boil'd,
Draw them with clubs like maules & full of stains,
Like *Vulcans* anvilling *New-Englands* brains.
Let round be gloomy forrests with crag'd rocks
Where like to castles they may hide their flocks,
Till oppertunity their cautious friend
Shall jogge them fiery worship to attend.
Shew them like serpents in an avious path
Seeking to sow the fire-brands of their wrath.
Most like Æneas in his cloak of mist,
Who undiscover'd move where ere they list
Cupid they tell us hath too sorts of darts.
One sharp and one obtuse, one causing wounds,
One piercing deep the other dull rebounds,
But we feel none but such as drill our hearts.
From Indian sheaves which to their shoulders cling,
Upon the word they quickly feel the string.
Let earth be made a screen to hide our woe
From Heavens Monarch and his Ladyes too;
And least our Jealousie think they partake,
For the red stage with clouds a curtain make.
Let dogs be gag'd and every quickning sound
Be charm'd to silence, here and there all round
The town to suffer, from a thousand holes
Let crawle these fiends with brands and fired poles,
Paint here the house & there there the barn on fire,
With holocausts ascending in a spire.
Here granaries, yonder the Churches smoak
Which vengeance on the actors doth invoke.
Let *Morpheus* with his leaden keyes have bound
In feather-beds some, some upon the ground,
That none may burst his drowsie shackles till
The bruitish pagans have obtain'd their will,
And *Vulcan* files them off then *Zeuxis* paint
The phrenzy glances of of the sinking saint.
Draw there the Pastor for his bible crying,
The souldier for his sword, The Glutton frying
With streams of glory-fat,[3] the thin-jaw'd Miser
Oh had I given this I had been wiser.
Let here the Mother seem a statue turn'd
At the sad object of her bowels burn'd.
Let the unstable weakling in belief

Be mounting *Ashurs* ⁴ horses for relief.
Let the half Convert seem suspended twixt
The dens of darkness, and the Plantes fixt,
Ready to quit his hold, and yet hold fast
By the great *Atlas* of the Heavens vast.
Paint Papists mutterring ore their apish beads
Whome the blind follow while the blind man leads.
Let *Ataxy* be mounted on a throne
Imposing her Commands on every one,
A many-headed monster without eyes
To see the wayes which wont to make men wise.
Give her a thousands tongues with wings and hands
To be ubiquitary in Commands,
But let the concave of her skull appear
Clean washt and empty quite of all but fear,
One she bids flee, another stay, a third
She bids betake him to his rusty sword,
This to his treasure, th'other to his knees,
Some counsels she to fry and some to freeze,
These to the garison, those to the road,
Some to run empty, some to take their load:
Thus while confusion most mens hearts divide
Fire doth their small exchecquer soon decide.
Thus all things seeming ope or secret foes,
An Infant may grow old before a close,
But yet my hopes abide in perfect strength.

The Town called *Providence*
Its Fate.

Why muse wee thus to see the wheeles run cross
Since *Providence* it self sustaines a loss:
And yet should *Providence* forget to watch
I fear the enemy would all dispatch;
Celestial lights would soon forget their line,
The wandering planets would forget to shine,
The stars run all out of their common spheres,
And quickly fall together by the eares:
Kingdoms would jostles out their Kings and set
The poor Mechanick up whome next they met,
Or rather would whole kingdoms with the world
Into a *Chaos* their first egge be hurl'd.
Ther's none this Providence of the Most High
Who can survive and write its Elegie:
But of a solitary town I write,
A place of darkness yet receiving light

From pagan hands, a miscellanious nest
Of errors Hectors, where they sought a rest.
Out of the reach of Lawes but not of God,
Since they have felt the smart of common rod.
Twas much I thought they did escape so long,
Who Gospel truth so manifestly wronge:
For one *Lots* sake perhaps, or else I think
Justice did at greatest offenders wink
But now the shott is paid, I hope the dross
Will be cashiered in this common loss.
Houses with substance feel uplifting wings,
The earth remains, the last of humane things:
But know the dismal day draws neer wherein
The fire shall earth it self dissolve and sin.

Seaconk Plain Engagement.

On our *Pharsalian Plaines*, comprizing space
For *Cæsars* host brave *Pompey* to outface,
An handfull of our men are walled round
With Indian swarmes; anon their pieces sound
A *Madrigal* like heav'ns artilery
Lightning and thunderbolts their bullets fly.
Her's hosts to handfulls, of a fevv they leave
Fewer to tell how many they bereave.
Fool-hardy fortitude it had been sure
Fierce storms of shot and arrows to endure
Without all hopes of some requital to
So numerous and pestilent a foe.
Some musing a retreat and thence to run,
Have in an instant all their business done,
They sink and all their sorrows ponderous weight
Down at their feet they cast and tumble straight.
Such who outliv'd the fate of others fly
Into the Irish bogs of misery.
Such who might dye like men like beasts do range
Uncertain whither for a better change,
These Natives hunt and chase with currish mind,
And plague with crueltyes such as they find.
   When shall this shower of Bloud be over? When?
   Quickly we pray oh Lord! say thou Amen.

Seaconk or *Rehoboths* Fate.

I once conjectur'd that those tygers hard
To reverend *Newmans* [5] bones would have regard,
But were all SAINTS they met twere all one case,

They have no rev'rence to an Angels face:
But where they fix their griping lions paws
They rend without remorse or heed to laws.
Rehoboth here in common english, Rest
They ransack, *Newmans* Relicts to molest.
Here all the town is made a publick stage
Whereon these *Nimrods* act their monstrous rage.
All crueltyes which paper stain'd before
Are acted to the life here ore and ore.

Chelmsfords Fate.

Ere famous *Winthrops* bones are laid to rest
The pagans *Chelmsford* with sad flames arrest,
Making an artificial day of night
By that plantations formidable light.
Here's midnight shrieks and Soul-amazing moanes,
Enough to melt the very marble stones:
Fire-brands and bullets, darts and deaths and wounds
Confusive outcryes every where resounds:
The natives shooting with the mixed cryes,
With all the crueltyes the foes devise
Might fill a volume, but I leave a space
For mercyes still successive in there place
Not doubting but the foes have done their worst,
And shall by heaven suddenly be curst.

> *Let this dear Lord the sad conclusion be*
> *Of poor* New-Englands *dismal tragedy.*
> *Let not the glory of thy former work*
> *Blasphemed be by pagan Jew or Turk:*
> *But in its funeral ashes write thy Name*
> *So fair all Nations may expound the same:*
> *Out of her ashes let a Phœnix rise*
> *That may outshine the first and be more wise.*

B. Tompson.

URIAN OAKES

[Most of the funeral verses and elegies which Puritan poets wrote
so facilely are better forgotten, but Urian Oakes's *An Elegy upon the
Death of the Reverend Mr. Thomas Shepard* (Cambridge, 1677), deserves
to survive on its own merits. Thomas Shepard (1635–1677) of Charlestown was a son of the famous Cambridge pastor of the same name.

He prepared the Almanac for 1656, and his election sermon for 1672, *Eye-Salve, Or A Watch-Word From our Lord Jesus Christ unto his Churches*, enunciated important views on toleration. For an account of Oakes, see p. 350. The text is from the original in the library of the Massachusetts Historical Society.]

AN ELEGY UPON THE DEATH OF THE REVEREND MR. THOMAS SHEPARD

(1)

OH! THAT I were a Poet now in grain!
   How would I invocate the Muses all
To deign their presence, lend their flowing Vein,
And help to grace dear *Shepard's* Funeral!
   How would I paint our griefs, and succours borrow
   From Art and Fancy, to limn out our sorrow!

(2)

Now could I wish (if wishing would obtain)
The sprightli'est Efforts of Poetick Rage,
To vent my Griefs, make others feel my pain,
For this loss of the Glory of our Age.
   Here is a subject for the loftiest Verse
   That ever waited on the bravest Hearse.

[3]

And could my Pen ingeniously distill
The purest Spirits of a sparkling wit
In rare conceits, the quintessence of skill
In *Elegiack Strains;* none like to it:
   I should think all too little to condole
   The fatal loss (to us) of such a Soul.

[4]

Could I take highest Flights of Fancy, soar
Aloft; If Wits Monopoly were mine:
All would be much too low, too light, too poor,
To pay due tribute to this great Divine.
   Ah! Wit avails not, when th'Heart's like to break,
   Great griefs are Tongue-ti'ed, when the lesser speak.

[5]

Away loose rein'd Careers of Poetry,
The celebrated Sisters may be gone;
We need no *Mourning Womens* Elegy,
No forc'd, affected, artificial Tone.
    Great and good *Shepard*'s Dead! Ah! this alone
    Will set our eyes abroach, dissolve a stone.

[6]

Poetick Raptures are of no esteem,
Daring *Hyperboles* have here no place,
Luxuriant Wits on such a copious Theme,
Would shame themselves, and blush to shew their face
    Here's worth enough to overmatch the skill
    Of the most stately Poet *Laureat's Quill.*

[7]

Exube'rant Fancies useless here I deem,
Transcendent vertue scorns feign'd Elogies:
He that gives *Shepard* half his due, may seem,
If Strangers hear it, to Hyperbolize.
    Let him that can, tell what his vertues were,
    And say, this Star mov'd in no common Sphere.

[8]

Here need no Spices, Odours, curious Arts,
No skill of *Egypt*, to embalm the Name
Of such a Worthy: let men speak their hearts,
They'l say, He merits an Immortal Fame.
    When *Shepard* is forgot, all must conclude,
    This is prodigious ingratitude.

[9]

But live he shall in many a gratefull Breast,
VVhere he hath rear'd himself a Monument,
A Monument more stately than the best,
On which Immensest Treasures have been spent.
    Could you but into th'Hearts of thousands peep,
    There would you read his Name engraven deep.

[10]

Oh! that my head were Waters, and mine Eyes
A flowing Spring of Tears, still issuing forth

In streams of bitterness, to solemnize
The *Obits* of this Man of matchless worth!
   Next to the Tears our sins do need and crave,
   I would bestow my Tears on *Shepards* Grave.

(11)

Not that he needs our Tears: for he hath dropt
His measure full; not one Tear more shall fall
Into God's Bottle from his eyes; *Death* stopt
That water-course, his sorrows ending all.
   He Fears, he Cares, he Sighs, he Weeps no more:
   Hee's past all storms, Arriv'd at th'wished Shoar.

[12]

Dear *Shepard* could we reach so high a strain
Of pure Seraphick love, as to devest
Our selves, and love, of self-respects, thy gain
Would joy us, though it cross our interest.
   Then would we silence all compaints with this,
   Our Dearest Friend is doubtless gone to Bliss.

(13)

Ah! but the Lesson's hard, thus to deny
Our own dear selves, to part with such a Loan
Of Heaven (in time of such necessity)
And love thy comforts better than our own.
   Then let us moan our loss, adjourn our glee,
   Till we come thither to rejoice with thee.

[14]

As when some formidable Comets blaze,
As when Portentous Prodigies appear,
Poor Mortals with amazement stand and gaze,
With hearts affrighted, and with trembling fear:
   So are we all amazed at this blow,
   Sadly portending some approaching woe.

[15]

We shall not summon bold Astrologers,
To tell us what the Stars say in the case,
(Those Cousin-Germans to black Conjurers)
We have a sacred Oracle that says,
   When th'Righteous perish, men of mercy go,
   It is a sure presage of coming wo.

[16]

He was (ah woful word! to say he was)
Our wrestling *Israel*, second unto none,
The man that stood i'th'gap, to keep the pass,
To stop the Troops of Judgments rushing on.
    This Man the honour had to hold the hand
    Of an incensed God against our Land.

[17]

When such a Pillar's faln (Oh such an one!)
When such a glorious, shining Light's put out,
When Chariot and Horsemen thus are gone;
Well may we fear some Downfal, Darkness, Rout.
    When such a Bank's broke down, there's sad occasion
    To wail, and dread some grievous Inundation.

[18]

What! must we with our God, and Glory part?
Lord! Is thy Treaty with *New-England* come
Thus to an end? And is War in thy Heart?
That this Ambassadour is called home.
    So Earthly Gods (Kings) when they War intend,
    Call home their Ministers, and Treaties end.

[19]

Oh for the Raptures, Transports, Inspirations
Of *Israel's Singers* when his *Jon'athan's* Fall
So tun'd his mourning Harp! what Lamentations
Then would I make for *Shepards* Funerall
    How truly can I say, as well as He?
    My *Dearest Brother I'am distress'd for thee.*

[20]

How Lovely, Worthy, Peerless, in my view?
How Precious, Pleasant hast thou been to me?
How Learned, Prudent, Pious, Grave, and True?
And what a Faithful Friend? who like to thee?
    Mine Eye's desire is vanish'd: who can tell
    Where lives my dearest *Shepard's* Parallel?

[21]

'Tis strange to think: but we may well believe,
That not a few of different Perswasions

From this great Worthy, do now truly grieve
I'th'Mourning croud, and joyn their Lamentations.
   Such Powers Magnetick had He to draw to Him
   The very Hearts, and Souls, of all that knew Him!

[22]

Art, Nature, Grace, in Him were all combin'd
To shew the World a matchless *Paragon:*
In whom of Radiant Virtues no less shin'd,
Than a whole Constellation: but hee's gone!
   Hee's gone alas! Down in the Dust must ly
   As much of this rare Person as could dy.

[23]

If to have solid Judgement, Pregnant Parts,
A piercing Wit, and comprehensive Brain;
If to have gone the *Round* of all the Arts,
Immunity from Deaths Arrest would gain,
   Shepard would have been Death-proof, and secure
   From that All conquering Hand, I'm very sure.

[24]

If Holy Life, and Deeds of Charity,
If Grace illustrious, and Virtue tri'ed,
If modest Carriage, rare Humility,
Could have brib'd Death, good *Shepard* had not di'ed.
   Oh! but inexorable Death attacks
   The best Men, and promiscu'ous havock makes.

[25]

Come tell me, Criticks, have you ever known
Such Zeal, so temper'd well with moderation?
Such Prudence, and such Inno'cence met in one?
Such Parts, so little Pride and Ostentation?
   Let *Momus* carp, and *Envy* do her worst,
   And swell with *Spleen* and *Rancour* till she burst.

[26]

To be descended well, doth *that* commend?
Can Sons their Fathers Glory call their own?
Our *Shepard* justly might to this pretend,
(His Blessed Father was of high Renown,
   Both *Englands* speak him great, admire his Name)
   But his own pers'onal worth's a better claim.

[27]

Great was the Father, once a glorious Light
Among us, Famous to an high Degree:
Great was this Son: indeed (to do him right)
As Great and Good (to say no more) as He.
  A double portion of his Fathers Spirit
  Did this (his Eldest) Son, through Grace, inherit.

[28]

His Look commanded Reverence and Awe,
Though Mild and Amiable, not Austere:
Well Humour'd was He (as I ever saw)
And rul'd by Love and Wisdome, more than Fear.
  The Muses, and the Graces too, conspir'd
  To set forth this Rare Piece, to be admir'd.

[29]

He govern'd well the Tongue (that busie thing,
Unruly, Lawless and Pragmatical)
Gravely Reserv'd, in Speech not lavishing,
Neither too sparing, nor too liberal.
  His Words were few, well season'd, wisely weigh'd,
  And in his Tongue the Law of kindness sway'd.

[30]

Learned he was beyond the common Size,
Befriended much by Nature in his Wit,
And Temper, (Sweet, Sedate, Ingenious, Wise)
And (which crown'd all) he was Heav'ens Favourite:
  On whom the God of all Grace did command,
  And show'r down Blessings with a lib'eral hand.

[31]

Wise He, not wily, was; Grave, not Morose;
Not stiffe, but steady; Seri'ous, but not Sowre;
Concern'd for all, as if he had no Foes;
(Strange if he had!) and would not wast an Hour.
  Thoughtful and Active for the common good:
  And yet his own place wisely understood.

[32]

Nothing could make him stray from Duty; Death
Was not so frightful to him, as Omission

Of Ministerial work; he fear'd no breath
Infecti'ous, i'th'discharge of his Commission.
   Rather than run from's work, he chose to dy,
   Boldly to run on Death, than duty fly.

[33]

(Cruel Disease! that didst (like *High-way-men*)
Assault the honest Trav'eller in his way,
And rob dear *Shepard* of his life (Ah!) then,
When he was on the Road, where Duty lay.
   Forbear, bold Pen! 'twas God that took him thus,
   To give him great Reward, and punish us.)

[34]

Zealous in God's cause, but meek in his own;
Modest of Nature, bold as any Lion,
Where Consc'ience was concern'd: and there were none
More constant Mourners for afflicted Sion:
   So gene'ral was his care for th'Churches all,
   His Spirit seemed Apostolical.

[35]

Large was his Heart, to spend without regret,
Rejoycing to do good: not like those *Moles*
That root i'th'Earth, or roam abroad, to get
All for themselves (those sorry, narrow Souls!)
   But He, like th'Sun (i'th'Center, as some say)
   Diffus'd his Rayes of Goodness every way.

[36]

He breath'd Love, and pursu'd Peace in his day,
As if his Soul were made of Harmony:
Scarce ever more of Goodness crouded lay
In such a piece of frail Mortality.
   Sure Father *Wilsons* genuine Son was he,
   New-England's Paul had such a *Timothy*.

[37]

No slave to th' Worlds grand *Idols;* but he flew
At *Fairer Quarries*, without stooping down
To Sublunary prey: his great Soul knew
Ambition none, but of the Heave'nly Crown.
   Now he hath won it, and shall wear't with Honour,
   Adoring Grace, and God in Christ, the Donour.

[38]

A Friend to Truth, a constant Foe to Errour,
Pow'erful i'th'*Pulpit*, and sweet in converse,
To weak ones gentle, to th'Profane a Terrour.
Who can his vertues, and good works rehearse?
  The Scripture-Bishops-Character read o'er,
  Say this was *Shepards:* what need I say more?

[39]

I say no more: let them that can declare
His rich and rare endowments, paint this Sun,
With all its dazling Rayes: But I despair,
Hopeless by any hand to see it done.
  They that can *Shepards* goodness well display,
  Must be as good as he: But who are they?

[40]

See where our Sister *Charlstown* sits and Moans!
Poor Widowed *Charlstown!* all in Dust, in Tears!
Mark how she wrings her hands! hear how she groans!
See how she weeps! what sorrow like to hers!
  Charlstown, that might for joy compare of late
  With all about her, now looks desolate.

[41]

As you have seen some Pale, Wan, Ghastly look,
When grisly Death, that will not be said nay,
Hath seiz'd all for it self, Possession took,
And turn'd the Soul out of its house of Clay:
  So Visag'd is poor *Charlstown* at this day;
  Shepard, her very Soul, is torn away.

[42]

Cambridge groans under this so heavy cross,
And Sympathizes with her Sister dear;
Renews her Griefs afresh for her old loss
Of her own *Shepard*, and drops many a Tear.
  Cambridge and *Charlstown* now joint Mourners are,
  And this tremendous loss between them share.

[43]

Must Learnings Friend (Ah! worth us all) go thus?
That Great Support to *Harvards* Nursery!

Our *Fellow* (that no Fellow had with us)
Is gone to Heave'ns great University.
   Our's now indeed's a lifeless *Corporation*,
   The Soul is fled, that gave it *Animation!*

[44]

Poor *Harvard's* Sons are in their Mourning Dress:
Their sure Friend's gone! their Hearts have *put on Mourning;*
Within their Walls are Sighs, Tears, Pensiveness;
Their new Foundations dread an overturning.
   Harvard! where's such a fast Friend left to thee!
   Unless thy great Friend, LEVERET, it be.[1]

[45]

We must not with our greatest Soveraign strive,
Who dare find fault with him that is most High?
That hath an absolute Prerogative,
And doth his pleasure: none may ask him, why?
   We're Clay-lumps, Dust-heaps, nothings in his sight:
   The Judge of all the Earth doth always right.

[46]

Ah! could not Prayers and Tears prevail with God!
Was there no warding off that dreadful Blow!
And was there no averting of that Rod!
Must *Shepard* dy! and that good Angel go!
   Alas! Our heinous sins (more than our haits)
   It seems, were louder, and out-crie'd our Prayers.

[47]

See what our sins have done! what Ruines wrought
And how they have pluck'd out our very eyes!
Our sins have slain our *Shepard!* we have bought,
And dearly paid for, our Enormities.
   Ah Cursed sins! that strike at God, and kill
   His *Servants*, and the Blood of *Prophets* spill.

[48]

As you would loath the Sword that's warm and red,
As you would hate the hands that are embru'd
I'th'Hearts-blood of your dearest Friends: so dread,
And hate your sins; Oh! let them be pursu'd:
   Revenges take on bloody sins: for there's
   No Refuge-City for these Murtherers.

[49]

In vain we build the Prophets Sepulchers,
In vain bedew their Tombs with Tears, when Dead;
In vain bewail the Deaths of Ministers,
Whilst Prophet-killing sins are harboured.
   Those that these Murth'erous Traitors favour, hide;
   Are with the blood of Prophets deeply di'ed.

[50]

New-England! know thy Heart-plague: feel this blow;
A blow that sorely wounds both Head and Heart,
A blow that reaches All, both high and low,
A blow that may be felt in every part.
   Mourn that this *Great Man's* faln in *Israel:*
   Lest it be said, *with him New-England fell!*

[51]

Farewel, Dear *Shepard!* Thou art gone before,
Made free of *Heaven,* where thou shalt sing loud *Hymns*
Of *High triumphant Praises* evermore,
In the sweet Quire of *Saints* and *Seraphims.*
   Lord! look on us here, clogg'd with sin and clay,
   And we, through Grace, shall be as happy as they.

[52]

My Dearest, Inmost, Bosome-Friend, is Gone!
Gone is my sweet Companion, Soul's delight!
Now in an Huddling Croud I'm all alone,
And almost could bid all the World *Goodnight:*
   Blest be my Rock! God lives: Oh let him be,
   As He is, so All in All to me.

                         The Bereaved, Sorrowful
                              Urian Oakes.

EDWARD TAYLOR (*ca.* 1645–1729)

In this 1963 reissue of *The Puritans,* the section on Edward Taylor
has been recast, a change made necessary by the fact that since the
discovery of Taylor's poetry twenty-five years ago, Taylor has taken
rank as a major American poet. Significantly, the first critical examination of the manuscript "Poetical Works" (a gift to the Yale University
Library by a Taylor descendant in 1883) was made during the course

Poetry

of preparing the 1936 edition of *The Puritans*. The text of all but
the selections here added is from *The Poetical Works of Edward*
(1939); that of "Upon a Sweeping Flood" is from *New England
Quarterly*, XVI (1943), 284.

After the Restoration, Parliament by an Act of Uniformity (1662)
required clergymen, college fellows, and schoolmasters to accept everything in the Book of Common Prayers. The Taylor family were
Nonconformists, living in Leicestershire near Coventry, and Edward
Taylor was a staunch Congregationalist evidently determined to enter
the ministry. He therefore migrated to the Bay Colony, was immediately
admitted to Harvard, and after graduation (1671) accepted a call to
organize a church in the frontier village of Westfield, Massachusetts,
where he remained as pastor and physician throughout his long life.
He was twice married and the father of thirteen children, and by will he
left an impressive library of some two hundred volumes (including his
400-page "Poetical Works") to his grandson Ezra Stiles, later president
of Yale.

Except for a few short lyrics (of which the "Three Poems" here
included are a part) and some topical verses, the "Poetical Works"
divide into two major groups: "Gods Determinations Touching His
Elect," and "Preparatory Meditations before my Approach to the
Lords Supper." "Gods Determinations," written before 1690, is an
extended verse sequence, medieval in structure, and thus it probably
reflects Taylor's grammar schooling. In idiom it is a semi-dramatic
dialogue about sin and redemption, and ends with Christ's limitless
power to defeat Satan. Its lyrical ardor, couched in homely language,
can be felt in the six concluding poems, here presented as a unit. The
joy of the Soul's achievement is refracted through the illuminated faith
of the poet, and displayed with metaphoric skill.

Taylor's "Preparatory Meditations" were written, approximately
once every two months, over a period of forty-three years, from 1682 to
1725. They are dated and numbered in two series (respectively 49 and
165), and composed in six-line stanzas, each preceded by a text from
scriptures. A belated metaphysical poet writing in the manner of Donne
and Herbert, Taylor links incongruities by stressing a paradox: balanc-
ing the concrete and the abstract, the minute and the transcendent,
the comic and the serious, the commonplace and the shocking. Thus in
Meditation Eight the soul, a bird of paradise, tweedles praise to God
from its wicker cage; and God grinds the bread of life, his Son, to serve
as "Heavens Sugar Cake," a food too fine for angels. These associa-
tions produce, as they are intended to do, almost unbearable tensions.

In addition to metaphors and other tropes, Taylor employs the "type" to create images. Types in theology are foreshadowings of things to come (the antitype). Typographical exegesis fascinated Puritan preachers, who used it as a way to link the historical events of the Bible. They intended thereby to present the solid core of facts, and not to bemuse their hearers by tropes, mere figures of speech which could mean to each listener what his imagination conjured. Thus Joseph, envied by his brothers (in Meditation Seven, second series) is said to foreshadow the treatment of Christ by the Pharisees. What gives vitality to such poems by Taylor is not the device he used, but the intensity of his love for the world God made and for the God who made it.

Indeed, this quality of intensity involved something of a dilemma for a colonial Puritan who happened to be a poet. The book of the Bible to which Taylor turned most often for inspiration was Canticles, the Song of Songs, for which the poet seems to have felt a humanly vigorous fascination. The fact that Taylor's ecstatic moods, quite literally redolent of altar incense, overleaped the limits of the doctrines he professed, must account in large part for his injunction that his heirs should never publish his verses. In Taylor's love of language for itself, he commands an eminence unique among Puritan writers in America, and today critical assessment gives him first rank among American poets before the nineteenth century.

From GODS DETERMINATIONS . . .

THE PREFACE

Infinity, when all things it beheld,
In Nothing, and of Nothing all did build,
Upon what Base was fixt the Lath[e] wherein
He turn'd this Globe, and riggalld[1] it so trim?
Who blew the Bellows of his Furnace Vast?
Or held the Mould wherein the world was Cast?
Who laid its Corner Stone? Or whose Command?
Where stand the Pillars upon which it stands?
Who Lac'de and Fillitted the earth so fine,
With Rivers like green Ribbons Smaragdine?[2]
Who made the Sea's its Selvedge, and it locks
Like a Quilt Ball within a Silver Box?
Who Spread its Canopy? Or Curtains Spun?
Who in this Bowling Alley bowld the Sun?
Who made it always when it rises set:
To go at once both down, and up to get?

Who th'Curtain rods made for this Tapistry?
Who hung the twinckling Lanthorns in the Sky?
Who? who did this? or who is he? Why, know
It's Onely Might Almighty this did doe.
His hand hath made this noble worke which Stands
His Glorious Handywork not made by hands.
Who spake all things from nothing; and with ease
Can speake all things to nothing, if he please.
Whose Little finger at his pleasure Can
Out mete ten thousand worlds with halfe a Span:
Whose Might Almighty can by half a looks
Root up the rocks and rock the hills by th'roots.
Can take this mighty World up in his hande,
And shake it like a Squitchen³ or a Wand.
Whose single Frown will make the Heavens shake
Like as an aspen leafe the Winde makes quake.
Oh! what a might is this! Whose single frown
Doth shake the world as it would shake it down?
Which All from Nothing fet, from Nothing, All:
Hath All on Nothing set, lets Nothing fall.
Gave All to nothing Man indeed, whereby
Through nothing man all might him Glorify.
In Nothing is imbosst the brightest Gem
More pretious than all pretiousness in them.
But Nothing man did throw down all by sin:
And darkened that lightsom Gem in him,
    That now his Brightest Diamond is grown
    Darker by far than any Coalpit Stone.

OUR INSUFFICIENCY TO PRAISE GOD SUITABLY FOR HIS MERCY

Should all the World so wide to atoms fall,
    Should th'Aire be shred to motes; should we
    Se[e] all the Earth hackt here so small
        That none Could smaller bee?
Should Heaven and Earth be Atomizd, we guess
The Number of these Motes were numberless.

But should we then a World each Atom deem,
    Where dwell as many pious men
    As all these Motes the world Could teem,
        Were it shred into them?
Each Atom would the World surmount, wee guess,
Whose men in number would be numberless.

But had each pious man as many Tongues
  At singing all together then
  The Praise that to the Lord belongs,
    As all these Atoms men?
Each man would sing a World of Praise, we guess,
Whose Tongues in number would be numberless.

And had each Tongue, as many Songs of Praise
  To sing to the Almighty ALL;
  As all these men have Tongues to raise
    To him their Holy Call?
Each Tongue would tune a World of Praise, we guess,
Whose songs in number would be numberless.

Nay, had each song as many Tunes most sweet,
  Or one intwisting in't as many,
  As all these Tongues have songs most meet
    Unparallelld by any?
Each song a world of Musick makes, we guess,
Whose Tunes in number would be numberless.

Now should all these Conspire in us, that we
  Could breath such Praise to thee, Most High:
  Should we thy Sounding Organs be
    To ring such Melody?
Our Musick would the World of Worlds outring,
Yet be unfit within thine Ears to ting.

Thou didst us mould, and us new mould when wee
  Were worse than mould we tread upon.
  Nay, Nettles made by Sin wee bee:
    Yet hadst Compassion.
Thou hast pluckt out our Stings; and by degrees
Hast of us, lately Wasps, made Lady-Bees.

Though e're our Tongues thy Praises due can fan,
  A Weevle with the World may fly,
  Yea fly away: and with a span
    We may out mete the sky.
Though what we can is but a Lisp, we pray
Accept thereof. We have no better pay.

THE SOULE SEEKING CHURCH-FELLOWSHIP

The Soul refresht with gracious Steams, behold,
  Christs royall Spirit richly tended
With all the guard of Graces manifold
  Throngs in to solace it amended
  And by the Trinity befriended.

Befriended thus! It lives a Life indeed.
  A Life! as if it Liv'd for Life,
For Life Eternall: wherefore with all heed,
  It trims the same with Graces rife
  To be the Lambs espoused Wife.

Yea like a Bride all Gloriously arraide
  It is arrai'de, Whose dayly ware
Is an Imbrodery with Grace inlaide,
  Of Sanctuary White most Faire:
  Its drest in Heavens fashion rare.

Each Ordinance and Instrument of Grace
  Grace doth instruct are Usefull here;
They're Golden Pipes where Holy Waters trace
  Into the spirits spicebed Deare,
  To vivify what withering were.

Hence do their Hearts like Civit-Boxes sweet
  Evaporate their Love full pure,
Which through the Chincks of their Affection reech
  To God, Christ, Christians all, though more:
  To such whose Counsills made their Cure.

Hence now Christ[s] Curious Garden fenced in
  With Solid Walls of Discipline
Well wed, and watered, and made full trim:
  The Allies all Laid out by line:
  Walks for the Spirit all Divine.

Whereby Corruptions are kept out, whereby
  Corrupters also get not in,
Unless the Lyons Carkass secretly
  Lies lapt up in a Lamblike skin,
  Which Holy seems, yet's full of sin.

For on the Towers of these Walls there stand
   Just Watchmen Watching day and night,
And Porter[s] at each Gate, who have Command
    To open onely to the right.
    And all within may have a sight.

Whose Zeale, should it along a Channell slide
   Not banckt with Knowledg right and Good,
Nor Bottomed with Love: nor wiers ti'de
    To hinder prejudiciall Blood,
    The Currant will be full of mud.

But yet this Curious Garden richly set,
   The Soul accounts Christs Paradise
Set with Choice slips and flowers, and longs to get
    Itself set here: and by advice
    To grow herein and so rejoyce.

The˙ Soul admiring the Grace of the Church
Enters into Church-Fellowship

How is this City, Lord, of thine bespangled
   With Graces shine?
With Ordinances alli'de ·and inam'led
   Which are Divine?
Wall'd in with Discipline her Gates obtaine
Just Centinalls with Love Imbellisht plain.

Hence glorious and terrible she stands;
   That Converts new
Seeing her Centinalls, of all demand
   The Word to shew;
Stand gazing much between two Passions Crusht:
Desire and Feare at once, which both wayes thrust.

Thus are they wrackt. Desire doth forward screw
   To get them in,
But Feare doth backward thrust, that lies purdue,
   And slicks that Pin.
You cannot give the word, Quoth she, which though
You stumble on't, its more than yet you know.

But yet Desires Screw Pin doth not slack:
   It still holds fast.
But Fears Screw Pin thrusts back, or Screw doth **Crack,**
   And breaks at last.
Hence on they go, and in they enter: where
Desire Converts to joy, joy Conquours Fear.

They now encovenant with God, and His;
   They thus indent
The Charters Seals belonging unto this,
   The Sacrament.
So God is theirs avoucht, they his in Christ,
In whom all things they have, with Grace are splic'te.

Thus in the usuall Coach of Gods Decree
   They bowle and swim
To Glory bright, if no Hypocrisie
   Handed them in.
For such must shake their handmaid off, lest they
Be shakt out of this Coach, or dy in th'way.

THE GLORY OF AND GRACE IN

THE CHURCH SET OUT

   Come now behold
  Within this Knot what Flowers do grow:
    Spanglde like gold:
  Whence Wreaths of all Perfumes do flow.
Most Curious Colours of all sorts you shall
With all Sweet Spirits s[c]ent. Yet thats not all.

   Oh! Look, and finde
  These Choicest Flowers most richly sweet
    Are Disciplinde
  With Artificiall Angells meet.
An heap of Pearls is precious: but they shall
When set by Art Excell. Yet that's not all.

   Christ's Spirit showers
  Down in his Word and Sacraments
    Upon these Flowers,
  The Clouds of Grace Divine Contents.
Such things of Wealthy Blessings on them fall
As make them sweetly thrive. Yet that's not all.

Yet still behold!
All flourish not at once. We see
 While some Unfold
Their blushing Leaves, some buds there bee:
Here's Faith, Hope, Charity in flower, which call
On yonders in the Bud. Yet that's not all.

But as they stand
Like Beauties reeching in perfume
 A Divine Hand
Doth hand them up to Glories room:
Where Each in sweet'ned Songs of Praises shall
Sing all ore heaven for aye. And that's but all.

THE SOULS ADMIRATION HEREUPON

What! I such Praises sing? How can it bee?
 Shall I in Heaven sing?
What! I that scarce durst hope to see,
 Lord, such a thing?
 Though nothing is too hard for thee,
 One Hope hereof seems hard to mee.

What! Can I ever tune those Melodies,
 Who have no tune at all?
Not knowing where to stop nor Rise,
 Nor when to Fall.
 To sing thy Praise I am unfit:
 I have not learn'd my Gam-ut yet.

But should these Praises on string'd Instruments
 Be sweetly tun'de? I finde
I nonplust am, for no Consents
 I ever minde.
 My Tongue is neither Quill nor Bow:
 Nor Can my Fingers Quavers show.

But was it otherwise, I have no Kit:
 Which though I had, I could
Not tune the strings, which soon would slip,
 Thqugh others should.
 But should they not, I cannot play,
 But for an F should strike an A.

And should thy Praise upon Winde Instruments
    Sound all o're Heaven Shrill?
My Breath will hardly through such Vents
    A Whistle fill:
    Which though it should, its past my spell
    By Stops and Falls to sound it Well.

How should I then, joyn in such Exercise?
    One Sight of thee'l intice
Mine Eyes to heft: whose Extasies
    Will stob my Voice.
    Hereby mine Eyes will bind my Tongue,
    Unless thou, Lord, do Cut the thong.

What use of Uselesse mee then there, poore snake?
    There Saints and Angels sing
Thy Praise in full Cariere, which make
    The Heavens to ring.
    Yet if thou wilt, thou Can'st me raise
    With Angels bright to sing thy Praise.

THE JOY OF CHURCH FELLOWSHIP
RIGHTLY ATTENDED

In Heaven soaring up, I dropt an Eare
    On Earth: and oh! sweet Melody!
And listening, found it was the Saints who were
    Encoacht for Heaven that sang for Joy.
    For in Christs Coach they sweetly sing,
    As they to Glory ride therein.

Oh! joyous hearts! Enfir'de with holy Flame!
    Is speech thus tasseled with praise?
Will not your inward fire of Joy contain,
    That it in open flames doth blaze?
    For in Christ[s] Coach Saints sweetly sing,
    As they to Glory ride therein.

And if a string do slip by Chance, they soon
    Do screw it up again: whereby
They set it in a more melodious Tune
    And a Diviner Harmony.
    For in Christs Coach they sweetly sing,
    As they to Glory ride therein.

In all their Acts, publick and private, nay,
   And secret too, they praise impart.
But in their Acts Divine, and Worship, they
   With Hymns do offer up their Heart.
   Thus in Christs Coach they sweetly sing,
   As they to Glory ride therein.

Some few not in; and some whose Time and Place
   Block up this Coaches way, do goe
As Travellers afoot: and so do trace
   The Road that gives them right thereto;
   While in this Coach these sweetly sing
   As they to Glory ride therein.

THREE POEMS

HUSWIFERY

Make me, O Lord, thy Spin[n]ing Wheele compleat;
   Thy Holy Worde my Distaff make for mee.
Make mine Affections thy Swift Flyers neate,
   And make my Soule thy holy Spoole to bee.
   My Conversation make to be thy Reele,
   And reele the yarn thereon spun of thy Wheele.

Make me thy Loome then, knit therein this Twine:
   And make thy Holy Spirit, Lord, winde quills:
Then weave the Web thyselfe. The yarn is fine.
   Thine Ordinances make my Fulling Mills,
   Then dy the same in Heavenly Colours Choice,
   All pinkt with Varnish't Flowers of Paradise.

Then cloath therewith mine Understanding, Will,
   Affections, Judgment, Conscience, Memory;
My Words and Actions, that their shine may fill
   My wayes with glory and thee glorify,
   Then mine apparell shall display before yee
   That I am Cloathd in Holy robes for glory.

THE EBB AND FLOW

When first thou on me, Lord, wrought'st thy Sweet Print,
   My heart was made thy tinder box.
   My 'ffections were thy tinder in't:
     Where fell thy Sparkes by drops.
Those holy Sparks of Heavenly fire that came
Did ever catch and often out would flame.

But now my Heart is made thy Censar trim,
  Full of thy golden Altars fire,
    To offer up Sweet Incense in
      Unto thyselfe intire:
I finde my tinder scarce thy sparks can feel
That drop out from thy Holy flint and Steel.

Hence doubts out bud for feare thy fire in mee
  'S a mocking Ignis Fatuus,
    Or lest thine Altars fire out bee,
      It's hid in ashes thus.
Yet when the bellows of thy Spirit blow
Away mine ashes, then thy fire doth glow.

Upon the Sweeping Flood[4]

O! that I'd had a tear to've quencht that flame
  Which did dissolve the Heavens above
    Into those liquid drops that Came
      To drown our Carnal love.
Our cheeks were dry and eyes refusde to weep.
Tears bursting out ran down the skies darke Cheek.

Were th'Heavens sick? must wee their Doctors bee
  And Physick them with pills, our sin?
    To make them purge and vomit; see:
      And Excrements out fling?
We've griev'd them by such Physick that they shed
Their Excrements upon our lofty heads.

From *PREPARATORY MEDITATIONS*

Meditation One

What love is this of thine, that Cannot bee
  In thine Infinity, O Lord, Confinde,
Unless it in thy very Person see
  Infinity and Finity Conjoyn'd?
  What! hath thy Godhead, as not satisfi'de,
  Marri'de our Manhood, making it its Bride?

Oh, Matchless Love! Filling Heaven to the brim!
  O'rerunning it: all running o're beside
This World! Nay, Overflowing Hell, wherein
  For thine Elect, there rose a mighty Tide!
  That there our Veans might through thy Person bleed,
  To quench those flames, that else would on us feed.

Oh! that thy love might overflow my Heart!
 To fire the same with Love: for Love I would.
But oh! my streight'ned Breast! my Lifeless Sparke!
 My Fireless Flame! What Chilly Love, and Cold?
 In measure small! In Manner Chilly! See!
 Lord, blow the Coal: Thy Love Enflame in mee.

THE EXPERIENCE

Canticles I:3: . . . thy name is as ointment poured forth.

Oh, that I always breath'd in such an aire
 As I suck't in, feeding on sweet Content!
Disht up unto my Soul ev'n in that pray're
 Pour'de out to God over last Sacrament.
 What Beam of Light wrapt up my sight to finde
 Me neerer God than ere Came in my minde?

Most strange it was! But yet more strange that shine
 Which fill'd my Soul then to the brim to spy
My nature with thy Nature all Divine
 Together joyn'd in Him that's Thou, and I.
 Flesh of my Flesh, Bone of my Bone: there's run
 Thy Godhead and my Manhood in thy Son.

Oh! that that Flame which thou didst on me Cast
 Might me enflame, and Lighten ery where.
Then Heaven to me would be less at last,
 So much of heaven I should have while here.
 Oh! Sweet though Short! I'le not forget the same.
 My neerness, Lord, to thee did me Enflame.

I'le Claim my Right: Give place ye Angells Bright.
 Ye further from the Godhead stande than I.
My Nature is your Lord; and doth Unite
 Better than Yours unto the Deity.
 Gods Throne is first and mine is next: to you
 Onely the place of Waiting-men is due.

Oh! that my Heart, thy Golden Harp might bee
 Well tun'd by Glorious Grace, that e'ry string
Screw'd to the highest pitch, might unto thee
 All Praises wrapt in sweetest Musick bring.
 I praise thee, Lord, and better praise thee would,
 If what I had, my heart might ever hold.

The Reflexion

Canticles II:1: I am the rose of Sharon.

Lord, art thou at the Table Head above
    Meat, Med'cine, Sweetness, sparkling Beautys, to
Enamour Souls with Flaming Flakes of Love,
    And not my Trencher, nor my Cup o'reflow?
    Ben't I a bidden guest? Oh! sweat mine Eye:
    O'reflow with Teares: Oh! draw thy fountains dry.

Shall I not smell thy sweet, oh! Sharons Rose?
    Shall not mine Eye salute thy Beauty? Why?
Shall thy sweet leaves their Beautious sweets upclose?
    As halfe ashamde my sight should on them ly?
    Woe's me! For this my sighs shall be in grain,
    Offer'd on Sorrows Altar for the same.

Had not my Soule's, thy Conduit, Pipes stopt bin
    With mud, what Ravishment would'st thou Convay?
Let Graces Golden Spade dig till the Spring
    Of tears arise, and cleare this filth away.
    Lord, let thy Spirit raise my sighings till
    These Pipes my soule do with thy sweetness fill.

Earth once was Paradise of Heaven below,
    Till inkefac'd sin had it with poyson stockt;
And Chast this Paradise away into
    Heav'ns upmost Loft, and it in Glory Lockt.
    But thou, sweet Lord, hast with thy golden Key
    Unlock[t] the Doore, and made a golden day.

Once at thy Feast, I saw thee Pearle-like stand
    'Tween Heaven and Earth, where Heavens Bright glory all
In streams fell on thee, as a floodgate and,
    Like Sun Beams through thee on the World to Fall.
    Oh! Sugar sweet then! My Deare sweet Lord, I see
    Saints Heaven-lost Happiness restor'd by thee.

Shall Heaven and Earth's bright Glory all up lie,
    Like Sun Beams bundled in the sun in thee?
Dost thou sit Rose at Table Head, where I
    Do sit, and Carv'st no morsell sweet for mee?
    So much before, so little now! Sprindge,[5] Lord,
    Thy Rosie Leaves, and me their Glee afford.

Shall not thy Rose my Garden fresh perfume?
  Shall not thy Beauty my dull Heart assaile?
Shall not thy golden gleams run through this gloom?
  Shall my black Velvet Mask thy fair Face Vaile?
  Pass o're my Faults; shine forth, bright sun; arise!
  Enthrone thy Rosy-selfe within mine Eyes.

MEDITATION EIGHT

John VI:51: I am the living bread.

I ken[n]ing through Astronomy Divine
  The Worlds bright Battlement, wherein I spy
A Golden Path my Pencill cannot line
  From that bright Throne unto my Threshold ly.
  And while my puzzled thoughts about it pore,
  I find the Bread of Life in't at my doore.

When that this Bird of Paradise put in
  This Wicker Cage (my Corps) to tweedle praise
Had peckt the Fruite forbid: and so did fling
  Away its Food, and lost its golden dayes,
  It fell into Celestiall Famine sore,
  And never could attain a morsell more.

Alas! alas! Poore Bird, what wilt thou doe?
  The Creatures field no food for Souls e're gave:
And if thou knock at Angells dores, they show
  An Empty Barrell: they no soul bread have.
  Alas! Poore Bird, the Worlds White Loafe is done,
  And cannot yield thee here the smallest Crumb.

In this sad state, Gods Tender Bowells run
  Out streams of Grace: And he to end all strife,
The Purest Wheate in Heaven, his deare-dear Son
  Grinds, and kneads up into this Bread of Life:
  Which Bread of Life from Heaven down came and stands
  Disht on thy Table up by Angells Hands.

Did God mould up this Bread in Heaven, and bake,
  Which from his Table came, and to thine goeth?
Doth he bespeake thee thus: This Soule Bread take;
  Come, Eate thy fill of this, thy Gods White Loafe?
  Its Food too fine for Angells; yet come, take
  And Eate thy fill! Its Heavens Sugar Cake.

What Grace is this knead in this Loafe? This thing
  Souls are but petty things it to admire.
Yee Angells, help: This fill would to the brim
  Heav'ns whelm'd-down Chrystall meele Bowle, yea and higher.
  This Bread of Life dropt in thy mouth doth Cry:
  Eate, Eate me, Soul, and thou shalt never dy.

MEDITATION THIRTY-EIGHT

I John II: 1: And if any man sin, we have an
advocate with the Father.

Oh! What a thing is Man? Lord, Who am I?
  That thou shouldst give him Law (Oh! golden Line)
To regulate his Thoughts, Words, Life thereby:
  And judge him wilt thereby too in thy time.
  A Court of Justice thou in heaven holdst,
  To try his Case while he's here housd on mould.

How do thy Angells lay before thine eye
  My Deeds both White and Black I dayly doe?
How doth thy Court thou Pannellst there them try?
  But flesh complains. What right for this? let's know!
  For right or wrong, I can't appeare unto't.
  And shall a sentence Pass on such a suite?

Soft; blemish not this golden Bench, or place.
  Here is no Bribe, nor Colourings to hide,
Nor Pettifogger to befog the Case;
  But Justice hath her Glory here well tri'de:
  Her spotless Law all spotted Cases tends;
  Without Respect or Disrespect them ends.

God's Judge himselfe, and Christ Atturny is;
  The Holy Ghost Regesterer is founde.
Angells the sergeants are, all Creatures kiss
  The booke, and doe as Evidence abounde.
  All Cases pass according to pure Law,
  And in the sentence is no Fret nor flaw.

What saith, my soule? Here all thy Deeds are tri'de.
  Is Christ thy Advocate to pleade thy Cause?
Art thou his Client? Such shall never slide.
  He never lost his Case: he pleads such Laws
  As Carry do the same, nor doth refuse
  The Vilest sinners Case that doth him Choose.

This is his Honour, not Dishonour: nay,
  No Habeas-Corpus 'gainst his Clients came;
For all their Fines his Purse doth make down pay.
    He Non-Suites Satan's suite or Casts the same.
    He'l plead thy Case, and not accept a Fee.
    He'l plead Sub Forma Pauperis for thee.

My Case is bad. Lord, be my Advocate.
  My sin is red: I'me under Gods Arrest.
Thou hast the Hit of Pleading; plead my state.
    Although it's bad, thy Plea will make it best.
    If thou wilt plead my Case before the King,
    I'le Waggon Loads of Love and Glory bring.

MEDITATION FORTY-NINE

Matthew XXV: 21: Enter thou into the joy of thy lord.

Lord, do away my Motes and Mountains great.
  My nut is vitiate. Its kirnell rots:
Come, kill the Worm that doth its kirnell eate,
    And strike thy sparkes within my tinderbox.
    Drill through my metall heart an hole, wherein
    With graces Cotters to thyselfe it pin.

A Lock of Steel upon my Soule, whose key
  The serpent keeps, I feare, doth lock my doore:
O pick 't: and through the key-hole make thy way,
    And enter in, and let thy joyes run o're.
    My Wards are rusty. Oyle them till they trig
    Before thy golden key: thy Oyle makes glib.

Take out the Splinters of the World that stick
  Do in my heart. Friends, Honours, Riches, and
The Shivers in't of Hell whose venoms quick
    And firy, make it swoln and ranckling stand.
    These wound and kill: those shackle strongly to
    Poore knobs of Clay, my heart; hence sorrows grow.

Cleanse and enlarge my kask: it is too small:
  And tartariz'd with worldly dregs dri'de in't.
It's bad mouth'd too: and though thy joyes do Call
    That boundless are, it ever doth them stint.
    Make me thy Chrystall Caske: those wines in't tun
    That in the Rivers of thy joyes do run.

Lord, make me, though suck't through a straw or Quill,
Tast of the Rivers of thy joyes, some drop.
'Twill sweeten me: and all my Love distill
Into thy glass; and me for joy make hop.
'Twill turn my water into wine, and fill
My harp with Songs my Masters joyes distill.

MEDITATION THREE

(Second series)

Romans V:14: [Adam:] who is the figure of him that
was to come.

Like to the Marigold, I blushing close
My golden blossoms when thy sun goes down:
Moist'ning my leaves with Dewy Sighs, half frose
By the nocturnall Cold, that hoares my Crown.
Mine Apples ashes are in apple shells
And dirty too: strange and bewitching spells!

When Lord, mine Eye doth spie thy Grace to beame
Thy Mediatoriall glory in the shine
Out Sprouted so from Adams typick streame
And Emblemiz'd in Noahs pollisht shrine
Thine theirs outshines so far it makes their glory
In brightest Colours, seem a smoaky story.

But when mine Eye full of these beams, doth cast
Its rayes upon my dusty essence thin
Impregnate with a Sparke Divine, defacde,
All candi[e]d o're with Leprosie of Sin,
Such Influences on my Spirits light,
Which them as bitter gall, or Cold ice smite.

My brissled sins hence do so horrid peare,
None but thyselfe, (and thou deckt up must bee
In thy Transcendent glory sparkling cleare)
A Mediator unto God for mee.
So high they rise, Faith scarce can toss a Sight
Over their heads upon thyselfe to light.

Is't possible such glory, Lord, ere should
Center its Love on me Sins Dunghill else?
My Case up take? make it its own? Who would
Wash with his blood my blots out? Crown his shelfe
Or Dress his golden Cupboard with such ware?
This makes my pale facde Hope almost despare.

Yet let my Titmouses Quill suck in
  Thy Graces milk Pails some small drop: or Cart
A Bit, or Splinter of some Ray, the wing
  Of Grace's sun sprindgd out, into my heart:
  To build there Wonders Chappell where thy Praise
  Shall be the Psalms sung forth in gracious layes.

MEDITATION SEVEN

(Second series)

Psalms CV: 17: He sent a man before them, even Joseph,
       who was sold for a servant.

All Dull, my Lord, my Spirits, flat and dead;
  All water sockt and sapless to the skin.
Oh! Screw mee up, and make my Spirits bed
  Thy quickening vertue, for my inke is dim;
  My pencill blunt. Doth Joseph type out thee?
  Haraulds of Angells sing out, Bow the Knee.

Is Josephs glorious shine a Type of thee?
  How bright art thou? He envi'de was as well.
And so wast thou. He's stript and pick't, poore hee,
  Into the pit. And so was thou. They shell
  Thee of thy kirnell. He by Judah's sold
  For twenty bits: thirty for thee [we're] told.

Joseph was tempted by his Mistress vile;
  Thou by the Divell, but both shame the foe.
Joseph was cast into the jayle awhile,
  And so was thou. Sweet apples mellow so.
  Joseph did from his jayle to glory run:
  Thou from Death's pallot rose like morning sun.

Joseph layes in against the Famine, and
  Thou dost prepare the Bread of Life for thine;
He bought with Corn for Pharaoh men and Land;
  Thou with thy Bread mak'st such themselves Consign
  Over to thee, that eate it. Joseph makes
  His brethren bow before him. Thine too quake.

Joseph constrains his Brethren till their sins
  Do gall their Souls. Repentence babbles fresh.
Thou treatest sinners till Repentance springs.
  Then with him sendst a Benjamin-like messe.
  Joseph doth Cheare his humble brethren. Thou
  Dost stud with joy the mourning Saints that bow.

Josephs bright shine th'Eleven Tribes must preach,
    And thine Apostles now Eleven, thine.
They beare his presents to his Friends: thine reach
    Thine unto thine, thus now behold a shine.
    How hast thou pensild out, my Lord, most bright
    Thy glorious Image here, on Josephs Light.

This I bewaile, in me under this shine,
    To see so dull a Colour in my Skin.
Lord, lay thy brightsome Colours on me: thine;
    Scoure thou my pipes, then play thy tunes therein.
    I will not hang my Harp in Willows by,
    While thy sweet praise, my Tunes doth glorify.

MEDITATION ONE HUNDRED TEN
(Second series)

Matthew XXVI: 30: And when they had sung an hymn,
                    they went out into the mount of Olives.

The Angells sung a Carole at thy Birth,
    My Lord, and thou thyselfe didst sweetly sing
An Epinicioum[6] at thy Death on Earth.
    And order'st thine, in memory of this thing,
    Thy Holy Supper, closing it at last
    Up with an Hymn, and Choakst the foe thou hast.

This Feast thou madst in memory of thy death:
    Which is disht up most graciously: and towers
Of reeching vapours from thy Grave (Sweet breath)
    Aromatize the Skies: That sweetest Showers,
    Richly perfumed by the Holy Ghost,
    Are rained thence upon the Churches Coast.

Thy Grave beares flowers to dress thy Church withall,
    In which thou dost thy Table dress for thine.
With Gospell Carpet, Chargers, Festivall
    And Spirituall Venison, White Bread and Wine:
    Being the Fruits thy Grave brings forth and hands
    Upon thy Table where thou waiting standst.

Dainties most rich, all spiced o're with Grace,
    That grow out of thy Grave do deck thy Table.
To entertain thy Guests, thou callst, and place
    Allowst, with welcome: (and this is no Fable)
    And with these Guests I am invited to't
    And this rich banquet makes me thus a Poet.

Thy Cross planted within thy Coffin beares
　　Sweet Blossoms and rich Fruits, Whose steams do rise
Out of thy Sepulcher and purge the aire
　　Of all Sins damps and fogs that Choake the Skies.
　　This Fume perfumes Saints hearts as it out peeps
　　Ascending up to bury thee in th'reechs.

Joy stands on tiptoes all the while thy Guests
　　Sit at thy Table, ready forth to sing
Its Hallilujahs in sweet musicks dress,
　　Waiting for Organs to imploy herein.
　　Here matter is allowd to all, rich, high,
　　My Lord, to tune thee Hymns melodiously.

Oh! make my heart thy Pipe: the Holy Ghost
　　The Breath that fills the same and Spiritually.
Then play on mee thy pipe that is almost
　　Worn out with piping tunes of Vanity.
　　Winde musick is the best if thou delight
　　To play the same thyselfe, upon my pipe.

Hence make me, Lord, thy Golden Trumpet Choice,
　　And trumpet thou thyselfe upon the same
Thy heart enravishing Hymns with Sweetest Voice.
　　When thou thy Trumpet soundst, thy tunes will flame.
　　My heart shall then sing forth thy praises sweet
　　When sounded thus with thy Sepulcher reech.

Make too my Soul thy Cittern, and its wyers
　　Make my affections: and rub off their rust
With thy bright Grace: and screw my Strings up higher,
　　And tune the same to tune thy praise most Just.
　　Ile close thy Supper then with Hymns most sweet,
　　Burr'ing thy Grave in thy Sepulcher's reech.

ROGER WOLCOTT, 1679–1767

[*Poetical Meditations, being the Improvement of some Vacant Hours* was published in New London in 1725 by Roger Wolcott of Windsor, Connecticut. Apprenticed to a weaver at twelve, Wolcott, without formal schooling, by industry and thrift acquired a competent fortune and distinguished himself in public affairs: as Major General he was second in command at the capture of Louisburg; successively he became legislator, county judge, chief-justice of the Supreme Court, and governor (1751-1754) of Connecticut. Though his verse is not intrinsically important, in one poem, "A Brief Account of the Agency Of the Honourable John Winthrop, Esq; in the Court of King Charles the Second, Anno Dom. 1662. When he Obtained for the Colony of Connecticut His Majesty's Gracious Charter," Wolcott attempted an epic in celebration of his native land. See his "Journal at the Siege of Louisburg," *Collections of the Connecticut Historical Society*, I (1860), 131-161; "Wolcott Papers, 1750-1754," 2 vols.; *ibid.*, XV, XVI. *Poetical Meditations* was reprinted in *Collections of the Massachusetts Historical Society*, first series, IV (1795), 262-298; also by the Club of Odd Volumes (Boston, 1898). The text is from the first edition, pp. 11-35, with omissions indicated.]

POETICAL MEDITATION

PROVERBS XXXI. 10.

Who can find a Vertuous Woman, for her Price is far above Rubies.

VERTUE's a Babe, first born in Paradice,
  And hath by birth priority of Vice.
Vertue is all that's good we brought from thence
The dear remains of our first Innocence.
Vertue still makes the Vertuous to shine,
Like those that Liv'd in the first week of time.
Vertue hath force the vile to cleanse again,
So being like clear shining after Rain.
A Kind and Constant, Chearful Vertuous Life,
Becomes each Man, and most Adorns a Wife.
    But such a Vertue, ah, where shall we find,
That's Bright, especially in Woman Kind?
If such an one had been on Earth, no doubt
Searching King *Solomon* had found her out.
    But stay my Muse, nor may we thence Conclude,
There is not One in all their Multitude:
For tho' it be too True, that *Solomon*
Amongst a Thousand found not such an one;
It follows not at all but such an one
Amongst an Hundred Thousand may be shown;
Which if she may, her Price beyond Compare,
Excels the Price of Rubies very fair.

PSALM LXIV. 6.

The Heart is Deep.

He that can trace a Ship making her way,
Amidst the threatening Surges on the Sea;
Or track a Towering Eagle in the Air,
Or on a Rock find the Impressions there
Made by a Serpents Footsteps. Who Surveys
The Subtile Intreagues that a Young Man lays,

In his Sly Courtship of an harmless Maid,
Whereby his Wanton Amours are Convey'd
Into her Breast; Tis he alone that can
Find out the Cursed Policies of Man.

A BRIEF ACCOUNT OF . . . WINTHROP[1]

THE KING IS RESTORED TO THE THRONE

THESE happy Tidings soon found out their way,
    Unto the *English* in *America;*
Who join with *Britain* in the Celebration,
Of their just Princes happy Restauration.
The Sages of *Connecticut* do meet,
To pay their Homage at their Princes Feet;
To whom they seek to hasten an Address,
To shew their Duty and their Joys Excess.
Learned *WINTHROP* then by general Consent,
Sat at the Helm to sway the Government;
Who prudently the People doth Advise,
To ask the King for CHARTER Liberties.

All like his Counsel well; and all reply,
Sir, You must undertake our Agency;
For there is none but You we may expect,
Can make the thing you Counsel take Effect:
Your Serving us in this Important Thing,
And Personating Us before the KING,
Will sure Endear a *WINTHROP*'s Memory
To Us, and to our Last Posterity.

His Mind, vast as the Heavenly Spheres above,
Was all bespangled with the Stars of Love;

And Zealous Care for their Posterity,
Of all his Acts the *Primum Mobile;*
Led on by these bright Stars kind Influence,
He hastens to the Palace of his Prince;
　There waiting for an Opportunity,——

E're long, Great CHARLES was in his Council sat
With some Choice Nobles of his Cabinet:
His Royal Mind Intent on his Affairs,
He thus Unbosoms to his Counsellers;

What News, My Lords? *How go Affairs Abroad?*
What more Remains to do for Englands *Good?*
Do distant Parts of our Dominion
Want farther Help or Favour from the Throne?

At this arose one of the Lords of Trade,
And to his Majesty this Answer made,
An Agent from *Connecticut* doth wait,
With an Address before your Palace Gate.

Let him come in, says CHARLES, *and let us Hear,*
What has been done, and what's a doing there?

Winthrop brought in before his Princes Feet,
Prostrates himself with Reverence, the *King* to *Greet;*
And thanks His Majesty for his Access:
Then for his People offers this Address;

"*GREAT SIR,* Since Reconciled Heaven Restores
You to the Throne of Your High Ancestors,
See how each Subject Emulating tries,
To Express our National Felicities:
The Joy of Your Accession to the Throne,
Is like the Lustre of the Morning Sun;
Which from the East Salutes the Western Shores,
Still trampling under foot Nights horrid Powers:
So the loud Accents of this boundless Joy,
Ecchoing in our Ears from *Britanny,*
Gave Light & Gladness where-so'ere it came,
And fill'd our joyful Hearts with equal Flame.
The sad Remembrance of those days of Wo,
Which in Your Absence we did undergo,
Transports our present Joys to that Excess,
As passeth all Expressions to express.

May Heaven preserve Your Majesty, and Bless
Your Reign with Honour, & with Length of Days;
And in Your Line the Regal Power extend,
Until the Suns last Revolution end.

"And since we are at mighty *Cæsar*'s Feet,
O may He Pardon us, while we Entreat,
Your Royal Favour in the thing we want;
T' Incorporate us by Your CHARTER-Grant.
The Land we've Purchas'd, or Subdu'd by Fight,
And Bought of *Fenwick* what was *Warwick*'s Right,
And all at the Endeavour of our Own,
Without the least Dis-bursement from the Throne."

Rise up, Quoth *Charles; My Liberal Hand Supplies,
All needful Help to every One that Cries;
Nor shall I be Illiberal to You:
But, Prithee,* Winthrop, *Please to let me Know,
By whom it was your Place did first Commence,
Your Patriarchs that Led your Tribes from Hence? . . .*

[After an account of the trials of the early settlers, Winthrop thus describes the Connecticut Valley:]

"After the *Meadows* thus have took their Place,
The Champion Plains draw up to fill the space.
Fair in their Prospect, Pleasant, Fruitful, Wide,
Here *Tellus* may be seen in all his Pride.
Cloud kissing Pines in stately Man groves stand,
Firm *Oaks* fair *Branches* wide and large extend.
The *Fir*, the *Box*, the *Balm-Tree* here stand mute,
So do the *Nut-Trees* Laden down with Fruit.
In shady Vales the Fruitful *Vine* o're whelms,
The Weaving Branches of the bending *Elms*.

"Within the Covert of these shady Boughs,
The Loving *Turtle* and his Lovely Spouse
From Bough to Bough in deep Affection move,
And with Chast Joy reciprocate their Love.
At the Cool Brooks, the *Beavers* and the *Minks*
Keep House, and here the *Hart* & *Panther* Drinks.
And *Partridges* here keep in Memory,
How to their Loss they soared once too high.

"Within these Spacious Forests, Fresh & Green,

No Monsters of Burn *Africk* may be seen.
No hissing *Bassalisk* stands to affright.
Nor *Seps*, nor *Hemorhus* with Mortal bite,
The Lybian *Lyon* ne'er set Footing here,
Nor *Tygers* of *Numedia* do appear.
But here the *Moose* his spreading *Antlers* sways,
And bears down Stubborn standels with their *sprays*,
These sport themselves within these *Woods*, & here
The Fatted *Roe-Buck* and the *Fallow Deer*,
Yield Venison as good as that which won
The Partriarchial Benediction.
  "Each Plain is bounded at its utmost Edge
With a long Chain of Mountains in a ridge,
Whose Azure tops advance themselves so high
They seem like Pendants hanging in the Skie.
Twenty Four Miles, Surveyers do account
Between the *Eastern* and the *Western* Mount;
In which vast Interspace, Pleasant and Fair,
Zephirus Whispers a Delightful Air.
These Mountains stand at Equi-distant space,
From the fair Flood in such Majestick Grace.
Their looks alone are able to Inspire
An Active Brain with a Mercurial Fire.
The Muses hence their ample Dews Distil,
More than was Feigned from the [tree] topt Hill.
And if those Witty Men that have us told
Strange Tales of Mountains in the Days of Old,
Had they but seen how these are Elevated,
We should have found them far more Celebrated,
In the Fine Works that they have left to us,
Than high *Olimpus* or long *Caucassus;*
Or *Latmos* which *Diana* stops upon,
There to Salute her dear *Endimion.*"

MATHER BYLES, 1706/7–1788

[Were it not that in background, training, and subsequent influence
the Reverend Mr. Mather Byles of Boston was an orthodox Calvinist,
he would hardly be considered among the Puritans. He is remembered
today as a wit, a Tory, and a lover of good society and polite letters.
But as a grandson of Increase Mather, trained up by his uncle Cotton
Mather, and as first pastor of the Hollis Street Congregational Church
from 1732 till the Revolution, he is perhaps the last link with the Puritan
tradition in letters. The discomforts he suffered because of his Loyalist

sympathies were mitigated somewhat by the fame he won as writer, preacher, and scholar. Much of his poetry was issued in the *New England Weekly Journal*. For the rest, *Poems on Several Occasions* (Boston, 1744) and *The Conflagration* (1755) contain most of his verses.

His poems, modeled upon the verses of Pope, Thomson, and Watts, reflect current literary fashions. "An Hymn to Christ" is written in the manner of the last named, and is taken from the last page of *Mr. Byle's Two Sermons at Dorchester* (Boston, 1732). See Tyler, *A History of American Literature*, II, 55–57, 192–198; and Arthur W. H. Eaton, *The Famous Mather Byles* (Boston, 1914). See also *Dictionary of American Biography* for a good biographical account and for further biographical material.]

AN HYMN *TO* CHRIST *FOR OUR* REGENERATION *AND* RESURRECTION.

I.

To THEE, my LORD, I lift the Song,
    Awake, my tuneful Pow'rs:
In constant Praise my grateful Tongue
Shall fill my foll'wing Hours.

II.

Guilty, condemn'd, undone I stood;
I bid my GOD depart:
He took my Sins, and paid his Blood,
And *turn'd* this wand'ring Heart.

III.

Death, the grim Tyrant, seiz'd my Fame,
Vile, loathsome and accurst:
His Breath renews the vital Flame,
And Glories *change* the Dust.

IV.

Now, SAVIOUR, shall thy Praise commence;
My Soul by Thee brought Home,
And ev'ry Member, ev'ry Sense,
Recover'd from the Tomb.

v.

To Thee my Reason I submit,
My Love, my Mem'ry, LORD,
My Eyes to read, my Hands to write,
My Lips to preach thy Word.

46.

Page of Edward Taylor's Manuscript. (For text, see p. 653.)

LITERARY THEORY

THOUGH it is evident that the Puritans as a group never developed a lively aesthetic sense in their appreciation of music, painting, and sculpture, yet they left on record a great number of brief comments upon the art of writing, as well as a few extended essays. In each instance the writer is concerned with the question: How can prose or verse be made more useful to the preacher, historian, poet, or controversialist? Usually the remarks are incidental to some broader aim. The motive behind Puritan writing was utilitarian: the author might chronicle the story of his times, attack unwelcome schools of thought, discourse upon man's duties, narrate the lives of famous men, or hymn praises to God, but the end he purposed was never merely an enjoyment of belles-lettres or of literature for its own sake. This is not to say that he was devoid of literary sensibilities. On the contrary, Michael Wigglesworth's college declamation praises eloquence because it is an art which "gives new luster and bewty, new strength new vigour, new life unto trueth" (see p. 674). The interest is utilitarian in the finest sense, for it does not limit eloquence to the service of one type or class of men; it is conceived rather as the art behind which other arts are hidden.

The early Puritan authors in this country were almost without exception college graduates who could look back upon a classical training acquired by seven years of grammar school study, concluded by four college years wherein the students were intensively drilled in rhetoric. They were, to begin with, inheritors of such Elizabethan training and rhetorical theory as had been in vogue at the English universities; they knew what Erasmus, Peacham, and Florio had to say on the art of writing well,—they further studied apophthegms culled from the rhetoric texts of Farnaby, Dugard, Draxe, and Buchler. Rapin's works, especially his *Reflections upon the Eloquence of these Times; particularly of the Barr and Pulpit* (London, 1672), and the usual *artes concionandi* [1] of Keckermann, Chappell, and others were the standard texts for divinity students. The consciousness of literary style was clearly a matter not left to chance; the gentlemen who came to establish a *"Plantation Religious"* were steeped in the humanistic tradition, and believed that the key to "truth" lay in advancement of learning. They believed therefore that such art was reckoned best which was clearest, most convincing, ingratiating, and appropriate.

[1] Manuals designed to teach the art of stirring the emotions.

Pulpit eloquence, especially the florid oratory, the figured, harmonious, "Ciceronian" periods of Hooker, Andrewes, and Donne had won high favor during the first quarter of the seventeenth century; and some few Puritans there were who defended the older tradition. "And where are there such high straines of all sorts of *Rhetoricall Tropes, & figures,* to be found in any Author," asks Charles Chauncy in 1655, "as there are in the writings of the *Prophets & Apostles?*" [1] Chauncy's apology for the fashions of an earlier day is the more striking since his voice was raised too late to win a hearing. After Perkins's *The Art of Prophesying* (1631), with its emphasis upon plainness, achieved wide currency, "high style" fell into disrepute. In 1642 John Cotton disparaged "affecting carnall eloquence" in the pulpit, on the grounds that "swelling words of humane wisedome make mens preaching seeme to Christ (as it were) a blubber-lipt Ministry." [2] It is a point of view even more elaborately stated by Thomas Hooker (see p. 672). The view held by Puritans that Holy Writ needed not the profane intermingling of human embellishment is echoed in the preface to the Bay Psalm Book (see p. 670), and Roger Williams, whose literary art was really not so uninspired as he would have his readers believe, asks: "And yet, is the *Language* plaine? it is the liker *Christs:* Is the composure rude? such was his outward *Beauty.*" [3]

Plain style was not confined to pulpit eloquence or to theological treatises alone. Historians like Daniel Gookin and William Bradford take pains to see that their narratives were adapted to their audience. Gookin remarks that his stories are "not clothed in elegancy of words and accurate sentences," but rather that he has "endeavoured all plainness . . . that the most vulgar capacity might understand; [4] Governor Bradford commends "Of Plimmoth Plantation" by saying in

---

[1] *Gods Mercy, shewed to his people in giving them a faithful Ministry,* p. 37. The example of the court and university preachers is cited by W. Fraser Mitchell, *English Pulpit Oratory,* p. 106, as the reason for the ornate fashion in rhetoric. Richard F. Jones, "The Attack on Pulpit Eloquence in the Restoration: An Episode in the Development of the Neo-Classical Standards for Prose," *Journal of English and Germanic Philology,* XXX (1931), 188–217, notes the turn to plainness after 1660, and in "Science and Language in England in the Midseventeenth Century," *ibid.,* XXXI (1932), 315–331, he remarks on the great influence of Bacon and Boyle in bringing about a simpler prose style. See also his "Science and English Prose Style in the Third Quarter of the Seventeenth Century," *Publications of the Modern Language Association,* XLV (1930), 977–1009.

[2] *A Brief Exposition Of the whole Book Of Canticles* (London, 1642), p. 112.

[3] *Experiments of Spiritual Life & Health* (London, 1652). Dedicatory address to Lady Vane the Younger.

[4] Preface to *Historical Collections of the Indians in New-England, Collections of the Massachusetts Historical Society,* first series, I (1792), 141–226. Preface dated November, 1674.

his brief preface that he is about to narrate events "in a plaine stile; with singuler regard unto yᵉ simple trueth in all things."[1] Indeed, the belief that truth was integral with well-written history was so firmly established by the second quarter of the seventeenth century that Hobbes assumed its acceptance in his preface to *Homer's Odysses* (1675): "For both the Poet and the Historian writeth only (or should do) matter of Fact."[2]

As we have already seen,[3] the Puritan held to a belief in the poet's high calling, but thought that the danger of poetry lay in its magic spell,—that it tempted men away from truth to fable; Sprat and other members of the Royal Society expressed the view that too much fictional nonsense achieved the dignity of poetic treatment. Yet the fact that danger lurked within the form in no way meant that men should shun it, providing they exhibited skill and high seriousness in handling their theme. The gentlemen who compiled *The Whole Booke of Psalmes*, saying that "Gods Altar needs not our pollishings," were employing poetry the better to honor God, while at the same time modestly deprecating their ability to write verse,—assuming God's gracious acceptance of their poor offering. Edward Taylor throughout his life chose verse to express his ardent love of Christ (see p. 650); Wigglesworth told the story of judgment day in monotonous fourteeners, though he "attended Conscience rather than Elegance, fidelity rather than poetry,"[4] thus sensibly acknowledging his inadequacy as a poet, for "every good minister hath not a gift of spiritual poetry";[5] and Jonathan Mitchell stated the case very clearly by saying: "Great Truths to dress in Meeter; Becomes a Preacher," adding,

> No Cost too great, no Care too curious is
> To set forth Truth, and win mens Souls to bliss.[6]

Along with the conception of the poet's high calling a further view obtained. Puritan schoolboys, like their Anglican cousins, were set the task of composing verse merely as rhetorical exercises. John Wilson's *Song of Deliverance* had been written in doggerel staves that children might more easily memorize history. Richard Steere's *Monumental Memorial* is recommended to the reader as a narrative which "in the Attire of *Measure* and *Cadency*, whose even and easie Pace being more

---

[1] MS (*ca.* 1650) in Massachusetts State Library, Boston. See Facsimile, ed. John A. Doyle (London, 1896).

[2] Ed. J. E. Spingarn, *Critical Essays of the Seventeenth Century*, II, 70.

[3] See p. 547.

[4] Preface, *The Day of Doom* (1662), sig. xx3ᵛ.

[5] *Ibid.*, sig. x3ᵛ.   [6] *Ibid.*, sig. B1.

Alluring and Captivating (Especially with youth, or the Crittically Ingenious of this Age) than the Elaborate *Volumes* of *Prose* left to us by our Worthy Ancestors, may probably the sooner *Decoy* or Invite thy Perusal." [1] Though the emphasis is still upon the matter, we are given to believe that a pleasing manner will do no harm. To none of the earlier generation, however, would Addison's conception of poetry as a mental relaxation, an indulgence of the imagination, have been adequate. Not until the eighteenth century did the urbane appreciation of poetry as a social accomplishment supersede an enthusiasm for verse as a means of expressing great truths in exalted moods.

The more critical dissection of "polite letters" gained no headway among Puritans until after Dryden's famous prefaces had appeared; nor indeed until Blackmore, Addison, and Pope, by calling attention to the neglected beauties in classic literature and by their example and analysis of epic poetry, had awakened a literary consciousness. The eighteenth century was well advanced in its first quarter before Cotton Mather in his preface to *Psalterium Americanum* attempted to defend the new idiom of blank verse by translating the Psalms (see p. 678). It is clear that Mather did not grasp the meaning of "blank verse," for each Bible stave is fashioned into an unrimed septinary couplet, lacking even the naïve charm of the Bay Psalm versions. Here, for example, is one stanza:

> Smooth were his Mouth's fine butter'd Words;
> but war was in his heart;
> much softer were his words than oil;
> and yet drawn Swords they were. [2]

But whether he understood the character of blank verse or not, his defense of it and of a good English idiom in the preface is a very conscious attempt to explore the possibilities of language, as well as to liberate colonial writers from the charge of provincialism. It is all the more significant in view of the fact that even in England blank verse was by no means established as a poetic form in 1718. Between *Paradise Lost* (1667) and Thomson's *Winter* (1726), few poets had used it and fewer still had discussed it; indeed, Addison's famous Spectator essays on the great Puritan epic barely touch upon blank verse. [3] By the time

---

[1] Address "To the Reader," *A Monumental Memorial of Marine Mercy Being an Acknowledgement of an High Hand of Divine Deliverance on the Deep in the Time of distress* (Boston, 1684).

[2] Psalm LV, verse 21 (Boston, 1718), p. 135.

[3] Cf. *Spectator* 285: ". . . Where the verse is not built upon rhymes, there pomp of sound and energy of expression are indispensably necessary to support the style.

John Bulkley came to write his preface to Wolcott's *Poetical Meditations* (see p. 680) the Puritan era was at its close. Bulkley's definition of wit, his discrimination between "the *Accomplish'd Poet* and the *Great Man*," and his apology for the poet as one who, by choosing a verse medium, has "Diverted some of his Leisure Hours" were the common-places that might be uttered by any eighteenth-century gentleman. In the same year Cotton Mather was preparing his handbook for divinity students, *Manuductio ad Ministerium*, with its essay "Of Poetry and Style" (see p. 684), which in its catholicity of taste and urbanity suggests the spirit of current periodical essays rather than the utilitarian aim of a preaching manual. It was not until 1745 that a literary essay, written solely for entertainment, was published in the colonies. The satire on style which Mather Byles printed in *The American Magazine* "to cultivate *polite* Writing" (see p. 689) really ushers in a new era of conscious literary feeling; here is an essay wherein the art of writing is conceived as an end in itself, one in which the utilitarian motive for presentation is forgotten and the artfulness of a cultivated style is extolled. Though serviceability still remained the criterion of good writing for mid-eighteenth-century colonial writers, there was often bound with it too great a literary self-consciousness to be characteristically Puritan. The idea of "taste" that Byles implies is one far removed from that ex-pressed by Richard Mather a century before in his preface to the Bay Psalm Book. The eighteenth-century minister, witty and urbane, was guided by very different literary standards from those in fashion during his great-grandfather's day, for Byles's writing indicate that God's altar received from his hands very solicitous "pollishings."

PREFACE TO THE BAY PSALM BOOK

[The original draft of the preface to the Bay Psalm Book, written by Richard Mather (1596–1669), has been recently discovered among the papers of the Prince Collection in the Boston Public Library. See

---

and keep it from falling into the flatness of prose," ed. Chalmers (Boston, 1854), p. 275. It is worth notice that a Richard Steere published at Boston in 1713 a poem, *The Daniel Catcher*, "To which is Added, Earth's Felicities, Heaven's Allowances, A Blank Poem." It opens thus:

> Upon the Earth there are so many Treasures
> Various Abounding objects of Delight,
> That to Enumerate, would be a Task
> Too ponderous for my Imperfect Skill,
> Or Pen, to Charactise Effect'ally.

"The Preface to *The Bay Psalm Book*," *More Books*, IV (1929), 223–229.
See the introduction to selections from the Bay Psalm Book, p. 555.]

THE PREFACE.

THE singing of Psalmes, though it breath forth nothing but holy harmony, and melody: yet such is the subtilty of the enemie, and the enmity of our nature against the Lord, & his wayes, that our hearts can finde matter of discord in this harmony, and crotchets of division in this holy melody.-for- There have been three questions especially stirring concerning singing. First. what psalmes are to be sung in churches? whether Davids and other scripture psalmes, or the psalmes invented by the gifts of godly men in every age of the church. Secondly, if scripture psalmes, whether in their owne words, or in such meter as english poetry is wont to run in? Thirdly. by whom are they to be sung? whether by the whole churches together with their voices? or by one man singing alone and the rest joyning in silence, & in the close saying amen.

Touching the first, certainly the singing of Davids psalmes was an acceptable worship of God, not only in his owne, but in succeeding times. . . .

As for the scruple that some take at the translation of the book of psalmes into meeter, because Davids psalmes were sung in his owne words without meeter: wee answer- First. There are many verses together in several psalmes of David which run in rithmes (as those that know the hebrew and as Buxtorf shews [1] *Thesau.* pa. 629.) which shews at least the lawfullnes of singing psalmes in english rithmes.

Secondly. The psalmes are penned in such verses as are sutable to the poetry of the hebrew language, and not in the common style of such other bookes of the old Testament as are not poeticall; now no protestant doubteth but that all the bookes of the scripture should by Gods ordinance be extant in the mother tongue of each nation, that they may be understood of all, hence the psalmes are to be translated into our english tongue; and is in our english tongue wee are to sing them, then as all our english songs (according to the course of our english poetry) do run in metre, soe ought Davids psalmes to be translated into meeter, that soe wee may sing the Lords songs, as in our english tongue soe in such verses as are familar to an english eare which are commonly metricall: and as it can be no just offence to any good conscience, to sing Davids hebrew songs in english words, soe neither to sing his poeticall verses in english poeticall metre: men might as well stumble at singing the hebrew psalmes in our english tunes (and not in the hebrew tunes) as at singing them in english meeter, (which are our verses) and not in such verses as are' generally used by David according to the poetry of the hebrew language: but the truth is, as the Lord hath hid from us the hebrew tunes, lest wee should think our selves bound to imitate them; soe also the course and frame (for the most part) of their hebrew poetry, that wee might not think our selves bound to imitate that, but that every nation without scruple might follow as the grave sort of tunes of their owne country songs, soe the graver sort of verses of their owne country poetry.

Neither let any think, that for the meetre sake wee have taken liberty or poeticall licence to depart from the true and proper sence of Davids words in the hebrew verses, noe; but it hath beene one part of our religious care and faithfull indeavour, to keepe close to the originall text. . . .

For although wee have cause to bless God in many respects for the religious indeavours of the translaters of the psalmes into meetre usually annexed to our Bibles, yet it is not unknowne to the godly learned that they have rather presented a paraphrase then the words of David translated according to the rule 2 *chron.* 29. 30. and that their addition to the words, detractions from the words are not seldome and rare, but very frequent and many times needles, (which we suppose would not be approved of if the psalmes were so translated into prose) and that their variations of the sense, and alterations of the sacred text too frequently, may iustly minister matter of offence to them that are able to compare the translation with the text; of which failings, some iudicious have oft complained, others have been grieved, wherupon it hath bin generally desired, that as wee doe inioye other, soe (if it were the Lords will) wee might inioye this ordinance also in its native purity: wee have therefore done our indeavour to make a plaine and familiar translation of the psalmes and words of David into english metre, and have not soe much as presumed to paraphrase to give the sense of his meaning in other words; we have therefore attended heerin as our chief guide the originall, shunning all additions, except such as even the best translators of them in prose supply, avoiding all materiall detractions from words or sence. . . .

As for our translations, wee have with our english Bibles (to which next to the Originall wee have had respect) used the Idioms of our owne tongue in stead of Hebraismes, lest they might seeme english barbarismes.

Synonimaes wee use indifferently: as *folk* for *people*, and *Lord* for

Iehovah, and sometime (though seldome) *God* for *Iehovah;* for which (as for some other interpretations of places cited in the new Testament) we have the scriptures authority ps. 14. with 53. Heb. 1. 6. with psalme 97. 7. Where a phrase is doubtfull wee have followed that which (in our owne apprehension) is most genuine & edifying:

Somtime wee have contracted, somtime dilated the same hebrew word, both for the sence and the verse sake: which dilatation wee conceive to be no paraphrasticall addition no more then the contraction of a true and full translation to be any unfaithfull detraction or diminution: as when wee dilate *who healeth* and say *he it is who healeth;* soe when wee contract, *those that stand in awe of God* and say *Gods fearers.*

Lastly. Because some hebrew words have a more full and emphaticall signification then any one english word can or doth somtime expresse, hence wee have done that somtime which faithfull translators may doe, *viz.* not only to translate the word but the emphasis of it. . . .

As for all other changes of numbers, tenses, and characters of speech, they are such as either the hebrew will unforcedly beare, or our english forceably calls for, or they no way change the sence; and such are printed usually in an other character.

If therefore the verses are not alwayes so smooth and elegant as some may desire or expect; let them consider that Gods Altar needs not our pollishings: Ex. 20. for wee have respected rather a plaine translation, then to smooth our verses with the sweetnes of any paraphrase, and soe have attended Conscience rather then Elegance, fidelity rather then poetry, in translating the hebrew words into english language, and Davids poetry into english meetre; that soe wee may sing in Sion the Lords songs of prayse according to his owne will; untill hee take us from hence, and wipe away all our teares, & bid us enter into our masters ioye to sing eternall Halleluiahs.

THOMAS HOOKER

[For a discussion of Thomas Hooker, see p. 290. The text is from the original edition (London, 1648).]

FROM PREFACE TO A SURVEY OF THE SUMME
OF CHURCH–DISCIPLINE

THAT the discourse comes forth in such a homely dresse and course habit, the Reader must be desired to consider. It comes *out of the wildernesse*, where curiosity is not studied. Planters if they can provide cloth to go warm, they leave the cutts and lace to those that study to go fine.

As it is beyond my skill, so I professe it is beyond my care to please the nicenesse of mens palates, with any quaintnesse of language. They who covet more sauce then meat, they must provide cooks to their minde. It was a cavill cast upon *Hierom*,[1] that in his writings he was *Ciceronianus non Christianus:* My rudenesse frees me wholly from this exception, for being Λόγῳ I'διώτης,[2] as the Apostle hath it, if I would, I could not lavish out in the loosenesse of language, and as the case stands, if I could answer any mans desire in that daintinesse of speech, I would not do the matter that Injury which is now under my hand: *Ornari res ipsa negat.*[3] The substance and solidity of the frame is that, which pleaseth the builder, its the painters work to provide varnish.

Erasmus in vita Hier.

If the manner of the discourse should occasion any disrellish in the apprehension of the weaker Reader, because it may seem too *Logicall, or Scholasticall,* in regard of the *terms* I use, or the way of dispute that I proceed in, in some places: I have these two things to professe,

1. That plainesse and perspicuity, both for matter and manner of expression, are the things, that I have conscientiously indeavoured in the whole debate: for I have ever thought writings that come abroad, they are not to dazle, but direct the apprehension of the meanest, and I have accounted it the chiefest part of Iudicious learning, to make a hard point easy and familiar in explication. *Qui non vult intelligi, debet negligi.*[4]

MICHAEL WIGGLESWORTH

[College undergraduates were required to deliver orations as part of their training in rhetoric. Michael Wigglesworth's declamation, "The prayse of Eloquence," was delivered in 1650, early in his senior bachelor year. Though it nowhere mentions pulpit oratory as the chief end of eloquence, we must keep in mind that Wigglesworth would assume, as well as his listeners, that sermonizing was indeed the chiefest part of oratory. The passage expounds the Protestant theory that oratory is the "means" of conviction; that the principal use of public speaking as a "means" was for working conversion by the sermon. For an account of Wigglesworth, see p. 548. The selection is from Samuel E. Morison, *Harvard College in the Seventeenth Century*, pp. 180–183,

passages transcribed from the manuscript original in the library of the
New England Historical Genealogical Society, and used by permission.]

THE PRAYSE OF ELOQUENCE

HOW SWEETLY doth eloquence even inforce trueth upon the understanding, and subtly convay knowledge into the minde be it
never so dull of conceiving, and sluggish in yeelding its assente. So
that let a good Oratour put forth the utmost of his skill, and you shall
hear him so lay open and unfould, so evidence and demonstrate from
point to point what he hath in hand, that he wil make a very block
understand his discourse. Let him be to giue a description of something
absent or unknown; how strangely doth he realize and make it present
to his hearers apprehensions, framing in their mindes as exact an idea
of that which they never saw, as they can possibly have of any thing
that they have bin longest and best acquainted with. Or doth he take
upon him to personate some others in word or deedes why he presents
his hearers not with a lifeless picture, but with the living persons of
those concerning whom he speaks. They see, they hear, they handle
them, they walk they talk with them, and what not? Or is he to speak
about such things as are already known? Why should he here discourse
after the vulgar manner, and deliver his mind as a cobler would doe:
his hearers might then have some ground to say they knew as much
as their oratour could teach them. But by the power of eloquence
ould truth receivs a new habit. though its essence be the same yet its
visage is so altered that it may currently pass and be accepted as a
novelty. The same verity is again and again perhaps set before the
same guests but drest and disht up after a new manner, and every
manner season'd so well that the intellectuall parts may both without
nauseating receiv, and so oft as it doth receiv it still draw some fresh
nourishing virtue from it. So that Eloquence giues new luster and
bewty, new strength new vigour, new life unto trueth; presenting it
with such variety as refresheth, actuating it with such hidden powerful
energy, that a few languid sparks are blown up to a shining flame.

And which is yet more: Eloquence doth not onely reviue the things
known but secretly convay life into the hearers understanding rousing
it out of its former slumber, quickning it beyond its naturall vigour,
elevating it aboue its ordinary conception. There are not onely objects
set before it, but ey's (after a sort) giuen it to see these objects in such
wise as it never saw. Yea it is strengthened as to apprehend that which
is taught it, so of it self with enlargment to comprehend many things

which are not made known unto it. Hence it comes to pass that after the hearing of a wel-composed speech livelily exprest the understanding of the Auditor is so framed into the mould of Eloquence, that he could almost goe away and compose the like himself either upon the same or another subject. And whats the reason of this? why his mind is transported with a kind of rapture, and inspired with a certain oratoric fury, as if the oratour together with his words had breathed his soul and spirit into those that hear him.

These and the like effects hath Eloquence upon the understanding. But furthermore 'tis a fit bait to catch the will and affections. For hereby they are not onely layd in wait for, but surprized: nor onely surprized, but subdued; nor onely subdued, but triumphed over. Yet Eloquence beguil's with such honesty, subdues with such mildness, triumphs with such sweetness: that here to be surprized is nothing dangerous, here to be subject is the best freedom, this kind of servitude is more desireable then liberty. For whereas our untractable nature refuseth to be drawn, and a stiff will scorn's to be compel'd: yet by the power of wel-composed speech nature is drawn against the stream with delight, and the will after a sort compelled with its owne consent. Altho: for a time it struggle and make resistance, yet at length it suffer's it self to be vanquish't, and takes a secret contentment in being overcome.

In like manner, for the affections. Look as a mighty river augmented with excessiue rains or winter snows swelling above its wonted channel bear's down banks and bridges, overflows feilds and hedges, sweeps away all before it, that might obstruct its passage: so Eloquence overturn's, overturn's all things that stand in its way, and carrys them down with the irresistible stream of its all controuling power. Wonderful it were to speak of the severall discoverys of the power in severall affections: wonderfull but to think in generall, how like a blustering tempest it one while driues before it the raging billow's of this troubled Ocean: how other whiles (as though it had them in fetters it curb's and calm's the fury at a word. And all this without offering violence to the party's so affected; nay with a secret pleasure and delight it stirs men up to the greatest displeasure and distast. Doth it affect with grief? why to be so grieved is no grievance. doth it kindle coales, nay flames of fiery indignation? why those flames burn not, but rather cherish. doth it draw tears from the eys? why even tears flow with pleasure. For as is wel sayd by one upon this point In omni animi motu etiam in dolore est quaedam jucunditas.[1] So potently, so sweetly doth Eloquence command. and of a skilfull orator in point of the affections that may be spoken really, which the Poet affirmeth fabulously of Æolus god of the winds. . . .

But I need instance no more. some of you I hope will by this time assent unto what has bin hitherto prov'd that Eloquence is of such useful concernment and powerfull operation. But methinks I hear some still objecting. 'Tis very true Eloquence is a desirable thing, but what are we the better for knowing its worth unless we could hope our selues to attain it? It is indeed a right excellent indowment but 'tis not every capacity, nay scarce one of a hundreth that can reach it. How many men of good parts do we find that yet excel not here? Cicero indeed, a man in whom vast understanding and naturall fluent facility of speech conspire together; no marvail if he make judges weep and princes tremble. But to what purpose is it for a man of weak parts and mean abilitys to labour after that which he is never like to compass? Had we not as good toss our caps against the wind as weary out our selves in the pursuit of that which so few can reach to?

An. To these I would answer first, the reason why so few attain it is because there [are] few that indeed desire it. hence they run not as if they ment to win, they pursue not as if they hop't to overtake. But 2ly let me answer them with Turner's [2] words upon this very argument Negligentiam nostram arguit, qui cum non possimus. quod debemus, optimus, nolumus quod possimus, benè. we cannot do what we would therefore will not doe what we may. This savours of a slouthfull sistem. Because we cannot keep pace with the horsemen, shall we refuse to accompany the footmen? Because we cannot run, shall we sit down and refuse to goe? we cannot reach so far as our selues desire and as some others it may be attain, shall we not therefore reach as far as our endeavours may carry us? Because we cannot be Oratores optimi, do we content our selues to be Oratores Pessimi?

And as for those that have most excell'd in this kind, whence had they their excellency? they did not come declaming into the world: they were not born with orations in their mouths: eloquence did not sit upon their lips whilest they lay in their cradles: neither did they suck it in from their mothers brests. But if you examine the matter you shall find that by incredible paines and daly exercise, they even turn'd the cours of nature into another channel, and cut out a way for the gentle stream of Eloquence, where naturall impediments seem'd altogether to deny it passage: thereby effecting as much as another could bragg, viam aut inveniam aut faciam: [3] Eminent in this respect is the example of the two best oratours that fame has brought to our ears. Of Cicero, who when he had naturally a shrill, screaming, ill-tun'd voyce rising to such a note that it indanger'd his very life: yet by art and industry he acquired such a commendable habit, as none with ease could speak more sweetly than he. And Demosthenes, though he were naturally of a stammering tongue crasy-body'd and broken-winded, and withall had accustom'd himself to a jetting uncomely deportment of his body, or some part of it at least: when to conclude he had scarce any part of an oratour, saue onely an ardent desire to be an oratour: yet by his indefatigable paines he so overcame these naturall defects, as that he came to be reputed prince of the Græcian Eloquence. Though this was not gotten without some further difficulty and seeming vain attempts. Insomuch as he was severall times quite discouraged, and once threw all aside, dispairing ever to become an oratour because the people laught at his orations. yet notwithstanding being heartned to it again by some of his welwillers, he never left striving till he had won the prize.

Go too therefore my fellow-students (for to you I address my speech, my superiours I attempt not to speak to, desiring rather to learn of them more of this nature, but) to you giue me leav to say: Let no man hereafter tel me I despair of excelling in the oratoricall faculty, there-fore 'tis bootless to endeavour. Who more unlike to make an oratour than Demosthenes except it were one who had no tongue in his head? yet Demosthenes became orator optimus. Tell me not "I have made trial once and again, but find my labour fruitless." Thou art not the first that hast made an onset, and bin repelled; neither canst thou presage what renew'd endeavors may produce. Would you then obtain this skill? take Demosthenes his course; gird up your loines, put to your shoulders, and to it again, and again, and agen, let nothing discourage you. Know that to be a dunce, to be a stammerer, unable to bring forth three or four sentences hanging well together, this is an easy matter: but to become an able speaker, hic labor, hoc opus est.[4] Would you haue your orations pleas, such as need not be laughts at? why follow him in that also. Let them be such as smell of the lamp, as was sayd of his. Not slovenly I mean, but elaborate, diurnam in-dustriam et nocturnis lucubrationibus elaboratæ,[5] such as savour, of some paines taken with them. A good oration is not made at the first thought, nor scarce at the first writing over. Nor is true Eloquence wont to hurry it out thick and threefould, as if each word were running for a wadger: nor yet to mutter or whisper it out of a book after a dreaming manner, with such a voyce as the oratour can scantly heare himself speak; but to utter it with lively affection, to pronounce it distinctly with audible voyce.

But I shall burden your patience no further at the present. Those and the like vices in declaming that are contrary to Eloquence, were the chief motives that drew me first into thoughts of this discourse. But I see I cannot reach at this season to speak of them particularly. wherefore with your good leav and gods assistance I shall rather treat of them at another opportunity. . . .

COTTON MATHER

[Cotton Mather published his translations of the Psalms, *Psalterium Americanum* (Boston, 1718), because, as the selection from his preface states, he felt all previous renderings had not kept faithfully enough to the Hebrew original. His attempt to use what he calls "blank verse" sets the translation apart and gives special interest to the introduction (see p. 668). The text is from the preface, pp. vii–xiii, with omissions indicated. For Mather, see p. 162.]

PREFACE TO PSALTERIUM AMERICANUM

§. 3. OUR Poetry has attempted many Versions of the PSALMS, in such *Numbers* and *Measures*, as might render them capable of being *Sung*, in those grave *Tunes*, which have been prepared and received for our *Christian Psalmody*. But of all the more than twice Seven Versions which I have seen, it must be affirmed, That they *leave out* a vast heap of those rich things, which the Holy SPIRIT of GOD speaks in the Original Hebrew; and that they *put in* as large an Heap of poor Things, which are intirely *their own*. All this has been meerly for the sake of preserving the *Clink* of the *Rhime:* Which after all, is of small consequence unto a Generous *Poem;* and of none at all unto the Melody of *Singing;* But of how little then, in *Singing unto the* LORD! Some famous pieces of Poetry, which this Refining Age has been treated withal, have been offered us in 𝕭𝖑𝖆𝖓𝖐 𝖁𝖊𝖗𝖘𝖊. And in 𝕭𝖑𝖆𝖓𝖐 𝖁𝖊𝖗𝖘𝖊 we now have the Glorious Book of PSALMS presented unto us: The PSALMS fitted unto the *Tunes* commonly used in the Assembles of our *Zion:* But so fitted, that the *Christian Singer* has his Devotions now supplied, with ALL that the Holy SPIRIT of GOD has dictated, in this Illustrious and Cælestial Bestowment upon His Church in the World; and there is NOTHING BESIDES the pure Dictates of that Holy SPIRIT imposed on him. Now, True PIETY, Thou shalt be Judge, whether such a *Divine matter* for thy *Songs* thus disencumbered from every thing that may give them any *Humane Debasements*, be not really to be preferred before any Compositions thou hast ever yet been entertain'd withal. Doubtless, the more that any are desirous to offer unto the Glorious GOD what is purely *His Own*, and the more concerned that any are to have their *Worship* entirely Regulated and Animated, by the SPIRIT OF GOD, the more agreeable to them, will be such an *Instrument of Devotion*, as is here prepared. Tho' the *Hymns* have not the Trifle of *Rhime*, as a Lace to set them off, yet they are *all Glorious within*, which is the thing that *Manly Christianity* has its eye most upon; and in the *Spiritual Songs* thus enjoyed and improved, thou mayst most hope to have the Holy SPIRIT of GOD, who indited them, *speaking* unto thee, even such Things as *cannot be uttered*.

BUT that our 𝕮𝖆𝖓𝖙𝖎𝖔𝖓𝖆𝖑 [1] may be furnished with a superabundance, and the Faithful be plentifully feasted with *Angels Food*, Behold, an Addition of Passages Collected in Metre, (but still as exactly translated) from some *other parts* of the Sacred Scriptures, to answer the various occasions of Christianity.

§. 4. FOR the *New Translation* of the PSALMS, which is here endeavoured, an *Appeal* may be with much Assurance made, unto all that are Masters of the 𝕳𝖊𝖇𝖗𝖊𝖜 𝕿𝖔𝖓𝖌𝖚𝖊, whether it be not much more agreeable to the *Original*, than the *Old* one, or than any that has yet been offered unto the World. Perhaps there is more Liberty taken here in Translating the *First Verse* of the *Psalter*, than almost any Verse in the whole Book beside. It keeps close to the *Original;* and even when a *word of supply* is introduced, it is usually a needless Complement unto the *care of exactness*, to distinguish it at all, as we have done, with an *Italica-Character;* for it is really in the Intention and Emphasis of the *Original*. Yea, the just *Laws of Translation* had not been at all violated, if a much greater Liberty had been taken, for the beating out of the Golden and Massy *Hebrew* into a more *Extended English*. For, it may be observed, if you Translate a *French Book*, suppose, into *English*, you turn it into *English Phrase*, and make not a *French English* of it; For, *Il fait froid*, for instance, you do not say, *It makes Cold*, but, *It is Cold*. We have tied our selves to *Hebraisms*, more scrupulously, than there is real occasion for. . . .

§. 5. MOST certainly, our Translation of the PSALMS, without the Fetters of *Rhime* upon it, can be justly esteemed no prejudice to the Character of *Poetry* in the performance. For indeed, however it is now appropriated, according to the true sense of the Term, to *Rhythme* it self a *Similis Desinentia*, or, a *likeness of sound* in the last Syllables of the Verse, is not essential. Old *Bede* will give you such a Definition of *Rhythme*, and bring other Authorities besides *Austins* for it, that *Scaliger* thereupon holds, all *Verses* wherein Regard is had unto the *Number*

of Syllables, to have a claim unto it. Be that as the Criticks on the Term
shall please, our *Translation* is all in *Metre;* and really more tied unto
Measure, than the *Original* appears to have been, by all the Examinations
that have as yet been employ'd upon it. . . .

I am therefore strongly of the Opinion, That the *Poesie* of the Ancient
Hebrews, knew no *Measure*, but that of the unknown *Music*, wherein it
was to be accommodated. Our Psalms in the *Hebrew*, are not so much
Metrical as *Musical;* And hence, the very Inscriptions of them sometimes
intimate, that there was a sort of *Melody*, unto which they were adapted.
It is true, the *Oriental Nations* at this day, have their *Metred Poetry;*
But it is of a late Original. However, 'tis very certain, that all the skill
in the World, will hardly find the Rules of that *Metred Poetry* observed
with any exactness in the Songs of the Sacred Scriptures. There is
little value to be set on the Authority, of either *Philo*, or *Josephus*, and
and after them, of *Jerom*, who quotes *Origen* and *Eusebius* for it, when
they go to resolve the *Hebrew Poesie*, into I know not what, *Lyricks* and
Hexameters. And therefore it may be hoped, that our Version may be
released from the *Chime* of a, *Similis Desinentia*, without being censured
for *Unpoetical*. The *Sublime Thought*, and the *Divine Flame*, alone is
enough, to challenge the Character of *Poetry* for these Holy Composures.
And if any *Beauties* be wanting, 'tis owing to the lowness of the *Language*,
whereinto a strict and close *Translation*, is what we are here tied unto.

JOHN BULKLEY, 1679–1731

[The Reverend Mr. John Bulkley of Colchester, Connecticut, was the
brilliant son of the Reverend Mr. Gershom Bulkley. He was graduated from Harvard College in 1699, and like his more famous father
devoted his life to medicine as well as to the service of Christ. Isolation only whetted the curiosity of this orthodox Calvinist, in philosophy, politics, and polite letters. He was reckoned by Charles Chauncy
(1705–1787) one of "the three first for extent and strength of genius
and powers New-England has ever yet produced" (*Collections of the
Massachusetts Historical Society*, first series, X, 155).

Bulkley's preface to the *Poetical Meditations* (1725) of Roger Wolcott
(see p. 657) is both an essay upon poetry and upon the rights of man.
It was reprinted in part as "An Inquiry into the Right of the Aborigi-
nal Natives to the Lands in America," in *Collections of the Massachusetts
Historical Society*, first series, IV (1795), 159–181. For biographical
data, see Sibley, *Biographical Sketches*, IV, 450–454. The text following
is from the 1725 edition, pp. i–x, with omissions indicated.]

PREFACE TO WOLCOTT'S POETICAL MEDITATIONS

§ 1. The buisy and restless Soul of Man which in all Ages has been Fruitful in *Many Inventions*, as it has been greatly Disserviceable to the Good and Comfort of Humane Life by the Discovery of things Prejudicial to it; so at the same time may we not say, has made some Compensation by the Invention of others of a Proportionable Advantage and Benefit. It were easy by a detail of some of the many Useful Arts found out by Man to give Evidence of this, but it must Suffice at Present, to Instance in one only, *viz.* That *Art of Writing* or Expressing all Sounds, and Consequently the Conceptions of our Minds, by a *Few Letters Variously Disposed or Plac'd*, the Commodity or Profit of which to Mankin'd is so Various & Extensive as not to be easily accounted for. This Art is stiled by One *Admirandarum Omnium inventionum humanarum Signaculum. i. e.* The Wonder or Master-piece of all Humane Inventions: And how deservedly is it so, whether we Speak with Reference to the *Strangeness* or the *Benefit* of it? How Strange is it that by the Various Disposition of so *Few Letters* as Our *Alphabet* contains, *all Sounds* should be express'd, and thereby all the Conceptions or Ideals of our Minds! And as for the *Commodity* of it; not to mention others, from hence it comes to pass that we are Furnish'd with so much Useful History, which bringing into our View both Persons and Things most distant from us in time and place, does greatly delight and entertain us, and at the same time Instruct or Teach and Furnish us with a main part of our most useful Knowledge.

§ 2 In the Early Ages of the World, before this most certain way of Communicating the Knowledge of things was found out; other *Mediums* were made use of for that end, the Principal of which seems to have been Representative *Symbols* or *Hieroglyphicks*, which way or Method of Communication every one knows still Obtains among many *Unletter'd Nations* in the World. But this as its very uncertain on the Account of that great Variety of *Interpretations* such *Symbols* are liable to, and as the Misconstruction of them, its reasonable to think, has been none of the least Prolifick Fountains of the *Heathen Mythology*, by which the Antient & True Tradition of the First Ages of the World has been so much Corrupted and Alter'd, so is now out of use with such Nations, as among whom the *Use of Letters* has been Introduced. I said above that to this we are Debtors for the useful History we are Furnish'd with: and I must observe on this Occasion that there are two ways in which those who have Oblig'd us with it, according to

*Galileo. [*Wolcott's note.*]

their different Genius and Humours, have Improv'd this Noble Invention in Composing the Historys they have put into our Hands; that some therein have Confin'd themselves to *Poetical Numbers* and *Measures*, others not so restricting themselves, have Written in *Prose*, which last in latter Ages has been the more common way. That a considerable part, especially of our more *Ancient History*, is delivered to us in the former of these ways, is known to most that are not Strangers to Books, a considerable part of the Writings both of the *Latin* and *Greek* Poets what are they but *Poemata Historica?* Among the former, *Ovid* assures us his Book *METAMORPHOSEON*, in part, at least is no other; when in the beginning of it he Invokes the Gods in these Words, *viz.*

> ——*Dij Cæptis* (——)
> *Adspirate meis, Primaque ab Origine Mundi*
> *Ad mea Perpetuum deducite Tempora carmen,*

In English thus rendred by one,[1]

> Ye Gods Vouchsafe (——————
> ——————————)
> To further this mine Enterprise;
>   and from the World begun,
> Grant that my Verse may to my time
>   his Course directly run.

And whoever has read it with understanding can't but see its so. . . .

. . . Its true he Writes in the Strain and Manner of others of his Tribe, who are wont generally to mingle a great deal of *Mythology* with the Truth; yet notwithstanding how easy is it for every Intelligent Reader to trace in him the Footsteps of the Sacred History, particularly in its accounts of the most Early Times?

§ 4. And may we not with equal Truth say the same of *Virgils* Æneids? which seem to be no other than a *Mythological* History of the Affairs of *Æneas*, or the Various Occurrences of his Life; to which *Homer* his *Iliads* with others from the *Greeks* might be added. Its Observed by some Learned Men, that this was the most Antient way of Writing, and that *Prose* is only an Imitation of *Poetry*, and that the *Grecians* in particular at their first delivery from *Barbarism*, had all their Phylosophy and Instruction from the *Poets*, such as *Orpheus*, *Hesiod*, *Parmenides*, *Xenophanes*, &c.—which seems to have Occasion'd those Lines of *Horace, Cap. de Arte Poetica*

——Fuit hæc sapientia quondam
Publica privatis Sacernere, sacra Profanis:
Concubitu Prohibere Vago; dare jura Maritis:
Oppida moliri: leges incidere ligno.
Sic honor & nomen Divinis Vatibus atque
Carminibus venit.

The sum of which is this, *viz.*

That in Old Time *Poets* were the Lights and Instructors of the World, and gave Laws to Men for their Conduct in their several Relations and Affairs of Life.

And Finally, To this seems to agree that of *Cato* in his Distichs,

Si Deus est Animus nobis ut carmina dicunt,

If God a Spirit be as Poets Teach, *&c.*

§ 5. I have premis'd this in way of *Apology* for the manner in which this *Worthy Person* has given us the *Ensuing History*, in Composing which he has Diverted some of his *Leisure Hours.* And from hence tis evident he has for a Precedent some of the most *Antient History,* and has trod in the steps of many of the most Eminent *Sages,* and earliest *Writers* History gives us any Knowledge of, who have taken that same way to raise up Monuments to, and eternize the Names and Actions of their Admired *Heroes.*

§ 6. Its undoubtedly true that as the Minds of Men have a very different *Cast, Disposition* or *Genius* leading to & accomplishing for very differing Improvements, so generally speaking, those are the most Accomplished to make a Judgment on any Performance that have by Nature a Genius Leading to and Accomplishing for the same: And it being so, and withal there being none among the *whole number of Mortals* less furnish'd for a Performance of this Nature *than my self,* I may well be excus'd in Omitting the part of a *Censor* or *Judge* upon it, further than to say that the Intelligent Reader will herein discern an uncommon *Vigour* of *Mind,* considerable *Reading,* and see reason to say, that herein we have a *Specimen* what good parts cultivated with a laudable Ambition to Improve in Knowledge will do, tho' not Assisted with those Advantages of *Education* which some are favoured withal.

§ 7. Some there are that have remark't, That the *Accomplish'd Poet* and the *Great Man* are things seldom meeting together *in one Person,* Or that its rare those Powers of Mind that *make* the one, are found *United* with those that Constitute the other. And perhaps it may be a Truth which for the main holds true. For whereas what is properly call'd *Wit,* (which is no other than a ready Assemblage of Ideas, or a putting those together with quickness & variety wherein there can be found any *Congruity* or *Resemblance;* or to speak more plain, an aptness at Metaphor and Allusion) is what, as I take it, makes the *Accomplish'd Poet;* exactness of Judgment, or Clearness of reason (which we commonly and truly say makes *the Great Man*) on the other hand lies in an Ability of Mind nicely to distinguish its Ideas the one from the other, where there is but the least difference thereby avoiding being misled by Similitude, and by Affinity to take one thing from another. And the process of the Mind in these two things being so *contrary* the one to the other, tis not strange if they are Powers not ever *United* in the same Subject, yet this notwithstanding, all must say, this is not a Remark that universally and without exception will hold true; but that how contrary and inconsistent soever the process of the mind in the exercise of these two Powers may seem to be, yet there are *Instances* wherein they are United in a Wonderful Measure: And many Men in whom we find a great deal of *Pleasantry* or *Wit*, are notwithstanding very *Judicious* and *Rational*. And tho' Modesty forbids me to say this of the *Author*, yet this I shall venture to say, *viz.* That whatever may be said in Commendation of this Performance by the Accomplished for a Judgment upon it; yet that there will not that Honour be done him thereby, as I conceive may with a great deal of Truth and Justice otherwise.

COTTON MATHER

[Undoubtedly the best essay "of poetry and style" written in the American colonies came from the pen of Cotton Mather (*q.v.*, p. 162). In 1726 he published at Boston a handbook for divinity students, *Manuductio ad Ministerium,* wherein he discusses science, experimental philosophy, the classics, modern languages, and polite letters with remarkable acumen. It was reprinted in London in 1781, and again in 1789 under the title *Dr. Cotton Mather's Student and Preacher.* The text of the chapter following is from the 1789 edition, pp. 110–120.]

OF POETRY AND STYLE.

Poetry, whereof we have now even an *Antediluvian* piece in our hands, has from the beginning been in such request, that I must needs recommend unto you some acquaintance with it. Though some have had a soul so unmusical, that they have decried all verse as being but a meer playing and fiddling upon words; all versifying, as if it were more unnatural than if we should chuse dancing instead of walking;

and rhyme, as if it were but a sort of morisce-dancing with bells: yet I cannot wish you a soul that shall be wholly unpoetical. An old Horace has left us an art of poetry, which you may do well to bestow a perusal on. And besides your lyric hours, I wish you may so far understand an epic poem, that the beauties of an Homer and a Virgil may be discerned with you. As to the moral part of Homer, it is true, and let me not be counted a Zoilus [1] for saying so, that by first exhibiting their gods as no better than rogues, he set open the flood-gates for a prodigious inundation of wickedness to break in upon the nations, and was one of the greatest apostles the devil ever had in the world. Among the rest that felt the ill impressions of this universal corrupter, (as men of the best sentiments have called him,) one was that overgrown robber, of execrable memory, whom we celebrate under the name of Alexander the Great; who by his continual admiring and studying of his Iliad, and by following that false model of heroic virtue set before him in his Achilles, became one of the worst of men, and at length inflated with the ridiculous pride of being himself a deity, exposed himself to all the scorn that could belong to a lunatic. And hence, notwithstanding the veneration which this idol has had, yet Plato banishes him out of a common-wealth, the welfare whereof he was concerned for. Nevertheless, custom or conscience obliges him to bear testimonies unto many points of morality. And it is especially observable, that he commonly propounds prayer to heaven as a most necessary preface unto all important enterprizes; and when the action comes on too suddenly for a more extended supplication, he yet will not let it come on without an ejaculation; and he never speaks of any supplication but he brings in a gracious answer to it. I have seen a travesteering high-flier, not much to our dishonour, scoff at Homer for this; as making his actors to be like those whom the English call dissenters. . . .

. . . Nevertheless, it is observed, that the Pagans had no rules of manners that were more laudable and regular than what are to be found in him. And some have said, it is hardly possible seriously to read his works without being more disposed unto goodness, as well as being greatly entertained. To be sure, had Virgil writ before Plato, his works had not been any of the books prohibited. But then, this poet also has abundance of rare antiquities for us: and such things, as others besides a Servius, have imagined that they have instructed and obliged mankind, by employing all their days upon. Wherefore if his Æneid, (which though it were once near twenty times as big as he has left it, yet he has left it unfinished,) may not appear so valuable to you, that you may think twenty-seven verses of the part that is the most finished in it, worth one and twenty hundred pounds and odd money, yet his Georgics, which he put his last hand to, will furnish you with many things far from despicable. But after all, when I said, I was willing that the beauties of these two poets might become visible to your visive faculty in poetry, I did not mean that you should judge nothing to be admittable into an epic poem, which is not authorized by their example; but I perfectly concur with one who is inexpressibly more capable to be a judge of such a matter than I can be; that it is a false critic who, with a petulant air, will insult reason itself, if it presumes to oppose such authority.

I proceed now to say, that if (under the guidance of a Vida [2]) you try your young wings now and then to see what flights you can make, at least for an epigram, it may a little sharpen your sense, and polish your style for more important performances; for this purpose you are now even overstocked with patterns, and——*Poemata passim,*[3] you may, like Nazianzen,[4] all your days make a little recreation of poetry in the midst of your painful studies. Nevertheless, I cannot but advise you. Withhold thy throat from thirst. Be not so set upon poetry, as to be always poring on the passionate and measured pages. Let not what should be sauce, rather than food for you, engross all your application. Beware of a boundless and sickly appetite for the reading of the poems which now the rickety nation swarms withal; and let not the Circæan cup intoxicate you. But especially preserve the chastity of your soul from the dangers you may incur, by a conversation with muses that are no better than harlots: among which are others besides Ovid's Epistles, which for their tendency to excite and foment impure flames, and cast coals into your bosom, deserve rather to be thrown into the fire, than to be laid before the eye which a covenant should be made withal. Indeed, not merely for the impurities which they convey, but also on some other accounts; the powers of darkness have a library among us, whereof the poets have been the most numerous as well as the most venemous authors. Most of the modern plays, as well as the romances, and novels and fictions, which are a sort of poems, do belong to the catalogue of this cursed library. The plays, I say, in which there are so many passages that have a tendency to overthrow all piety, that one, whose name is Bedford,[5] has extracted near seven thousand instances of them, from the plays chiefly of but five years preceding; and says awfully upon them, They are national sins, and therefore call for national plagues; and if God should enter into judgment, all the blood in the nation would not be able to atone for them. How much do I wish that such pestilences, and indeed all those worse than

Egyptian toads, (the spawns of a Butler, a Brown, and a Ward,[6] and a company whose name is legion!) might never crawl into your chamber! The unclean spirits that come like frogs out of the mouth of the dragon, and of the beast; which go forth unto the young people of the earth, and expose them to be dealt withal as the enemies of God, in the battle of the great day of the Almighty. As for those wretched scribbles of madmen, my son, touch them not, taste them not, handle them not: thou wilt perish in the using of them. They are the dragons, whose contagious breath peoples the dark retreats of death. To much better purpose will an excellent but an envied Blackmore [7] feast you, than those vile rhapsodies (of that *Vinum dæmonum*) [8] which you will find always leave a taint upon your mind, and among other ill effects, will sensibly indispose you to converse with the holy oracles of God your Saviour.

But there is, what I may rather call a parenthesis than a digression, which this may be not altogether an improper place for the introducing of.

There has been a deal of a-do about a style; so much, that I must offer you my sentiments upon it. There is a way of writing, wherein the author endeavours that the reader may have something to the purpose in every paragraph. There is not only a vigour sensible in every sentence, but the paragraph is embellished with profitable references, even to something beyond what is directly spoken. Formal and painful quotations are not studied; yet all that could be learnt from them is insinuated. The writer pretends not unto reading, yet he could not have writ as he does if he had not read very much in his time; and his composures are not only a cloth of gold, but also stuck with as many jewels as the gown of a Russian ambassador. This way of writing has been decried by many, and is at this day more than ever so, for the same reason that, in the old story, the grapes were decried, that they were not ripe. A lazy, ignorant, conceited set of authors, would persuade the whole tribe to lay aside that way of writing, for the same reason that one would have persuaded his brethren to part with the incumbrance of their bushy tails. But however fashion and humour may prevail, they must not think that the club at their coffee-house is all the world; but there will always be those, who will in this case be governed by indisputable reason: and who will think that the real excellency of a book will never lie in saying of little; that the less one has for his money in a book, it is really the more valuable for it: and the less one is instructed in a book, and the more superfluous margin and superficial harangue, and the less of substantial matter one has in it, the more it is to be accounted of. And if a more massy way of writing be ever so much disgusted at this day, a better gust will come on, as will some other thing, *quæ jam cecidere*.[9] In the mean time, nothing appears to me more impertinent and ridiculous than the modern way (I cannot say, rule; for they have none!) of criticising. The blades that set up for critics, I know not who constituted or commissioned them!— they appear to me, for the most part, as contemptible as they are a supercilious generation. For indeed no two of them have the same stile; and they are as intolerably cross-grained, and severe in their censures upon one another, as they are upon the rest of mankind. But while each of them, conceitedly enough, sets up for the standard of perfection, we are entirely at a loss which fire to follow. Nor can you easily find any one thing wherein they agree for their stile, except perhaps a perpetual care to give us jejune and empty pages, without such touches of erudition (to speak in the stile of an ingenious traveller) as may make the discourses less tedious, and more enriching to the mind of him that peruses them. There is much talk of a florid stile obtaining among the pens that are most in vogue; but how often would it puzzle one, even with the best glasses, to find the flowers! And if they were to be chastised for it, it would be with much the same kind of justice as Jerom was, for being a Ciceronian.[10] After all, every man will have his own stile, which will distinguish him as much as his gait: and if you can attain to that which I have newly described, but always writing so as to give an easy conveyance unto your ideas, I would not have you by any scourging be driven out of your gait; but if you must confess a fault in it, make a confession like that of the lad unto his father while he was beating him for his versifying.

However, since every man will have his own stile, I would pray that we may learn to treat one another with mutual civilities and conde- scensions, and handsomely indulge one another in this as gentlemen do in other matters.

I wonder what ails people that they cannot let Cicero write in the stile of Cicero, and Seneca write in the (much other!) stile of Seneca; and own that both may please in their several ways.—But I will freely tell you, what has made me consider the humourists that set up for critics upon stile as the most unregardable set of mortals in the world, is this! Far more illustrious critics than any of those to whom I am now bidding defiance, and no less men than your Erasmus's and your Gro- tius's, have taxed the Greek stile of the New Testament with I know not what solecisms and barbarisms; and how many learned folks have obsequiously run away with the notion! whereas it is an ignorant and an insolent whimsey which they have been guilty of. It may be (and particularly by an ingenious Blackwall,[11] it has been) demonstrated, that the gentlemen are mistaken in every one of their pretended instances; all the unquestionable classics may be brought in to convince them of their mistakes. Those glorious oracles are as pure Greek as ever was written in the world; and so correct, so noble, so sublime is their stile, that never any thing under the cope of Heaven, but the Old Testament, has equalled it.

MATHER BYLES

[By 1745 the literary essay was a commonplace. A variety of English periodicals had found an increasingly large circle of readers ever since *The Tatler* had appeared thirty-six years before. English literary magazines had circulated in the colonies for many years, but not until 1741 did American publishers themselves initiate such productions. In that year Benjamin Franklin and Andrew Bradford each ventured periodicals in Philadelphia, largely extracts from British counterparts, or from newspapers and recent books. Both attempts proved short-lived. In 1743 Joshua Gridley (1702–1767) published *The American Magazine and Historical Chronicle* in Boston. It appeared monthly for three years. Though most of its essays were extracted ·from English periodicals, it occasionally gave a place to local productions. In January 1745 (pp. 1–4) appeared an essay in light vein on "the *Bombastick* and the *Grubstreet*" style. It is signed "L," and is identified by Lyon N. Richardson (*A History of Early American Magazines, 1741–1789*, New York, 1931, p. 54, note) as the work of Mather Byles (*q.v.*, p. 662).]

BOMBASTIC AND GRUBSTREET STYLE: A SATIRE.

As one great Design of many of the Entertainments in our *Magazine*, is to cultivate *polite* Writing, and form and embellish the Style of our ingenious Countrymen: So, Instead of a Preface to this Volume, we ask Leave to give the following Piece of *Criticism*.

> *Clamorem immensum tollit, quo pontus et omnes*
> *Intremuere undæ, penitusque exterrita tellus*
> *Italiæ, curvisque immugiit Ætna cavernis.*   Virg. Æneid.[1]

THERE have been innumerable Authors, from *Aristotle's Rhetorick* to *Longinus's Treatise of the Sublime*, and from thence down to the Compiler of our modern *Horn-book*, who have written Introductions to the Art of Polite Writing. Every one that can just distinguish his

Twenty Four Letters sets up for a Judge of it; as all who are able to flourish a Goose's Quill, pretend to be Masters of that Secret. The noblest Productions have given Birth to many a supercillious Caveller; Criticks of all Sizes and Dimensions have nibled round the divinest Pages; and Ignorance and Conceit have endeavoured to shake down the most beautiful Structures, in order to build themselves a Reputation out of the Ruins. A superiour Genius, though he seems to kindle a wide Horizon of Light all about him, and is admired by the understanding Part of Mankind, yet he must expect to be the Occasion of a great many Absurdities, with which the unknowing and envious will strive to satyrize him: As the Sun scatters Day through a whole Frame of Worlds, but yet may, in some particular Spots, raise a Fog, or hatch a Nest of Vermin. To conclude, the Science of correct Writing having been a Subject exhausted by so many able Hands, and seeing all the Rabble of Scriblers are such indisputable Proficients in it; not to mention my own Incapacity for such an Undertaking; I shall not be so vain as to offer my Thoughts upon it: But I shall apply my Labours at this Time, to an Ornament of a contrary Nature, which is a Theme intirely New, Namely, *The Art of writing Incorrectly.*

This, I take it, is a Work that I am excellently well qualified for, and I doubt not but to convince the World that I am a perfect Master of my Subject. In the Prosecution of this useful Design, I shall show the Excellency of Incorrect Writing in general; I shall lay open the several Artifices, by which a Man of competent Abilities, may, with proper Application, attain to a tolerable Degree of Perfection in it; I shall produce pertinent Examples from Writers of undoubted Eminence in that improving Science: And in the last place, I may possibly address the World with a very pathetick Exhortation, to follow the Instructions which I shall give them, in order to accomplish themselves in the Art of Incorrect Writing. In short, I intend to entertain the Publick, with a regular Criticism upon Nonsense.

Authors of this Kind may be divided into two Classes, generally known under the Denomination of the *Bombastick* and the *Grubstreet.* The latter of these Characters is easily attained, provided a Man can but keep himself from thinking, and yĕt so contrive Matters, as to let his Pen run along unmolested over a Sheet of White Paper, and drop a convenient Quantity of Words, at proper Intervals on it. A Person who is acquainted with this Secret, may, with great Facility and Composure of Mind, furnish himself with a comfortable Stock of Reputation, as often as he finds it requisite. This he might do, as without any Ruffle to his own Tranquility, so neither would it prove the least Disturbance to his Readers: For while he flow'd along with that unmeaning Softness, every one within the Warble of his Accents would undoubtedly dissolve away in a supine Indolence, and, (as a late Musical Author of this Species has very tenderly expressed it) be *hush'd into lulling Dreams.*

I shall, perhaps, dedicate some future Essay to the Incouragement of these worthy Gentlemen, but at this Time I intend to consider those my ingenious Fellow-Labourers, who deviate into the contrary Extream; I mean the Admirers of Bombast and Fustian.

These Writers, to avoid the Imputation of low and flat, blow up every Subject they take in Hand beyond its natural Dimensions; and nothing will please them that is not big and boisterous, wild and irregular. They wonderfully delight in Noise and Clamour; a Rattle of Words, and an Extravagance of Imagination, they look upon as the Perfection of Rhetorick; and are Transported beyond themselves, at the Tumult and Confusion that bellows through a Hurricane of Nonsense. In short, that which Men of this Turn applaud as the Masterpiece of good Writing, differs from the *true Sublime,* as a Boy's artificial Kite, wadling among the Clouds at the End of a Skein of Pack-thread, does from the natural Flight of an Eagle, towering with steddy Pinions up the Sky, and bearing full upon the Sun.

If this false Taste prevails amongst us, we shall quickly prove such a Generation of Blusterers, that our Country will resemble the Cave of *Æolus,* where the Winds make their general Rendezvous, and battel and clash together in an eternal Din and Uproar. For my own Part, I look upon it to be the Duty of every one, as far as in him lies, to lend his Assistance in banking out this Inundation of Sound, which, if it finds a clear Passage, will not fail to overwhelm us in a Deluge of Folly and Absurdity.

A Friend of mine who writes in this exorbitant Style, Mr. *Richard Stentor* by Name, shall be the Hero of the present Essay. Mr. *Stentor* as to his exterior Figure, is one of the portliest Mortals that have flourished in our World, since *Goliah* over-top'd the *Philistian* Army. He is moderately speaking, Nine Foot high, and Four in Diameter. His Voice is not unlike the Roar and Rapidity of a Torrent foaming down a Mountain, and reverberated amongst the neighbouring Rocks. The Hurry of Vociferation with which he drives along in the Heat of an Argument, imitates the Thunder of a Cart-load of Stones poured out upon a Pavement. He was educated in a Ship of War, and one would imagine he learnt the Notes of his Gamut, from the various Whistlings of a Tempest thro' the Rigging of his Vessel. I was once so unadvised as to offer my Dissent from one of his Opinions; but I had better have held my Tongue: He turned upon me, and rung me such a Peal of Eloquence, that had I not made off with the greatest Precipitation, would have gone near to have stun'd, and made me deaf all my Days. Nay, I have cause to think my Hearing has been never the better for it to this Moment.

This is a short Description of his external Accomplishments; as to the Qualifications of his Mind, they will be best perceived, by a Transcript I shall here make, from an Oration he formerly composed in *Praise* of *Beacon Hill.* I must inform my Readers, that it was conceived as he stood upon the Summit of that little Mount, one Training-Day, when, as he has since owned to me, the Drums and Musquets assisted his Inspiration, and augmented and deepend the Rumbling of his Periods. It begins in the following Manner—

THE gloriously-transcendent, and highly-exalted Precipice, from which the sonorous Accents of my Lungs resound with repeated Echoes, is so pompous, magnificent, illustrious, and loftily-towering, that, as I twirl around my Arm with the artful Flourish of an Orator, I seem to feel my Knucles rebound from the blew Vault of Heaven, which just arches over my Head. I stand upon an amazing Eminence that heaves itself up, on both sides steep and stupendous! high and horrendous! The spiry Teneriffe, *the unshaken* Atlas, *or* Olympus *divine and celestial, when compared to this prodigious Mountain, sink to Sands, and dwindle to Atoms. It is deep-rooted in its ever-during Foundations, firm as the Earth, lasting as the Sun, immoveable as the Pillars of Nature! I behold from this awful and astonishing Scituation, the concave Expanse of uncreated Space, stretch itself above: and the Land and Ocean below, spreading an Infinitude of Extension all about me. But what daring Tropes and flaming Metaphores shall I select, O aspiring Beacon! to celebrate Thee with a suitable Grandeur, or exalt thee to a becoming Dignity? How does it shoot up its inconceivable Pinnacle into the superior Regions, and blend itself with the cerulian circum-ambient Æther! It mocks the fiercest Efforts of the most piercing Sight, to reach to its impenetrable Sublimities. It looks down upon the diminish'd Spheres; the fixt Stars twinkle at an immeasurable Distance beneath it; while the Planets roll away, unperceived, in a vast, a fathomless Profound!* *****

By this little Quotation from Mr. *Stentor's* Panegyrick on Beacon Hill, my Reader will in some Measure be able to judge of his Manner of thinking, and expressing himself. It appears plainly that he heaps his Subject with improper and foreign Thoughts; that he strains those Thoughts into the most unnatural and ridiculous Distortions; and, last of all, that he clouds them with so many needless supernumerary Epithets, as to fling the whole Piece into this unaccountable Huddle of Impertinence and Inconsistency. *Richard* is mighty fond of great sounding Words, and, let his Topick be what it will, he has perpetual Recourse to them upon all Emergencies. He once took it in his Head to be in Love, and wrote a Poem to his Mistress on that delicate Passion: But instead of the gentle Flow of Harmony which any one would reasonably have expected, and which is indeed essential to Compositions of that Kind, his Numbers stalked along as sturdy and outragious as in any other of his Performances. I my self counted in Fifty Six Lines of it, three *Celestials*, eight *Immortals*, eleven *Unboundeds*, six *Everlastings*, four *Eternities*, and thirteen *Infinites;* Besides *Bellowings, Ravings, Yellings, Horrors, Terribles, Rackets, Hubbubs,* and *Clutterings,* without Number. But what pleased me the most of any of my Friend's Compositions, was, *A Poetical Description of a Game at Push-pin.* Sure, thought I, when I read the Title, there can be nothing very loud and impetuous upon so trivial a Matter as This. How I was surprized out of my mistake, my Reader will in some Measure conceive, when he understands that the first Distich of the Poem runs thus,

> *Rage, fire, and fury in my bosom roll,*
> *And all the gods rush headlong on my soul.*

He then proceeded to compare the Pins to two Comets, whose Heads, as he expressed it, enlightned the boundless Desarts of the Skies with a bloody Glare, and threw behind them the ruddy Volumes of their tremendous Trains, into the tractless Wastes of Immensity. When the Pins met in the Progress of the Game, for a Similitude, he supposed the two Continents to be tossed from their Foundations, and encounter, with a direful Concussion, in the midst of the briny *Atlantick:* or rather, *says he,* as if two Systems of Worlds, Suns, Planets and all, should be hurled resistless one against another, and dash a horrible *Chaos,* from the general Ruins of Matter, and Wrecks of a whole Universe. He concluded the Poem with the following Lines, which I look upon to be the most finished Pattern of this Sort of Productions, that I have any where met with; whether I consider, the Uncouthness of the Language, the Ruggedness of the Style, or the Disproportion and Extravagance of the Images. Speaking of the Pins he says,

> *The Bars of Brass, harsh-crashing, loud resound,*
> *And jarring discords rend th' astonish'd ground.*
> *So when aloft dire hurricanes arise,*
> *And with horrendous shatterings burst the skies,*
> *Dread ghastly terrors drive along in crowds,*
> *And hideous thunder howls amongst the clouds;*
> *Eternal whirlwinds on the ocean roar,*
> *Infinite earth-quakes rock the bounding shore.*

I shall conclude these **Remarks upon** Bombast, with an Observation which I ought in Justice to make, in favour of those who fall into it; *viz. That no Person can be a considerable Proficient this way, who has not a good Share of natural Powers and Abilities.* Hence, when we see a Young Man delivering himself in this warm Manner, he is to be regarded as a good *Genius* run wild, for want of Cultivation from Study, and the **Rules** of Art: And it follows, that should such a juvenile Writer, take **proper** Methods to improve his Mind, in innuring himself to a close **Way** of Reasoning, and by conversing with the best Authors, however defective he might be in this Particular at first, he would in the End make a chaste and excellent Writer. Thus it happened to the immortal *Virgil*, whose divine *Æneid* once shot itself into so great a Luxuriance, as to be near twenty Times as Large as it appears at this Day. As his Imagination cooled by Years, and his Judgment ripened, and hasted on to Maturity, his Style dropped the false Glare of Ornaments, and shone with an equal Purity and Elegance; His Thoughts learned to proportion themselves to his Subject, and cast themselves into that exact Symmetry of Arrangement and Disposition, in which they now charm us; And, in a word, a new Beauty began to dawn in every·Line of that exquisite Work which consecrates his deathless Fame to the Admiration of all Posterity.

L.

Chapter VIII

EDUCATION [1]

EVEN as the Puritans, "dreading to leave an illiterate Ministry to the Churches," [2] demanded that their clergy be well trained, so they expected the laity should receive at least enough instruction to understand the ministers' exposition of doctrine. To that end Massachusetts passed an Act in 1647, which was adopted by Connecticut three years later, requiring that every town of one hundred families or more should provide free common and grammar school instruction. The provision was designed to give children enough training to enable them to read, whether the teaching were conducted privately or in public school, and the cost was met by funds taken from the taxes or raised by tuition. The Puritans preserved in secondary education a humanistic standard—a classical training—which in England was being supplanted by courses with a more utilitarian end in view; and it is noteworthy that they required a longer elementary schooling than the Anglicans. The higher education of the Puritans was erected on the splendid foundation of learning that had obtained in the Church since the Middle Ages,—one to which Renaissance and Reformation traditions had brought renewed vitality. It is well, nevertheless, to make two points clear at the start. One is that in no sense did the Puritans foster church schools; the other is that of all English peoples those with Puritan leanings were most concerned for proper education.

No phase of Puritan manners is more difficult to reconstruct than that which traces the method, aims, discipline, curriculum, and support of the elementary schools. From the very first, we may be sure, something was done to provide common schools, though the records are meager. Until a formal provision was made, we imagine that the child was taught at home by his parents or by the older children. Cotton Mather's "Special Points" relating to the education of his children were probably not substantially different from those of all intelligent parents (see p. 724). The child was first introduced to his studies by way of the "reading-schools"—later known as dame schools, since they were conducted by women. Here boys and girls together as a

---

[1] This account is frequently indebted to Robert F. Seybolt, *The Public Schools of Colonial Boston* (Cambridge, 1935); *idem*, "The Private Schools of Seventeenth-Century Boston," *New England Quarterly*, VIII (1935), 418–424; and chapters II–IV of Samuel E. Morison, *The Puritan Pronaos* (New York, 1936), wherein is briefly digested much that the author's Harvard History has already presented in detail.

[2] *New Englands First Fruits*, p. 12.

group were taught spelling, reading, writing, and ciphering. At this stage also—that is, while they were not over five years old—girls were started in needlework. If the child were moderately apt, he was advanced to the "writing-schools," kept by a man, where he was prepared for the grammar schools at the age of seven or eight. Such advancement depended, however, upon his capacity to wrestle with Latin and Greek, the only subjects taught in the secondary schools; if he lacked the ability, his formal education was over. The reading-schools, as the name indicates, barely carried children beyond the most rudimentary disciplines:—writing and ciphering came later. It is quite possible that many who learned to read were never taught to write, and that therefore such literacy data as are based upon writing ability do not tell the whole story.

The child began his reading with that time-honored device, the hornbook—a printed alphabet list of one syllable words, together with the Lord's Prayer, held in a wooded frame, the whole covered by a sheet of horn. He was advanced next to a spelling book, and thence to a primer and a catechism. "In Adam's Fall/ We sinned all" begins that most famous of American readers, *The New England Primer or Milk for Babes,* of which it is estimated that seven million copies were printed before 1840. If the first issue was printed, as we have reason to think, in 1683, we can readily understand the hard usage to which the primers were put, when we consider that the earliest known copy dates only from 1727, and that the total number surviving is very small.

All available records yield but scant information regarding the number of private schools or their curriculum before 1700. Boys' education could be continued in the free grammar schools, but the training of girls must either stop after their reading-school days were over, or be conducted privately. During the eighteenth century, records show that such private school instruction included for girls not only the rudiments, but instruction in English diction and grammar, and in "polite accomplishments"—French, vocal and instrumental music, dancing, needlework, painting, and drawing. For boys, there was also training in bookkeeping, shorthand, history, dancing, music and horsemanship; and those who could not spare time during the day might attend evening schools. Whether such instruction was offered in or about Boston during the seventeenth century cannot be definitely stated, though the subjects listed are such that it would not be reasonable to think they were introduced only after the turn of the century.

One of the oldest secondary or grammar schools in the country, and the only one in Boston until 1713, was the "Free Grammar School," better known as the Boston Latin School, opened in 1635. Here innumerable generations have been prepared for college, and here, after 1709, they were annually exhibited on a certain day before the clergy and other notables:—a group of sixty who attended school exercises in a body to pronounce upon the excellence of the year's accomplishments. The schoolmaster in Boston and elsewhere was a man of some standing. He was at times exempt from poll and estate taxes, his house was furnished him by the town, his salary was higher than most of the local officials, and upon retirement he might be granted a pension or allowance. But such provisions were not always forthcoming, and a master's tenure was usually brief; he remained as schoolmaster in a town only while he awaited a more lucrative call to some near-by pulpit. The most famous colonial schoolmaster was Ezekiel Cheever, who taught continuously in and about Boston for seventy years. The veneration in which he was held is charmingly told by Cotton Mather in *Corderius Americanus*, and the picture therein sketched of master and pupils is one that deserves to be remembered (see p. 722).

As we suggested earlier, grammar schools were designed only for the training of boys, and such of them as could handle Latin and Greek. To enter, a student must be at least seven years of age and be able to read. The requirements satisfied, the student faced a seven-years' curriculum which, like that of the Elizabethan grammar schools, was exclusively devoted to a study of the classics, with no place for modern language, history, or science. The purpose was humanistic: to achieve a mastery of the classics and a wide knowledge of the best authors in those tongues. Thus the student was provided with a general education and incidentally fitted for college, though probably less than half of any one graduating class went further with his education. It is noticeable that the religious element was relatively small. The student doubtless went to church on Sunday and attended the Thursday "lecture," even as his Anglican cousin was expected to do, but there was no law whereby the ministers' approval of teachers or curriculum was required until 1701, and evidently then simply to assure the town of sufficiently high teaching standards.

The only seventeenth-century grammar school curriculum which has come down to us is that of the Boston Latin School, which may perhaps serve as typical. The entering students were taught their Latin accidence and grammar. When their vocabulary was sufficient and the rudiments mastered, they passed on to Aesop's Fables. By their fourth year they were reading Erasmus's Colloquies and undertaking Greek. At the same time they were supposed to be ready for Ovid's *de Tristibus* and

Metamorphosis, and Cicero's Letters. By the end of the sixth year they would have completed Cicero's *de Officiis,* and the *Aeneid.* In their seventh and final year, with the language difficulties fairly mastered, they could approach classic literature with some ease: more Cicero, and Vergil, then Horace, Juvenal, Persius, Isocrates, Hesiod, and the New Testament. They composed Latin verse, and studied rhetoric and Roman history and antiquities. It is possible that some especially capable may have begun a study of Hebrew. Thus we see that the grammar-school boy was subjected to a stiff but none the less broadening course in the classics, and that he was well prepared to enter college if he satisfactorily concluded his seven years of preparation.

It is clear that religious training in the Puritan colonies was vastly important in the educational scheme, even though the curriculum and administration of the schools were completely free from church interference. All knowledge was, of course, from God, and all training pursued that His ways might be more clearly manifested:—it was a point of view common to educational systems of Europe, and in no way peculiar to Puritanism. Such an approach continued to be true for the boy who went on to college. Actually no more than half of all Harvard graduates during the seventeenth century became ministers.[1] Those intent upon professional theology remained in residence after they had been granted their Bachelor of Arts degree to study further, and thereby obtain such specialized learning as would qualify them for the pulpit; only by such application could they secure the degree of Master of Arts.

Provision was made for higher education almost as soon as grammar schools were established. Harvard College was founded by the Massachusetts Legislature—the General Court—in October, 1636, and the purpose expressed in the Charter of 1650 was "The aduancement and education of youth in all manner of good literature Artes and Sciences" —that is, in "polite letters" and the seven arts and the three philosophies of the Middle Ages: Grammar, Logic, Rhetoric, Arithmetic, Geometry, Astronomy; Metaphysics, Ethics, and Natural Science. It was actually a course in the mediaeval *trivium* and *quadrivium* with music omitted, geometry slighted, the philosophies stressed, with the Renaissance subjects, history, Greek, and Hebrew added. Not only was Hebrew considered the foundation for an exact understanding of the Old Testament, but it was then as later thought to be the mother of languages; a knowledge of it therefore was believed to advance learning in the best sense.

[1] See Samuel E. Morison, *Harvard College in the Seventeenth Century,* p. 562.

Students entered as freshmen and remained four years, living much as students do today, in a dormitory with a roommate, under the supervision of tutors who shared their commons and gave them instruction. For admission to the freshman class the student must be interviewed by the President or by a tutor under the President's eye. If the interview, conducted in Latin, terminated satisfactorily, the boy was then assigned a subject for a theme; if the composition won presidential approval, the boy was entered as a member of the freshman class. The pursuit of higher education then as now often depended upon the ability of a family to raise money enough to pay for it. Tuition and board, which totaled in mid-seventeenth century about £50 to £75 for the four years, might be paid in produce, for the college ran the commons. His financial obligations discharged, the student, with his classmates, was put in charge of one of the two or three tutors, who acted as instructor in all subjects and as "class officer" for that group throughout their four years.

The curriculum at some points was a continuation of the work undertaken in grammar school, although broadened and deepened. Hesiod was read, as well as Sophocles, Euripides, Homer, and Theocritus. The boy was expected to dispute syllogistically at stated intervals, and at the end of his senior year he must demonstrate his ability to defend a thesis: some philosophical problem which would bring to bear all the arts of persuasion, logic, and rhetoric which he had studied. This final exercise took place at Commencement, and like all other elements of college life—recitations, reports, and even informal conversations—must be delivered in Latin. The training that the colonial college offered, both formally in the classroom and informally in close association with the tutors, was liberal in the true sense of the term—the education of gentlemen. Whoever fears that the Puritan boy had no time to play or lacked red blood must look more closely at the record, for in his free moments we find him copying or imitating the amorous verses of Spenser, Sidney, or Herrick; we see him too consuming much beef, bread, and beer; and we wonder how many fathers must have taken their sons into conference to inquire why the bill for broken window-glass mounted so high.

In its own day President Chauncy's commencement address in 1655 (see p. 705) was no doubt considered sufficient answer to those who thought that the provincial college should serve only the church by training men for the ministry; and the letter of Leonard Hoar to his freshman nephew (see p. 708), written six years later, is warrant enough that a study of the cultural past alone was not thought to advance learning—that a study of the sciences must be cultivated. When at the end of the century President Mather addressed the undergraduates, urging them to search for truth even though the way led through new and disturbing fields of thought (see p. 721), he was enunciating the central theme of Puritan scholarship. Such statements justify the conclusion that in matters of education the Puritans were leaders not reactionaries, as resolute as they were sincere.

NEW ENGLANDS FIRST FRUITS

[No other colonizers in the English-speaking world have provided for higher education so soon upon their arrival as those in Massachusetts Bay. In October, 1636, the General Court voted £400 "towards a schoale or colledge," and by 1642 the first class of nine members was graduated from Harvard College. In the following year a twenty-six-page tract was published in London: *New Englands First Fruits*. It pictured attractively the natural resources, the benefits of climate, the opportunities for converting the heathen, and it made a special point of describing the thriving young college. The promoters of New England took this way to ask for money, and at the same time spread propaganda abroad to counter that which was "selling" the West Indies.

The material for the part "In respect of the Colledge, and the proceedings of *Learning* therein" was very likely supplied by Henry Dunster (1609–1659), the young minister who, emigrating in 1640, served the college as President for fourteen years. Its list of rules by which the students lived and its outline of curriculum furnishes important data about the Puritan educational ideal.

See Worthington C. Ford, "The Authorship of 'New Englands First Fruits,'" *Publications of the Massachusetts Historical Society*, XLII (1909), 259–266. The tract has twice been reprinted in full: Sabin Reprints, Quarto series, No. vii (New York, 1865); Samuel E. Morison, *The Founding of Harvard College* (Cambridge, 1935), Appendix D (where it is given an accurate line-for-line and word-for-word transcription). See further, *ibid.*, pp. 304, 305. The best brief summary of "The Beginnings of Higher Education" in America is in Samuel E. Morison, *The Puritan Pronaos* (New York, 1936), chapter II.

The text which follows is from a copy of the 1643 edition in the New York Public Library, pp. 12–16.]

NEW ENGLANDS FIRST FRUITS:

2. In Respect of the Colledge, and the proceedings of *Learning* therein.

1. After God had carried us safe to *New-England*, and wee had builded our houses, provided necessaries for our liveli-hood, rear'd convenient places for Gods worship, and setled the Civill Government: One of the next things we longed for, and looked after was to advance *Learning* and perpetuate it to Posterity; dreading to leave an illiterate Ministery to the Churches, when our present Ministers shall lie in the Dust. And as wee were thinking and consulting how to effect this great Work; it pleased God to stir up the heart of one Mr. *Harvard* (a godly Gentleman, and a lover of Learning, there living amongst us) to give the one halfe of his Estate (it being in all about 1700. l.) towards the erecting of a Colledge, and all his Library: after him another gave 300. l. others after them cast in more, and the publique hand of the State added the rest: the Colledge was, by common consent, appointed to be at *Cambridge*, (a place very pleasant and accommodate) and is called (according to the name of the first founder) *Harvard Colledge*.

The Edifice is very faire and comely within and without, having in it a spacious Hall; (where they daily meet at Common Lectures) Exercises, and a large Library with some Bookes to it, the gifts of diverse of our friends, their Chambers and studies also fitted for, and possessed by the Students, and all other roomes of Office necessary and convenient, with all needfull Offices thereto belonging: And by the side of the Colledge a faire *Grammar* Schoole, for the training up of young Schollars, and fitting of them for *Academicall Learning*, that still as they are judged ripe, they may be received into the Colledge of this Schoole: Master *Corlet* is the Mr., who hath very well approved himselfe for his abilities, dexterity and painfulnesse, in teaching and education of the youth under him.[1]

Over the Colledge is master *Dunster* placed, as President, a learned conscionable and industrious man, who hath so trained up, his Pupills in the tongues and Arts, and so seasoned them with the principles of Divinity and Christianity, that we have to our great comfort, (and in truth) beyond our hopes, beheld their progresse in Learning and god-linesse also; the former of these hath appeared in their publique declamations in *Latine* and *Greeke*, and Disputations Logicall and Philo-sophicall, which they have beene wonted (besides their ordinary Exer-cises in the Colledge-Hall) in the audience of the Magistrates, Ministers, and other Schollars, for the probation of their growth in Learning, upon set dayes, constantly once every moneth to **make** and uphold: The latter hath been manifested in sundry of them by the savoury breathings of their Spirits in their godly conversation. Insomuch that we are confident, if these early blossomes may be cherished and warmed with the influence of the friends of Learning and lovers of this pious worke, they will by the help of God, come to happy maturity in a short time.

Over the Colledge are twelve Overseers chosen by the generall Court, six of them are of the Magistrates, the other six of the Ministers, who are to promote the best good of it, and (having a power of influence into all persons in it) are to see that every one be diligent and proficient in his proper place.

2. *Rules, and Precepts that are observed in the Colledge.*

1. When any Schollar is able to understand *Tully*,[2] or such like classical Latine Author *extempore*, and make and speake true Latine in Verse and Prose, *suo ut aiunt Marte;*[3] And decline perfectly the Paradigm's of *Nounes* and *Verbes* in the *Greek* tongue: Let him then and not before be capable of admission into the Colledge.

2. Let every Student be plainly instructed, and earnestly pressed to consider well, the maine end of his life and studies is, *to know God and Iesus Christ which is eternall life*, Joh. 17. 3. and therefore to lay *Christ* in the bottome, as the only foundation of all sound knowledge and Learning.

And seeing the Lord only giveth wisedome, Let every one seriously set himselfe by prayer in secret to seeke it of him *Prov* 2, 3.

3. Every one shall so exercise himselfe in reading the Scriptures twice a day, that he shall be ready to give such an account of his proficiency therein, both in *Theoretticall* observations of the Language, and *Logick*, and in *Practicall* and spirituall truths, as his Tutor shall require, according to his ability; seeing *the entrance of the word giveth light, it giveth understanding to the simple*, Psalm. 119. 130.

4. That they eshewing all profanation of Gods Name, Attributes, Word, Ordinances and times of Worship, doe studie with good conscience, carefully to retaine God, and the love of his truth in their mindes, else let them know, that (notwithstanding their Learning) God may give them up *to strong delusions*, and in the end *to a reprobate minde*, 2 Thes. 2. 11, 12. Rom. 1. 28.

5. That they studiously redeeme the time; observe the generall houres appointed for all the Students, and the speciall houres for their owne *Classes:* and then diligently attend the Lectures, without any

disturbance by word or gesture. And if in anything they doubt, they shall enquire, as of their fellowes, so, (in case of *Non satisfaction*) modestly of their Tutors.

6. None shall under any pretence whatsoever, frequent the company and society of such men as lead an unfit, and dissolute life.

Nor shall any without his Tutors leave, or (in his absence) the call of Parents or Guardians, goe abroad to other Townes.

7. Every Schollar shall be present in his Tutors chamber at the 7th. houre in the morning, immediately after the sound of the Bell, at his opening the Scripture and prayer, so also at the 5th. houre at night, and then give account of his owne private reading, as aforesaid in Particular the third, and constantly attend Lectures in the Hall at the houres appointed? But if any (without necessary impediment) shall absent himself from prayer or Lectures, he shall bee lyable to Admonition, if he offend above once a weeke.

8. If any Schollar shall be found to transgresse any of the Lawes of God, or the Schoole, after twice Admonition, he shall be lyable, if not *adultus*, to correction, if *adultus*, his name shall be given up to the Overseers of the Colledge, that he may bee admonished at the publick monethly Act.

3. *The times and order of their Studies, unlesse experience shall shew cause to alter.*

The second and third day of the weeke, read Lectures, as followeth.

To the first yeare at 8th. of the clock in the morning *Logick*, the first three quarters, *Physicks* the last quarter.

To the second yeare, at the 9th. houre, *Ethicks* and *Politicks*, at convenient distances of time.

To the third yeare at the 10th. *Arithmetick* and *Geometry*, the three first quarters, *Astronomy* the last.

Afternoone.

The first yeare disputes at the second houre.

The 2d. yeare at the 3d. houre.

The 3d. yeare at the 4th. every one in his Art.

The 4th. day reads Greeke.

To the first yeare the *Etymologie* and *Syntax* at the eighth houre.

To the 2d. at the 9th. houre, *Prosodia* and *Dialects*.

Afternoone.

The first yeare at 2d. houre practice the precepts of *Grammar* in such Authors as have variety of words.

The 2d. yeare at 3d. houre practice in *Poësy*, [with] *Nonnus, Duport*,[4] or the like.

The 3d. yeare perfect their *Theory* before noone, and exercise *Style, Composition, Imitation, Epitome,* both in Prose and Verse, afternoone.

The fift[h] day reads Hebrew, and the Easterne Tongues.
Grammar to the first yeare houre the 8th.
To the 2d. *Chaldee* [*i.e.* Aramaic] at the 9th. houre.
To the 3d. *Syriack* at the 10th. houre.

Afternoone.

The first yeare practice in the Bible at the 2d. houre.
The 2d. in *Ezra* and *Dan[i]el* at the 3d. houre.
The 3d. at the 4th. houre in *Trostius* [5] New Testament.

The 6th. day reads Rhetorick to all at the 8th houre.

Declamations at the 9th. So ordered that every Scholler may de-claime once a moneth. The rest of the day *vacat Rhetoricis studiis.*[6] *The 7th. day reads Divinity Catecheticall at the 8th. houre, Common places at the 9th. houre.*

Afternoone.

The first houre reads history in the Winter,
The nature of plants in the Summer
The summe of every Lecture shall be examined, before the new Lecture be read.

Every Schollar, that on proofe is found able to read the Originalls of the *Old* and *New Testament* into the Latine tongue, and to resolve them *Logically;* withall being of godly life and conversation; And at any publick Act hath the Approbation of the Overseers and Master of the Colledge, is fit to be dignified with his first Degree.

Every Schollar that giveth up in writing a *System*, or *Synopsis*, or summe of *Logick*, Naturall and Morall *Phylosophy, Arithmetick, Geometry* and *Astronomy:* and is ready to defend his *Theses* or positions: withall skilled in the Originalls as abovesaid: and of godly life & conversa-tion: and so approved by the Overseers and Master of the Colledge, at any publique *Act*, is fit to be dignified with his 2d. Degree.

CHARLES CHAUNCY, 1591–1671/2

[With Cotton and Hooker, Charles Chauncy was reckoned one of the most learned men of his day. Silenced in England, he emigrated to New England in 1638, and was settled as pastor first at Plymouth and later at Scituate; but his somewhat truculent casuistry—principally his defense of "total immersion"—made him unwelcome to orthodox Puritans. He was on his way through Boston to return to England in 1654, when he was offered the presidency of Harvard College. He accepted the post, promising to keep his unorthodox ideas to himself, and continued in office till his death.

Gods Mercy, shewed to his people in giving them a faithful Ministry and schooles of Learning for the continual supplyes thereof (Cambridge, 1655), delivered as a Commencement sermon, is a defense of liberal education for ministers. Coming from the pen of the leading colonial educator, it significantly answers the tracts which were advocating a purely Christian and Scriptural curriculum for divinity students. See *Dictionary of American Biography*, and Samuel E. Morison, *Harvard College in the Seventeenth Century*, chap. XVI. The text is from a copy in the New York Public Library, pp. 32–38, with omissions indicated.]

A COMMENCEMENT SERMON

. . . But now it is not a verball thankfulness that will serve our turn, (that would be gross hypocrisie) but it must be really expressed, towards the education of youth, & the incouragement of the ministry, and the propagation of the Gospel.

The reality of your thankfulness let it be expressed in your future care,

1. To do (if it be in your power) as *Hezekiah did* 2 Chron: 30. 22. *that spake to the heart of all the Levites, that taught the good knowledg of the Lord* Yea do as *Nehemiah did chap:* 13. 11. *See that sufficient portions be allotted & contributed unto them.*

2. Do as *Jehoshaphat did* 2 Chron: 19. 8. *reach forth thine hand to send Levites* into the blind and dark places of the country.

3. Be at the cost *to trayn up thy towardly children in good literature:* parents are commanded to *trayn up their children Ephes.* 6. 4. *in putting understanding & instruction* into them: as if children were like bruit beasts without it.

4. In *relieving the sons of the Prophets,* and the *Colledg,* as *Elishah did* 1 Kings 4. 34. In setting up of free schools, as the Lord inables you.

5. If ye be poor, yet *pray for posterity* and means of education, and *pray for the peace of Jerusalem;* and that *Bethel,* the house of God may not be turned into *Bethaven* the house of iniquity, that schools of learning be not poysoned, or the fountains corrupted.

Vse 4. This point may serve for Information, To teach us, that Schools of learning are approved and appointed of God, and of great importance for the benefit of Gods people: Seeing that the Lord works with, & blesseth this means, for the laying up of provision, & making of supplys for the work of the ministry; and the Lord here reckons it up as the chiefest of all the blessings mentioned: and this was always one way (even when there were extraordinary Prophets) of raising up of Prophets &c: And there is much more need of schools now, when those extrardinary Prophets are wanting. . . .

. . . I do much desire that the opposers of schools & universityes would speak plainly what they mean by humane learning, then wee should easily come to some conclusion. Therfore let this distinction be premised, that humane learning may either be taken for all that learning that the heathen Authours or philosophers have delivered in their writings: or else all other Arts besides Theology, as they call *physicks, ethicks, politicks* &c: take in also the grounds of languages, *Latine Greek & Hebrew*. Now in the former sense, if *Mr. D.*[1] do mean by humane learning, all that learning that the heathen men have uttered out of the light of nature: It will be a great oversight to pass such a sentence upon it. 1. Because we find in Scriptures, some testimonies out of humane writers, as *Tit:* 1. 12. *Acts* 17. 28. 1 *Cor:* 15. 33. &c: which the Spirit of God would not have alledged, if their writings had been utterly unlawfull to read. 2. There are certain principles of trueth written, even in corrupt nature, which heathen authors have delivered unto us, that doe not cross the holy writ, 1 *Cor:* 11. 14. *doth not nature it self teach you &c:* and it cannot be denyed that all trueth, whosoever it be that speakes it, comes from the God of truth. as he is called several times And who can deny but that there are found many excellent & divine morall truths in *Plato, Aristotle, Plutarch, Seneca &c:* and to condemn all pel-mel, will be an hard censure, especially to call universities Antichrists for reading of them. Besides they have treated of the works of God, most excellently in many places, and the works of God ought to be *declared by parents to their children,* Psal. 78. 2–6. Besides they have delivered many excellent sayings of God, and have attested many Scripture historyes, as might be shewed by severall instances, out of *Justine, Tacitus &c:* and *Mr. D.* is not ignorant of them, shall all these be thrown away as antichristian, or as lyes?

Object. But they have much profaness and filthiness in them, and besides they are made idolls of in our universities, when as *ipse dixit,* and their authority goeth for currant, as Scripture it self amongst them.

Answ. But 1. All heathenish writers, have not such profaness in them. 2. Those that have, let them be condemned & abhored, & let not youth be poysoned by them. 3. Let God be true & every man a lyer, and let not man, especially any heathen be deified, or his authority be accounted on, or go cheek by jowle with the speaking in the Scriptures: this is indeed to be abhored whersoever it is received, but *abusus non tollit usum.*[2]

II. But now if humane learning be taken in the second sense, for all those Arts that are commonly taught in Universities, as *Physicks, Ethicks, Politicks Oeconomicks, Rhetorick, Astronomy &c:* or also for learned tongues of *Latine, Greek, and Hebrew &c:*

1. I will be bold to affirm, that these in the true sense and right meaning therof are Theologicall & Scripture learning, and are not to be accounted of as humane learning. For who can deny, that the first & second chapters of *Genesis*, and many chapters in *Job*, and the *Psalms*, and diverse other places of holy Scripture, do afford excellent and sure grounds for natural Philosophy, and a just systeme thereof: which *Mr. Zanchy*,[3] *Daneus*, and diverse other eminent Divines have opened & declared unto us? And where are there to be found such *Ethicall, Politicall*, or *Morall* precepts, as are to be found in holy Scriptures? or such principles for the ordering of our lifes, families, or common weals? let any man declare it unto us. And where are there such high straines of all sorts of *Rhetoricall Tropes, & figures*, to be found in any Author, as there are in the writings of the *Prophets & Apostles?* and who can imagine, but that the best & surest Chronology in the world, is to bee found in holy Scriptures, upon which all the computation of times in all ages in the world depends?

LEONARD HOAR, *ca.* 1630–1675

[Born in England, Leonard Hoar was brought by his widowed mother to Braintree, Massachusetts. Soon after graduation from college in 1650, he returned to England to preach, but he was silenced in 1660. During the next ten years he cultivated the friendship of scholars, studied botany, and was created "Doctor of Physick" by the University of Cambridge. He returned to New England in 1672 on invitation from the Third Church in Boston (the Old South), but was never ordained, for he accepted an offer of the presidency of his alma mater to succeed Charles Chauncy. Within three years he was forced to resign for reasons still obscure, but certainly not to his discredit. He died within the year.

The letter to Josiah Flynt was written during his stay abroad, and emphasizes Hoar's conviction that higher education should not merely preserve the cultural past, but should advance learning as well, especially by developing the sciences.

See *Dictionary of American Biography*, and Sibley, *Biographical Sketches*, I, 228–252. See especially Samuel E. Morison, *Harvard College in the Seventeenth Century*, pp. 392–414, and 639–644, from which the text, along with the accompanying notes, has been taken by generous permission.]

LETTER OF LEONARD HOAR

To his Freshman Nephew, Josiah Flynt [1]

[London] March 27, 1661

Cozen Josiah Flint,

Your first second and 3d are before me in answer to one of mine to you the last year: the which you esteemed somewhat sharp but I thought and still doe fear that it was scarce so much as was needfull: and I am sure yourself would be of the same mind if with me you knew the unutterable misery and irreparable mischeif that follows upon the mispense of those Halcyon dayes which you do yet enjoy. The which letter, whilst you fence withall in your first by those seven or eight thin-sculd-paper-put-byes And as many empty excuses; you did but lay more open your own blame-worthinesse and augment my greif insted of giving me satisfaction.

But your two latter epistles are better Containing some acknowledgment of those grand defects, discerned in you, and those errors committed by you: together with your promises of reparation and amendment by redoubling your diligence in your studyes for the time to come. Only remember to doe what you have promised, and I thereupon have believed; that I may see some testimonyes of it in all your succeeding letters; And also hear it testyfyed by others, that shall write to me concerning you. By all things that you can either revere or desire I adjure you that you doe not æmulate those unhappy youths that reckon it a high point of their wisdom to elude the expectations of their friends for a little while; whereby they indeed not only delude, but destroy themselves for ever.

Your account of the course of your studyes, as now ordered, under the worthy Mr. Chancey, is far short of my desire; for its only of what you were then about; Wheras it should have bin a delineation of your whole method and authors, from your matriculation till commencement. Therfore I can still touch but upon a few generalls for your direction.

The first is this that you would not content yourself with the doing that only which you are tasked to; Nor to doe that, meerly as much as needs must, and is expected of you: But dayly somthing more than your task: and that task also somthing better than ordinary. Thus when the classis study only Logick or Nature you may spend some one or two spare houres in Languages Rhetorique History or Mathematiques or the like, And when they recite only the text of an author read you some other of the same subject or some commentator upon it at the same time. Also in your accustomed disputations doe not satisfy yourself only to theiv an argument but study the question before hand and if possible draw in a book on purpose a summary of the arguments and answers on all hands: unto which you may briefly subjoyn any thing choice and accurate which you have heard in the hall upon the debate of it in publick.

Nextly as you must read much that your head may be stored with notion so you must be free and much in all kinds of discourse of what you read: that your tongue may be apt to a good expression of what you doe understand. And further; of most things you must wr[ite] to; wherby you may render yourself exact in judging of what you hear or read and faithfull in remembering of what you once have known. Touching your writing take a few hints of many which I had thought to have given you. 1. let it not be in loose papers for it will prove for the most part lost labour. Secondly, nor in a fortuitous vagrant way But in distinct bookes designed for every severall purpose And the heads of all, wrote aforehand in every page with intermediate spaces left (as well as you can guesse) proportionable to the matter they are like to contain.

3. Let all those heads be in the method of the incomparable P. Ramus, as to every art which he hath wrot upon. Get his definitions and distributions into your mind and memory. Let thesse be the titles of your severall pages and repositoryes in the books aforesaid. He that is ready in these of P. Ramus, may refer all things to them And he may know where again to fetch any thing that he hath judiciously referred; for there is not one axiom of truth ever uttered, that doth not fall under some speciall rule of art.

The Genus on any page, you may (having paged your book before hand) by a figure set before it direct from what page it came: And the species thereof, one or more which, for method and understanding sake shall be set down under it, but not handled there: you may by figures after them direct to the severall pages that are made the repositoryes for the matters referrible to each of them And so need no childish confused Alphabetical indices.

Mr Alexander Richardson's Tables would be as an Ariadne's thred to you in this labyrinth. Which with other his Manuscripts in Logick Physick and Theology, by transcribing, have bin continued in your colledg ever since the foundation thereof among most that were reckoned students indeed. And if you have now lost them I know no way to recover them but of some that were of that society in former times. I suppose Mr Danforth Mr Mitchell and others have them.[2] Mr Hancock a quondam pupil of Mr. Chaunceyes hath his Divinity. But in the utter defect of this, you may make use of the grand Mr Ramus in Grammar Rhetorique Logick (the Mathematiques must be left to your industry and memory unlesse it should be some practicall branches of it, of which you may take short notes) and then for Theology (which you may yet let alone) you have Dr Ames Medulla: Of this Theme I shall be larger: when you shall give me encouragement thereunto by attending to what I have written on the rest fore going.

4ly. As to the authors you should distill into your paper bookes in generall let them not be such as are already methodicall concise and pithy as possible: for it would be but to transcribe them: which is very tedious and uncouth. Rather keep such bookes by you for immediate perusall. But let them be such as are voluminous; intricate and more jejune: Or else those tractabuli that touch only on some smaller tendrells of any science. Especially if they be bookes that you doe only borrow, or hire to read. By this mean I have kept my library in a little compasse: (scarce yet having more bookes then my self can carry in my arms at once my paper bookes only excepted) and yet I have not quite lost any thing that did occur in my multifarious wandring readings. Were a man sure of a stable abode in a place for the whole time of his life, and had an estate also to expend; then indeed the bookes themselves in specie were the better way and only an index to be made of them all. But this was not like to be nor hath bin my condition: and it may be may not be yours. Wherefore, though it be somewhat laborious yet be not discouraged in prosecuting it. It is the surest way and most ready for use in all places and times, yielding the greatest evidences of your growth in knowledge and therefore also the greatest delight. It comprehends the other way of an index to: If for the bookes you read you keep a catalogue of their names authors scope and manner of handling and edition. And so for every severall tract you devise a certain mark, by which you may breifly quote the author from whence you had those collected notes and refer to him for more ample satisfaction in any article when as it shall be to[o] tedious to transcribe him word for word.

5t. For bookes into which you should thus hoard your store Take at present only some quires of paper stitct together, which you may encrease or substract from, as you shall see occasion upon experience. Only let them that concern one thing be all ruld after one fashion; and let them be sewed and written so as that afterwards they may be bound into one volume, in case that you should never have time to digest them again into more handsome order. At least no further then a succinct epitome: or Synopsis.

6. One paper book more adde of the names of all philosophicall authors and divines of ordinary note: of all the severall sects in the schooles and in the Church. Of all the nations famed in the world; of all and singular the most misterious arts and sciences: And of them all write a Latine Alphabeticall Index which by figures shall direct to the severall pages in a book where you have noted or will note the characters commendations and censures which any of them doe give of other and some of the charriteristick differences by which they were known, the time of their rise their progresse subdivisions and several ends. I mean such fragments as shall occur of these things, to you by the by in your reading: and would for most part be lost, if not thus laid up. As for the full history of them wherever that is found, tran-scribe nothing out of it, for its to laborious and endlesse: but only refer to it. Much lesse doe you doe offer to gather any thing out of the workes of authors who have written volumes to this very purpose, such as are Possewine,[3] Sextus Senensis,[4] Gesner,[5] Draudius,[6] and the like. The great use of this is to preserve these fragments that yourself shall find in your studyes, and could not be otherwise referred. Like-wise, that you may know and compare their thoughts of each other especially the moderns; and that accordingly you may be directed and cautioned in the perusal of any of them. Finally that you may have of your own store those characters and lineaments by which you may presently pencill any of them at pleasure: And this not as usually upon prejudice and peradventures; but the testimonyes of some or other that you may also produce. for alway be sure in this, that you note down the author whence you excepted any thing of this nature. But this you will judg so vast as never to be accomplished, and therefore vain to be attempted, you never having heard the names of $\frac{1}{10}$ of those things and persons that I have proposed so that you know not how so much as to begin this platform. I answer that for the progresse or compleating of this work you need not take care: Let it but grow as you studyes grow; you never need seek any thing on purpose to put into this book. And for the entrance I shall shew

it easy. For if you take but one quire of paper and divide the first 2
sheets into 24 narrow columnes, and every page of the rest into two:
which also must be paged. Then mark the narrow columnes each
with one letter of the Alphabet. And it is ready for use: for tis but
to write the name of seid place or person that next occurs into your
index with the figure J at it: and again that name, with what is there
said of it in your first page of the quire, with the author whence you
had it, and its done. And the like of the second in the second. When
the index shall grow full tis but write it over again leaving larger
spaces where needed. And when that quire shall grow full tis but to
take up another and carry on the same columnes and numbers. And
when they grow to be five or 6 quires to this one index, why then,
if that on any name swell to big for its column, tis but to refer it to
some other column further forwards. On the contrary if any others
have not nor are not like to yeild any thing much upon them, when
more titles occur tis but croud those into them, referring them also,
as the former, by the index and its figures. Thus I think I have made
it facile and plain enough And beleiv me you will find it beyond your
estimation, both pleasant and profitable.

7. One more Quire you may take and rule each leaf into 4 columnes
And therin also note Alphabetically all those curious criticismes Ety-
mologyes and derivations that you shall meet withall in the English
Latin Greek and Hebrew tongues. I still mean by the by: while you
are seeking other matters. Not which you may gather out of vocabu-
laryes and Criticks that have purposely written on such subjects. for
that were but actum agere.

8. Be forward and frequent in the use of all those things which
you have read, and which you have collected: judiciously molding
them up with others of your own fancy and memory according to
the proposed occasions. Whether it be in the penning of epistles orations Theses or Antitheses, or determinations upon a question. Analyses
of any part of an author, or imitations of him, *per modum genésews.*[7]
For so much only have you profited in your studyes as you are able
to doe these. And all the contemplations and collection in the world,
will but only fit you for thesse: tis practise and only your own practise
that will be able to perfect you.

My charg of your choyce of company I need not inculcate: nor I
hope that for your constant use of the Latine tongue in all your converse together: and that in the purest phrase of Terence and Erasmus
etc Musick I had almost forgot I suspect you seek it both to soon, and
to much. This be assured of that if you be not excellent at it Its worth

nothing at all. And if you be excellent it will take up so much of your mind and time that you will be worth little else: And when all that excellence is attained your acquest will prove little or nothing of real profit to you unlesse you intend to take upon you the trade of fidling. Howbeit hearing your mother's desires were for it for your sisters for whom tis more proper and they also have more leisure to looke after it: For them I say I had provided the Instruments desired, But I cannot now attend the sending them being hurrying away from London by this unexpected providence of your unkle Daniells sicknesse: which with some other circumst: with which its acc[ompanied] dt. nt. a ltl dist. me.[8]

My deservedly honoured friend and colleague Mr Stoughton is coming over. he hath promised me to doe you any civill courtesy either for advice or loan of a book or the like. Therfore to him I wish you modestly to apply your self and hearken to: whom as I am sure you will find able, so I am perswaded that you will find both free and faithfull, to assist you as is meet.

I shall adde but one thing more for a conclusion: But that the crown and perfection of all the rest: which only can make your endeavours succesfull and your end blessed: And that is som thing of the dayly practice of piety and the study of the true and highest wisdome And for gods sake, and your own both present and æternall welfares sake, let me not only entereat, but enjoyn, and obtain of you, that you doe not neglect it: No not a day. For it must be constancy, constancy, as well as labour, that compleats any such work. And if you will take me for an admonitor doe it thus. Read every morning a chapter in the old Test: and every evning one in the new: using your self alwayes as much as you can to one edition of the bible. And as you read, note lightly with your pen in the margent the severall places of remarque, with severall marks. Those I use are: for such as have any thing in them new to me, notable and evident, this sign ‹' for those that are obscure and worthy to consult an interpreter upon: this ‹ For those that are seemingly contradictory to some others, this + For those that must be compared with others this > For those golden sayings that are full of the soul and power of the Gospell; worthy of highest consideration and admiration, thus ∾. And if any 3 or 4 or 10 verses together be of like import I upon the first of them set down the proper mark and double it as ″ ‶ ≫.

2. Out of these latter most eminent sentences cull one or two for to expatiate upon in your own thoughts, half a quarter of an houre by way of meditation. There use your Rhetoricque, your utmost ra-

tionation, or rather indeed your sanctifyed affections: Love faith fear hope joy etc: For your direction and encouragement in this exercise, you may read the practique of Augustine Bernard or Gerard. Or our more modern worthyes I Ambrose, R Baxter, B[isho]p Hall or mr Watson,[9] as to the Theoreticall part.

3ly and lastly, those 2 being premised, close with Prayer. for this I præscribe not whether it should be linguall or mentall longer or breifer: Only let it as wel as its two preparatives, be most solemn and secret: and as tis said of Hannah, the speech of your heart. The barrenest ground, and with but mean tillage, being thus watered with these dews of heaven, will bring forth abundantly: and that, the most excellent fruites. Doe but seriously try these 3 last things, for some good while: and reckon me a Lyar in all the rest, if you find not their most sensible sweet effects. yea (as that Christian Seneca, B[isho]p Hall, said before me so I boldly say again) Doe you curse me from your death-bed, if you doe not reckon these amongst your best spent houres.

Touching the other items about your studyes, either mind them or mend them and follow better. So we shall be freinds and rejoyce in each other. But if you will neither: then (tho I am no prophet, yet) I will fortell you the certain issue of all: viz: that ere a very few years be over, with inconceivable indignation that you will call your self fool and caitif: And then, (then when it is to no purpose) [call] me what I now subscribe my self

Your faithfull freind, and loving unkle

LEON HOAR.

THOMAS SHEPARD, JR. (1635–1677)

[The advice which Leonard Hoar offered his nephew, Josiah Flynt, primarily concerned matters of curriculum. Thomas Shepard, Jr., son of the first minister at Cambridge, emphasized quite different points in the letter to his son Thomas (1658–1685). Shepard had served the College as Tutor shortly after his graduation in 1653, hence his advice was especially apt. Son Thomas was graduated in 1676, and four years later he was ordained pastor of the same church in Charlestown, Massachusetts, which his father served as teacher.

For an account of Thomas Shepard, Jr., see Sibley, *Biographical Sketches*, I, 327–335; for the son, see Sibley, *ibid.*, II, 482–488. The letter was inaccurately printed in Cotton Mather, *Magnalia* (1702), IV, 202–203; also in *American Quarterly Register*, IX (1836), 116–117. The text, together with the notes, is from *Publications of the Colonial Society of Massachusetts*, XIV (1913), 192–198.]

A LETTER FROM THE REV^D M^R THO^S SHEPHARD
To His Son att His Admission into the College.

D EAR Son, I think meet (partly from the advice of your renowned Grandfather to myself att my admission into the College, and partly from some other observations I have had respecting studies in that society) to leave the Remembrances and advice following with you, in this great Change of your life, rather in writing, than viva voce only; that so they may be the better considered and improved by you, and may abide upon your heart when I shall be (and that may be sooner than you are aware) taken from thee, and speak no more: requiring you frequently to read over, and seriously to ponder, and digest, as also conscientiously to putt in practice the same through the Lords assistance.

I. Remember the end of your life, which is acoming back again to God, and fellowship with God; for as your great misery is your separation, and estrangement from him, so your happiness, or last end, is your Return again to him; and because there is no coming to God but by Christs Righteousness, and no Christ to be had but by faith, and no Faith without humiliation or sense of your misery, hence therefore let all your Prayers, and tears be, that God would first humble you, that so you may fly by faith to Christ, and come by Christ to God.

II. Remember the End of this turn of your life, vizt your coming into the College, it is to fitt you for the most Glorious work, which God can call you to, vizt the Holy Ministry; that you may declare the Name of God to the Conversion and salvation of souls; for this End, your Father has sett you apart with many Tears, and hath given you up unto God, that he may accept of you; and that he would delight in you.

III. Remember therefore that God looks for and calls for much holiness from you: I had rather see you buried in your Grave, than grow light, loose, wanton, or prophane. God's secretts in the holy scriptures, which are left to instruct Ministers, are never made known to common and prophane Spirits: and therefore be sure you begin, and end every Day wherein you study with Earnest prayer to God, lamenting after the favour of God; reading some part of the Scriptures daily; and setting apart some time every Day (tho' but one Quarter of an hour) for meditation of the things of God.

IV. Remember therefore, that tho' you have spent your time in the vanity of Childhood; sports and mirth, little minding better things, yet that now, when come to this ripeness of Admission to the College, that now God and man expects you should putt away Childish things: now is the time come, wherein you are to be serious, and to learn sobriety, and wisdom in all your ways which concern God and man.

V. Remember that these are times and Days of much Light and Knowledge and that therefore you had as good be no Scholar as not excell in Knowledge and Learning. Abhorr therefore one hour of idleness as you would be ashamed of one hour of Drunkenness: Look that you loose not your precious time by falling in with Idle Companions, or by growing weary of your Studies, or by Love of any filthy lust; or by discouragement of heart that you shall never attain to any excellency of Knowledge, or by thinking too well of your self, that you have gott as much as is needfull for you, when you have gott as much as your Equals in the same year; no verily, the Spirit of God will not communicate much to you in a way of Idleness, but will curse your Soul, while this sin is nourished, which hath spoiled so many hopefull youths in their first blossoming in the College: And therefore tho' I would not have you neglect seasons of recreation a little before and after meals (and altho' I would not have you Study late in the night usually, yet look that you rise early and loose not your morning thoughts, when your mind is most fresh, and fitt for Study) but be no wicked example all the Day to any of your Fellows in spending your time Idly: And do not content yourself to do as much as your Tutor setts you about, but know that you will never excell in Learning, unless you do Somewhat else in private Hours, wherein his Care cannot reach you: and do not think that Idling away your time is no great Sin, if so be you think you can hide it from the Eyes of others: but Consider that God, who always sees you, and observes how you Spend your time, will be provoked for every hour of that precious time you now mispend, which you are like never to find the like to this in the College, all your Life after.

VI. Remember that in ordering your Studies you make them as pleasant as may be, and as fruitfull as possibly you are able, that so you may not be weary in the work God setts you about: and for this End remember these Rules, vizt

1, Single out two or three scholars most Godly, Learned and studious, and whom you can most love, and who love you best, to be helps to you in your Studies; Gett therefore into the acquaintance of some of your Equalls, to spend some time with them often in discoursing and disputing about the things you hear and read and learn; as also grow acquainted with some that are your Superiours, of whom you may often ask questions and from whom you may learn more than by your Equals only.

2, Mark every mans Disputations and Conferences, and study to gett some Good by every thing: and if your memory be not very strong, committ every notion this way gained unto Paper as soon as you gett into your Study.

3, Lett your studies be so ordered as to have variety of Studies before you, that when you are weary of one book, you may take pleasure (through this variety) in another: and for this End read some Histories often, which (they Say) make men wise, as Poets make witty;[1] both which are pleasant things in the midst of more difficult studies.

4, Lett not your Studies be prosecuted in an immethodicall or Disorderly way; but (for the Generality) keep a fixed order of Studies Suited to your own Genius, and Circumstances of things, which in each year, att least, notwithstanding, there will be occasion of some variation of: Fix your Course, and the season for each kind of Study, and suffer no other matters, or Persons needlessly to interrupt you, or take you off therefrom.

5, Lett difficult studies have the strength and flower of your time and thoughts: and therein suffer no difficulty to pass unresolved, but either by your own labour, or by enquiry of others, or by both, master it before you pass from it; pass not cursorily or heedlessly over such things (rivet the knottyest place you meet with) 'tis not so much *multa Lectio sed sedula et attenta*[2] that makes a scholar, as our Phrase speaks.

6, Come to your Studies with an Appetite, and weary not your body, mind, or Eyes with long poreing on your book, but break off & meditate on what you have read, and then to it again; or (if it be in fitt season) recreate your Self a little, and so to your work afresh; let your recreation be such as may stir the Body chiefly, yet not violent, and whether such or sedentry, let it be never more than may Serve to make your Spirit the more free and lively in your Studies.

7, Such books, as it is proper to read over, if they are very choice and not overlarge, read them over oftener than once: if it be not your own and that you are not like to procure it, then collect out of such book what is worthy to be noted therein: in which Collections take these Directions, (1) Write not in loose Papers, but in a fair Paper-book paged thro'out. (2) Write faithfully the words of your Author. (3) Sett down in your Paper-book the name of your Author, with the title of his book, and the page, where you find the Collection. (4) Allow a margin to your paper-book no broader than wherein you may write the letters. a. b. c. d. e. f &c. vizt att the beginning of each observable Collection, if you have more Collections than two or three in a side. (5) When you have written out such a book being marked with some distinguishing character (as 1. 2. 3. 4. &c. or α, β, γ, δ, &c.) prepare another of the same dimensions as near as you can, and improve that as the former, and so onwards: which book may be (as the Merchants Journal is to his principal Ledger) preparatory for your Common-place book, as your reason and fancy will easily Suggest how, by Short reference of any subject to be handled, found in, (suppose) the paper book, β. page 10. margine f. Suppose the subject be [Faith] you need only write in your Common place book [Faith] vide β. 10, f: if the Subject be [hope] write [hope, γ 10 d.] which signifies that there is some Description of that Subject [hope] or some sentence about hope that is observable, or some story concerning that Vertue, & ye like; In the third paper book marked with [γ] and in the tenth page of that book, begun in the margin at the letter [d] [b] as you have leisure, read over your paper books, wherein you have writen your Collections at large, the frequent perusal thereof will many ways be useful to you as your Experience will in time witness.

8, Choose rather to confess your Ignorance in any matter of Learning, that you may [be] instructed by your Tutor, or another, as there may be occasion for it, than to pass from it, and so continue in your Ignorance thereof, or in any Errour about it; malo te doctum esse quam haberi.[3]

9, Suffer not too much to be spent, and break away in visits (visiting, or being visited) let them be Such as may be a whett to you in your studies, and for your profitt in Learning some way of other, so that you be imparting to others or imparted to from them, or both, in some notion of other, upon all Such occasions.

10, Study the art of reducing all you read to practice in your orations &c: turning and improving elegantly to words and notions, and fancy of your authour to Sett of quite another subject; a delicate example whereof you have in your Chrystiados, whereof Ross is the author, causing Virgil to Evangelize:[4] and as in your orations, so in all you do, labour for exactness, and acurateness, let not crude, lame, bungling Stuff come out of your Study: and for that end, see that you neither play nor sleep, nor idle away a moments time within your Study door, but remember your Study is your work-house only, and place of prayer.

11, So frame an order your Studies, that the one may be a further-ance to the other (the Tongues to the arts and the arts to the Tongues) and endeavour that your first years Studies may become a Clue to lead you on the more clearly, strongly, profitably, & chearfully to the Studies of the years following, making all still usefull, and subservient to Divinity, and so will your profiting in all be the more Perspicuous and methodicall.

12, Be sparing in your Diet, as to meat and drink, that so after any repast your body may be a servant to your mind, and not a Clogg and Burden.

13, Take pains in, and time for preparing in private for your recitations, declamations, disputations, and such other exercises as you are called to attend before your Tutor or others; do not hurry them off indigestly, no not under pretence of Studying some other matter first: but first (I Say in the first place) attend those (straiten not your self in time for the thorough dispatch thereof) and then afterwards you may apply yourself as aforesaid to your private and more proper Studies; In all which, mind that reading without meditation will be in a great measure unprofitable, and rawness and forgetfulness will be the Event: but meditation without reading will be barren soon; therefore read much that so you may have plenty of matter for meditation to work upon; and here I would not have you forgett a speech of your precious Grandfather to a Scholar that complained to him of a bad memory, which did discourage him from reading much in History, or other books, his answer was, [Lege! lege! aliquid haerebit] So I say to you read! read! something will stick in the mind, be diligent and good will come of it: and that Sentence in Prov. 14. 23. deserves to be written in letters of Gold upon your study-table [in all labour there is profitt &c] yet also know that reading, and meditation without prayer, will in the End be both blasted by the holy God, and therefore,

VII. Remember that not only heavenly and spiritual and Supernatural knowledge descends from God, but also all naturall, and humane learning, and abilities; and therefore pray much, not only for the one but also for the other from the Father of Lights, and mercies; and remember that prayer att Christs feet for all the learning you want, shall fetch you in more in an hour, than possibly you may gett by all the books, and helps you have otherwise in many years.

VIII. Remember to be Grave (not Childish) and amiable and loving toward all the Scholars, that you may win their hearts and Honour.

IX. Remember now to be watchful against the two great Sins of many Scholars; the first is youthful Lusts, speculative wantoness, and secret filthiness, which God sees in the Dark, and for which God hardens and blinds young mens hearts, his holy Spirit departing from such, unclean Styes. The second is malignancy and secret distaste of Holiness and the Power of Godliness, and the Professors of it, both these sins you will quickly fall into, unto your own perdition, if you be not carefull of your Company, for there are and will be such in every Scholasticall Society for the most part, as will teach you how to be filthy and how to jest, and Scorn at Godliness, and the professors thereof, whose Company I charge you to fly from as from the Devil, and abhor: and that you may be kept from these, read often that Scripture Prov. 2. 10. 11. 12, 16.

X. Remember to intreat God with Tears before you come to hear any Sermon, that thereby God would powerfully speak to your heart, and make his truth precious to you: neglect not to write after the preacher always, and write not in loose sheets but in handsome Paperbooks; and be carefull to preserve and peruse the Same. And upon the Sabbath days make exceeding Conscience of Sanctification; mix not your other Studies, much less Idleness, or vain and casual discourses with the Duties of that holy Day; but remember that Command Lev. 19. 30. Ye shall keep my Sabbaths and reverence my Sanctuary, I am the Lord.

XI. Remember that whensoever you read, hear or conceive of any Divine truth, you Study to affect your heart with it and the Goodness of it. Take heed of receiving Truth into your head without the Love of it in your heart, lest God give you up to strong Delusions to believe lyes, and that in the Conclusion all your learning shall make you more fitt to decieve your Self and others. Take heed lest by seing things with a form of Knowledge, the Lord do not bind you by that Knowledge the more, that in seing you shall not see: If therefore God revealeth any truth to you att any time, be sure you be humbly and deeply thankfull: and when he hides any truth from you, be sure you lie down, and loath yourself, and be humble: the first degree of wisdom is to know and feel your own folly.

2 Tim. 2. 7. Consider what I say and the Lord give thee understanding in all things.

Prov. 23. 15. My Son, if thine heart be wise, my heart shall rejoice, even mine.

Pater tuus

T. SHEPARD

INCREASE MATHER

[One popular misconception too often repeated has been the belief that Puritan educators were interested in higher learning only as it prepared students by means of a curriculum preponderantly theological. The presidential address delivered in Latin by Increase Mather sometime before 1697, counseling the pupils to search for Truth with evidence derived from the new and disturbing scientific discoveries, is in the finest tradition of humane learning.

For Increase Mather, see p. 334. The English text is from Samuel E. Morison, *Harvard College in the Seventeenth Century*, p. 167, by generous permission.]

A PRESIDENTIAL ADDRESS

IT PLEASETH me greatly that you, who have been initiated in the Liberal Arts, seem to savour a liberal mode of philosophizing, rather than the Peripatetic. I doubt not that the *Exercitationes* of Gassendi [1] are familiar to you; in which he sheweth with many proofs that there are many deficiencies in Aristotle, many excesses, and many errors. It is a trite saying, *He who desireth not to be intelligible, should be negligible;* moreover there are some matters in the books of Aristotle which no mortal can comprehend. Wherefore it is alleged of Hermolaus Barbarus,[2] that he raised a demon from hell, to explain what Aristotle meant by ἐντελέχεια.[3] A right proper interpreter of Aristotle, forsooth! How much in his writings are redolent of their author's paganism! He would have the world uncreated; he denieth a possible resurrection of the dead, he declareth the soul mortal. To Aristotle some prefer Pyrrho, father of the Sceptics; others, Zeno, father of the Stoics; many prefer Plato, father of the Academics. You who are wont to philosophize in a liberal spirit, are pledged to the words of no particular master, yet I would have you hold fast to that one truly golden saying of Aristotle: *Find a friend in Plato, a friend in Socrates* (and I say a friend in Aristotle), *but above all find a friend in* TRUTH.

COTTON MATHER

[Upon the death of Ezekiel Cheever (1615/16–1708), Cotton Mather wrote a biographical sketch of that beloved teacher: *Corderius Americanus. An Essay upon the Good Education of Children.* The tribute to the most famous schoolmaster of the period, with its accompanying verse elegy, bespeaks the esteem in which the venerable master was held. It indicates as well the training which boys received for seven years in Latin and Greek—the only subjects studied in grammar school.

Cheever, a graduate of Emmanuel College, Cambridge, emigrated in 1637. He taught continuously for seventy years, at New Haven, Ipswich, Charlestown, and finally for the last thirty-eight years of his life as master of the Boston Latin School. His Latin Accidence was used as a text for two centuries. Hawthorne's *Grandfather's Chair* pictures him vividly. See also Elizabeth P. Gould, *Ezekiel Cheever, Schoolmaster* (Boston, 1904); and *Dictionary of American Biography*.

Elijah Corlet (1610?–1687/8) was likewise a distinguished schoolmaster. He received his A.B. degree at Oxford in 1631, and emigrated to Cambridge, Massachusetts, where he was master of the Grammar School from 1642 till his death. See William C. Lane, "Nehemiah Walter's Elegy on Elijah Corlet," *Proceedings of the Cambridge Historical Society*, II (1906), 13–20; George E. Littlefield, "Elijah Corlet and the 'Faire Grammar Schoole' at Cambridge," *Publications of the Colonial Society of Massachusetts*, XVII (1915), 131–140. The Elegy is reprinted in *Early American Poetry*, ed. James F. Hunnewell, Boston, 1896. For account of Cotton Mather, see p. 162.

We cannot know how Mather's children reacted to the sententiousness of the "Special Points" relating to their education. The plan was well enough, and doubtless one which all good Puritans strove to execute in some degree. Had Mather been mindful of the principle enunciated by Jonathan Swift in his "Resolutions"—not to apply them all for fear of observing none—he might have been spared the shame brought upon him by his unfilial scapegrace "Cressy."

The text of *An Elegy on Ezekiel Cheever* is from *Corderius Americanus;* that of "Some Special Points" is from *The Diary of Cotton Mather*, ed. by Worthington C. Ford in *Massachusetts Historical Society Collections*, series 7, VII (1911), 534–537, dated February, 1705/6.]

AN ELEGY ON EZEKIEL CHEEVER

YOU THAT are *Men*, & Thoughts of *Manhood* know,
    Be Just now to the *Man* that made you so.
Martyr'd by *Scholars* the stabb'd *Cassian* dies,
    And falls to cursed Lads a Sacrifice.
Not so my CHEEVER; Not by *Scholars* slain,
But Prais'd, and Lov'd, and wish'd to *Life* again.
A mighty *Tribe* of Well-instructed Youth
Tell what they owe to him, and Tell with Truth.
All the *Eight parts of Speech* he taught to them
They now Employ to *Trumpet* his Esteem.
They fill *Fames Trumpet*, and they spread a Fame
To last till the *Last Trumpet* drown the same. . . .

A Learned Master of the *Languages*
Which to Rich *Stores* of Learning are the *Keyes*
He taught us first *Good Sense* to understand
And put the *Golden Keyes* into our Hand,
We but for him had been for Learning *Dumb*,
And had a sort of *Turkish Mutes* become.
Were *Grammar* quite Extinct, yet at his Brain
The *Candle* might have well been lit again.
If *Rhet'rick* had been stript of all her *Pride*
She from his *Wardrobe* might have been Supply'd,
Do but Name CHEEVER, and the *Echo* straight
Upon that Name, *Good Latin*, will Repeat.
A *Christian Terence*, Master of the *File*
That arms the Curious to Reform their *Style*.
Now *Rome* and *Athens* from their Ashes rise;
See their *Platonick Year* with vast surprize:
And in our *School* a *Miracle* is wrought;
For the *Dead Languages* to *Life* are brought.
   His *Work* he Lov'd: Oh! had we done the same:
Our *Play-dayes* still to him ungrateful came.
And yet so well our *Work* adjusted Lay,
We came to *Work*, as if we came to *Play*.
   Our *Lads* had been, but for his wondrous Cares,
Boyes of my Lady *Mores* [1] unquiet Pray'rs.
Sure were it not for such informing *Schools*,
Our *Lat'ran* too would soon be fill'd with *Owles*.
Tis CORLET's pains, & CHEEVER's, we must own,
That thou, *New-England*, art not *Scythia* grown.
The *Isles* of S*illy* [2] had o're-run this Day
The *Continent* of our *America*.
Grammar he taught, which 'twas his work to do:
But he would *Hagar* [3] have her place to know.
   The *Bible* is the Sacred *Grammar*, where
   The *Rules of speaking well*, contained are.
He taught us *Lilly*,[4] and he *Gospel* taught;
And us poor Children to our *Saviour* brought.
Master of Sentences, he gave us more
The [5] we in our *Sententia* had before.
We Learn't Good Things in *Tullies Offices;*
But we from *him* Learn't Better things than these,
With *Cato's* he to us the *Higher* gave
Lessons of JESUS, that our Souls do save.
We Constru'd *Ovid's Metamorphosis*,
But on our selves charg'd, not a *Change* to miss.
Young *Austin* wept,[6] when he saw *Dido* dead,

Tho' not a Tear for a *Lost Soul* he had:
Our Master would not let us be so vain,
But us from *Virgil* did to *David* train,
Textors Epistles [7] would not *Cloathe* our Souls;
Pauls too we heard; we *went to School at Pauls.* . . .
Death gently cut the *Stalk*, and kindly laid
Him, where our God His *Granary* has made.
    Who at *New-Haven* first began to Teach,
Dying *Unshipwreck'd*, does *White-Haven* reach.
At that *Fair Haven* they all Storms forget;
He there his DAVENPORT [8] with Love does meet.
    The *Luminons Robe*, the *Less* whereof with *Shame*
Our Parents wept, when *Naked* they became;
Those Lovely *Spirits* wear it, and therein
Serve God with *Priestly Glory*, free from Sin.
    But in his *Paradisian Rest* above,
To *Us* does the Blest Shade retain his Love.
With *Rip'ned Thoughts* Above concern'd for Us,
We can't but hear him dart his Wishes, thus.
    "TUTORS, Be *Strict;* But yet be *Gentle* too:
Don't by fierce *Cruelties* fair *Hopes* undo.
Dream not, that they who are to Learning slow,
Will mend by Arguments in *Ferio*.
Who keeps the *Golden Fleece*, Oh, let him not
A *Dragon* be, tho' he *Three Tongues* have got.
Why can you not to Learning find the way,
But thro' the Province of *Severia?*
Twas *Moderatus*, who taught *Origen;* [9]
A *Youth* which prov'd one of the Best of men.
The Lads with *Honour* first, and *Reason* Rule;
Blowes are but for the *Refractory Fool*.

SOME SPECIAL POINTS, RELATING TO THE EDUCATION OF MY CHILDREN.

I. I pour out continual Prayers and Cries to the God of all Grace for them, that He will be a Father to my Children, and bestow His Christ and His Grace upon them, and guide them with His Councils, and bring them to His Glory.

And in this Action, I mention them distinctly, every one by Name unto the Lord.

II. I begin betimes to entertain them with delightful Stories, especially *scriptural* ones. And still conclude with some *Lesson* of Piety; bidding them to learn that *Lesson* from the *Story*.

And thus, every Day at the *Table*, I have used myself to tell a *Story* before I rise; and make the *Story* useful to the *Olive Plants about the Table*.

III. When the Children at any time accidentally come in my way, it is my custome to lett fall some *Sentence* or other, that may be monitory and profitable to them.

This Matter proves to me, a Matter of some Study, and Labour, and Contrivance. But who can tell, what may be the Effect of a *continual Dropping?*

IV. I essay betimes, to engage the Children, in Exercises of Piety; and especially *secret Prayer*, for which I give them very plain and brief *Directions*, and suggest unto them the *Petitions*, which I would have them to make before the Lord, and which I therefore explain to their Apprehension and Capacity. And I often call upon them; *Child, Don't you forgett every Day, to go alone, and pray as I have directed you!*

V. Betimes I try to form in the Children a Temper of *Benignity*. I putt them upon doing of Services and Kindnesses for one another, and for other Children. I applaud them, when I see them Delight in it. I upbraid all Aversion to it. I caution them exquisitely against all Revenges of Injuries. I instruct them, to return good Offices for evil Ones. I show them, how they will by this *Goodness* become like to the Good GOD, and His Glorious CHRIST. I lett them discern, that I am not satisfied, except when they have a Sweetness of Temper shining in them.

VI. As soon as tis possible, I make the Children learn to *write*. And when they can *write*, I employ them in Writing out the most agreeable and profitable Things, that I can invent for them. In this way, I propose to fraight their minds with *excellent Things*, and have a deep Impression made upon their Minds by such Things.

VII. I mightily endeavour it, that the Children may betimes, be acted by Principles of *Reason* and *Honour*.

I first begett in them an high Opinion of their Father's Love to them, and of his being best able to judge, what shall be good for them.

Then I make them sensible, tis a Folly for them to pretend unto any Witt and Will of their own; they must resign all to me, who will be sure to do what is best; my word must be their Law.

I cause them to understand, that it is an *hurtful* and a *shameful* thing to do amiss. I aggravate this, on all Occasions; and lett them see how *amiable* they will render themselves by well doing.

The *first Chastisement*, which I inflict for an ordinary Fault, is, to lett the Child see and hear me in an Astonishment, and hardly able to beleeve that the Child could do so *base* a Thing, but beleeving that they will never do it again.

I would never come, to give a child a *Blow;* except in Case of *Obstinacy:* or some gross Enormity.

To be chased for a while out of *my Presence,* I would make to be look'd upon, as the sorest Punishment in the Family.

I would by all possible Insinuations gain this Point upon them, that for them to learn all the brave Things in the world, is the bravest Thing in the world. I am not fond of proposing *Play* to them, as a Reward of any diligent Application to learn what is good; lest they should think *Diversion* to be a better and a nobler Thing than *Diligence.*

I would have them come to propound and expect, at this rate, *I have done well, and now I will go to my Father; He will teach me some curious Thing for it.* I must have them count it a *Priviledge,* to be taught; and I sometimes manage the Matter so, that my Refusing to teach them Something, is their *Punishment.*

The *slavish* way of *Education,* carried on with raving and kicking and scourging (in *Schools* as well as *Families,*) tis abominable; and a dreadful Judgment of God upon the World.

VIII. Tho' I find it a marvellous Advantage to have the Children strongly biased by Principles of *Reason* and *Honour,* (which, I find, Children will feel sooner than is commonly thought for:) yett I would neglect no Endeavours, to have *higher Principles* infused into them.

I therefore betimes awe them with the *Eye* of God upon them.

I show them, how they must love JESUS CHRIST; and show it, by doing what their Parents require of them.

I often tell them of the *good Angels,* who love them, and help them, and guard them; and who take Notice of them: and therefore must not be disobliged.

Heaven and *Hell,* I sett before them, as the Consequences of their Behaviour here.

IX. When the Children are capable of it, I take them *alone,* one by one; and after my Charges unto them, to fear God, and serve Christ, and shun Sin, *I pray with them* in my Study and make them the Witnesses of the Agonies, with which I address the Throne of Grace on their behalf.

X. I find much Benefit, by a particular Method, as of *Catechising* the Children, so of carrying the *Repetition* of the public Sermons unto them.

The Answers of the *Catechism* I still explain with abundance of brief

Quaestions, which make them to take in the Meaning of it, and I see, that they do so.

And when the Sermons are to be *Repeated*, I chuse to putt every *Truth*, into a *Quæstion*, to be answered still, with, *Yes*, or, *No*. In this way I awaken their *Attention*, as well as enlighten their *Understanding*. And in this way I have an Opportunity, to ask, *Do you desire such, or such a Grace of God?* and the like. Yea, I have an Opportunity to demand, and perhaps, to obtain their *Consent* unto the glorious Articles of the *New Covenant*. The Spirit of Grace may fall upon them in this Action; and they may be siez'd by Him, and Held as His *Temples*, thro' eternal Ages.

Broadside of Theses for a Harvard Commencement, 1678.

Chapter IX

SCIENCE

S UBSEQUENT generations have generally assumed that the Puritans in their day were hostile to experimental philosophy. "Science," as we have understood it, portrays a world subject to immutable natural laws, and at first sight there would seem to be nothing in common between it and the Puritan conception of a universe in the control of an unpredictable deity. Yet the fact is that the Puritans were no more negligent in fostering scientific inquiry than any other group, and were as ready as others to accept the implications of the great scientific discoveries of the century. Even as late as 1650, it was the "absence of mathematical training in Oxford and Cambridge, not any imaginary hostility of Puritanism to mathematics," [1] that prevented students of science from establishing a firm basis for research. Both in the English universities and at Harvard algebra was not studied, geometry was slighted, and physics taught by way of commentaries on Aristotle. Free inquiry into natural phenomena was hindered much more by lack of adequate equipment than by theological opposition.

There was indeed a religious reason for not giving the study of nature too exalted an importance in the Puritan scale of values. The principal business of man in this life, as the Puritans saw it, was the salvation of his soul, not the investigation of curious phenomena or the accumulation of irrelevant data. We must remember that in the seventeenth century natural science had not yet demonstrated its utility by the invention of time- and labor-saving devices, and that the best body of scientific theory available to educated persons still explained very little and provided no indubitable certainty. Consequently John Cotton warned his hearers that the pursuit of scientific knowledge was a very unsatisfying occupation:

> . . . the study of these natural things, is not available to the attainment of true happinesse; For how should that which is restlesse . . . procure us setled rest and tranquillity, which accompanieth true happinesse? . . . In particular, the Study and Knowledge of the passing away of one Generation after another, sheweth us our mortality and misery, and thereby yeildeth us grief and vexation, but no reliefe if we rest there. [2]

[1] Samuel E. Morison, *The Puritan Pronaos*, p. 236.
[2] *A Briefe Exposition . . . upon . . . Ecclesiastes* (London, 1654), p. 13.

However, in such a passage Cotton was not speaking merely as a Puritan, he was voicing the traditional sense of Christian culture. He was actually far from condemning scientific inquiry altogether. Indeed, it is demonstrable that the very tenets of Puritanism favored such inquiry, and that the Puritans therefore welcomed phenomenal proof of natural law in the universe.

The key to the Puritan conception of nature was the doctrine of providence, of which Urian Oakes's sermon is an excellent exposition (pp. 350–367). The natural world was God's providence in operation. Man was free to study nature and arrive at such conclusions as his observations warranted, but the facts should not interest him as facts merely. The Puritan felt that unless he could see the divine purpose in the phenomenal world he had failed to interpret his facts correctly. For him nature was a revelation of the divine order which had pre-existed in the mind of God before it was incarnated in matter, and its highest value was symbolic. "The stately theater of heaven and earth," said Thomas Shepard, is a visible manifestation of the invisible wisdom:

> Every creature in Heaven and Earth is a loud preacher of this truth: Who set those candles, those torches of heaven on the table? Who hung out those lanthorns in heaven to enlighten a dark world? . . . Who taught the Birds to build their nests, and the Bees to set up and order their commonwealth?[1]

John Cotton expounded the Puritan attitude in a sermon upon Christ's rebuke to the Pharisees, wherein he censured those who were versed in the signs of the weather, but not in the evidences of their salvation. A red sky at sunset generally does foretell a fine day, Cotton explained; there is some possibility of ascertaining a few natural sequences, and erecting the facts into a "law." For this particular law Cotton offered his congregation the best scientific account he had been able to discover. A red cloud, he said, is a thin one into which the rays of the sun can penetrate, thereby dissipating "the matter or cause of foule weather." But in all explanations of this sort, "every man that observes them to bee evident, yet findes them not alwaies certain"; the best of philosophers "are not able to say that the event hath and will always follow." [2] Furthermore, to what end is this knowledge? Only the lowest practical

---

[1] *The Sincere Convert* (London, 1652), p. 4.

[2] It is interesting to note that even when declaring that natural causes are unreliable, Cotton suggests a natural explanation for this one failing to create its effect: "yet who can tell, but that the Sunne may gather up new clouds, from the other side of the Heaven, before it rise to us in the next morning."

interest is served. It affects what business a man intends to do the next day, and "if he be crossed, it is not greatly material with him," whereas the signs of his own spiritual condition involve his eternal welfare. Hence he who seeks scientific knowledge for its own sake alone, who is "very quick sighted in points of nature, but very dull and heavy in matters of Religion and grace," endangers his soul. Yet a man who is not heavy and dull in matters of grace, who studies laws of the weather not to rest content with mechanistic solutions but to behold the workings of God within them, will secure true knowledge, "God having usually made this world to be a mappe and shadow of the spiritual estate of the soules of men." It is not the study of nature that is dangerous, it is the study of nature in the wrong spirit; if the visible world is seen correctly, as the map and shadow of the spiritual estate of the beholder, as a means of divine communication with the devout worshiper, then the understanding of its laws and workings becomes an essential part of Christian knowledge:

This serves to shew you, that it is not utterly unlawfull for men to make observation of the estate of the weather, and face of the sky; our Saviour doth not reproove it in them, but onely reprooves this, in that they were better skilled in the face of the sky, and signes of the weather, then in the signes of the times . . . hee rejects not such kind of conjectures, there is a workemanship of God in them, nor doth hee mislike the study of nature.[1]

Indeed, not only did Cotton say that the investigation of nature was lawful, but in another connection he actually declared it to be the positive duty of all men:

To study the nature and course, and use of all Gods works, is a duty imposed by God upon all sorts of men; from the King that sitteth upon the Throne to the Artificer.[2]

Since nature was under God's direction, God was responsible for the order, and it was the duty of the philosopher and theologian alike to formulate this order into "laws" of nature.

Puritans did not forbid the teachings of the "new science" during the seventeenth century, and often they were enthusiastic exponents of it; but the student of today must keep in mind that they never abandoned the assumption that God was sovereign and therefore reserved to himself the right to reverse or interrupt the laws of nature, which though usual, customary, and ordinary, were not inevitable. God

---

[1] *Gods Mercie Mixed with His Iustice* (London, 1641), pp. 113–134.
[2] *A Briefe Exposition . . . upon . . . Ecclesiastes*, p. 23.

could and sometimes did warn men by fire, flood, earthquake, and "blazing star," by apparition and providential intervention, in order that He might chasten whom He wished, condemn or save at will. Yet from the first, Puritans were disposed to place more emphasis upon the rules than upon the exceptions. John Cotton said that miracles were not to be multiplied without necessity.[1] Almost all the "special providences" by which men were saved from drowning or punished by plagues or conflagrations were viewed not as miracles, rending the appointed order, but as instances of God's skillful management of causes to produce the proper effects in accordance with the laws of nature. "God can work miracles, but when ordinary means may be had, he will not work miracles." [2] God will still deliver his faithful children out of Egypt, but not often by such a defiance of His own order as the division of the Red Sea: "we in these days have no promise of such a miraculous & immediate assistance; God works now by men and meanes, not by miracles." [3] As the seventeenth century progressed, the conviction grew that God abided by His laws. Though all phenomena were still investigated for their spiritual meaning, still the Puritan became more and more assured that God almost without exception works within the frame of nature and not by doing violence to it. When Samuel Danforth points out to the general public in the 1665 almanac—the only periodical literature that circulated at the time—that the comet of 1664 is a divine portent of disaster, he is stating a traditional theory of honorable antiquity. When at the same time he holds it to be subject to natural law (see p. 738), he is expressing belief in the Copernican system,[4] whereas European

---

[1] *Way of the Congregational Churches Cleared* (London, 1648), Pt. I, 42

[2] Samuel Nowell, *Abraham in Arms* (Boston, 1678), p. 11.

[3] John Richardson, *The Necessity of a Well Experienced Souldiery* (Cambridge, 1679), p. 6. The interdependence of the religious beliefs and the scientific can be further illustrated from the fact that once Mrs. Hutchinson started on the road to theological heresy she was compelled to make rash assertions about the unimportance of second-ary causes. She horrified the Court by declaring that she had immediate revelations from God, and she sealed her doom in their opinion by asserting that God Himself had promised her He would deliver her from their persecution. They immediately asked her if she expected this deliverance by a miracle, "a work above nature," or "from the hand of God by his providence." John Cotton labored heroically to force her to confine herself to the second sort of expectation, and said before all the assembled people that if she believed she would be saved by a miracle, "I do not assent to, but look at it as a delusion." She would not accept Cotton's distinction, and was banished, among other reasons, for attributing to the deity too free a dis-position to work miracles in opposition to the laws of nature and of probability (Hutchinson, *History*, ed. Mayo, II, 384-391).

[4] Zechariah Brigden, a graduate of Harvard in 1657, brought out the almanac for 1659, wherein he eagerly displayed his acquaintance with Vincent Wing's *As-*

astronomers were usually forbidden to teach such doctrine until the end of the century:—here is the "new science" which the young college graduates were so excitedly disseminating into every household through the medium of the yearly almanac (see p. 744). They had gleaned their information from their college textbooks: Robert Boyle's *Usefulness of Experimental Natural Philosophy* (1663); Charles Morton's *Compendium Physicae*—a manuscript text in use at Harvard till 1725; and especially from the popular Copernican expositions of Vincent Wing and Adrian Heereboord, whose works had acquainted the students with Galileo, Kepler, and Gassendi, even before the epochal discoveries of Halley and Newton.

The Newtonian triumph established the concept of a necessary and inviolable system of law which God Himself cannot break even though he created it. All deists were followers of Newton, and there are deistic tendencies perceptible in Puritan writings, though the more central orthodoxy strove to reconcile God's sovereign freedom and the reign of law. Perhaps the New England orthodox rationalism is most clearly seen in Cotton Mather's *The Christian Philosopher* (see p. 750). Mather therein attempts to show how divine order manifests itself throughout the phenomenal universe; he sees God as a creating force in the world of nature as well as a Divine Original for man's spirit and mind. A pedant rather than a learned scholar, Mather depended upon a few intermediary works for his array of data; he quoted erudite sources at second hand, but the resulting compendium is enriched by observations of his own which enunciate the deistic principle that God's benevolence is manifested in the well-ordered beauty of Nature, apparent to man through his Reason. Such a point of view marks the beginning in America of the "enlightenment" which, first expounded by Franklin, Paine, and Jefferson, later flowered in Emerson and Thoreau. But Mather did not abandon his essentially Puritan view that Jehovah is a jealous God who can set all law aside to intervene directly in man's affairs. If he realized the antinomy, he took no step to resolve it.[1]

The colonists were as alert to the new discoveries in science as their English contemporaries who, under the aegis of Boyle, Pepys, Evelyn,

---

tronomia instaurata (1656), the first work in English to popularize Copernicus, and a book already adopted as a text at Harvard.

[1] Evidently Mather was considered by the older generation somewhat "advanced," for on December 23, 1714, Sewall notes: "Dr. C. Mather preaches excellently from Ps. 37. Trust in the Lord &c. only spake of the Sun in the centre of our System. I think it inconvenient to assert such Problems" (*Diary*, III, 31).

and Sprat were stimulating scientific inquiry by founding the Royal Society of London, membership in which body was conferred only for substantial scientific achievement. Governor John Winthrop, Jr., of Connecticut, was chosen fellow at the first regular election of the Society in 1663. He had brought with him to the colonies in the same year a three-and-one-half-foot telescope which he presented to Harvard College in 1672; Newton was assisted by observations made with it in arriving at his laws of gravitation. Winthrop's further active scientific inquiries and his communications of them to the Society (see p. 740), establish for him an important role in the history of American science. No other New Englanders were chosen members of the Society during the seventeenth century, though in 1683 a Philosophical Society was formed in Boston, modeled on the English counterpart; it met fortnightly for about ten years—the first of many scientific clubs in the English-speaking world founded on the plans of the "Illustrious Body" in London. Cotton Mather was elected to the Royal Society probably in 1713, though as he never went to London to sign the constitution, he could never qualify as member in full standing. At the time of Thomas Brattle's death in 1713 the Royal Society desired "his mss. relating to Astronomy, Musick and other parts of ye Mathematicks" so eagerly that they elected his brother William a member in the following year the more gracefully to procure them,[1] but William Brattle declined in modest deprecation of his own talents. The contributions of Winthrop and Thomas Brattle to pure science (see p. 739) were more substantial than those made by any other Americans of their day (see p. 758), though Paul Dudley, elected in 1721, was a frequent correspondent of the London body (see p. 747). John Leverett, elected in 1714, and Thomas Brattle are spoken of as having "many years since perus'd with delight their Transactions & recommended 'em to their Pupils as the best standards of Natural Philosophy now extant";[2] and in truth, there were no higher scientific standards at that time.

A discussion of the Puritan's concern in science must inevitably touch upon the tragic witchcraft trials of 1692. One point must be clearly understood at the start: witches were creatures whose existence was questioned by no one in his right senses, and even as late as the

[1] Letter of Henry Newman to John Chamberlayne, *Publications of the Colonial Society of Massachusetts*, XXVIII (1935), 223.

[2] *Ibid.* Of the nine members from the American colonies elected before 1740, only William Byrd of Virginia was not a New Englander; Thomas Robie was elected in 1725; Zabdiel Boylston, 1726; Fitz-John Winthrop, 1734. The list of eighteen, carried to 1795, is in Samuel E. Morison, *The Puritan Pronaos*, p. 266.

close of the seventeenth century hardly a scientist of repute in England but accepted certain phenomena as due to witchcraft. Three factors conjoined to start the trouble in New England,—where after all it played but a small role in the drama of a great delusion. First, since God could intervene directly in the natural order of events, He therefore could manifest His power against His adversaries in the invisible world; in the second place, no class of literature at the time more deeply impressed all classes of men than chronicles and narratives written to demonstrate remarkable providences wherein God interposed Himself in man's affairs; finally, it was not only the privilege but the duty of ministers to record such providences, for by their scholarly training and priestly office they were peculiarly fitted to perceive, interpret, and justify God's way to man. Now to observe the fatal conjunction of these separately reasonable views.[1]

Four children in Boston were seized by convulsions, and accused an old woman of bewitching them; the woman confessed her guilt, was tried, condemned, and executed by a most orderly procedure of law. The children still being "sadly molested with Evil Spirits," their minister Cotton Mather gave them spiritual consolation—psychiatric ministrations perhaps—to such good effect that they recovered. Elated by his success, Mather immediately published *Memorable Providences, Relating to Witchcrafts and Possessions* (1689), but his book, with its lurid details, instead of leading readers to see that God's power once again had triumphed over Satan, was seized upon by some of the more emotionally unstable as an exciting manual for the practice of witchcraft. Undue prominence was therefore given to abnormal states of mind. The situation was badly out of hand by 1692, when an outburst of accusations against witches gained headway in Salem Village (Danvers)—a parish that evidently had more than its share of neurotic women and hysterical children, and less than it needed of understanding leaders. By September, twenty people and two dogs had been executed as witches, one hundred and fifty were in prison awaiting trial, and two hundred more stood accused. Yet the Court, chosen by Governor Phips, and composed of distinguished citizens, had reviewed

[1] Two books especially should be noted among the great number that deal with the history of witchcraft in New England: George L. Burr, ed., *Narratives of the Witchcraft Cases* (New York, 1914), a reprint of essential documents with an introduction that discusses many details; and George L. Kittredge, *Witchcraft in Old and New England* (Cambridge, 1929), a work that treats the history of the subject in its wider implications. A brief summary of "Witchcraft" is included in Samuel E. Morison, *The Puritan Pronaos*, pp. 248–257, to which this summary is at a few points indebted.

the cases according to established law and had proceeded against the accused only after deliberation among themselves and upon the advice of leading ministers.

The point at issue was this: alleged victims claimed they were attacked by spirits in the likeness of some resident whom they identified. Was the evidence of mere allegation sufficient to convict the accused? If it was, who could escape hanging once the accusation were made? In Europe the best legal opinion, available to the New England court, advised that such "spectral evidence" was not adequate by itself to convict, yet those sitting in judgment at Salem continued to admit it as sole basis for conviction. The position in which even the most conservative and clear-headed gentlemen found themselves is well expressed by Thomas Brattle in "A Full and Candid Account of the Delusion called Witchcraft" (see p. 758). The tragedy is not difficult to comprehend when we recognize the frenzy and mass madness which confused even the wisest. As soon as the enormity of the panic became evident, the ministers gathered to find a way to stop it. That way seemed clearly to attack "spectral evidence"—the one real flaw in the legal machinery. Increase Mather therefore wrote a pamphlet, *Cases of Conscience concerning Evil Spirits* (1693), at first circulated in manuscript, in which he affirms his belief that witches exist, prays that none will think him unfair to the judges, who "are wise and good men, and have acted with all Fidelity according to their Light";[1] but he states positively, "This notwithstanding, I will add; It were better that Ten Suspected Witches should escape, than that one Innocent Person should be Condemned."[2] The Governor harkened especially to the opinion presented by twelve ministers therein added as a Postscript, which condemned the uses that the Court had made of spectral evidence; he ruled such evidence out, and without it the cases fell through; accusations were dropped, and the condemned—if they recanted—were free. But a great blot remained, even though indemnities were granted bereaved families. Five years later the noblest among the deliberative body, Samuel Sewall, rose in church to make public confession and ask humble forgiveness for the part he had taken in supporting a procedure which he had good reason to know was not sound.[3]

In the dispassion of a long-range view of the facts we do not entirely credit Robert Calef's prejudiced tirade directed against the part which the ministers played in the affair, headed by Increase Mather, —who, mistaken, yet was honest. We can only realize that eminently

---

[1] Page 70.   [2] Page 66.   [3] *Diary*, I, 445.

sane leaders of church and state, acting in accordance with the accepted scientific beliefs of their day, became momentarily victims of mass frenzy; they soon came to their senses and revised their legal and sociological viewpoint toward the wonders of the invisible world. Witches were never again brought to trial in New England, even though witchcraft trial continued in England till well into the eighteenth century.

It is pleasant to turn from the misty mid-regions of demonology to relate in a few words the story of the role played by Puritans in the development of preventive medicine. The place of medicine in the New England colonies is elsewhere briefly discussed (see p. 386), but one phase of it, the introduction of smallpox inoculation, deserves special record. In April, 1721, an epidemic of smallpox spread through Boston and vicinity, and by June had struck down nearly fifty-nine hundred persons; eight hundred and forty-four died. Cotton Mather, whose essays to do good were never more productive of beneficial results, recalled that he had not only read about the favorable outcome of inoculation as reported in the Transactions of the Royal Society,[1] but that his slave Onesimus claimed to have recovered from the dread disease after some such treatment in Africa. Mather suggested to the Boston physicians that they might profitably give inoculation a trial, but only Zabdiel Boylston among them agreed with him. To be sure, it was a risky undertaking, for the method in use was still untested. Boylston had been attacked by the disease some years before, hence it was useless to experiment on himself. He therefore tried out the method on his willing children and servants. The town was horrified and ready to cry murder if any of them died. A pamphlet war started between the proponents of inoculation, led by Increase and Cotton Mather, Boylston, and Benjamin Colman on the one side, and on the other a very much aroused opposition headed by the physician William Douglass. Feeling rose to such a pitch that the lives of Boylston and Cotton Mather were actually endangered by mob violence. But the good effects of inoculation became apparent —of two hundred and forty-one persons treated, only six died—and a bill introduced in the legislature aiming to forbid inoculation by law failed to pass. In November, 1721, a report of the treatment of cases—the first clinical treatise ever written on the subject—was communicated to the Royal Society and published in their Transactions[2] (see p. 763). It is a document of prime importance in medical history,

[1] See Vol. XXIX (1714–1716).
[2] Vol. XXXII (1721), 33–35, No. 370.

and one which appropriately closes the first period of scientific inquiry in this country.[1]

SAMUEL DANFORTH, 1626–1674

[The significance of *An Astronomical Description of the Late Comet or Blazing Star . . .* (Cambridge, 1665), by Samuel Danforth, lies in the fact that though it holds comets to be divine portents of disaster, it recognizes that they are not "Exhalations," but stellar phenomena, subject to natural law.

Danforth was born in Cambridge and graduated from Harvard in 1643. For some years he devoted his time to astronomical studies, and prepared the yearly Almanacs from 1645 to 1649. In them he presented descriptions of heavenly bodies as well as specimens of his poetry. He was ordained at Roxbury as assistant to John Eliot in 1650, and remained there as pastor for twenty-four years—until he "passed from *Natural Health*, to *Eternal Peace*."

See Cotton Mather, *Magnalia*, IV, 153 (whence the quotation); Sibley, *Biographical Sketches*, I, 88–92. For an account of astronomy in early New England, see Samuel E. Morison, *Harvard College in the Seventeenth Century*, chap. X.]

AN ASTRONOMICAL DESCRIPTION

I. *This Comet is no sublunary Meteor or sulphureous Exhalation, but a Celestial Luminary, moving in the starry Heavens.*

The Truth hereof may be demonstrated, 1. *By the vast Dimensions of it's body.* Some Comets have been observed by Astronomers to be halfe as big as the *Moon*, some bigger then the *Moon*, yea some bigger then the *Earth*. The exact Dimensions of this Comet, I may not presume to determine, but it seemeth not to be of the smallest size. Now 'tis not easy to imagine how the *Earth* should afford matter for a *Meteor* of such a huge magnitude, except we grant the greater part of the lower World, to be turned into an exhalation. 2. *By the smalness of it's Parallax.* The Parallax is the Distance between the *true* place of a

---

[1] An interest in natural history and botany was very slow to develop in New England, and the fact is surprising in view of the alertness of Puritans to physical science. Fitz-John Winthrop, F.R.S., was the only New Englander to win a place for himself as a naturalist before 1750. The greatest colonial naturalist was John Bartram of Pennsylvania, called by Linnaeus the greatest botanist in the world. Others who made contributions of value on the fauna and flora of the country were John Banister, William Byrd, Mark Catesby, John Clayton, and John Mitchell— all of Virginia.

Planet and the *apparent*. The lower and neerer any *Planet* is to the Earth, it hath the greater *Parallax*. . . .

IV. *This Comet is not a new fixed Star, but a Planetick or Erratick Body, wandring up & down in the etherial firmament under the fixed stars.*

Some learned Astronomers distinguish these more noble and celestial *Phænomena* or *Appearances* into *Fixed* and *Erratick*. Several new Stars have appeared which are fixed, *i.e.* they keep the same place in the *Heavens*, and the same distance from the *fixed Stars*. One in *Cassiopeia* Anno 1572. which continued a year and four months. . . .

Iuly 20 1663. That bright and radiant Star, a Star of the first magnitude, Mr. *Samuel Stone*,[1] the strength and glory of *Connecticut*, rested from his labours and sorrows, and fell a sleep sweetly and placidly in the Lord. A little before Him, Mr *Iohn Miller* [2] and Mr. *Samuel Newman*,[3] faithful, painful and affectionate Preachers of the Gospel, were also taken from us by death. Thus our Pillars are cut down, our strongest Stakes pluck't up, and our breaches not repaired. Is it a small thing in our eyes, our principal Congregations & Head-townes, should be so badly bereaved, as they are at this day?

3. The sad *Mildew* and *Blasting*, whereby we have been greatly afflicted the last Summer, and some of us the Summer before: our principal grain being turned into an husk & rotteness.

4. Severe *Drought* this last Summer, which burnt up the Pastures and the latter growth.

5. Early *Frosts*, which smote our *Indian Corn*, and greatly impoverished our latter Harvest.

Unto these and some other no less threatning Visitations, is superadded this strange and fearful Appearance in the Heavens, which is now seconded by a new Appearance this Spring, concomitant to the translation of our Honoured and Aged Governour, Mr. *John Endicot*,[4] from hence to a better World: By all which doubtless the Lord calls upon *New-England* to awake and to repent.

To this End Consider.

1. What a jealous eye the Lord hath upon us, observing how we carry and behave our selves at such a time as this.

JOHN WINTHROP, JR., 1605/6–1676

[John Winthrop, Jr., eldest son of Governor Winthrop, was probably the most versatile colonial figure in the seventeenth century. After attending Trinity College, Dublin, for two years, he was admitted to

the Inner Temple, London, in 1624. He traveled widely before emigrating to New England in 1631, where he founded Ipswich and New
London. As governor of Connecticut he secured exceptional privileges
for the Colony. His business acumen and public benefactions in both
colonies earned for him the respect and affection of all men. Even
though far removed from England, he remained in terms of warm
intimacy with Wren, Boyle, Stirk, Digby, and Newton. Indeed, he
may rightly be claimed as the first American scientist. As physician
he explored the composition of plants and minerals, took notes on his
investigations, and communicated the results to the Royal Society of
London. In 1663 he was elected a Fellow of that body, the first colonial
so honored. The remains of his library, rich in scientific lore, are now
in the New York Society Library.

The letter here quoted from the *Philosophical Transactions* of the Royal
Society of London was published in 1670 (V, 1151–1153), and is a
fair sample of the scientific observations then being gathered. See *Dictionary of American Biography;* Tyler, *A History of American Literature*, I,
99–103; II, 311–312. See especially Samuel E. Morison, *Builders of the
Bay Colony*, chap. IX.]

AN EXTRACT OF A LETTER,

WRITTEN BY JOHN WINTHROP ESQ; GOVERNOUR OF CONNECTICUT IN
   NEW ENGLAND, TO THE PUBLISHER, CONCERNING SOME NATURAL
   CURIOSITIES OF THOSE PARTS, ESPECIALLY A VERY STRANGE AND VERY
   CURIOUSLY CONTRIVED FISH, SENT FOR THE REPOSITORY OF THE
   R. SOCIETY.

I KNOW not, whether I may recommend some of the productions
of this Wilderness as rarities or novelties, but they are such as
the place affords. There are, amongst the rest, 2. or 3. smal Oaks,
which though so slender and low (as you may see, if they come safe)
have yet Acorns and cups upon them, so that it may be truly said,
that there is a Country, where Hoggs are so tall, that they eat acorns
upon the standing growing Oakes. This is every year visible in many
parts here, there being of this sort of dwarf-Oak whole Forrests in
the Inland Country; too many for the Husband-man, who finds that
sort of land most difficult to break. up at first with his plough, in regard that the whole surface is fill'd with spreading strong roots of
this sort of Oak. Neither must it be thought, that they are small shoots,
which in time would grow big trees; for, where these grow, there are
no great Oaks, or very few amongst them. But whether it be a novelty

to see such kind of dwarf-trees bearing acorns, I know not: It was to me, having not seen the like (as far as I remember,) in *England* or *France*, or other parts. Mean time I have observed, that in some Plains, full of these shrubs, there have been no acorns on most of them; but whether in other years they were not fruitful, I know not. Some years, we know, even the great Oaks bear no fruit, which are very full at other times; but this year throughout the whole Country there is plenty of acorns; and I should be glad to be informed, whether this year they have been also abounding in *England*, or other parts of Europe; and if so, or not so, possibly something not altogether inconsiderable may be thence inferr'd. Besides, if such dwarfish Oakes, as these, should be found in other parts of the World, it were not amiss, me thinks, to inquire, Whether it be not some Mineral ground, where these grow; and if so, what sorts of Minerals those places afford?

There are also sent you some pieces of the Bark of a Tree, which grows in *Nova-Scotia*, and (as I hear) in the more Easterly parts of N. *England*. Upon this bark there are little knobs, within which there is a liquid matter like Turpentine (which will run out, the knob being cut open) of a very sanative nature, as I am informed by those, who affirm, that they have often tryed it.

In the same Box are Pods of a Vegetable, we call *Silk-grass*, which are full of a kind of most fine down-like Cotton-wool, many such flocks in one and the same pod ending in a flat Seed. 'Tis used to stuff up Pillows and Cushions; being tryed to spin, it proves not strong enough. The Seeds 'tis like may grow with you, if set in some Garden; whereby the whole Plant may be seen.

You'l find also a Branch of the Tree, call'd the Cotton-tree, bearing a kind of Down which also is not fit to spin. The Trees grow high and big. At the bottom of some of the Leaves, next to the stalk of them, is a knob, which is hollow, and a certain fly, some-what like a pis-mire-fly, is bred therein.

More-over, there are some of the *Matrices*, in which those Shels are bred, of which the *Indians* make the white *Wampanpeage*, one sort of their mony: They grow on the bottom of Sea-bays, and the shels are like Periwinkles, but greater. Whilst they are very smal, and first growing, many of them are within one of the concave receptacles of these *Matrices*, which are very tough, and strong, so contrived, that they are separate from one another, yet so, that each of them is fastned to a kind of skin, subtended all along to all these cases or baggs.

There is, besides, in a large round Box, a strange kind of *Fish*, which was taken by a Fisherman, when he was fishing for Codfish in that

Sea, which is without *Massachuset* Bay in N. *England*. It was living, when it was taken, which was done, I think, by an hook. The name of it I know not, nor can I write more particularly of it, because I could not yet speak with the Fisherman, who brough it from Sea. I have not seen the like. The Mouth is in the middle; and they say, that all the Arms, you see round about, were in motion, when it was first taken. . . .

LEONARD HOAR

[Though Leonard Hoar is remembered primarily as an educator (see p. 707), he had the born scientist's love for investigating natural phenomena at first hand. The letter here reproduced is from Boyle, *Works* (1744), V, 642, 643. Robert Boyle (1627–1691), natural philosopher and chemist, was a founder of the Royal Society of London, a voluminous writer, and one of the greatest scientists of his day. He was deeply interested in theology, and a student of Hebrew, Greek, Chaldee, and Syriac. The letter has been reprinted in Sibley, *Biographical Sketches*, I, 588–590; and in Samuel E. Morison, *Harvard College in the Seventeenth Century*, 644–646.]

MR. *LEONARD HOAR* TO MR. *ROBERT BOYLE*.

Cambridge, New-England, December the 13th, 1672.

RIGHT honourable,

Your freedom and courteous treating me, when hither coming, giveth me the hardiness to present you with my acknowledgments, although it be but your interpellation; judging it better, that I were censured for troublesomness, than for ingratitude. Yea the chiefest of this colony, a poor, but yet pious and industrious people, know and acknowledge your kindness often and on considerable occasions expressed towards them, in their just defences, *&c.* although they know not where or how to publish their tabula votiva, or memorials of it unto your acceptation, but still do gratefully recommend you and your well-devoted labours in their prayers to God; and any publick affair them concerning, that shall unexpectedly, emerge unto your prudence, love and candor, hoping, that nothing shall ever be believed or concluded against them before that they be heard.

Noble Sir, I am not unmindful of your desires to see what rarities the country might yield; and have taken course, that now be presented to you, first, a sort of berries, that grow closely conglomerated unto the stalk of a shrub, in its leaf, smell and taste, like the broadest leaved myrtle, or to a dwarf-bay; which, by plain distillation, yields an almost unctuous matter; and by decoction, not a resina, nor oil, but a kind of serum, such as I have not known ordinarily for any vegetables. I believe it excels for the wind-colick.

Though I thought myself an indifferent botanist for any thing could grow in *England*, yet here in our wild plants I am presently [at a loss] but I hope I shall in season search out their pedigrees; and would be free to gratify any person valuing them with their seeds, or bodies dried. Mr. *Alexander Balaam*,[1] my master in those studies, and a person well known to Mr. *Charles Howard* and Dr. *Morrison*,[2] are now in your land.

Also (pardon, I beseech you, the confidence) I make bold to present your honour with a model of our natives ships. With one of them twenty foot long they will carry six or eight persons, their house and furniture and provisions, by one padling her forwards in the stern, swifter than any sculler. And when they come to falls, or would go over the land, [the passengers] load themselves away with the ship and her freight too.

I doubt they are not for the wars; for if you but stamp hard, you may strike out the bottom; and if you lay your tongue on one side of your mouth, it may over-set.

Also Sir, a piece of their plate, a fish I call the sea-spider, and some stones, I doubt more ponderous than precious; but that your honour will prove.

It hath pleased even all to assign the college for my Sparta. I desire I may adorn it; and thereby encourage the country in its utmost throws for its resuscitation from its ruins. And we still hope some helpers from our native land; of which your honoured self, Mr. *A.*[3] and some others have given a pledge.

A large well-sheltered garden and orchard for students addicted to planting; an ergasterium for mechanick fancies; and a laboratory chemical for those philosophers, that by their senses would culture their understandings, are in our design, for the students to spend their times of recreation in them; for readings or notions only are but husky provender.

And, Sir, if you will please of your mature judgment and great experience to deign us any other advice or device, by which we may become not only nominal, but real scholars, it shall, I hope, be as precious seed, of which both you and me and many by us shall have uberous provent at the great day of reckoning, which I know you do respect above all.

If I durst, I would beg one of a sort of all your printed monuments, to enrich our library, and encourage our attempts this way.

ı know nothing so stunting our hopes and labours in this way, as that we want one of a sort of the books of the learned, that come forth daily in *Europe*, of whose very names we are therefore ignorant.

To Mr. *Ashhurst* I have written more. Let not, I beseech you, my prolixity tire or deter your acception of things hinted, or your honour's condonation of

Your devoted humble servant,

Leonard Hoar.

NOADIAH RUSSELL AND WILLIAM WILLIAMS

[The *Cambridge Ephemeris* for 1684 was brought out by Noadiah Russell (1659–1713), a graduate of Harvard in 1681, who after teaching at Ipswich for three and one-half years, returned in 1688 to his birthplace, Middletown, Connecticut, as minister where he thenceforth remained. He was a founder and trustee of Yale College, and among the framers of the Saybrook Platform. (See Sibley, *Biographical Sketches*, III, 216–222.)

William Williams (1665–1741) prepared the Cambridge almanac for 1685. Born in Newton, he was graduated from Harvard in 1683, and was later settled as pastor in Hatfield, where he died. Among his published discourses is the Massachusetts Election Sermon for 1719. (See Sibley, *ibid.*, III, 263–269.)

The almanac science of 1684 and 1685 is quaint only in relation to present-day knowledge. It was alert to the latest advancements and free from religious cant. For a summary of developments of astronomy, see Samuel E. Morison, *Harvard College in the Seventeenth Century*, 216–222. The text for both selections is from photostat copies of the unique originals in possession of the Massachusetts Historical Society.]

FROM THE ALMANAC FOR 1684.

Concerning Lightning, and Thunder, with some Observations and Cautions touching the same.

LIGHTNING is an exhalation hot and dry, as also hot and moist; which being Elevated by the Sun to the middle Region of the Air, is there included or shut up within a cloud and cannot ascend; but by an Antiperistasis grows hotter and is enkindled, attenuated, and so seeks for more room, which it not finding in the cloud, violently rends the same, breaks out of it, and continues burning so long that it comes to the very ground.—By its rending of the cloud, there is caused a most dreadful noise or rumbling, and this we call Thunder: So that Thunder is improperly reckoned among the kinds or *species* of *Meteors*.

Of Lightning, [*fulmen*] there are three sorts, *viz*. piercing, [*Terebrans*], dashing in pieces [*disentiens*] and burning [*urens*] Piercing Lightning (which is also called white Lightning,) does consist of a most Subtile and thin exhalation and is very penetrating.

Observ. By reason of its subtile nature, many strange effects are produced thereby; A sword blade will be melted in its scabbard, and the scabbard not hurt at all: The pores in the scabbard are so great, that this Lightning passeth through them without any hurt, but coming to a more solid body (as the sword blade is) it meets with opposition there, and so through its heat melts it.

The *Second* sort of Lightning, is such as consists of a more fat and thick exhalation, which meeting with things, burnes not to ashes, but blasts and scorcheth them.

Observ. With this Lightning, there happens to be (yet seldome) a Stone, that is called a Thunderbolt, which breaketh forth with the exhalation, (as a bullet out of a gun) and breaks into pieces whatever it meets. When it strikes the earth it is reported to go not above five foot deep.

The *Third* sort of Lightning is fulmen urens [*burning Lightning*] and is more fiery then flamy; of a more grosse and earthy substance then the preceding sorts.

Observ. If Lightning kill one in his sleep, he dyes with his eyes opened, the Reason is because it just wakes him and kills him before he can shut his eyes again: If it kills one waking his eyes will be found to be shut, because it so amaseth him, that he winketh and dyes before he can open his eyes again.

Caution. It is not good to stand looking on the lightning at any time, for if it hurts no otherway, yet it may dry up or so waste the Chrystalline Humour of the eyes that it may cause the sight to perish, or it may swell the face, making it to break out with scabs, caused by a kind of poyson in the exhalation which the pores of the face and eyes do admit.

Finis.

FROM THE ALMANAC FOR 1685.

Concerning the nature of *Comets*, &c.

COMETS are judged by many excellent Philosophers to be *Meteors*, whose matter is an Exhalation, hot and dry, fat and clammy; drawn by vertue of the heavenly bodies into the highest part of the

Air, (and sometimes into the Starry region) where it is closely con-
glutinated into a great Lump, by reason of supply that it hath from
below, so long as there is a working to exhale: and being thus compacted, it is set on fire in convenient time by the excessive heat of
the place where it resteth: Sometimes they continue burning long,
sometimes but a little time, seven dayes is reckoned to be the least,
whereas some have continued 6 months and more, all which commeth
to pass by reason of the paucity or plenty of the matter whereof it
consisteth.

There are 2 things observable in Comets. The colour and the form
or Fashion, both which proceed from the diverse disposing of the
matter.

Their colours are principally 3. White, which comes to pass when
the matter is thin 2. Ruddy, looking like fire when the matter is
meanly thick. 3 Of a blew colour when the matter is very thick.

Their forms or Fashions are principally. 2. 1 Roundish, having
beams round about them, which happens when the matter is thin on
the edges and thick every there else 2 They appear with a beard or
tail, which happens when the matter is but meanly thick towards
some one side or other and rather long then round.

Thus are Comets made to be meteors, and certain it is that there
are difficulties which will arise from the other notion which some
have of them, which may be as difficult yea far more difficult to a
rational head then any that will proceed from this notion we have
here presented you with.

The cheifest objections against this opinion seem to me to be two.
The one is the greatness and duration or long continuance of Comets
sometimes. The other objection is grounded upon the place of the
Comets existence sometimes, it being found to be above the Moon.

As for the first objection (which might have been made two) Certain it is that a spoonfull of water will yield a vapor an 100 times as
big as to its dilation, and since so why may not the like be rationally
asserted of fumes or earthy exhalations, that tho' in themselves they
may be very large yet originally very small: and if this is considered
we need not wonder that the earth yields so much of exhalations as
to cause such vast beings as Comets are and yet to the eye loose nothing
of its bigness.

As for the other objection; all the answer, I shall give to it, may be
seen in tendring to consideration these two things.

1 That after Comets are above the highest region of the air, or
the Moon yet they are under the starry heaven which hath an at-

tractive power 2 That the nature of the place aboue the Moon is falsly concieved of, if imagined to be really different from [the] place below the Moon, Now if thus why may not Comets ascend above the Moon as well as up to the Moon.

FINIS.

PAUL DUDLEY, 1675–1750/51

[Paul Dudley, son of Governor Joseph Dudley of Massachusetts, began life after graduation from Harvard College in 1690 as a lawyer. Soon appointed attorney-general, he later became Chief Justice of Massachusetts. Intellectually curious, he was alive to every cultural development, especially in natural philosophy. His unbending mannerisms, aristocratic background, wealth, and religious bigotry lent easy target during his lifetime and after for the opprobrious detractions which his high office made inevitable. The dispassionate judgment of time, however, reveals him as a jurist of probity and courage. By his will Harvard received the endowment of what were soon known as the Dudleian Lectures, for which incumbents are still annually chosen.

After contributing his account of maple-sugar making in New England to the Royal Society of London in 1720, Dudley was elected a Fellow of that learned body. During the course of the next fifteen years he submitted eleven more papers—all published in due course—ranging from accounts of the rattlesnake and of Niagara Falls to "An Essay upon the Natural History of Whales."

See *Dictionary of American Biography;* and especially Sibley, *Biographical Sketches*, IV, 42–54. The text of the essay on sugar making is from *Philosophical Transactions* of the Royal Society of London, XXXI (1720), No. 364 (pp. 27, 28); that of the essay on hiving of bees, *ibid.*, No. 367 (pp. 148–150).]

VII. *AN ACCOUNT OF THE METHOD OF MAKING SUGAR FROM THE JUICE OF THE* MAPLE TREE *IN* NEW ENGLAND.

By PAUL DUDLEY, Esq; F.R.S.

MAPLE Sugar is made of the Juice of Upland Maple, or Maple Trees that grow upon the Highlands. You box the Tree, as we call it, *i.e.* make a hole with an Axe, or Chizzel, into the Side of the Tree, within a Foot of the Ground; the Box you make may hold about a Pint, and therefore it must shelve inwards, or towards the bottom of the Tree; you must also bark the Tree above the Box, to steer or direct the Juice to the Box.

You must also Tap the Tree with a small Gimblet below your Box, so as to draw the Liquor off. When you have pierced or tapp'd your Tree, or Box, you put in a Reed, or Pipe, or a bit of Cedar scored with a Channel, and put a Bowl, Tray, or small Cask at the Foot of the Tree, to receive your Liquor, and so tend the Vessels as they are full.

After you have got your Liquor, you boil it in a Pot, Kettle, or Copper. Ten Gallons will make somewhat better than a pound of Sugar.

It becomes Sugar by the thin part evaporating in the boiling, for you must boil it till it is as thick as Treacle. Ten Gallons must boil till it comes to a pint and half.

A Kettle of twenty Gallons will be near 16 Hours in boiling, before you can reduce it to three Pints; a good Fire may do it sooner.

When you take it off, you must keep almost continually stirring it, in order to make it Sugar: otherwise it will candy as hard as a Rock.

Some put in a little Beef Sewet, as big as a Walnut, when they take it off the Fire, to make it turn the better to Sugar, and to prevent its candying, but it will do without. A good large Tree will yield twenty Gallons. The Season of the Year is from the beginning of *February* to the beginning of *April*.

Mr. Dudley *in a following Letter adds this Note.*

I have nothing to add to my Chapter of Maple Sugar, but that our Physicians look upon it not only to be as good for common use as the *West India* Sugar, but to exceed all other for its Medicinal Virtue.

VII. *AN ACCOUNT OF A METHOD LATELY FOUND OUT IN* NEW–ENGLAND, *FOR DISCOVERING WHERE THE BEES HIVE IN THE WOODS, IN ORDER TO GET THEIR HONEY.*

By the same Mr. Dudley.

THE HUNTER in a clear Sun-shiny day, takes a Plate or Trencher, with a little Sugar, Honey or Molosses spread on it, and when got into the Woods, sets it down on a Rock or Stump in the Woods: this the Bees soon scent and find out; for 'tis generally supposed a Bee will scent Honey or Wax above a Mile's distance. The Hunter secures in a Box or other Conveniency, one or more of the Bees as they fill themselves, and after a little time, lets one of them go, observing very carefully the Course the Bee steers; for after he rises in the Air, he flies directly, or upon a streight Course to the Tree where the Hive is.

In order to this, the Hunter carries with him his Pocket Compass, his Rule, and other Implements, with a Sheet of Paper, and sets down the Course, suppose it be West; by this he is sure the Tree must be somewhere in a West Line from where he is, but wants to know the exact Distance from his Station; in order to determine that, he makes an off-set either South or North (we'll suppose North) an hundred Perch or Rod, (if it be more, it will still be more exact, because the Angle will not be so acute) then he takes out another Bee and lets him go, observing his Course also very carefully, for he being loaded will, as the first, (after he is mounted a convenient height) fly directly to the Hive; this second Course, (as I must call it) the Hunter finds to be South, 54 Degrees West; then there remains nothing but to find out where the two Courses intersect, or, which is the same thing, the Distance from B to A, or from C to A, as in the Figure, Tab. 3d. for there the Honey-Tree is.

For which Reason, if the Course of the second Bee from C had been South-west, and by South, *viz.* to D, then the Hive-Tree must have been there, for there the Lines are found to intersect.

The Foundation of all this is the streight or direct motion of Bees, when bound home with their Honey, and this is found to be certain by the Observation and Experience of our Hunters every Year, and especially of late Years, since this Mathematical way of finding Honey in the Woods has been used with such Success.

An ingenious Man of my Acquaintance the last Year took two or three of his Neighbours that knew nothing of the matter, and after he had taken his Bees, set the Courses the first and second Bee steered, made the off-set, and taken the Distance from the two Stations to the Intersection, he have orders to cut down such a Tree, pointing to it; the Labourers smiled, and were confident there was no Honey there, for they could not perceive the Tree to be hollow, or to have any hole for the Bees to enter by, and would have disswaded the Gentleman from felling the Tree, but he insisted on it, and offered to lay them any Wager that the Hive was there, and so it proved to the great surprize of the Country-men.

I cannot dismiss this Subject, without acquainting you, that all the Bees we have in our Gardens, or in our Woods, and which now are in great numbers, are the produce of such as were brought in Hives from *England* near a hundred Years ago, and not the natural produce of this part of *America;* for the first Planters of *New England* never observed a Bee in the Woods, until many Years after the Country was settled; but that which proves it beyond question is, that the *Aborigines* (the *Indians*) have no word in their Language for a Bee, as they have for all Animals whatsoever proper to, or aboriginally of the Country, and therefore for many Years called a Bee by the name of *English Man's Fly.*

Our People formerly used to find out Honey in the Woods, by surprizing and following one Bee after another by the Eye, till at length they found out where the Bees hived.

I will mention another thing with respect to Bees, tho' I don't know but it may have been commonly observed; and that is, when they Swarm they never go to the Northward, but move Southward, or inclining that way.

I should have taken notice in the proper place, that when one Bee goes home from the Sugar-plate, he returns with a considerable number from the Hive.

COTTON MATHER

[No Puritan more clearly represents the temper of seventeenth-century curiosity in the phenomenal universe than Cotton Mather (see p. 162). One encounters his ubiquitous mind at every turn, sometimes trivial and credulous, often pedantic, but never unresponsive to intellectual stimuli. He planned *The Christian Philosopher: A Collection of the Best Discoveries in Nature, with Religious Improvements* (London, 1721) to reconcile science and religion. One should not overlook Mather's skill throughout as a literary craftsman.

The text here reproduced is from the original edition: "Of the Vegetables," pp. 122–127, 130, 131, 134–139; "Of Man," pp. 301, 303, 304. These and further selected essays may be found in *Selections from Cotton Mather,* ed. Murdock (New York, 1926). The notes for this text correspond, with some additions and variations, to those in the *Selections.* See especially the introduction to *Selections,* pp. xlviii–liv.]

FROM *THE CHRISTIAN PHILOSOPHER*

Essay XXVI. Of the Vegetables.

THE CONTRIVANCE of our most Glorious Creator, in the VEGETABLES growing upon this Globe, cannot be wisely observed without Admiration and Astonishment.

We will single out some Remarkables, and glorify our GOD!

First, In *what manner* is *Vegetation* performed? And how is the Growth of *Plants* and the Increase of their *Parts* carried on? The excellent and ingenious Dr. *John Woodward* [1] has, in the way of nice Experiment, brought this thing under a close Examination. It is evident that *Water* is necessary to *Vegetation;* there is a *Water* which ascends the Vessels of the *Plants*, much after the way of a *Filtration;* and the Plants take up a larger or lesser Quantity of this Fluid, according to their Dimensions. The much greater part of that *fluid Mass* which is conveyed to the Plants, does not abide there, but exhale thro them up into the *Atmosphere*. Hence Countries that abound with *bigger Plants* are obnoxious to greater Damps, and Rains, and inconvenient Humidities. But there is also a *terrestrial Matter* which is mixed with this *Water*, and ascends up into the *Plants* with the *Water:* Something of this Matter will attend *Water* in all it motions, and stick by it after all its Percolations. Indeed the Quantity of this *terrestrial Matter*, which the Vapours carry up into the *Atmosphere*, is very *fine*, and not very *much*, but it is the truest and the best prepared *vegetable Matter;* for which cause it is that *Rain-Water* is of such a singular Fertility. 'Tis true there is in *Water* a *mineral Matter* also, which is usually too scabrous, and ponderous, and inflexible, to enter the Pores of the *Roots*. Be the *Earth* ever so rich, 'tis observed little good will come of it, unless the Parts of it be loosened a little, and separated. And this probably is all the use of *Nitre* and other *Salts* to Plants, to loosen the Earth, and separate the Parts of it. It is this *terrestrial Matter* which fills the *Plants;* they are more or less nourished and augmented in proportion, as their *Water* conveys a greater or lesser quantity of proper *terrestrial Matter* to them. Nevertheless 'tis also probable that in this there is a variety; and all Plants are not formed and filled from the same sort of *Corpuscles*. Every *Vegetable* seems to require a *peculiar and specifick Matter* for its Formation and Nourishment. If the Soil wherein a Seed is planted, have not all or most of the Ingredients necessary for the *Vegetable* to subsist upon, it will suffer accordingly. Thus *Wheat* sown upon a Tract of Land well furnish'd for the Supply of that *Grain*, will succeed very well, perhaps for divers Years, or, as the Husbandman expresses it, *as long as the Ground is in heart;* but anon it will produce no more of that *Corn;* it will of some other, perhaps of *Barley:* and when it will subsist this no more, still *Oats* will thrive there; and perhaps *Pease* after these. When the Ground has lain fallow some time, the *Rain* will pour down a fresh Stock upon it; and the care of the *Tiller* in manuring of it, lays upon it such things as are most impregnated with a Supply for *Vegetation*. It is observ'd that *Spring-*

water and *Rain-water* contain pretty near an equal charge of the *vege-table Matter*, but *River-water* much more than either of them; and hence the Inundations of *Rivers* leave upon their Banks the fairest Crops in the World. It is now plain that *Water* is not the *Matter* that composes *Vegetables*, but the *Agent* that conveys that *Matter* to them, and introduces it into the several parts of them. Wherefore the plentiful provision of this Fluid supplied to all Parts of the Earth, is by our *Woodward* justly celebrated with a pious Acknowledgment of that *natural Providence* that superintends over the Globe which we inhabit. The Parts of *Water* being exactly spherical, and subtile beyond all expression, the Surfaces perfectly polite, and the Intervals being there-fore the largest, and so the most fitting to receive a *foreign Matter* into them, it is the most proper Instrument imaginable for the Service now assign'd to it. And yet *Water* would not perform this Office and Service to the *Plants*, if it be not assisted with a due quantity of *Heat;* *Heat* must concur, or *Vegetation* will not succeed. Hence as the *Heat* of several *Seasons* affords a different face of things, the same does the *Heat* of several *Climates*. The *hotter* Countries usually yield the *larger Trees*, and in a greater variety. And in *warmer* Countries, if there be a remission of the *usual Heat*, the Production will in proportion be diminish'd.

That I may a little contribute my *two Mites* to the illustration of the way wherein *Vegetation* is carried on, I will here communicate a couple of Experiments lately made in my Neighbourhood.

My Neighbour planted a Row of Hills in his Field with our *Indian Corn*, but such a Grain as was colour'd *red* and *blue;* the rest of the Field he planted with Corn of the most usual Colour, which is *yellow*. To the most *Windward-side* this Row infected *four* of the next neighbouring Rows, and part of the fifth, and some of the sixth, to render them colour'd like what grew on itself. But on the *Leeward-side* no less than seven or eight Rows were so colour'd, and some smaller impressions were made on those that were yet further distant.

The same Neighbour having his Garden often robb'd of the *Squashes* growing in it, planted some *Gourds* among them, which are to ap-pearance very like them, and which he distinguish'd by certain ad-jacent marks, that he might not be himself imposed upon; by this means the Thieves 'tis true found a very *bitter Sauce*, but then all the *Squashes* were so infected and embitter'd, that he was not himself able to eat what the Thieves had left of them.

That most accurate and experienc'd Botanist Mr. *Ray* [2] has given us the *Plants* that are more commonly met withal, with certain characteristick Notes, wherein he establishes *twenty-five Genders* of them. These *Plants* are to be rather stiled *Herbs*.

But then of the *Trees* and *Shrubs*, he distinguishes *five Classes* that have their *Flower* disjoined and remote from the *Fruit*, and as many that have their *Fruit* and *Flower* contiguous.

How unaccountably is the *Figure* of *Plants* preserved? And how unaccountably their *Growth* determined? Our excellent *Ray* flies to an intelligent *plastick Nature*, which must understand and regulate the whole Oeconomy.

Every particular *part* of the *Plant* has its astonishing Uses. The *Roots* give it a Stability, and fetch the Nourishment into it, which lies in the Earth ready for it. The *Fibres* contain and convey the Sap which carries up that Nourishment. The *Plant* has also larger Vessels, which entertain the proper and specifick Juice of it; and others to carry the Air for its necessary respiration. The outer and inner *Bark* defend it from Annoyances, and contribute to its Augmentation. The *Leaves* embrace and preserve the *Flower* and *Fruit* as they come to their explication. But the principal use of them, as *Malpighi*, and *Perault*, and *Mariotte*,[3] have observed, is, to concoct and prepare the *Sap* for the Nourishment of the *Fruit*, and of the whole *Plant;* not only that which ascends from the Root, but also what they take in from without, from the Dew, and from the Rain. For there is a *regress* of the *Sap* in Plants from above downwards; and this descendent Juice is that which principally nourishes both Fruit and Plant, as has been clearly proved by the Experiments of Signior *Malpighi* and Mr. *Brotherton*.

How agreeable the *Shade* of *Plants*, let every Man say that *sits under his own Vine, and under his own Fig-tree!*

How charming the Proportion and Pulchritude of the *Leaves*, the *Flowers*, the *Fruits*, he who confesses not, must be, as Dr. *More* says, *one sunk into a forlorn pitch of Degeneracy, and stupid as a Beast.*

Our Saviour says of the *Lillies* (which some, not without reason, suppose to be *Tulips*) *that* Solomon *in all his Glory was not arrayed like one of these*. And it is observed by *Spigelius*, that the Art of the most skilful Painter cannot so mingle and temper his *Colours*, as exactly to imitate or counterfeit the *native* ones of the *Flowers* or *Vegetables*.

Mr. *Ray* thinks it worthy a very particular Observation, that *Wheat*, which is the best sort of Grain, and affords the wholesomest Bread, is in a singular manner patient of both Extremes, both Heat and Cold, and will grow to maturity as well in *Scotland*, and in *Denmark*, as in *Egypt*, and *Guiney*, and *Madagascar*. It scarce refuses any Climate. And the exceeding *Fertility* of it is by a Pagan *Pliny* acknowledged as an

Instance of the Divine Bounty to Man, *Quod eo maxime Hominem alat;* [4]
one Bushel in a fit Soil, he says, yielding one hundred and fifty. **A**
German Divine so far plays the Philosopher on this Occasion, as to
propose it for a Singularity in *Bread,* that *totum Corpus sustentat, adeo,*
ut in unicâ Bucellâ, omnium Membrorum totius externi Corporis, nutrimentum
contineatur, illiusque Vis per totum Corpus sese diffundat. [5] A Friend of mine
had *thirty-six Ears* of Rye growing from *one Grain,* and on *one Stalk.*

But of our *Indian Corn,* one Grain of *Corn* will produce above a
thousand. And of *Guiney Corn,* one Grain has been known to produce
ten thousand.

The *Anatomy of Plants,* as it has been exhibited by the incomparable
Curiosity of Dr. *Grew,* what a vast *Field of Wonders* does it lead us into!

The most inimitable *Structure* of the Parts!

The particular *Canals,* and most adapted ones, for the conveyance
of the lymphatick and essential Juices!

The *Air-Vessels* in all their curious Coylings!

The *Coverings* which befriend them, a Work unspeakably more curious in reality than in appearance!

The strange Texture of the *Leaves,* the angular or circular, but always most orderly Position of their *Fibres;* the various *Foldings,* with
a *Duplicature,* a *Multiplicature,* the *Fore-rowl,* the *Back-rowl,* the *Tre-rowl;*
the noble Guard of the *Films* interposed!

The *Flowers,* their Gaiety and Fragrancy; the *Perianthium* or *Em-*
palement of them; their curious Foldings in the *Calyx* before their Expansion, with a *close Couch* or a *concave Couch,* a *single Plait* or a *double*
Plait, or a *Plait* and *Couch* together, or a *Rowl,* or a *Spire,* or *Plait*
and *Spire* together; and their luxuriant Colours after their *Foliation,*
and the expanding of their *Petala!*

The *Stamina,* with their *Apices;* and the *Stylus* (called the *Attire* by
Dr. *Grew*) which is found a sort of *Male Sperm,* to impregnate and
fructify the Seed!

At last the whole Rudiments and Lineaments of the *Parent-Vegetable,*
surprizingly lock'd up in the little compass of the *Fruit* or *Seed!* [6]

Gentlemen of Leisure, consult my illustrious Doctor, peruse his *Anatomy*
of Plants, ponder his numberless Discoveries; but all the while consider that rare Person as inviting you to join with him in adoring
the *God of his Father,* and the God who has *done these excellent things,*
which ought to be *known in all the Earth. . . .*

The peculiar Care which the great God of Nature has taken for the
Safety of the *Seed* and *Fruit,* and so for the Conservation of the *Plant,* is
by my ingenious *Derham* considered as a loud Invitation to His Praises.

They which dare shew their Heads all the Year, how securely is their *Seed* or *Fruit* lock'd up in the Winter in their *Gems*,[7] and well cover'd with neat and close *Tunicks* there!

Such as dare not expose themselves, how are they preserved under the Coverture of the *Earth*, till invited out by the kindly Warmth of the Spring!

When the *Vegetable Race* comes abroad, what strange Methods of Nature are there to *guard* them from Inconveniences, by making some to lie down prostrate, by making others, which were by the Antients called *Æschynomenæ*, to close themselves up at the Touch of Animals, and by making the most of them to shut up under their guard in the cool of the Evening, especially if there be foul Weather approaching; which is by *Gerhard*[8] therefore called, *The Countryman's Weather-wiser!*

What various ways has Nature for the *scattering* and the *sowing* of the *Seed!* Some are for this end winged with a light sort of a *Down*, to be carried about with the *Seed* by the Wind. Some are laid in springy cases, which when they burst and crack, dart their Seed to a distance, performing therein the part of an Husbandman. Others by their good Qualities invite themselves to be swallowed by the Birds, and being fertiliz'd by passing thro their Bodies, they are by them transferred to places where they fructify. *Theophrastus* affirms this of the *Misletoe;* and *Tavernier* of the *Nutmeg*. Others not thus taken care for, do, by their Usefulness to *us*, oblige us to look after them.

It is a little surprizing, that *Seeds* found in the *Gizzards* of *Wild-fowl*, have afterwards sprouted in the Earth; and *Seeds* left in the *Dung* of the *Cattel*. The Seeds of *Marjoram* and *Strammonium*, carelesly kept, have grown after seven Years.

How nice the provision of Nature for their Support in *standing* and *growing*, that they may keep their Heads above ground, and administer to our Intentions! There are some who stand by their own Strength; and the ligneous parts of these, tho' like our Bones, yet are not, like them, inflexible, but of an elastick nature, that they may dodge the Violence of the Winds: and their Branches at the top very commodiously have a tendency to an hemispherical Dilatation, but within such an Angle as makes an Æquilibration there. An ingenious Observer upon this one Circumstance, cannot forbear this just Reflection: *A visible Argument that the plastick Capacities of Matter are govern'd by an all-wise and infinite Agent, the native Strictnesses and Regularities of them plainly shewing from whose Hand they come.* And then such as are too weak to stand of *themselves*, 'tis wonderful to see how they use the

Help of their *Neighbours,* address them, embrace them, climb up about
them, some twisting themselves with a strange *convolving* Faculty, some
catching hold with *Claspers* and *Tendrels,* which are like Hands to them;
some striking in rooty *Feet,* and some emitting a natural *Glue,* by which
they adhere to their Supporters.

But, Oh! the glorious *Goodness* of our GOD in all these things! . . .

The Persuasion which Mankind has imbib'd of *Tobacco* being good
for us, has in a surprizing manner prevail'd! What incredible Millions
have *suck'd in* an Opinion, that it is an *useful* as well as a *pleasant* thing,
for them to spend much of their Time in drawing thro a Pipe the
Smoke of that lighted Weed! It was in the Year 1585, that one Mr. *Lane* [9]
carried over from *Virginia* some *Tobacco,* which was the first that had
ever been seen in *Europe;* and within an hundred Years the *smoking*
of it grew so much into fashion, that the very Customs of it brought
four hundred thousand Pounds a Year into the *English* Treasury.

It is doubtless a *Plant* of many Virtues. The *Ointment* made of it is
one of the best in the Dispensatory. The Practice of *smoking* it, tho
a great part of them that use it might very truly say, *they find neither
Good nor Hurt by it;* yet it may be fear'd it rather does more *Hurt* than
Good.

"May God preserve me from the indecent, ignoble, criminal *Slavery,*
to the mean Delight of *smoking a Weed,* which I see so many carried
away with. And if ever I should *smoke* it, let me be so wise as to do it,
not only with *Moderation,* but also with such Employments of my Mind,
as I may make that Action afford me a Leisure for!"

Methinks *Tobacco* is but a poor *Nepenthe,* tho the Takers thereof take
it for such an one. It is to be feared the *caustick Salt* in the *Smoke* of
this Plant, convey'd by the *Salival Juice* into the Blood, and also the
Vellication [10] which the continual use of it in *Snuff* gives to the *Nerves,*
may lay Foundations for Diseases in Millions of unadvised People,
which may be commonly and erroneously ascribed to some other
Original. . . .

But then we have one *far-fetch'd* and *dear-bought* Plant, on which
we have so many Volumes written, that they alone almost threaten
to become a *Library.* TEA is that charming Plant. Read *Pecklinus's* [11]
Book *de Potu Theæ,* and believe the medicinal and balsamick Virtues
of it; it strengthens the *Stomach,* it sweetens the *Blood,* it revives the
Heart, and it refreshes the *Spirits,* and is a Remedy against a World
of Distempers. Then go to *Waldschmidt,* [12] and you'll find it also to
brighten the *Intellectuals.* When *Prose* has done its part, our *Tate* [13] will
bring in *Verse* to celebrate the sovereign Virtues of it. . . .

Essay XXXII. Of Man

. . . Nor may we lay aside a grateful Sense of this, that as the *Son* of God is *the Upholder of all Things in all Worlds*, thus, that it is owing to his potent *Intercession* that the *Sin of Man* has made no more havock on this *our World*. This *our World* has been by the *Sin of Man* so perverted from the *true Ends* of it, and rendred full of such loathsome and hateful Regions, and such *Scelerata Castra*,[14] that the Revenges of God would have long since rendred it as a *fiery Oven*, if our blessed JESUS had not *interceded* for it: *O my Saviour, what would have become of me, and of all that comforts me, if thy Interposition had not preserved us!* . . .

I will finish with a Speculation, which my most valuable Dr. *Cheyne*[15] has a little more largely prosecuted and cultivated.

All *intelligent compound Beings* have their whole Entertainment in these three Principles, the DESIRE, the OBJECT, and the SENSATION arising from the *Congruity* between them; this *Analogy* is preserved full and clear thro the *Spiritual World*, yea, and thro the *material* also; so *universal* and *perpetual* an *Analogy* can arise from nothing but its *Pattern* and *Archetype* in the infinite God or Maker; and could we carry it up to the Source of it, we should find the TRINITY of Persons in the eternal GODHEAD admirably exhibited to us. In the GODHEAD we may first apprehend a *Desire*, an infinitely active, ardent, powerful *Thought*, proposing of *Satisfaction;* let this represent GOD the FATHER: but it is not possible for any Object but God Himself, to *satisfy Himself*, and fill His *Desire* of Happiness; therefore HE Himself *reflected* in upon Himself and contemplating His own infinite Perfections, even the *Brightness of His Glory*, and the *express Image of His Person*, must answer this glorious Intention; and this may represent to us GOD the SON. Upon this Contemplation, wherein GOD Himself does behold, and possess, and enjoy Himself, there cannot but arise a *Love*, a *Joy*, an *Acquiescence* of God Himself within Himself, and worthy of a God; this may shadow out to us the third and the last of the Principles in this *mysterious Ternary*, that is to say, the Holy SPIRIT. Tho these *three Relations* of the Godhead in itself, when derived analogically down to Creatures, may appear but *Modifications* of a *real Subsistence*, yet in the supreme Infinitude of the Divine Nature, they must be infinitely *real* and *living* Principles. Those which are but *Relations*, when transferred to *created Beings*, are glorious *Relatives* in the infinite God. And in this View of the Holy Trinity, low as it is, it is impossible the SON should be without the FATHER, or the FATHER without the SON, or both without the Holy SPIRIT; it is impossible the SON should not be necessarily and eternally ien of the FATHER, or that the Holy SPIRIT should not necessarily eternally proceed both from Him and from the SON. Thus from what occurs throughout the whole Creation, *Reason* forms an imperfect Idea of this incomprehensible Mystery.

But it is time to stop here, and indeed how can we go any further!

THOMAS BRATTLE, 1658–1713

[Thomas Brattle of Boston was a scion of the wealthiest family in New England. In 1676 he was graduated from Harvard College where he had developed a marked skill in mathematical sciences. After travel abroad he settled in Boston, and served the College as treasurer for twenty years. He never married. In 1698 he was the chief organizer of the Brattle Street Church where the liberal principles of its members under the Reverend Benjamin Colman brought down the outspoken scorn of Increase Mather and his son Cotton. Brattle declined a judgeship in 1712. By will he left his organ—the first in New England—to the church he had founded, provided the institution should "procure a Sober person [to] play skilfully thereon with a loud noise" (Sibley, II, 496). The instrument was declined for reasons of church polity.

Brattle wrote out "A Full and Candid Account of the Delusion called Witchcraft, which prevailed in New England; and of the Judicial Trials and Executions at Salem, in the County of Essex, of that Pretended Crime, in 1692" in October of the same year. It was circulated as a private letter, and remained in manuscript for over a century. The criticisms directed against it in recent years blame the author, together with such other disapproving leaders as Saltonstall, Willard, Bradstreet, and Increase Mather, for not speaking out against the judges. But the modern reader must bear in mind that while the rage was at its height, any outspoken critic of the court would have been answered with an accusation of complicity in the crime.

See *Dictionary of American Biography;* and Sibley, *Biographical Sketches*, II, 489–498. For thoughtful discussion of "Dolefull Witchcraft," see Kenneth B. Murdock, *Increase Mather, Foremost American Puritan* (Cambridge, 1926), chap. XVII. The text here is from *Collections of the Massachusetts Historical Society*, series I, V (1798), 61–80, with omissions indicated.]

THE WITCHCRAFT DELUSION

. . . This Salem philosophy, some men may call the new philosophy; but I think it rather deserves the name of Salem superstition and sorcery, and it is not fit to be named in a land of such light as New-England is. I think the matter might be better solved another way; but I shall not make any attempt that way, further than to say, that these afflicted children, as they are called, do hold correspondence with the devil even in the esteem and account of the S[alem] G[entlemen]; for when the black man, i.e. say these gentlemen, the devil, does appear to them, they ask him many questions, and accordingly give information to the inquirer; and if this is not holding correspondence with the devil, and something worse, I know not what is.

But furthermore, I would fain know of these Salem justices what need there is of further proof and evidence to convict and condemn these apprehended persons, than this look and touch, if so be they are so certain that this falling down and arising up, when there is a look and a touch, are natural effects of the said look and touch, and so a perfect demonstration and proof of witchcraft in those persons. What can the jury or judges desire more, to convict any man of witchcraft, than a plain demonstration, that the said man is a witch? Now if this look and touch, circumstanced as before, be a plain demonstration, as their philosophy teaches, what need they seek for further evidences, when, after all, it can be but a demonstration? But let this pass with the S. G. for never so plain and natural a demonstration; yet certain is it, that the reasonable part of the world, when acquainted herewith, will laugh at the demonstration, and conclude that the said S. G. are actually possessed, at least, with ignorance and folly.

I most admire that Mr. N[icholas] N[oyes] the Reverend Teacher at Salem, who was educated at the school of knowledge, and is certainly a learned, a charitable, and a good man, though all the devils in Hell, and all the possessed girls in Salem, should say to the contrary; at him, I say, I do most admire; that he should cry up the above mentioned philosophy after the manner that he does. I can assure you, that I can bring you more than two, or twice two, (very credible persons), that will affirm, that they have heard him vindicate the above mentioned demonstration as very reasonable.

Secondly, with respect to the confessors, as they are improperly called, or such as confess themselves to be witches, (the second thing you inquire into in your letter), there are now about fifty of them in prison; many of which I have again and again seen and heard; and I cannot but tell you, that my faith is strong concerning them, that they are deluded, imposed upon, and under the influence of some evil spirit; and therefore unfit to be evidences either against themselves, or any one else. . . .

The great cry of many of our neighbours now is, What, will you not believe the confessors? Will you not believe men and women who confess that they have signed to the devil's book? that they were baptized by the devil; and that they were at the mock-sacrament once and again? What! will you not believe that this is witchcraft, and that such and such men are witches, although the confessors do own and assert it?

Thus, I say, many of our good neighbours do argue; but methinks they might soon be convinced that there is nothing at all in all these their arguings, if they would but duly consider of the premises. . . .

Now for the proof of the said sorcery and witchcraft, the prisoner at the bar pleading not guilty.

1. The afflicted persons are brought into court; and after much patience and pains taken with them, do take their oaths, that the prisoner at the bar did afflict them: And here I think it very observable, that often, when the afflicted do mean and intend only the appearance and shape of such an one, (say G. Proctor), yet they positively swear that G. Proctor did afflict them; and they have been allowed so to do; as though there was no real difference between G. Proctor and the shape of G. Proctor. This, methinks, may readily prove a stumbling block to the jury, lead them into a very fundamental error, and occasion innocent blood, yea the innocentest blood imaginable, to be in great danger. Whom it belongs unto, to be eyes unto the blind, and to remove such stumbling blocks, I know full well; and yet you, and every one else, do know as well as I who do not.

2. The confessors do declare what they know of the said prisoner; and some of the confessors are allowed to give their oaths; a thing which I believe was never heard of in this world; that such as confess themselves to be witches, to have renounced God and Christ, and all that is sacred, should yet be allowed and ordered to swear by the name of the great God! This indeed seemeth to me to be a gross taking of God's name in vain. I know the S. G. do say, that there is hope that the said confessors have repented: I shall only say, that if they have repented, it is well for themselves; but if they have not, it is very ill for you know who. But then,

3. Whoever can be an evidence against the prisoner at the bar is ordered to come into court; and here it scarce ever fails but that evidences, of one nature and another, are brought in, though, I think, all of them altogether alien to the matter of indictment; for they none of them do respect witchcraft upon the bodies of the afflicted, which is the alone matter of charge in the indictment.

4. They are searched by a jury; and as to some of them, the jury brought in, that on such or such a place there was a preternatural excrescence. And I wonder what person there is, whether man or woman, of whom it cannot be said but that, in some part of their body or other, there is a preternatural excrescence. The term is a very general and inclusive term.

Some of the S. G. are very forward to censure and condemn the poor prisoner at the bar, because he sheds no tears: but such betray great ignorance in the nature of passion, and as great heedlessness as to common passages of a man's life. Some there are who never shed tears; others there are that ordinarily shed tears upon light occasions, and yet for their lives cannot shed a tear when the deepest sorrow is upon their hearts; and who is there that knows not these things? Who knows not that an ecstacy of joy will sometimes fetch tears, when as the quite contrary passion will shut them close up? Why then should any be so silly and foolish as to take an argument from this appearance? But this is by the by. In short, the prisoner at the bar is indicted for sorcery and witchcraft acted upon the bodies of the afflicted. Now, for the proof of this, I reckon that the only pertinent evidences brought in are the evidences of the said afflicted.

. . . I cannot but admire that the justices, whom I think to be well-meaning men, should so far give ear to the devil, as merely upon his authority to issue out their warrants, and apprehend people. Liberty was evermore accounted the great privilege of an Englishman; but certainly, if the devil will be heard against us, and his testimony taken, to the seizing and apprehending of us, our liberty vanishes, and we are fools if we boast of our liberty. Now, that the justices have thus far given ear to the devil, I think may be mathematically demonstrated to any man of common sense: And for the demonstration and proof hereof, I desire, only, that these two things may be duly considered, viz.

1. That several persons have been apprehended purely upon the complaints of these afflicted, to whom the afflicted were perfect strangers, and had not the least knowledge of imaginable, before they were apprehended.

2. That the afflicted do own and assert, and the justices do grant, that the devil does inform and tell the afflicted the names of those persons that are thus unknown unto them. Now these two things being duly considered, I think it will appear evident to any one, that the devil's information is the fundamental testimony that is gone upon in the apprehending of the aforesaid people.

If I believe such or such an assertion as comes immediately from the minister of God in the pulpit, because it is the word of the ever-living God, I build my faith on God's testimony: and if I practise upon it, this my practice is properly built on the word of God: even so in the case before us.

If I believe the afflicted persons as informed by the devil, and act thereupon, this my act may properly be said to be grounded upon the testimony or information of the devil. And now, if things are thus, I think it ought to be for a lamentation to you and me, and all such as would be accounted good christians. . . .

What will be the issue of these troubles, God only knows; I am afraid that ages will not wear off that reproach and those stains which these things will leave behind them upon our land. I pray God pity us, humble us, forgive us, and appear mercifully for us in this our mount of distress: herewith I conclude, and subscribe myself,

Reverend sir, your real friend and humble servant,

T. B.

[N. B. *As there is no superscription on the copy of this letter, it is not known to whom it was addressed.*]

ZABDIEL BOYLSTON, 1680–1766

[Cotton Mather very possibly wrote up the anonymous account here presented from information gathered by Boylston. See George L. Kittredge, "Some Lost Works of Cotton Mather," *Proceedings of the Massachusetts Historical Society*, XLV (1912), 418–479. Zabdiel Boylston, great-uncle of President Adams, never procured a medical degree, though he enjoyed an enviable reputation as a physician. His work during the smallpox epidemic of 1721 was recognized five years later by a Fellowship in the Royal Society. See account of him in *Dictionary of American Biography;* see also Reginald H. Fitz, "Zabdiel Boylston, Inoculator, and the Epidemic of Smallpox in Boston in 1721," *Johns Hopkins Hospital Bulletin*, XXII (1911), 315–327.

Henry Newman (1670–*ca.* 1750) of Rehoboth, Massachusetts, was graduated from Harvard in 1687. He published the Cambridge almanac for 1691 and served as college librarian from 1690 to 1693. Before 1700 he went to England, where he resided till his death. Though he conformed to the Established Church, he remained on intimate terms with several New Englanders, acting as agent in England for the Corporation of Harvard College, agent for New Hampshire, and secretary for the Society for Promotion of Christian Knowledge. See Sibley, *Biographical Sketches*, III, 389–394; see also George L.

Kittredge, introduction to the Cleveland 1921 reprint of Increase Mather, *Severall Reasons Proving that Inoculation . . . is a Lawful Practice* (Boston, 1721). The text is from the *Philosophical Transactions* of the Royal Society of London, XXXII (1721), 33-35.]

THE WAY OF PROCEEDING IN THE SMALL POX INOCULATED IN NEW ENGLAND.

COMMUNICATED BY HENRY NEWMAN, ESQ; OF THE MIDDLE TEMPLE.

1. We make usually a Couple of *Incisions* in the *Arms* where we make our *Issues*, but somewhat larger than for them, some times in one *Arm*, and one *Leg*.

2. Into these we put bits of *Lint*, (the patient at the same time turning his Face another way, and guarding his Nostrils) which have been dipt in some of the *Variolus Matter*[1] taken in a Vial, from the Pustules of one that has the *Small Pox* of the more laudable Sort, now turning upon him, and so we cover them with a Plaister of *Diachylon*.[2]

3. Yet we find the *Variolous Matter* fetched from those, that have the *inoculated Small Pox*, altogether as agreeable and effectual as any other. And so we do what is taken from them that have the *Confluent Sort*.

4. Within Four and Twenty Hours, we throw away the *Lint*, and the *Sores* are dressed once or twice every Four and Twenty Hours, with warmed *Cabbage Leaves*.

5. The Patient continues to do all Things, *as at other times*, only he exposes not himself unto the Injuries of the *Weather*, if that be at all Tempestuous.

6. About the Seventh Day the Patient feels the usual Symptoms of the *Small Pox* coming upon him; and he is now managed as in an ordinary *Putrid Fever*. If he cannot hold up, he goes to *Bed;* If his *Head ach* too much, we put the common *Poultice* to his *Feet*, if he be very Sick at the *Stomach*, we give him a *gentle Vomit*, yea, we commonly do these Things *almost of Course*, whether we find the Patient want them or no. And we reckon the *sooner* we do these Things, the *better*. If the *Fever* be too high, in some Constitutions, we *Bleed* a little: And finally, to hasten the Eruption, we put on a Couple of *Blisters*.

7. On or about the Third Day from the Decumbiture the *Eruption* begins. The Number of the *Pustules* is not alike in all, in some they are a *very few*, in others they amount to an *Hundred* yea, in many they

amount unto *several Hundreds;* frequently unto more than what the Accounts from the *Levant* say is usual there.

8. The *Eruption* being made, *all Illness* vanishes; except perhaps a little of the *Vapours* in those that are troubled with them; there is nothing more to do, but to *keep Warm,* drink proper Teas, eat Gruel, Milk Pottage, Panada, Bread, Butter, and almost any thing equally Simple and Innocent.

9. Ordinarily the Patient *sits* up every Day, and entertains his Friends yea, ventures upon a *Glass of Wine* with them. If he be too Intent upon hard *Reading* and *Study* we take him off.

10. Sometimes, tho' the Patient be on other Accounts easy enough, yet he *can't Sleep* for divers Nights together. In this Case we do not give him *Anodynes* or *Opiates,* because we find, That they who have taken these Things in the *Small Pox* are generally pestered with miserable *Biles* after their being recovered. So we *let them alone;* their *Sleep* will come of it self, as their *Strength* is coming on.

11. On the Seventh Day the *Pustules* usually come to their Maturity; *and soon after* this they go away, as those of the *Small Pox* in the *Distinct Sort* use to do.

12. The Patient gets abroad quickly, and is most sensibly *Stronger,* and in *better* Health than he was before. The Transplantation has been given to *Women in Child-bed,* Eight or Nine Days after their Delivery; and they have got earlier out of their Child-bed, and in better Circumstances, than ever in their Lives. Those that have had ugly *Ulcers* long running upon them, have had them healed on, and by this *Transplantation.* Some very feeble, crazy, *Consumptive* People, have upon this *Transplantation,* grown hearty and got rid of their former Maladies.

13. The *Sores* of the *Incision* do seem to dry a little in Three or Four Days of the Feverish Preparation for *Eruption.* After this there is a *plentiful Discharge* at them. The discharge may continue a little while after the Patient is quite well on other Accounts; But the *Sores* will soon enough dry up of themselves; but the *later,* the *better,* as we think. If they happen to be *inflamed,* or otherwise Troublesome, we presently help them in the ways we do any *Ordinary Sores.*

Chapter IV—Manners, Customs, and Behavior

JOHN SMITH

1. *neare* = nearer. Obsolete comparative of "nigh."

﹑ 2. *secure* = careless.

3. Son of Sir Humphrey Mildmay (*d.* 1613), and grandson of Sir Walter Mildmay, chancellor of the exchequer under Elizabeth and founder of Emmanuel College, Cambridge.

4. For an account of Winthrop, see p. 125.

THOMAS LECHFORD

1. A perennial herb growing in the northern part of both Europe and America. Powerfully astringent, its root was often employed medicinally.

2. This may refer to the land about Providence, Rhode Island, though there seems to be no record of any "Lords Isle."

JASPER DANCKAERTS

These notes on Danckaerts's *Journal* are from the James and Jameson edition of 1913 (see p. 404).

1. This seems to mean the creek which made in from the cove at the foot of Milk Street.

2. Simon Bradstreet, elected in May, 1679, was governor of Massachusetts till 1686—the last governor under the old charter. He had come out in 1630, and was now seventy years old.

3. Original, "Jan Tayller of [Dutch for *or*] Marchand Tayller." No John Taylor of Boston answering to the description has been identified.

4. Sluyter was from Wesel, on the Rhine. Though it was a German town, many of its inhabitants were Dutch (like Peter Minuit) and Walloon.

5. Captain John Foy appears in the records of the court of assistants, as still master of the *Dolphin*, in 1691.

6. A Dutch settlement in Guiana, owned at the time by the province of Zeeland: the present Dutch Guiana.

7. In the Azores.

8. The Thursday Lecture.

9. This fast is not noted in the elaborate list in Mr. Love's *Fast and Thanksgiving Days of New England*. The Old South Church had a fast on June 29, O.S., but this was June 28, N.S.

10. Rev. John Eliot (1604–1690), the Apostle to the Indians, came over to Massachusetts in 1631, and in 1632 was ordained as "teacher" of the church of Roxbury. He soon engaged in efforts to Christianize the Indians, and in 1646 began to preach to them in their own tongue. He formed a community and church of "praying Indians" at Natick, and others elsewhere. His translation of the Bible into the dialect of the Massachusetts Indians was completed in 1658. The first edition of the New Testament, printed at Cambridge, was issued in 1661, the whole Bible (Old Testament of 1663, New Testament of 1661 imprint, and metrical version of the Psalms) in 1663.

11. Eliot was not quite seventy-six.

12. The first edition of the whole Bible seems to have been 1040 copies; of the separate New Testament, 500. Many copies were lost or destroyed in the Indian war of 1675–1676; but 16 copies now existing of the New Testament, and 39 of the Bible, in this first edition, are listed in Mr. Wilberforce Eames's bibliography. In 1677 Eliot began to prepare a revised edition of the whole work. It was published in 1685. The printing of the New Testament portion was begun in 1680 and finished in the autumn or winter of 1681; the printing of the Old Testament was not begun until 1682.

Wonderful to relate, the identical copy of the Old Testament (edition of 1663, and metrical Psalms) which Eliot presented to Danckaerts and Sluyter is still in existence, in the library of the Zeeland Academy of Sciences at Middelburg in the Netherlands. It lacks the title-page, but in its place contains the following

manuscript note. See the *Proceedings* of
the Massachusetts Historical Society,
XIII, 307–310, and the Dutch pamphlet
there named.

"All Bibles of the Christian Indians
were burned or destroyed by these heathen
savages. This one alone was saved; and
from it a new edition, with improvements,
and an entirely new translation of the
New Testament, was undertaken. I saw
at Roccsberri, about an hour's ride from
Boston, this Old Testament printed, and
some sheets of the New. The printing-
office was at Cambridge, three hours' ride
from Boston, where also there was a college of students, whether of savages or
of other nations. The Psalms of David
are added in the same metre.

"At Roccsberri dwelt Mr. Hailot, a
very godly preacher there. He was at
this time about seventy years old. His
son was a preacher at Boston. This good
old man was one of the first Independent
preachers to settle in these parts, seeking
freedom. He was the principal translator
and director of the printing of both the
first and second editions of this Indian
Bible. Out of special zeal and love he
gave me this copy of the first edition,
for which I was, and shall continue,
grateful to him. This was in June, 1680.

"Jasper Danckaerts."

13. The first building of Harvard College, the building "thought by some to
be too gorgeous for a Wilderness, and
yet too mean in others apprehensions for
a Colledg" (Johnson, *Wonder-working
Providence*, p. 201), had partly tumbled
down in 1677. The building now visited
was the "New College," the second Harvard Hall, built with difficulty 1672–1682
and destroyed by fire in 1764. Edward
Randolph, in a report of October 12,
1676, writes: "New-colledge, built at the
publick charge, is a fair pile of brick
building covered with tiles, by reason of
the late Indian warre not yet finished.
It contains 20 chambers for students, two
in a chamber; a large hall which serves
for a chappel; over that a convenient
library." A picture of the building may
be seen in the *Proceedings* of the Massachusetts Historical Society, XVIII, 318.

14. Rev. Urian Oakes, minister of

Cambridge, was at this time acting president, and was installed as president in
the next month. There were apparently
seventeen students in the college at this
time who subsequently graduated, and
perhaps a few others. The library no
doubt contained more than a thousand,
perhaps more than fifteen hundred books.

15. The allusion is to the printing-
office at Wieuwerd, which Dittelbach,
Verval en Val der Labadisten (Amsterdam,
1692), p. 50, says was a very costly one.
The Labadists had everywhere maintained their own printer, Louriens Autein
going with them in that capacity from
Amsterdam to Herford. As to the building occupied by the famous Cambridge
press, Randolph mentions "a small brick
building called the Indian colledge,
where some few Indians did study, but
now it is a printing house." Printing
here was this year at a low ebb; nothing
is known to have been printed but the
second edition of Eliot's Indian New
Testament.

16. This is to ignore the voyages of
Gosnold, Pring, Weymouth, etc., and the
settlement at Fort St. George in 1607.

17. The Connecticut.

18. The reading is *eer*, but *heer* was of
course intended. The control by the English king was much more real than is
here indicated. The next sentence alludes
to the Navigation Acts and their evasion.
As to customs, Edward Randolph had in
1678 been appointed collector for New
England, and had begun his conflict with
the Massachusetts authorities, but with
little success thus far. Land-taxes did in
fact exist.

19. On Endicott's [*sic*] cutting of the
cross from the flag, in 1634, see Winthrop's *Journal*, in this series, I, 137, 174,
182. Since the decision then reached
(1636), the cross had been left out of
all ensigns in Massachusetts bay except
that on Castle Island.

JOHN DUNTON

1. Now Court Street, Boston.
2. Increase Mather, *A Sermon . . . of
   Murder* (Boston, 1687).
   Cotton Mather, *The Call of the
   Gospel* (Boston, 1687).

Joshua Moody, *An Exhortation to a Condemned Malefactor* (Boston, 1687).

See also Cotton Mather, *Magnalia* (1702), for Morgan's edifying speeches.

3. Samuel Willard was teacher of the Third (Old South) Church in Boston. The "New Church" probably refers to the Second (Old North) Church, of which the Mathers were co-ministers. It had been rebuilt after the Boston conflagration of 1676. These were the two largest auditoriums in Boston.

4. About 1690, Major Jonathan Wade built a tavern in Medford, which was kept by Nathaniel Pierce.

5. John Cotton (1658–1710), eldest son of Seaborn, and grandson of the first John Cotton, was graduated from Harvard College, along with his cousin Cotton Mather, in 1678. Three years later he was chosen a Fellow and Librarian of the College. In 1696 he was ordained as pastor of Hampton, New Hampshire.

6. John Eliot, who was eighty-two at the time, lived until 1690.

SARAH KEMBLE KNIGHT

1. The Reverend Joseph Belcher (1669–1723).

2. I.e., Madam Belcher, wife of the pastor. She was a daughter of the poet Benjamin Tompson, *q.v.* p. 635.

3. The works of the Elizabethan romancer, Emmanuel Ford. *The most Famous, Delectable, and pleasant, History of Parismus, the most renowned Prince of Bohemia* . . . (1598) went through twenty-six printings before the middle of the eighteenth century. It is listed by Francis Meres, *Palladis Tamia* (1598) as one of the books that should be forbid youth, as tending to corrupt morals. *The Famous History of Montelion, Knight of the Oracle* (earliest extant edition, 1633) is less known today. It is worth noting that Madam Knight speaks of both romances as if they were well known in her day.

4. That the word clearly means a pipe for smoking is evident from its use on p. 433; see below, note 9. Such a meaning for *junk* is not recorded in the *New English Dictionary*.

5. Prov. Eng.: ringed; having a ring through the snout.

6. A lean-to room; that is, one having a low, slanting roof.

7. Lieutenant. Sometimes still pronounced, and formerly spelled, *leftenant*.

8. English proverb: "Bare walls make gadding housewives."

9. See above, note 4.

10. Gurdon Saltonstall (1666–1724), minister at New London, was a celebrated preacher. He sat at one time as Chief Justice of the Supreme Court of the Connecticut Colony.

11. Pumpkins.

12. The regular midweek religious lecture was held on Thursdays. Training days were those appointed for militia drill.

13. "The law of merchants": the system of usages of commerce in force and recognized by law.

14. Spanish saddlebags. Here facetiously used of cheeks.

15. Genteel.

16. I.e., election days are ceremoniously observed.

17. Fitz-John Winthrop (1638–1707), eldest son of Governor John Winthrop, Jr. of Connecticut. He was educated at Harvard, but took no degree. After some time spent in the army in England, he returned to New England and served as a major-general in the expedition against Canada, 1690. He was the Connecticut agent in London, 1693–1697. He filled the office of governor of Connecticut from 1698 till his death.

18. That is, "paid our tavern reckoning."

19. Place of public sale or auction.

20. Beams and joints.

21. Edward Hyde, Lord Cornbury, governor of New York, 1702–1708. He was the disreputable son of the famous Earl of Clarendon.

22. A beverage, usually fermented, of honey and water.

23. Spuyten Duyvil Creek, at Kingsbridge. The creek divides Manhattan Island from the mainland, and connects the Harlem River with the Hudson.

24. Joseph Webb (1666–1732), pastor in Fairfield from 1694 till his death. He was one of the first Fellows of Yale College.

25. James Pierpont (1660–1714), father-in-law of Jonathan Edwards, was an original trustee of Yale College and a Professor of Moral Philosophy.

JOSEPH GREEN

1. A small island near the tip of Long Island, settled by Lion Gardiner in 1639, and owned by direct descent until it was sold out of the family in 1936. It was originally in the township of East Hampton.

2. East Hampton was originally bought from the Indians in 1648, and settled by residents from Lynn, Massachusetts.

3. Probably the Reverend Mr. Ebenezer White (1672–1756), pastor of Sagg. Sag Harbor was a New England settlement with as many Indians and negroes as whites; largely a whaling village.

4. The Reverend Mr. Joseph Whiting (1641–1723), called by Cotton Mather "a Worthy and Painful Minister of the Gospel" (*Magnalia*, III, 157).

5. Joseph Coit, shipbuilder and deacon of the church at New London. His son Joseph had graduated from college two years later than Green.

6. Thomas Blowers (1677–1729), classmate of Green and pastor at Beverly.

7. Samuel Gerrish of Boston, bookseller and Town Clerk, was Green's brother-in-law.

8. Probably Increase Mather.

9. The Reverend Mr. Benjamin Wadsworth (1670–1737) was later president of Harvard College. He was an influential Boston preacher. In his youth, as a college tutor, he had been one of three who contributed money to help pay for Green's education.

10. The Reverend Mr. John Rogers (1666–1745), pastor at Ipswich, the eldest son of President Rogers of Harvard.

11. The Reverend Mr. Nicholas Noyes (1647–1717), pastor at Salem.

COTTON MATHER

1. The metrical version of the Psalms, published in 1562, that remained in use into the eighteenth century, though generally supplanted in New England by the *Bay Psalm Book*, *q.v.* p. 555.

2. Abenezra or Ibn Ezra (1092–1167), distinguished Spanish Jew whose Old Testament commentaries were notable.

SOLOMON STODDARD

1. Thomas Fuller (1608–1661).

2. Henry Hammond (1605–1660), English scholar and divine, a writer of controversial tracts.

3. "The long-haired Greeks."

4. "An empty habitation."

Chapter V—Biographies and Letters

JOHN WINTHROP

1. The first hint of a possible emigration in Winthrop's correspondence.

THOMAS SHEPARD

1. Lawrence Chadderton (1536–1640), Master of Emmanuel College, a majestic figure, who exerted a great influence on all Puritans of the early seventeenth century through his teaching and preaching, his splendid personality, and his amazing longevity.

2. The Pequot War.

ROGER WILLIAMS

1. *Experiments of Spiritual Life & Health* (London, 1652).

2. Cromwell.

3. "The King's Book" is the *Eikon Basilike*. The sermons of Bishop Launcelot Andrewes were the arch-embodiment of the High Church ideal of pulpit style and doctrine, as opposed to plain sermon and the Calvinist doctrine of the Puritan variety. Jackson and Taylor were Anglican authors, but Jeremy Taylor had recently advocated toleration in *The Liberty of Prophesying*, so that in citing him Mrs. Sadleir gave Williams an opening, of which he did not hesitate to avail himself.

4. *Eikonoklastes*, 1649.

5. Andrew Marvell (1621–1678), the poet, a friend of Milton, whom Milton recommended for assistant secretary in 1653, though he was not appointed to the post until 1657; he was identified with Milton's group, but that he helped Milton write *Eikonoklastes* is not true.

6. John Winthrop, Jr., married a

daugher of Hugh Peter.

7. Edward Winslow (1595–1655), a leader among the Plymouth settlers, agent for the colony in England, governor in 1633, 1636, and 1644, to relieve Bradford. It is probably a commentary upon the personality of Williams that both Winthrop and Bradford should think him a true saint even when they condemned his opinions, and that both Winthrop and Winslow, men of broad, statesmanlike qualities, should take pains to give him secret advices and even encouragements, but would not have him within their own jurisdictions.

INCREASE MATHER

1. Puritans objected to stated holy days and fixed days for celebrations because they believed them pagan in origin, because they almost always became occasions for dissipation and profanity among the people, and because they believed that God desired men to observe days of thanksgiving or of humiliation as events seemed to indicate from time to time, or as the spirit seemed to dictate.

2. "Hence the custom of praising the dead, to which we are enslaved."

3. "No one can acquire a great fame and a great quiet at the same time," Quintillian.

4. Thomas Cartwright (1535–1603) was the foremost spokesman for the Puritan cause in Elizabeth's reign. Robert Parker (1564–1614), Paul Baynes (d. 1617), and William Ames (1576–1633) were Puritan theologians and writers who worked out in common the draft of the non-separating Congregational church polity and were the true fathers of the New England ecclesiastical order.

5. William Prynne (1600–1669), Puritan agitator and pamphleteer, pilloried and his ears cut off by sentence of Laud for his attack upon the Queen's theatricals and upon the Laudian bishops.

6. "A wise man foresees."

7. Thus Increase Mather married his father's step-daughter.

8. Girolamo Zanchius, Italian Protestant theologian, whose works were textbooks in New England.

9. "Good diet is better than any Hippocrates," i.e., than any physician.

10. "The flail of the studious."

11. A quarrel in the First Church of Boston over the introduction of the Half-Way Covenant and the calling of the aged John Davenport from New Haven; the issue became a political one and resulted in the secession of half the congregation from the First Church to form the Third, or Old South.

12. "We have prospered in Synods, and now we die in this one."

13. Richard Mather was pleading on his deathbed with his son to embrace the decision of the Synod of 1662 setting up the Half-Way Covenant, the device by which it was determined that the children of persons who had been baptized but had never yet had an experience that could be ascertainably recognized as regeneration could be baptized on the strength of their parents' being "Half-Way" members of the churches. Increase had publicly opposed his father on this question, and that he should print his father's dying injunction to maintain the Half-Way Covenant was a handsome and pious manner of serving notice of his own conversion.

14. "Strange things familiarly and familiar things unusually."

15. "The art is to conceal the art."

16. Arthur Hildersham (1563–1632), Puritan divine and controversialist.

COTTON MATHER

1. "I scarcely call them mine," Ovid, *Metamor.*, 13, 141.

2. Thomas Wilson (1525–1581), author of *The Arte of Rhetorique;* quotation from Clark's *Lives,* ed. 1683, p. 19.

3. "A dusty and most troublesome vocation, but by far the most favoured of God."

4. "Grotian" means of the opinion of Grotius, the great lawyer and theologian of the Arminian party in Holland; Grotius was read widely in New England, though his theories of the freedom of the will and of the atonement were considered heretical.

5. "Impart no life, because they have none," reference to a knotty and threadbare dispute in scholastic philosophy.

6. Published Boston, 1678.

7. Edward Winslow, in *The Glorious Progress of the Gospel amongst the Indians of New England*, 1649 (*Collections of the Massachusetts Historical Society*, Series 3, IV, 89).

8. Cf. Cambden's *Remains* (1637), p. 357: "His conceit was obscure to me which painted a savadge of America pointing toward the sun, with Tibi accessu, Mihi Recessu." Mather either deliberately or unwittingly transposes the motto to read "As I approach, you recede"; he means that though Cambden could not understand this "device," it might well serve as the emblem for the life of Eliot.

9. "Interminable words."

10. "Soldier emeritus."

11. "When the luminaries undergo an eclipse, it is a bad sign for the world."

12. "Two fortresses stand against the visage of the foe."

SAMUEL SEWALL

1. "We have come even to Cambridge to stabilize and correct manners."

EBENEZER TURELL

1. William Whiston (1667–1752), theologian, divine, professor and free-lance popularizer of knowledge, friend of Newton, in trouble for supposedly being an Arian, a brilliant but eccentric mind, ranging over the fields of theology, church history, astronomy, physics, and chemistry.

2. "Long nocturnal studies are most dangerous."

3. "No day without letters."

Chapter VI—Poetry

JOHN WILSON

1. In 1625 occurred the great London plague during which in the capital alone 35,417 souls perished. Wilson's figures are exaggerated. The "Bills of Mortality" issued in London, on which his figures are based, were compiled on the evidence of ignorant people. The first great plague in 1603 destroyed as great a number as that of 1625; that of 1609 about half as many.

2. Surrounding districts over which London exercised jurisdiction.

3. Obsolete form of "more" (O.E. adverb *ma*), used of number rather than size.

ANNE BRADSTREET

1. The glede is the common European kite.

2. Small wooden casks for butter, lard, etc.

3. Hebrew *fleeing*. The land into which Cain fled, Genesis 4 : 16.

4. The ocean. Thetis was one of the Nereids.

5. The nightingale. Here Mistress Bradstreet is following poetic convention, for nightingales have never been native to America.

6. Precede; anticipate (L. *praevenire*). The original meaning, but now obsolete.

7. Revelation 2 : 17: He that hath an ear let him hear what the Spirit saith unto the churches; To him that overcometh will I give to eat of the hidden manna, and will give him a white stone, and in the stone a new name written, which no man knoweth saving he that receiveth it.

8. The poem seems to be based upon the idea of St. Paul (Romans 8), of the strife between the Flesh and the Spirit, or the law of the members and the law of the mind.

9. Revelation 21 : 10–27; 22 : 1–5.

10. I.e., winter. The tenth sign of the Zodiac, which the sun enters about December 21.

11. I.e., summer. The fourth sign of the Zodiac, which the sun enters about June 21.

NATHANIEL WARD, JOHN ROGERS, AND JOHN NORTON

1. Joshua Sylvester (1563–1618) translated Du Bartas's *Divine Weeks and Works* (collected ed., 1605).

2. "for weariness."

3. "marvel."

4. "shod by."

5. I.e., lying in the shelter.

6. Pertaining to a town in Samnium (Maronea), famous for its wines.

7. Mount Hybla in Sicily, famed for its honey.

8. Dreary(?).

9. Affrays.

10. Site.

11. Leave-takings; congés.

12. Peneus, the chief river in Sicily. Also the name of the river god.

13. Greek: "all-virtuous."

14. Perhaps a reference to Ormazd, the supreme deity of Zoroastrianism.

15. Publius Vergilius Maro.

16. Marcus Tullius Cicero.

17. Cf. Francis Beaumont *Ad Comitissam Rutlandiae:*

"Although I know whate'er my verses be,
  They will like the most servile flattery
  show,
If I write truth, and make the subject
  you."

18. "Let all the people of Rome be silent before this marvel."

MICHAEL WIGGLESWORTH

1. Careless. (Obsolete.)

2. Practice or condition. (Obsolete.)

3. The text reads "Gold."

4. As the 1715 edition and later. The text here reads "cush."

5. The spiritually reborn; regenerate.

6. As the 1715 edition and later. The text here reads "where."

7. Assistant or helper. (Obsolete.)

8. Know how to.

9. Obsolete form of "more."

10. As the 1715 edition and later. The text here reads "chaste."

11. Ceases.

12. Would not.

13. "All things pass except the love of God."

14. Judges 14 : 14: And he said unto them, Out of the eater came forth meat, and out of the strong came forth sweetness. And they could not in three days expound the riddle.

15. Cf. with Anne Bradstreet's poem "The Flesh and the Spirit." This and all the following selections of Wigglesworth's verse are from a group of poems printed with the 1689 edition of *Meat out of the Eater* (pp. [51]–208), but bearing a separate title-page: *Riddles unriddled, or*

Christian Paradoxes Broke open, smelling like sweet Spice New taken out of Boxes.

SAMUEL BRADSTREET AND DANIEL RUSSELL

1. "Everything that lies concealed will be manifest in due time."

2. *Tellus mater* was the ancient Italian earth deity of marriage and fertility.

3. Apollo is invoked as sun-god.

4. Personifying Heaven.

5. Archaic: "holds perforce."

6. Until 1752 in the British colonies in America the new year was reckoned as beginning in March.

7. Lat. *Hiems:* "stormy weather."

8. Cancer, the fourth sign of the Zodiac, which ushers in summer.

9. The sun enters Virgo, the sixth sign of the Zodiac, about August 22.

10. "Stable, yet always in motion."

BENJAMIN TOMPSON

1. During King Philip's Narraganset war the Indians attacked Marlborough, Groton, Rehoboth, and Chelmsford, Massachusetts, and Providence, Rhode Island, in February and March, 1676, burning houses and barns, destroying cattle, and slaying the inhabitants.

2. Official statistics recording the number of deaths.

3. Glory-fat or gloar-fat: especially dirty or unrefined fat.

4. Asshur was the chief god of the Assyrians, usually depicted as a war deity.

5. Samuel Newman (1600–1663), first minister of Rehoboth. His concordance of the Bible (London, 1643) was one of the best known prior to Cruden's.

URIAN OAKES

1. John Leverett (1662–1724), president of Harvard College, 1707–1724.

EDWARD TAYLOR

1. *riggal:* to make a groove for (archaic).

2. *smaragdine:* L. *smaragdus,* emerald.

3. *squitchen:* possibly a switch or stick.

4. Taylor dated this poem "Aug. 13. 14. 1683."

5. *sprindge:* to spread out.

6. An *epinicioum* is a song of triumph.

ROGER WOLCOTT

1. For a sketch of John Winthrop, Jr., see p. 739. In 1661, while Winthrop was governor of Connecticut, he was appointed agent to go to England to procure a charter from the King. By astute diplomacy Winthrop secured a charter so liberal that it served the colony and state until 1818.

The selection opens with the arrival of news that the monarchy has been reestablished under King Charles, 1660.

Chapter VII—Literary Theory

PREFACE TO THE BAY PSALM BOOK

1. Johannes Buxtorf (1564–1629), German Hebrew and Rabbinic scholar; author of *Thesaurus Grammaticus Linguae Sanctae Hebraeae* (1629).

THOMAS HOOKER

1. St. Jerome. His Life is included in Erasmus's Complete Works (9 vols., Basel, 1516–1520).

2. "Ignorant of the Word."

3. "That a work needs decoration argues weakness of structure."

4. "He who does not wish to be understood (clearly) ought to be passed over."

MICHAEL WIGGLESWORTH

1. "In every activity of the spirit, yea even in sorrow, there is a certain pleasure."

2. Robert Turner, *Orationes Septemdecim* (1602). "It is proof of our slothfulness that since we are not able at best to do that which we ought, we are unwilling to do well that which we could."

3. "I shall either find a way or make one."

4. "This is the task, this is the work."

5. "By day hard work, by night unending toil, such as savor of some pains."

COTTON MATHER

1. Pertaining to song (obsolete).

JOHN BULKLEY

1. Arthur Golding (*ca.* 1536–*ca.* 1605). His chief work was his translation of Ovid. A man of strong Puritan sympathies, he also translated many of the works of Calvin.

COTTON MATHER: "OF POETRY AND STYLE"

1. I.e., a spiteful critic. Zoïlus (*ca.* 400–320 B.C.) was a Greek grammarian, remembered chiefly for splenetic attacks on Homeric mythology.

2. Marco Girolamo Vida (1490–1566), Italian epic poet and critic.

3. "(writing) poetry now and then."

4. St. Gregory Nazianzen (329–389), a father of the Eastern church, bishop of Sasima. He devoted his later life to literary pursuits.

5. Arthur Bedford, *The Evil and Danger of Stage Plays* (1706).

6. Samuel Butler (1612–1680), author of *Hudibras* (1663–1668), a satire on Puritans.

Thomas Brown (1663–1704), schoolmaster near London whose satires were witty, coarse, and abusive.

Edward ("Ned") Ward (1667–1731), humorist who wrote coarse satires upon the Whigs and Low Church. He was pilloried for his *Hudibras Redivivus* (1705).

7. Sir Richard Blackmore (1650–1729), physician and author of voluminous and turgid epics that were immensely popular with the Puritans.

8. "Heady wine."

9. "Which (discourse) now to cut short."

10. See Hooker's comment on St. Jerome, p. 673.

11. Anthony Blackwall (1674–1730), classical scholar. Among his writings were *The Sacred Classics* (1725) and *Introduction to the Classics* (1718), a scholarly description of the beauties of ancient writers.

MATHER BYLES

1. "He raises a mighty roar, whereat

the sea and all its waves shuddered and the land of Italy was affrighted far within, and Aetna bellowed in its winding caverns" (Aeneid, III, 672–674).

Chapter VIII—Education

NEW ENGLANDS FIRST FRUITS

1. Elijah Corlet (1610–1688), master of the Grammar School at Cambridge from 1642 until his death. See p. 722.

2. Marcus Tullius Cicero.

3. "To stand, as they say, on his own feet."

4. Both are little known today and not used long at Harvard. Nonnus, an Alexandrian Christian of the fifth century, was author of *Paraphrase of St. John*. James Duport, colleague of Charles Chauncy at Trinity College, Cambridge. The reference is either to his paraphrase in Homeric verse of the Bible poetry, or to his *Homeri Gnomologia*, aphorisms collected from Homer.

5. Martin Trost, Professor of Theology at Wittenberg, was the editor (1621–1622) of the Syriac New Testament.

6. ". . . is given over to the study of rhetoric."

CHARLES CHAUNCY

1. William Dell, *The tryal of spirits* (London, 1653).

2. "The evil use of a thing does not destroy its good."

3. Girolamo Zanchi (Zanchius), *Opera Theologica* (Geneva, 1605).

LEONARD HOAR

1. M.H.S., "Papers 1636–75," fol. 4. Printed inaccurately in 1 *Coll. M.H.S.*, VI, 100–108. The then (1799) editor of the Society touched up the original letter in ink, and used it for printer's copy, thus making the establishment of the original text somewhat difficult. For a discussion of Peter Ramus, see pp. 28–41.

2. Evidence that Jonathan Mitchell (A.B. 1647) had the Theses Logicae at least, is found in his MS theses, Mass. Archives, CCXL, 141. 5a. Richardson was the author of *The Logicians School-Master* (1657).

3. Antonio Possevino, *Bibliotheca de Ratione Studiorum* (1607).

4. The *Bibliotheca Sancta* (Venice, 1566; and later editions to 1626), by Sixtus of Siena (1520–1569), a converted Jew and Dominican. See article "Sixtus von Siena" in Wetzer and Welte, *Kirchenlexikon*.

5. Conrad Gesner (1516–1565), the Swiss botanist, physician, universal savant, and pioneer Alpinist (cf. Arnold Lunn, *The Alps*, pp. 33–39). Hoar doubtless refers to his remarkable, though incompleted, *Bibliotheca Universalis* (Zürich, 1545–1549, and later editions and epitomes), a catalogue in the three learned tongues of all known writers and books.

6. Georg Draud (1573–1635?), *Bibliotheca Classica* (Frankfort-am-Main, 1611 and 1625), a catalogue of books and authors that was superseded by Bayle's *Dictionnaire* in 1697.

7. "by way of birth."

8. "doth not a little distress me."

9. Isaac Ambrose, nonconformist, writer of *Looking unto Jesus* (1658) and other devotional works; Richard Baxter, author of *The Saints Everlasting Rest* (1650); Bishop Joseph Hall of *Epistles* fame, author of *Christian Moderation* (1640); and, probably, Thomas Watson (d. 1686), Rector of St. Stephen's, Walbrook, whose *Three Treatises* reached a sixth edition in 1660.

THOMAS SHEPARD, JR.

1. "*Histories* make Men Wise; *Poets* Witty; The *Mathematicks* Subtill; *Naturall Philosophy* deepe; *Morall* Graue; *Logick* and *Rhetorick* Able to Contend" (Bacon, "Of Studies," in *Essayes*, 1625, p. 294).

2. "Frequent perusal, but rather diligence and industry."

3. "I prefer that you *be* educated rather than be so esteemed."

4. *Virgilii Evangelisantis Christiados Libri XIII. . . . Instante Alexandro Rosæo Aberdonese*. Londini, 1638. There is a copy of this edition in the Boston Athenaeum. A notice of the Rev. Alexander Ross (1591–1654) will be found in the *Dictionary of National Biography*.

INCREASE MATHER

1. Pierre Gassendi (1592–1655), French

philosopher, scientist, and mathematician, whose texts were widely used by students. Mather probably refers to *Exerciattiones Paradoxicae adversus Aristoteles* (Grenoble, 1624).

2. Ermolao Barbaro (1454–1495), Italian scholar and diplomat. He translated the paraphrase of Themistius on Aristotle at the age of nineteen.

3. "Complete reality."

COTTON MATHER: ELEGY ON CHEEVER

1. Gr. folly.

2. A group of wild and picturesque islands 25 miles southwest of Cornwall, England.

3. Abraham's concubine; mother of Ishmael. A type of bondservant.

4. William Lily (*ca.* 1460–1522). His *Eton Latin Grammar* was a common text for generations of school boys.

5. Then (than).

6. St. Augustine in his youth studied at Carthage, devoting his time to Latin poets. See *Confessio*, xiii, 21.

7. Jean Tixier de Ravisi (*ca.* 1480–1524), French humanist, whose works were widely used throughout Europe as texts for a century and a half.

8. John Davenport (1597–1670), founder of the New Haven Colony.

9. Probably the most famous and influential of all theologians of the ancient Christians.

Chapter IX—Science

SAMUEL DANFORTH

1. Samuel Stone (1602–1663), a founder of Connecticut, and teacher of the church at Hartford.

2. John Miller (1604–1663), pastor of Yarmouth and later of Groton.

3. Samuel Newman (1600–1663), first minister of Rehoboth. He is said to have predicted the exact moment of his death.

4. John Endecott (1589–1665), bigoted and fanatical persecutor of the Quakers. He was many times elected governor of the Massachusetts Bay Colony.

LEONARD HOAR

1. Alexander Balaam (*fl.* 1656–1680),

English merchant, traveler, and amateur botanist.

2. Dr. Robert Morison (1620–1683), senior physician to Charles II, and first Professor of Botany at Oxford University.

3. Henry Ashurst, merchant of London, treasurer of the New England Company; not to be confused with his son Sir Henry Ashurst, friend of Increase Mather.

COTTON MATHER: THE CHRISTIAN PHILOSOPHER

1. John Woodward (1665–1728), English naturalist and geologist. See his contribution "Some Thoughts and Experiments concerning Vegetation," *Philosophical Transactions*, XXI.

2. John Ray (or Wray) (1628–1705) was a pioneer in English natural history.

3. Mather is drawing from John Ray's sermon *Wisdom of God in the Creation*, Pt. I, for his references to other botanists.

4. "Because he feeds man chiefly with it"; quoted from Ray.

5. "It sustains all the body, to such a degree that in one bushel is contained nutriment for all the members of the whole body, and its strength is spread through all the body." Mather adds this quotation to what he has read in Ray.

6. The nine preceding paragraphs are taken directly from William Derham's *Physico-Theology* (1713), wherein Mather found references to Grew. The work is a teleological argument for God, used by Paley a hundred years later.

7. Buds.

8. John Gerard (1545–1612), English herbalist. Quoted from Derham.

9. Ralph Lane was the first governor of Virginia. Said to be the first smoker in England, he brought from Virginia tobacco and pipes which he gave to Sir Walter Raleigh.

10. Irritation.

11. Johannes Pechlin (1646–1706), Dutch physician.

12. Probably Johann Jacob Waldschmidt (1644–1689), German physician and medical writer.

13. Nahum Tate (1652–1715).

14. "Wicked settlements."

15. Mather refers to Dr. George Cheyne, *Philosophical Principles of Religion, Natural and Revealed* (London, 1715).

ZABDIEL BOYLSTON

1. Pertaining to pits caused by small-pox.

2. A plaster containing lead salts of the fatty acids, used for wounds.

IV. MANNERS

This section is designed to list items that shed light upon the diversions and vocations of Puritans, their daily lives and behavior. The student will find further essential material listed under Section V (Biography), especially in the part dealing with diaries, journals, and personal papers. See also Section I A.

A. PRIMARY SOURCES

The bibliography could be indefinitely extended, for good pastors never wearied of advising their flocks in matters of conduct.

Allin, James, *Serious Advice to Delivered Ones From Sickness*, Boston, 1679.

Belcher, Joseph, *Duty of Parents*, Boston, 1710.

Bridge, William, *Word to the Aged*, Boston, 1679.

Colman, Benjamin, *The Government & Improvement of Mirth*, Boston, 1707.

—— *The Hainous Nature of the Sin of Murder*, Boston, 1713.

—— "Letter to Mrs. John George" (1701), *Publications of the Colonial Society of Massachusetts*, VIII (1906), 246–250. (Advice on women's apparel.)

Constables Pocket-Book, The, 2nd ed., Boston, 1727.

Danckaerts, Jasper, *Journal of Jasper Danckaerts [and Peter Sluyter], 1679–1680*, printed from manuscript by the Long Island Historical Society, 1867; also in Original Narratives Series, ed. B. B. James and J. F. Jameson, New York, 1913. (Contains notes on a visit to Cambridge and Boston, together with sketches of some of the residents.)

Danforth, Samuel, *The Woful Effects of Drunkenness*, Boston, 1710.

Dunton, John, *John Dunton's Letters from New-England [ca.* 1686], ed. W. H. Whitmore, Boston, Prince Society, 1867. (Agreeable but unreliable; see C. N. Greenough, "John Dunton's Letters," *Publications of the Colonial Society of Massachusetts*, XIV (1913), 213–257.)

Gay, Ebenezer, *Ministers are Men of Like Passions with Others*, Boston, 1725.

Hubbard, William, *The Benefit of a Well-Ordered Conversation*, Boston, 1684.

Mather, Cotton, *The Accomplished Singer*, Boston, 1721.

—— *Agricola; Or, the Religious Husbandman*, Boston, 1727.

—— *Bonifacius*, Boston, 1710; reprinted as *Essays to do Good* in many subsequent eighteenth- and nineteenth-century editions published in Boston and London.

—— *A Family Well-Ordered*, Boston, 1699.

—— *Gospel for the Poor*, Boston, 1697.

—— *Lex Mercatoria; Or, The Just Rules of Commerce Declared*, Boston, 1704.

—— *Ornaments for the Daughters of Zion*, Boston, 1692. (The position of women in society and the code of feminine deportment.)

—— *The Religious Marriner*, Boston, 1700.

—— *Sober Considerations, on a growing Flood of Iniquity: . . . the Woful Consequences [of] the Prevailing Abuse of Rum*, Boston, 1708.

—— *The Way to Prosperity*, Boston, 1690.

Mather, Increase, *An Arrow against Profane and Promiscuous Dancing. Drawn out of the Quiver of the Scriptures*, Boston, 1684; 1686.

—— *Meditations on the Glory of the Heavenly World*, Boston, 1711.

—— *The Original Rights of Mankind Freely to Subdue and Improve the Earth*, Boston, 1722.

—— *Seasonable Meditations Both for Winter & Summer*, Boston, 1712. (Orthodox views on Sabbath-keeping.)

—— *A Testimony against several Prophane*

and Superstitious Customs, Now practised by some in New-England, London, 1687; ed. with critical comment by William Peden, Charlottesville, 1953.

Mather, Samuel, An Essay Concerning Gratitude, Boston, 1732.

Moody, Samuel, The Debtor's Monitor, Boston, 1715.

New Husbandry to New-England, Philadelphia, 1692.

Pemberton, Ebenezer, Advice to a Son: A Sermon Preached at the Request of a Gentleman . . . Upon his Son's going to Europe, Boston, 1705.

Prince, Thomas, The Vade Mecum for America; Or, A Companion for Traders and Travellers, Boston, 1732. (A manual for travel, with tables of weights, charts of distance, etc., prepared by the learned Boston minister.)

Salva Conducta; Or, A Safe Conduct for the Increase of Trade in New-England, Boston, 1699. (Issued 13 times before 1700.)

School of Good Manners, The, New London, 1715.

Sewall, Samuel, The Selling of Joseph, Boston, 1700. (The earliest antislavery pamphlet in America.)

Shepard, Thomas, Jr., Wine for Gospel Wantons, Cambridge, 1668.

Stoddard, Solomon, An Answer to Some Cases of Conscience Respecting the Country, Boston, 1722.

Symmes, Thomas, The Reasonableness of Regular Singing, Boston, 1720.

Twichell, Joseph H., ed., Some Old Puritan Love-Letters, John and Margaret Winthrop, 1618–1638, New York, 1893.

Wadsworth, Benjamin, The Well-Ordered Family, Boston, 1712.

Walter, Thomas, The Grounds and Rules of Musick Explained, Boston, 1721.

—— The Sweet Psalmist of Israel, Boston, 1722.

Whitman, Samuel, Practical Godliness the Way to Prosperity, New London, 1714.

Wise, John, A Word of Comfort to a Melancholy Country, Boston, 1721. (A plea for paper money and "inflation" against the "sound money" merchants of Boston.)

B. Secondary Works

The customs and behavior of Puritans have long been a subject for discussion and comment, all too often misleadingly presented.

1. Almanacs

The most widely distributed item to be issued from the colonial press, the almanac today is also the scarcest; it took the place of a newspaper during the seventeenth century, and like a newspaper was discarded when out of date. See Section IX-B for a chronological checklist dealing with "Popular Science in the Almanacs."

Bates, Albert C., "Check List of Connecticut Almanacs, 1709–1850, with Introduction and Notes," Proceedings of the American Antiquarian Society, N.S. XXIV (1914), 93–215.

—— "Part of an Almanack," Proceedings of the American Antiquarian Society, LII (1942), 38–44.

Briggs, Samuel, The Essays, Humor, and Poems of Nathaniel Ames, Father and Son . . . from their Almanacks, 1726–1775, Cleveland, 1891.

—— "The Origin and Development of the Almanack," Western Reserve and Northern Ohio Historical Society, Tract No. 69 (1887), 435–477.

Brigham, Clarence S., "An Account

of American Almanacs and their Value for Historical Study," Proceedings of the American Antiquarian Society, N.S. XXXV (1925), 1–25, 194–209.

Chapin, Howard M., "Check List of Rhode Island Almanacs, 1643–1850, with Introduction and Notes," Proceedings of the American Antiquarian Society, N.S. XXV (1915), 19–54.

Denker, David D., "American Almanacs in the Eighteenth Century," Journal of the Rutgers University Library, XVIII No. 2 (June, 1955), 12–55.

Eisenger, Chester E., "The Farmer in the Eighteenth Century Almanac," Agricultural History, July, 1954.

Gummere, Richard M., "The Classical

Element in Early New England Almanacs," *Harvard Library Bulletin*, IX (1955), 181–196. (Allusions to the classics were second only to those to Scripture.)

Kittredge, George L., *The Old Farmer and his Almanack*, Boston, 1904.

Littlefield, George E., "Notes on the Calendar and the Almanac," *Proceedings of the American Antiquarian Society*, N.S. XXIV (1914), 11–64.

Lovely, Napoleon W., "Notes on New England Almanacs," *New England Quarterly*, VIII (1935), 264–277.

Morrison, Hugh A., *Preliminary Check List of American Almanacs, 1639–1800*, Washington, 1907.

Nichols, Charles L., "Checklist of Maine, New Hampshire and Vermont Almanacs," *Proceedings of the American Antiquarian Society*, N.S. XXXVIII (1928) 63–163.

—— "Notes on the Almanacs of Massachusetts," *Proceedings of the American Antiquarian Society*, N.S. XXII (1912), 15–134.

Perry, Amos, "New England Almanacs, with Special Mention of Those Published in Rhode Island," *Narragansett Historical Register*, IV (1885), 27–39.

Stickney, Matthew A., "Almanacs and their Authors," *Essex Institute Historical Collections*, VIII (1866), 28–32, 75, 101–104, 158–164, 193–205; XIV (1877), 81–93, 212–223, 242–248.

2. Daily Life and Behavior

In addition to the items listed below, the student should consult town histories and family genealogies.

Adams, Charles F., "Some Phases of Sexual Morality and Church Discipline in Colonial New England," *Proceedings of the Massachusetts Historical Society*, XXVI (1891), 477–516. (For a counter-statement, see H. B. Parker, *New England Quarterly*, III (1930), 133–135.

Adams, James Truslow, *Provincial Society, 1690–1763*, New York, 1927. (Volume III of *A History of American Life*, ed. Arthur M. Schlesinger and Dixon R. Fox. A substantial description of general culture and social and economic life in the colonies. The "Critical Essay on Authorities," pp. 324–356, is of great value.)

——, and others, eds., *Album of American History: Colonial Period*, New York, 1944. (A good pictorial miscellany, but disregard the text.)

Albertson, Dean, "Puritan Liquor in the Planting of New England," *New England Quarterly*, XXIII (1950), 477–490. (Drinking habits of Puritans and the attempt to regulate them. No taint of immorality was attached to drinking, and prodigious amounts were consumed in comparative sobriety.)

Andrews, Charles McL., *Colonial Folkways: A Chronicle of American Life in the Reign of the Georges*, New Haven, 1919. (*The Chronicle of America*, Vol. IX. Excellent, readable survey.)

Bardsley, Charles W., *Curiosities of Puritan Nomenclature*, London, 1880.

Benton, Josiah H., *Warning out in New England, 1656–1817*, Boston, 1911. (A history of poor-relief.)

Bliss, William R., *Side Glimpses from the Colonial Meeting-House*, Boston, 1894. (Chatty and informative.)

Bridenbaugh, Carl, *Cities in Revolt: Urban Life in America 1743–1776*, New York, 1955. (A continuation of *Cities in the Wilderness*, documenting the rise of urban culture.)

—— *Cities in the Wilderness: The First Century of Urban Life in America 1625–1742*, New York, 1938; 1955. (Contains, among others, intensive studies of Boston and Newport, and shows them to be mature cities by the European standards of the day.)

—— "The New England Town: A Way of Life," *Proceedings of the American Antiquarian Society*, LVI (1946), 19–48.

Buffinton, Arthur H., "Sir Thomas Temple in Boston, a Case of Benevolent Assimilation," *Publications of the Colonial Society of Massachusetts*, XXVII (1932), 308–319.

Bushnell, David, "The Treatment of the Indians in Plymouth Colony," *New England Quarterly*, XXVI (1953), 193–218.

Calhoun, Arthur W., *A Social History of the American Family from Colonial Times to the Present*, Cleveland, 1917–1919, 3 vols. (The first seven chapters of Vol. I, "Colonial Period," relate to New England. Stimulating.)

Caulfield, Ernest, "Pediatric Aspects of the Salem Witchcraft Tragedy: A Lesson in Mental Health," *American Journal of Diseases of Children*, LXV (1943), 788–802. (Argues that the child-accusers were hysterics, not frauds, and that their hysteria was a by-product of Puritan piety and theology.)

—— "The Pursuit of a Pestilence," *Proceedings of the American Antiquarian Society*, LX (1950), 21–52. (Influenza in the colonies.)

—— "Some Common Diseases of Colonial Children," *Publications of the Colonial Society of Massachusetts*, XXXV (1942–1946), 1951, 4–65.

Chapman, Clayton Harding, "Benjamin Colman's Daughters (1708–1745)," *New England Quarterly*, XXVI (1953), 162–192. (Family life in early New England.)

Chase, Gilbert, *America's Music: From the Pilgrims to the Present*, New York, 1955; 1960. (The most scholarly general history of music in the United States.)

Child, Frank S., *The Colonial Parson of New England*, New York, 1896.

"Colonial Scene 1602–1800, The," *Proceedings of the American Antiquarian Society*, LX (1950), 53–160. (An invaluable annotated list of books, broadsides, prints and maps revealing daily life and occupations of the colonists, compiled by the staffs of the A. A. S. and of the John Carter Brown Library.)

Covey, Cyclone, "Puritanism and Music in Colonial America," *William and Mary Quarterly*, VIII (1951), 378–388.

Cowell, Henry J., *John Winthrop: A Seventeenth Century Puritan Romance*, Colchester, Eng., 1949. (A brief pamphlet on John and Margaret Winthrop, containing a collection of their love letters.)

Crawford, Mary C., *In the Days of the Pilgrim Fathers*, Boston, 1920.

—— *Little Pilgrimages among Old New England Inns*, Boston, 1907.

—— *The Romance of Old New England Churches*, Boston, 1904.

—— *Social Life in Old New England*, Boston, 1914.

Cutler, U. Waldo, "Tools, Trades and an Honest Living in Early New England," *Publications of the Worcester Historical Society*, N.S. I (1935), 479–486.

Davis, Andrew McF., "Hints of Contemporary Life in the Writings of Thomas Shepard," *Publications of the Colonial Society of Massachusetts*, XII (1911), 136–163.

—— "John Harvard's Life in America," *Publications of the Colonial Society of Massachusetts*, XII (1911), 4–45. (Life and manners in the first decades.)

Dawes, Norman H., "Titles as Symbols of Prestige in Seventeenth-Century New England," *William and Mary Quarterly*, VI (1949), 69–83.

Day, Clive H., "Capitalistic Tendencies in the Puritan Colonies," *Annual Report of the American Historical Association*, Washington, 1925, 225–235.

Deutch, Albert, "The Sick Poor in Colonial Times," *American Historical Review*, XLVI (1941), 560–579.

Dexter, Elizabeth A., *Colonial Women of Affairs: Women in Business and the Professions in America before 1776*, 2nd ed., Boston, 1931.

Dodge, Daniel K., "Puritan Names," *New England Quarterly*, I (1928), 467–475.

Dow, George F., *Domestic Life in New England in the Seventeenth Century*, Topsfield, Mass., 1925.

—— *Every Day Life in the Massachusetts Bay Colony*, Boston, 1935.

Drake, Samuel A., *A Book of New England Legends and Folk Lore*, Boston, 1884.

—— *Old Boston Taverns and Tavern Clubs*, Boston, 1917.

Duffy, John, *Epidemics in Colonial America*, Baton Rouge, 1953.

Dulles, Foster Rhea, *America Learns to Play: A History of Popular Recreation, 1607–1940*, New York, 1940.

Earle, Alice M., *Child Life in Colonial Days*, 2nd ed., New York, 1927.

—— *Colonial Dames and Good Wives*, New York, 1895.

—— *Costume of Colonial Times*, New York, 1894.

—— *Customs and Fashions in Old New England*, New York, 1894.

—— *Home Life in Colonial Days*, New York, 1898.

—— *The Sabbath in Puritan New England*, New York, 1891.

—— *Stage-Coach and Tavern Days*, New York, 1900.

—— *Two Centuries of Costume in America*, New York, 1903.

Eggleston, Edward, *The Beginners of a Nation*, New York, 1896.

—— *The Transit of Civilization from England to America*, New York, 1901.

Englishmen at Rest and Play, 1558–1714, by members of Wadham College, Oxford, 1931. (Important for background of New England society.)

Ezell, John Samuel, *Fortune's Merry Wheel: The Lottery in America*, Cambridge, 1960.

Felt, Joseph B., *The Customs of New England*, Boston, 1853.

Ferguson, J. DeLancey, "The Roots of American Humor," *American Scholar*, IV (1935), 41–48.

Field, Edward, *The Colonial Tavern: A Glimpse of New England Town Life in the Seventeenth and Eighteenth Centuries*, Providence, 1897.

Fisher, Sydney G., *Men, Women and Manners in Colonial Times*, Philadelphia, 1898, 2 vols.

Fitzpatrick, Kathleen, "The Puritans and the Theatre," *Historical Studies of Australia and New Zealand*, III (1944–1949), 253–276.

Fleming, Sandford, *Children & Puritanism: The Place of Children in the Life and Thought of the New England Churches, 1620–1847*, New Haven, 1933.

Foote, Henry Wilder, *Three Centuries of American Hymnody*, Cambridge, 1940; Hamden, 1961. (Important and authoritative. Contains, for example, the best brief account of the Bay Psalm Book.)

Forbes, Esther, *Paradise*, New York, 1937. (A brilliant novel of seventeenth century Boston and vicinity. The manners of the Bay Colony settlers, especially of those living in the countryside, are portrayed with authentic vigor.)

Ford, Edwin H., "Colonial Pamphleteers," *Journalism Quarterly*, XIII (1936), 24–36.

Ford, Worthington C., "Samuel Sewall and Nicholas Noyes on Wigs," *Publications of the Colonial Society of Massachusetts*, XX (1920), 109–128.

Gabriel, Ralph H., ed., *The Pageant of America*, New Haven, 1925–1929, 15 vols. (A useful collection of social and cultural remains.)

Gretton, Richard H., *The English Middle Class*, London, 1917. (Important backgrounds.)

Griswold, A. Whitney, "Three Puritans on Prosperity, *New England Quarterly*, VII (1934), 475–493.

Haller, William and Malleville Haller, "The Puritan Art of Love," *Huntington Library Quarterly*, V (1942), 235–272. (An account of the teachings of the Puritan pulpit concerning love and marriage.)

Hanscom, Elizabeth D., ed., *The Heart of the Puritan; Selections from Letters and Journals*, New York, 1917.

Haynes, Henry W., "Cotton Mather and His Slaves," *Proceedings of the American Antiquarian Society*, N.S. VI (1889–1890), 191–195.

Holliday, Carl, *Woman's Life in Colonial Days*, Boston, 1922.

—— *The Wit and Humor of Colonial Days (1607–1800)*, Philadelphia, 1912.

Hooker, Roland M., *The Colonial Trade of Connecticut*, Publications of the Tercentenary Commission of the State of Connecticut, New Haven, 1936.

Howard, John T., *Our American Music: Three Hundred Years of It*, 4th ed. rev., New York, 1955.

Jameson, John F., ed., *Privateering and Piracy in the Colonial Period; Illustrative Documents*, New York, 1923.

Jewett, Amos E., "Deacon John Pearson and his Fulling Mill at Rowley," *Publications of the Rowley Historical Society*, 1948, 24–26.

—— "A New England Shoemaker's Shop," *Ibid.*, 27–29.

—— "The Tidal Marshes of Rowley and Vicinity with an Account of the Old-Time Methods of Marshing," *Essex Institute Historical Collections*, LXXXV (1949), 272–291.

Jones, Matt B., 'Some Bibliographical Notes on Cotton Mather's 'The Accomplished Singer,' " *Publications of the Colonial Society of Massachusetts*, XXVIII (1935), 186–193.

—— "Bibliographical Notes on Thomas Walter's 'Grounds and Rules of Musick Explained,' " *Proceedings of the*

American Antiquarian Society, N.S. XLII (1932), 235–246.

Kelly, J. Frederick, "Raising Connecticut Meeting-Houses," *Old-Time New England*, XXVII (1936), 3–9.

Kelso, Robert W., *The History of Public Poor Relief in Massachusetts, 1620–1920*, Boston, 1922.

Kouwenhoven, John A., "Some Unfamiliar Aspects of Singing in New England, 1620–1810," *New England Quarterly*, VI (1933), 567–588.

Langdon, William Chauncy, *Everyday Things in American Life, 1607–1776*, New York, 1937.

Lawrence, Henry W., *The Not-Quite Puritans*, Boston, 1928. (A labored striving to present the peccadilloes of Puritans with humor.)

—— "Puritan Scandals—Courtship, Marriage and Divorce Three Centuries Ago," *Yankee*, III (1937), 7–9, 29.

Lawrence, Robert M., *New England Colonial Life*, Cambridge, 1927.

Love, William de L., *The Fast and Thanksgiving Days of New England*, Boston, 1895.

Lovell, John, Jr., "The Beginnings of the American Theatre," *Theatre Annual*, X (1952), 7–19. (Finds the beginnings of the American theatre in the colonial meetinghouse.)

McClusker, Honor, "Scholars, Rogues, and Puritans," *More Books*, XIII (1938), 1–8.

Mangler, Joyce Ellen, and William Dinneen, "Early Music in Rhode Island Churches," *Rhode Island History*, XVII (1958), 1–9, 33–44, 73–84, 108–118.

Morgan, Edmund S., *The Puritan Family: Essays on Religion and Domestic Relations in Seventeenth Century New England*, Boston, 1944. (A valuable collection of literate scholarly essays, most of which originally appeared in *More Books*, published by the Boston Public Library.)

Muzzey, David S., "The Heritage of the Puritans," *Annual Report of the American Historical Association*, 1925, 239–249. (Stresses the point that they educated for responsibility.)

Myers, Gustavus, *Ye Olden Blue Laws*, New York, 1921.

Nordell, Philip G., "Cotton Mather in Love," *Harper's Magazine*, CLIII (1926), 556–572.

Oberholzer, Emil, Jr., "The Church in New England Society," *Seventeenth Century America: Studies in Colonial History*, ed. James Morton Smith, Chapel Hill, 1959, 143–165. (A study in the ecclesiastical regulation of social behavior.)

—— *Delinquent Saints: Disciplinary Action in the Early Congregational Churches of Massachusetts*, New York, 1950.

Parkes, Henry B., "Morals and Law Enforcement in Colonial New England," *New England Quarterly*, V (1932), 431–452.

—— "New England in the Seventeen Thirties," *New England Quarterly*, III (1930), 397–419. (A picture of affairs, books, reading, and trends.)

—— "Sexual Morals and the Great Awakening," *New England Quarterly*, III (1930), 133–135.

Porter, Katherine A., "Affection of Praehiminincies," *Accent*, II (1942), 131–138, 226–232. (A fragment of a domestic biography of Cotton Mather.)

—— "A Bright Particular Faith, A.D. 1700. A Portrait of Cotton Mather," *Perspectives USA*, No. 7 (Spring 1954), 83–92. (An imaginative study of Mather's conflicting emotions during the long illness of his wife, Abigail, and after her death.)

Powell, Chilton L., "Marriage in Early New England," *New England Quarterly*, I (1928), 323–334.

Schafer, Joseph, *The Social History of American Agriculture*, New York, 1936.

Schlesinger, Elizabeth Bancroft, "Cotton Mather and His Children," *William and Mary Quarterly*, X (1953), 181–189.

Scholes, Percy A., *The Puritans and Music in England and New England*, London, 1934. (An authoritative work, even though prone to special pleading.)

—— "The Truth about the New England Puritans and Music," *Musical Quarterly*, XIX (1933), 1–17.

Sonneck, Oscar G., *Early Concert Life in America, 1731–1800*, Leipzig, 1907.

Sprott, S. E., "The Puritan Problem of Suicide," *Dalhousie Review*, XXXVIII (1958), 222–233.

Stetson, Sarah Pattee, "American Garden Books Transplanted and Native Before 1807," *William and Mary Quarterly*, III (1946), 343–369.

Stevenson, Noel C., "Marital Rights in

the Colonial Period," *New England Historical and Genealogical Register*, CIX (1955), 84–91.

Stewart, George R., "Men's Names in Plymouth and Massachusetts in the Seventeenth Century," *University of California Publications in English*, Vol. VII, No. 2, 109–137.

Stiles, Henry R., *Bundling; its Origin, Progress and Decline in America*, Albany, 1871; Harrisburg, Pa., 1928.

Thwing, Leroy L., "Lighting in Early Colonial Massachusetts," *New England Quarterly*, XI (1938), 166–170.

Trewartha, Glenn T., "Types of Rural Settlement in Colonial America," *Geographical Review*, XXXVI (1946), 568–596. (Social desiderata determined the settlement pattern in New England.)

Walcott, Robert R., "Husbandry in Colonial New England," *New England Quarterly*, IX (1936), 218–252.

Weeden, William B., *Early Rhode Island, A Social History of the People*, New York, 1910.

—— "Ideal Newport in the 18th Century," *Proceedings of the American Antiquarian Society*, N.S. XVIII (1906), 106–117.

Weld, Ralph F., *Slavery in Connecticut*, Hartford, 1935.

Wendell, Barrett, "Some Neglected Characteristics of the New England Puritans," *Annual Report of the American Historical Association*, 1891, 245–253.

Wertenbaker, Thomas J., *The First Americans, 1607–1690*, New York, 1927. Volume II of *A History of American Life*.

—— *The Golden Age of Colonial Culture*, New York, 1942. (Eighteenth-century cultural interests in Boston, New York, Philadelphia, Annapolis, Williamsburg, and Charleston.)

Wharton, Anne H., *Colonial Days and Dames*, Philadelphia, 1895.

Woodhouse, Julia, "Judge Sewall and Antislavery Sentiment in Colonial New England," *Negro Historical Bulletin*, VI (1943), 125, 143.

Wright, Harry A., "Those Human Puritans," *Proceedings of the American Antiquarian Society*, L (1940), 80–90.

Wright, Louis B., "The Colonial Struggle Against Barbarism," *Culture on the Moving Frontier*, Bloomington, 1955; Harper Torchbook edition, 1961, 11–45.

—— *The Cultural Life of the American Colonies*, New York, 1957; Harper Torchbook edition, 1962. (This admirably concise, immensely valuable little book has chapters on "Zeal for Education," "Books, Libraries and Learning," "Literary Production," "Drama, Music and Other Diversions," etc., and could well be listed under a half dozen rubrics of this bibliography.)

V. BIOGRAPHY

Only a few "Lives" were published as such during the first century of the settlements. Eventually, when the funeral sermons, historical essays, diaries, journals, and the large collections of personal papers (usually in manuscript) have been consulted, the amount of biographical material covering the period will prove enormous. This bibliography is confined to printed sources only. Such libraries as those of the New England Historical Genealogical Society, Congregational Library, and Massachusetts Historical Society in Boston; as well as those of Harvard and Yale Universities, and of the American Antiquarian Society in Worcester, are especially rich in manuscript material.

A. PURITAN BIOGRAPHIES

Certain items, often biographical in nature, are more properly classified elsewhere. Such historical narratives, for instance, as John Williams's *The Redeemed Captive*, Cotton Mather's *Magnalia*, John Winthrop's *Journal*, will be found in section I A. See also section IV A.

Barnard, John, *Ashton's Memorial. An History of the Strange Adventures, and Signal Deliverances, of Mr. Philip Ashton*, Boston, 1725.

Colman, Benjamin, *Reliquiae Turellae, et Lachrymae Paternae*, Boston, 1735; London, 1741.

—— *The Prophet's Death Lamented and*

Improved, Boston, 1723. (Funeral sermon on Increase Mather.)

Mather, Cotton, *Chrysostomus Nov-Anglorum*, Boston, 1695. (Life of John Davenport.)

—— *Ecclesiastes*, Boston, 1697. (Life of Jonathan Mitchell.)

—— *Johannes in Eremo. Memoirs, Relating to The Lives, Of . . . John Cotton, . . . John Norton*, Boston, 1695.

—— *The Life of Mr. Thomas Dudley*, ed. Charles Deane, Cambridge, 1870.

—— *Memoria Wilsonia*, Boston, 1695. (Life of John Wilson.)

Mather, Samuel, *The Life of . . . Cotton Mather*, Boston, 1729.

Mather, Samuel (of Witney), *Memoirs of the Life of the Late Reverend Increase Mather*, London, 1725.

Norton, John, *Abel being dead yet speaketh*, Cambridge, 1657; London, 1658; ed. E. Pond, 1842. (Life of John Cotton; see Dana K. Merrill, in part D of this section.)

Turell, Ebenezer, *The Life and Character of the Reverend Benjamin Colman*, Boston, 1749.

—— *Memoirs of the Life and Death Of the Pious and Ingenious Mrs. Jane Turell*, Boston, 1735; London, 1741. (Jane Turell was a daughter of Benjamin Colman.)

—— *Observanda*, Boston, 1695. (Life of Queen Mary.)

—— *Parentator*, Boston, 1724. (Life of Increase Mather.)

—— *Pietas in Patriam*, Boston, 1697. (Life of Sir William Phips.)

—— *Piscator Evangelicus. Or, The Life of Mr. Thomas Hooker*, Boston, 1695.

—— *The Triumphs of the Reformed Religion, in America*, Boston, 1691. Subsequently published as *The Life and Death Of The Renown'd Mr. John Eliot*, London, 1691, 1694, 1820.

Mather, Increase, *The Life and Death Of That Reverend Man of God, Mr. Richard Mather*, Cambridge, 1670; reprinted in *Collections of the Dorchester Antiquarian and Historical Society*, No. 3, Boston, 1850.

B. Diaries, Journals, and Collections of Personal Papers

Thousands of Puritans kept diaries, and many also preserved their correspondence and papers. For a bibliography of diaries, see Harriette M. Forbes, *New England Diaries, 1602–1800*, Topsfield, Mass., 1923.

Aspinwall Papers, The, Collections of the Massachusetts Historical Society, fourth series, Vols. IX and X (1871).

Barnard, John, "Autobiography," *Collections of the Massachusetts Historical Society*, third series, V (1836), 177–243.

—— "Memoranda Quotidiana, 1715–1735," *Congregational Quarterly*, IV (1862), 376 ff.

Belcher Papers, The, Collections of the Massachusetts Historical Society, sixth series, Vols. VI and VII (1893–1894).

Bradford, William, "Letter Book," *Collections of the Massachusetts Historical Society*, first series, III (1794), 27–76.

Brainerd, David, *An Account of the Life of the Late Reverend Mr. Brainerd*, ed. by Jonathan Edwards, Boston, 1749; numerous editions, the latest *The Life and Diary of David Brainerd with a Biographical Sketch of President Edwards* by Philip E. Howard, Jr., Chicago, 1949.

Brock, John, "The Autobiographical Memoranda of John Brock, 1636–1659," ed. by Clifford K. Shipton, *Proceedings of the American Antiquarian Society*, LIII (1943), 96–105.

Burr, Esther, "Journal," ed. Josephine Fisher, *New England Quarterly*, III (1930), 297–315.

Calder, Isabel M., ed., *Letters of John Davenport, Puritan Divine*, New Haven, 1937.

Dow, George F., ed., *The Holyoke Diaries, 1709–1856*, Salem, Mass., 1911.

Green, Joseph, "The Commonplace Book of Joseph Green (1675–1715)," ed. by Samuel E. Morison, *Publications of the Colonial Society of Massachusetts*, XXXIV (1943), 191–253.

—— "Diary," (together with a biographical sketch of Green by Samuel P. Fowler), *Essex Institute Historical Collections*, VIII (1868), 91–96, 105–174, 215–224; X (1870), pt. I, 73–104; XXXVI (1900), 325–330.

Hinckley Papers, The, Collections of the Massachusetts Historical Society, fourth series, Vol. V (1861).

Homes, William, "Diary of Rev. William Homes of Chilmark, Martha's Vineyard, 1689-1746." New England Historical and Genealogical Register, XLVIII (1894), 446-453; XLIX (1895), 413-416; L (1896), 155-166.

Hull, John, "The Diaries of John Hull," Transactions and Collections of the American Antiquarian Society, III (1857), 109-316.

Jones, Matt B., "Thomas Maule, the Salem Quaker, and Free Speech in Massachusetts Bay," Essex Institute Historical Collections, LXXII (1936), 1-42.

Knight, Sarah Kemble, The Journals of Madam Knight, and Rev. Mr. Buckingham, New York, 1825; The Journal of Madam Knight, ed. George P. Winship, Boston, 1920.

Lynde, Benjamin, The Dairies of Benjamin Lynde and Benjamin Lynde, Jr., [1690-1780], Boston, 1880.

Mather, Cotton, Diary of Cotton Mather, [1681-1724], Collections of the Massachusetts Historical Society, seventh series, Vols. VII and VIII (1911, 1912); New York, 1957, 2 vols.

Mather, Increase, Diary, with Introduction by Samuel A. Green, Cambridge, 1900. (Brief extracts.)

Mather, Richard, Journal, Collections of the Dorchester Antiquarian and Historical Society, No. 3 (1850).

Mather Papers, The, Collections of the Massachusetts Historical Society, fourth series, Vol. VIII (1868).

[Sewall, Joseph], "Sins and Mercies of a Harvard Student," More Books, XI (1936), 277-285. (Sewall's Diary ca. 1707).

Sewall, Samuel, Diary of Samuel Sewall, 1674-1729, Collections of the Massachusetts Historical Society, fifth series, Vols. V-VII (1878-1882). Selections from the Diary in convenient form in Samuel Sewall's Diary, ed. Mark Van Doren, New York, 1927.

—— Letter-Book of Samuel Sewall, Collections of the Massachusetts Historical Society, sixth series, Vols. I-II (1886-1888).

Shepard, Thomas, "The Autobiography of Thomas Shepard," Publications of the Colonial Society of Massachusetts, XXVII (1932), 345-400. (Prefaced by a complete bibliography.)

Stearns, Raymond P., ed., "Letters and Documents by or Relating to Hugh Peter," Essex Institute Historical Collections, LXXI (1935), 303-318; LXXII (1936), 43-72, 117-134, 208-232, 303-349; LXXIII (1937), 130-157.

Thacher, Peter, "The Diary of a Colonial Clergyman: Peter Thacher of Milton," ed. by Edward Pierce Hamilton, Proceedings of the Massachusetts Historical Society, LXXI (1953-1957), 1959, 50-63. (A revealing account of day to day life of a well-to-do clergyman.)

Trumbull Papers, The, Collections of the Massachusetts Historical Society, fifth series, Vols. IX and X (1885, 1888); seventh series, Vols. II and III (1902).

Wigglesworth, Michael, "The Diary of Michael Wigglesworth (1653-1657)," ed. by Edmund S. Morgan, Publications of the Colonial Society of Massachusetts, XXXV (1942-1946), 1951, 311-444.

Williams, Roger, Letters of Roger Williams, 1632-1682, ed. John R. Bartlett, Providence, 1874.

—— Letters and Papers of Roger Williams, 1629-1682, Boston, 1924.

Winthrop Papers, The, Collections of the Massachusetts Historical Society, fourth series, Vols. VI and VII (1863, 1865); fifth series, Vols. I and VIII (1871, 1882); sixth series, Vols. III and V (1889, 1892). The "Papers" are now being re-edited, with copious notes, by the Society (Vols. III, IV and V, ed. by Allyn Bailey Forbes): Vol. I, 1929; Vol. II, 1931; Vol. III, 1943; Vol. IV, 1944; Vol. V, 1947. (Rich in details of everyday life for Puritans in England and Massachusetts Bay.)

"Winthrop-Davenport Papers," Bulletin of the New York Public Library, III (1899), 393-408.

C. COLLECTIONS

First of all, the student should consult the *Dictionary of American Biography* (containing bibliographies), and the *Dictionary of National Biography*; secondly, such repositories of genealogical information as James Savage, *Genealogical Dictionary of the First Settlers of New England*, Boston, 1860–1862, 4 vols., or the pages of *The New England Historical and Genealogical Register*, Boston, 1847—current. In addition the following are useful:

Brook, Benjamin, *Lives of the Puritans*, London, 1813, 3 vols.

Calamy, Edmund, *Calamy Revised*, ed. A. G. Matthews, Oxford, 1934; London, 1959, with a revision of the original introduction. (Revision of Calamy's *Account of the Ministers and Others Ejected and Silenced, 1660–1662*. Biographies of the English Puritans, some of them New England figures.)

Chauncy, Charles, "A Sketch of Eminent Men in New England," *Collections of the Massachusetts Historical Society*, first series, X (1809), 154–165. (A letter to Ezra Stiles, written in 1768, giving sketches of twenty-two Puritan divines.)

Dexter, Franklin B., *Biographical Sketches of the Graduates of Yale College with Annals of the College History*, New York, 1885–1912, 6 vols.

Foster, Joseph, *Alumni Oxonienses, 1500–1714*, Oxford, 1891–1892, 4 vols.

Lives of the Chief Fathers of New England, Boston, 1846–1849, 6 vols. (Cotton, Wilson, Norton, Davenport, Eliot, Shepard, I. Mather, Hooker.)

Peel, Albert, *The Congregational Two Hundred*, London, 1948. (A short biographical guide to two hundred leaders of Congregational thought and polity, with emphasis on the earlier leaders.)

Sibley, John L., *Biographical Sketches of Graduates of Harvard University in Cambridge, Massachusetts*, Cambridge, 1873–1885, 3 vols. (Includes Harvard classes 1642–1689.) Vol. IV, Cambridge, 1933, and Vols. V–XI, Boston, 1937–1960 (Harvard classes 1699–1745), ed. Clifford K. Shipton. (The series is a joy to read and an indispensable biographical and bibliographical guide for the period and subjects covered.)

Sprague, William B., *Annals of the American Pulpit*, New York, 1857–1869, 9 vols.

Venn, John, and J. A. Venn, *Alumni Cantabrigienses*, Cambridge, Eng., 1922–1927, 4 vols.

Walker, Williston, *Ten New England Leaders*, New York, 1901. (Bradford, Cotton, R. Mather, Eliot, I. Mather, Edwards, Chauncy.)

Wendell, Barrett, *Stelligeri, and Other Essays Concerning America*, New York, 1893.

Wood, Anthony, *Athenae Oxonienses*, ed. Philip Bliss, 1813–1820, 4 vols. (The best edition.)

D. SECONDARY WORKS

This list is far from complete. The student should consult the bibliography appended to the articles in *Dictionary of American Biography*. Further biographical material will be found listed throughout the text of this book in the brief notices which introduce the selections.

Allen, Alexander V. G., *Jonathan Edwards*, Boston, 1889. (An able analysis of Edwards' position as a theologian.)

Augur, Helen, *An American Jezebel: The Life of Anne Hutchinson*, New York, 1930. (Novelized invective.)

Bingham, Hiram, "Elihu Yale, Governor, Collector and Benefactor," *Proceedings of the American Antiquarian Society*, XLVII (1937), 93–144.

Boas, Ralph P., and Louise Boas, *Cotton Mather: Keeper of the Puritan Conscience*, New York, 1928. (Somewhat journalistic.)

Bradford, Alden, *Memoir of the Life and Writings of Rev. Jonathan Mayhew*, Boston, 1838.

Burgess, Walter H., *John Robinson, Pastor of the Pilgrim Fathers*, London, 1920.

Campbell, Helen S., *Anne Bradstreet and Her Time*, Boston, 1891.

Carpenter, Edmund J., *Roger Williams;*

A Study of the Life, Times and Character of a Political Pioneer, New York, 1909.

Chamberlain, Nathan H., *Samuel Sewall and the World He Lived In*, Boston, 1897.

Clarke, Hermann Frederick, *John Hull: A Builder of the Bay Colony*, Portland, 1940.

Curtis, Edith, *Anne Hutchinson: A Biography*, Cambridge, 1930.

Cavis, Richard B., *George Sandys, Poet Adventurer: A Study in Anglo-American Culture in the Seventeenth Century*, New York, 1955.

Dean, John W., *A Memoir of the Rev. Nathaniel Ward*, Albany, 1868.

—— *Memoir of Rev. Michael Wigglesworth*, Albany, 1871.

De Levie, Dagobert, "Cotton Mather, Theologian and Scientist," *American Quarterly*, III (1951), 362–365.

Earle, Alice M., *Margaret Winthrop*, New York, 1895.

Easton, Emily, *Roger Williams, Prophet and Pioneer*, New York, 1930. (A popular work, stressing the early and little-known years.)

Eaton, Arthur W. H., *The Famous Mather Byles*, Boston, 1914.

Ernst, James E., *Roger Williams: New England Firebrand*, New York, 1932. (Overenthusiastic and inaccurate.)

—— "Roger Williams and the English Revolution," *Collections of the Rhode Island Historical Society*, XXIV (1931), 1–58, 118–128.

—— "New Light on Roger Williams' Life in England," *Collections of the Rhode Island Historical Society*, XXII (1929), 97–103.

Foote, Henry W., "George Phillips, First Minister of Watertown," *Proceedings of the Massachusetts Historical Society*, LXIII (1931), 193–227.

Freiberg, Malcolm, "Thomas Hutchinson: The First Fifty Years (1711–1761)," *William and Mary Quarterly*, XV (1958), 35–55.

—— "William Bollan, Agent of Massachusetts, "*More Books*, XXIII (1948), 43–53, 90–100, 135–146, 168–182, 212–220.

Gookin, Frederick W., *Daniel Gookin, 1612–1687*, Chicago, 1912.

Gorton, Adelos, *The Life and Times of Samuel Gorton*, Philadelphia, 1907.

Gould Elizabeth P., *Ezekiel Cheever, Schoolmaster*, Boston, 1904.

Green, Samuel A., *Benjamin Tompson*, Boston, 1895.

Gummere, Richard, "John Wise, A Classical Controversialist," *Essex Institute Historical Collections*, XCII (1956), 265–278.

Hare, Lloyd C. M., *Thomas Mayhew, Patriarch to the Indians, 1593–1682*, New York, 1932.

Harkness, Reuben E. E., "Roger Williams—Prophet of Tomorrow," *Journal of Religion*, XV (1935), 400–425.

Holmes, Thomas J., "Samuel Mather of Witney, 1674–1733," *Publications of the Colonial Society of Massachusetts*, XXVI (1927), 312–322.

Hornberger, Theodore, "Samuel Lee (1625–1691), A Clerical Channel for the Flow of New Ideas to Seventeenth-Century New England," *Osiris*, I (1936), 341–355.

Hosmer, James K., *The Life of Young Sir Henry Vane*, Boston, 1888.

Kimball, Everett, *The Public Life of Joseph Dudley*, New York, 1911.

Kittredge, George L., *Doctor Robert Child the Remonstrant*, Cambridge, 1919. (Reprinted from *Publications of the Colonial Society of Massachusetts*, XXI (1920), 1–146.

Marvin, Abijah P., *The Life and Times of Cotton Mather*, Boston, 1892.

Mason, Louis B., *The Life and Times of Major John Mason of Connecticut: 1600–1672*, New York, 1935.

Matthews, Albert, "Samuel Mather," *Publications of the Colonial Society of Massachusetts*, XVIII (1917), 206–228.

Mayo, Lawrence S., *John Endecott*, Cambridge, 1936.

—— *The Winthrop Family in America*, Boston, 1948.

Merrill, Dana K., "The First American Biography," *New England Quarterly*, XI (1938), 152–154. (A sketchy account of John Norton's life of John Cotton.)

Miller, Perry, *Jonathan Edwards*, New York, 1948; Meridian paperback. (A full-bodied presentation of Edwards as a great theologian, philosopher and intellect.)

—— "Jonathan Edwards and the Great Awakening," *America in Crisis*, ed. Daniel Aaron, New York, 1952. Reprinted in Perry Miller, *Errand into the Wilderness*, Cambridge, 1956, 153–166.

—— Roger Williams: His Contribution to the American Tradition, Indianapolis, 1953. (Combines selections and comment.)

Mood, Fulmer, "Notes on John Josselyn, Gent.," Publications of the Colonial Society of Massachusetts, XXVIII (1935), 24–36.

—— The Puritan Dilemma: The Story of John Winthrop, Boston, 1958. (The Reconciliation of the Puritan ethic to political life.)

Morison, Samuel E., "William Pynchon, The Founder of Springfield," Proceedings of the Massachusetts Historical Society, LXIV (1932), 67–107.

Morris, Maxwell H., "Roger Williams and the Jews," American Jewish Archives, III (1951), 24–27.

Murdock, Kenneth B., Increase Mather, the Foremost American Puritan, Cambridge, 1925. (A definitive biography and an authoritative study of the period.)

Nickerson, Philip Tillinghast, "More about Reverend John Mayo of Cape Cod and Boston," New England Historical and Genealogical Register, CIII (1949), 32–42.

—— "Rev. John Mayo, First Minister of the Second Church in Boston, Massachusetts," New England Historical and Genealogical Register, XCV (1941), 39–49, 100–108.

Patrick, J. Max, "The Arrest of Hugh Peters," Huntington Library Quarterly, XIX (1955–1956), 343–351.

—— Hugh Peters, A Study in Puritanism, The University of Buffalo Studies, XVII, 4, Buffalo, 1946.

Porter, Kenneth W., "Samuel Gorton, New England Firebrand," New England Quarterly, VII (1934), 405–444.

Powicke, Frederick J., John Robinson, London, 1920.

Preston, Richard Arthur, Gorges of Plymouth Fort: A Life of Sir Fernando Gorges, Captain of Plymouth Fort, Governor of New England, and Lord of the Province of Maine, Toronto, 1953.

Reuter, Karl, Wilhelm Amesius, Neukirchen, 1940. (The only full-scale study of Ames.)

Rice, Howard C., "Cotton Mather Speaks to France," New England Quarterly, XVI (1943), 198–233. (Mather's Une Grande Voix du Ciel a la France 1725, a plea for French Protestants, reveals his energy as a propagandist.)

Rose-Troupe, Frances, John White, the Patriarch of Dorchester and the Founder of Massachusetts, 1575–1648, New York, 1930. (Detailed but injudicious.)

Rugg, Winifred K., Unafraid: A Life of Anne Hutchinson, Boston, 1930. (Somewhat sentimentalized, but careful and fairminded.)

Shipton, Clifford K., Roger Conant: A Founder of Massachusetts, Cambridge, 1944.

Stearns, Raymond P., "Hugh Peter and his Biographers," Proceedings of the Bostonian Society (1935), 27–50.

—— The Strenuous Puritan: Hugh Peters, 1598–1660, Urbana, 1954.

Straus, Oscar S., Roger Williams: The Pioneer of Religious Liberty, New York, 1894.

Swan, Bradford F., Gregory Dexter of London and New England, 1610–1700, Rochester, N.Y., 1949.

Titus, Anson, "Madam Sarah Knight, Her Diary and Her Times," Bostonian Society Publications, IX (1912), 99–126.

Turnbull, G. H., "George Stirk, Philosopher by Fire (1628?–1665)," Publications of the Colonial Society of Massachusetts, XXXVIII (1947–1951), 1959, 219–251. (A fascinating account of a New England doctor and alchemist.)

—— "Robert Child," Publications of the Colonial Society of Massachusetts, XXXVIII (1947–1951), 1959, 21–53. (Supplements Kittredge's article supra with new information based on Hartlib's papers.)

Tuttle, Charles W., Captain John Mason, Boston, 1887.

Updike, Daniel, Richard Smith, First English Settler of Narragansett Country, Rhode Island, With a Series of Letters written by his son Richard Smith to members of the Winthrop Family . . . , Boston, 1937. (The letters are of interest for the light they shed on the politics of speculation in the Narragansett lands.)

Walker, George L., Thomas Hooker, New York, 1891.

Wendell, Barrett, Cotton Mather, the Puritan Priest, New York, 1891.

Wiener, Frederick B., "Roger Williams' Contribution to Modern Thought," Collections of the Rhode Island Historical Society, XXVIII (1935), 1–20.

Willcock, John, *Life of Sir Henry Vane the Younger*, London, 1913.

Winslow, Ola E., *Jonathan Edwards, 1703–1758*, New York, 1940. (A straightforward, reliable biography.)

—— *Master Roger Williams: A Biography*, New York, 1957.

Winthrop, Robert C., *Life and Letters of John Winthrop*, Boston, 1864–1867, 2 vols. (Contains many important original papers.)

Wolkins, George C., "Edward Winslow (O. V. 1606–1611), King's Scholar and Printer," *Proceedings of the American Antiquarian Society*, LX (1950), 237–266.

VI. LITERARY THEORY

Literature as a separate and self-sufficient art did not exist for Puritans. The art of writing, either in prose or verse, was first and foremost a means to the end of expressing some truth, theological, historical, or philosophical. Yet Puritans wrote voluminously, and no study of their ideology would be complete without a careful presentation of such theory as they expressed, or some attempt at an evaluation of their artistry in prose and verse.

A. Primary Sources

Puritans almost never discussed literature as *belles lettres*, and very seldom devoted a whole discussion to theories of rhetoric and composition. Consequently, a list of passages in which the Puritan standards of composition, vocabulary, and style are proclaimed almost always will be found as incidental remarks in passing, or in prefaces of commendation. The following list cannot have exhausted all such passages, but it gives at least a representative selection. No list of secondary works has been added to this section, since so few studies of the literary theories of Puritans have been made. All appropriate items have been assembled in Section VII B, under the general heading: "Puritan Literature—Secondary Works."

Adams, Eliphalet, *A Funeral Discourse*, New London, 1724, Sig. K3 verso.

—— Preface to Nehemiah Hobart, *The Absence of the Comforter Described and Lamented*, New London, 1717.

Adams, John, *Poems on Several Occasions*, Boston, 1745, "The Publisher to the Reader."

Allen, James, *New-Englands choicest Blessing*, Boston, 1679, "To the Reader."

—— *Serious Advice to delivered Ones from Sickness*, Boston, 1679, "To the Reader."

Allen, Thomas, Preface to John Cotton, *An Exposition upon . . . Revelation*, London, 1656.

Ames, William, *The Marrow of Sacred Divinity*, London, 1643, Sig. A4 verso; pp. 157–162.

Appleton, Nathaniel, *The Great Apostle Paul exhibited, and recommended as a Pattern of true Gospel Preaching*, Boston, 1751, pp. 26–30.

—— *Faithful Ministers of Christ*, Boston, 1743, p. 25.

—— *Superior Skill and Wisdom necessary for Winning Souls*, Boston, 1737, pp. 26, 32.

Barnard, John, *Elijah's Mantle*, Boston, 1724, p. 36.

—— *Sermons on Several Subjects*, London, 1727, Dedication; and pp. 11, 38.

[*Bay Psalm Book*,] *The Whole Book of Psalmes*, Cambridge, 1640, preface.

Belcher, Jonathan, Manuscript commonplace book, Harvard College Library ca. 1725–1728.

Bradford, William, "Of Plimmoth Plantation," Manuscript in Massachusetts State Library; Facsimile, London, 1896, p. 19.

Brocklesby, Richard [?], *Private Vertue and Public Spirit display'd. In a Succinct Essay on the Character of Captain Thomas Coram*, Boston, 1751, p. 15. (Reprinted in *Proceedings of the Massachusetts Historical Society*, LVI (1922), 15.

Bulkley, John, Preface to Roger Wolcott, *Poetical Meditations*, New London, 1725.

Byles, Mather, *A Discourse on the Present Vileness of the Body*, Boston, 1732, preface.

—— An essay on style in *The American Magazine and Historical Chronicle*, Boston,

January, 1745, pp. 1–4. (Signed "L," and identified as Byles's by Lyon N. Richardson, *A History of Early American Magazines, 1741–1789*, p. 54 note.)

—— Letter to Alexander Pope, October 7, 1727. Manuscript in New England Historical Genealogical Society, Boston. (Printed in Arthur W. H. Eaton, *The Famous Mather Byles*, Boston, 1914, p. 233.)

Chappell, William, *Methodus Concionandi*, London, 1648; translated as *The Preacher, or The Art and Method of Preaching*, London, 1656. (One of the best manuals of sermon style and practice.)

Chauncy, Charles (1592–1672), *Gods Mercy*, Cambridge, 1655, p. 37.

Chauncy, Charles (1705–1787), *Ministers cautioned against the Occasions of Contempt*, Boston, 1744, pp. 29, 35.

A Collection of Poems. By Several Hands, Boston, 1744. (Incidental critical phrases throughout, in poems by Mather Byles, John Adams, John Perkins, Matthew Adams, and Jonathan Belcher.)

Colman, Benjamin, Preface to Josiah Smith, *A Discourse*, Boston, 1726.

—— *The Government & Improvement of Mirth*, Boston, 1707, p. 45.

—— *Practical Discourses*, London, 1707, p. 57.

—— *The Prophet's Death Lamented*, Boston, 1723, p. 32.

—— *Reliquiae Turellae*, London, 1741, p. 153.

Cooke, William, *The Great Duty of Ministers*, Boston, 1742, p. 7.

Cotton, John, *A brief exposition with practical observations upon the whole book of Canticles*, London, 1655, p. 92.

—— *A Brief Exposition Of the whole Book of Canticles*, London, 1642, pp. 7–9, 112.

—— *A Briefe Exposition with Practicall Observations upon the Whole Book of Ecclesiastes*, London, 1654, pp. 265–266, 269, 272.

Douglass, William, *A Summary, Historical and Political, Of the first Planting*, Boston, 1749–1752, 2 vols. Vol. I, p. 1; Vol. II, title-page and p. 1.

Edwards, Jonathan, Rules on the cover of "Notes on Natural Science," *ca.* 1719. (Manuscript in Yale University Library; see C. H. Faust and T. H. Johnson, *Jonathan Edwards, Representative Selections*, New York, 1935.)

—— *Five Discourses*, Boston, 1738, preface.

—— *An Humble Inquiry*, Boston, 1749, conclusion.

—— *The Life of President Edwards*, by Sereno E. Dwight, New York, 1829, p. 601.

Eliot, Andrew, *A burning and shining Light*, Boston, 1750, p. 31.

Eliot, Jared, *Essays upon Field-Husbandry*, New York, 1748, preface.

Fitch, James, *Peace The End of the Perfect and Upright*, Cambridge, 1672, preface.

Foxcroft, Thomas, *The day of a godly Man's Death*, Boston, 1722, preface.

—— *A practical Discourse*, Boston, 1718, pp. 24–40. (One of the best discussions of style, delivered in a sermon at his own ordination by a minister who throughout his career was preoccupied with the problem of style and form.)

—— *Some seasonable Thoughts on Evangelic Preaching*, Boston, 1740, pp. 4, 5.

—— Preface to Jonathan Dickinson, *The True Scripture-Doctrine*, Boston, 1741.

Gookin, Daniel, *Historical Collections of the Indians in New-England, ca.* 1675, first printed in *Collections of the Massachusetts Historical Society*, first series, I (1792), p. 143.

Hobby, William, *An Inquiry*, Boston, 1745, pp. 19, 24.

Hooker, Thomas, *The Soules Exaltation*, London, 1638, pp. 26, 110.

—— *The Soules Preparation*, London, 1632, p. 66.

—— *A Survey of the Summe*, London, 1648, preface.

Hubbard, William, *The Happiness of a People*, Boston, 1676, pp. 8–15, 36–38.

Knapp, Francis, *Gloria Britannorum*, Boston, 1723, p. 11.

Lawson, Deodat, *The Duty & Property of a Religious Hous[e]holder Opened*, Boston, 1693, Sig. A4.

Mather, Cotton, *The A. B. C. of Religion*, Boston, 1713, p. 4.

—— *Bonifacius*, Boston, 1710, preface.

—— *Brethren*, Boston, 1718, pp. 21, 23.

—— *Corderius Americanus*, Boston, 1708, Introduction, and pp. 28, 29.

—— *Duodecennium Luctuosum*, Boston, 1714, Introduction, and p. 12.

—— *Just Commemorations*, Boston, 1715, preface and p. 34.

—— *Magnalia*, London, 1702. (See *Selections from Cotton Mather*, ed. K. B. Murdock, New York, 1926, pp. 1, 6, 13, 14, 18, 19, 26, 27.)

—— *Malachi*, Boston, 1717, pp. 27, 73.

—— *Manuductio*, Boston, 1726, pp. 28–35, 42, 44–50. (The section "Of Poetry and Style" is the only essay on the subject in America before Mather Byles's essay on style in *The American Magazine* for January, 1745, and it is the best treatment of the subject before Franklin's *Autobiography*.)

—— *Parentator*, Boston, 1724, Introduction, and p. 215.

—— *Psalterium Americanum*, Boston, 1718, Introduction. (Very important for the statement of his theories of translation and his conception of blank verse.)

Mather, Increase, *A Call from Heaven*, Boston, 1679, "To the Reader."

—— *Some Important Truths*, London, 1674, "To the Reader."

Mather, Richard, in Increase Mather, *The Life . . . of Richard Mather*, Cambridge, 1670, p. 85.

Mather, Samuel, *The Life of . . . Cotton Mather*, Boston, 1729, pp. 33, 68, 69, 72.

Mayhew, Experience, *Indian Converts*, Boston, 1727, Introduction.

Mitchell, Jonathan, Poem prefacing Michael Wigglesworth, *The Day of Doom*, Cambridge, 1662.

Morgan, Joseph, *Sin its own Punishment*, Boston, 1728, "To the Reader."

Morrell, William, *New-England*, London, 1625, "To the Reader."

Morton, William, preface to John Cotton, *The way of Life*, London, 1641.

Norton, John, *The Heart of N-England rent*, Cambridge, 1659, pp. 6, 58.

Noyes, Nicholas, Prefatory poem to Cotton Mather, *Magnalia*, London, 1702.

Oakes, Urian, *An Elegie upon . . . Shepard*, Cambridge, 1677, "To the Reader."

Penhallow, Samuel, *The History of the Wars of New-England*, Boston, 1726, preface.

Perkins, William, *The Art of Prophecying* (1592), *Works*, London, 1631, II, 670 ff. (A work regarded as the authoritative manual of sermon style and practice in New England.)

Pigot, George, *A Vindication*, Boston, 1731, preface.

Prince, Thomas, *A Chronological History of New-England*, Boston, 1736, preface.

—— Preface to Thomas Hooker, *The Poor Doubting Christian*, Boston, 1743.

—— Introduction to *Meditations and Spiritual Experiences of Mr. Thomas Shepard*, Boston, 1749.

Prince, Thomas, and Joseph Sewall, Preface to Samuel Willard, *A Compleat Body of Divinity*, Boston, 1726.

Saffin, John, Dedicatory poem in William Hubbard, *A Narrative of the Troubles with the Indians*, Boston, 1677.

—— *John Saffin His Book*, ed., with introduction by Caroline Hazard, New York, 1928, pp. 2, 47, 60.

Seccomb, Joseph, *On the Death Of the Reverend Benjamin Colman*, Boston 1747, p. 8.

Select Essays, With some few Miscellaneous Copies of Verses, Boston [?]. 1714, pp. 10, 11. (Unique copy in library of Massachusetts Historical Society.)

Shepard, Thomas, "Subjection to Christ," *Works*, ed. Albro, 1853, III, 278. (Preface by William Greenhill and Samuel Mather.)

Steere, Richard, *A Monumental Memorial of Marine Mercy*, Boston, 1684, "To the Reader," and p. 1.

Symmes, Thomas, *Lovewell Lamented*, Boston, 1725, pp. 5, 6.

"To Mr. B[yles] occasioned by his verses to Mr. Smibert on seeing his Pictures," *Proceedings of the Massachusetts Historical Society*, LIII (1920), 59.

Turell, Ebenezer, *The Life and Character of the Reverend Benjamin Colman*, Boston, 1749, pp. 167–169.

—— *Memoir of . . . Mrs. Jane Turell*, London, 1741, pp. 15, 25–31.

—— *Ministers should carefully avoid giving Offence*, Boston, 1740, pp. 14, 15.

Walter, Thomas, *The Sweet Psalmist of Israel*, Boston, 1722, Dedication and pp. 1–15.

Webb, John, *The Duty of Survivers*, Boston, 1739, p. 27.

White, John, *The Planters Plea*, London, 1630, "To the Reader."

Wigglesworth, Michael, *The Day of Doom*, Boston, 1701, Invocation.

—— "The prayse of Eloquence," in Samuel E. Morison, *Harvard College in the Seventeenth Century*, Cambridge, 1936, pp. 180–183. (From manuscript notebook in possession of the New England Historical Genealogical Society.)

Wilkins, John, *Ecclesiastes, or A Discourse concerning the Gift of Preaching*, London, 1646.

Willard, Samuel, *Ne Sutor*, Boston, 1681, p. 2.

—— "Particular Application, the best way of teaching," *The Truly Blessed Man*, Boston, 1700, pp. 423–434.

Wise, John, and Jonathan Mitchell, Preface to Samuel Whiting, *A Discourse of the Last Judgment*, Cambridge, 1664.

VII.   PURITAN POETRY

Though the Puritans remained relatively indifferent to poetry as an art, there were many among them who chose it as a vehicle to express their deepest feelings, and a few who achieved in it some measure of excellence. Elegies, memorial odes, satires and hymns (or stanzas designed for congregational singing) make up the largest portion of the Puritan verses.

A.   PRIMARY SOURCES

No attempt is made to list the great number of elegies which were written, and all too often printed, during the first century of the New England settlements. Such items are usually found in broadsides. Occasionally they were appended to funeral sermons, or scattered through such histories as Johnson's *Wonder-working Providence*, Morton's *New-Englands Memoriall*, or Mather's *Magnalia*. (See Ford and Winslow below.)

Adams, John, *Poems on Several Occasions, Original and Translated*, Boston, 1745.

[*The Bay Psalm Book.*] *The White Booke of Psalmes Faithfully Translated into English Metre*, Cambridge, 1640. Many editions; the latest, a facsimile reprint, Chicago, 1956.

Bradstreet, Anne, *The Tenth Muse Lately sprung up in America*, London, 1650. Second edition published with title *Several Poems Compiled with great variety of Wit and Learning, full of delight*, Boston, 1678; 1758. *Works*, ed. John H. Ellis, Charlestown, Mass., 1867; ed. Charles E. Norton, New York, 1897.

Bradstreet, Samuel, *An Almanack for ... 1657*, Cambridge, 1657.

Byles, Mather, *The Comet*, Boston, 1744.

—— *On the Death of the Queen: A Poem*, Boston, 1738.

—— *A Poem on the Death of His Late Majesty, King George*, Boston, 1727.

—— *Poems. The Conflagration*, Boston, 1755.

—— *Poems on Several Occasions*, Boston, 1736; 1744.

—— *To His Excellency Governor Belcher on the Death of his Lady*, Boston, 1736.

Byles, Mather, Joseph Green, John Adams, and others, *A Collection of Poems. By Several Hands*, Boston, 1744.

Colman, Benjamin, *A Poem on Elijah's Translation*, Boston, 1707.

Folger, Peter, *A Looking Glass For the Times*, Cambridge, 1676; 1763. (No Puritan, Folger was a Nantucket Quaker, grandfather of Benjamin Franklin.)

Ford, Worthington C., ed., "Epitaphs on Nowell, Endicott, Withington and Pole," *Publications of the Colonial Society of Massachusetts*, VIII (1906), 224–233.

Green, Joseph, *Entertainment for a Winter's Evening*, Boston, 1750.

—— *The Grand Arcanum Debated*, Boston, 1755.

—— *A Mournfull Lamentation for the Death of Mr. Old Tenor*, Boston, 1750.

Handkerchiefs from Paul, ed. K. B. Murdock, Cambridge, 1927. (Poems from six seventeenth-century Puritans. This well-edited volume contains the best introduction on Puritan poetry to be found.)

Harvard Heroics: A Collection of Eighteenth Century Verse Descriptions of Harvard College, ed. Robert A. Aubin, Cambridge, 1934. (Contains Mather Byles's Hogarthian sketch of a public Commencement.)

Hubbard, John, *A Monumental Gratitude Attempted, In a Poetical Relation of the Danger and Deliverance of Several of the Members of Yale-College in Passing the Sound, from Southold to New-Haven*, New London, 1727.

Johnson, Edward, *Wonder-working Providence.* [See section II A.] (Johnson's history is interspersed with many epitaphs and poetic memorials.)

Oakes, Urian, *An Elegy upon The Death of the Reverend Mr. Thomas Shepard,* Cambridge, 1677. Reprinted Boston, 1896. (Perhaps the best elegy written by a colonial Puritan.)

Pain, Philip, *Daily Meditations; or, Quotidian Preparations for and Considerations of Death and Eternity,* Cambridge, 1670. Reprinted with an Introduction by Leon Howard, San Marino, Calif., 1936.

Russell, Daniel, *An Almanack,* Cambridge, 1671.

Seccombe, John, "Father Abbey's Will," Cambridge, 1730; ed. John L. Sibley, 1854. (Verses on the college bedmaker.)

Select Essays, Boston, 1714. (A collection of poems and prose essays, written perhaps by young Harvard graduates.)

Steere, Richard, *The Daniel Catcher. The Life Of the Prophet Daniel: in a Poem. To which is Added, Earth's Felicities, Heaven's Allowances, A Blank Poem. With several other Poems,* Boston, 1713. (The earliest attempt in America to write black verse.)

—— *A Monumental Memorial of Marine Mercy Being An Acknowledgment of an High Hand of Divine Deliverance on the Deep in the Time of distress, in A Late Voyage from Boston in New-England To London,* Boston, 1684.

Taylor, Edward, "The Earliest Pcems of Edward Taylor," ed. Donald E. Stanford, *New England Quarterly,* XXXIII (1960), 136–151. (Early poems not included in Stanford's *Poems of Edward Taylor,* 1960.

—— "Nineteen Unpublished Poems by Edward Taylor," ed. Donald E. Stanford, *American Literature,* XXIX (1957),

18–46. (The essential Calvinism of Taylor's thought appears in these selections from "Sacramental Meditations.")

—— *The Poems of Edward Taylor,* ed. Donald E. Stanford, New Haven, 1960. (A full edition.)

—— "Poetical Works," Manuscript in Yale University Library. Selections ed. Thomas H. Johnson, *New England Quarterly,* X (1937), 290–322.

—— *The Poetical Works of Edward Taylor,* ed. Thomas H. Johnson with Introd. and Notes, New York, 1939. (Johnson's article in the *New England Quarterly* [above] and the publication of Taylor's collected works brought about a re-evaluation of the literature of the Puritans.)

—— "Some Edward Taylor Gleanings," *New England Quarterly,* XVI (1943), 280–295.

Tompson, Benjamin, *Works,* ed. Howard J. Hall, Boston, 1924.

Wigglesworth, Michael, "Gods Controversy with New England" (1662), *Proceedings of the Massachusetts Historical Society,* XII (1873), 83–93.

—— *Meat out of the Eater,* Cambridge, 1670[?]; 6th ed., New London, 1770. (See *Yale University Gazette,* V (1931), 45–47.)

—— *The Day of Doom,* Cambridge, 1662; ed. Kenneth B. Murdock, New York, 1929.

Wilson, John, *A Song or, Story, For the Lasting Remembrance of divers famous works,* London, 1626. (The same. Boston, 1680, *A Song of Deliverance.)*

Winslow, Ola E., ed., *American Broadside Verse from Imprints of the 17th and 18th Centuries,* New Haven, 1930.

Wolcott, Roger, *Poetical Meditations, being the Improvement of Some Vacant Hours,* New London, 1725; reprinted Boston, 1898.

B. PURITAN LITERATURE—SECONDARY WORKS

No general history of colonial literature has yet superseded Tyler's account, undertaken in the last quarter of the nineteenth century. The two-volume Duyckinck *Cyclopædia,* issued over a century ago, contains a large gathering of prose and verse; Stedman and Hutchinson's *Library* devotes three volumes to literature in the American colonial period, and remains the most extensive anthology.

Adams, Charles, F., "Milton's Impress on the Provincial Literature of New England," *Proceedings of the Massachusetts Historical Society,* XLII (1909), 154–170.

Barbeau, Marius, "Indian Captivities," *Proceedings of the American Philosophical Society*, XCIV (1950), 522–548.

Black, Mindele, "Edward Taylor: Heaven's Sugar Cake," *New England Quarterly*, XXIX (1956), 159–181.

Blau, Herbert, "Heaven's Sugar Cake: Theology and Imagery in the Poetry of Edward Taylor," *New England Quarterly*, XXVI (1953), 337–360.

Bleyer, Willard G., *Main Currents in the History of American Journalism*, Boston, 1927.

Bowden, Edwin T., "Benjamin Church's *Choice* and American Colonial Poetry," *New England Quarterly*, XXXII (1959), 170–184.

Boys, Richard C., "The Beginnings of the American Poetical Miscellany, 1714–1800," *American Literature*, XVII (1945), 127–139.

——— "The English Poetical Miscellany in Colonial America," *Studies in Philology*, XLII (1945), 114–130. (An annotated list of English miscellanies in American libraries, together with critical notes on the reception of poetic miscellanies in the American colonies.)

Bradford, Eugene F., "Conscious Art in Bradford's *History of Plymouth Plantation*," *New England Quarterly*, I (1928), 133–157.

Brown, Wallace C., "Edward Taylor, American Metaphysical," *American Literature*, XVI (1944), 186–197.

Cady, Edwin H., "The Artistry of Jonathan Edwards," *New England Quarterly*, XXII (1949), 61–72.

Cambridge History of American Literature, The, ed. William P. Trent and others, New York, 1917–1921, 4 vols.; 1933, 3 vols.; 1954, 3 vols. in one without the useful bibliographies of the earlier editions. (Vol. I covers the colonial period.)

Carleton, Phillips D., "The Indian Captivity," *American Literature*, XV (1943), 169–180. (Revaluation of the place of "captivity literature" in the social and literary history of America.)

Cook, Elizabeth C., *Literary Influences in Colonial Newspapers, 1704–1750*, New York, 1912.

Duyckinck, Evert A., and George L., eds., *Cyclopædia of American Literature*, New York, 1855, 2 vols. (Still useful.)

Dykema, Karl W., "Samuel Sewall Reads John Dryden," *American Literature*, XIV (1942), 157–161.

Fisch, Harold, "The Puritans and the Reform of Prose Style," *Journal of English Literary History*, XIX (1952), 229–248. (Influences of sermons and other writings of the Puritans in shaping plain prose.)

Fussell, Edwin S., "Benjamin Thompson, Public Poet," *New England Quarterly*, XXVI (1953), 494–511.

Galinsky, Hans, "Anne Bradstreet, Du Bartas, und Shakespeare in Zusammenhang kolonial Verpflanzung und Umformung europäischer Literatur: Ein forschungsbericht und eine Hypothese," *Festschrift fur Walther Fischer*, ed. Carl Winter, Heidelberg, 1959.

Goodman, William B., "Edward Taylor Writes His Love," *New England Quarterly*, XXVII (1954), 510–515.

Grabo, Norman S., "Catholic Tradition, Puritan Literature, and Edward Taylor," *Papers in Michigan Academy of Science, Arts, and Letters*, XLV (1959), 395–402.

——— "Edward Taylor on the Lord's Supper," *Boston Public Library Quarterly*, XII (1960), 22–36.

Greenough, Chester N., "The Publication of Cotton Mather's *Magnalia*," *Publications of the Colonial Society of Massachusetts*, XXVI (1927), 296–312.

Grierson, Herbert J. C., *Cross Currents in English Literature of the Seventeenth Century*, London, 1929.

Gummere, Richard M., "The Classics in a Brave New World," *Harvard Studies in Classical Philology*, LXII (1957), 118–139.

——— "The Heritage of the Classics in Colonial North America, an Essay in the Greco-Roman Tradition," *Proceedings of the American Philosophical Society*, XCIX (15 April, 1955), 68–78.

Haraszti, Zoltàn, *The Enigma of the Bay Psalm Book*, Chicago, 1956. (Attributes preface and a large part of the translations to John Cotton.)

Hart, James D., *The Oxford Companion to American Literature*, New York, 1956, 3rd edn. (A standard handbook.)

——— "A Puritan Bookshelf," *New Colophon*, I (1948), 13–26. (Reading and love of books among the New England colonists.)

Henson, Robert, "Form and Content of the Puritan Funeral Elegy," *American Literature*, XXXII (1960), 11–27.

Holden, William P., *Anti-Puritan Satire, 1572–1642*, New Haven, 1954.

Hornberger, Theodore, "A Note on Eighteenth-Century American Prose Style," *American Literature*, X (1938), 77–78. (Cites an early example (1708) of an American author being charged with provinciality in style.)

Howell, W. S., *Logic and Rhetorics in England, 1500–1700*, Princeton, 1956.

Jantz, Harold S., "The First Century of New England Verse," *Proceedings of the American Antiquarian Society*, LIII (1943), 219–258; reprinted Worcester, Mass., 1945. (Contains a critical and descriptive survey, selections, and an annotated, inclusive bibliography of early New England verse.)

—— "A Funeral Elegy for Thomas Danforth, Treasurer of Harvard," *Harvard Library Bulletin*, I (1947), 113–115.

Johnson, Thomas H., "The Discovery of Edward Taylor's Poetry," *Colophon, New Graphic Series* I, No. 2 (1939).

—— "A Seventeenth Century Printing of Some Verses of Edward Taylor," *New England Quarterly*, XIV (1941), 139–141. (Taylor exercised true poetic craftsmanship in giving his verses form.)

Jones, Howard M., "American Prose Style: 1700–1770," *Huntington Library Bulletin*, No. 6, 1934, 115–151.

—— "Desiderata in Colonial Literary History," *Publications of the Colonial Society of Massachusetts*, XXXII (1938), 428–439.

Jones, Richard F., "The Attack on Pulpit Eloquence in the Restoration: An Episode in the Development of the Neoclassical Standards for Prose," *Journal of English and Germanic Philology*, XXX (1931), 188–217. (A much neglected essay; essential reading for anyone with ideas about "Puritan Plain Style.")

—— "Science and English Prose Style in the Third Quarter of the Seventeenth Century," *Publications of the Modern Language Association*, XLV (1930), 977–1009.

—— "Science and Language in England of the Mid-seventeenth Century," *Journal of English and Germanic Philology*, XXXI (1932), 315–331. (The preceding three essays were republished in *The Seventeenth Century: Studies in the History of English Thought*, Stanford, 1948.)

—— *The Triumph of the English Language*, Stanford, 1953. (For Puritan views on Language, see especially Chapter X, "The Useful Language.")

Jordan, Philip D., "The Funeral Sermon; A Phase of American Journalism," *American Book Collector*, IV (1933), 177–188.

Koller, Kathrine, "The Puritan Preacher's Contribution to Fiction," *Huntington Library Quarterly*, XI (1948), 321–340.

Lee, James M., *History of American Journalism*, rev. ed., Boston, 1923.

Lind, S. E., "Edward Taylor, A Revaluation," *New England Quarterly*, XXI (1948), 518–530.

MacDougall, Hamilton C., *Early New England Psalmody: An Historical Appreciation, 1620–1820*, Brattleboro, 1940.

Manierre, William Reid, "Some Characteristic Mather Redactions," *New England Quarterly*, XXXI (1958), 496–505. (Mather's use of sources in the *Magnalia Christi Americana*.)

Matthiessen, Francis O., "Michael Wigglesworth, A Puritan Artist," *New England Quarterly*, I (1928), 491–504.

Miller, Perry, "The Rhetoric of Sensation," *Perspectives of Criticism*, ed. H. Levin, Cambridge, 1950; reprinted in P. Miller, *Errand into the Wilderness*, Cambridge, 1956, 167–183. (Edward's rhetoric of the naked idea.)

Mitchell, W. Fraser, *English Pulpit Oratory from Andrewes to Tillotson: A Study of its Literary Aspects*, London, 1932. (Indispensable for literary forms and values of sermons; excellent bibliography.)

Morison, Samuel E., "The Reverend Seaborn Cotton's Commonplace Book," *Publications of the Colonial Society of Massachusetts*, XXXII (1938), 320–352. (Family and church records interspersed with extracts from Sidney's *Arcadia*, and verses from ballads and amorous poetry.)

Murdock, Kenneth B., "The Colonial Experience in the Literature of the United States," *Papers of the American Philosophical Society*, C (1956), 129–132.

—— *Literature and Theology in Colonial*

New England, Cambridge, 1949; Harper Torchbook edition, 1962.

Nichols, Charles L., "The Holy Bible in Verse," *Proceedings of the American Antiquarian Society*, N.S. XXXVI (1926), 71–82. (Earliest written, 1699; earliest extant, 1717.)

Owst, Gerald R., *Literature and Pulpit in Medieval England*, Cambridge, Eng., 1933. (Important background.)

Pearce, Roy Harvey, "Edward Taylor: The Poet as Puritan," *New England Quarterly*, XXIII (1950), 31–46.

—— "The Significance of the Captivity Narrative," *American Literature*, XIX (1947), 1–20.

Peckham, Howard H., ed., *Captured by Indians: True Tales of Pioneer Survivors*, New Brunswick, N. J., 1954. (A popular retelling of fourteen "captivity" stories.)

Piercy, Josephine K., "The Character in the Literature of Early New England," *New England Quarterly*, XII (1939), 470–476.

—— *Studies in Literary Types in Seventeenth-Century America (1607–1710)*, New Haven, 1939.

Putnam, Michael C. J., ed., "The Story of the Storm," *New England Quarterly*, XXXIII (1960), 489–501. (Latin verse, c. 1706–1707; perhaps Sewall's.)

Quinn, Arthur Hobson, *et al.*, *The Literature of the American People: An Historical and Critical Survey*, New York, 1951. ("The Colonial and Revolutionary Period" by Kenneth B. Murdock is a valuable survey, but does not supplant *Literature and Theology in Colonial New England*. A useful bibliography with critical comments.)

Richardson, Caroline F., *English Preachers and Preaching, 1640–1670. A Secular Study*, New York, 1928. (Very useful for understanding the character of sermon literature.)

Richardson, Lyon N., *A History of Early American Magazines, 1741–1789*, New York, 1931. (Best history of the subject; immense bibliography.)

Rosenbach, Abraham S. W., *Early American Children's Books*, Portland, Me., 1933.

Russell, Jason A., "The Narratives of the Indian Captivities," *Education*, LI (1930), 84–88.

Shaaber, Matthias A., "Forerunners of the Newspaper in the United States," *Journalism Quarterly*, XI (1934), 339–347.

Shipton, Clifford K., "Literary Leaven in Provincial New England," *New England Quarterly*, IX (1936), 203–217.

Spiller, Robert E., *et al.*, *Literary History of the United States*, New York, 1948; 2 vols., with 3rd vol. of bibliographies, comp. by Thomas H. Johnson; revised one vol. edn., New York, 1953. (The best work of its kind.) *Bibliographical Supplement*, ed. Richard M. Ludwig, New York, 1959. (Earlier bibliographical vol. by Thomas H. Johnson continued through 1957 with some listings for 1958, and supplementary entries throughout.)

Stanford, Donald E., "Edward Taylor and the Lord's Supper," *American Literature*, XXVII (1955), 172–178. (Asserts Taylor's orthodoxy in this sacrament.)

—— "The Puritan Poet as Preacher, an Edward Taylor Sermon," *Studies in American Literature*, ed. Waldo McNeir and Leo B. Levy, Baton Rouge, 1960, 1–10.

Stedman, Edmund C., and Ellen M. Hutchinson, eds., *A Library of American Literature from the Earliest Settlement to the Present Time*, New York, 1888–1890, 11 vols. (Vols. I, II, and III cover the colonial period; the most extensive anthology.)

Stewart, Randall, "Puritan Literature and the Flowering of New England," *William and Mary Quarterly*, III (1946), 319–342.

Strange, Arthur, "Michael Wigglesworth Reads the Poets," *American Literature*, XXXI (1959), 325–326.

Svendsen, J. Kester, "Anne Bradstreet in England: A Bibliographical Note," *American Literature*, XIII (1941), 63–65. (Evidence of Anne's popularity in England during her lifetime.)

Swan, Bradford F., "Some Thoughts on the Bay Psalm Book of 1640, with a Census of Copies," *Yale University Library Gazette*, XXII (1948), 56–76.

Thayer, William R., "Pen Portraiture in Seventeenth Century Colonial Historians," *Proceedings of the American Antiquarian Society*, N.S., XXXI (1921), 61–69.

Thompson, W. Lawrence, "Classical Echoes in Sewall's Diaries (1674–1729),"

New England Quarterly, XXIV (1951), 374-377. (A temporary decline in the classical tradition revealed by "primitive" specimens of colonial Latin verse.)

Titus, Anson, "Madam Sarah Knight, Her Diary and Her Times," *Bostonian Society Publications*, IX (1912), 99-126.

Tyler, Moses C., *A History of American Literature during the Colonial Period, 1607-1765*, New York, 1878, 2 vols.; rev. ed., 1897; Ithaca, New York, 1949. (Still the best discussion of colonial American literature. Should be consulted in the 1949 edn., a reprint of the 1878 edn. with the changes made in the three later edns. indicated in footnotes containing Tyler's own marginal notes to the first edn. Introduction by Howard Mumford Jones.)

Vail, Robert W. G., "Certain Indian Captives of New England," *Proceedings of the Massachusetts Historical Society*, LXVIII (1944-1947), 1952, 113-131.

Warren, Austin, "Edward Taylor's Poetry: Colonial Baroque," *Kenyon Review*, III (1941), 355-371. Reprinted in Warren's *Rage for Order*, Chicago, 1947, 1-18.

Watters, Reginald E., "Biographical Technique in Cotton Mather's *Magnalia*," *William and Mary Quarterly*, II (1945), 154-163.

Weathers, Willie T., "Edward Taylor, Hellenistic Puritan," *American Literature*, XVIII (1946), 18-26.

—— "Edward Taylor and the Cambridge Platonists," *American Literature*, XXVI (1954), 1-31. (His large debt to the Southern Renaissance and the Platonists explains why he could be both a good New England Puritan and a good poet.)

Wendell, Barrett, *A Literary History of America*, 6th ed., New York, 1911. (Heavily biased in favor of the Puritan tradition, but written on the basis of deep knowledge of the seventeenth century.)

—— *The Temper of the Seventeenth Century in English Literature*, New York, 1904.

White, Elizabeth Wade, "The Tenth Muse—A Tercentenary Appraisal of Anne Bradstreet," *William and Mary Quarterly*, VIII (July, 1951), 355-377.

White, Helen C., *English Devotional Literature, 1600-1640*, Madison, Wis., 1931. (Valuable study of religious prose.)

White, Trentwell M., and Paul W. Lehmann, *Writers of Colonial New England*, Boston, 1929.

Winship, George Parker, *The Cambridge Press, 1638-1692. A Reexamination of the Evidence Concerning the Bay Psalm Book and the Eliot Indian Bible as well as other Contemporary Books and People*, Philadelphia, 1945.

Wright, Nathalia, "The Morality Tradition in the Poetry of Edward Taylor," *American Literature*, XVIII (1946), 1-17.

Wroth, Lawrence C., "John Maylem: Poet and Warrior," *Publications of the Colonial Society of Massachusetts*, XXXII (1938), 87-120.

VIII. EDUCATION

No colonizing Puritan wrote formal discourses on education; his theories for the training of youth are expressed in funeral sermons, diaries, letters, and public addresses. Further bibliographical data is supplied in the headings throughout the chapter on Education.

A. PRIMARY SOURCES

Puritans, like other cultivated Englishmen of the time, were deeply concerned in acquiring an education, as their incidental remarks make sufficiently clear.

Chauncy, Charles, *Gods Mercy, shewed to his people in giving them a faithful Ministry and schooles of Learning for the continual supplyes thereof*, Cambridge, 1655.

Colman, Benjamin, *The Master Taken up from the Sons of the Prophets*, Boston, 1724. (Funeral sermon on President Leverett.)

Hancock, John, *The Danger of an Unqualified Ministry*, Boston, 1743. (A sermon directed against itinerant preachers and an illiterate clergy.)

Harvard College Records, Publications of the Colonial Society of Massachusetts, Vols. XV, XVI, XXXI (1925-1935).

Hoar, Leonard, "[Letter] To his

Freshman Nephew, Josiah Flynt," 1661, in Samuel E. Morison, *Harvard College in the Seventeenth Century*, Cambridge, 1936, 639–644.

Keach, Benjamin, *The Protestant Tutor for Children*, Boston, 1685.

Mather, Cotton, *Corderius Americanus. An Essay upon the Good Education of Children*, Boston, 1708. (A funeral sermon upon Ezekiel Cheever.)

—— "Special Points," *The Diary of Cotton Mather*, ed. Worthington C. Ford, *Collections of the Massachusetts Historical Society*, seventh series, VII (1911), 534–537. (An outline, dated February 1705/06, relating to the education of his children.)

Mather, Increase, "Presidential Address," *ca.* 1696, in Samuel E. Morison, *Harvard College in the Seventeenth Century*, Cambridge, 1936, p. 167.

New Englands First Fruits, London, 1643. Reprinted various times: most recently in a line-for-line and word-for-word reprint in Samuel E. Morison, *The Founding of Harvard College*, Cambridge, 1935, 419–447. (An account of the first commencement at Harvard in 1642; classic statement of the Puritan educational ideal.)

Shepard, Thomas, Jr., "A Letter . . . to his Son at his Admission into the College," *Publications of the Colonial Society of Massachusetts*, XIV (1913), 192–198.

B. Secondary Works

Detailed and accurate studies of Puritan education, necessarily slow in appearing, are still in progress. The works in this field by Morison and Seybolt are especially noteworthy.

Adamson, John W., *Pioneers of Modern Education, 1600–1700*, Cambridge, Eng., 1905.

Allen, Phyllis, "Medical Education in Seventeenth Century England," *Journal of the History of Medicine and Allied Sciences*, I (1946), 115–143.

—— "Scientific Studies in Seventeenth Century English Universities," *Journal of the History of Ideas*, X (1949), 219–253.

Bainton, Roland H., *Yale and the Ministry: A History of Education for the Christian Ministry at Yale from the Founding in 1701*, New York, 1957.

Cairns, Earle E., "The Puritan Philosophy of Education," *Biblioteca Sacra*, CIV (1947), 326–336.

Chamberlain, Joshua L., and others, *Yale University*, Boston, 1900.

Chaplin, Jeremiah, *Life of Henry Dunster*, Boston, 1872. (Contains many important documents.)

Clapp, Clifford B., "Christo et Ecclesiae," *Publications of the Colonial Society of Massachusetts*, XXV (1924), 59–83.

Costello, William T., *The Scholastic Curriculum of Early Seventeenth-Century Cambridge*, Cambridge, 1958.

Cubberley, E. P., *Public Education in the United States*, Boston, 1919. (Convenient bibliographies.)

Dexter, Franklin B., *Documentary History of Yale University, 1701–1745*, New Haven, 1916.

Ford, Paul L., *The New-England Primer*, New York, 1897.

Gambrell, Mary L., *Ministerial Training in Eighteenth-Century New England*, New York, 1937.

Hale, Richard Walden, "The First Independent School in America," *Publications of the Colonial Society of Massachusetts*, XXXV (1942–1946), 1951, 225–297. (Early history of Roxbury Latin School, and some records of the Ipswich Grammar School.)

—— *History of the Roxbury Latin School*, Cambridge, 1946.

Hansen, Allen O., *Liberalism and American Education in the Eighteenth Century*, New York, 1926. (The emphasis is mainly on the latter half of the century; well documented, with a good bibliography of primary sources.)

Hazlitt, William C., *Schools, School-books and Schoolmasters*, London, 1888.

Holmes, Pauline, *A Tercentenary History of the Boston Public Latin School, 1635–1935*, Cambridge, 1935.

Hudson, Winthrop S., "The Morison Myth Concerning the Founding of Harvard College," *Church History*, VIII (1939), 148–159. (Morison "represents the establishment of Harvard College as a great adventure in secular education," rather than as an effort to provide for the training of ministers.)

Johnson, Clifton, *Old-Time Schools and School-Books*, New York, 1904.

Klain, Zora, *Educational Activities of New England Quakers*, Philadelphia, 1928.

Lane, William C., "Early Harvard Broadsides," *Proceedings of the American Antiquarian Society*, N.S. XXIV (1914), 264–304.

Latimer, John F. and Kenneth B. Murdock, "The 'Author' of Cheever's Accidence," *Classical Journal*, XLVI (1951), 391–397. (Establishes that Nathaniel Williams was "Author" or editor of the first five editions of the first Latin text written and published in America.)

Littlefield, George E., *Early Schools and School-Books of New England*, Boston, 1904.

—— "Elijah Corlet and the 'Faire Grammar Schoole' at Cambridge," *Publications of the Colonial Society of Massachusetts*, XVII (1915), 131–140.

McAnear, Beverly, "The Raising of Funds by the Colonial Colleges," *Mississippi Valley Historical Review*, XXXVIII (1951–1952), 591–612.

Matthews, Albert, "A Proposal for the Enlargement of University Learning in New England, 1658–1660," *Proceedings of the Massachusetts Historical Society*, XLI (1908), 301–308.

Meriwether, Colyer, *Our Colonial Curriculum, 1607–1776*, Washington, 1907.

Meyer, Isidore S., "Hebrew at Harvard, 1636–1760," *Publications of the American Jewish Historical Society*, No. 35, 145–170.

Middlekauff, Robert, "The Classical Curriculum in Eighteenth Century New England," *William and Mary Quarterly*, XVIII (1961), 54–67.

Morgan, Edmund S., "Ezra Stiles: The Education of a Yale Man, 1742–1746," *Huntington Library Quarterly*, XVII (1953–1954), 251–268.

Morison, Samuel E., *The Founding of Harvard College*, Cambridge, 1935. (A history of intellectual backgrounds and movements as well as of Harvard, the volume presents the college as a school of culture, not simply as a theological seminary.)

—— *Harvard College in the Seventeenth Century*, Cambridge, 1936, 2 vols.

—— "Precedence at Harvard College in the Seventeenth Century," *Proceedings of the American Antiquarian Society*, N.S. XLII (1932), 371–431.

Murdock, Kenneth B., "The Teaching of Latin and Greek at the Boston Latin School in 1712," *Publications of the Colonial Society of Massachusetts*, XXVII (1932), 21–29.

—— "Cotton Mather and the Rectorship of Yale College," *Publications of the Colonial Society of Massachusetts*, XXVI (1927), 388–401.

Nash, Roy, "Abiah Holbrook and His 'Writing-Master's Amusement'," *Harvard Library Bulletin*, VII (1953), 88–104.

—— "A Colonial Writing Master's Collection of English Copybooks," *Harvard Library Bulletin*, XIV (1960), 12–19.

Oviatt, Edwin, *The Beginnings of Yale, 1701–1726*, New Haven, 1916.

Parker, Irene, *Dissenting Academies in England*, Cambridge, Eng., 1914.

Pears, Thomas Clinton, Jr., "Colonial Education among Presbyterians," *Journal of Presbyterian History*, XXX (1952), 115–126, 165–174.

Perrin, Porter G., "Possible Sources of *Technologia* at Early Harvard," *New England Quarterly*, VII (1934), 718–724.

—— "The Teaching of Rhetoric in American Colleges before 1750," Manuscript dissertation, University of Chicago, 1936.

Pfeiffer, Robert H., "The Teaching of Hebrew in Colonial America," *Jewish Quarterly Review*, XLV (1955), 363–373.

Plimpton, George A., "The Hornbook and Its Use in America," *Proceedings of the American Antiquarian Society*, N.S. XXVI (1916), 264–272.

Pool, David de S., "Hebrew Learning Among the Puritans of New England Prior to 1700," *Publications of the American Jewish Historical Society*, XX (1911), 31–83.

Potter, David, *Debating in the Colonial Chartered Colleges: 1642–1900*, New York, 1944.

Rand, Benjamin, "Philosophical Instruction in Harvard University from 1636 to 1906," *Harvard Graduates' Magazine*, XXXVII (1928), 29–47, 188–200, 296–311.

Rand, Edward K., "Liberal Education in Seventeenth-Century Harvard," *New England Quarterly*, VI (1933), 525–551.

Rashdall, Hastings, *The Universities of Europe in the Middle Ages*, revised by F. M. Powicke and A. B. Emden, Oxford, 1936. (Essential for backgrounds of Puritan education and culture.)

Robbins, Fred G., "Salaries of School-teachers in Colonial America," *Monthly Labor Review*, XXVIII (1929), 27–31.

Seybolt, Robert F., *Apprenticeship & Apprenticeship Education in Colonial New England & New York*, New York, 1917.

——— *The Evening School in Colonial America*, Urbana, Ill., 1925.

——— *The Private Schools of Colonial Boston*, Cambridge, 1935.

——— "The Private Schools of Seventeenth-Century Boston," *New England Quarterly*, VIII (1935), 418–424.

——— *The Public Schools of Colonial Boston, 1635–1775*, Cambridge, 1935.

——— "Schoolmasters of Colonial Boston," *Publications of the Colonial Society of Massachusetts*, XXVII (1932), 130–156.

Shipton, Clifford K., "Secondary Education in the Puritan Colonies," *New England Quarterly*, VII (1934), 646–661.

(During the eighteenth century public schools improved in quality.)

Small, Walter H., *Early New England Schools*, Boston, 1914.

Steiner, Bernard C., *The History of Education in Connecticut*, Washington, 1893.

Tucker, Louis Leonard, "President Thomas Clap and the Rise of Yale College, 1740–1766," *The Historian*, XIX (1956–1957), 66–81.

Tuer, Andrew W., *The History of the Horn-Book*, London, 1896.

Updegraff, Harlan, *The Origin of the Moving School in Massachusetts*, New York, 1907.

Vincent, W. A. L., *The State and School Education 1640–1660 in England and Wales*, London, 1950.

Walsh, James J., "Scholasticism in the Colonial Colleges," *New England Quarterly*, V (1932), 483–532.

Williams, George H., *Wilderness and Paradise in Christian Thought*, New York, 1961. (Part Two, a revision of "Excursus" from *Harvard Divinity School*, Boston, 1954, traces the Christian tradition in the Puritan idea of education.)

Wood, Norman, *The Reformation and English Education*, London, 1931.

IX. SCIENCE

The speculative nature of the Puritan made him keenly alert to developments in the scientific field. As long as he saw the shaping hand of God in the phenomenal universe, he not only accepted scientific inquiry but sought to advance it. He gathered data on earthquakes, thunderstorms, comets; on farming and the natural history of New England; on medical prodigies and physical disease. Most notably of all, he advanced the cause of inoculation for smallpox.

A. PRIMARY SOURCES

The student should note particularly the number of contributions made by Puritans to the *Philosophical Transactions* of the Royal Society of London.

Boylston, Zabdiel, "The way of proceeding in the Small Pox inoculated in New England," *Philosophical Transactions*, Royal Society of London, XXXII (1721), No. 370, pp. 33–35. (Written in collaboration with Cotton Mather.)

Brattle, William, *Sundry Rules and Regulations for Drawing up a Regiment*, Boston, 1733.

A Brief Rule To guide the Common-People of New-England How to order themselves and theirs in the Small Pocks, or Measles, Boston,

1677. (A broadside; the earliest medical treatise printed in the colonies.)

Colman, Benjamin, *Some Observations on the New Method of Receiving the Small-Pox, by ingrafting or inoculating*, Boston, 1721.

Cooper, William, *A Letter . . . Attempting a Solution of the Objections . . . Against the New Way of Receiving the Small-Pox*, Boston, 1721.

Danforth, Samuel, *An Astronomical Description of the Late Comet or Blazing Star, As it appeared in New-England in the 9th,*

10th, 11th and in the beginning of the 12th Moneth, 1664. Together With a brief Theological Application thereof, Cambridge, 1665.

Doolittle, Thomas, *Earthquakes Explained and practically Improved*, London, 1693.

Dudley, Paul, "An Account of the Method of Making Sugar from the Juice of the Maple Tree in New England," *Philosophical Transactions*, Royal Society of London, XXXI (1720), No. 364, pp. 27, 28. (Dudley contributed in all, twelve scientific essays to the *Philosophical Transactions*. For a bibliography, see Sibley's *Biographical Sketches*, IV, 54.)

Edwards, Jonathan, "Some Early Writings of Jonathan Edwards," ed. Egbert C. Smyth, *Proceedings of the American Antiquarian Society*, N.S. X (1895), 212–247; XI (1896), 251–252.

—— "Of Insects," ed. Egbert C. Smyth, *Andover Review*, XIII (1890), 1–19.

Greenwood, Isaac, *An Experimental Course on Mechanical Philosophy*, Boston, 1726.

—— *A Friendly Debate; or, A Dialogue Between Academicus; and Sawny & Mundungus, Two Eminent Physicians, About some of their Late Performances*, Boston, 1722. (A satire.)

—— *A Philosophical Discourse concerning the Mutability and Changes of the Material World*, Boston, 1731.

Hoar, Leonard, "Letter to Mr. Robert Boyle," in Boyle's *Works* (London, 1744, 6 vols.), V, 642, 643; reprinted in S. E. Morison, *Harvard College in the Seventeenth Century*, Cambridge, 1936, pp. 644–646.

Lee, Samuel, 'Ελεοριαμβος. *Or the Triumph of Mercy in the Chariot of Praise. A Treatise Of Preventing secret & unexpected Mercies*, Boston, 1718.

A Letter from One in the Country, to His Friend in the City; in Relation to the Distress Occasioned by . . . Inoculation, Boston, 1721.

Mather, Cotton, "Account of a great storm, 1723," *Collections of the Massachusetts Historical Society*, first series, II, (1810), 11.

—— *A Letter to a Friend in the Country, Attempting a Solution of the Scruples . . . against the New Way of receiving the Small-Pox*, Boston, 1721.

—— *The Christian Philosopher: A Collection of the Best Discoveries in Nature, with Religious Improvements*, London, 1721. (The most important indication of New England's familiarity with the scientific advance.)

—— *Ignorantia Scientifica*, Boston, 1727.

Mather, Increase, *A Discourse Concerning Earthquakes*, Boston, 1706.

—— *An Essay for the Recording of Illustrious Providences*, Boston, 1684. Reprinted with introduction by George Offor, under the title *Remarkable Providences*, London, 1856; 1890.

—— ΚΟΜΗΤΟΓΡΑΦΙΑ. *Or A Discourse Concerning Comets*, Boston, 1683; London, 1811.

—— *The Latter-Sign Discoursed of*. Paged separately in the second edition of *Heavens Alarm to the World*, Boston, 1682.

—— *Severall Reasons Proving that Inoculation . . . is a Lawful Practice*, Boston, 1721; ed. with introduction by George L. Kittredge, Cleveland, 1921.

—— *The Voice of God, in Stormy Winds*, Boston, 1704.

Mather, Samuel, *A Letter to Doctor Zabdiel Boylston; Occasion'd by a late Dissertation concerning Inoculation*, Boston, 1730.

Morton, Charles, *Compendium Physicae*, ed. Theodore Hornberger with introd. by Samuel Eliot Morison. Publications, Colonial Society of Massachusetts, XXXIII (*Collections*), Boston, 1940. (In manuscript, this was the standard textbook of natural science at Harvard College at the end of the seventeenth century.)

Paine, Thomas, *The Doctrine of Earthquakes*, Boston, 1728.

Prince, Thomas, "Account of the Northern Lights, when first seen in England, 1716," *Collections of the Massachusetts Historical Society*, first series, II (1793), 14–20.

—— *Earthquakes the Works of God*, Boston, 1727.

Robie, Thomas, *A Letter to a Certain Gentleman desiring a particular Account may be given of a wonderful meteor*, Boston, 1719.

Thatcher, Thomas, *A Brief Rule to Guide the Common-people of New-England how to Order Themselves and Theirs in the Small Pocks, or Measles*, Boston, 1677; reprinted with a valuable introd. by Henry R. Viets, Baltimore, 1937.

Williams, John, *Several Arguments Proving that the Inoculating of the Small-Pox is* not Contained in the Law of Physick, Either Natural or Divine, and therefore Unlawful, Boston, 1721.

—— An Answer to a Late Pamphlet, intitled, A Letter to a Friend in the Country, Boston, 1722.

Winthrop, John, Jr., "Correspondence with Members of the Royal Society," Proceedings of the Massachusetts Historical Society, XVI (1878), 206–251.

—— "An Extract of a Letter . . . concerning some Natural Curiosities," Philosophical Transactions, Royal Society of London, V (1670), 1151–1153.

Winthrop, John (1681–1747), "Account of the Winter, 1717," Collections of the Massachusetts Historical Society, first series, II (1793), 11, 12. (This John Winthrop of Boston, as well as his uncle, John Winthrop, Jr., governor of Connecticut, was a member of the Royal Society of London.)

B. POPULAR SCIENCE IN THE ALMANACS

The almanacs of New England, edited by a series of young Harvard graduates, often contain a page or two of scientific information especially designed for popular instruction. Even though brief, the articles indicate on the one hand the knowledge of the authors, and on the other the interest of the people. See Samuel E. Morison, Harvard College in the Seventeenth Century, pp. 216–219; see also in this bibliography Section IV B 1. The arrangement here is chronological.

T. S. [Thomas Shepard, Jr.?], "A Brief Explication of the most observable Circles in the Heavens," Almanack, Cambridge, 1656.

Brigden, Zechariah, "A breif Explication and proof of the Philolaick Systeme," Almanack, Cambridge, 1659; reprinted in New England Quarterly, VII (1934), 9–12. (The first recorded exposition of the Copernican system in New England.)

Cheever, Samuel, "A breif discourse concerning the various Periods of time," Almanack, Cambridge, 1660.

—— "A breif Discourse of the Rise and Progress of Astronomy," Almanack, Cambridge, 1661.

Chauncy, Nathaniel, "The primum mobile," Almanack, Cambridge, 1662.

Chauncy, Israel, "The Theory of Planetary Orbs," Almanack, Cambridge, 1663.

Nowell, Alexander, "The Suns Prerogative Vindicated," Almanack, Cambridge, 1665.

J. S. [John Sherman or Jeremiah Shepard?], "A Postscript to the preceding Kalender," Almanack, Cambridge, 1674.

Foster, J[ohn], "A brief Description of the Coelestial Orbs according to the Opinion of that Ancient Philosopher Pythagoras, and of all later Astronomers," Almanack, Boston, 1675. (Foster was the first printer in Boston.)

Sherman, John, "Of Eclipses of the Sun and Moon," Almanack, Cambridge, 1676.

J. F. [John Foster], "The Course of the Spring-tides this year," Almanack, Boston, 1678.

J. D. [John Danforth], "A Brief Memorial of some few Remarkable Occurrences in the 6 preceding yeares," Almanack, Cambridge, 1679.

Foster, John, "Postscript," Almanack, Boston, 1679. (An explanation of leap-year.)

—— "The Natures and Operations of the seven Planets," Almanack, Boston, 1680.

—— "Of Comets, Their Motion, Distance & Magnitude," followed by "Observations of a Comet seen this last Winter 1680, and how it appeared at Boston," Almanack, Boston, 1681.

Brattle, William, "An Explanation of the Preceding Ephemeris," Ephemeris, Cambridge, 1682. (A series of philosophical and scientific observations on Reason, the calendar, eclipses, and the planets.)

Mather, Cotton, "A Description of the Last Years Comet," Ephemeris, Boston, 1683.

Russell, N[oadiah], "Concerning Lightning, and Thunder," Ephemeris, Cambridge, 1684.

Williams, W[illiam], "Concerning a Rainbow"; "Concerning the nature of Comets," Ephemeris, Cambridge, 1685.

Mather, Nathaniel, "A short view of the Discoveries that have been made in the Heavens with, and since the invention of the Telescope," *Ephemeris*, Boston, 1685.

—— "Concerning some late discoveries respecting the fixed Stars"; "Concerning late marvellous Astronomical Discoveries in the Planets," *Ephemeris*, Boston, 1686.

Danforth, Samuel, "Ad Librum," *New-England Almanack*, Cambridge, 1686. (Dedicatory poem, with defence of astronomy.)

Tulley, John, "Of the Rain-bow: Whence it is, and what it signifieth"; "Of Thunder and Lightning," *Almanack*, Boston, 1690.

Newman, Henry, "A Postscript Exhibiting somewhat Touching the Earth's Motion," *Harvard's Ephemeris, or Almanack*, Cambridge, 1690.

—— "Of Telescopes," *News from the Stars, An Almanack*, Boston, 1691.

Tulley, John, "Astronomicall Observations of the Weather & Winds from the Planets & their Aspects," *Almanack*, Cambridge, 1692.

Brattle, William, "A Postscript concerning the Tides, Weather, etc.," *Almanack*, Boston, 1694.

Lodowick, C[hristian], Concerning "certain Impieties and Absurdities" in the "Astrological Predictions" of Tulley: "As for Meteorology, it is meerly conjectural," *New-England Almanack*, Boston, 1695.

Tulley, John, "Concerning Astrology & Meteorology," *Almanack*, Boston, 1696. (An answer to the attack of Lodowick.)

C. WITCHCRAFT

Material concerning witchcraft is also to be found in the *Diary* of Cotton Mather and the *Diary* of Samuel Sewall. See also Justin Winsor, *The Memorial History of Boston*, Vol. II; John G. Palfrey, *A Compendious History of New England*, IV, 96 ff; John Fiske, *New France and New England* (New York, 1902).

1. Primary Sources

The number of items here listed is limited to such as are historically important; the list is by no means exhaustive.

Brattle, Thomas, "A Full and Candid Account of the Delusion called Witchcraft which prevailed in New England," (MS. ca. 1692), *Collections of the Massachusetts Historical Society*, first series, V (1798), 61–80.

Burr, George L., ed., *Narratives of the Witchcraft Cases, 1648–1706*, New York, 1914; 1959. (The volume includes the essential portions of works concerned with Salem witchcraft: Cotton Mather, *Late Memorable Providences*, 1691; Deodat Lawson, *Brief and True Narrative*, 1692; Thomas Brattle, *A Full and Candid Account of the Delusions*, 1692; Cotton Mather, *Wonders of the Invisible World*, 1693; Cotton Mather, *A Brand Pluck'd out of the Burning*, 1693; Robert Calef, *More Wonders*, 1700.)

Hale, John, *A Modest Enquiry into the Nature of Witchcraft*, Boston, 1702.

Hutchinson, Francis, *An Historical Essay concerning Witchcraft*, London, 1718.

Hutchinson, Thomas, *The Witchcraft Delusion of 1692*, ed. W. F. Poole, Boston, 1870.

Lawson, Deodat, *Christs Fidelity the Only Shield Against Satans Malignity*, Boston, 1693. (A terrifying sermon, delivered at Danvers (Salem Village), March 24, 1692, at the height of the panic; an explicit statement of the Puritan conception of the character and role of the devil.)

Mather, Increase, *Cases of Conscience Concerning Evil Spirits Personating Men; Witchcrafts, Infallible Proofs of Guilt in such as are Accused with that Crime*, Boston, 1693; London, 1693; 1862. (The statement of rules and procedure in the examination of witches which, had it been followed by the Court at Salem, would have prevented the craze and the executions. See Kenneth B. Murdock, *Increase Mather*, pp. 287–316.)

—— *A Disquisition Concerning Angelical-Apparitions*, Boston, 1696.

Turell, Ebenezer, "Detection of Witchcraft," *Collections of the Massachusetts Historical Society*, second series, X (1823), 6–22.

Woodward, William E., ed., *Records of Salem Witchcraft*, Roxbury, Mass., 1864, 2 vols.

2. Secondary Works (Witchcraft)

Because of the fierceness of the controversy, the witchcraft delusion has often been disproportionately emphasized in Puritan history. Actually it played but a small part in affairs and was soon over.

Coffin, Joshua, *A Sketch of the History of Newbury, [Massachusetts], . . . from 1635 to 1845*, Boston, 1845.

Drake, Samuel G., *Annals of Witchcraft in New England, and Elsewhere in the United States*, Boston, 1869.

—— *The Witchcraft Delusion in New England*, Roxbury, Mass., 1866, 3 vols. (Contains original records and depositions.)

Fowler, Samuel P., *An Account of the Life . . . of the Rev. Samuel Parris*, Salem, 1857.

Fuess, Claude Moore, "Witches at Andover," *Proceedings of the Massachusetts Historical Society*, LXX (1950–1953), 1957, 8–20.

Greene, Samuel A., *Groton in Witchcraft Times*, Groton, Mass., 1883.

Gummere, Amelia M., *Witchcraft and Quakerism*, Philadelphia, 1908.

Haraszti, Zoltán, "Cotton Mather and the Witchcraft Trials," *More Books*, XV (1940), 179–184. (In a letter of Cotton Mather to John Cotton, Mather betrays sensitiveness to criticism of the judges of the witchcraft cases.)

Haven, Samuel F., *The Mathers and the Witchcraft Delusions*, Worcester, 1874.

Holmes, Thomas J., "Cotton Mather and His Writings on Witchcraft," *Papers of the Bibliographical Society of America*, XVIII (1925), 30–59.

Kittredge, George L., *Witchcraft in Old and New England*, Cambridge, 1929. (The chapter on witchcraft in New England is the definitive analysis, based upon exhaustive knowledge of the whole history of witchcraft in Europe.)

Lea, Henry Charles, *Materials toward a History of Witchcraft, collected by Henry Charles Lea*, arranged and edited by Arthur C. Howland, Philadelphia, 1939. (Provides a background for the American student with its exposition of the logical system that directed popular opinion and guided the actions of ecclesiastical and secular authorities in witchcraft cases. Describes methods of trial and court procedures.)

Levermore, Charles H., "Witchcraft in Connecticut," *New England Magazine*, N.S. VI (1892), 636–644.

Nevins, Winfield S., *Witchcraft in Salem Village in 1692*, Salem, 1916.

Notestein, Wallace, *A History of Witchcraft in England from 1558 to 1718*, Washington, 1911.

Poole, William F., "Cotton Mather and Salem Witchcraft," *North American Review*, CVIII (1869), 337–397. (Defense of Mather against C. W. Upham.)

Starkey, Marion L., *The Devil in Massachusetts: A Modern Inquiry Into the Salem Witch Trials*, New York, 1949. (A triumph of historical reconstruction; makes the trials, confessions, hysteria, and repentances credible.)

Summers, Montague, *The Geography of Witchcraft*, New York, 1927.

—— *The History of Witchcraft and Demonology*, New York, 1926.

Tapley, Charles S., *Rebecca Nurse, Saint but Witch Victim*, Boston, 1930.

Taylor, John M., *The Witchcraft Delusion in Colonial Connecticut, 1647–1697*, New York, 1908.

Upham, Charles W., *Salem Witchcraft and Cotton Mather*, Morrisania, N.Y., 1869. (Reply to Poole's defense.)

—— *Salem Witchcraft; with an Account of Salem Village, and a History of Opinions on Witchcraft and Kindred Subjects*, Boston, 1867, 2 vols.

Williams, Charles, *Witchcraft*, London, 1941; Forest Hills, 1944. (A history of witchcraft in Christendom.)

Winsor, Justin, "The Literature of Witchcraft in New England," *Proceedings of the American Antiquarian Society*, N.S. X (1895), 351–373.

D. SECONDARY WORKS

In addition to the items here listed, the student should consult Samuel E. Morison, *Harvard College in the Seventeenth Century*, chapters X, XI, and XIII, dealing with the teaching of mathematics, astronomy, physics, and medicine.

Bates, Ralph S., *Scientific Societies in the United States*, New York, 1945.

Beall, Otho T., Jr., "Cotton Mather's Early 'Curiosa Americana' and the Boston Philosophical Society of 1683," *William and Mary Quarterly*, XVIII (1961), 360–372. (Reports of a short-lived scientific society, the earliest in America.)

——, and Richard H. Shryock, *Cotton Mather: First Significant Figure in American Medicine*, Baltimore, 1954. (An important contribution to our understanding of colonial medical thought; contains generous selections from Cotton Mather's *Angel of Bethesda*.)

Bedinfeld, Malcolm S., "The Early New England Doctor: An Adaptation to a Provincial Environment," *Yale Journal of Biology and Medicine*, XV (1942–1943), 99–132, 271–288. (A Senior Thesis in History, Yale University, based on printed records and other literature.)

Bell, Whitfield J., "Medical Practice in Colonial America," *Bulletin of the History of Medicine*, XXXI (1957), 442–453.

Bernstein, Solon S., "Smallpox: Its Historical Significance in American Colonies," *Autograph Collectors' Journal*, V (1953), 14–23.

Blake, John R., *Public Health in the Town of Boston, 1630–1822*, Cambridge, 1959. (Illustrates and illuminates the attitudes of the time not only toward disease and death but also toward other basic social and political questions.)

Brasch, Frederick E., *John Winthrop (1714–1779), America's First Astronomer, and the Science of His Period*, San Francisco, 1916.

—— "The Newtonian Epoch in the American Colonies [1680–1783]," *Proceedings of the American Antiquarian Society*, XLIX (1939), 314–332.

—— "Newton's First Critical Disciple in the American Colonies—John Winthrop [Jr.]," in *Sir Isaac Newton, 1727–1927*, Baltimore, 1928, 301–338.

—— "The Royal Society of London and Its Influence upon Scientific Thought in the American Colonies," *Scientific Monthly*, XXXIII (1931), 336–355, 448–469.

Bronfenbrenner, Martha (Ornstein), *The Role of the Scientific Societies in the Seventeenth Century*, New York, 1913. (A key book for the study of the influence of science on general thought.)

Brown, Francis H., "The Practice of Medicine in New England Before the Year 1700," *Bostonian Society Publications*, VIII (1911), 93–120.

Browne, Charles A., "Scientific notes from the books and letters of John Winthrop, Jr.," *Isis*, XI (1928), 325–342.

Buck, Albert H., *The Growth of Medicine from the Earliest Times to about 1800*, New Haven, 1917.

Bush, Douglas, "Two Roads to Truth: Science and Religion in the Early Seventeenth Century," *Journal of English Literary History*, VIII (1941), 81–102.

Butterfield, Herbert, *The Origins of Modern Science 1300–1800*, London and New York, 1949.

Cohen, I. Bernard, *Some Early Tools of American Science: An Account of Early Scientific Instruments and Mineralogical and Biological Collections in Harvard College*, Cambridge, 1950.

Farmer, Laurence, "When Cotton Mather Fought the Smallpox," *American Heritage*, VIII (1957), 40–43, 109.

Fitz, Reginald H., "Zabdiel Boylston, Inoculator, and the Epidemic of Smallpox in Boston in 1721," *John Hopkins Hospital Bulletin*, XXII (1911), 315–327.

Forbes, Allyn B., "William Brattle and John Leverett, F.R.S.," *Publications of the Colonial Society of Massachusetts*, XXVIII (1935), 222–224.

Gordon, Maurice Bear, *Aesculapius Comes to the Colonies: The Story of the Early Days of Medicine in the Thirteen Original Colonies*, Ventnor, N. J., 1949. (Little original research, occasionally inaccurate.)

Green, Samuel A., *History of Medicine in Massachusetts*, Boston, 1881.

Guerra, F., "Harvey and the Circulation of Blood in America during the Colonial Period," *Bulletin of the History of Medicine*, XXXIII (1959), 212–229.

Hornberger, Theodore, "American Puritanism and the Rise of the Scientific Mind," unpublished dissertation, University of Michigan, 1934.

—— "Cotton Mather's Annotations on the First Chapter of Genesis," *University of Texas Publications*, 3826 (July 8, 1938), *Studies in English*, 112–122. (The annotations reveal Cotton Mather's reading and his interest in Newtonian science.)

—— "The Date, the Source, and the Significance of Cotton Mather's Interest in Science," *American Literature*, VI (1935), 413–420.

—— "The Effect of the New Science upon the Thought of Jonathan Edwards," *American Literature*, IX (1937), 196–207.

—— "Puritanism and Science: The Relationship Revealed in the Writings of John Cotton," *New England Quarterly*, X (1937), 503–515.

—— "Samuel Johnson of Yale and King's College. A Note on the Relation of Science and Religion in Provincial America," *New England Quarterly*, VIII (1935), 378–397.

—— "Science and the New World," *Catalogue of the Huntington Library* (1937), 3–18. (Refers especially to the Mathers and Winthrops.)

—— "The Science of Thomas Prince," *New England Quarterly*, IX (1936), 26–42.

—— *Scientific Thought in the American Colleges, 1638–1800*, Austin, 1945.

Jones, Richard F., *Ancients and Moderns: A Study of the Background of the Battle of the Books*, St. Louis, 1936; reprinted with some revisions in *The Seventeenth Century Studies in the History of English Thought and Literature from Bacon to Pope*, R. F. Jones and others, Stanford, 1951. (A discussion of the rise and progress of experimental philosophy during the seventeenth century in England. See also bibliography section V, C above.)

Jorgenson, Chester E., "The New Science in the Almanacs of Ames and Franklin," *New England Quarterly*, VIII (1935), 555–561.

Kincheloe, Isabel, "Nature and the New England Puritan," *Americana*, XXXI (1937), 569–588.

Kittredge, George L., "Some Lost Works of Cotton Mather," *Proceedings of the Massachusetts Historical Society*, XLV (1912), 418–479. (Important for the inoculation controversy.)

—— "Cotton Mather's Election into the Royal Society," *Publications of the Colonial Society of Massachusetts*, XIV (1913), 81–114, 281–292.

—— "Cotton Mather's Scientific Communications to the Royal Society," *Proceedings of the American Antiquarian Society*, N.S. XXVI (1916), 18–57.

Mason, S. F., "Science and Religion in 17th Century England," *Past and Present*, 3 (Feb. 1953), 28–44. (The contribution of Calvinism to the development of seventeenth century science.)

Matthews, Albert, "Notes on Early Autopsies and Anatomical Lectures," *Publications of the Colonial Society of Massachusetts*, XIX (1918), 273–290.

Mood, Fulmer, "John Winthrop, Jr., on Indian Corn," *New England Quarterly*, X (1937), 121–133.

Morison, Samuel E., "The Harvard School of Astronomy in the Seventeenth Century," *New England Quarterly*, VII (1934), 3–24.

Packard, Francis R., *The History of Medicine in the United States before 1800*, Philadelphia, 1901.

"Thomas Prince, Scientist and Historian," *Publications of the Colonial Society of Massachusetts*, XXVIII (1935), 100–104.

Russell, Gurdon W., *Early Medicine and Early Medical Men in Connecticut*, Hartford, 1892.

Shryock, Richard Harrison, *Medicine and Society in America, 1660–1860*, New York, 1960. (An analysis of concepts and movements in medical history.)

Stahlman, William D., "Astrology in Colonial America: An Extended Query," *William and Mary Quarterly*, XIII (1956), 551–563.

Stearns, Raymond P., "Colonial Fellows of the Royal Society of London, 1661–1788," *William and Mary Quarterly*, III (1946), 208–268.

Steiner, Walter R., "Governor John Winthrop, Jr., of Connecticut as a

Physician," *Johns Hopkins Hospital Bulletin*, XIV (1903), 294–302.

—— "The Reverend Gershom Bulkeley, of Connecticut, an Eminent Clerical Physician," *Johns Hopkins Hospital Bulletin*, XVII (1906), 48–53.

Stimson, Dorothy, "Puritanism and the New Philosophy in Seventeenth Century England," *Bulletin of the Institute of the History of Medicine*, III (1935), 321–334.

Streeter, John W., "John Winthrop, Junior, and the Fifth Satellite of Jupiter," *Isis*, XXXIX (1948), 159–163.

Thoms, Herbert, "The Beginnings of Obstetrics in America," *Yale Journal of Biology and Medicine*, IV (1932), 665–675.

Thorndike, Lynn, "Medieval Magic and Science in the Seventeenth Century," *Speculum*, XXVIII (1953), 692–704.

Viets, Henry R., *A Brief History of Medicine in Massachusetts*, Boston, 1930.

—— "Some Features of the History of Medicine in Massachusetts during the Colonial Period, 1620–1770," *Isis*, XXIII (1935), 389–405.

Westfall, Richard S., *Science and Religion in Seventeenth Century England*, New Haven, 1958.

White, Andrew D., *A History of the Warfare of Science with Theology in Christendom*, New York, 1896, 2 vols. (Interesting but not too trustworthy.)

Wilson, William J. and C. A. Browne, "Robert Child's Chemical Book List of 1641," *Journal of Chemical Education*, XX, 123–129.

Zirkle, Conway, "The Theory of Concentric Spheres: Edmund Halley, Cotton Mather, and John Cleves Symmes," *Isis*, XXXVII (1947), 155–157.

X. PURITAN LIBRARIES, BOOKS, AND READING

Omnivorous readers, the cultivated Puritans collected libraries whenever their means allowed. Students of colonial history are now undertaking to examine inventories of libraries and estates, and are culling diaries and other source material in order to present a picture of colonial books and reading.

[Adams, William,] "Acc^t of Books y^t William Adams put up to carry to College, Nov. 5, 1726," *Collections of the Massachusetts Historical Society*, fourth series, I (1852), 43, 44.

Bacon, Edwin M., and Lyman H. Weeks, *An Historical Digest of the Provincial Press* [*1689–1707*], Boston, 1908.

Bates, Albert C., "Some Notes on Early Connecticut Printing," *Papers of the Bibliographical Society of America*, XXVII (1933), pt. I.

Baxter, Joseph, "Catalogue of Books in his library," Congregational Library, Boston (*ca.* 1745.)

Baxter, William T., "Daniel Henchman [1689–1761], A Colonial Bookseller," *Essex Institute Historical Collections*, LXX (1934), 1–30.

Belcher, Jonathan (1710–1776), Manuscript Commonplace Book in Harvard College Library. (Extracts from his reading during his college years.)

Bowman, George E., "Governor Thomas Prence's [*sic*] Will and Inventory, and the Records of His Death," *Mayflower*

Descendents, III (1901), 203–216. (A list of books is itemized to a value of more than £13.)

Boynton, Henry W., *Annals of American Bookselling, 1638–1850*, London, 1932.

Brayton, Susan S., "The Library of an Eighteenth-Century Gentleman of Rhode Island," *New England Quarterly*, VIII (1935), 277–283.

Brigham, Clarence S., "Harvard College Library Duplicates, 1682," *Publications of the Colonial Society of Massachusetts*, XVIII (1917), 407–417.

—— *History and Bibliography of American Newspapers, 1690–1820*, 1947, 2 vols. First installment appeared in *Proceedings of the American Antiquarian Society*, XXIII (1913), 207–403.

—— "History of Book Auctions in America," *Bulletin of the New York Public Library*, XXXIX (1935), 55–90.

—— *Journals and Journeymen: A Contribution to the History of Early American Newspapers*, Philadelphia, 1950.

Cadbury, Henry J., "Bishop Berkeley's Gifts to Harvard Library," *Harvard*

Library Bulletin, VII (1953), 75–87; 196–207.

—— "Harvard College Library and the Libraries of the Mathers," *Proceedings of the American Antiquarian Society*, L (1940), 20–48.

—— "John Harvard's Library," *Publications of the Colonial Society of Massachusetts*, XXXIV (1937–1942), 353–377. (An identifying list, supplementing the list of Alfred C. Potter, listed below.)

Cannon, Carl L., *American Book Collectors and Collecting from Colonial Times to the Present*, New York, 1941. (See chapter on Thomas Prince.)

Clapp, Thomas, *Manuscript catalogue of books in the Yale Library*, Yale College Library. (A list of over 700 books given by Jeremiah Dummer in 1714; over 400 given by Elihu Yale in 1718.)

Cotton, Rowland, and Nathaniel Rogers, *A Catalogue of Curious and Valueable Books, Being the greatest part of the Libraries of the Reverend and Learned Mr. Rowland Cotton, . . . and Mr. Nathaniel Rogers . . . To be Sold by Auction*, Boston, 1725. (Six hundred and ninety-five titles; unique copy in the Boston Public Library.)

Curwin, George, *Catalogue of the Greatest Part of the Library of the Reverend Mr. George Curwen [sic], Late of Salem . . . to be sold by auction*, Boston, 1718. (Nearly 600 titles; unique copy in Harvard College Library.)

Dexter, Franklin B., "Early Private Libraries in New England," *Proceedings of the American Antiquarian Society*, N.S. XVIII (1907), 135–147.

—— "The First Public Library in New Haven," *Papers of the New Haven Colony Historical Society*, VI (1900), 301–313. (Library of Samuel Eaton, 1658.)

Dexter, Henry M., "Elder Brewster's Library," *Proceedings of the Massachusetts Historical Society*, XXV (1890), 37–85.

Duniway, Clyde A., *The Development of Freedom of the Press in Massachusetts*, New York, 1906.

Ernle, Rowland E., *The Light Reading of our Ancestors*, London, 1921. (Popular in treatment.)

Evans, Evan A., Jr., *Literary References in New England Diaries, 1700–1730*, unpublished thesis in Harvard College Library.

Ford, Worthington C., *The Boston Book Market, 1679–1700*, Boston, 1917.

—— *Broadsides, Ballads, &c. Printed in Massachusetts, 1639–1800*, Boston, 1922. (Check list, with short introduction.)

Gilman, D. C., "Bishop Berkeley's Gifts to Yale College," *New Haven Colony Historical Society Papers*, I (1865), 146–170.

Green, Samuel A., *John Foster, the Earliest American Engraver and the First Boston Printer*, Boston, 1909.

—— *Ten Fac-simile Reproductions Relating to Old Boston and Neighborhood*, Boston, 1901.

—— *Ten Fac-simile Reproductions Relating to New England*, Boston, 1902.

—— *Ten Fac-simile Reproductions Relating to Various Subjects*, Boston, 1903.

Greenberg, Herbert, "The Authenticity of the Library of John Winthrop the Younger," *American Literature*, VIII (1937), 449–452.

Hall, Howard J., "Two Book-Lists: 1668 and 1728," *Publications of the Colonial Society of Massachusetts*, XXIV (1923), 64–71.

Harris, J. Rendel, and S. K. Jones, *The Pilgrim Press*, Cambridge, Eng., 1922.

Harvard University, *Catalogus Librorum Bibliothecae Collegii Harvardiani*, Boston, 1723. (Two *Continuatio* published before 1730.)

Harvard University, Library of, "Books given to the Library by John Harvard, Peter Bulkley, Sir Kenelme Digby, and Governor Bellingham," *Bibliographical Contributions*, No. 27 (1888), 5–14.

Herrick, C. A., "The Early New-Englanders: What Did They Read?" *Library*, third series, IX (1918), 1–17.

Howard, Leon, "Early American Copies of Milton," *Huntington Library Bulletin*, No. 7, 1935, 169–179.

—— "The Influence of Milton on Colonial American Poetry," *Huntington Library Bulletin*, No. 9, 1936, 63–89.

"Hubbard's Narrative, 1677," *Colophon*, I (1936), 456–457.

Jantz, Harold S., "German Thought and Literature in New England, 1620–1820," *Journal of English and German Philology*, XLI (1942), 1–45. (Contains important material on early colonial libraries.)

—— "Unrecorded Verse Broadsides of

Seventeenth-Century New England," *Papers of the Bibliographical Society of America*, XXXIX (1945), 1–19. (Adds sixteen broadsides to the list of those already known.)

Johnson, Thomas H., "Jonathan Edwards' Background of Reading," *Publications of the Colonial Society of Massachusetts*, XXVIII (1935), 193–222.

Kimber, Sydney A., *Cambridge Press Title-pages, 1640–1665*, Takoma Park, Md., 1954. (A pictorial representation of the work done in the first printing office in British North America.)

Kittredge, George L., "A Harvard Salutatory Oration of 1662," *Publications of the Colonial Society of Massachusetts*, XXVIII (1935), 1–24. (Analysis of the commonplace book of Elnathan Chauncy, Harvard A.B. 1661; a record of taste in reading and poetry.)

Kobre, Sidney, *The Development of the Colonial Newspaper*, Pittsburgh, 1944.

Lee, Samuel, *The Library of . . . Mr. Samuel Lee . . . Exposed . . . to Sale*, Boston, 1693. (Unique copy in Boston Public Library. See also chapter VI, "The Earliest Book-Catalogue Printed in this Country, 1693," in Samuel A. Green, *Ten Fac-simile Reproductions Relating to Old Boston and Neighborhood*, Boston, 1901.)

Lehmann-Haupt, Helmut, and others, *The Book in America: A History of the Making, the Selling, and the Collecting of Books in the United States*, New York, 1939; revised edn. 1951. (A primer first published in Germany, 1937, this is primarily a book of facts. Laurence Wroth has contributed for the period 1638–1860.)

Littlefield, George E., *Early Boston Booksellers, 1642–1711*, Boston, 1900. (Superseded by Worthington C. Ford, *The Boston Book Market, q.v.*)

—— *The Early Massachusetts Press, 1638–1711*, Boston, 1907, 2 vols. (To be used with care; very inaccurate.)

McKay, George L., comp., "American Book Auction Catalogues, 1713–1934," *Bulletin of the New York Public Library*, XXXIX (1935), 141–166. (Part I lists catalogues to 1800.)

Matthews, Albert, "Knowledge of Milton in Early New England," *Nation* (New York), LXXXVII (1908), 624, 625, 650.

Mayflower Descendant, The: A Quarterly Magazine of Pilgrim Genealogy and History, Boston, 1899—1940. (Often lists inventories of private libraries, or brief diary comments on reading.)

Moody, Joshua, and Daniel Gookin, *A Catalogue of Rare and Valuable Books . . . of . . . Moodey, and . . . Gookin . . .*, Boston, 1718. (A list of 780 items put up for auction sale; unique copy in the library of the American Antiquarian Society, Worcester, Mass.)

Morgan, Edmund S., "The Colonial Scene, 1602–1800," *Proceedings of the American Antiquarian Society*, LX (1950), 53–160. (An annotated list of books, broadsides, prints and maps.)

Morison, Samuel E., "The Library of George Alcock, Medical Student, 1676," *Publications of the Colonial Society of Massachusetts*, XXVIII (1935), 350–357.

Morris, Edward P., "A Library of 1742," *Yale University Library Gazette*, IX (1935), 1–11. (Notes on a Yale Library Catalogue of 1742.)

Mott, Frank Luther, *American Journalism: A History of Newspapers in the United States Through 260 Years: 1690–1950*, revised ed., New York, 1950.

Murdock, Kenneth B., "The Puritans and the New Testament," *Publications of the Colonial Society of Massachusetts*, XXV (1924), 239–243. (A denial that the Puritans used the Old Testament rather than the New.)

Myres, J. N. L., "Oxford Libraries in the Seventeenth and Eighteenth Centuries," *The English Library before 1700: Studies in its History*, ed. Francis Wormald and C. E. Wright, London, Toronto, New York; 1958; 236–255.

Norton, Arthur O., "Harvard Textbooks and Reference Books of the Seventeenth Century," *Publications of the Colonial Society of Massachusetts*, XXVIII (1935), 361–438.

Oates, J. C. T., "The Libraries of Cambridge, 1570–1700," *The English Library Before 1700: Studies in its History*, London, Toronto, New York; 1958; 213–235.

Paltsits, Victor Hugo, "New Light on *Publick Occurences*: America's First Newspaper," *Proceedings of the Massachusetts Historical Society*, LIX (1949), 75–88.

(Cotton Mather's letter of October 17, 1690, here for the first time printed, calls the paper noble, useful, laudable.)

Pemberton, Ebenezer, *A Catalogue Of Curious and Valuable Books*, Boston, 1717. (A list of about a thousand items put up for auction sale, principally Pemberton's library; unique copy in the New York Public Library.)

Perry, Michael, "Inventory of the estate of Michael Perry, a Boston bookseller, taken A.D. 1700," *John Dunton's Letters*, Boston, 1867, Appendix B, 314–319.

Potter, Alfred C., "Catalogue of John Harvard's Library," *Publications of the Colonial Society of Massachusetts*, XXI (1920), 190–230. (See supplementary list of H. J. Cadbury, above.)

—— "The Harvard College Library, 1723–1735," *Publications of the Colonial Society of Massachusetts*, XXV (1924), 1–14.

Powell, William S., "Books in the Virginia Colony Before 1624," *William and Mary Quarterly*, 3rd series, V (1948), 177–184. (Interesting for inclusion of works by H. Smith, Perkins, and other Puritan favorites.)

Pratt, Ann Stokely, *Isaac Watts and His Gift of Books to Yale College*, New Haven, 1938.

Prince, Thomas, *Catalogue of The American Portion of the Library of the Rev. Thomas Prince*, ed. W. W. Whitmore, Boston, 1868.

Robbins, Caroline, "Library of Liberty —Assembled for Thomas Hollis of Lincoln's Inn," *Harvard Library Bulletin*, V (1951), 5–23, 181–196. (A valuable study of the significant contribution of books made by Hollis to Harvard College and eighteenth-century New England.)

Robinson, Charles F., and Robin Robinson, "Three Early Massachusetts Libraries," *Publications of the Colonial Society of Massachusetts*, XXVIII (1935), 107–175. (A list of 565 items from three seventeenth-century libraries.)

Roden, Robert F., *The Cambridge Press, 1638–1692*, New York, 1905.

Salisbury, Stephen, "Early Books and Libraries," *Proceedings of the American Antiquarian Society*, N.S. V (1887–1888), 183–215.

Seybolt, Robert F., "Student Libraries at Harvard, 1763–1764," *Publications of the Colonial Society of Massachusetts*, XXVIII (1935), 449–461.

Shera, Jesse H., "The Beginnings of Systematic Bibliography in America, 1642–1799," *Essays Honoring Lawrence C. Wroth*, Portland, Me., 1951.

Silver, Rollo G., "Government Printing in Massachusetts-Bay, 1700–1750," *Proceedings of the American Antiquarian Society*, LXVIII (1958), 135–162.

—— "Publishing in Boston, 1726–1757: The Accounts of Daniel Henchman," *Proceedings of the American Antiquarian Society*, LXVI (1956), 17–36.

Sloane, William, *Children's Books in England and America in the Seventeenth Century: A History and Checklist*, New York, 1955.

Thomas, Isaiah, *The History of Printing in America*, Worcester, Mass., 1810, 2 vols.

Thompson, Lawrence, "Notes on Some Collectors in Colonial Massachusetts," *Colophon*, N.S. II (1936), 82–100.

Tuttle, Julius H., "The Library of Dr. William Ames," *Publications of the Colonial Society of Massachusetts*, XIV (1913), 63–66.

—— "Early New England Libraries": Manuscript card catalogue in the library of the Massachusetts Historical Society, Boston. See "Early Libraries in New England," *Publications of the Colonial Society of Massachusetts*, XIII (1912), 288–292.

—— "The Libraries of the Mathers," *Proceedings of the American Antiquarian Society*, N.S. XX (1910), 269–356.

Vail, Robert W. G., "Seventeenth Century American Book Labels," *American Book Collector*, IV (1933), 164–176.

Whitehill, Walter Muir, "The King's Chapel Library, 1698–1948," *Athenaeum Items*, June, 1948, 1–2.

Wigglesworth, Michael, "Catalogue of Mr. Wigglesworth's Books Taken Oct. 22, 1705," in John W. Dean, *Memoir of Rev. Michael Wigglesworth*, 2nd ed., Albany, 1871, Appendix III (pp. 151–152); reprinted from *New England Historical and Genealogical Register*, XVII (1863), 129ff.

Winship, George Parker, *The Cambridge Press*. (See VII, B.)

—— *The Literature of the History of Printing in the United States*, London, 1923.

—— "Old Auction Catalogues," *American Collector*, IV (1927), 188–193.

Winterich, John T., *Early American Books and Printing*, Boston, 1933.

Winthrop, John, Jr., "Library of John Winthrop, Jr.," *Catalogue of the New York Society Library*, New York, 1850, 491–505.

Wright, Louis B., "Pious Reading in Colonial Virginia," *Journal of Southern History*, VI (1940), 383–392.

—— "The Purposeful Reading of Our Colonial Ancestors," *English Literary History*, IV (1937), 85–111. (Emphasizes the general culture of Puritans as demonstrated in their reading.)

Wright, Thomas G., *Literary Culture in Early New England, 1620–1730*, New Haven, 1920. (The best comprehensive survey of Puritan reading and book business; needs to be supplemented by subsequent work done on the subject.)

Wroth, Lawrence C., *An American Bookshelf, 1755*, Philadelphia, 1934. (An examination of the books that might be found in the library of a cultivated gentleman in the mid-eighteenth century.)

—— *The Colonial Printer*, New York, 1931; Portland, 1938. (The best book on the subject.)

—— "The First Press in Providence: A Study in Social Development," *Proceedings of the American Antiquarian Society*, LI (1941), 351–383. (A study of the printer in colonial America.)

—— *The Oath of a Free-Man*, with a Historical Study by Lawrence C. Wroth and a Note on the Stephen Daye Press by Melbert B. Cary, New York, 1939. (A reprinting of the first work done in confines of what is now the United States.)

XI. ARTS AND CRAFTS

The Puritans were little concerned with aesthetic problems. They produced no sculpture or statuary; painting was confined to portrait likenesses. For many decades after the founding of New England, artistic creations—household necessities, textiles, and decorations—were generally imported. The craftsmanship of the architects, cabinetmakers, and silversmiths became evident in larger centers as soon as money was plentiful enough to commission their services. The Puritans were by no means constitutionally incapable of displaying good taste, but because of their relative indifference to the arts they did not write critiques upon the subject. In recent years the *Magazine of Antiques* has shown an increasing interest in early American arts and crafts. For further items that might have been listed here, see Section IV, B-2.

American Church Silver of the Seventeenth and Eighteenth Centuries . . . Exhibited at the [*Boston*] *Museum of Fine Arts*, Introduction by George N. Curtis, Boston, 1911.

American Silver . . . Exhibited at the [*Boston*] *Museum of Fine Arts*, Introduction by Richard T. H. Halsey, Boston, 1906.

Ayars, Christine M., *Contributions to the Art of Music in America by the Music Industries of Boston, 1640–1936*, New York, 1936.

Bach, Richard F., "Early American Architecture and the Allied Arts: a Bibliography," *Architectural Record*, LIX (1926), 265–273, 328–334, 483–488, 525–532; LX (1926), 65–70; LXIII (1928), 577–580; LXIV (1928), 70–72, 150–152, 190–192.

Bagg, Ernest N., "The Psalms, Tune Books and Music of the Forefathers,"

Proceedings of the Bostonian Society, V (Jan., 1904), 38–57.

Baker, C. H. Collins, "Notes on Joseph Blackburn and Nathaniel Dance," *Huntington Library Quarterly*, IX (1945–1946), 33–47. (Early American portrait painters.)

Barker, Virgil, *American Painting: History and Interpretation*, New York, 1950.

Bayley, Frank W., *Five Colonial Artists of New England*, Boston, 1929. (Reproductions of portraits of many colonial leaders.)

—— *Little Known Early American Portrait Painters*, Boston, n.d.

Belknap, Henry W., *Artists and Craftsmen of Essex County, Massachusetts*, Salem, 1927.

Belknap, Waldron P., *American Colonial*

Painting; Materials for a History, Cambridge, 1955. (See especially "The Identity of Robert Feke," pp. 3–34, and "English Mezzotint as Prototype of American Colonial Portraiture," pp. 273–322.)

Bigelow, Francis H., Historic Silver of the Colonies and Its Makers, New York, 1917.

Bolton, Charles K., The Founders; Portraits of Persons born abroad who came to the Colonies . . . [to] 1701, Boston, 1919–1926, 3 vols.

Bolton, Ethel S., and Eva J. Coe, American Samplers, Boston, 1921.

Bridenbaugh, Carl, The Colonial Craftsman, New York, 1950. (Social and economic history.)

—— Peter Harrison, First American Architect, Chapel Hill, 1949.

Briggs, Martin S., The Homes of the Pilgrim Fathers in England and America, 1620–1685, London, 1932. (Illustrated in detail.)

Brown, Madelaine R., "Rhode Island Pewterers," Collections of the Rhode Island Historical Society, XXXI (1938), 1–8.

Burroughs, Alan, Limners and Likenesses; Three Centuries of American Painting, Cambridge, 1936.

Caffin, C. H., The Story of American Painting; the Evolution of Painting in America from Colonial Times to the Present, London, 1907.

Casey, Dorothy N., "Rhode Island Silversmiths," Collections of the Rhode Island Historical Society, XXXIII (1940), 49–64.

Chandler, Joseph E., The Colonial House, New York, 1916.

Christensen, Erwin O., Early American Wood Carving, Cleveland, 1952.

Clarke, Herman Frederick, "The Craft of Silversmith in Early New England," New England Quarterly, XII (1939), 68–79.

Coburn, Frederick W., "Artistic Puritans," American Magazine of Art, XXI (1930), 481–496. (A description of portraits of the Puritan era.)

Colonial Dames of America, National Society of the, Old Houses in the South County of Rhode Island, Providence, 1933.

Crouch, Joseph, Puritanism and Art, An Inquiry into a Popular Fallacy, London, 1910.

Dorsey, Stephen, Early English Churches in America, 1607–1807, New York, 1952.

Dow, George F., The Arts and Crafts in New England, 1704–1775, Topsfield, Mass., 1927.

Downs, Joseph, American Furniture: Queen Anne and Chippendale Periods in the Henry Francis Du Pont Winterthur Museum, New York, 1952.

—— "Three Early New England Rooms," The New York Historical Society, XXXV (1951), 141–155. (Late seventeenth and early eighteenth-century rooms of The New York Historical Society.)

Dresser, Louisa, Likeness of America, 1680–1820; Catalogue, Colorado Springs [1949].

Dunlap, William, History of the Rise and Progress of the Arts of Design in the United States, New York, 1834, 2 vols.; reprinted Boston, 1918, 3 vols.

Eberlein, Harold D., The Architecture of Colonial America, Boston, 1915; 1927.

——, and Abbot McClure, The Practical Book of Early American Arts and Crafts, Philadelphia, 1916.

Ensko, Stephen G. C., American Silversmiths and Their Marks, New York, 1927.

"Fabrics, Clothing and Tools Purchased in England, in 1639–1642, for Governor George Wyllys of Hartford, Connecticut," Old Time New England, XXVI (1936), 142–145.

Flexner, James Thomas, American Painting: First Flowers of our Wilderness, Boston, 1947. (A good general work in the subject, but marred by broad, unsubstantiated generalizations.)

Foote, Henry Wilder, "Benjamin Blyth of Salem: Eighteenth Century Artist," Proceedings of the Massachusetts Historical Society, LXXI (1953–1957), 1959, 64–107.

—— John Smibert, Painter, Cambridge, 1950.

—— "Mr. Smibert Shows His Pictures, March, 1730," New England Quarterly, VIII (1935), 14–28. ("John Smibert was the first professional portrait-painter to settle in Boston.")

Forbes, Hariette M., Gravestones of Early New England and the Men Who Made Them, 1653–1800, Boston, 1927.

French, Hollis, A List of Early American Silversmiths and their Marks, New York, 1917.

Garvan, Anthony, Architecture and Town Planning in Colonial Connecticut, New Haven,

1951. (A broad and scholarly view of the work involved in planning domains, and designing settlements, towns, dwelling houses and meeting-houses.)

Grace, George C., and David H. Wallace, *The New York Historical Society Dictionary of Artists in America*, New Haven, 1957. (A biographical dictionary of American artists.)

Griffin, Gillett, "John Foster's Woodcut of Richard Mather," *Printing and Graphic Arts*, (Lunenberg, Va.), VII (1959), 1–19. (Technical but also critical.)

Guyol, Philip N., "The Prentis Collection," *Historical New Hampshire*, XIV (Dec., 1958), 9–17. (Description of the furnishings of a suite of early New England rooms of the New Hampshire Historical Society. Excellent photographs.)

Haddon, Rawson, *A Tourist's Guide to Connecticut*, Waterbury, 1923.

Hamilton, Sinclair, "Portrait of a Puritan: John Foster's Woodcut of Richard Mather," *Princeton University Library Catalogue*, XVIII (1957), 43–48.

Hipkiss, Edwin J., "Boston's Earliest Silversmiths: The Philip Leffingwell Spalding Collection," *Bulletin of the Museum of Fine Arts*, XL (1942), 82–86.

—— *Eighteenth-Century American Arts: The M. & M. Karolik Collection of Paintings, Drawings, Engravings, Furniture, Silver, Needlework, and Incidental Objects . . . , 1720 to 1820*, Cambridge, 1941.

Isham, Norman M., *Early American Houses*, Boston, 1928.

——, and Albert F. Brown, *Early Connecticut Houses*, Providence, 1900.

——, and Albert F. Brown, *Early Rhode Island Houses*, Providence, 1895.

Jackson, Russell Leigh, "Essex Institute Museum Collections, Silver," *Essex Institute Historical Collections*, LXXXI (1945), 97–104.

Jones, Edward Alfred, *The Old Silver of American Churches*, Letchworth, Eng., 1913.

Kelly, John Frederick, *Early Connecticut Meetinghouses*, New York, 1948; 2 vols. (A scholarly study; invaluable for the history of architecture, state and religion, of early America.)

—— *The Early Domestic Architecture of Connecticut*, New Haven, 1924.

—— *Architectural Guide for Connecticut*, Hartford, 1936.

Kettell, Russell H., ed., *Early American Rooms, 1650–1858: A Consideration of the Changes in Style Between the Arrival of the Mayflower and the Civil War in the Regions Originally Settled by the English and the Dutch*, Portland, Me., 1936.

—— *The Pine Furniture of Early New England*, New York, 1949.

Kimball, Sidney F., *Domestic Architecture of the American Colonies and of the Early Republic*, New York, 1922; 1927. (Authoritative and standard.)

Knittle, Rhea M., *Early American Glass*, New York, 1927.

Langdon, William C., *Everyday Things in American Life, 1607–1776*, New York, 1937.

Larkin, Oliver W., *Art and Life in America*, New York, 1949. (The best one volume historical survey; contains useful illustrations and bibliographies.)

Lee, Cuthbert, *Early American Portrait Painters*, New Haven, 1929.

Lockwood, Luke V., *Colonial Furniture in America*, New York, 1921, 2 vols.

Lyon, Irving W., *The Colonial Furniture of New England*, Boston, 1891.

McCausland, Elizabeth, "A Selected Bibliography of American Painting and Sculpture from Colonial Times to the Present," *Magazine of Art*, XXXIX (1946), 329–349.

McClellan, Elizabeth, *Historic Dress in America, 1607–1800*, Philadelphia, 1904. New ed., New York, 1937, with title *History of American Costume, 1607–1870*.

Mendelowitz, Daniel M., *A History of American Art*, New York, 1960. (A popular general introduction.)

Mixer, Knowlton, *Old Houses of New England*, New York, 1927. (Pleasant, but unreliable in details.)

Monograph Series Recording the Architecture of the American Colonies and Early Republic, The, ed. Russell V. Whitehead. Vols. 15–18 (1929–1932), N. Y. Vols. 1–14 (1915–1928) called *White Pine Series of Architectural Monographs*. Vols. 19–26 (1933–1940) published in *Pencil Points*. (A valuable series which presents classified illustrations of the more beautiful and suggestive examples of early American architecture together with a critical description by modern architects.)

Morgan, John H., *Early American Painters*, New York, 1921.

Morrison, Hugh, *Early American Architecture, from the First Colonial Settlements to the National Period*, New York, 1952. (The best of its kind; a judicious compilation largely from secondary sources. Contains five chapters on seventeenth-century buildings.)

Northend, Mary H., *Historic Homes of New England*, Boston, 1914.

Nutting, Wallace, *Furniture of the Pilgrim Century, 1620–1720*, Boston, 1921.

Old Time New England, Boston, 1910-current. Published by the Society for the Preservation of New England Antiquities. (Repository for articles on New England antiquities and monuments; the student of Puritan culture should search its pages carefully.)

Phillips, John Marshall, "Gold and Silver in the Prentis Collection (New York)", *The New York Historical Society Quarterly*, XXXV (1951), 165–169.

—— "Portraits in the Prentis Collection, (New York)," *The New York Historical Society Quarterly*, XXXV (1951), 157–164. (Seventeenth-century portraits.)

Poor, Alfred E., *Colonial Architecture of Cape Cod, Nantucket and Martha's Vineyard*, New York, 1932.

Rawson, Marion N., *Candleday Art*, New York, 1938. (A broadly informal and sketchy survey of American fold art.)

—— *Handwrought Ancestors: The Story of Early American Shops and Those Who Worked Therein*, New York, 1936.

Robinson, A. G., *Old New England Doorways*, New York, 1920.

—— *Old New England Houses*, New York, 1920.

Scott, Kenneth, "Daniel Greenough, Colonial Silversmith of Portsmouth," *Historical New Hampshire*, XV (Nov., 1960), 26–31.

Seventeenth-Century Painting in New England. A Catalogue of an Exhibition held at the Worcester Art Museum in Collaboration with the American Antiquarian Society, July and August, 1934, ed. Louisa Dresser and Alan Burroughs, Worcester, 1935.

Shurtleff, Harold R., *The Log Cabin Myth: A Study of the Early Dwellings of the English Colonies in North America*, ed. with an Introduction by Samuel Eliot Morison, Cambridge, 1939.

Singleton, Esther, *The Furniture of Our Forefathers*, New York, 1901, 2 vols.

Starkey, Laurence G., "Benefactors of the Cambridge Press: A Reconsideration," *Studies in Bibliography*, III (1950), 267–269.

—— A Descriptive and Analytical Bibliography of the Cambridge, Massachusetts, Press from its Beginnings to the Publication of Eliot's Indian Bible in 1663, Lexington, Ky., 1955. (Ten microcards.)

—— "The Last Broadside on the Quakers from the Cambridge Press in Massachusetts," *English Studies in Honor of James Southall Wilson*, Charlottesville, 1951.

Stow, Charles M., *Seventeenth and Eighteenth Century American Silver*, New York, 1934.

Sweet, Frederick A., Hans Huth and others, eds., *From Colony to Nation: An Exhibition of American Painting, Silver, and Architecture from 1650 to the War of 1812*, Chicago Art Institute, 1949.

Vanderpoel, Emily N., *American Lace and Lace-Makers*, New Haven, 1924.

Waterman, Thomas T., *The Dwellings of Colonial America*, Chapel Hill, 1950.

Watkins, Lura Woodside, *Early New England Potters and Their Wares*, Cambridge, 1950. (A definitive study.)

Whitmore, William H., "The Early Painters and Engravers of New England," *Proceedings of the Massachusetts Historical Society*, IX (1867), 197–216.

Yale University Portrait Index, 1701–1951, New Haven, 1951.

XII. BIBLIOGRAPHY

Current publications on the Puritan period are listed in the issues of *Isis*, in the quarterly bibliographies in *American Literature*, and the annual bibliographies in *Publications of the Modern Language Association* and the *New England Quarterly*, in the bulletins of the Modern Humanities Research Association, and in the *Writings on American History*, 1902—. (Vols. for the years 1904–1905, 1941–1947, have not been published; latest vol., 1953, appeared in 1960.)

The following list contains the principal bibliographies of source material for the period. Several secondary works listed contain further bibliographical material.

Adams, James Truslow, ed., *Atlas of American History*, New York, 1943. (A companion volume to the *Dictionary of American History*, below.)

——, and others, eds., *Dictionary of American History*, 6 vols., New York, 1940.

Allison, William H., *Inventory of Unpublished Material for American Religious History in Protestant Church Archives and Other Repositories*, Washington, 1910.

American Literary Manuscripts: A Checklist of Holdings in Academic, Historical, and Public Libraries in the United States, Compiled and Published under the Auspices of the American Literature Group, Modern Language Association of America, Committee on Manuscripts, Austin, 1961.

Ayer, Mary F., *Check-List of Boston Newspapers, 1704–1780*, Boston, 1907. (Bibliographical notes by Albert Matthews.)

Baginsky, Paul, *German Works Relating to America, 1493–1800: A List Compiled from the Collections of the New York Public Library*, New York, 1942.

Basler, Roy D., and others, *A Guide to the Study of the United States of America*, Washington, 1960.

Beers, Henry P., *Bibliographies in American History: Guide to Materials for Research*, 2nd ed., New York, 1942.

Bibliotheca Americana: Catalogue of the John Carter Brown Library in Brown University, 3 vols., Providence, 1919–1931. (Lists by year of publication *Americana* published before 1675, and acquired by the Library before 1931.)

Billington, Roy Allen, "Guide to American Historical Manuscript Collections in Libraries of the United States," New York, 1952; reprinted from *Mississippi Valley Historical Review*, XXXVIII (1951–1952), 467–496.

Blanck, Jacob, *Bibliography of American Literature*, New Haven; Vol. I, 1955;

Vol. II, 1957; Vol. III, 1959. (Full bibliographies of American authors whose work, primarily belles-lettres, was at one time read and considered significant. To date three volumes have been published.)

Bowen, Richard Le Baron, *Massachusetts Records. A Handbook for Genealogists, Historians, and Other Researchers*, Rehoboth, Mass., 1957.

Bradford, Thomas L., and Stanley V. Henkels, *The Bibliographer's Manual of American History*, Philadelphia, 1907–1910, 5 vols. (For state and county histories.)

Brigham, Clarence S., "Bibliography of American Newspapers: Massachusetts," *Proceedings of the American Antiquarian Society*, XXV (1915), 193–293, 398–501. (The definitive check list; for other states consult Vols. XXIII–XXX, XXXII, XXXIV, XXXV, XXXVII.)

Cambridge History of American Literature, The. (See in section VII, B. Bibliographies covering Puritan New England, I, 363–442, 452–467.)

Channing, Edward, Albert B. Hart, and Frederick J. Turner, *Guide to the Study and Reading of American History*, Boston, revised edition, 1912.

Child, Sargent B., and others, *Check List of Historical Records Survey Publications; W. P. A. Technical Series, Research and Records. Bibliography No. 7*, Washington, 1943.

Cuthbert, Norma B., *American Manuscripts Collections in the Huntington Library for the History of the Seventeenth and Eighteenth Centuries*, San Marino, 1941.

Dissertation Abstracts; A Guide to Dissertations and Monographs Available in Microfilm, Ann Arbor, 1938—. (Beginning with vol. 16 the last number of each volume contains an "Index to American Doctoral Dissertations.")

Dorgan, Marion, *Guide to American Biography. Part I: 1607–1815*, Albuquerque, 1949. (A working bibliography more extensive than exhaustive.)

Early Catholic Americana 1729–1830, comp. Wilfred Parsons, New York, 1939.

—— *Additions and Corrections to*, comp. Forrest Bowe, New York, 1952.

Emerson, Everett H., "Notes on the Thomas Hooker Canon," *American Literature*, XXVII (1956), 554–555. (Some false ascriptions and some overlooked titles.)

Evans, Charles, *American Bibliography, 1639–1820*, Chicago, 1903–1934, 12 vols.; New York, 1942. (The most exhaustive; compiled by years, well indexed.) Vol. 13, *Index*, comp. by Roger Pattrell Bristol, Worcester, 1959.

—— "American Imprints before 1801 in the University of Pennsylvania Library and not in Evans," comp. Thomas R. Adams, *Library Chronicle of the University of Pennsylvania*, XXII (1956), 41–57.

Flagg, Charles A., *A Guide to Massachusetts Local History*, Salem, 1907.

—— "Reference List on Connecticut Local History," *New York State Library Bulletin*, No. 53, Albany, 1900.

Gohdes, Clarence, *Bibliographical Guide to the Study of the Literature of the United States of America*, Durham, 1959.

Haller, William, *The Rise of Puritanism*. (See Section III, B. Contains a useful bibliography of sermons and other works of English Puritan preachers.)

Hamer, Philip M., *A Guide to Archives and Manuscripts in the United States*, New Haven, 1961. (Compiled for the National Historical Publications Commission; it lists manuscript and archival holdings of 1300 depositories.)

Handbook of the Massachusetts Historical Society, 1791–1948, Foreword and Historical Sketch by Stewart Mitchell, Boston, 1949. (Contains a check-list of publications and another of the major manuscript collections in the Society's library.)

Harvard Guide to American History, ed. Oscar Handlin and others, Cambridge, 1954.

Hill, Robert W., "Resources on Colonial History in the New York Public Library," *New York History*, XL (1959), 387–413.

Holmes, Thomas J., *Cotton Mather: A Bibliography of His Works*, 3 vols., Cambridge, 1940. (A landmark in American bibliographical scholarship.)

—— *Increase Mather: A Bibliography of His Works*, Cleveland, 1931, 2 vols. (A superlative work; contains summaries and extracts from the volumes.)

—— *The Minor Mathers: A List of Their Works*, Cambridge, 1940.

Henry E. Huntington Library and Art Gallery, *American Imprints, 1648–1797, in the Huntington Library*, Cambridge, 1933.

Jefferey, William, and Zechariah Chaffee, Jr., "Early New England Court Records: A Bibliography of Published Materials," *Boston Public Library Quarterly*, VI (1954), 160–184.

Jensen, Merrill, *English Historical Documents*, Vol. IX. See Section I, A.

Johnson, Thomas H., ed., *Literary History of the United States*, Vol. 3, New York, 1948; 1953. (The most extensive bibliography of the subject. See also *Literary History of the United States. Bibliography Supplement*, comp. Richard M. Ludwig, New York, 1959, which adds materials published since 1948.)

—— *The Printed Works of Jonathan Edwards*, Princeton, 1940.

Lancour, A. Harold, *Passenger Lists of Ships Coming to North America 1607–1825; A Bibliography*, New York, 1937.

Larned, Josephus N., *The Literature of American History, A Bibliography*, Boston, 1902.

Leary, Lewis, *Articles on American Literature Appearing in Current Periodicals, 1920–1945*, Durham, 1947. (Edited from materials supplied by the Committee on Bibliography of the American Literature group of the Modern Language Association and the University of Pennsylvania Library. Bibliography of current articles in American literature appear quarterly in *American Literature*.)

List of Doctoral Dissertations in History Completed or in Progress at Colleges and Universities in the United States since 1955, Washington, 1958. (Published triennially by the American Historical Association.)

Lord, Clifford, and Elizabeth H. Lord, *Historical Atlas of the United States*, New

York, 1944. (Section II, "Colonial Period.")

Matteson, D. M., and others, *Index to Writings on American History, 1902–1940*, Washington, 1956.

Matthews, William, *British Diaries: An Annotated Bibliography of British Diaries Written Between 1442 and 1942*, Berkeley, 1950.

——, and Roy Harvey Pearce, *American Diaries: An Annotated Bibliography of American Diaries Written Prior to 1861*, Berkeley and Los Angeles, 1945. (List restricted to published diaries; arranged chronologically by date of first entries published.)

Mode, Peter G., *Source Book and Bibliographical Guide for American Church History*, Menasha, Wisconsin, 1921.

Morey, Verne D., "American Congregationalism: A Critical Bibliography 1900–1952," *Church History*, XXI (1952), 323–329.

Morris, Richard B., *Encyclopædia of American History*, New York, 1953.

Morse, Jarvis M., *American Beginnings*, Washington, 1952. (A critical commentary on writings on British America published before 1775.)

Otis, William B., *American Verse, 1625–1807*, New York, 1909. (Valuable bibliography.)

Pauldin, Charles Oscar, *Atlas of the Historical Geography of the United States*, ed. John K. Wright, Baltimore, 1932. (The standard work; a monumental achievement.)

Prager, Herta, and William W. Price, "A Bibliography on the History of the Courts of the Thirteen Original Colonies, Maine, Ohio, and Vermont," *American Journal of Legal History*, I (1957), 336–362; II (1958), 35–52, 148–154.

Quinn, Arthur H., ed., *The Literature of the American People*. See VII, B. (Has a useful bibliography of colonial literature with critical comments.)

Riley, Stephen T., "The Manuscript Collections of the Massachusetts Historical Society: A Brief Listing," *Massachusetts Historical Society Miscellany*, No. 5, December, 1958, 1–15.

Ring, Elizabeth, and others, *A Reference List of Manuscripts Relating to the History of Maine*. Part I, Orono, 1938; Part II, 1939 (with an introduction and Maine maps by Fannie Hardy Eckstrom); Part III, 1941.

Sabin, Joseph, *Bibliotheca Americana: A Dictionary of Books Relating to America, from its Discovery to the Present Time*, New York, 1867–1936. 29 vols. (Trustworthy and exhaustive; later volumes continued by Wilberforce Eames.)

Starr, Edward C., *A Baptist Bibliography; Being a Register of Printed Materials By and About Baptists, Including Works Written Against the Baptists*. Vol. I, Philadelphia, 1947; Vols. II, III, IV, Chester, 1952–1954; Vol. V, Rochester, 1955. (An author and title index; present volumes, A–Cz.)

Stillwell, Margaret B., *Incunabula and Americana, 1450–1800: A Key to Bibliographical Study*, New York, 1931. (Important check lists.)

Trumbull, James H., *List of Books Printed in Connecticut, 1709–1800*, Hartford, 1904.

Vail, R. W. G., *The Voice of the Old Frontier*, Philadelphia, 1949. (Valuable for its bibliography of works "written before 1800 by those living on the frontier ... principally stories of Indian captivity, and promotion tracts by agents for the sale of frontier lands ...".)

Waldman, Milton, *Americana; the Literature of American History*, New York, 1925.

Walker, Williston, *The Creeds and Platforms of Congregationalism*, New York, 1893. (The principal documents in New England ecclesiastical disputes, with full bibliographies for the background of each episode.)

Watkins, George T., *American Typographical Bibliography, being a list of brief titles of books and pamphlets relating to the history of Printing in America*, Indianapolis, 1898.

—— *Bibliography of Printing in the United States*, Boston, 1906.

Watt, Robert, *Bibliotheca Britannica*, Edinburgh, 1824, 4 vols. (Often extremely useful, particularly the subject index of the last two volumes.)

Wegelin, Oscar, *Early American Poetry*, second edition revised and enlarged, New York, 1930, 2 vols. (Vol. I, 1650–1799.)

Weimer, David R., ed., *Bibliography of*

American Culture, 1493–1875, Ann Arbor. University micro-films.

Whitley, W. T., *A Baptist Bibliography; Being a Register of the chief materials for Baptist history, whether in manuscript or in print, preserved in Great Britain, Ireland and the Colonies*, London, 1916. Vol. I, 1526–1776. (Chronologically arranged.)

Wing, Donald, *Short-title Catalogue of Books Printed in England, Scotland, Ireland, Wales, and British America and of English Books Printed in Other Countries, 1641–1700*, 3 vols., New York, 1945–1951.

Woodress, James; *Dissertations in American Literature, 1891–1955*, Durham, N.C., 1957. (Subsequent lists of dissertations completed or in progress appear annually in *American Literature*.)

HARPER TORCHBOOKS / The University Library

John R. Alden	THE AMERICAN REVOLUTION: 1775–1783. Illus. TB/3011
Ray A. Billington	THE FAR WESTERN FRONTIER: 1830–1860. Illus. TB/3012
Kenneth E. Boulding	CONFLICT AND DEFENSE: *A General Theory* TB/3024
Crane Brinton	A DECADE OF REVOLUTION: 1789–1799. Illus. TB/3018
J. Bronowski & Bruce Mazlish	THE WESTERN INTELLECTUAL TRADITION: *From Leonardo to Hegel* TB/3001
Edward P. Cheyney	THE DAWN OF A NEW ERA: 1250–1453. Illus. TB/3002
Foster Rhea Dulles	AMERICA'S RISE TO WORLD POWER: 1898–1954. Illus. TB/3021
Harold U. Faulkner	POLITICS, REFORM AND EXPANSION: 1890–1900. Illus. TB/3020
Carl J. Friedrich	THE AGE OF THE BAROQUE: 1610–1660. Illus. TB/3004
Leo Gershoy	FROM DESPOTISM TO REVOLUTION: 1763–1789. Illus. TB/3017
Myron P. Gilmore	THE WORLD OF HUMANISM: 1453–1517. Illus. TB/3003
Lawrence Henry Gipson	THE COMING OF THE [AMERICAN] REVOLUTION: 1763–1775. Illus. TB/3007
L. C. Goodrich	A SHORT HISTORY OF THE CHINESE PEOPLE. Illus. TB/3015
Arthur S. Link	WOODROW WILSON AND THE PROGRESSIVE ERA: 1910–1917. Illus. TB/3023
George E. Mowry	THE ERA OF THEODORE ROOSEVELT AND THE BIRTH OF MODERN AMERICA: 1900–1912. Illus. TB/3022
Wallace Notestein	THE ENGLISH PEOPLE ON THE EVE OF COLONIZATION: 1603–1630. Illus. TB/3006
Joseph A. Schumpeter	CAPITALISM, SOCIALISM AND DEMOCRACY. Third edition. TB/3008
Frederick L. Nussbaum	THE TRIUMPH OF SCIENCE AND REASON: 1660–1685. Illus. TB/3009
Penfield Roberts	THE QUEST FOR SECURITY: 1715–1740. Illus. TB/3016
John B. Wolf	THE EMERGENCE OF THE GREAT POWERS: 1685–1715. Illus. TB/3010
John B. Wolf	FRANCE: 1814–1919: *The Rise of a Liberal-Democratic Society.* TB/3019
Louis B. Wright	THE CULTURAL LIFE OF THE AMERICAN COLONIES: 1607–1763. Illus. TB/3005
M. D. Zabel, *Ed.*	LITERARY OPINION IN AMERICA. 3rd Edition. *Vol. I*, TB/3013; *Vol. II*, TB/3014

HARPER TORCHBOOKS / The Academy Library

[Selected Titles]

Jacques Barzun	THE HOUSE OF INTELLECT TB/1051
H. J. Blackham	SIX EXISTENTIALIST THINKERS TB/1002
Crane Brinton	ENGLISH POLITICAL THOUGHT IN THE NINETEENTH CENTURY TB/1071
Ernst Cassirer	ROUSSEAU, KANT AND GOETHE. Intro. by Peter Gay. TB/1092
Cochran & Miller	THE AGE OF ENTERPRISE: *A Social History of Industrial America* TB/1054
G. G. Coulton	MEDIEVAL VILLAGE, MANOR, AND MONASTERY TB/1022
St. Clair Drake & Horace Cayton	BLACK METROPOLIS: *Negro Life in a Northern City.* *Vol. I*, TB/1086; *Vol. II*, TB/1087. Intros. by Richard Wright & E. C. Hughes
Peter F. Drucker	THE NEW SOCIETY: *The Anatomy of Industrial Order* TB/1082
W. K. Ferguson, et al.	THE RENAISSANCE: *Six Essays* TB/1084
F. L. Ganshof	FEUDALISM TB/1058
Etienne Gilson	DANTE AND PHILOSOPHY TB/1089
W. K. C. Guthrie	THE GREEK PHILOSOPHERS: *From Thales to Aristotle* TB/1008
John Higham, *Ed.*	THE RECONSTRUCTION OF AMERICAN HISTORY TB/1068
Dan N. Jacobs, *Ed.*	THE NEW COMMUNIST MANIFESTO *and related documents* TB/1078
Hans Kohn, *Ed.*	THE MIND OF MODERN RUSSIA TB/1065
Samuel Noah Kramer	SUMERIAN MYTHOLOGY. Illustrated TB/1055
Paul Oskar Kristeller	RENAISSANCE THOUGHT: *Classic, Scholastic, Humanist Strains* TB/1048
Arthur O. Lovejoy	THE GREAT CHAIN OF BEING: *A Study of the History of an Idea* TB/1009
Paul Mantoux	THE INDUSTRIAL REVOLUTION IN THE EIGHTEENTH CENTURY TB/1079
Miller & Johnson, *Eds.*	THE PURITANS: *A Sourcebook of Their Writings.* *Vol. I*, TB/1093; *Vol. II*, TB/1094
Sir Lewis Namier	VANISHED SUPREMACIES: *Essays on European History*, 1812–1918 TB/1088
Erwin Panofsky	STUDIES IN ICONOLOGY: *Humanistic Themes in Renaissance Art.* Illus. TB/1077
Priscilla Robertson	REVOLUTIONS OF 1848: *A Social History* TB/1025
Ferdinand Schevill	THE MEDICI. Illustrated TB/1010
Ferdinand Schevill	MEDIEVAL AND RENAISSANCE FLORENCE. Illus. *Vol. I*, TB/1090; *Vol. II*, TB/1091
C. P. Snow	TIME OF HOPE. A novel. TB/1040
Paul A. Schilpp, *Ed.*	PHILOSOPHY OF BERTRAND RUSSELL. *Vol. I*, TB/1095; *Vol. II*, TB/1096
Dorothy Van Ghent	THE ENGLISH NOVEL: *Form and Function* TB/1050
W. Lloyd Warner	SOCIAL CLASS IN AMERICA: *The Evaluation of Status* TB/1013

HARPER TORCHBOOKS / The Bollingen Library

HARPER TORCHBOOKS / The Cloister Library

HARPER TORCHBOOKS / The Science Library